OLD TESTAMENT STUDIES

Volume 2

The Study Companion To Old Testament Literature

An Approach to the Writings of Pre-Exilic and Exilic Israel

by

Antony F. Campbell, S.J.

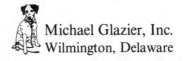
Michael Glazier, Inc.
Wilmington, Delaware

*"You are precious in my eyes
and honored, and I love you."
Isaiah 43:4*

About the Author

Antony F. Campbell, S.J., teaches Old Testament at Jesuit
Theological College, within the United Faculty of Theology,
Parkville, in Melbourne. He has taught in graduate institutions
in the U.S., lectured widely in renewal courses and worked
diligently to share the riches of the Old Testament with a wider
public. His publications include *The Ark Narrative* and *Of
Prophets and Kings.*

*First published in 1989 by Michael Glazier, Inc., 1935 West Fourth Street,
Wilmington, Delaware 19805. Copyright* © 1989 by Michael Glazier, Inc. All
rights reserved. No part of this publication may be reproduced or transmitted in
any form or by any means, electronic or mechanical, including photocopy,
recording, or any information storage and retrieval system, without permission
in writing from the publisher: Michael Glazier, 1935 West Fourth Street,
Wilmington, Delaware 19805. The Scripture quotations contained herein are
from the Revised Standard Version of the Bible, copyrighted © 1946, 1952,
1971 by the Division of Christian Education of the National Council of the
Churches of Christ in the U.S.A., and are used by permission. All rights reserved.
Library of Congress Cataloging-in-Publication Data
Campbell, Antony F.
The study companion to Old Testament literature.
Bibliography. Includes index. 1. Bible, O.T.—Criticism, interpretation, etc.
I. Title. BS1171.2.C35   1988   221.6   86-45319
ISBN 0-89453-586-2
ISBN, *Old Testament Studies* Series: 0-89453-654-0
Typography by Edith Warren
Printed in the United States of America

Contents

Pre-Exilic Prophets

Jonah and Job

Acknowledgments

A book like this which seeks to cover a wide sweep of the Old Testament draws on the contributions of so many people who can hardly be acknowledged adequately: those who have taught me; those I have taught in turn, whose needs and questions have driven me deeper into the biblical text; those who, in renewal groups and study seminars, have shared in probing the meaning and illumination offered by the scriptures. To them, my deepest thanks.

Special thanks are due to the Jesuit School of Theology at Berkeley where the bulk of the writing was done during a sabbatical leave. Above all, my thanks to Fr. John Endres, S.J., whose generosity in putting his books at my disposal was invaluable. Also to Michael Glazier and the editors at Michael Glazier Inc. whose suggestions have been an important influence on the final shape of the book.

At home in Parkville (Melbourne), my gratitude in particular to Dr. Lawrence McIntosh, director of the Joint Theological Library, for constant help and encouragement; to Mrs. Leonie Hudson, secretary of Jesuit Theological College, for typing a substantial part of the manuscript at a critical stage; to Fr. John Scullion, S.J. who read and commented on the whole manuscript most helpfully; and to those who generously shared in the proofreading.

A quite different acknowledgment may also be in order. Not all the Old Testament is treated in this book. Proverbs and Psalms are absent because they could hardly be dealt with as larger literary works. Chronicles, the post-exilic prophets, and others are absent because I do not know them well enough to be passionately engaged by them. Rather than bone up on them for the purposes of apparent completeness, it seemed more fitting simply to acknowledge that fact.

An Avowal

It is my belief that a thorough understanding of the Old Testament, entering fully into the richness of its communication, is a source of profound intellectual pleasure and intense theological stimulation.

It is the endeavor of this book to bring its reader into continuous contact with the text of the Old Testament, opening up insights into the creativity and sophistication of its principal literary works.

This involves the demanding task of reading the Old Testament texts closely. The understanding which is gained makes the task an enjoyable one. It involves the challenging effort to follow the thinking and explore the faith of the Old Testament authors. The benefit for personal faith makes the effort well worthwhile.

I do not want this book to be a substitute for reading the Old Testament. I hope that, as a companion along the way of inquiry, it may help readers of the Old Testament to discover there generations of thinkers and poets and believers, struggling to make sense of their human lives before the mystery of the experience of God. I believe that the application and study needed for that discovery can only bring a deeper joy in the Old Testament text, a greater awe before the power of its thought, and a more sympathetic appreciation of the God of the Judeo-Christian tradition.

Introduction

The aim of this book is to deal with the Old Testament at the level of its literary structures and with an eye to its contribution for contemporary theology. Literature is produced in order to communicate meaning or to generate emotion. Literature, as communication, always addresses an audience. It is conceived in a particular situation and speaks to that situation. Especially in traditional societies, it draws on and is fuelled by the past traditions of the community, the beliefs and experiences which have been articulated, accepted, and passed into the heritage of the community.

Within the Old Testament, this has been a long process. Where written form is concerned, it began, at the latest, at the courts of David and Solomon, in rough figures, from around the year 1000 B.C.E. And it continued for seven or eight centuries. The Old Testament was shaped within a strongly traditional society. So, before major complexes were given written form in the period of David and Solomon, experience was brought to expression as oral literature and began to constitute the community's heritage, the heritage of Israel.

When we talk about the literary structures of the Old Testament, we are therefore talking about a number of things. We are talking about the early literary works at the beginning of the process which led up to the Old Testament. We are talking about later generations' use of these works, expanding them and combining them to form new works of literature, addressing new situations. And we are talking about the end product of all this process, the Old Testament itself.

Two tendencies are present in Old Testament scholarship today. One gives priority in its researches to recovering the stages in the history of the Old Testament before it became the present canonical text we possess. One might summarize: we have the present text already; we need in our study to recover the earlier stages which are not immediately accessible to us. The other tendency gives priority in its researches to studying the present text as we have it. One might summarize: we are only certain of the present text and anything else is hypothetical and too uncertain for fruitful study.

This book endeavors to pay appropriate attention to both the present text and to the stages which can be recovered behind it. The present text has to be given serious attention. It is all we have with certainty. It is the foundation for any attempt to recover its past history. As the sacred scriptures of the Jewish and Christian faiths, it deserves close and proper study. On the other hand, the nature of the present text cannot be properly understood if we are unaware of the processes by which it has been shaped and formed. Without study of the earlier stages which lie behind the present text, it is impossible to grasp the full richness and depth of the changing attitudes and theologies which marked Israel's faith over generations and centuries. In this book, we will begin with the present text, but where it is appropriate we will also examine the earlier stages at which texts can be identified.

The Old Testament is, of course, a collection of the traditions of Israel: it encompasses storytelling and narrative, laws and customs, wisdom sayings, songs and prayers, the sayings of the prophets, and much else. These have been brought together within the Old Testament in much the same way that the literature of a community or a country is brought together within a library. And that raises questions about literary structures in the Old Testament text. The Old Testament had become the repository of Israel's traditions, the storehouse in which traditions were preserved. But as texts were placed side by side in this storehouse, and so came to occupy the same or adjoining pages in the Old Testament, they did not necessarily form literary structures. Three volumes on a library shelf may be three parts of a trilogy, forming a literary whole; or they may be three separate works, by separate authors, having nothing more in common than that they belong together within the classification system of the library. When dealing with the present text of the Old Testament, that is the text as we find it now in printed Bibles, we always have to ask whether we are dealing with a literary structure or with a simple collection.

By a literary structure, I mean a text which has been artfully composed for the purpose of communication or expression. It has an author, whether an individual or a group; it has an audience in mind; it has something to say. It may be as small a unit as a single psalm; it may be as large as the Pentateuch. What is essential is that it was composed or assembled with a view to communication. In this aspect, it differs from collections of traditions which have been put together with a view to their preservation. When we look at texts like a prophetic book, or even the Pentateuch, the question has to be asked: has a literary structure been formed, or do we simply have a collection? The question cannot be taken for granted. It must be asked. And we can only answer that question by a careful study of the text itself.

There are plenty of books available on a general level which deal with the Old Testament, its history and its literature. They may give a good picture of the results of modern scholarship, but often they do not set themselves the task of showing how these results flow out of the phenomena which are found in the biblical text. For that reason, they do not present a sense of the compelling fidelity to the biblical text which is a driving force of all responsible biblical scholarship. There are plenty of books available on an academic level which deal with the Old Testament. Often, they are concerned with particular areas, or with a breadth of coverage, or at a level of detail, which leaves little scope for the exploration of literary structures and the meaning which they seek to convey.

This particular book seeks to plot a path through the middle ground. Its endeavor is to come to terms with the literary structures—with the Old Testament at the various levels where its texts form literary wholes. What shape do these texts have, and why? Why were they written and what situations did they respond to? What did they want to say to the community? At the same time, the effort will be made to keep the conclusions of scholarship in touch with the phenomena in the text which justify and legitimate those conclusions. What in the text obliges us to speak of a Yahwist or a Priestly Writer? What in the text justifies us in speaking of the Pentateuch, or a particular prophetic book, as a literary whole? And the final concern, which justifies all the rest, is: what is the significance of all this for our own faith and theology today?

At this point, it is worth noting that there are two widespread attitudes to the Bible which are poles apart. One we might call "iconic," borrowing the term from Martin Marty. Marty exemplifies this iconic attitude with a quotation from President Grover Cleveland: "The Bible is good enough for me, just the old book under which I was brought up. I do not want notes or criticisms or explanations about authorship or origin or even cross-references. I do not need them or understand them, and they confuse me."[1] Where the Bible has become such an icon, a conviction has become ingrained about the nature of the biblical text. A particular understanding of what it means for the Bible to be God's inspired word has become unshakably associated with very deep and vital convictions about the meaning and worth of life. Consciously or unconsciously, for people with this attitude, anything which appears to alter their conviction about the nature of the biblical text will be sensed as threatening their convictions about the meaning and worth of life—convictions which alone make life possible. Change in such attitudes will not be the result of simple biblical study.

On the other hand, there is what I would call an "inquiring" attitude. It is one that is delighted by explorations into the nature of the biblical text. Here, often, two experiences have been in tension. There has been the experience of receiving and accepting the Bible as the word of God, the foundation document of the Jewish and Christian communities, and the primary and authoritative source of God's revelation. In tension with this is the experience that much that has been received as biblical sits uncomfortably with the proper attitudes and outlook of a modern believer. For example, the wonder-working, self-revealing biblical God is at a pretty considerable distance from the God of modern experience. Or there is the discovery that a lot of what was thought to be the biblical picture of history does not sit comfortably with modern historical findings. Then there is the experience of realizing that biblical chronology and portrayals of creation do not square with the accepted scientific consensus

[1]Quoted in M. Marty, "America's Iconic Book," *Humanizing America's Iconic Book: Society of Biblical Literature Centennial Addresses 1980* (ed. G.M. Tucker and D.A. Knight; Chico: Scholars Press, 1980) 1-23, see p. 3.

or that biblical stories share much in common with the myths and legends of other ancient Near Eastern cultures. Consciously or unconsciously, the tension can verge on the intolerable: if the foundation document of faith is shaky, what is the fate of faith itself?

For people tormented by this tension, inquiry into the biblical text is a source of delight, of relief, and of a renewed affirmation of faith—because they discover there deeply intelligent minds, wrestling with human experiences not dissimilar from their own, and they find there too contrasting theologies struggling in their different ways to give expression to the encounter with the divine in human life. Experiences are discovered in the biblical text which are not so different from our own. A God is revealed in the biblical text who is not so distant from the God of our own experience. Authors are encountered in the biblical text who turn out to be powerful theologians, splendid storytellers, committed visionaries, and great religious poets. It is not difficult to see the spirit of God moving in their work and words.

It may be that one of the fundamental differences between these two groups of people is to be found in their attitude toward what we may call "the nature of the biblical text." For those whose attitude to the Bible is iconic, their conviction about the nature of the biblical text is one of the primary givens of their lives; any change in it would be equivalent to a betrayal of their God. For those whose attitude to the Bible is inquiring, their conviction about the nature of the biblical text is open to modification by their experience of the biblical text itself. Intuitively, they accept that the "how" of God's self-revelation to humankind cannot be determined in advance. Only through a deep and open encounter with its sources can one ascertain how that self-revelation of God has taken place. An understanding of the nature of the biblical text is, therefore, of critical importance, because through it we come to an understanding of the nature of God's communication with us. To help in this pursuit is the primary aim of this book.

The pursuit of all the avenues for understanding the biblical text is what makes up the task of biblical exegesis, biblical interpretation. There is an immense panoply of scientific research at the disposal of the interpreter: archaeology and history, languages and ancient Near Eastern literatures, and so on. But at the end of all this science, interpretation remains an art—and one that is often insufficiently practised. Gerhard von Rad expresses it well.

> We know a considerable amount about the literary forms of Old Testaments texts. We have learned how to visualise the text in an earlier, that is to say pre-literary, shape. We have a whole arsenal supplying the history of terms and concepts which is of the utmost service for the elucidation of details. *But when someone then goes on to ask what, with all its details, the text is saying, whether, or how, it is to be interpreted in the light of its context, he generally finds himself alone.* It would be a great mistake to regard this establishment of the meaning of a text, *which is the final stage and crown of exposition,* as something simple, a thing which dawns as it were automatically on the expositor's mind. Here again the latter needs all the acumen he possesses, for he will very soon be brought to see that there is more than simply one possible way of interpreting the text taken as a whole, and that it is often difficult to decide for one way as against another. Yet here is one of the most important decisions which Old Testament theologians would have to make.[2]

This task of establishing the meaning of a text is obligatory on the interpreter, not only at the level of the final text, but also wherever, at earlier levels, a text can be identified. The question of the extent to which a scholar may dismember the present text and reconstitute an earlier text is one that requires great sensitivity.

It is rare that the phenomena of a text present themselves with such clarity that their significance imposes itself from the outset.[3]

---

[2] G. von Rad, *Old Testament Theology*, vol. 2 (New York: Harper & Row, 1965) 416, emphasis mine.

[3] By these "phenomena of the text" are meant all the little signals in the text which contribute to its interpretation and the understanding of its history and meaning. They may be matters of syntax, such as a change from singular to plural or from second person to third person. They may be matters of style, such as an overloaded sentence or a clause in the wrong place. They may be occurrences of repetition, where the communication is doubled up for some reason or other. They may be issues of continuity or discontinuity, whether a text flows smoothly or not. All these and many more are the basic elements

How far, for example, should the exegete go in pursuing the inner tensions and irregularities of a text? Sometimes, pursued with ruthless logic to the bitter end, all that is left of the text is a meaningless accumulation of fragments, allegedly the work of a veritable posse of redactors. In my judgment, as a rule of thumb, the phenomena of a text have to be pursued as long as their pursuit illuminates the text, its origin and growth and meaning. The art of interpretation includes knowing how to balance the uncertainties and fragilities of human knowledge, and how best to marshal what is known about a text in order to bring this knowledge fruitfully to bear in its interpretation.

The phenomena of a text are not always so many pieces of self-evident data. The estimation of their significance is often a matter for subtle and informed judgment. In one situation, the phenomena observed—such as continuity/discontinuity, repetitions, style, syntax, vocabulary—may be most significant for understanding a text and revealing the process of growth behind it. But in other situations, similar phenomena may be judged to have been roughnesses which were acceptable to the author and have no significant bearing on the text's process of growth. On each occasion, the question has to be judiciously weighed.

The phenomena of the text are explained by hypotheses. Hypotheses are the lifeblood of research and discovery. In the Old Testament, they give us access to insight into the riches of Israel's theology, the trajectory of Israel's struggle constantly to understand itself and its life in the encounter with its God. They cannot be dismissed because of their fragility. Nor can they be endowed with a certainty beyond the clarity of the observations on which they are based. In this book, we will endeavor to quarry the hypotheses of biblical scholarship for the wealth of insight they have to yield. And we will try, too, to shore up that quarrying through constant reference to the phenomena in the text which underpin the hypotheses.

The study of the literary structures of the Old Testament begins with the present text. That is the one certain datum on which all

around which the interpretation of a text is built. They can be pointers to its history and the way in which it has been composed. They can be pointers to its meaning and the way in which it should be interpreted.

else rests. Even the decision as to where this constitutes a literary unit and where it does not is, in the final analysis, a hypothetical judgment. The study of the Pentateuch is greatly enriched by the exploration of the work of the Yahwist and the Priestly Writer(s). This is well into the realm of hypothesis; even more so when we ask the question, "What was the central communicative thrust which drove these authors?" But without venturing into these areas, we cannot give the Old Testament a decent chance to speak to us with all of its potential eloquence and power. The risks must be taken. They must also be recognized. And the fruits must be enjoyed.

There are also other risks to be run. Interpretation is not an exact science. It is an art. It is exacting, however, and it demands much care and precision; but it remains in the high realm of human art. It is a risky business, for it intimately involves the interpreter. Interpretation is the outcome of a process, a sustained encounter between the interpreter and the text. It is the endeavor to lay bare the results of that process. The process involves the text being laid bare by the interpreter. It also involves the person being laid bare by the text—and that is a risk the interpreter must always run.

The process involves the submission of the interpreter to the authority of the text. This is the case for all texts. Such authority need not be that of a biblical or classical text; it may be the authority of a lover's utterance to express and declare the lover's feelings or state of mind. This submission means that, at a certain point, the text is master of the interpreter. Yet the process involves the mastery of the text by the interpreter, in the effort to understand. To greater or less degree, the interpreter will be transformed in this process. The text has its own way of working its will upon the interpreter, baring convictions, exposing prejudice, seducing or repelling. In this process, again to greater or less degree, the interpreter brings to the text personal experience, sensibility, and purpose, and through them may endow the text with clarity of meaning.

The meaning of a text is seldom exhausted in a single interpretation. The being of an interpreter is seldom transformed by a single text.

The venture which this book invites us to undertake is that of exploring the Old Testament in its literary structures. There is a vast wealth to be exploited: the messages conveyed by literary creation, the past recalled and rehearsed in liturgy and literature, the emotions felt and celebrated. The exploration cannot be undertaken responsibly without considerable hard work. There is an asceticism required too. It is all too easy and too tempting, and too irresponsible, to seize on the results we find attractive and to exploit them, without due regard to the qualifications or reserves that have to be voiced. The fragility and uncertainty of much that is said has to be borne in mind. But the gains to be won are great, and the risks have to be run.

RECOMMENDED READING AS BACKGROUND TO THIS BOOK

Bernhard W. Anderson, *Understanding the Old Testament*. 4th ed. Englewood Cliffs: Prentice-Hall, 1986 (UK edition: *The Living World of the Old Testament*).

John Barton, *Reading the Old Testament: Method in Biblical Study*. London: Darton, Longman and Todd, 1984.

Lawrence Boadt, *Reading the Old Testament: An Introduction*. New York: Paulist, 1984.

Norman K. Gottwald, *The Hebrew Bible: A Socio-Literary Introduction*. Philadelphia: Fortress, 1985.

Chronology

THE TIME OF THE EVENTS

18th-14th cent.	PATRIARCHS
13th cent.	EXODUS
1000	DAVID'S kingship (c. 1004 in Hebron, 996 in Jerusalem)
922	DIVISION of kingdom after the death of Solomon (1 Kgs 12)
722	DEFEAT of Samaria: end of northern kingdom (2 Kgs 17)
622	DEUTERONOMIC reform under Josiah (2 Kgs 22-23)
587	DESTRUCTION of Jerusalem: end of southern kingdom (2 Kgs 25)
538	EDICT of Cyrus: end of exile (Ezra 1)
c. 450-400	NEHEMIAH and EZRA: reorganization of Jewish community

THE TIME OF THE TEXTS (very approximate in most cases)

11th century	Some songs: e.g., Genesis 49, Exodus 15, Judges 5
10th century	Yahwist, Story of David's Rise, Succession Narrative
9th century	Prophetic Record
8th century	Amos, Hosea, Micah, Isaiah 1-39
7th century	Jeremiah, Deuteronomistic History (1st edition)
6th century	Ezekiel, Priestly Document, Deuteronomistic History (later editions), Isaiah 40-55, Haggai, Zechariah 1-8
Late 6th/5th	Isaiah 56-66
5th-3rd cent.	Job
Late 4th/3rd	Chronicles, Ezra-Nehemiah, Jonah
2nd century	Daniel

Genesis
to
Deuteronomy

1

The Pentateuch as Literary Work

Recommended preliminary reading

Before reading the body of the chapter, it will be helpful to have read the following passages to get a feel for some of the text:
Genesis 1:26-31; 8:20-9:7; 12:1-4a; 49:28-33; 50:15-21
Exodus 1:1-14; 14:21-31; 19:1-6; 40:34-38
Leviticus 26:40-45
Numbers 9:15-23
Deuteronomy 7:6-11; 26:5-11

The first part of the Bible to be received as sacred scripture was the Torah, the five books from Genesis to Deuteronomy. These books can be looked at as a collection, containing a huge amount of very different traditions from the storehouse of Israel's past. In them, the Yahwist's narrative,[1] the Priestly Document,[2] Israel's legal collections, and other traditions besides, have been stored and preserved. As such, it would hardly be proper to treat the resulting text as a literary work. Rather, it would be a repository of cherished and valued traditions. Yet its components have not been simply classified and shelved. They have been blended and

---

[1]For an understanding of the Yahwist's narrative, see chap. 3.

[2]For an understanding of the Priestly Document, see chap. 2.

intermingled in a remarkably creative way. Over the generations, authors and redactors have given shape to these traditions; the Torah has come to be recognized as having a particular unity of its own, as being a whole in a way which sets it apart from the rest of the Bible.

The question is there to be asked: whether it makes sense to look at this whole as a literary work. In the arc which extends from creation to the death of Moses, has a sense of unity and purpose been achieved? Is there an intention that informs the whole, a communication that is expressed in all this composite text? In the final analysis, does it spring from the urgency of a communication to be made about human beings and their reflective struggle to come to grips with their lives and their God—not in the surface level of day-to-day living, but in the powerful and mysterious depths of religious faith and passion?

These questions can only be answered by looking at the text. There cannot be a theoretical or a dogmatic answer. The question whether the vast variety of traditions contained in the Pentateuch forms a literary work or not cannot be answered "It is so sacred it must have," nor can it be answered "It is so diverse it could not have." The only way to answer the question is by close study of the text itself. Yet the text of the Pentateuch is so vast, and so manifold in its forms, that it must in some way be brought into focus, to provide a manageable point of reference. This must be our first task. As far as possible, repetition from later chapters will be kept to a minimum.

Survey of the Text

The Pentateuch falls into three major sections: stories of humankind (Genesis 1-11); stories of Israel's ancestors (Genesis 12-50); stories of the generation which, under Moses, first emerged as a nation on the stage of history (Exodus-Deuteronomy). In all of these, the goodness of God's purpose and promise is engaged in subtle interplay with human fragility in all of its potential for failure as well as its capacity to be open to renewal, to new beginnings and fresh hope.

GENESIS 1-11: THE WHOLE HUMAN RACE

In Genesis 1-11, the mythic stories from a common and distant past, before Israel existed, have been blended into the story of humankind—and it is a sorry story. God's purpose is visible in the majestic account of creation with which it opens: it is punctuated by the constant refrain, "It was good, it was good, it was good," and it culminates in the sabbath rest and its blessing. Yet it sweeps almost immediately into the story of human fragility, human failure. The tender recognition of human complementarity— "and they become one flesh" (Gen 2:24)—is swiftly followed by one of the partner's being deceived—"And you will be like God" (Gen 3:5)—and in turn leading the other astray, so that both are expelled from the mythic garden. The existence of two brothers leads to the death of one (Gen 4:1-16). The development of cultural skills only leads to an expansion of the capacity to satisfy the human potential for violence (Gen 4:17-24). As the generations roll on, evil intensifies and the annihilation of the flood follows (Gen 6-9). As nations spread across the earth again, the sorry pattern is repeated and human pride—"Let us make a name for ourselves" (Gen 11:4)—leads to the scattering, division, and alienation which is characteristic of much of Israel's world, and ours.

The God who, in creation, separated the waters to make living space for the human race to flourish (Gen 1:6) is experienced as the God who let those waters flow back to obliterate that created life (Gen 7:11). The God who walked with the man and his wife in the cool of the day (Gen 3:8) is experienced as the God who scattered the human race in confused incommunicability over the face of the earth (Gen 11:1-9). There are hopeful touches along the way: God fashioning garments and clothing the first couple (Gen 3:21); God protecting the guilt-burdened Cain (Gen 4:14); God coming to terms with human fragility and giving assurance that never again would the created order be catastrophically disturbed (Gen 8:21-22; 9:8-17). For all that, the picture is a dark one: distorted relationships and domination, death and violence, division, and the shattering of the innate human passion for unity and peace.

It is a picture which we can recognize easily enough in ourselves: fragile and needy, driven by jealousy, longing, and fear. There is the sense of the image of God, felt deep within us, yet fractured and rendered unrecognizable in the turbulence of living. Israel felt it and portrayed it in these stories. It becomes the backdrop against which the quest for identity is pursued, the search for the meaning of existence.

GENESIS 12-50: THE ANCESTORS OF ISRAEL

In Genesis 12-50, the second great section of the Pentateuch, the story of Israel's ancestors unfolds under the shadow of this failure of humankind to achieve its destiny: the failure to live as stewards of creation, the failure to find the full experience of blessing, the failure to exist in the image and likeness of God.

For a moment, the darkness of this shadow is dispelled by a shaft of light that comes with Abraham's call to enter into history. Abraham is called to find blessing and to be a source of blessing for all the families of the earth (Gen 12:1-3). Here an articulation of Israel's traditions, which we attribute to the Yahwist, an earlier narrative embedded in the Pentateuch, has left its determining mark on the final form of the text.

It is one of the great thematic moments of the Old Testament. Its sweep reaches down into the New, both in the impact of fulfillment, and in the echo of thought (cf., Gal 3:8). Here, in the call of Abraham, universal human history and need are brought into conjunction with the destiny of a single people. In an act of remarkable theological vision, the stories of Israel are aligned with the stories of humankind: Israel is to become a great nation and be blessed, and—much more than that—Israel is to be a source of blessing available to all the families of the earth.

This is a forceful text. It is the pivot between the picture of the human race and the portrayal of the beginnings of the people of Israel. The human race is pictured as endowed with an initial blessing (Gen 1:28) and doing precious little with it. The theme of blessing is strong at the start: the fish of the sea and the birds of the air (1:21), the first human pair (1:28), the sabbath (2:3); the theme returns when the text swings back to the beginning again with the first genealogy (5:2). After the annihilation of the flood, the world is pictured getting a fresh start, and the theme of blessing returns. Noah and his family are blessed, with a strong echo of Gen 1:28 (Gen 9:1); yet a negative tone has come in, there is fear and dread, there will be animal slaughter (9:2-3), homicide is penalized, hence foreshadowed (Gen 9:5-6). Blessing is there, too, for Noah's son, Shem (9:26); a negative tone remains in the curse on Canaan. So the theme of blessing in these chapters is linked to the beginning, which is creation, and to the fresh beginning after the flood. Apart from that, expulsion, murder, violence, annihilation, and dispersion paint an emphatically unblessed picture.

When the focus of the narrative shifts dramatically from the universal vision of Genesis 1-11 to zero in on the people of Israel, the theme of blessing again comes strongly to the fore. Abraham will be blessed, and will be a blessing; those who bless him will be blessed; in him all the families of the earth shall be blessed, or, in him all the families of the earth shall get blessing for themselves (Gen 12:1-3). The blessing bestowed on Abraham is to overflow to the benefit of the whole human family.

At almost any stage in Israel's history, it is a fantastic claim to have made. It is scarcely a historical or a national claim; it transcends such limits. It is a theological claim, based on an understanding of God. The God Israel has experienced is a God whose goal is blessing, a blessing destined for the whole human race. When the initial power of that blessing appears to have faltered and failed (Gen 1-11), God takes a new initiative to achieve the goal of blessing. The individual Abraham is called to leave all that is secure and familiar to him—country, kindred, and father's house—and to venture forth into an unknown of which he has simply the assurance that it will be shown him (12:1). From him will come a great nation: through him, blessing will once again be available to all. It is a magnificent statement of faith about God. It is also a remarkable understanding of the destiny of Israel. Israel, to spring from the descendants of Abraham, is to be the vehicle by which God will make blessing effective again in the sphere of human life.

The Pentateuch is the beginning of Israel's story. Here, with the combination of the Yahwist narrative (= J) and the Priestly Document (= P), the theme of blessing is given special weight. With P, it is present at the start of the human race, but is rapidly displaced by strife and violence; it is present again after the flood, and again displaced. With J, it is present again, still available to the world, but this time through the mediating presence of Abraham's descendants.

The stories of Abraham form a varied collection. There is firstly his obedience, "Go ... and he went" (12:1, 4a). There is his belief in the promise made to him (15:1-6). There are the stories of the covenant made with him (15:7-21; 17:1-8). The existence of the promised son, and the blessing which is dependent on it, are under threat. First the human powerlessness of a barren womb: "Is anything too hard for the LORD?" (Gen 18:14). The fulfillment of the blessing in the gift of a son, Isaac, is bracketed by the stories which bring out the shadow side—the expulsion of Hagar and Ishmael (Gen 16:1-16; 21:8-21). Then there is the strange threat from a mysteriously demanding God: "Take your son ... and offer him as a burnt offering" (Gen 22:2). Interspersed among these, the promise of blessing remains in view: before Abraham's persistent intercession for Sodom and Gomorrah (Gen 18:18), and after the story of the sacrifice of Isaac (Gen 22:16-18). The promise of a son has been fulfilled. The fulfillment of the promise of land is adumbrated: Abraham has successfully purchased property for a burying place (chap. 23).

From the first ancestor, the narrative moves on to the larger scale of the family. The theme of blessing is still there, but the shadows of conflict will fall across it. "After the death of Abraham, God blessed Isaac his son" (Gen 25:11). The barren Rebekah conceived, and the two children struggled in her womb (25:21-23). The conflict begun there, in the womb, is not just that of individuals; it mirrors the conflict in the destinies of nations (25:23), the conflict in human life.

The story of Isaac is little more than the background against which this family conflict unfolds. The blessing is not forgotten. Despite famine, Isaac is not to go down to Egypt, but to dwell in the land of which God will tell him (Gen 26:2, parallel to Abraham's instructions in 12:1-3). Isaac's descendants will be many and the blessing will come, through them, to all the nations of the earth (26:4-5). The blessing brings Isaac prosperity (26:12-14). It brings him the blessing of peace with the Philistines, the archenemy of Israel, later one of the greatest threats to its survival (26:26-31). But Jacob, who earlier had taken his brother's birthright (25:29-34), now moves to action and takes his father's blessing (27:1-40). With this, the conflict reaches breaking point, and Jacob must take to flight to save his life (27:41-45).

The blessing is still with Jacob in his flight (Gen 28:13-15). His eventual bride will be the lovely Rachel. Yet flight from his brother first leads him into conflict with Laban, his uncle. He is duped by the substitution of Leah for Rachel (29:15-30). The blessing brings prosperity to Laban (30:27-30). In his turn, Jacob dupes Laban, in the first exercise of selective breeding in the flock (30:31-43). The conflict again comes to the point of flight (chap. 31). Within the narrative, in the meantime, there has been the conflict of Jacob's wives, the bitter rivalry of Leah and Rachel in the bearing of his sons (29:31-30:24). Jacob's flight brings him back to the land of his fathers. Before he enters it, there is one last mighty conflict: he must struggle with God. In the strange mystery of a night of wrestling, alone on the far side of a dividing stream, his name and his destiny are changed (32:22-32). He is called Israel, because he has struggled with God and men and has prevailed (v 28). As he limps past the place of the encounter, crippled by the struggle, the sun rises upon him (v 31), a powerful image of the new life bestowed by the blessing. So Jacob comes home, survives the encounter with his brother Esau (33:1-17), and the old Isaac dies and is buried by his sons (35:27-35).

The story moves toward a wider focus again. Reaching beyond the struggles within the family, the narrative now involves this family of Jacob's with the great nation of Egypt, and even with the fate of "all the earth" (Gen 41:57). Once again, family conflict is the moving force which powers the story. Joseph is favored by his father and indiscreetly free with his dreams. The urge to which Cain succumbed rises again. What Esau said to himself (27:41), Joseph's brothers say to one another: "Kill him" (37:20). Joseph, the first born of Rachel, has his life saved by the intervention of his eldest brother, Reuben, the firstborn of Leah (37:22; cf., the less benign proposal of Judah, 37:26-27). And so the story takes Joseph into Egypt, into slavery (39:1), and finally into a position of great power (41:37-45).

The theme of blessing is not totally absent from the story. Potiphar's house is blessed by God, for Joseph's sake (Gen 39:5). In the way that stories function, the theme is present still when "all the earth came to Egypt to Joseph to buy grain" (41:57). For the survival of all the earth is procured by the wise management of this man, blessed of God. The narrative has a bridging function to perform too. The whole of Jacob's family must be brought to Egypt—for from there they are to be delivered by the power of

God. Like Abraham and Isaac, Jacob is given his instructions and obeys (46:1-5); the whole extended family moves down into Egypt.

The stories of the ancestors of Israel come to an end with the death of Jacob. With his twelve sons gathered around him, he gives them his last charge: to take his body back to Canaan, and there to bury him with Abraham and Sarah, with Isaac and Rebekah, there were he had buried Leah. And so he breathed his last (Gen 49:28-33). As the narrative moves inexorably toward the slavery in Egypt, already anticipated (Gen 15:13-14), a pledge of their return is lodged in the promised land. The resting place of the three patriarchs is Israel's surety for the future.

EXODUS-DEUTERONOMY: THE GENERATION LED BY MOSES

The third great section of the Pentateuch moves the story from the sphere of the family to that of a nation among the nations (Exodus-Deuteronomy). It begins with the list of the sons of Israel, the patriarch, who increase and multiply to become the sons of Israel, the nation, the people (Exod 1:1-9). Generations pass; the narrative is not concerned with their number. Israel has become a nation, and nation now confronts nation (1:8-14). A people enslaved and oppressed is no people. For Israel to exist as nation in its own right, it must have freedom. With freedom comes the responsibility, under God, of being in control of its own destiny. That is the burden of the story which follows. It is the story of the constitutive generation of Israel. It unfolds from the birth of Moses to his death, from the oppression of Israel to its deliverance, from the repeated failure of Israel to its standing in new hope on the brink of the promised land. The new hope arises out of the shadow of death. The generation that had experienced slavery and liberation, exodus and wandering, was to die in the desert (Num 14:26-35; 26:63-65). The death of Moses will seal the end of that generation, and with it bring the end of the story. It is an end that is indeed a beginning.

It is the story of a people brought into existence in freedom (Exod 1:1-15:21). It charts the people's relationship with God within that freedom (Exod 15:22-24:11), both the fragility of

Israel (15:22-18:27) and the charter of Israel's relationship with God (19:1-24:11). It dwells in detail on the mystery of God's visible presence among the people (Exod 25-40): the divine instructions for a sanctuary (25-31), the renewed fragility and restored hope (32-34), the compliance with God's instructions and God's presence to the people (35-40). It details the consequences of God's presence to the people, the implications of living with the holy (Leviticus). Finally, it follows Israel in the march into the future, the continued fragility of their journeying, and the renewal of hope in the midst of all their failure (Numbers-Deuteronomy). At Moses' death, Israel lives in freedom, constituted a people, within sight of the promised land in which their history with God will unfold (Deut 34:1-12).

It is the figure of Moses which holds all these traditions within the focus of a single narrative—the narrative of the generation in which Israel came to be a free and independent people. If Abraham, Isaac, and Jacob are the ancestors of Israel, Moses is its founding father. When the narrative lays him to rest in an unknown grave, at the end of Deuteronomy, Israel has been constituted as a people, a covenantal relationship has been established between God and people, the laws needed to maintain this relationship have been proclaimed, the leadership succession has been secured, and all that remains is for the people to move into the promised land. It is as if the core experiences of Israel have been encapsulated within that desert generation. The new generation, led by Joshua, is able to make a fresh start in the land, buoyed up by the experience of the past but unburdened by its failures (cf., Josh 5:2-12).

So the narrative gives us Moses' birth story, his call by the God of Abraham, of Isaac, and of Jacob, his commission to bring out the people of Israel from Egypt, and his carrying out of that commission. This first section, the bringing of the people from oppression and slavery into freedom, concludes with the exultant triumph of the Song of Miriam (Exod 15:1-18,19-21).

From then on, the story of Israel is a story of journeying: of putting distance between themselves and Egypt, of deepening and endangering their relationship with God, and of moving closer toward the land of promise. The stages of the narrative follow the stages of this journey.

The first stage of the narrative, the journey toward Sinai (Exod

15:22-18:27) is very carefully structured. There are three stages in the journey: Marah, the wilderness of Sin, and Rephidim. Thirst, hunger, and thirst again bring the people to murmur against Moses. There is a calculated intensification in this rebellious murmuring: they murmur against Moses (15:24); they murmur against Moses and Aaron and deplore their departure from Egypt (16:2-3); they find fault with Moses, putting God to the proof, ready to put Moses to death (17:2-4). It is a most remarkable portrayal, by Israel's narrator-theologians, of human fragility, juxtaposed so immediately to the great experience of deliverance. Each time, God supplies the people's need. These are stories of the self-destructive forces within the people, and of the God who does not let those forces destroy them. The desire for death is expressed rhetorically by the people (16:3; 17:3); there is no menace or threat of it from God.

Still at Rephidim, destructive forces come against the people from without, namely, the armed might of Amalek. And again, God does not let that force either destroy the people (17:8-16). The story of Jethro (chap. 18) might seem out of place in this context. But it is not. It, too, is concerned with destructive forces: it tells how Moses is prevented from being destroyed by the burden of his office. And, by delineating Moses' role as mediator between the people of God (18:19-20), it prepares the way for the stories of Sinai.

The next stage of the narrative begins with the formally dated move to Sinai (19:1-2). Its concern is the relationship between God and Israel: "you shall be my own possession among all peoples" (19:5). The people have experienced the saving power of God, the archetypal experience of the exodus, the subsequent experiences in the desert. This is now to climax in the people's encounter with God, mediated by Moses (19:9). Yet, for the first time, a warning note is struck. The encounter with God is a dangerous moment, and the people are both to be prepared for it and to be warned to keep a safe distance (19:10-25). It is a fascinating insight, both from the point of view of narrative and theology, that the encounter with God is expressed simply in the words of the ten commandments. There is a density of thought here which must be pondered. Despite thunderings and lightnings, trumpets and smoking mountain (20:18), there is no attempt to describe or portray the God who is encountered. There is God's statement: "I am the LORD your God" (20:2), and the fleshing out of this in terms of the human experience which the people have just been through, "who brought you out of the land of Egypt, out of the land of bondage." The commandments, which follow this statement, spell out what it implies: what it means for them that the LORD is their God (vv 3-7); what it means for them that they are God's people (vv 8-17). In these words, and in the life which they so succinctly circumscribe, Israel has met its God (cf., 20:22). The laws which follow in the Covenant Code (Exod 20:22-23:19) are a first spelling out of the lapidary commands of the decalogue.

An understanding of what all this is about is given in 23:20-33. These are not conditions for establishing a relationship with God. They are guidance for living within the relationship with God that has already been established by God's action—action begun in the call of Abraham, action climaxed in the deliverance from Egypt, action continued in the desert. They are commands to be observed in order that the favorable action of God may continue to be experienced in Israel, that Israel may be protected from its own fragility. They are neglected at Israel's peril (cf., 23:20-22, 33).

The first phase of this Sinai experience concludes with the covenantal sacrifice and the covenantal meal (24:1-11). God's words are presented to the people, and the people's acceptance of them is made explicit (v 3). What has been said in word is then symbolized in the ritual of sacrifice and meal.

A second phase in the narrative opens with Moses' ascent of the mountain again (24:12-18). Vv 12-15a prepare the way for the later stories of Exodus 32-34; there is no mention of the "tables of stone" until 31:18. For six chapters, the text is concerned with the exact details of the sanctuary to be constructed according to the heavenly model shown to Moses, in order that God may dwell in the midst of Israel (25:8-9). A further six chapters will describe, in equal detail, the exact compliance with all of these instructions (Exodus 35-40; note that in the execution of the commands, the tent is made first, before the sacred articles it is to house). The essential concern here is the way in which God is to be present to the people.

God's presence to the people, up till now, has been manifest through appearances—to the ancestors, to Moses at the burning bush, and, above all, to Moses and the people at Sinai. Up till now, there has been no continuous presence of God to the people.

The sanctuary of Exodus 25-40 is to change all that. It brings together the two theologies of presence and appearance. The sanctuary is where God will *dwell* in their midst (25:8); from above the ark, God will *meet* with Moses and speak with him (25:22). Basically, the tent tradition in Israel was one of meeting, of appearance, and the ark tradition in Israel one of presence. Here these two traditions, these two ways of symbolizing contact with God, are brought together to securely assure God's presence.[3] The presence of God cannot be controlled by creatures, nor are its circumstances a matter for human design. Hence the minute instructions from God about every detail of this desert tent-sanctuary (chaps. 25-30). The presence of God cannot be taken lightly; the ritual surrounding it is treated with immense seriousness. Hence the equally detailed account of the carrying out of God's instructions (chaps. 35-40). The whole proceeding reaches its climax when the cloud covers the tent and the glory of God fills the tabernacle (40:34-35), and God is present to Israel in their continuing journey, wherever they go (40:36-38). (Note the care with which Israel's theologians avoid imaging God's presence in too anthropomorphic a fashion; it is the cloud and the glory which symbolize the presence of God.)

Sandwiched between God's instructions for the sanctuary and Israel's compliance with them, there is the episode of the golden calf (Exodus 32-34). It is an extraordinary episode, which any rightminded narrators, with half a sense of national honor, would have omitted. It is a sign of the theological seriousness of Israel's narrative traditions that it has been retained. For it is indeed extraordinary. Israel is fresh out of Egypt, with its needs cared for in its wandering; this great act of deliverance is only a couple of months in the past. Israel has met its God at Sinai in awe-inspiring spectacle and mighty word. Israel's leader is still on the mountain, in receipt of God's revelation. And Israel's narrators take this moment to portray the people leaping joyously into apostasy. As theology through narrative, it can only signify two things: the fragility of belief in the God of Israel; the seductive power of other understandings of the world.

---

[3]For aspects of these traditions, see Samuel Terrien, *The Elusive Presence: Toward a New Biblical Theology* (Religious Perspectives 26; San Francisco: Harper & Row, 1978).

The name of Israel's God, the LORD (YHWH),[4] names a specific experience and understanding of the transcendent being of God. The other names given to the divine, whether Baal or Yam, Anat or Astarte, or many others, evoke other understandings of God and world. The experience of the LORD, the God of Israel, is a fragile one, delicate in its drawing of the human experience toward the limit of its comprehension. There are always in life elements more tangible, more powerfully present to the senses, more immediately attractive, and apparently more life-giving. The movement of the spirit is always deep within the human being, easily stilled, easily ignored, at least for a time. Yet it alone gives life; what deviates from it, leads toward death and the denial of life. This Israel knew and remembered.

What sense, then, do these chapters make in their present place? Are they there simply because that is how and when it happened? Do they have anything to contribute to the overall narrative structure of the Pentateuch? They combine quite a number of traditions. The tent of meeting, for example, is already in use (33:7-11). It would seem that these traditions, clustered around the episode of the golden calf, have been placed here as the most appropriate place for them, despite the tensions with the surrounding text on the sanctuary.

However, as is so often the case, such a view fails to reckon with the subtlety of the Hebrew narrators. We have already seen that the encounter with God is fraught with danger. The mountain of Sinai was put out of bounds, under penalty of death (19:10-25). It is precisely this threat of death which permeates the traditions of Exodus 32-34. The apostasy of the golden calf threatens to bring the annihilation of Israel in its train: "Now therefore let me alone, that my wrath may burn hot against them and I may consume them; but of you I will make a great nation" (32:10). The echo of Gen 12:2a is unmistakable; not only their present existence, but a whole sweep of their history is under threat. Only

---

[4]While Yahweh is used as the name for God in the *Jerusalem Bible* and elsewhere, the practice is offensive to many Jews and those who respect the Jewish tradition of the unpronounceable name of God; it also forces an undesirable separation from the usage of the New Testament which follows the Septuagint, using *kyrios*, the Lord, to represent the name of God. From the point of view of inclusive language, "the Lord" is unsatisfactory; where it cannot be avoided, small capitals—the LORD—will be used, as in the *RSV*, to indicate that it is substituting for the personal name.

Moses' intercession averts this fate (32:11-14). Extermination is also threatened through a plague (32:33-35). And then, turning toward the future, God refuses to go up with the people into the promised land, "lest I consume you in the way" (33:3); since, "if for a single moment I should go up among you, I would consume you" (33:5). In a remarkable dialogue, Moses again intercedes: God's presence is to go with the people and give them rest; this presence of God's will set them apart from all other people on the face of the earth (33:14-16). The culmination comes with Moses' prayer, after he has been granted a unique personal vision of God. He prays: "if now I have found favor in thy sight, O Lord, let the Lord, I pray thee, *go in the midst of us,* although it is a stiff-necked people; and pardon our iniquity and our sin, and take us for thy inheritance" (34:9). Again, a degree of tolerance is established between the all-holy God and the sinful fragility of God's creatures. God's steadfast love is stronger than the creatures' iniquity and transgression and sin (cf., 34:7). Given the context, it is natural that the commandments Moses brings down the mountain with him this time are concerned, almost exclusively, with matters of worship and cult (34:11-28).

Just as immediately after the exodus, Israel's potential for self-destruction is brought to the fore, so here, immediately after the great experience of God's revelation at Sinai, Israel's potential for self-destructive apostasy is brought under scrutiny. The presence of God, so soon to be made real in Israel's midst through the tent-sanctuary, is awesome and mysterious, a sign of special favor and protection, yet in some strange way, also possessed of a menacing potential for bringing death. Israel has encountered this menace and survived. By Moses' intercession, God will be present in the midst of this stiff-necked people, pardoning iniquity and sin, and taking this people for God's own inheritance. And the commandments for the proper worship of God and sanctification of life—the so-called "ritual decalogue"—give guidance to Israel as to how to live in harmony with this God.

So the sanctuary is built. The cloud covers the tent instead of the mountain. The glory of God, previously settled on Mount Sinai, as a devouring fire on the top of the mountain (Exod 24:16-17), now fills the tent-tabernacle (40:34-35). The continued journey of God with Israel is foreshadowed: when the cloud was taken up from over the tabernacle, the people went forward;

when the cloud stayed put, the people stayed put; and God was present to them, guiding them throughout all their journeys (40:36-38). The second phase of the Sinai narrative is complete.

Before Israel's journey can be resumed, a third phase is still to be dealt with. The presence of God in their midst has consequences for Israel. In manifold ways, humankind relates to God. With the special closeness of God to Israel, expressed now by God's presence in their midst, this relationship must be regulated with special care. So the regulations for offerings and sacrifices are laid down (Leviticus 1-7). Once they have been promulgated, it is possible to consecrate the sanctuary and its ministers, with all the offerings and sacrifices involved in that celebration (Leviticus 8-10).

Once again, the theme of the menace of death comes to the fore. First for Aaron and his sons. Their ordination ceremony is to be performed as charged—"lest you die" (Lev 8:35). Then the threat becomes actuality for Nadab and Abihu, who breached the regulations, offering unholy fire—"and they died before the LORD" (Lev 10:1-2). The mortal peril remains (10:6-7). Then one of the primary priestly tasks is spelled out for Aaron: to distinguish between the holy and the common, and between the unclean and the clean; and to teach the people of Israel all the statutes of God (10:8-11). These laws follow in two great collections: the laws of impurity (Leviticus 11-16), and the laws of holiness (Leviticus 17-26). A key theme runs through these laws: "You shall therefore be holy, for I am holy" (11:45). With the holiness of God constantly in its midst, Israel must also be holy. And the implications of this holiness are spelled out in almost embarrassingly intimate detail. The significance of this minute priestly regulation of so many spheres of life into holy and profane, clean and unclean, needs deeper consideration than we are able to give it here.[5] In our context, it is enough to see how they fit into the

---

[5]A valuable treatment is given in Mary Douglas, *Purity and Danger: An Analysis of Concepts of Pollution and Taboo* (New York: Praeger, 1966). Since cultural condescension and prejudice are rife in this area, some selected quotations may be helpful. "So primitive religious fear, . . . seems to be a false trail for understanding these religions" (p. 2). "In this sense I emphatically deny that a proliferation of ideas about purity and contagion imply a rigid mental outlook or rigid social institutions" (p. 5). "Even if some of Moses's dietary rules were hygienically beneficial it is a pity to treat him as an enlightened public health administrator, rather than as a spiritual leader" (p. 29). "The more deeply we go into this

context of the narrative of the Pentateuch. They follow on the establishment of the relationship with God and the establishment of God's presence to the people. They are for the protection of the people, "lest they die in their uncleanness by defiling my tabernacle that is in their midst" (Lev 15:31). Once again, Israel's fragility is catered for. There will be a ceremony of atonement, to atone for the uncleannesses of the people, so that the tent is able to abide in their midst (Leviticus 16; esp. v 16, also vv 1-2, 13).

This concern for the life-and-death seriousness of the holiness of Israel is very strong in the collection of laws in Leviticus 17-26. In its existence in freedom and in its relationship with God, Israel has been given a gift which brings life. It is a precious gift, but it is held in fragile vessels. It is enshrined in a way of life which is not that of Egypt or Canaan (Lev 18:1-5). The fragility of that way of life is a constant threat to the gift, and to the life which it brings. Hence observance of the laws which ensure the continuance of that way of life is utterly vital to Israel; it is a matter, literally, of life and death. Since breach of the law threatens to erode the life of the people, lawbreakers shall be cut off from among the people (e.g. Lev 17:4, 9, 10, 14; 18:29; 19:8; 20:17, 18; 22:3); the death penalty shall be inflicted (e.g. Lev 20:2-6, 9-16; 21:9; 24:16, 17, 21). Counterbalancing this negative side, there is the even more emphatic stress on the positive. Israel is to be holy as its God is holy. The quality of the God who brought Israel out from Egypt is a quality that is to inhere in Israel itself. It recurs again and again, among the vast diversity of the laws—from sexual disorder to social security—bringing a unity of conception to them all: the holiness required of Israel because of the encounter with God (e.g.

---

and similar rules, the more obvious it becomes that we are studying symbolic systems" (p. 34). "We can conclude that holiness is exemplified by completeness. Holiness requires that individuals shall conform to the class to which they belong. And holiness requires that different classes of things shall not be confused" (p. 53). "But in general the underlying principle of cleanness in animals is that they shall conform fully to their class. Those species are unclean which are imperfect members of their class, or whose class itself confounds the general scheme of the world" (p. 55). "If the proposed interpretation of the forbidden animals is correct, the dietary laws would have been like signs which at every turn inspired meditation on the oneness, purity and completeness of God. By rules of avoidance holiness was given a physical expression in every encounter with the animal kingdom and at every meal" (p. 57). "It is not too much to say that ritual is more to society than words are to thought" (p. 62).

Lev 19:2, 10, 11, 14, 16, 18, 25, 28, 30, 31, 32, 34, 36, 37; 20:7, 8, 24, 26; 21:12, 15, 23; 22:8, 9, 16, 30, 31, 32-33; 23:22, 43; 24:22; 25:17, 38,55; 26:13, 44-45).

The concern is one that is foreign to modern society. It is one that is clearly of critical importance to Israel. It will be very difficult for us to understand it, and to reconcile it with the God of Israel who guides, protects, and cares for the people, who says, "I bore you on eagles' wings and brought you to myself" (Exod 19:4). It is important to see how these extensive legal prescriptions bring to a close the establishment of God's relationship to the people at Sinai. God has delivered Israel, bringing them out of Egypt into freedom. Despite their human fragility, God's relationship has been established with them. Despite their fragility, God's presence has been established in their midst, to be with them in their journeying. And for the maintenance of that presence, safe and secure, for the maintenance of the life with which they have been gifted, these detailed prescriptions have been given them. Israel has become a people, with their freedom, with their God, with their charter for the preservation of that life in freedom. They are now ready to pursue their journey.

The next stage of the narrative, then, is the move from Sinai. It is carefully prepared, and the preparation again mirrors the concern for the holiness of the presence of God in the midst of the people. The census of the people is taken, beginning with Reuben, Israel's first-born (Num 1:20). The people are then arranged in travelling order, with the camp of Judah leading off toward the east and the promised land (Num 2:3). In the center of this great journeying procession, there is the presence of God in the tent of meeting (Num 2:17), surrounded by the Levites, as a protective buffer for the rest of the people (Num 1:51-53). When all of the last traditions which need to be gathered in under the Sinai rubric have been recounted, the preparations are complete and the people, and the narrative, are ready to move on. Something of the character of this journey is brought out by one of the final preparatory traditions (Num 9:15-23). It repeats what was said at Exod 40:34-38. This is one way of letting us know, narratively, that the intervening thirty-five chapters have been an aside in the story; they have not advanced its plot. They have merely specified the conditions under which it is possible for God to be present in the midst of Israel, to go with God's people in a way that makes them distinct from all other peoples (Exod 33:16). It is now time for that journey to be resumed.

Yet Num 9:15-23 goes beyond what was said at the end of Exodus. Again, it has something to do with the nature of this journey. It is under God's control and guidance; that is clear. "At the command of the LORD the people of Israel set out, and at the command of the LORD they encamped" (Num 9:18). That was also present in Exod 40:36-37. It is of particular interest that here, just before the journey is resumed, there is great emphasis on the aspect of waiting and not journeying. Vv 17-18a are evenhanded. The first sign of the emphasis occurs with v 18b: "as long as the cloud rested over the tabernacle, they remained in camp." V 18a is echoed again in v 23. In between, the emphasis is on Israel's waiting for its God. Whether the cloud remained over the tabernacle many days (v 19), a few days (v 20), overnight or a day and a night (v 21), a couple of days, a month, or a longer time (v 22), as long as the cloud remained over the tabernacle, the people of Israel stayed put and did not set out. We are not initiated into the inner meaning of these directions. We are simply left with the awareness that there is something special about this journey, that the initiative in it is with God, and that it can be expected to involve a considerable amount of waiting for God. The emphasis on waiting is too extensive to be anything other than intentional. Perhaps it is Israel's remembrance of this journey in particular that calls forth this measured emphasis on waiting for God; perhaps it is Israel's understanding of this journey as symbolic and expressive of the human journey through life; more probably it reflects the faith and hope of exiled Israel.

The departure is very formally narrated, according to the instructions of Numbers 2. The standard of Judah takes the lead (10:14), followed by the standards of Reuben (v 18), and Ephraim (22), while the standard of Dan brings up the rear (v 25). The order of march seems more linear than the four-points-of-the-compass plan of Numbers 2. Having seen the significance of Num 9:15-23, we may note the presence of other traditions as well. While the guidance from God has been emphasized, it is worth noting that Moses is shown hiring Hobab as a guide in the wilderness: "you will serve as eyes for us" (Num 10:29-32). Theology and reality intermesh. The issue of divine guidance is taken up a second time. Before, it was in terms of the tabernacle;

now it is expressed in terms of the ark of the covenant, not travelling in Israel's midst but going before them (10:33-36). These various traditions can be harmonized, but they should not be. Like so much else in this great complex of traditions, it is a matter of retaining different ways of expressing reality in language and symbol.

It is also in the little passage on the hiring of Hobab that the destination of the journey is mentioned again. Little has been said since Exod 3:8. Now it is described simply as: "the place of which the LORD said, 'I will give it to you'. . . . for the LORD has promised good to Israel" (Num 10:29). Such is to be the journey's end.

After all of this splendid preparation, the stories which follow come as a total surprise. Woven together from the store of Israel's tradition, they plunge Israel straight back into the depths of failure. Failure and rebellion are piled on murmuring and failure. Yet through it all, Israel survives and God provides. For all that, the narrative import of these stories cannot be passed over.

First, there are the complaints at Taberah, and "the fire of the LORD burned among them" (Num 11:1-3). There is the longing of some of the people to return to Egypt (11:4-6), and "the anger of the LORD blazed hotly" (11:10). Even the theme of the destructive burden of office, raised in Exodus 18, returns again here (11:11-17, 24-30). The people demand meat, and they are given the quails, but with a price to pay in divine anger (11:33).

Next, there is another in the series of challenges to Moses' leadership. It is mounted by Miriam and Aaron, and is put down in dramatic fashion (Numbers 12).

Then the episode of the spying out of the land brings together failures of a number of kinds. There is faintness of heart, lack of courage, lack of faith (Num 13:25-33). Once more, the people want to go back into the servitude of Egypt, and the proposal is mooted to do just that (14:1-4). Moses' intercession again saves the people from destruction (14:10b-19). His intercession is heard, but the wilderness generation comes under sentence of death (14:20-23). The whole experience thus far is summed up as disobedient revolt: "(they) have put me to the proof these ten times and have not hearkened to my voice" (v 22). "Ten times" is surely intended to suggest totality. The narrative dwells on the "dead bodies" which shall lie in the wilderness (14:26-35). This is storytelling with a theological point to it, and it is highly unlikely that the point is restricted simply to the desert generation.

The episode of the spies ends with a shift from faintness of heart to foolhardy and disobedient rashness. The people decide to conquer the land on their own initiative—and they fail (14:39-45).

Numbers 15 presents sacrificial regulations, and regulations for atoning for unwitting sin. At first sight, they seem hugely out of place. But they relate to the time "when you come into the land you are to inherit, which I give you" (15:2), so they contain seeds of hope. And they deal with forgiveness of sin, so that, for all the failure, God's work with Israel goes on, and the journey can go on. But infringement of the sabbath brings death (15:32-36), and the commandments are recalled to preserve Israel's holiness (15:37-41). It is a brief summary of the whole of the Leviticus legislation (cf., v 41).

Even after this, failure and rebellion are still the order of the day, again over the issue of the leadership. The rebels, Korah and Dathan and Abiram, are either swallowed up by the earth (Num 16:31-33) or consumed by divine fire (16:35). The lesson is not learned. The rebellion continues (16:41), and it brings the threat of divine destruction once again (16:45). It is only averted through the intervention of Moses and Aaron.

The next chapters (Numbers 17-19) are a further example of the portrayal of God's coming to terms with human fragility and sinfulness. The issue of priestly leadership is settled (Num 17). Instructions are given for this priestly caste and their privileges prescribed (Num 18). The point of it all is "that there be wrath no more upon the the people of Israel" (18:5). Atonement for sin is regulated (Num 19:1-10), and regulations are also given for coping with the presence of death (19:11-22).

The seeds of hope fail to bear fruit. Murmuring breaks out again, and with it the rejection of life (Num 20:2-5). The issue is once more the absence of water, as at the outset. Moses sweetened water at Marah (Exod 15:22-25). At Rephidim, he produced water from the rock, earning the place the name of Massah/Meribah (Exod 17:1-8). Here, now at Kadesh, Moses produces water from the rock, and mysteriously incurs the condemnation which will lead to his own death outside the promised land (Num 20:2-13). This failure is followed by the rebuff at the hands of the king of Edom (20:14-21). Then, after the priestly succession has been assured, the death of Aaron brings on a sense of approaching end (20:22-29).

These have been stories of almost unmitigated failure. The only bright spots have come from Moses' intercession, and from the regulations which should enable Israel's relationship with God to continue, despite their failures. Beyond that, it has been an unhappy history.

The tide turns, for once, with a victory over the king of Arad (Num 21:1-3). Momentarily, failure rears its head again (21:4-9). Finally, with the approaching closeness of the promised land, Israel has success: first Sihon, then Og, are defeated (21:10-35). These are narrative prerequisites for the story of Balaam (Numbers 22-24).

The Balaam stories are truly remarkable, and theologically very weighty. Balaam is a non-Israelite prophet, from Pethor, "which is near the River (Euphrates), in the land of Amaw (Syria)" (Num 22:5). Balaam is hired to curse Israel, since he has the reputation of being a powerful operator: "for I know that he whom you bless is blessed, and he whom you curse is cursed" (22:6). However, the stories lay immense emphasis on the fact that Balaam can only speak the word that God gives him to speak. And he speaks blessing over Israel. His prophecies conclude with a promise of future hope.

> I see him, but not now;
>> I behold him, but not nigh:
> a star shall come forth out of Jacob,
>> and a scepter shall rise out of Israel;
> It shall crush the forehead of Moab,
>> and break down all the sons of Sheth. (Num 24:17)

The reference is understood to be to David. It brings hope to Israel that the promise, under which its existence began, will be fulfilled. The blessing, present in the call to Abraham, has not been cancelled by all the failure and disobedience of this desert generation—the very generation which had most intimately experienced the delivering and freeing power of God. The possibility of blessing is still with Israel: "Blessed be every one who blesses you, and cursed be every one who curses you" (Num 24:9; cf., Gen 12:3a). The blessing has not been annulled, not for Israel and, at least within that, not for others. But it lies in the future, not now and not nigh (Num 24:17). (We may also note that the blessing is not evident for Moab and Sheth. Here is a case where the tradition does not itself carry the full message which the Yahwist's redaction added to it. "All the families of the earth" are not in view here. It is to the credit of the Yahwist that they come into view at all.)

For all of the hope and blessing, Israel is once again plunged into apostasy. "So Israel yoked himself to the Baal of Peor" (Num 25:3). Here, in Moab, on the brink of the promised land, the deadly conflict with the force of Baal is begun. On this occasion, it costs the chiefs of the people their lives (25:4-5). It will become a major threat to Israel's life in the land.

At this point, a number of traditions are gathered together which concern the end of the journey (Numbers 26-36). Israel has arrived at the border of the promised land. From one point of view, Israel's journey is at an end. From another point of view, the journey has only just begun. It is a journey which cannot end in apostasy and failure. Balaam has pointed to the future hope and blessing. The last activities of Moses' life are dedicated to assuring that hope and that blessing (Deuteromony).

The book of Deuteronomy is presented as a series of speeches by Moses, on the last day or days of his life. They are addressed to all Israel, just across the Jordan from the promised land. They constitute Moses' testamentary activity, setting Israel's house in order before death takes him from them (cf., Genesis 49, for the portrayal of similar activity on Jacob's part, at a different stage in Israel's story).

Deuteronomy begins with a historical retrospect, tracing Israel's journey from Sinai to "the valley opposite Beth-peor." The goal of the journey is clear: the land promised to the patriarchs and their descendants (Deut 1:7-8). Surprisingly, after the command to leave Sinai, the very first passage returns to the theme of the overwhelming burden of Moses' office, in view of Israel's constant conflict: "how can I bear alone the weight and burden of you and your strife?" (1:12; cf., previously Exod 18:13-26; Num 11:10-30). Then the episode of Numbers 13-14 is recounted: the failure of nerve before the report of the promised land, and the ill-fated attempt to conquer the land on their own (1:19-45). It accounts for the death of the desert generation, all the men of war involved in this failure of nerve (2:14-16). There is peaceful passage through the territory of Esau and Moab, and military victory over Sihon and Og, forerunners of the victories to come (3:21-22). All this has brought Israel to "the valley opposite Beth-peor" (3:29). The recall of the apostasy of Beth-peor provides an opportunity for an exposition of deuteronomic theology: keeping the commandments brings life; departure from them brings death (4:1-4).

The law is to follow immediately: the decalogue (Deut 5:1-21), the Shema (6:4-9), and then the deuteronomic code (chaps. 12-26). This introductory exhortation in chap. 4 places great weight on the observance of the commandments: it will be Israel's wisdom and understanding (4:6); it will ensure for Israel that all goes well (4:40). The exhortation ends on the theme of God's elective love. It is a very significant one, because it can all too easily be overwhelmed by the emphasis on the keeping of the commandments as source of life. But God's love, God's election and action on behalf of the chosen people, precedes the giving of the commandments and all that follows from them. God took Israel from the midst of another nation (4:34); God communicated with them (4:36). And this was because God loved their fathers and chose their descendants after them (4:37). Therefore the commandments are to be observed, so that the favor God has already bestowed may be preserved (4:39-40; cf., 7:6-11).

When we look back over all the history of failure, between the Exodus and Sinai, at Sinai itself, during the journey onwards from Sinai, the significance of Moses' address becomes apparent. This history of failure is not forgotten; but it does not prevent Israel from making a new beginning. Symbolized by the apostasy at Beth-peor, it stands for Israel as a warning. Despite it all, Moses can still speak to the future. Despite it all, Israel's God is still so near (Deut 4:7). Despite it all, Israel has the incredible gift of the law (4:8). Life, therefore, lies before Israel. These speeches of Moses, and the laws they propose, have only one purpose: to enable Israel to choose life and good, and to avoid death and evil (cf., Deut 30:15-20). All the failures of the desert generation, privileged as they were, have not destroyed God's relationship with Israel. What was true at Sinai is still true here: Israel is a people loved by God (4:32-40). A generation of sin and rebellion has not changed that. What was offered at Sinai to Israel, and to Abraham long before that, is still offered now. It is a very significant reflection on the stories of the desert generation.

The history of failure is not forgotten, but it does not prevent Israel from making a new beginning. The new beginning starts with the new rehearsal of the decalogue. The sense of continuity-in-discontinuity is clear: "Not with our fathers did the LORD make this covenant, but with us who are all of us here alive this day" (Deut 5:3). The sin of the fathers has not annulled God's relationship with God's people; it is here taken as valid for those who, at the time, were too young to bear the responsibility for sin. And it will be equally valid for those in generations and centuries to come.

The theme of the danger constituted by the closeness of the presence of God is still there (Deut 5:23-27). Here it is invoked as a motivation for observation of the commandments (5:28-29). And the deuteronomic understanding of the purpose of the law is again made clear: "that you may live, and that it may go well with you, and that you may live long in the land which you shall possess" (5:33).

This standard deuteronomic language can be, and often is heard as saying: if you keep the law, then life and prosperity will be given you as reward. Such an interpretation does the Deuteronomists injustice. God's love and purpose for Israel have been made clear. Given proper order within the people, God's love will bring about God's purpose for the people. The law is to ensure the maintenance of that proper order, so that God's love may have its purposed effect. Any view which would deny the importance of that proper order in human affairs denies the seriousness of human life and misconstrues the manner of God's action in this world. To insist on the observance of the law, as the condition which maintains or creates a situation where God's action can be effective, is not to make of the law a means of winning God's favor or love. The later problems of the New Testament generations should not be imported into Deuteronomy. At the same time, the potential in the deuteronomic rhetoric for misunderstanding ought not be overlooked.

The same understanding of the law and its purpose is reiterated (Deut 6:1-3), as an introduction to the Shema: "Hear O Israel, the LORD our God is one LORD; and you shall love the LORD your God with all your heart, and with all your soul, and with all your might"—and this you shall cherish and teach, inside your house and outside; to conclude each day and to begin it, and so throughout the livelong day; bound to your hand, and so to all you do; placed between your eyes, and so before you in all that you see and think (6:4-9). It is the most incredible internalization of the law and, at the same time, extension of it to include the totality of human activity. The liturgical answer to the child's question keeps the meaning of this law constantly before the community (6:20-25); "for our good always, that he might preserve us alive, as at this day" (v 24). Death, disaster, and failure form a constant threat, engendered by disorder when right order breaks down. The law is a bulwark against that threat. "And it will be righteousness (şĕdāqâ = being in the enlivening web of right relationships) for us, if we are careful to do all this commandment before the LORD our God, as he has commanded us" (v 25).

In Deut 7:6-11, there is one of the beautiful Old Testament passages on divine grace. "You are a people holy to the LORD your God; the LORD your God has chosen you to be a people for his own possession ... not because you were more in number than any other people ... for you were the fewest of all peoples; but it is because the LORD loves you, and is keeping the oath which he swore to your fathers" (7:6-8). The expression of that love may echo treaty fidelity rather than romantic attachment, but it is based not on the might of Israel but on their powerlessness. It is grace. Yet it is juxtaposed with other elements of the rhetoric of the deuteronomic preacher: Israel's God is "the faithful God who keeps covenant and steadfast love with those who love him and keep his commandments, to a thousand generations, and requites to their face those who hate him, by destroying them" (vv 9-10). This can be personalized as the vengeful and destroying God, even if set within the formulas of treaty language; it can also be understood as bringing to expression the experience of the destructive and destroying force of sin and evil.

What preceded these verses, however, is one of the classic sources for those who fear or despise the God of the Old Testament (i.e., Deut 7:1-5). The command is indeed horrendous: "you must utterly destroy them; you shall make no covenant with them, and show no mercy to them" (v 2). The Yahwist's hope of blessing for "all the families of the earth" is far away. This is the ban, the annihilating of all that is pagan. The shudders and revulsion evoked demand an extensive study, which is beyond our present scope. Two points, at least, need to be made. Firstly, the motivation for it: "For they would turn away your sons from following me, to serve other gods" (v 4). Israel has been given a very special gift, and contamination from the peoples in their midst and around them would destroy that gift—and did, indeed, destroy it in its form of free and independent national survival. What is at stake, therefore, is a grave and vital issue: self-preservation. Secondly, its use in Israel's literature is very largely a theological construct. By this, I mean a reflection on the contaminating seeds of destruction sown in Israel's midst, and a conclusion drawn as to what they should have done about them. There is scarcely a story that gives clear and unequivocal evidence of any historical carrying out of the ban. The practice existed; Israel may have done it.[6] But the stories we have demonstrate theological tendencies rather than historical accuracy. It may be that, to the preachers of the seventh century, looking back over centuries of failure in faith, it might have seemed an obvious conclusion that the ban should have been practised at the beginning. The stories, such as Achan at Jericho (Joshua 7) and Samuel, Saul, and Agag (1 Samuel 15), could have given rise to the belief that this had indeed been commanded. It may be that it was also an expression of the life and death quality of faith. As martyrs have always known, faith is to be preserved at all costs, even the cost of death. The ban, placing the cost on others, may be a most radical expression of this quality; it is certainly one of the most unfortunate.

These chapters which precede the deuteronomic law code of chaps. 12-26, give expression to various theologies providing motivation for keeping the law and living by it. So the desert period can become symbolic for Israel: it was a time of testing, to know what was in Israel's heart (Deut 8:2). So, too, the manna becomes symbolic of the human condition, life lived not out of human power alone but out of the gift of God's grace (8:3). "As a

---

[6]There is a reference to the practice, using the same word *herem* in the Moabite Stone, c. 830. Mesha, king of Moab, says in his inscription: "And Chemosh said to me, 'Go, take Nebo from Israel?' So I went by night and fought against it from the break of dawn until noon, taking it and slaying all, seven thousand men, boys, women, girls and maid-servants, for I had *devoted them to destruction* for (the god) Ashtar-Chemosh" (*ANET*, 320, emphasis mine). For something of the context, see 2 Kings 3.

man disciplines his son, the LORD your God disciplines you" (8:5). A highly anthropomorphic theology, and one we may not find attractive. Yet, if its expression is refined, it can echo much of the reality of human life; in the created order, much of the time, our errors tend to cause us pain, and what we do well tends to heighten the quality of our lives. The theme of God's power undergirding human life returns: "Beware lest you say in your heart, 'My power and the might of my hand have gotten me this wealth.' You shall remember the LORD your God, for it is he who gives you power to get wealth. And if you forget the LORD your God and go after other gods ... I solemnly warn you this day that you shall surely perish" (8:17-19). A variant of this theology appears in 9:4-5.

The story of the desert generation is then laid out before Israel as a model for their understanding of their existence, as symbol for the generation still to come (Deut 9:6-10:22). The land is not given Israel because of their righteousness, "for you are a stubborn people" (9:6). Says Moses, "You have been rebellious against the LORD from the day that I knew you" (9:24). This stubbornness and rebelliousness—surely not Israel's prerogative, but a mark of the human condition—is a constant threat to Israel's existence, just as the force of evil is a constant threat to human existence. Throughout this powerful passage, this theme is constantly expressed in terms of God's anger being provoked to the point where God is ready to destroy Israel (cf., 9:8, 14, 19, 20, 25, 26, 28); only Moses' repeated intercession spared Israel from this fate (9:18-19, 20, 25-29; 10:10).

How, then, is Israel to escape this fate? "And now, Israel, what does the LORD your God require of you, but to fear the LORD your God, to walk in all his ways, to love him, to serve the LORD your God with all your heart and with all your soul, and to keep the commandments and statutes of the LORD which I command you this day for your good?" (Deut 10:12-13). It is the law, then, that is Israel's protection; its observance is their guarantee of life. The wisdom of the law makes this a statement in considerable conformity with much of the reality of existence. It is also filled out theologically. Existence is wholly supported by God, and the reality of God is awesome. "The LORD your God is God of gods and LORD of lords, the great, the mighty, and the terrible God, who is not partial and takes no bribe" (10:17). When the awesome reality of God is reckoned with, the law is Israel's charter which will give them continued life in their relationship with their God.

These introductory chapters to the final rehearsal of the law conclude with the presentation of that life as available to Israel in their now (Deut 11:26-32). This day, blessing and curse are set before them (v 26). This is the language of the international treaties of the day: observance brings blessing; violation incurs curse. It is a theology expressed in the language of the legal structures and international diplomacy of its time. Like any language, it requires interpretation. What it seeks to make clear is that the choice of life remains open to Israel. The desert generation, the constitutive generation of the nation Israel, has died in the desert (cf., Num 26:63-65; 32:13-15; Deut 2:14-16; 5:3). The cost of disobedience is clear. The choice of life is still open.

The implications of that choice for life are spelled out in the laws of Deuteronomy 12-26. The code concludes with the ceremony of Deuteronomy 26. With it, Israel's choice is consummated.

> You have declared this day concerning the LORD
> that he is your God,
> and that you will walk in his ways, and keep
>   his statutes and his commandments
>   and his ordinances, and will obey his voice;
> and the LORD has declared this day concerning you
> that you are a people for his own possession,
>   as he has promised you,
> and that you are to keep all his commandments
> that he will set you high above all nations that he has made,
>   in praise and in fame and in honor,
> and that you shall be a people holy to the LORD
>   your God, as he has spoken. (Deut 26:16-19)[7]

---

[7]For careful treatment of the complexities of this passage—though without particular attention to whether the obedience functions as condition or consequence of the relationship—see N. Lohfink, "Dt 26, 17-19 und die 'Bundesformel,'" *ZKT* 91 (1969) 517-53 and D.J. McCarthy, *Treaty and Covenant* (new ed.; AnBib 21a; Rome: Biblical Institute, 1978) 182-87.

The blessings and curses follow, as in the international treaties (Deuteronomy 27-28). The emphasis is predominantly on curse, a sad commentary on the predilection of humankind to be motivated out of fear rather than led "with reins of kindness, with leading-strings of love" (Hos 11:4).

The theme of choice is put before Israel once more in Deut 30:15-20. It is prefixed by the claim that the law "is not too hard for you, neither is it far off" (v 11). "The word is very near you; it is in your mouth and in your heart, so that you can do it" (v 14). With that assurance, and Moses' exhortation to his people, "therefore choose life ... loving the LORD your God, obeying his voice and cleaving to him; for that means life to you and length of days" (vv 19-20), we may bring this review of the Pentateuch to a close.

Moses has set Israel's house in order. He has brought Israel through the perils of initial existence and can leave it on the verge of new life. The cycle, which was to serve as archetype and model for Israel in its subsequent generations, has been completed. Like a patriarch taking leave of his family, Moses takes leave of his people. There is his song (Deuteronomy 32); there is his blessing (Deuteronomy 33). He is permitted to view the promised land. He dies and is buried in an unknown grave. The leadership passes to Joshua. With Moses' passing an era has passed for Israel; there shall never be another like him (Deut 34:10-12). For Israel, the beginning is at an end.

The *Jerusalem Bible* has given a most unfortunately over-emphatic nuance to the translation of this important passage. Twice, in place of the "and" of the Hebrew, correctly rendered by the *RSV*, it translates "but only if." Thus God's commitment to Israel and Israel's commitment to God are both made explicitly conditional on the observance of the law. This is a regrettable injection of a translator's theology into a text which does not make such a condition explicit. The declarations of commitment have observance of the law associated with them as complementary. It is significant that there is no assertion here that the commitment will be void if the complementary obligations are not observed. The *NAB* slips in an equally unjustified "provided" in the second case (v 18). The nature of the link between commitment and commandment is not spelled out in the text and should not be imposed by the translator—above all in a text of such solemnity where every word is weighed.

In the same context, against the *Jerusalem Bible's* note, the following comment by Dennis McCarthy should be noted as much more representative of recent scholarship: "Covenant is not contract, as we have had occasion to repeat more than once. It is personal union pledged by symbol and/or oath. The relationship comes first" (ibid., 297).

Unity

Looking back over the trajectory of this survey, it seems to be clear that there is a sense in which the Pentateuch may reasonably be called a literary work. The combination of its sources has been carefully and artistically done. The additions made to the combined text have been intelligently and appropriately inserted. The resulting text has certain clear points of focus and unity. It has a beginning, a middle and an end. It begins with the story of humankind. It moves from there to the story of the ancestors of Israel, and after that, to the story of the constitutive generation of Israel. It concludes at the end of a journey and at the end of that constitutive generation. It makes a whole.

Furthermore, it seems that the final text is more than merely the sum of its sources. While, as we will see later, the central message of both the Yahwist and the Priestly Writer are quite strongly preserved, their combination and the addition of the great legal complexes have changed the nature of the work. The basic communication of the final text is worth careful study.

We can now return to the implications of our initial question: does it make sense and is it legitimate to speak of the final text of the Pentateuch as a literary work?[8] What is its meaning, what message does it communicate? When trying to answer these questions, we will need to bear in mind the limits and finite nature of our language, and the impossibility of identifying in single themes the immense and manifold richness of human experience which has been distilled, over the generations, into these texts. Interpretation can only point and highlight; in realms such as these, it cannot hope to be complete.

As we have just noted, it seems legitimate to speak of the Pentateuch as a literary entity. There is a unity of progression in the text, from beginning, through middle, to end. There is a unity of focus in its various stages, which gives coherence to the whole. There is even a certain unity of understanding

---

[8]An affirmative answer raises the further question: how has it happened that such an extraordinary collection should have ended up forming a literary entity? Since this involves deeper consideration of the Priestly Document and the Yahwist, it will be dealt with in chap. 4, "Reflection on Method in the Study of the Pentateuch."

which permeates it all. We can look, first, at these aspects of unity; then we can essay the task of interpretation.

There is a unity of progression, from one world, to one people, to one generation. The three stages are linked to one another, and the imbalance in the first is brought to equilibrium in the third. In the first stage, the world is brought into existence, not just the world as God's creation, but the world as we know and experience it, with all that human activity has added to distort the creator's art. In the second stage, the people of Israel is brought into existence, a family and a clan, existing among others, in Canaan, the land of their sojourning. In the third stage, from Egypt, this people is brought into national existence and into a life of independence and freedom. In this third stage, Israel is on a journey back toward the promised land, to be not a land of sojourning but their own land. The journey is incomplete at the end of Deuteronomy. Nevertheless, at the end of Deuteronomy, a thread of the narrative is complete and closure is possible.

The imbalance set up in the first stage (Gen 1-11) is between the goodness of creation, as it came from the hand of God, and the distortion suffered by God's handiwork as the result of human activity. God's creation was marked with blessing. After the flood, blessing is repeated. Yet humankind ends up scattered, separated, and alienated. That is the imbalance: humankind that was created, blessed, and found good, and that has been scattered abroad over the face of the earth and has left off building the city (Gen 11:8). God moves to restore equilibrium in the call of Abraham. For through Abraham, blessing is to be mediated to all the families of the earth. This concept of blessing survives fragilely alongside the close-to-internecine strife of the pairs of human relatives (i.e., Abraham and Lot, Isaac and Ishmael, Jacob and Esau, Joseph and his brothers). It disappears almost entirely with the rebellious murmuring of Israel in the wilderness, longing to turn back salvation history and return to Egypt. Yet in the book of Deuteronomy, an equilibrium is created in which Israel stands freely before the choice for life or death—with the exhortation to choose life.

There is another sense of progression, less closely linked to the narrative text, yet there all the same. It is the sense of God's growing closeness. In the beginning, God walked in the garden in the cool of the day, and, for the first time, the man and the woman—humanity's representatives—hid from God (Gen 3:8). From then on, the story of salvation is the story of "God's love seeking its lost company."[9] From the outset, people began "to call upon the name of the LORD" (Gen 4:26). But to Israel's ancestors, God was identified as "El Shaddai" (Gen 17:1; 35:11; 48:3; cf., 28:3; 43:14; and 49:25). These of course are from P, and so constitute only a thread within the total story; but they carry enough weight to be felt (for comparison, see Gen 28:13). To Moses, in Egypt at the moment of liberation, the name is made doubly special. For all the mystery of its meaning, there is obviously great weight attached to this revelation: "I am who I am. . . . Say this to the people of Israel, 'I AM has sent me to you.'. . . Say this to the people of Israel, 'the LORD, the God of your fathers, the God of Abraham, the God of Isaac, and the God of Jacob, has sent me to you': this is my name forever, and thus I am to be remembered throughout all generations" (Exod 3:14-15). In its own way, this connotes what is explicit in the P tradition: "I am the LORD [YHWH]. I appeared to Abraham, to Isaac, and to Jacob, as El Shaddai, but by my name the LORD [YHWH] I did not make myself known to them" (Exod 6:2-3). From the revelation of the name of God, the narrative moves to the presence of God to the people, and through them to all creation. That presence, at Sinai and in the sanctuary, is experienced as both saving and endangering. In narrative fashion, Israel is brought through the danger. By the end of Deuteronomy, the narrative has reached a certain balance. There is the mutuality of the declarations by Israel and by God (Deut 26:17-19); there is the ancient poem's assurance that God is at work in the world through Israel, God's people and allotted heritage.

> When the Most High gave to the nations their inheritance,
>   when he separated the sons of men,
> he fixed the bounds of the peoples
>   according to the number of the sons of Israel (*RSV,*
>   sons of God).

---

[9]The phrase is from C.S. Song, *Third Eye Theology: Theology in Formation in Asian Settings* (Maryknoll: Orbis, 1979) 64.

> For the LORD's portion is his people,
>> Jacob his allotted heritage.
> He found him in a desert land,
>> and in the howling waste of the wilderness;
> he encircled him, he cared for him,
>> he kept him as the apple of his eye. (Deut 32:8-10)

This is reinforced and rounded off by the entire blessing, with which Moses the man of God blessed the people of Israel before his death (Deuteronomy 33).

> Happy are you, O Israel! Who is like you,
>> a people saved by the LORD! (Deut 33:29)[10]

The unity of focus is threefold. At first there is the focus on one world, created, blessed, and fractured. Then there is the focus on one people, emerging in the midst of that fractured world. Finally, there is one generation, brought into freedom and enduring the formative experiences of a nation. There is a centering in this movement, which gives it an overall unity. The fractured world is in need; it no longer enjoys the blessing with which it began. The one people is called into being to be bearer of that blessing. The one generation gives to that people its foundational experience of God.

The unity of understanding is not easily expressed. Put most simply and most baldly, in twentieth-century language, the unity of understanding which helps bind the Pentateuch together is that of a God whose commitment endures, who is unconditionally loving. This is not to deny the portrayal of anger, threat, and punishment. It is a rocky relationship, but not a fragile one—the commitment is never withdrawn. In the mythic beginnings, despite the mystery of the flood, God's commitment to creation remains eternal (Gen 8:21-22; 9:8-17). Perhaps one may say that, in the strange grammar of narrative, the catastrophe of the flood and the change which it involved made possible an unconditional

---

[10]The last half of the verse, "Your enemies shall come fawning to you; and you shall tread upon their high places"(33:29b), has its focus on Israel alone and not on all creation. Looked at in the light of Gen 12:3, its quality may be transmuted.

commitment from the all-holy creator to the less-than-perfect creation. The call of Abraham is continued evidence of that commitment of God to "all the families of the earth" (Gen 12:1-3). The relationship of God to Abraham is fundamentally uncondi- tional, whether in his call or the covenants made with him (Genesis 15 and 17). In all of the bitterness and strife which runs through the stories of Abraham's descendants, the theme of blessing is never completely absent. There, Joseph has the last word, a summary of it all: "You meant evil against me; but God meant it for good, to bring it about that many people should be kept alive, as they are today" (Gen 50:20).

Seen in its entirety, not scrutinized in its individual episodes and stories, but looked at as a whole, even the third phase of the Pentateuch witnesses to God's unconditional commitment to Israel. There is law there in plenty, but it is not a condition of God's commitment to Israel. If it were, Israel would never have made it past Sinai (cf., Exodus 32). It is more exact to speak of the law as articulating the conditions which best permit God's overwhelming love to reach its full flowering and bear its best fruit among the people. Israel's first generation breaks with God again and again and again—before Sinai, at Sinai, after Sinai. While God's wrath may flare, God's faithful commitment remains. The very dialogues with Moses, in which God is portrayed as ready and willing to annul the commitment made to Israel, are themselves evidence that the commitment continued. Finally, Moses' speeches to Israel, in the book of Deuteronomy, explore the unresolvable paradox of unconditional love, on the part of God, and responsibility for human existence, on the part of Israel. What is paradox is not impossible: "The word is very near you; it is in your mouth and in your heart, so that you can do it" (Deut 30:14) and "The LORD your God will circumcise your heart and the heart of your offspring, so that you will love the LORD your God with all your heart and with all your soul, that you may live" (Deut 30:6).[11]

---

[11]These verses express, of course, two different theologies, tending toward different poles of the paradox. V 14 presumes that human existence can be lived responsibly; v 6, with the context of exile, assumes that fullness of human life can only come from God's gift.

The overarching and unifying understanding of God in the Pentateuch, then, is of a God of enduring and loving commitment. The actions of God in creation, after the flood, and in the call of Abraham, witness to God's love and have as their object the whole human race. After the call of Abraham, the actions of God within history witness to enduring love and commitment to Israel, as people of God's election. This election is initiated in the call of Abraham, in a context of blessing for all the families of the earth, so that the relationship of Israel to humankind can never be left out of consideration. What is experienced by Israel may be archetypal too for the experience of humanity.

Interpretation

The Pentateuch moves from the universal toward the particular. From the cosmic sweep of its creation account, it moves to the mythic originating moments of humankind, to a single people, to a single generation, even to a single individual—Moses, the representative figure of that generation. Yet there is also present a reverse movement, from inward to outward. The generation of the exodus and the desert is paradigmatic for Israel. They are the archetype and model for the experience of later Israel. Their experiences contain and foreshadow the destiny of Israel. Yet, since in Israel all the families of the earth are to find blessing, there is a sense in which Israel's experience of God is paradigmatic for humankind. The movement outward has rejoined the universal.

The Pentateuch is too rich to be encompassed by any single theme or any one pattern of interpretation. There is not only the movement from universal to particular and back to universal, which we have just traced. There are also threads which seem to explore in narrative the relationship between God's love and human responsibility in existence, the interplay of promised blessing with the bitter experience of human fragility and sin. One aspect of this can be traced through the thread of conflict in relationships. After the initial establishment of order and creation, the first couple come into conflict with God; Cain and Abel come into conflict with each other; Lamech comes into conflict with a wider circle; and the human race closes the circle by coming into conflict with God.

The flood is the resolution of this conflict, radically wiping the slate clean. Paradoxically, it leaves an apparently strengthened relationship to God. Yet it is ineffectual, insofar as humankind is once again in conflict with God, in the story of the tower of Babel.

At this point, the text moves from mythic to historical time, and the conflict is continued. It is present between Abraham and Lot, though to a relatively mild degree. Between Jacob and Esau, it is sporadic but potentially deadly. Between Joseph and his brothers, the conflict is deadly, but it leads eventually to life. It also leads to a qualitative change in the nature of the conflict portrayed. The very blessing of Israel brings Israel and Egypt into conflict.

The resolution of this conflict in Israel's favor by God leads to a further qualitative change. The conflict advances to the point where it is conflict between Israel and God. At this point, it picks up in history what the first couple portrayed in myth: the human condition of rebellious frailty in relationship with God. In this sense, Israel is paradigm for humanity.

The conflict begins to operate in the area of obedience and faith. It is explored in Exod 15:22-17:15. There is God's self-understanding: "I am the LORD, your healer" (15:26). This is developed in terms of law (cf., Exod 16:4, 28). There is question of death on Israel's lips, but it is only on Israel's lips. There is no sign of any corresponding threat from God. The question emerging out of this conflict is: "Is the LORD among us or not?" (Exod 17:7). The presence of God is manifest at Sinai, and law is given there. There the presence of God is made permanent among the people of Israel.

At this stage, there seems to be another qualitative shift. As God has drawn closer to Israel, a danger emerges. There is talk now of death for the people. It begins with the episode of the golden calf. It is continued in the stories of the murmuring in the wilderness. It is intensified by the motivation to be found in the legal complexes, which insist on observance, "lest you die," "lest God break out upon you." Israel and God are involved in a relationship which is not without conflict and has potential for death. Much of the law seems to be directed at survival through protection against the dangerous force in Israel's midst.

What reality of experience is being expressed here? Evil is certainly a power to be reckoned with. In the form of distrust, fear, selfishness, ruthlessness, ambition and greed, evil can be a widely pervasive force, corrupting the fabric of society. Holiness is also a force; it too can powerfully affect society. Among other things, it can be a challenge to complacency and mediocrity—and such a challenge can be deeply threatening. A vision abandoned is worse than no vision at all.

For Israel, there is immense benefit in the picture of life lived in close companionship with God. The abandonment of that vision and that life can only lead to a destructive level of materialism, at best, and, at worst, of cynicism and despair. The promise is always in tension with human fragility. When the promise is nearest to fulfillment, then the destructive and self-destructive forces of human evil are at their most dangerous. It is as though it were as natural to fear the demands of blessing as it is to fear those of intimacy.

The lesson of Israel's wilderness stories is of continued rejection and rebellion on the human side, and of continued sustained relationship on God's side. The resolution of this pattern of conflict comes with Moses' final discourse. The movement returns to the nature of the relationship between God and Israel and its implications for Israel. The deuteronomic law code has a much stronger social and community dimension than that of the cultic and liturgical laws. The deuteronomic insistence on blessing and curse puts clearly before Israel the choices it must inescapably make. And all the power of the deuteronomic rhetoric is bent toward bringing Israel to choose life. The ultimate resolution of the conflict between God and creature is a combination of the creature's recognition of God's free gift of love and of the creature's response in choosing life.

The archetypal or paradigmatic elements are very strong and too manifold to be more than touched on here. Israel in the desert is a paradigm for later Israel, and more broadly for life. Gifted with water and manna, they murmur and rebel. Graced with forgiveness time and time again, they fall back. They encounter a God who is not meek and mild, but capable of destructive anger. Yet pushed to the extreme limit, God's commitment to Israel stands. The God Israel encounters is not untouched by the happenings of human life. At its most severe, a generation dies in the desert, short of their goal. In responsibility for their existence, what they turn away from they cannot achieve. But their descendants are not prevented from it. "But your little ones, who you said would become a prey, I will bring in, and they shall know the land which you have despised" (Num 14:31). God's commitment is not broken by human fragility.

There is the experience of intimacy with God and of the danger in it. The intimacy of Sinai: "For what great nation is there that has a god so near to it as the LORD our God is to us" (Deut 4:7); "For ask now of the days that are past, . . . ask from one end of heaven to the other. . . . Did any people ever hear the voice of a god speaking out of the midst of the fire, as you have heard, and still live?" (Deut 4:32-33). The danger of it: "Now therefore let me alone, that my wrath may burn hot against them and I may consume them; but of you I will make a great nation" (Exod 32:10); "You are a stiff-necked people; if for a single moment I should go up among you, I would consume you" (Exod 34:5). Yet in the working of the narrative, as well as in the regulations of the liturgical law, this tension finds its reconciliation.

There is the experience of the journey, with its waiting for God (above all, Num 9:15-23). Whether for a day, two days, a few days, many days, a month, or longer time, when the cloud did not move, Israel did not move. "How long, O God, how long?" is an oft-heard, plaintive cry. In exile, Israel must often have asked: How long, O God, how long? And in life, one asks.

There is the experience of failure. Israel's narrators painted it with a heavy brush. Almost on the verge of the promised land, at Beth-peor, Israel commits apostasy and turns to the worship of Baal (Num 25:1-5; cf., Deut 3:29; 4:3, 46). While it brings its consequences in its train, it does not prevent Israel being brought into a situation where they can be challenged to choose life. God's unconditional love does not take away the consequences of choice in the dimensions of human life. But it keeps the option for life open always. It creates a context of assurance in which that choice is possible.

In the experience of failure, there is also the reality of fear. Human fragility, individual and social, is cause for fear. Order seems fragile against the threat of disorder. The limited creature is threatened by the infiniteness of the creator, the sinful by the all-holy. Yet in the laws which hedge the holy around, there is a strongly positive element. "Be holy as I am holy" is an awesome challenge, but also a call to a fullness of human life, lived at depth.

"Remember that you were a slave" and are enslaved no longer, is a call to cherish the freedom that has been God's gift. Somehow, Deuteronomy holds in balance the dignity of human choice and the passion of divine love.

It is precisely in the area of fear and love that we might review briefly the aspect of the dangerousness of God which surfaced so often in the survey of the laws. The intimate presence of God among Israel appeared as a danger. How real was this to Israel? How applicable is this to us? It is always a risky enterprise to psychologize the rites and customs of another culture. It is equally risky to assume primitive religious fear as a forceful factor in ancient religion (cf., above, footnote 5).

At least two aspects seem to me significant. One is the raw awesomeness of the creator of the universe. Israel did not have our knowledge of solar systems, and galaxies, and an expanding universe. But Israel was well aware of the mysteries of nature, and the vastness of the world stretched before them. Second Isaiah does not appeal to the creator for nothing. The poet of Job does not bring in the creator and conserver of the universe for nothing. Both psalms and wisdom hymn the creator's power and might. "When I look at your heavens, the work of your fingers, the moon and the stars which you have established; what is man that you are mindful of him and the son of man that you care for him?" (Ps 8:3-4). The awesomeness of the creator could not escape Israel and cannot escape us.

When we turn our gaze inward rather than outward, and when we ponder the overwhelming love of God, is the reality of danger there too? How much this can or should be tied to the aspect of the cultic presence of God in Israel, I do not know and will not speculate. It is enough, for the present, that it can be symbolic of another presence of God to us. Love calls for intimacy and closeness. Intimacy and closeness require the opening of oneself to another and, therefore, call for vulnerability. In this lies the conflict between the universal human desire for intimacy and closeness and the almost equally universal fear of intimacy and closeness. Furthermore, it is of the nature of unconditional love that ultimately it is going to call forth total vulnerability. So it is not surprising that deep human longing for God will also be met by deep human fear.

Deuteronomy, as the culmination of the Pentateuch, is in its own way a meditation on the dilemma of unconditional divine love and full human responsibility. But at the beginning of the Pentateuch, two of the stories of the ancestors point to the mystery of the experience of an unconditionally loving God. Genesis 22, the sacrifice of Isaac, can only make sense as the response of basic trust to unconditional love. The only acceptable context for unconditional obedience is the absolute certainty that the one who commands loves unconditionally. Abraham's "God will provide" (22:8) can only be an expression of Abraham's acceptance of God's unconditional love, experienced in call and covenant (Gen 12; 15; 17). Genesis 32 has the strange story of Jacob's night-long wrestling with God (vv 22-32). The story's dark of night shrouds the mystery of the encounter. Only slowly does the man emerge as spirit and as God. And he only wins by cheating. And Israel remembers God's cheating by a dietary custom (v 32). Somehow, radically deep in this story is the experience that when God lames, God blesses. The radical encounter with God, of life lived at real depth, risks at least that laming and finds that blessing. It is expressed in image in the final sentence of the story: "The sun rose upon him as he passed Penuel, limping because of his thigh" (v 31). It is expressed in words by Jesus: "Unless a grain of wheat falls into the earth and dies, it remains alone; but if it dies, it bears much fruit" (Jn 12:24). It is expressed in symbol in the cross. The Pentateuch as a whole tells not only Israel's story but also the human story and the story of God's love seeking its lost company.

Today

The Pentateuch has the potential for generating many and various reflections today. Here we will touch on three: the view of creation, the understanding of law as guidance for life, and the mystery of a loving God.

CREATION

It is immediately clear from the opening of the Pentateuch that Israel believed in creation and a creator God. Far too many people, unfortunately, are quite unaware that Israel's theologians operated with a number of views of how the world was created. The background imagery of the ancient Near Eastern myths, in which creation involved combat by the gods, is used in a number of biblical texts and is of central importance to some of them. Isaiah is using such combat creation mythology when saying of God:

> Was it not you that cut Rahab in pieces,
>   that pierced the dragon?
> Was it not you that dried up the sea,
>   the waters of the great deep;
> that made the depths of the sea a way
>   for the redeemed to pass over? (Isa 51:9-10)

The reference to Rahab, the dragon, is to the portrayals of creation as a battle between God and the primeval sea monsters. For Isaiah, the image is central to the message of the text. The divided sea monster (creation) blends with the divided sea (Exodus: redemption), thus evoking the power of the creator as the guarantee of the power of God to redeem exiled Israel. There are echoes of similar understandings of creation in Job (Rahab, Job 9:13; 26:12-13; Yamm, Job 7:12), as well as in the Psalms (e.g., Ps 74:12-17).

Genesis 1:1-2:4a presents a creation account of a very different order, devoid of all combat motifs. It belongs to the cluster of myths which deal with the creation of the world. The narrative of creation in Gen 2:4b-25 is about as different from Genesis 1 as chalk from cheese. It belongs to the cluster of myths which deal with the creation of a human being. The radical difference between the two biblical texts is so marked it takes a massive effort to overlook it. Gen 1:1-2:4a begins in the dark and wet (1:2); among other elements, plants and trees are created on the third day (1:11-12) and birds and animals on the fifth and sixth days (1:20-25); finally man and woman are created together (1:26-27); and the image of the creator God, named God, is one of distance and majestic power. On the other hand, Gen 2:4b-25 begins in barren dryness, without a plant or herb (2:5); the first act of creation is the creature to be called man (2:7); after that, plants and trees are created (2:8-9) and then all the animals and birds (2:19-20); finally woman is created to bring humanity to completeness (2:21-23); and the image of the creator God, named the LORD God, is one of nearness and cooperative intimacy.

Without utterly fixed dogmatic preconceptions, these texts portray pictures of creation as different from one another as they both are from the images of the creation-through-combat mythology. It is one of the foibles of modern creationism that the battles are fought on the fields of evolution and physics, and not where they belong—over the texts of the Old Testament itself. The only explanation for the preservation and juxtaposition of such different pictures of creation is that Israel believed firmly *that* God created the world and was perfectly ready to entertain a variety of presentations as to *how* God created the world. To that degree, Israel was wiser by far than the creationists! The mystery of creation is not unlocked in a single metaphor.

Israel looked on creation with warmth and benevolence. In Genesis 2, there is an understanding of the world as essentially right and in right relationship, with God. It is in right relationship, with God: there is a comfortable and cooperative relationship between the creator God and the first human creature— the birds and the animals were brought to the man who named them. It is a world that is essentially right: in the garden, surrounded by the animals he has named, it is not good for the man to be alone; the goal is to find a partner, and that goal is achieved—there is a sense of complementarity and wholeness to the picture. It sits as one pole in the Yahwist's portrayal of Israel's story. It is the ideal from which humankind steadily deviated (Genesis 2-11); it contains germs of the blessing which is the goal of humankind, and which it is Israel's destiny to mediate.

The picture in Genesis 1 is not dissimilar. Clearly the world is perceived as good. The refrain echoes through the chapter: everything on earth is evaluated by God as good (only the firmament lacks it), and the whole is viewed as very good. There is a clear sense of order in the portrayal, with everything in the world disposed according to God's will. These two perceptions are remarkable against the background of the Priestly Document. It is believed to have been composed during the time of the exile, when Israel's independent existence as a sovereign nation had been crushed. With the promised land in the power of others, with the temple in ruins and the king in prison, the world for a believing Israelite might have well seemed the turbulent battle-ground of the forces of evil. Instead the Priestly picture is a remarkable act of faith and insight. The structuring of the account over seven days and its culmination in God's rest is equally remarkable. Their sabbath related exiled Israel to their God, the creator of their world.

The Yahwist, structuring a narrative around the increasing distance between creator and creature and the need to reverse that trend, chose to begin the narrative with a story of creation that emphasized the intimacy with God and the human wholeness of creation. The Priestly Writer, confronted with a world that threatened to shake the foundation of faith, composed an account of that world's creation which emphasized its total dependence on God's will, expressed through the pattern of command and compliance. It is an account which moves with stately progress from the initial chaos to the final divine declaration that it was very good. Common to both is the perception of creation as the sovereign work of God's freedom, that is good in its result and benign in its intention. There is no battle here, no struggle for victory over other forces; there is no hint here of the ancient Near Eastern theme of the human creature being at the service of the gods that they might be at ease. In both accounts, human beings are the culmination of creation, echoing the sentiments of Psalm 8: you have made them little less than God, crowned them with glory and honor.

LAW

For whatever reason, law in the Old Testament is often given a bad press. An overview of the Pentateuch as a whole, such as we have undertaken, helps put Old Testament law in better and more accurate perspective. It is important to realize that there is no trace of law until a firm relationship has been established between God and Israel. Law as a means of winning one's way into God's favor is a travesty of Old Testament theology.

When one reflects on the role of law in life, a variety of understandings is likely to exist in any given culture. It is just as true that a variety of understandings exists in the Old Testament. The extremes can be found in one and the same chapter of Ezekiel: "I gave them my statutes and showed them my ordinances, by whose observance man shall live" (Ezek 20:11) and "I gave them statutes that were not good and ordinances by which they could not have life" (Ezek 20:25). My own understanding of law is based on the fundamental idea of the ordering of society toward the common good. "Common good," in this sense, may be understood as the preservation and furthering of life in society.

There is much muddled thinking today about law in the Old Testament, just as there is much muddled thinking about God's justice and the ups and downs of human life. For some, law in the Old Testament comes close to being an arbitrary test: if the law is kept, there will be reward; and if the law is not kept, there will be punishment. At its crudest, the link between obedience and reward or disobedience and punishment is no more nor less than the divine power of God. There are expressions in the wisdom literature which can tend in this direction; the deuteronomic language of blessing and curse can lend credence to it too. However, it may be that such a view does profound injustice to God.

In the study of ancient documents, we must always maintain a clear distinction between the convictions we find expressed in the documents and the convictions we cling to as our own today. One of my convictions, which will surface now and again in this book, is that the ordinary rhythm of fortune and misfortune in life is not to be linked directly to the intervention of God's justice; it may be the consequence of human choice, of chance interaction, or of simple natural phenomena. To link such fortune or misfortune directly to God is to do God an injustice. The perception that human actions bore their consequences in their train, for better or for worse, is quite clear in the Old Testament. What is less clear is the extent to which the Old Testament linking of goodness with reward and of evil with punishment is attributed to the direct action of God or rather indirectly to God through the natural order established and maintained by God (see below, chap. 13).

In the Pentateuch, it can be argued that law has as its aim the preservation and furthering of life. The action of God in calling Abraham and in leading Israel out of the bondage of Egypt has given Israel the gift of life in freedom and in independence. The further gift of the law is portrayed as guidance for the full living of that life.

We can see this in the content of the laws. Of the ten

commandments, for example, no other gods, no images, not taking the name of God in vain, and observing the sabbath are all ways of keeping alive, in the reality of day-to-day living, the life-giving relationship with God. Honor your father and your mother protects the relationship between generations; it is pointed specifically toward life—"that your days may be long in the land" (Exod 20:12). You shall not kill, commit adultery, steal, bear false witness, or covet are all protective of social living in community, protecting life, family, property, and the fabric of society. And so, in their various ways, do the vast bulk of the other laws.

We can see this too in some of the motivation given for the laws. For example: "You shall therefore keep my statutes and my ordinances, by doing which a man shall live: I am the LORD" (Lev 18:5). It is very clear in a liturgical formulation, responding directly to the question, "What is the meaning of the testimonies and the statutes and the ordinances which the LORD our God has commanded?", which gives the answer:

> And the LORD commanded us to do all these statutes, to fear the LORD our God, for our good always, to preserve us alive, as at this day. (Deut 6:24)[12]

The same understanding is found in the grand peroration toward the end of Deuteronomy (Deut 30:15-20):

> Therefore choose life, that you and your descendants may live, loving the LORD your God, obeying his voice, and cleaving to him; for that means life to you and length of days, that you may dwell in the land which the LORD swore to your fathers, to Abraham, to Isaac, and to Jacob, to give them. (Deut 30:19-20)

In this view, the law is not condition, but direction pointing to the attainment and preservation of full human living, of peace, prosperity, and happiness.[13]

---

[12]My own translation. The *RSV* "that he might preserve us alive" introduces a potential ambiguity not expressed in the simple Hebrew infinitive.

[13]As we have noted, a variety of understandings of law existed in the Old Testament. It is not possible to explore them all here. It is worth noting though that the rather different

LOVE

The idea of a loving God, unconditionally committed to that love, is the ultimate mystery of Christian faith. It evoked exclamations of wonder long ago: when I look at your heavens, the work of your fingers, the moon and the stars which you have established, what are we that you are mindful of us, what are we that you care for us? Yet you have made us little less than God, and you crown us with glory and honor (cf., Ps 8:3-5). At the heart of this mystery is the experience of human misery. How can this be compatible with the love of an all-powerful God? To the great mysteries of life there are no ultimate answers, only insights and approaches.

The Pentateuch is a rich vein in the exploration of the mystery of a loving God. The enigma of divine action lurks in many places among the patriarchal narratives. The right of primogeniture, the favoring of the firstborn, would have been seen as God's law, and yet God's action passes through Isaac and Jacob and Joseph. In a patriarchal society, believed to be divinely ordained, "Isaac loved Esau ... but Rebekah loved Jacob" (Gen 25:28), and the line of divine action passed through Jacob. The manner of that passage is extremely strange. It is begun in a divine oracle to Rebekah that the elder of her twins would serve the younger (Gen 25:23). Then Jacob, the second son, bargained for the birthright of his elder brother when Esau was a victim of the hunger of his own appetite (Gen 25:29-34).[14] By outright deceit, at the prompting of Rebekah, Jacob wins the blessing of his aged father (Gen 27:1-40). The biblical narrative, in its own oblique way, rebukes this conduct. Jacob, in search of a bride, agrees to serve seven years for the lovely Rachel, the younger of his kinsman's two daughters. On

---

view expressed in Exod 19:5 is in an unusual and singular passage (vv 3b-8). Exod 19:5 is clearly conditional, but perhaps mitigated by the use of the term *sĕgulâ* (= valued property, peculiar treasure; cf., M. Weinfeld, *Deuteronomy and the Deuteronomic School*[Oxford: Clarendon, 1972] 226-27). The condition may not be intended to determine the relationship as such between God and Israel but rather the quality of that relationship ("a kingdom of priests and a holy nation"). It is noteworthy here that the consequences of breach of covenant are not spelled out.

[14]For a number of valuable insights into the Genesis narratives, see Robert Alter, *The Art of Biblical Narrative* (New York: Basic Books, 1981) passim; on Gen 25:29-34, see pp. 42-45.

the wedding night, Laban substitutes the elder daughter. Jacob's protest is met with the stern rebuke: "It is not so done in our country, to give the younger before the firstborn" (Gen 29:26). Yet for all this, it is through Jacob that the line of God's action passes in the thread of the narrative.

There is enigma enough in stories like the sacrifice of Isaac (Gen 22, prepared for in the story of Hagar in Gen 21:9-21) and Jacob's wrestling with God at the Jabbok (Gen 32). Yet the willingness to sacrifice "your son, your only son whom you love, Isaac" elicits a renewal of the promise of descendants, as many as the stars of heaven and the sand on the seashore, and of the blessing for all the nations of the earth (Gen 22:16-18). And the stubbornness of Jacob in his wrestling is rewarded with blessing, and the sun of new life rose upon him as he limped across the place of his struggle (Gen 32:29-31). The Genesis text itself may be given the last word on the enigmatic experience of God in all these stories: "But God meant it for good, to bring it about that many people should be kept alive, as they are today" (Gen 50:20). The mystery remains.

There is mystery in belief in a loving God coupled with the experience of all too unholy human behavior. The Pentateuch struggles with this at length. So very early, right at the end of the flood narrative, there is the guarantee of continued human existence, despite the recognition that "the imagination of man's heart is evil from his youth" (Gen 8:20-22). The covenant with Noah knows no condition. The covenants with Abraham too are unconditional (Genesis 15 and 17; if circumcision was thought to be a condition, Israel has never been accused of breaching it). The covenant at Sinai is conditioned and breach of it brings consequences in its train. But most remarkable: one of these consequences is not irreparable breach in Israel's relationship with God. The covenant may be broken; the relationship is not. Time and again in the desert Israel disobeys; time and again God is portrayed as furious. Always Israel remains God's people. Throughout the stories of Israel in the wilderness, there is the paradox of God's deliverance and Israel's rejection of the deliverer. God may be portrayed as angry, fulminating, and threatening; but God is never portrayed as giving up. The presence of the All-Holy in the midst of Israel is both source of life and strength and a danger to their existence; but the danger can be circumscribed and overcome. The rhetoric of blessing and curse used in the covenant of Deuteronomy brings Israel face to face with the choice of life or death. But at no point is it said that breach of this covenant would put an end to God's relationship with Israel.[15]

Acts have their consequences. Immutably, breach of the covenant laws entails the consequences which flow from the structures of created order. But irreparable rupture of the relationship with God is not one of those consequences. God's commitment is stronger than the creature's frailty. As Israel will later sing:

> Love is strong as death,
>   passionate love as adamant as the grave.
> Its flashes are flashes of fire,
>   a most vehement flame. (Song of Songs 8:16)[16]

The Pentateuch portrays a God who is capable of threatening and dangerous anger, but a God whose love is stronger than anger, whose commitment endures.

---

[15]Only in Hos 1:9 is it said, "You are not my people and I am not your God," to be immediately revoked in the following verse, "where it was said to them, 'You are not my people,' it shall be said to them, 'Sons of the living God'" (Hos 1:10, *RSV*).

[16]Translation adapted from the *RSV*.

RECOMMENDED FURTHER READING

Brevard S. Childs, *Introduction to the Old Testament as Scripture* (Philadelphia: Fortress, 1979) 127-32.

David J.A. Clines, *The Theme of the Pentateuch* (JSOTSup 10; Sheffield: JSOT, 1978).

Rolf P. Knierim, "The Composition of the Pentateuch." Pp. 393-415 in *Society of Biblical Literature 1985 Seminar Papers*, edited by Kent H. Richards (Atlanta: Scholars Press, 1985)—with reserves, however, about the genre suggested for the Pentateuch.

Still valuable:

Gerhard von Rad, *Genesis.* Rev. ed. Philadelphia: Westminster, 1972.

Bruce Vawter, *On Genesis: A New Reading.* Garden City: Doubleday, 1977.

Particularly theological:
Walter Brueggemann, *Genesis.* Interpretation. Atlanta: John Knox, 1982.

Vastly comprehensive:
Claus Westermann, *Genesis.* 3 vols. Minneapolis: Augsburg, 1984-86. German original, 1974-82.

2

The Priestly Document

Recommended preliminary reading

Before reading the body of the chapter, it will be helpful to have read the following passages:
Genesis 1:1-8; 9:1-17; 17:1-8
Exodus 6:2-9; 24:15 – 25:22; 40:33b-35
Numbers 1:1-3; 2:34; 10:11-12; 13:1-3, 32: 14:1-10; 20:10-12
Deuteronomy 34:7-9

🌿

Our study of the Pentateuch, even looked at from the point of view of literary unity, had to take account of the great variety of traditions and collections which are brought together in the pentateuchal text. An enormously complex process of growth is presumed, reflecting the theological thought and activity in ancient Israel and culminating in the text of the Pentateuch as we now have it. Two great and quite different strands of activity have contributed to this process; we need to be aware of both of them. One strand we can call vertical: it is the passing on from generation to generation of specific traditions or blocks of tradition. Such traditions might be stories about a patriarchal figure or traditions from a particular sanctuary or collections of law or traditions related to a specific theme (e.g., exodus, wilderness, conquest, or deliverance, etc). As such traditions were handed down, they were adjusted and adapted to express current theological views or to speak more powerfully to their contemporary situation. This was an ongoing process within Israel. The other strand we can call horizontal: it is the gathering together of a selection of Israel's traditions in one generation or one moment in time to present a picture of the whole. Such a picture is composed by taking a cross-section of all or many of the traditions being handed down vertically in Israel. Except that it is a cross-section only in retrospect. At the time of its creation, it is an arrangement of a selection of Israel's traditions at the point which they have reached in this particular generation.

In the understanding of the growth of Israel's traditions which will be favored in this book, there are basically two of these horizontal strands in the Pentateuch. One is the Yahwist narrative (J), to which a considerable amount of similar narrative material has been added. The other is the Priestly Document (P), to which a great deal of supplementary material has also been added. In this understanding, when the Pentateuch was finally put together, the Priestly Document was taken as the basic structure and was retained almost in its entirety. The traditions of the Yahwist narrative were blended into the structure provided by the Priestly Document, sacrificed to it here and there, but for the most part filling it out as well as providing color and texture. The understanding of this process will be studied more closely in Chapter 4.

We began with the present text of the Pentateuch. We move now to the level of text which preceded the Pentateuch—the Priestly Document. Within the pentateuchal text, it is identifiable through characteristic language, characteristic concerns, and a narrative or structuring thread which can be followed step by step. Our task will be to look at the Priestly Document as a literary work and to discover what it was saying to the Israel of its day, before reflecting on what it might have to say to us. The most commonly held view puts the composition of the Priestly Document during the exile or the immediate post-exilic period, somewhere between the mid-sixth and early fifth centuries. The understanding expounded here makes most sense in the time of exile, but it would be equally applicable to the period of uncertainty and of fragile and often disappointed hope which followed shortly on the exile or, indeed, to the period of ominous threat which immediately preceded it.

This chapter is written with the conviction that the Priestly Document was indeed a document. This view is disputed by some scholars, who regard the Priestly Writer(s) as late editors in the long growth of the Pentateuch, editors who simply added their own particular traditions to the mass of material already constituted by the Yahwist and the Elohist (= JE). The position taken on this issue is fundamental for any understanding of P, since it controls the shape and structure of P's work. As in the case of the Pentateuch, in the previous chapter, the grounds for decision are close inspection of the P text itself. It will be seen that, unlike the flowing stream of the Yahwist's narrative, which we will look at in the next chapter, the Priestly Document might be likened to a necklace. Its stories are often separate and encapsulated; they are like the beads of the necklace. Its thread, on which the stories are strung, consists primarily of genealogies, moving the narrative focus from generation to generation, and of itineraries, moving the narrative focus from place to place along the route of Israel's journey.

The text of the Priestly Document is not as extensive as that of the Yahwist, so that it is possible to look more closely at it here. The appendix to this chapter provides a comparative listing, setting out the text attributed to P by Martin Noth,[1] Karl Elliger,[2] and Norbert Lohfink.[3] At first sight, a great mass of figures of this kind seems horrendously complicated, baffling, and boring. Closer inspection will reveal that, for all the apparent complication, the picture is really simple enough, and it provides the base for useful insights into the processes of such literary critical analysis.

The first impression, on comparing the three analyses, is of the extensive unanimity on the material to be attributed to P. This substantial agreement on the text of P is just as well, for

---

[1] M. Noth, *A History of Pentateuchal Traditions* (Englewood Cliffs, N.J.: Prentice-Hall, 1972) 17-19.

[2] K. Elliger, "Sinn und Ursprung der priesterlichen Geschichtserzählung," *ZTK* 49 (1952) 121-43, see pp. 121-22. In my judgment, this is the best treatment of the narrative horizon in P.

[3] N. Lohfink, "Die Priesterschrift und die Geschichte," *Congress Volume: Göttingen, 1977*, (VTSup 29; Leiden: Brill, 1978) 189-225, see p. 198. This is a masterful article, with a wealth of documentation and argument clarifying issues connected with P, and providing some extremely valuable insights into the deeper levels of meaning in P.

unfortunately, there is not a similar degree of consensus among scholars as to the central message of P. An understanding of the communication intended by P can only be achieved in confrontation with the P text as a whole. To this end, an inventory of the contours of P will be helpful.

Creation	Gen 1:1-2:4a
Genealogy: Adam to Noah	Gen 5:1 ff
Flood	Gen 6-9*
Genealogy: Noah to Abram	Gen 10:1 ff.
Abraham	
Coming to the land	Gen 12:4b ff.
Hagar and Ishmael	Gen 16:1a ff.
COVENANT & CIRCUMCISION[4]	Gen 17:1-27
Genealogy: birth of Isaac	Gen 21:1b ff.
BURIAL OF SARAH: MACHPELAH	Gen 23:1-20
Death of Abraham: burial at Machpelah	Gen 25:7 ff.
Genealogy: descendants of Ishmael	Gen 25:12 ff.
Isaac	
Genealogy: descendants of Isaac	Gen 25:19 ff.
Strictures against Canaanite wives	Gen 26:34 ff.
Jacob	
Journey of Jacob in search of a wife	Mainly JE
PROMISE TO JACOB/ISRAEL AT BETHEL	Gen 35:6 ff.
Genealogy: twelve sons of Jacob	Gen 35:22b ff.
Death of Isaac	Gen 35:28 ff.
Genealogy: descendants of Esau	Gen 36:1 ff.

---

[4]In this listing, CAPITALS will be used as a pointer to the beads on P's necklace. By this, I mean the stories P appears to have lingered over, rather than the material which simply moves the narrative along. This is necessarily a rather subjective judgment. To give it some appearance of objectivity, approximately ten verses are taken as the lower limit. The promise to Jacob (Gen 35:6ff) may be an exception, because of its intrinsic significance. Lohfink uses the criterion of the presence of divine speech (coupled with the Toledoth formulas and the itinerary notices) to identify a similar series of about a dozen theologically significant passages ("Priesterschrift," 205-6).

Joseph Story

Journey into Egypt	Mainly JE
Jacob's blessing of Joseph	Gen 48:3 ff.
Death of Jacob: burial at Machpelah	Gen 49:1a ff.

Exodus

Genealogy: names of the sons of Israel	Exod 1:1 ff.
Oppression of Israel	Exod 1:13 ff
REVELATION OF GOD TO MOSES	Exod 6:2 ff.
CONFRONTATION WITH PHARAOH: PLAGUES	Exod 7:1 ff.
PASSOVER (?)	Exod 12:1-28*
Exodus	Exod 12:40 ff.
DELIVERANCE AT THE REED SEA	Exod 14:1-29*
Itinerary: from Reed Sea to Elim	Exod 15:22aα ff.
MANNA (quail & sabbath)	Exod 16:1-35*
Itinerary: from Sin to Rephidim to Sinai	Exod 17:abα ff.

Sinai

Ascent of mountain by Moses	Exod 24:15b ff.
INSTRUCTIONS CONCERNING THE SANCTUARY	Exod 25-29*
The two tables of the Law	Exod 31:18
CONSTRUCTION OF THE SANCTUARY	Exod 35-40*
COMMISSIONING OF THE SANCTUARY	Lev 8-9*
ORGANIZATION OF ISRAEL AROUND THE SANCTUARY	Num 1-9*

Wilderness

Itinerary: from Sinai to Paran	Num 10:11-12
SPYING OUT THE LAND	Num 13-14*
Itinerary: to Zin and Kadesh	Num 20:1 ff.
WATER FROM THE ROCK	Num 20:2-12*
Itinerary: to Mount Hor	Num 20:22 ff.
DEATH OF AARON & SUCCESSION	Num 20:25 ff.
Itinerary: from Mount Hor to Edom to Moab	Num 21:4ff.
DEATH OF MOSES & SUCCESSION	Deut 32-34*

[*Conquest of the Land* (?)	Joshua*]

These are simply the bare bones of the Priestly Document. It will very soon be time to put some flesh on them, but one rather technical observation remains to be made.

It concerns the absence of the laws. Law bulks large in the Pentateuch; it is not for nothing that it is known as "the Law." Yet, in the outline above, the laws are conspicuous by their absence. Since the legal sections of the Pentateuch share much the same language, style, and thought world as P, and since they probably come from the same priestly circles, it is important to recognize why, from a literary point of view, they do not belong in the P document.[5]

The sacrifice laws in Leviticus 1-7 are appropriately located before the P account of the first sacrifices (Lev 8-9). But they break the narrative connection between the instructions (Exod 25-29), their execution (Exod 35-40), and the commissioning of the sanctuary (Lev 8-9). Lev 16:1 is explicitly connected to Lev 10:1-7 (both being already part of the supplements to P), suggesting that the laws on ritual cleanliness (Lev 11-15) have been inserted in the same way, at what is an appropriate place. The collection of laws in Leviticus 17-26 (the Holiness Code) is appropriately located after the treatment of the Day of Atonement in Leviticus 16. Much the same can be argued for the smaller groups of laws occurring in Numbers. While these various additions are clearly priestly supplements, they may have been added to the combined text of the Pentateuch, rather than to the independent P narrative. Chap. 1, on the pentateuchal text as a whole, showed that these additions produce a marked change in the overall tone and message of the text.

Once these points have been grasped, it is possible to read the text of the Priestly Document and recognize that it is a coherently structured document with an identity and an integrity of its own.[6]

---

[5]For these issues, see Noth, *Pentateuchal Traditions*, 8-10.

[6]Noth is rightly insistent on the character of P as a *narrative work*, although I would prefer to place the emphasis on "independent" rather than "narrative." This is denied by F.M. Cross, in his influential *Canaanite Myth and Hebrew Epic* (Cambridge: Harvard, 1973). Cross gives his position without any attempt at full discussion. He writes: "The P 'narrative' of the Tetrateuch as put together by Noth is a rather strange document. Its 'narrative' is nothing like the narrative of saga" (p. 294). Against Cross, while P is clearly different from J or JE, this in no way impugns its integrity or independence as a document—it is a different sort of narrative. It has to be looked at in its own right. Cross,

Its message has to be assessed on the basis of the Priestly text alone, without including the traditions P appears to have excluded. This is not to say that P was ignorant of the other traditions of Israel. To the contrary, it is assumed here that P knew of these traditions. The intriguing factor in the puzzle of P is to take account of the meaning of P in such a way as to explain these omissions.

Survey of the Text of P

It is time now to turn to the text of the Priestly Document itself. The priestly creation account, in Gen 1:1-2:4a, is an extraordinary text with which to preface even a document, to say nothing of the whole biblical tradition. With immense and stately majesty, through the steady progress of command and fulfillment, it imposes order on the chaotic and awesome forces of nature, and it declares creation good. In a placid, static world, this might be taken for granted; in a shaky and uncertain one, it is a massive affirmation of faith. Yet, the world of P was a world of exile, in which all of Israel's certainties had gone by the board: their temple was in ruins, their king was dethroned, and their land was in alien hands. It was a very uncertain world.

The stately progress of the creation account moves toward the seventh day. Whether it was imposed on an earlier account,[7] or

apparently, has found it wanting: "In fact, if we are to suppose that the Priestly strata were ever an independent narrative source, we must suppose also that a redactor has used only a précis of P to frame the Epic tradition" (p. 294). This view, of course, is in direct opposition to Noth's understanding of the process. It is by no means clear to me that the text identified by Noth is inadequate or unsatisfactory. Regrettably, the reasons on which Cross founds his opinion are not provided. Readers will have to study Noth's text (or equivalents), as identified and discussed in this chapter, and then make their judgment. Against Cross, Rendtorff, and others, Lohfink argues: P must not be judged by the literary form of JE; it is an unfounded assumption that P must relate everything contained in JE; it is self-evident that P and his readers were familiar with JE; the attribution to P of passages necessary for its narrative continuity, but which lack the characteristics of P language, should only be denied when a more satisfactory hypothesis can be provided. Only an independent P document accounts for the type of redactional combination found in texts like the stories of the flood or the spies; for the remarkably strong structure in P; for the important theological statements which depend on this structure (Lohfink, "Priesterschrift", 199, n. 31).

[7]See Werner H. Schmidt, *Die Schöpfungsgeschichte der Priesterschrift: Zur Überlieferungsgeschichte von Genesis 1.1-2.4a und 2.4b-3.24* (WMANT 17; 2nd ed.; Neukirchen: Neukirchener Verlag, 1967).

whether it reflects P's creative artistry,[8] it is crowned by the institution of the sabbath.[9] The crown of all creation is the sabbath, blessed and hallowed by God. Imagination is needed to sense the liberating power of such a view. With the temple and its liturgies gone, with the king and his court gone, with the land and its seasons gone, what is left to exiled Israel to maintain contact with their God? P seizes on the sabbath. All the power of the creator and all the steadfast order of creation is distilled into that one day. When, on sabbath, Israel is still, it participates in the very life of God; the rhythm of Israel's existence is the divine rhythm of the created universe. It is the creator God of all this vast universe whose sabbath is the distinguishing mark of Israel alone. From the outset, then, there is an unbroken relationship with God, and there is a deep sense of divine order in the universe.

Out of all the traditions available, it is remarkable that P should have selected just the flood story to precede the beginnings of human history. For P, the flood must have had special meaning. P's picture of the flood is very different from J's. J's flood was a massive downpour, a forty-day disaster which disrupted the sequence of the seasons (cf., Gen 8:22). P's flood has almost cosmic dimensions. In creation, God had separated the waters and gathered them, in order that there might be room for dry land and life. In P's flood, this separation collapses: "all the fountains of the great deep burst forth, and the windows of the heavens were opened" (Gen 7:11; cf., 8:2). From below and from above, the waters rush in to reverse creation. For P, it started in the 600th year of Noah's life; not till a year and ten days later was it all over (see 7:11 and 8:14).

In the 601st year of Noah's life, on the first day of the year, Noah looked out and saw dry ground (8:13). There is something very significant about this moment: the first day of the year, the first year of Noah's seventh century. It is a new start to the human race. For a modern anthropologist, this has particular significance.

---

[8]See Odil Hannes Steck, *Der Schöpfungsbericht der Priesterschrift: Studien zur literarkritischen und überlieferungsgeschichtlichen Problematik von Genesis 1.1-2.4a* (FRLANT 115; Göttingen: Vandenhoeck & Ruprecht, 1975).

[9]The reader who is using a translation has to be alerted to the linguistic echoes of the Hebrew in Gen 2:2-3. The *RSV*'s "rested" (twice) translates the verb *šābaṭ*, with its clear echo of sabbath; the three occurrences of "work" use the same term that occurs in the sabbath laws (*mĕlā'kâ*, in Exod 20:9-10; Lev 23:3; Deut 5:13-14).

> It is a characteristic of flood stories that the survivors become
> the ancestors of all humankind.... What is common to
> almost all the stories is that the survivors are ordinary human
> beings who have been born in an ordinary way. They are thus
> quite unlike the first parents in the first creation.... The
> function of flood stories is to destroy the first creation and its
> ambiguities and to start again. The end of the Flood marks the
> beginning of true time.[10]

This may well be part of the deep structure of flood stories. It has
its echoes in the surface structure of P's document.

There is the covenant with Noah (parallel with 8:21-22 in J). It
is God's unconditional promise that never again shall a flood
destroy all flesh (Gen 9:11). The sign of the covenant is associated
with the threatening phenomenon itself; it is the rainbow, in the
storm clouds (9:12-16). It is not so much disaster itself as the fear
of it which can be humanly crippling. At the level of myth,
technically understood, the flood story says that the worst
possible disaster has occurred, and we have survived, and we need
not fear again.

We are, in some strange way, freed from the fear of the holiness
of God. Just as in J there is a coming to terms with human evil on
the part of God (cf., the discussion of Gen 6:5 and 8:21 in chap. 3),
so, too, in P something of the same phenomenon is visible. With a
strong echo of the first creation, "God blessed Noah and his sons,
and said to them, 'Be fruitful and multiply, and fill the earth'"
(9:1, cf., 1:28). But then the fourth element of the first blessing in
Gen 1:28 has been replaced. Instead of subduing the earth (1:28),
fear and dread is now imposed on the animal kingdom, the
vegetarian era is over, and a reckoning for the violent shedding of
human blood has to be foreshadowed (9:2-6). There is a twofold
intimation of stability here: God's unconditional promise to
Noah, and the fact of God's acceptance of a less than perfect
world.

The covenant with Abraham is also significant. It, too, is

---

[10]Edmund Leach, "Anthropological Approaches to the Study of the Bible during the
Twentieth Century," *Humanizing America's Iconic Book: Society of Biblical Literature
Centennial Addresses 1980* (ed. G.M. Tucker and D.A. Knight; Chico: Scholars Press,
1982) 73-94, see p. 80.

unconditional. As an everlasting covenant, it guarantees the relationship with God, and it guarantees possession of the land.

> I will make you exceedingly fruitful; . . . And I will establish my covenant between me and you and your descendants after you throughout their generations for an everlasting covenant, to be God to you and to your descendants after you. And I will give to you and to your descendants after you, the land of your sojournings, all the land of Canaan, for an everlasting possession; and I will be their God.   (Gen 17:6-8)

The blessing of creation is to be realized in Abraham, exceedingly. The relationship with God is pledged. The relationship to the land is changed from temporary to permanent. It is an unconditional covenant. Circumcision is its sign, rather than a condition of it (17:11). Even if circumcision were viewed as in some way a condition, it is one that Israel fulfilled. There is no cause for insecurity here. Rather, a relationship with both God and land is guaranteed.

The relationship to the land is immediately tied down in contractual form. In open and public negotiations, Abraham buys a field near Hebron and there buries Sarah in the cave of Machpelah. There, for P, Abraham and Sarah, Isaac and Rebekah, and Jacob and Leah were to be buried (Gen 49:29-32). From the beginning to the end of the patriarchal narratives, the security of Israel's tenure in its land is emphasized. No exiled Israelite could hear these stories, without either the bitterness of cynical disappointment or the glow of the kindling of renewed hope.

The strictures against Canaanite wives (Gen 26:34-35: 27:46-28:9) also hold lessons for the exiles, with all the temptation to marry into a foreign environment and put down roots in foreign soil. Jacob, who goes through so much to win his brides among his kin, and who returns to the promised land, can hardly be less than a model for the exiles. It may also be that P wished to delay the overt theme of sin until the wilderness period (see Num 13-14; 20); therefore, he avoids making use of the Jacob-Esau conflict in this context.[11]

---

[11]So Lohfink, "Priesterschrift," 208.

When P portrays God's self-revelation to Moses, in the servitude of Egypt, he has God refer back to the covenant with the patriarchs. It is in the name of this covenant that Israel will be delivered from Egypt. They shall be brought to the land promised to Abraham, Isaac, and Jacob (Exod 6:2-8). The significance of the covenant with Abraham is held up to the exiles, in the context of a situation not unlike their own.

The significance given to the covenant with Abraham, extended to Isaac and Jacob, is extremely important in the context of P's treatment of the Sinai traditions. For Sinai is one of the enigmas of the P document. The fact of the matter is simple: there is no narrative in P language of a covenant at Sinai. The P account begins with the glory of God covering the mountain, and, on the seventh day, Moses being summoned to ascend (Exod 24:15b-18). What Moses receives from God on the mountain are the instructions concerning the sanctuary. The two tables of the law are mentioned (Exod 31:18; possibly 34:29-32); but there is no mention of any covenant.

These are the facts, the phenomena in the text. What do they mean? For those for whom P is not an independent document, but the last redactional level of the Pentateuch, there is no problem. The Sinai covenant is there, in the JE sources; they are all part of the final level of the text. Even in that hypothesis, however, it remains surprising that, if the Sinai covenant were significant to P, he should have left it as he found it in the JE sources, without a word of comment or interpretation of his own. On the other hand, for those who advocate an independent P document, it is possible to surmise that the P account of the Sinai covenant was suppressed in favor of the JE account by some later redactor. Given the prominence of P at Sinai, this is not entirely plausible. The other possibility is that P chose not to mention the covenant at Sinai.[12] Could this make sense?

---

[12]Frank Cross is misleading at this point, He writes: "To suppose that the Priestly tradent simply had no tradition of the covenant rites at Sinai is incredible. To posit a theory that P had no covenant at all at Sinai is a fortiori beyond credence" *Canaanite Myth and Hebrew Epic*, 319-20). Against Cross, it is not suggested that P was unaware of JE. "To be sure, P is familiar with the traditions fixed in these old sources and presupposes such a familiarity also on the part of his readers; but it cannot be demonstrated that he ever used them as models, available to him in written form" (Noth, *Pentateuchal Traditions*, 11, n. 23). Why it should be "beyond credence" for P to pass over the covenant at Sinai

Writing for exiled Israel, in the sixth century, there is good reason why P might have chosen not to incorporate the Sinai covenant into his document. The Sinai covenant was heavily hedged around with law. The Sinai covenant was taken up by the deuteronomic movement, with its heavy emphasis on blessing and curse: "all these blessings/curses shall come upon you and overtake you" (see Deut 27-28, esp. 28:2, 15). There is deep truth in the deuteronomic theology, but its theological language is open to abuse. What might be said lightly enough in the context of a confident religious reform (cf., Deut 30:11-14, "the word is very near you . . . so that you can do it") may sound very different in the context of that reform's complete collapse. And that is what happened to Israel.

A theology of divine wrath and just judgment was certainly about in P's day: "Therefore the anger of the LORD was kindled against this land, bringing upon it all the curses written in this book; and the LORD uprooted them from their land in anger and fury and great wrath, and cast them into another land, as at this day" (Deut 29:27-28). There is no reason to insist, however, that P should share this theology. There is the witness of Second Isaiah to the possibility of other theologies. There is good reason for P—not in an opportunistic and time-serving theology, but out of deep theological conviction—to return to the unconditional promises of God to Noah and to Abraham.

It is important to see what P places at Sinai, instead of the old covenant. In any reconstruction, these are massive blocks of P material. It is not possible to interpret P adequately, without taking due account of the specifically P material at Sinai. It is impressive in its sheer mass; it is impressive in its location at the heart of divine revelation; and it is P's own work. So it cannot be ignored. But neither is it easy to interpret.

The sanctuary is to be made, on the heavenly model, in order "that I may dwell in their midst" (Exod 25:8). If the sanctuary

---

demands argument and not mere rhetorical assertion. Compare Zimmerli's careful treatment in W. Zimmerli, "Sinaibund und Abrahambund: Ein Beitrag zum Verständnis der Priesterschrift," in *Gottes Offenbarung: Gesammelte Aufsätze zum Alten Testament* (TBü 19; Munich: Kaiser, 1963) 205-16. In this connection, the recent characterization of the Holiness Code as a deliberate corrective polemic against P is important; see A. Cholewinski, *Heiligkeitsgesetz und Deuteronomium: Eine vergleichende Studie* (AnBib 66; Rome: Biblical Institute, 1976) esp. pp. 334-44.

were to have consisted only of the tent of meeting (so Lohfink), then God's presence to the people is one of meeting: "There I will meet with the people of Israel, and it shall be sanctified by my glory"(Exod 29:43). If the ark is included (with Noth and Elliger), then the modes of God's presence have been brilliantly blended: "There I will meet with you, and from above the mercy seat, from between the two cherubim that are upon the ark of the testimony, I will speak with you of all that I will give you in commandment for the people of Israel" (Exod 25:22). Here the occasional presence of meeting, at the tent, has been harmonized with the tradition of more permanent presence, represented by the ark.

In either case, P goes out of his way to ensure the presence of God to Israel. The instructions are from God. The execution is in accord with the instructions. And the glory of God filled the tabernacle (Exod 40:34). Israel is then organized painstakingly around this divine presence in their midst. (Numbers 1*, 2*, 4* especially). Judah is given preeminence in this material: Judah is the most numerous of the tribes (Num 1:27); Judah is encamped on the east of sanctuary, leading the way to the promised land (Num 2:3). In some way, this has to mirror the status of Judah in P's time and thinking; it does not reflect an earlier historical reality. The precise interpretation of P's symbolism here is not clear. This much can be said: P goes to great pains, within the sacred locus of Sinai, to assure the presence of God to Israel in a context connected with P's own time.

Finally, we may note that the episodes of the spying out of the land and of the production of water by striking the rock, although they are portrayals of grave sin, are stories which point to the need for absolute faith. The desert generation did not trust the power of God to bring them safely into Canaan; as a result of that disbelief, they will die outside the promised land (Num 13-14). Moses, apparently, did not trust the power of God to bring forth water from the rock by word alone; as a result, he too will die outside the promised land (Num 20:8-12). In the context of the exile, both stories could be read as a demand for strong faith in God. After these, Aaron dies and is succeeded by Eleazar (Num 20:25-29); when Moses dies, he is succeeded by Joshua (Num 27:12-23; Deut 34:7-9). Despite the failures, a secure succession in the priestly and national leadership is assured.

Interpretation of P

There are then numerous elements in P which point to a vision of a world which should be stable and secure, where God's promise is unconditional, where Israel's history has unfolded in the closest possible compliance with God's plan. There is the potential here for comfort and assurance for exiled or post-exilic Israel. Is it possible to be more precise in assessing the message and intention of the Priestly Document? What is needed is an interpretation which takes account of the particular context of the Priestly Document, of the kind of structure which is evident in P, and, above all, which comprehends the whole horizon of the text attributed here to P. The studies have been done which make such an interpretation possible.[13] Without preempting the possibility of an immediately pre-exilic date, we may focus here on a context in the exilic period.[14]

We begin with P's account of creation (Gen 1:1-2:4a). Since it is both his own and his beginning, it must have been important to him. As we have noted, it has a very strong sense of order, and it culminates in the first sabbath day. The order in the world emerges from the absolute compliance with the divine command: "And God said ... And it was so." As would be expected, creation is declared good, both throughout the process and in a final review, "behold, it was very good" (1:31). There is, in P's portrayal of the creating God, almost "a blessed rage for order."

[13]What follows will be based on Elliger ("Sinn und Ursprung"), supplemented from Lohfink ("Priesterschrift"). Elliger gives a very good account of the total narrative horizon of P; Lohfink sees powerfully into the depths of P. Other recent studies, available in English, are valuable for particular aspects but do not provide the same grasp of the whole P narrative: see Noth, *Pentateuchal Traditions*, 239-47; J. Blenkinsopp, "The Structure of P," *CBQ* 38 (1976) 275-92; W. Brueggemann, "The Kerygma of the Priestly Writers," *The Vitality of Old Testament Traditions* (ed. W. Brueggemann and H.W. Wolff; 2nd ed.; Atlanta: Knox, 1982) 101-13.

[14]See Lohfink, "Priesterschrift," 201, n. 33, who dates P to the first possibility of return from exile. For the linguistic evidence, see R. Polzin, *Late Biblical Hebrew: Toward an Historical Typology of Biblical Hebrew Prose* (Missoula: Scholars Press, 1976), and Avi Hurvitz, "The Evidence of Language in Dating the Priestly Code: A Linguistic Study in Technical Idioms and Terminology," *RB* 81 (1974) 24-56, and *A Linguistic Study of the Relationship between the Priestly Source and the Book of Ezekiel: A New Approach to an Old Problem* (CRB 20. Paris: Gabalda, 1982). In an immediately pre-exilic context, the loss of temple, king, and land would be threateningly imminent rather than having just happened.

The question, which the Israelites of the exile would have wanted answered, was whether God had maintained that order and what their place was in it.

The sense of order remains very strong throughout the Priestly Document. For example:

—There are ten generations between creation and the flood, ten generations between Noah and Abraham, and ten *toledoth* formulas.

—There are six days and a seventh at creation, and there are six days and a seventh before Moses went up Mt. Sinai (Exod 24:16).

—There are numerous pairs: creation and flood; the Noah and Abraham covenants; the appearances to two ancestors, Abraham and Jacob; the two leaders, Moses and Aaron; the establishment of sabbath (Exod 16) and the sanctuary (Exod 25-40); the two episodes of sin (the spies, Num 13-14); the rock, Num 20); the deaths of Aaron and Moses; the establishment of their two successors, Eleazar and Joshua.[15]

—There are other little details. The ages of the figures in the genealogy after the flood are arranged so that they all live to see Abraham's birth. According to the figures in the MT, Abraham was born in the year 1946 after creation; his forebears died between the years after creation 1994 (Peleg) and 2124 (Shelah), with Noah dying in 2006. Of the ten generations before the flood, if the figures of the Samaritan Pentateuch are adopted as the original ones, Jared, Methuselah, and Lamech all perish in the flood.[16] Lamech, at least, was known in the tradition as a violent man (cf., Gen 4:23-24); perhaps Jared and Methuselah shared a similar reputation. Certainly, the lives of all three come to a violent end in the same year. There is very careful structuring going on here, with a concern which is theological rather than historical.[17] Beyond these, there is P's constant care for dating by year, month, and day, wherever possible, and for providing ages at every opportunity.

[15]See Lohfink, "Priesterschrift," 207,

[16]The Samaritan figures are (from *BHS*): Jared fathered Enoch at 62, and lived to be 847; Enoch fathered Methuselah at 65, and lived to be 365, before being taken up to God; Methuselah fathered Lamech at 67, and lived to be 720; Lamech fathered Noah at 53, and lived to be 653. The flood, of course, began when Noah was 600.

[17]For this material, see Lohfink, "Priesterschrift," 210-11.

P is, then, concerned to portray a world which God has carefully ordered, from the beginning and throughout its history. An exiled generation, pondering this text, could not help but see its implications for their own time. The world is not chaotic; it has been divinely ordered since creation. Their fate in exile does not lie outside that order. Nothing escapes the dominion of the creator God of Gen 1:1-2:4a, a faith to which Second Isaiah also bears eloquent witness. Their future, too, is in the hands of that creator God. The creation culminated in sabbath. Exiled Israel observed sabbath. In this sabbath observance, there is a special bond between Israel and its creator; in that special bond, there is reason for faith and hope. From the beginning, this sense of the absolute power of God, the pervasiveness of order in creation and the significance of this for sabbath-observing Israel is a strong element in the P document.

A blessing is given to humankind, "Be fruitful and multiply, and fill the earth and subdue it" (Gen 1:28). It is given to the whole human race, not just to Israel. Yet, in this creation account which is directed toward sabbath, it must have a special resonance for Israel. Its various elements will recur through the P document.[18] They do not constitute the central assertion of P's message. [19] Rather they provide a context for the unfolding of the narrative; the patriarchs are seen embodying the creator's blessing in their own lives and destinies. The question whether this blessing is to be extended to include Israel's occupation of Canaan can be held over until the end of this discussion (see footnote 22).

The flood story, too, has to be significant for P. It is the only other story from mythic prehistory which he includes; it is given in his own version.[20] After it, the blessing of Gen 1:28 is repeated, but

[18]So Gen 9:1, 7 (be fruitful, multiply, fill the earth); Gen 17:2, 6, 16; 28:3; 35:9, 11; 48:3-4 (be fruitful, multiply). Fulfillment is noted in Gen 47:27 (were fruitful, multiplied); Exod 1:7 (were fruitful, multiplied, filled the land); and there is also Josh 18:1 (the land lay subdued). See Lohfink, "Priesterschrift," Table IV, p. 218.

[19]Against Brueggemann, "Kerygma of the Priestly Writers." I do not believe that it is prudent to try and apply one and the same particular interpretative approach to a series of different literary works. Each work has to be approached in its own right, and any adequate interpretation has to take account of the total horizon of the work (cf., E.D. Hirsch, Jr., *Validity in Interpretation* [New Haven: Yale University, 1967]) and *The Aims of Interpretation* [Chicago: University of Chicago, 1976]).

[20]P is careful to avoid anachronisms. The distinction between clean and unclean is associated with Moses, so J's seven pairs of clean animals and one pair of unclean have to

in a diminished form. As we have seen, fear and dread have entered the world; bloodshed has to be reckoned with. The new reality, after the flood, is a diminished reality, a sinful reality. Yet it is the reality which God pledges never again to destroy. The covenant with Noah is immensely significant: it is the expression of God's unconditional commitment to all creation; sinful though it is, it will never again be subject to destruction. The implications for exiled Israel are inescapable: if God so loves the whole world, surely God's love for Israel must be at least as strong. The catastrophe of the exile cannot mean the ultimate destruction of Israel. As there was an unconditional covenant with Noah, so there must be hope of a new dispensation for Israel. These two accounts of creation and flood, situated before historical time, set up a paradigm. The goodness of creation was corrupted by violence (Gen 6:11-12). God's response is one of annihilation. A new era emerges which is less than perfect, yet its survival is guaranteed by God. The perception of the world has changed. It is no longer a world which may be completely cut off by God; it has become a world in which no disaster is final. The guarantee of this stability is the covenant with Noah (Gen 9:8-17).

In the repeopling of the world after the flood, P has a recurrent note which exiled, landless Israel would not have overlooked. As the nations spread from Noah's sons, each has its land (Gen 10:5, 20, 31). There is the natural association of nation with land. If, for all the nations, possession of their land is natural, surely Israel cannot remain landless forever.

With the world properly peopled, P moves to the story of Israel's ancestors. Abraham and Lot come into Canaan together. Their wealth is such that they must separate; Lot chooses the valley, leaving Canaan to Abraham (Gen 13*). There in the land, God appears to Abraham and, in the covenant, stakes out the future of Israel. The covenant with Abraham has the same unconditional quality as the covenant with Noah. The covenant will be an everlasting covenant, and its primary element is the commitment "to be God to you and to your descendants after

---

be reduced to two of every sort (and then food taken aboard, Gen 6:21). Similarly, P is mindful of the withholding of God's name until its revelation to Moses, although he will allow himself to use it, as narrator, at the important moment of Gen 17:1. For J, the use of the LORD (YHWH) began about the third generation (see Gen 4:26).

you" (17:7). And to Abraham and his descendants, all the land of Canaan will be given as an everlasting possession (17:8). Two elements come through: descendants and land. Two qualities come through: unconditional and everlasting.

The fulfillment is begun promptly. The descendants are started with the birth of Isaac. The possession of the land is begun with the acquisition of the field near Hebron, with the cave of Machpelah. There Abraham buries Sarah; there Abraham is buried; there a claim on the land begins to accumulate. Isaac marries from within his kinsfolk. Esau marries two local Hittites, and they make life miserable for Isaac and Rebekah. Jacob goes in search of a wife among his kin, and on his return to Canaan, God appears to him. The blessing is reiterated: be fruitful and multiply; the promise is repeated: descendants and the land, given to Abraham and Isaac (Gen 35:11-12). For both Abraham and Jacob, the presence of God is merely temporary; when the theophany is over, P specifically notes that God went up from them (Gen 17:22; 35:13a). Again, at least partial fulfillment follows promptly: P lists the twelve sons of Jacob (35:22b-26). After Isaac's death, P has Esau remove himself from the land, so that, like Abraham after Lot's departure, Jacob remains in sole possession of Canaan.

At this point, P has put clear emphasis on the unconditional covenant with Abraham, and on the issues of descendants and land. The promise is unequivocal; the fulfillment has been begun. The inner-family conflict and strife, a strong note in J, is absent from P's narrative. It emerges only around the theme of inter-marriage. The order, evident in creation, is unfolding itself steadily and surely on Israel's behalf. The Joseph story brings the whole clan into Egypt. But there, Jacob repeats God's blessing for Joseph, with the descendants to be a company of peoples and the land to be an everlasting possession (Gen 48:3-4). With Jacob's burial, the claim on the land is twice repeated: through the dead who lie there (49:29-33); through the act of purchase (50:12-13).

With the oppression in Egypt, P has to come to terms with a difficult aspect of his traditions. It is the very blessing itself (Exod 1:7) which brings the oppression on Israel. In God's self-revelation and revelation of the divine name to Moses, there is double emphasis on the point of God's forthcoming action. It is to give Israel the land of Canaan (Exod 6:4,8). What is very clear throughout the following episodes is the power of God. Even Pharaoh's resistance is attributed to God hardening his heart. So supreme is God's power, that after coming out of Egypt (12:40-41), Israel is directed back within Pharaoh's reach, so that God's dominion will be unmistakably clear (14:1-4). The episode of the Red Sea is a climactic, brilliant display of that power.

After it, P's story differs markedly from J's. There is no water shortage, no murmuring or rebellion. God's power is succeeded by God's providence. Israel is guided by Moses to Elim, with its twelve springs and its seventy palm trees (Exod 15:27). With the move into the wilderness of Sin, there is murmuring from the people. Far from being punished, it is rewarded with the appearance of the glory of God and the gift of manna. In the course of the story, P establishes the law of sabbath (Exod 16*).

From the wilderness of Sin, the people reach Sinai, and P's narrative reaches the establishment of the tent sanctuary. We have already mentioned the potential for meaning in P's omission of the law-burdened covenant of Sinai. The significance of the sanctuary has to be explored. All too often, the high point of P is seen to lie in the establishment and regulation of Israel's cult. But in the basic P narrative, there is surprisingly little about cultic regulations. Even in the establishment of the sanctuary, not all the essential items are accounted for; much less, if only the tent belonged in the original narrative (so Lohfink). The material is very extensive; somewhere between a quarter and a third of P's total text, depending on how the text is attributed (though less if Lohfink is followed).

The extent of the text is in part accounted for by recognizing that it results from P's concern for exact compliance with God's commands. This pattern was begun in the creation account. It continues throughout P. It contributes considerably to the bulk of the sanctuary text. The central theme of this sanctuary text is unmistakable: it is the presence of God in Israel's midst. For the first time in P's document, the presence of God, whether through cloud or glory, is to be permanently assured in Israel. This is an enormous step. It accounts for the detail and precision of the P narrative at this point. The all-powerful God of the exodus is now present to Israel in a permanent and tangible way.

Once this has been established, P has Israel move off toward the promised land (Num 10:11-12). At this point, for the first time in P's narrative, things turn nasty for Israel. The episode of the spies is related as a crisis in Israel's faith. Despite all the evidence of God's power which they have experienced, and despite the presence of God among them, all the Israelites bar two are portrayed having greater fear of the inhabitants of the land than trust in God. The result, for the desert generation, is that they will not reach the land. But the land is still God's gift to Israel (cf., Num 13:2; 20:12; 27:12). Moses, too, is excluded from entry into the land, for the same reason—lack of faith (Num 20*). Yet he and Aaron are to be succeeded by Eleazar and Joshua.

Something has happened to P's stately march toward the promised land. That something has been Israel's failure, the failure of both the people and their leaders. God's goal remains; the land has been given them (Num 27:12; Deut 34:4). Joshua is in place to lead the people, whenever the command comes from God (Num 27:17, 21). The enterprise has not been abandoned. Human failure has delayed the execution of God's plans; it has not deflected God from them. What is played out in this, the first constitutive generation of Israel, is paradigmatic for Israel's destiny. Israel's rebellion and failure will not deflect God's plans. It may entail a delay. Those who have doubted may die outside the land. But when God's command comes, Israel will enter into the everlasting possession of its land.

Elliger concludes:

> He (P) is not so deeply concerned to portray the events of a gray past, but to show to his reader or listener the living God active in these events, the living God active in their own present moment, who this God is, and, above all, what he purposes and does. The being of this God is far more powerful than all gods and all earthly powers; the nature of this God is a wisely guiding and graciously protecting favor, extending to all peoples, but especially to the people of the covenant. Just as he has given all peoples their land, for the development of their stock and their life, so it is his will to give the entire land of Canaan to his people Israel, for all time. The one deadly sin is: in unbelief, to doubt God's power to accomplish this will.[21]

[21]Elliger, "Sinn und Ursprung," 141.

This is P's message to his people. Just as God has set the world in order, ordained toward sabbath, so too God has set Israel on the road toward Canaan, the promised land. God, the creator, has the power to achieve it. Israel's unbelief can delay the accomplishment of God's will; it cannot deflect God from it. God's love for Israel is unconditional; it will not bow to rejection. God's presence is set in Israel's midst; it will not be withdrawn.

It is not central to an understanding of P whether the tent sanctuary was intended as a program for the future or a retrojection into the past; in either case, the sense of God's commitment to Israel is the same. It is, also, not central to the interpretation of P whether an account of the occupation of Canaan belonged to it or not. It was known to P and to his audience, as it is to us, that Israel took possession of Canaan. Narrated or not, it does not change the message of the Priestly Document outlined here.[22]

Whatever uncertainties remain about the precise extent of the Priestly Document, the key elements of the total picture can be summarized with confidence. P's stately account of creation is followed by an annihilating flood and God's unconditional commitment to a diminished and less-than-wholly-good world. P's account of the covenant with Abraham portrays God's unconditional commitment to the relationship with the people of Abraham and a promise of their everlasting possession of the land. Outside of that land, they are powerfully delivered, God's presence in their midst is established in complete compliance with the divine command. Equally under God's guidance, the march toward the promised land is begun. In all of this, the fragility of Israel can only delay God's purpose; human fragility cannot cancel out the divine will. Whether or not P portrayed Israel's taking possession of the land, there can hardly be any justifiable

[22]The verses attributed to P by Lohfink (Josh 4:19*; 5:10-12; 14:1, 2*; 18:1; 19:51) could very well be the additions of a later hand (so Noth). Depending on the analysis of the levels in Joshua 13-22, they may be simply added subordinate clauses. It is hard to imagine that a substantial P account was suppressed. Lohfink argues that only a brief report would have been needed, on the analogy of Exod 12:40-42 ("Priesterschrift," 198, n. 30). While it seems all the more unlikely for a short report not to have been preserved along with the other fragments, it is also clear that such a short report would not substantially alter the contours of P. P knew Israel entered the land. P asserts God's intention of giving Israel the land. Whether P left them at Moses' death or brought them to the finished distribution at Shiloh does not change the substance of the message. See also Blenkinsopp, "Structure of P."

doubt that for P the everlasting possession of the land lay in the future, at the end of a stately march which had as its driving force the unswerving will of God.

Today

AWE

The measured progress of the Priestly account of creation in Gen 1:1-2:4a is a remarkable reflection of the awe-inspiring nature of God. A believer within either the Jewish or Christian traditions is inevitably torn between two attitudes. One is wonder at a God who is near, who says to bruised Israel, "You are precious in my eyes, and honored, and I love you" (Isa 43:4). The other is awe before a God the immensity of whose being is utterly beyond our comprehension—"When I look at your heavens, the work of your fingers..." (Ps 8:3). The Priestly Document can serve as a powerful reminder that the God we believe to be intimately close to us is at the same time the wholly other whose being is infinitely distanced from our own.

Apathy is all too often a modern reaction to the question of God. Yet apathy is about the only attitude which is completely out of place where God is concerned. There are certain indivisible "either-or" issues which do not permit of any middle ground. The existence of God is one of these. God either exists or God does not exist. There is simply no other option. If God does not exist, our universe is the outcome of an extraordinary act of chance, the encounter of clouds of gas in cosmic space, with a beginning or a being which is totally unaccounted for. One may reckon the odds in favor of creation at almost uncountable billions to one (as in a calculation by well-known astronomer Sir Fred Hoyle) or at a simple fifty-fifty. Either way, the precise odds do not matter very much. The possibility that God does not exist can never be wiped from the slate of human consciousness.[23] But if God does exist,

---

[23]"Both the believer and the unbeliever share, each in his own way, doubt *and* belief, if they do not hide away from themselves and from the truth of their being. Neither can quite escape either doubt or belief; for the one, faith is present *against* doubt, for the other *through* doubt and in the *form* of doubt. It is the basic pattern of man's destiny only to be allowed to find the finality of his existence in this unceasing rivalry between doubt and belief, temptation and certainty" (J. Ratzinger, *Introduction to Christianity* [London: Search, 1969] 21).

then there is a mysterious presence in our universe with whom we are inextricably involved—there is no place for apathy. Love or hate, yes. Cringing fear or confident integrity, yes. But apathy, no! The possibility that God does exist can never be wiped from the slate of human consciousness either.

If God does exist, we are confronted by the mystery of one whose dimensions are of a magnitude that utterly escapes the boundaries of human knowledge. God by very definition exhausts our frameworks of space and time, or any other dimensions yet undreamed of. Before there was a beginning, before time made sense, there was God. Beyond the most farflung expanses of the immense dynamic of our universe, if we dare use such spatial terms analogically, there is God. And God is more intimately present than any presence we can imagine. The God whose incarnation took place in a stable in Bethlehem is the God whose vastness and mystery can only inspire human awe and reverence.

The Priestly Document places the history and destiny of Israel within the context of such a God. The majesty of creation is matched by the measured dimensions of the flood story. P's God does not brew up a rain storm; the deeps are unleashed and the vault of heaven opened, and the expansive force of creation is reversed. The God of the Priestly Document deals in the long term, the prospect of the everlasting. The covenant with all humankind through Noah is everlasting (Gen 9:16); the covenant with all Israel through Abraham is everlasting (Gen 17:1-8). This God then establishes a presence within the midst of the people of Israel. Not an intimate presence, rather an intimidating one (Exod 40:35); a majestic presence in the midst of the serried ranks of a people on the march toward the everlasting possession of their land (Num 2:17, 34; 10:11-12). There is no doubt of P's reverential awe before God.

One of the surprising aspects of twentieth-century culture is that an ever-increasing knowledge of the complexity of the subatomic world and an equally ever-increasing knowledge of the immensity of the universe lead so many moderns to be rather blasé about God. It is as if, knowing all this, we do not need God. Yet we do not know the origins of our universe and we have not yet plumbed the unifying laws which govern its innermost being. We constantly discover more of the marvel of creation, without wondering at the marvel of the God who might be its creator. P knew the vastness of our local solar system and confessed a God whose word brought it into being, the two great lights of sun and moon and the stars as well (Gen 1:14-19). We know so much more and seem to think it sophistication to be unimpressed—even at the possibility that all of this comes ultimately from God.

COMMITMENT

The flood story is witness in its own strange way to the awesome holiness of the God of the Priestly Document: a corrupt and violent creation could not stand before this God (Gen 7:11-13). Equally strange, but vastly significant, is the re-established relationship after the flood. God makes an irreversible commitment to a creation which is clearly perceived to be less than holy (Gen 9:1-17). The all-holy God has come to terms with the less-than-holy creation in which there is fear and dread and homicidal violence. This is no flash-in-the-pan assertion of divine commitment. The whole movement of the Priestly Document asserts this commitment of God's to Israel.

This is a remarkable affirmation of faith when we consider the context within which the Priestly Document was composed: either in the exilic period or shortly afterwards, when in either case Israel's situation called for tears and weeping (cf., Ps 137:1; Ezra 3:12). In this situation, when all the high hopes of Israel had been laid low, the Priestly Document can assert the unconditional commitment of God to humankind, through Noah, and to Israel, through Abraham. Speaking to a broken Israel, P has no need to provide a catalogue of failures of Israel. The reality of failure was all too evident to P's contemporaries. As we will see in the next chapter, the Yahwist drew up such a catalogue of Israel's murmuring against God. But the Yahwist was probably addressing an Israel at the height of its power and prestige. All the more remarkable then that the Priestly Document, composed at the low point of Israel's fortunes, can still emphasize the irrevocability of God's commitment to this people, which in its fragility and failure typified so much of human experience.

There is in the Priestly Document a boldness of theological genius which can unfold the majestic holiness of God and, at the same time, assert the unshakable commitment of this all-holy God to a creation and a nation that had so deeply experienced its weakness and its failure.

RECOMMENDED FURTHER READING

Sue Boorer, "The Kerygmatic Intention of the Priestly Document." *Australian Biblical Review* 25 (1977) 12-20.

Walter Brueggemann, "The Kerygma of the Priestly Writers." Chap. 6 in *The Vitality of Old Testament Traditions,* edited by W. Brueggemann and H. W. Wolff. 2nd ed. Atlanta: Knox, 1982.

Ralph W. Klein, "When Memory is Hope: The Response to Exile in P. " Chap. 6 in *Israel in Exile.* Philadelphia: Fortress, 1979.

—————, "The Message of P." In *Die Botschaft und die Boten: Festschrift für Hans Walter Wolff zum 70. Geburtstag,* edited by Jörg Jeremias and Lothar Perlitt, 57-66. Neukirchen: Neukirchener Verlag, 1981.

Norbert Lohfink, "Creation and salvation in Priestly theology." *Theology Digest* 30 (1982) 3-6.

Sean McEvenue, *The Narrative Style of the Priestly Writer.* AnBib 50. Rome: Biblical Institute, 1971.

Claus Westermann, *Genesis 1-11,* 594-599. Minneapolis: Augsburg, 1984.

Appendix

The Text of the Priestly Document
(as identified by M. Noth, K. Elliger, and N. Lohfink)

The first impression, on comparing these three analyses, is of the extensive unanimity on the material to be attributed to P. In Genesis the differences are practically negligible. From Exodus 35 onwards, the text identified by Elliger differs from Noth's in attributing more of the material as perhaps belonging to the later additions to P, indicated here by parentheses, ( ). These later additions are usually designated P^s (= supplements to P).

The text identified by Lohfink differs from the other two in four areas.[24] Firstly, in Exodus 12, reference to the Passover is omitted. Secondly, the instructions given on Mt. Sinai for the construction of the sanctuary are restricted to the tent; hence the omissions in the instructions (Exodus 25-29), in the account of their execution (Exodus 37-40), and in the account of its consecration (Leviticus 8). Thirdly, in Numbers 1, 2, and 4, the wordy lists are reduced to their bare bones. In Numbers 1, this is basically the totals for each tribe, and the overall total; in Numbers 2, there is the camping order for the tribes, listed simply by name from east to south to west to north; and in Numbers 4, the focus is restricted to the tent of meeting, omitting the same details omitted earlier (e.g., the ark, the table, the seven-branched candlestick, etc). Fourthly, Lohfink's text extends P to include an account of the conquest of the land; hence the additions in Num 34:1-18, Deuteronomy, and Joshua.

There is remarkable unanimity on the overall picture. There is doubt about the extent of the original traditions about the sanctuary, the census, and the camping order; what is at stake is

---

[24]While based on Elliger, Lohfink's text incorporates results from his own investigations, from earlier commentaries, and from a number of recent studies (Lohfink, "Priesterschrift," 198).

largely a matter of emphasis. Lohfink's extension to include the conquest is a major variation from the picture of P painted by Noth and Elliger.

NOTH	ELLIGER	LOHFINK
GENESIS		
1:1-2:4a	1:1-2:4a	1:1-2:4a
5:1-32*	5:1-32*	5:1-32*
6:9-22	6:9-22	6:9-22
7:6,11,13-16a, 18-21,24	7:6,11,13-16a, 17a,18-21,24	7:6,11,13-16a, 17a,18-21,24
8:1-2a,3b-5,7,13a, 14-19	8:1-2a,3b-5,13a, 14-19	8:1-2a,3b-5,13a, 14-19
9:1-17,28-29	9:1-17,28-29	9:1-3,7-17,28-29
10:1-7,20,22,23, 31-32	10:1-4a,5aβ-7,20,22, 23,31-32	10:1-7,20,22,23, 31-32
11:10-27,31-32	11:10-27,31-32	11:10-27,31-32
12:4b-5	12:4b-5	12:4b-5
13:6,11b,12abα	13:6,11b,12abαβ	13:6,11b,12*
19:29	19:29	19:29
16:1a,3,15-16	16:1,3,15-16	16:1,3,15-16
17:1-27	17:1-27	17:1-13,14*,15-27
21:1b-5	21:1b-5	21:1b-5
23:1-20	23:1-20	23:1-20
25:7-11a,12-17, 19,20,26b	25:7-11a,12-17, 19,20,26b	25:7-11a,12-17, 26b
26:34-35	26:34-35	26:34-35
27:46-28:9	27:46-28:9	27:46-28:9
31:18*	31:18*	31:18*
33:18a	33:18a	33:18a
35:6,9-13a,15, 22b-29	35:6a,9-13,15, 22b-29	35:6a,9-15, 22b-29
36:1-14	36:1-14	36:1-2a,6-8,40-43
37:1,2aαb	37:1-2	37:1-2
41:46a	41:46a	41:46a
46:6-7	46:6-7	46:6-7
47:27b-28	47:27b-28	47:27b-28
48:3-6	48:3-6	48:3-6
49:1a,29-33	49:1a,28b-33	49:1a,28b-33
50:12-13	50:12-13	50:12-13

EXODUS

1:1-7,13-14	1:1-5,7,13-14	1:1-5,7,13-14
2:23aβb-25	2:23aγb-25	2:23*-25
6:2-12	6:2-12	6:2-12
7:1-13,19,20aα, 21b,22	7:1-13,19,20aα, 21b,22	7:1-13,19,20*, 21b,22
8:1-3,11aβb-15	8:1-3,11a*b-15	8:1-3,11*-15
9:8-12	9:8-12	9:8-12
		11:9-10
12:1,3-20,28,40-41	12:1,3-14,28,40-41	12:37a,40-42
		13:20
14:1-4,8,9aβb, 10abβ, 15-18,21aαb,22-23, 26,27aα,28-29	14:1-4,8a,10abγ, 15-18,21aαb,22-23, 26,27aα,28-29	14:1-4,8-9,10*, 15-18,21*,22-23, 26,27*,28-29
15:22aα,27	15:27	15:22*,27
16:1-3,6-7,9-27, 32-35a	16:1-3,6-7,9-13a, 14bα,16abγ-20, 22-26, 31a, 35b	16:1-3,6-7,9-12,13*, 14*,16*,17,18*, 19-21a, 22*, 23-26, 31a,35b
17:1abα	17:1abα	17:1*
19:2a,1	19:2a,1	19:2a,1
24:15b-18	24:15b-18a	24:15b-18a
25:1-29:46	25:1-27:19	25:1-2,8,9*
		26:1-30
	28:1-41	
	29:1-37,42b-46	29:43-46
31:18	31:18	31:18
		34:29-32
35:1a,4b-10,20-27, 29-31a,32-33	35:1a,4b-10,20-29, (30-33)	35:4-5a,10,20-22a,29
36:2-7	36:2	36:2-3a,8*
37:1-24	(37:1-24)	
36:8-38	(36:8-38)	
38:1-7,9-22,24-31	(38:1-7,9-20)	
39:1-32,43	39:(1-31),32,43	39:32-33a,42-43
40:1-2,9,17-25, 28-29a,33	40:17,33b-34,(35)	40:17,33b-35

LEVITICUS

8:1-6aα,7-10aα, 12-36	(8:1-10aα,12-36)	
9:1-7a,8-14,15b-23	9:1-24	9:1*,2-3,4b-7,8*, 12a,15a,21b-24

NUMBERS

1:1-47	1:1-3,(4-19a),19b-43, (44),45-47	1:1,2*,3*,19b, 21*,23*, 25*,27*,29*,31*,33*, 35*,37*,39*,41*,43*,46
2:1-34	(2:1-34)	2:1*,2,3*,5*,7a,10a, 12*,14a,18a,20a,22a, 25a,27*,29a,34
3:14-32a,33-51	3:14-16,(17-38), 39,(40-51)	
4:1-10,12-15,21-28a, 29-33a,34-39		4:1*,2*,3,34*,35-36, 37*,38-40,41*, 42-44,45*,46*,47-48
8:5-22	(8:5-10,12-15a,20)	
9:15-23	(9:15-18)	
10:11-12	10:11-12	10:11-13
		12:16b
13:1-3a,17aβ,21,25, 26*,32,33aαb	13:1-3a,17aβ,21,25, 26a,32	13:1-3a,17*,21,25, 26*,32
14:1a,2-3,5-10,26-27a, 26-29aα,35-38	14:1a,2,5-7,10, 26-29aα,	14:1a,2,5-7, 10, 26-28,29*, 35-38
20:1aαb,2,3bα,4,6-7, 8aβbβ,10,11b-12, 22b,23aα,25-29	20:1aα,2,3b,4,6-7, 8aβγbβ,10,11b-12, 22*,23aα,25-29	20:1*,2,3b-7, 8*,10,11b, 12*,22b,23*,25-29
21:4*	21:4aα *	21:4*,10-11
22:1b	22:1b	22:1
27:12-23	27:12-14a,15-23	27:12-14a,15-23
		34:1-18

DEUTERONOMY

		1:3
		32:48-52
34:1aα,7-9	34:1a,7-9	34:1*,7-9

JOSHUA

	4:19*
	5:10-12
	14:1,2*
	18:1
	19:51

3

The Yahwist

Recommended preliminary reading

Before reading the body of the chapter, it will be helpful to have read the following passages:
Genesis 12:1-3; 18:17-19 (and vv 20-33); 26:12-14, 26-31; 28:10-16; and also Genesis 22:15-18; 26:3-5
Numbers 23:1-20 (mainly Yahwist); 24:1-19

Our treatment of the Pentateuch began with a consideration of the present text, as it stands in our Bibles now (chap. 1). Next we moved back a stage to look at the Priestly Document (P), a document which formed quite a late strand in the evolution of what was to become the pentateuchal text (chap. 2). When the relatively easily identifiable priestly material is set to one side, the remaining text offers a substantially coherent presentation of the story of Israel. "Substantially coherent" because there are still duplications, repetitions, and interruptions to the thread of the story line. It is clear that in a number of places in the text, similar traditions have been combined to form a common text. In the course of scholarship, these have been identified as the Yahwist (J) and the Elohist (E) sources, and their combination is referred to as JE. In my judgment, the existence of the Elohist as an independent and coherent source is open to serious doubt. In this chapter, we will turn our attention to the literary work of the

Yahwist. The material usually attributed to the Elohist will be left aside; whether it derived from a single source or comprised a variety of different traditions supplementing J need not be resolved here.[1] The text attributed to the Yahwist by Martin Noth is identified in the appendix to this chapter. It has been common wisdom for some time to associate the Yahwist with the period of David and Solomon, in Jerusalem, while expressing cautious reserve in view of the uncertainty of any such dating. Recent views advocating a much later date will be mentioned in the note at the end of the chapter.

In looking at the Yahwist narrative or the work of the Yahwist, it is quite important to be aware of what we are talking about. The Yahwist, credited as the Bible's first theologian, is not a writer in the modern sense. The task we believe the Yahwist performed was that of organizing Israel's traditions—or better, a selection from them—into a literary whole. The genius of the Yahwist does not lie in the creative ability of his own writing. Rather, it lies in the ability to perceive meaning in his people's traditions, and to select and arrange those traditions in such a way as to bring out this meaning for others to see. Nor was the Yahwist the first to organize Israel's traditions; there is evidence for the work of predecessors. The Yahwist is the name we give to a particular stage in the development and organization of Israel's traditions, a stage that we believe to be identifiable and to bear the mark of a theological mind of genius.[2]

The traditions of Israel, then, can be presumed to have had a relatively long life before the Yahwist set out to shape them into a literary work. These would be traditions about the patriarchal figures, Abraham, Isaac, and Jacob. They would be traditions about Israel in Egypt, the exodus and the traverse of the

---

[1]Claus Westermann, for example, dismisses an independent E source in Genesis 12-36 (*Genesis 12-36* [Minneapolis: Augsburg, 1985] 571-72). H.W. Wolff's study, "The Elohistic Fragments in the Pentateuch" (in *The Vitality of Old Testament Traditions*, edited by W. Brueggemann and H.W. Wolff, 67-82 [2nd ed.; Atlanta: John Knox, 1982]) is far less convincing than his companion studies on the Yahwist and the Deuteronomistic History. My disappointment with A.W. Jenks. *The Elohist and North Israelite Traditions* (SBLMS 22; Missoula: Scholars Press, 1977) is expressed in *CBQ* 47 (1985) 131-33.

[2]Note Westermann's comment on the Yahwist in Genesis 12-36: "The whole . . . reveals a planned structure with a purpose; it is the work of a writer who is at the same time a transmitter, a storyteller, and a theologian" (*Genesis 12-36*, 571).

wilderness. They were traditions which were significant for Israel, and so they were surely retold from generation to generation. Precisely because of their significance, in that constant retelling they would also have been reshaped. And there lies the nub of a grave problem: in the retelling and reshaping of traditions, how do we know what is to be attributed to the Yahwist and what the Yahwist inherited from his forebears?

In earlier years of OT scholarship, there was a confidence that the actual text and contribution of the Yahwist could be identified by characteristics of style and vocabulary. In this understanding, it was not a difficult matter to identify the work of the Yahwist himself. More recently, the criteria of style and vocabulary have been seen to be much less reliable, so that the identification of the Yahwist, at least as a theologian, has become more problematic (see below, chap. 4.)

In the heyday of source critical analysis of the pentateuchal text, in the late nineteenth century, scholars were concerned principally with the accurate attribution of the text to the Yahwist, the Priestly Writer, and so on. The idea of looking for the shape of the literary works created by these authors and, therefore, of looking for the communication they were trying to express, appears not to have become a conscious endeavor until the early 1930's.

As a rough generalization, we may see three stages in the approach to the Yahwist. At a first stage, concern focused principally on Gen 12:1-3, as the immensely significant link between the traditions of Genesis 2-11 and the early patriarchal traditions of Israel. At a second stage, concern was focused on the movement of the stories within Genesis 2-11, throwing into sharp relief the significance of the Yahwist's linking verses in Gen 12:1-3. At a third stage, the focus shifted to the articulation of the theme of blessing throughout the patriarchal traditions.

FIRST STAGE

In the first stage, Gen 12:1-3 is recognized as the work of a compiler of Israel's traditions rather than being itself one of the ancient traditions. It does not bear the marks of the old traditions: it is not in story form, for example; it is not associated with a particular place or sanctuary. It is simply a divine speech from

God to Abraham. And it is a very dense and carefully structured speech. It begins with a command to Abraham to be on the move. The structure of the command reveals something of Israel's understanding of what it meant to move with their God. What Abraham is to leave is clearly named: "Go from your country and your kindred and your father's house"—a triad of the things which were near and dear to Abraham, and which would naturally have constituted his basic security. These he is to leave for "the land that I will show you"—a vague and uncertain assurance.

This is followed by a very carefully structured set of variations around the theme of blessing. The word itself occurs five times. Its first focus is on Abraham himself: "And I will make of you a great nation, and I will bless you." Then it begins a modulation in the direction of others, although still with the focus principally on Abraham: "And I will make your name great, so that you will be a blessing." The idea of the "great name" implies others who hear that name and respect it and bless themselves by it. The focus on others is intensified, when Abraham becomes the touchstone of the destiny of others: according as they behave toward Abraham, so will their destiny be. "I will bless those who bless you, and him who curses you I will curse." And finally, the focus is swung worldwide: "And by you all the families of the earth shall bless themselves."

It is a text of remarkable density, with single-minded concentration on the one theme of blessing. The blessing is given to Abraham, but it is given to Abraham eventually for others. It is a text which is the result of long reflection on the Abraham traditions and their significance. It is a text, too, which is the result of long reflection on humankind's need for blessing. In its own right, it is an extraordinary text. It implies that, after contemplation of the human scene and after contemplation of Israel's traditions, the Yahwist concluded that Israel's destiny was to be a bringer of blessing to "all the families of the earth." Not only is this a reflection on Israel's destiny; it is a reflection on the nature of God. The Yahwist understands God as a force moving to make blessing effective in the human world. And the Yahwist portrays God as making this move for no other reason than humanity's need for blessing. And finally, the Yahwist portrays a God who makes the move toward blessing, not with awesome divine directness, but through the mediation of human forces. This text, Gen 12:1-3, stands at the head of Israel's recorded traditions about itself; it puts a very special stamp on Israel's understanding of itself, of its world, and of its God, right from the outset. The world is in need of blessing. God is intent on blessing. Israel is chosen, in Abraham, to be the vehicle of that blessing—"for all the families of the earth."

Two comments need to be made at this point. One is a matter of the text. The Hebrew text in v 3 has: I will bless *those* who bless you, and *him* who curses you I will curse. The difference between the plural *those* and the singular *him* is only a *yod,* the jot of the "jot and tittle" in Mt 5:18. But its significance is considerable. As the Hebrew stands, the masses (the plural) will bless Abraham, and so be blessed by God. It is only the odd-one-out (the singular) who will be foolish enough to curse Abraham and so be cursed by God. It is regrettable that the *Jerusalem Bible* and the *New English Bible* should have emended the Hebrew text to make both occurrences plural and so obscure this otherwise important difference.

The second comment relates to those who might want to water down the significance of the blessing offered to all the families of the earth through Abraham. The *JB* notes on v 3b: "Its precise meaning is: 'the nations shall say to each other: May you be blessed as Abraham was' (cf. v 2 and 48:20; Jer 29:22)." This literally correct understanding opens the way to a possible belittling of the significance of this blessing for *all the families of the earth* by making it narrowly particularistic on Israel's part. Israel will be the object of others' vain longing. Other nations will long for blessing such as Israel has—but they will not receive it. Any such demeaning understanding would go against the plain meaning of the text. The text says that those who bless Abraham, God will bless. We may suppose, in the context, that those who wish to be blessed "as Abraham is blessed," would also bless Abraham. It would make little sense to curse Abraham and then ask to be blessed as he is. But the text assures us that those who bless Abraham will be blessed by God. The significance of this blessing can hardly be underestimated. The remarkable universalism of the text can hardly be denied.

SECOND STAGE

In the second stage, Gerhard von Rad brought the significance of this blessing into sharp focus by his analysis of the traditions of Genesis 2-11. He saw there a series of four stories : the fall, Cain and Abel, the flood, and the tower of Babel. In the first three of these, von Rad observed the presence of a note of grace—absent in the last one. In the story of the fall, as the first man and woman are being driven from the garden, their comfortable and intimate relationship with God ruptured, the storyteller shows that all is not lost: "And the LORD God made for Adam and for his wife garments of skins and clothed them" (Gen 3:21). All relationship with God is not lost. The creator, in a first sally into the garment industry, will still clothe the man and the woman.

In much the same way, the story of Cain ends on a note of grace. Adam and Eve were banished from the garden; more emphatically, Cain is banished from the presence of God (Gen 4:14,16). Yet not before God has put a mark on Cain—which, contrary to some popular usage, is a protective mark. Cain feared for his life, as the consequence of what he had done; the mark put on him is to protect him (cf. Gen 4:15b). Despite what Cain has done, therefore, some relationship with God continues.

Evil persists, and the story of the flood portrays its consequences as the annihilation of humankind. "And the LORD was sorry that he had made man on the earth, and it grieved him to his heart" (Gen 6:6). Yet despite this, and amidst all the mystery of the story of the flood, the storyteller still maintains the existence of the relationship with God. "I will never again curse the ground because of man.... While the earth remains, seedtime and harvest, cold and heat, summer and winter, day and night, shall not cease" (Gen 8:21-22).

In fact, it would seem that, in the Yahwist's flood story, the storyteller sets out to portray God as having become in some way reconciled to human fragility and sin. What other sense can we make of the motivation given in the two passages just quoted? In Gen 6:5, the reason given for the flood which is about to happen is: "The LORD saw that the wickedness of man was great in the earth, and that *every imagination of the thoughts of his heart was only evil continually.*" And in Gen 8:21, the reason given for why the flood, which has just happened, will never happen again is: "I will never again curse the ground because of man, for *the imagination of man's heart is evil from his youth."* The similarity of phrasing is far too striking to be overlooked. The direct opposition of thought is far too obvious to be accidental. This is storytelling, not theological discourse, but it is deep theology. And like much great theology, it is expressed in paradox. Somewhere between the opposites of Gen 6:5 and 8:21, the infinite distance between creator and creature has been bridged, the menacing tension between uncreated holiness and sinful creation has been reconciled.[3]

For all of this fresh start, humankind is still portrayed as unerringly estranging itself from God. The story of the Tower of Babel leaves the human race in a condition we can easily recognize: scattered, divided, and alienated. And this time, there is no note of grace. "And from there the LORD scattered them abroad over the face of all the earth" (Gen 11:9). That is it. It is into this situation that the Yahwist presents the call of Abraham, with its promise of blessing for all the families of the earth.

This is the significance of Gen 12:1-3, the key formulation of the Yahwist's theology: it presents the call of Abraham as God's response to human need. Von Rad's understanding of the Yahwist's prologue in Genesis 2-11 shows the increasing deterioration of the human plight. Three times, humankind distances itself from God; three times, God is still there with them. But the fourth time, there is nothing until the call of Abraham, which is the beginning of the destiny of Israel as chosen people. Von Rad's approach heightened the significance of Gen 12:1-3, since it brought the telling of the mythic stories of human beginnings into close correlation with God's action in the call of Abraham. The choice of Israel is the fourth action, the sign that God is still there with the human race—Immanuel in our midst.

THIRD STAGE

In the third stage, H. W. Wolff extended the study of the Yahwist in a different direction.[4] Wolff's question was whether

---

[3]See G. von Rad, *Genesis* (OTL, rev. ed.; Philadelphia: Westminster, 1972) 122-23.

[4]H.W. Wolff, "The Kerygma of the Yahwist," *The Vitality of Old Testament Traditions* (ed. W. Brueggemann and H.W. Wolff, 2nd ed.; Atlanta: John Knox, 1982) 41-66.

Gen 12:1-3 expressed the import of the entire Yahwistic work (p. 55). His response was to show that the theme of blessing for all nations had been introduced at key points throughout the narrative, with the assumption that this was the Yahwist's doing.

After Gen 12:1-3, the first of these key points is Gen 18:18. The traditional material on the destruction of Sodom and Gomorrah is about to be introduced. It will be prefaced by an incredibly lively scene in which Abraham haggles with God with remarkable success. From a starting point of fifty just men, Abraham beats God down to ten, "For the sake of ten I will not destroy it" (18:32). Of course, Abraham is unable to be portrayed as completely successful, for Sodom and Gomorrah had long been destroyed. The sense of the story, however, is clear: this Abraham, who has been chosen by God, is gifted with remarkable powers of intercession and uses them on behalf of others. What is important, in our context, is the reason why Abraham is given the information in the first place, thus enabling him to intercede. God's statement is given as: "Shall I hide from Abraham what I am about to do, seeing that Abraham shall become a great and mighty nation, *and all the nations of the earth shall bless themselves by him?*" The theme of Gen 12:1-3 is stirring in the narrative.

The theme returns in Gen 26:12-33 although in a different fashion. Here it is used within the flow of the narrative, rather than spelled out in terms of a speech. It reveals two further aspects of the significance of blessing. Isaac sowed in the region of Gerar, in Philistine territory, and reaped a hundredfold. The text notes: "The LORD blessed him, and the man became rich, and gained more and more until he became very wealthy" (vv 12-13). So prosperity is one of the aspects of blessing. But the prosperity of Isaac is depicted as arousing Philistine envy. A confrontation eventuates between Isaac and Abimelech, king of Gerar, along with his adviser and his army chief. These Philistines, of all people, are presented as saying: "We see plainly that the LORD is with you.... You are now the blessed of the LORD" (vv 28-29). The outcome is peace, peace between the Philistines and Israel (in the person of Isaac). In the Davidic-Solomonic period, the probable period of the Yahwist, this must have seemed a most impressive achievement. For in the time of Saul and David, the Philistines were Israel's constant enemies and a very real threat to Israel's national survival. So peace, even between archenemies, is another of the aspects of this blessing.

When Isaac blesses Jacob (Gen 27:27-29), there is again an echo of Gen 12:1-3 at the end, "Cursed be every one who curses you, and blessed be every one who blesses you." This is, in all probability, an older formulation and not the Yahwist's own work. If so, it is all the more significant that, in Gen 12:1-3, the Yahwist changed the curse from plural ("every one") to singular.

In Gen 28:14, the theme of blessing occurs again in a divine speech. Jacob's trickery and deceit have earned him his brother Esau's mortal hatred, and Jacob has to leave the land for his life (Gen 27:41-45). In search of a wife for Isaac, Abraham had earlier sent the senior servant of his house back to the land from which they had come. But he had been specific: on no account must the boy, the vehicle of the promise, go back there (Gen 24:6). Now, in the third generation, Jacob is about to go back to Haran, retracing Abraham's steps. From a narrative point of view, the movement of the promise is reversed. So, at this key point in the narrative, God is presented giving assurance to Jacob and re-affirming the promise of blessing. "And by you and your descendants shall *all the families of the earth bless themselves"*(28:14). Within the story, the blessing theme is again turned into the concrete reality of prosperity. Laban makes the fascinating avowal, "If you will allow me to say so, I have learned by divination that the LORD has blessed me because of you"(30:27). And Jacob unhesitatingly agrees, "The LORD has blessed you wherever I turned" (30:30).

Wolf sees these stories linking the theme of blessing to Israel's principal neighbors at the time of David. The story of Lot brings in the association with the Moabites and Ammonites (cf., Gen 19:30-38); the story of Isaac brings in the Philistines; and the story of Jacob and Laban brings in the Arameans.[5] In the Joseph story, the trace of the theme of blessing is slighter, but its focus is swung universally wide. The first pointer is in the blessing of the Egyptian's house (Gen 39:5). The theme, though without the language of blessing, is strongly present in Gen 41:55-57, for survival is the ultimate blessing, and "all the earth came to Egypt

[5]Wolff, "Kerygma," 59.

to Joseph to buy grain, because the famine was severe over all the earth" (v 57).

Before turning to the Balaam stories, where he sees the Yahwist's narrative ending, Wolff claims one more trace of the theme in the trajectory of the text. In Egypt, at the moment of the exodus, and despite an earlier fiery final encounter (Exod 10:28-29), the Pharaoh sends Israel out into the liberation of the exodus—and asks a blessing for himself. "Rise up, go forth from among my people, both you and the people of Israel; and go, serve the LORD . . . and bless me also!" (Exod 12:31-32).

Wolff regards the Balaam stories as the last major complex in the Yahwist's narrative.[6] Two themes are evident in these stories: firstly, Balaam's words are from God and no other source; secondly, instead of the expected curse, for which he was hired and paid, Balaam spoke blessing over Israel. So the word of blessing comes from God, and it has power enough to overcome curse. The formulation of this word of blessing points to David's time: "I see him, but not now; I behold him, but not nigh: a star shall come forth out of Jacob, and a scepter shall rise out of Israel; it shall crush the forehead of Moab, and break down all the sons of Sheth" (Num 24:17). The star and the scepter are David.

What Wolff's treatment of the Yahwist has done is to encompass the entire narrative within the vision of Gen 12:1-3. The world is in need (Genesis 2-11). And the whole of Israel's history is a story of God's response to that need (Genesis 12—Numbers 24). Before assessing the adequacy of this treatment, there are two further issues to be noted.

Firstly, there is the question of the Yahwist's authority for this view of Israel's destiny. Is this simply one person's vision, or is there some further authority for it? Wolff's response to that question may throw intriguing light on the theological procedures of ancient Israel. The Yahwist found the seed of his understanding already present in the tradition. Gen 12:3a, as we have seen, brings Abraham's destiny into relation with the destiny of others: "I will bless those who bless you, and him who curses you I will curse." And this is found already in Gen 27:29 and in Num 24:9b.[7]

[6]Wolff, "Kerygma," 43.

[7]Wolff, "Kerygma," 51-53.

In the tradition itself, the Yahwist may have found the key to perceiving the inner significance of that tradition.

Secondly, an idea does not lose its power simply because it has been expressed once. Nor is the theme of blessing for all nations the exclusive possession of the Yahwist. Later generations have added it into the text, at places where the Yahwist had left it unspoken. These are Gen 22:15-18; 26:3-5. They are both marked with the style and language and thought of the deuteronomic circles associated with the book of Deuteronomy and the reform of Josiah, in the late seventh century. The significance of these additions should not be overlooked. They are intelligently located. Gen 22:15-18 comes immediately after the testing of Abraham and the threat to the promise vested in Isaac, both involved in the story of the sacrifice of Isaac. There is need for the blessing to be reaffirmed. Gen 26:3-5 takes cognizance of the fact that a divine speech announced this theme of blessing at or near the beginning of the Abraham and Jacob cycles of stories; so a speech is inserted for Isaac as well. The significance of these insertions is that the centrality of the theme of blessing in the Yahwist's narrative was still understood and powerfully alive in the late seventh century. The blessing is universal: "and by your descendants all the nations of the earth shall bless themselves" (22:18a; 26:4b). Finally, we may note the extension of the theme of blessing into areas well beyond the Yahwist. The principal texts are: Ps 47:8-9 ("The princes of the peoples gather as *the people of the God of Abraham*"); Isa 19:23-25; Jer 4:1-2; Zech 8:13, 23; Acts 3:25; and Gal 3:8. The text from Isaiah is so remarkable, it deserves to be quoted in full:

> In that day Israel will be the third with Egypt and Assyria, a blessing in the midst of the earth, whom the LORD of hosts has blessed, saying, "Blessed be Egypt *my people*, and Assyria *the work of my hands*, and Israel *my heritage*." (Isa 19:24-25, emphasis mine)

Given the oppressive roles played by Egypt and Assyria in Israel's history, this a truly remarkable statement.

FURTHER CONSIDERATIONS

Wolff's admirable study has covered a wide sweep of the Yahwist's text. One area, however, remains untouched: the wilderness traditions. Wolff comments: "As thorough as the Yahwist has been in dealing with the patriarchal and exodus themes, he is positively stingy when it comes to the sojourn in Sinai. But how could it be otherwise in the light of his kerygma?"[8] However, it is unsatisfactory when an interpretation cannot cope with a major part of a text. It casts doubt on whether the interpretation has correctly seized the appropriate horizon of the text. In the present case, it is all the more worrying when we take into account the claim by both G. Coats and V. Fritz that it was the Yahwist himself who gave a negative tone to the wilderness traditions.[9] If this is the case, it becomes absolutely imperative to take the wilderness traditions into account in order to give an adequate interpretation of the Yahwist's text.

I believe that it is possible to provide an interpretation of the Yahwist in which the wilderness traditions find their proper place.[10] This interpretation relies on the existence, in the Jerusalem of David and Solomon, of a particular theological view of Israel's recent past history. I have argued that the theologian-authors of the Ark Narrative (1 Sam 4-6; 2 Sam 6) intended to draw a line through the history of Israel's relationship with God (see below, in chap. 6). This relationship is put into suspense with the departure of the ark in 1 Sam 4-6. Kiriath-jearim, to which the ark returned, was no more than a cultic backwater; the ark is not portrayed as returning to the mainstream of Israel's life. And the departure of the ark is narrated in such a way as to make clear that it was understood by the narrator as God's doing (1 Sam 4:1b-7:2aα)— "Yahweh's power and purpose is what the story is about."[11] The

---

[8]Wolff, "Kerygma," 61.

[9]G.E. Coats, *Rebellion in the Wilderness* (Nashville: Abingdon, 1968); V. Fritz, *Israel in der Wüste* (Marburger Theologische Studien 7; Marburg: N.G. Elwert, 1970). This view has been criticized by B.S. Childs, *Exodus* (London: SCM, 1974) 254-64.

[10]See A.F. Campbell, "The Yahwist Revisited," *AusBR* 27 (1979) 2-14.

[11]Forcefully expressed by P.D. Miller, Jr. and J.J.M. Roberts, although with a different understanding of the story (*The Hand of the Lord: A Reassessment of the "Ark Narrative" of 1 Samuel* [The Johns Hopkins Near Eastern Studies; Baltimore: Johns Hopkins, 1977]

relationship is not portrayed as fully resumed until David's time and the return of the ark to Jerusalem—and that too is portrayed as God's doing (2 Sam 6:2-23).[12]

Such a theological interpretation of history should not be thought of as accepted throughout all Israel. It overlooks the figure of Samuel and bypasses the era of Saul. Nevertheless, precisely this is done by Psalm 78, which moves directly from Shiloh to Jerusalem (see vv 59-72). In fact, Psalm 78 copes rather boldly with the period of Samuel and Saul by implying that, during it, God was as soundly asleep as a warrior with a hangover (v 65). What is important is the probability that the conviction was abroad in tenth-century Jerusalem that, with David's coming to power in Jerusalem, the slate of past failure had been wiped clean and God had begun something new in Israel.[13]

Interpretation

Both the Ark Narrative and Psalm 78 testify to the existence of the theological conviction that God departed with disfavor from the Israel of Shiloh and the Elides and that God returned with favor to the Israel of David. Combined with the earlier stages of interpretation, this view can give a particularly sharp contour to the interpretation of the Yahwist. In essence, it would run like this: the world was in dire need of blessing; God chose Israel to be vehicle of that blessing to all the families of the earth; throughout the patriarchal stories, Israel approximated fairly well to the demand of its destiny; in Egypt, the picture changed, with oppression becoming the dominant theme—inflicted by the Egyptians on the Israelites, and inflicted on the Egyptians in their turn in the form of the plagues; but at least the Pharaoh implored a blessing from Moses; Israel in the wilderness murmured against

---

60). Despite other differences, on this point Miller and Roberts and I are at one: the narrative is about the power and purpose of the God of Israel.

[12]See A.F. Campbell, *The Ark Narrative (1 Sam 4-6; 2 Sam 6): A Form-critical and Traditio-historical Investigation* (SBLDS 16; Missoula: Scholars Press, 1975); also, idem, "Yahweh and the Ark: A Case Study in Narrative," *JBL* 98 (1979) 31-43.

[13]See A.F. Campbell, "Psalm 78: A Contribution to the Theology of Tenth Century Israel," *CBQ* 41 (1979) 51-79.

God, wanting back into Egypt, living its life under the sign of curse rather than of blessing, symbolically expressive of our sinful world; but with Balaam blessing emerged out of curse—and it is a blessing which points to David.

So the Yahwist would have mustered Israel's traditions to portray a world in need of blessing, to portray the choice of Israel as being God's response to this need of the world, and to portray the various stages and phases of Israel's response, culminating in the picture of total failure in the wilderness—relieved only by Balaam's prophecy of future hope. That hope pointed to David's time, and the Yahwist addressed the Israel of David and Solomon. The message of the Yahwist to Israel: we have not been chosen for ourselves; the success which has been given us is not for ourselves alone; our destiny is to be bringers of salvation to all the families of the earth, in peace and prosperity. So far we have failed in this, both in the archetypal world of the wilderness, and in the history of the more recent generations of the period of the conquest. With the onset of God's new action in the Davidic era, we now have an opportunity to set things right and to be faithful to the call of our destiny. It is a noble claim.

There is fairly clear evidence for a certain interplay between the Yahwist's theme and the materials of Israel's tradition. A good case of this is the various levels within the patriarchal promises: of land, of a son, of descendants, and of blessing.[14] We cannot always be sure when the Yahwist is speaking and when it is rather the traditions he inherited coming to expression. But these traditions have been shaped into a literary whole; and it is a fundamentally coherent whole. While, therefore, we may fluctuate and hesitate on the attribution of verses or passages here or there, we can be secure in the basic thrust of the Yahwist: God's free action initiated to bring blessing to all the families of the earth.

The concept of the Yahwist remains hypothetical, as do all the constructions of Old Testament scholarship. The theological statement attributed to the Yahwist is magnificent. It must be used wisely, but it cannot be neglected. Whether it is attributed to the Yahwist or not, it is a given of the present text. If it can be

---

[14]See Claus Westermann, *The Promises to the Fathers: Studies on the Patriarchal Narratives* (Philadelphia: Fortress, 1976); also Rolf Rendtorff, *Das überlieferungsgeschichtliche Problem des Pentateuch* (BZAW 147; Berlin: de Gruyter, 1977).

situated within the horizon of a Yahwist narrative, it is given a sharpness and definition which is otherwise lacking.

It says a great deal about Israel. If it stems from the time of Solomon, then it comes from a period in Israel's history only a couple of generations removed from constant insecurity and a genuinely grave threat to survival. The stories of Samson and then of Saul reveal Israel in conflict with the Philistines, who occupied the southern section of the fertile coastal plain. Apparently, Israel's growth was attracting Philistine attention, to the point that Philistine garrisons were stationed in Israel's territory (cf., 1 Sam 13:3) and Philistine raiding parties menaced Israel (cf., 1 Sam 23:27). To add to the gravity of the threat, the Philistines were vastly superior to Israel in the quality of their weapons (cf., 1 Sam 13:19-22). There is good reason to see the emergence of the institution of kingship in Israel as due, at least in part, to Israel's need to defend itself against the threat of subjugation by the Philistines (cf., 1 Sam 4:9; 8:20; 9:16).

Final victory over the Philistines came with David. The time of Solomon is only the next generation. It is a truly remarkable intellectual and spiritual transition to move from a situation of near-subjugation to one of political and military dominance and to be able to enunciate one's national destiny in terms of bringing blessing to "all the families of the earth." This is not to say that all Israel shared the view. It is striking enough that anyone in Israel held it. It is more striking still that Israel canonized it, and took it to heart enough that it became part of the national literature.

It also speaks deeply of the God of Israel. It is not simply a witness to how Israel saw itself; it is also a witness to Israel's understanding of God. The Yahwist narrative portrays a God whose concern is with the well-being, the blessed state, of the whole human race. The Yahwist's God stays in relationship with humankind, despite their failures. The results of evil cannot be ignored, so the first couple leave the garden, Cain is a wanderer on the face of the earth, and so on. But God does not abandon the world. God's action, in Abraham, to bring blessing to the world, is one of purest grace. Abraham has done nothing to earn it. He exists   that is all. He exists—as part of a human world that is separated and scattered, far from the blessed state desired by its creator. So the Yahwist's God gives Abraham his marching orders, and sets history in motion in the direction of Israel, with a view to bringing blessing back into the mainstream of human life. The God of the Yahwist is intent on blessing, not unaware of human conflict and disharmony, but determined to bring about a world in which peace, well-being, and harmonious relationships might give reality to the ideal of blessing.

The Yahwist's structuring of the patriarchal stories and Israel's story around this central theme of blessing was an act of considerable theological courage. The stories of the patriarchs, constituting the traditions available to the Yahwist, were more marked by strife and discord than they were by blessing. It is no mean achievement to look at the traditions marked by much of the shadow side of human existence and, nevertheless, be able to impose upon them a claim unsurpassed in its humanity and its universalism. Only very deep insight into the wellsprings of human nature and a very profound confidence in the commitment of God to creation could enable the Yahwist to stake out this claim.

The tradition did not invite the interpretation, to say the least. Abraham was forced to separate from Lot (Gen 13:1-12*). Although occasioned by strife, the separation was portrayed as happening peacefully. But it was a reminder of the harsh realities of economics and the limited capacity of land to support a population. As regards the next generation, it was humanly speaking impossible to support the presence of Isaac and Ishmael. So Hagar and Ishmael were driven out into the desert (16:1-14*). As to the following generation, the strife between Esau and Jacob is well-known. While Jacob brought prosperity to Laban, there was also a strong element of discord in their relationship: Laban's initial deception of Jacob; Jacob's parting deception of Laban. In the last of the patriarchal generations, Jacob's sons, the discord between Joseph and his brothers reached murderous intent. It is remarkable that, against such a background, the Yahwist can see deeply enough into the needs of human nature and be confident enough of the benevolent intentions of God to be able to put forward the claim that Israel's destiny was to be mediator of blessing to all the families of the earth.

It is one thing to make a theological claim. It is another to have it recognized. The historians, the wise, and the prophets of the Old Testament do not seem, at first sight, to have accepted the Yahwist's view. Yet we must recognize that it has set its stamp upon the whole Pentateuch, upon Israel's Torah. To this degree it has been accepted. Secondly, we have noted the additions which later spelled out the same theme of blessing for all the nations of the earth (Gen 22:15-18; 26:3-5). These are marked with language close to that of the deuteronomic movement, three to four hundred years after the Yahwist. Clearly these editors were sufficiently convinced of the Yahwist's position that they reiterated it at two key points. Thirdly, a similar tradition lives in texts like Isa 19:23-25 (see above). The Yahwist's theology was not ignored.

The Yahwist's theology reveals a profound understanding of God. It can only have been distilled from long pondering and much contemplation of a store of rich experience of human life and its possibilities for meaning before God. It is an understanding of God that we need to make our own again today.

Today

The Yahwist put a strikingly challenging message before Israel. It is a message which is no less challenging today. The Yahwist has a vision of the world in which all nations are blessed and the Yahwist claims that vision is from God. Furthermore, Israel, the nation which is privileged by God, is to be the source through which all nations will find blessing.

Can we look at our world today with a less lofty gaze? We live in the age when the global village is closer to reality in terms of communications, travel, and trade than at any previous time. The Yahwist's claim on us is that our global village must be a source of blessing for all the families of the earth. There is no room for cultural superiority or notions of manifest destiny. Blessing is for all, in harmony, peace, and prosperity; the privileged people are to mediate God's blessing to all.

Our globe is no village when it comes to equality of living standards. Whether we look at north and south, or first and third worlds, or whether we look at the vast disparities between rich and poor within individual nations, there is nothing to be seen of the egalitarian quality of the village image. The Yahwist will not let us rest easy with the complacency that believes this is the way things are, that it has something to do with the way people have used their opportunities and talents, and that anyway there is not much that can be done about it. The Yahwist was not content to let Israel sit with the laurels of its newly won independence and prosperity. Israel was reminded that its destiny was as bringer of blessing to all. Can we settle for a vision that is less?

Our globe is moving slowly and haltingly, willingly or unwillingly, toward increasing economic interdependence. While it will certainly bring its problems, it may also provide the greatest hope for world peace, replacing the deterrent of mutual terror with the reality of mutual self-interest. This would be blessing indeed. But if it comes about, it will not come about easily. Economic interdependence, resulting from substantially free markets and free trade, necessarily makes nations and their people dependent on other nations and their peoples. In recent decades, the economies of many western nations have been dependent on the engine of the economy of the United States. In recent years the major western economies have been dependent on decisions being made by Japan, West Germany, and the United States. Behind all these moves, standards of living fluctuate and countries move up and down the lists which rank relative standards of living.

The Yahwist's challenge to us correlates directly with fluctuating standards of living. It would be blissful indeed if all the nations moved into steadily higher standards of living, with the poorer countries moving faster until all countries shared a substantial equality of living standards. But that is not the way it is. It only has to be enunciated for us to realize how far it is from reality. If there is to be "a substantial equality of living standards" in our world—blessing for all the families of the earth—there are going to have to be some sacrifices. Some of our nations may have to put their high standards of living on hold while others catch up. Some of our nations may have to watch their own living standards slip back to some degree while those of others move up. The Yahwist challenges us to lift our gaze beyond cramped self-interest to the wider greater vision of blessing for all the nations of the earth.

This is not the place for a treatise on global economics—and I am not the person to write one. It may be that global interdependence will be reduced to a struggle between the present major economic powers about relative rankings on top of the pile. If so, it would be disastrous for the Yahwist's dream—and ours. It may be that the economic notions implicit here are fanciful. If so, the reality remains that economic interdependence will not be achieved without sacrifices and shifts in standards of living.

Against this background, it would be good for us to be steeped in the Yahwist's vision of a world where all the nations of the earth find blessing. Self-interest, motivated by a longing for peace and security, would be a valuable motive for accepting sacrifices to achieve global interdependence. The vision and dream of the world in which the blessing of prosperity and peace is available to all can transform enlightened self-interest into motivation of a higher and more powerful order.

The Yahwist does not let us deal with all this exclusively on the inner-human level of economics and national interests. The Yahwist ties this vision into the understanding of God. For the Yahwist, it is evident that God wants all the nations of the earth to find blessing. And what God wants, Israel must want. Can we want less?

To return to the language used earlier in this book, if we accept God's love, if we accept God's unconditional commitment to us, can we be unconcerned by the fact of God's unconditional commitment to all others and can we be unconcerned by the fate of those others? The Yahwist has a vision of what the world should be. The Yahwist also has a vision of how God is: spontaneously concerned for the blessing of all the families of the earth. No people and no person can enter into a committed relationship with that God which excludes concern for all of those families of the earth. The God of the Yahwist—indeed the God of Israel and the God of the Jewish and Christian faiths—is a God whose purposes "are always entrammeled in history, dependent on the acts of individual men and women for their continuing realization."[15] To enter into relationship with such a God is to become inextricably involved in the working out of God's purposes. This is the challenge of the Yahwist narrative.

---

[15]Robert Alter, *The Art of Biblical Narrative* (New York: Basic Books, 1981) 12.

Note
The reader of this chapter needs to be aware that it is based on the classical understanding and positioning of the Yahwist. Over the last decade, several studies have been written which would place the Yahwist much later in the history of Israel's literature. Although some of these have been on the scholarly scene for a number of years, there has not yet been a thorough evaluation of the various arguments advanced, not all of which carry equal weight. Until the discussion has come into the mainstream of Old Testament scholarship, it is not appropriate to treat it in a book such as this. Such proposals cannot be dismissed, nor can their evaluation be taken lightly. The implications of these proposals are immense, and the work involved in their proper evaluation is equally immense.

Some discussion of these positions to date is to be found in the contributions to *JSOT* 3 (1977), in A.D.H. Mayes, *The Story of Israel between Settlement and Exile: A Redactional Study of the Deuteronomistic History* (London: SCM, 1983) 139-49, and in R. N. Whybray, *The Making of the Pentateuch: A Methodological Study* (JSOTSup 53; Sheffield: JSOT, 1987) esp. 221-42.

The following are the principal works, which contributed the initial stimulus for the current debate.

J. Van Seters, *Abraham in History and Tradition.* New Haven: Yale University, 1975.

H. H. Schmid, *Der sogenannte Jahwist: Beobachtungen und Fragen zur Pentateuchforschung.* Zurich: Theologischer Verlag, 1976.

R. Rendtorff, *Das überlieferungsgeschichtliche Problem des Pentateuch.* BZAW 147. Berlin: de Gruyter, 1977.

M. Rose, *Deuteronomist und Jahwist: Untersuchungen zu den Berührungspunkten beider Literaturwerke.* AThANT 67. Zurich: Theologischer Verlag, 1981.

A recent contribution in English is: T.L. Thompson, *The Origin Tradition of Ancient Israel: I. The Literary Formation of Genesis and Exodus 1-23.* JSOTSup 55. Sheffield: JSOT, 1987.

The evaluation of such proposals involves difficulties both in methodology and in scale. As to scale, it is a truism, that source-critical studies have to be carried out on the total material; this is particularly true of studies of source-critical method, but holds also in different degree for questions like dating. While good ideas may emerge from more partial studies, their evaluation and wider application has to take place in relation to the total text.

Where methodology is concerned, several points need to be made. The first is obvious, but easily overlooked. A view being contested should always be contested in its strongest presentation, never in its weakest. Failure in this regard is a weakness of Rendtorff's 1977 monograph. Secondly, it must be recognized that source-critical hypotheses are precisely that: hypotheses. There is evidence pointing to the possibility of multiple sources in the Pentateuch. A hypothesis seeks to present an understanding of the growth of the pentateuchal text which adequately accounts for this evidence, while making good sense of the text in its various stages. Of course hypotheses are to be compared, but it is absurd to compare one hypothesis with another as though they were simply identifying blocks of text by the cataloguing of criteria. The comparison of who puts what where is not, in itself, a justified ground for criticism. Where text has no clear distinguishing characteristics, its attribution to one or another source is a matter of intuitive plausibility in view of the process envisaged, the narrative thread of the resulting text, and the overall economy of the hypothesis. Thirdly, evidence from specific texts may have to be weighed differently against different hypotheses. Such evidence may have to be evaluated quite differently, according as the extent and intention of the sources vary in one or another hypothesis.

This is a major issue for the understanding of the Pentateuch and the history of Israel's literature and theology. It is unlikely to reach rapid resolution.

RECOMMENDED FURTHER READING

H. W. Wolff, "The Kerygma of the Yahwist." In *The Vitality of Old Testament Traditions* edited by W. Brueggemann and H. W. Wolff, 41-66. 2nd ed. Atlanta: John Knox, 1982.

A.F. Campbell, "The Yahwist Revisited," *AusBR* 27 (1979) 2-14.

Peter F. Ellis, *The Yahwist: The Bible's First Theologian.* Notre Dame, IN: Fides, 1968. The J text in the appendix must be used with extreme caution.

Gerhard von Rad, *Old Testament Theology.* 2 vols. Edinburgh: Oliver and Boyd, 1962-65, 1.148-65.

_____ *The Problem of the Hexateuch and Other Essays,* 50-74. Edinburgh: Oliver and Boyd, 1965.

C. Westermann, *The Promises to the Fathers: Studies on the Patriarchal Narratives,* esp. pp. 155-63. Philadelphia: Fortress, 1980.

Appendix

The Text of the Yahwist
(according to M. Noth)

GENESIS

2:4b-4:24; ... 5:29; ... 6:5-8; ... 7:1-2,3b,4-5,10,7*, 16b, 12,17b,22,23aαb; 8:6a, 2b, 3a ... 6b, 8-12, 13b ... 20-22; 9:18-27; 10: ... 8, (9), 10-19, 21, 25-30; 11:1-9 ... 28-30; ... 12:1-4a ... 6-20; 13:1-5, 7-11a, 12bβ, 13, (14-17), 18; 15:1abβ, 2a, 3b-4, 6-12, 17-18, (19-21); 16: ... 1b-2, 4-8, 11-14 ...; 18:1-18, (19), 20-33; 19:1-16, (17-22), 23-25, (26), 27-28, 30-38; 20:1a; 21:1a ... 7; 22:20-24; 24:1-6, (7), 8-24, (25), 26-29, (30), 31-40a (40b), 41-60, (61a), 61b-62a, (62b), 63-67; 25:5-6, 11b, 21-26a, 27-34; 26:1*, 2aα, (2aβb), 3abα, (3bβ-5), 6-14, (15), 16-17, (18), 19-23; (24-25a), 25b-33; 27:1-45; 28:10-11aα, 13-16, 19a, (19b); 29:1-35; 30:1aα ... 3bβ, 4-5, ... 7-16 ... 20aβb, (21) ... 24-43; 31:1, 3, 17, 18aα, 19a, 20, 21aαb, 22, 23, 25bα, (25bβ), 26aα, 27, 30a, 31 ... 36a, 38-40, 46, ([47], 48), (49), 51-53a; 32:4-14a ... 23-33; 33:13, 6-7, 12-17 ... 18b; 34:1-31*; 35:21-22a ... ;37:3a, 4-5a, 6-21, 25-27, 28aβb; 38:1-30; 39:1-23; 40:1 ... ; 41:34a, 35b,41-45a, (45b), 46b, 49, 55, (56a), 56bα, (56bβ), 57; 42:1b ... 4-5 ... 7bβ-9a ... bβ, 10-11a, 12 ... 27-28a ... 38; 43:1-13, 14aαb, 15-23a, 24-34; 44:1a, (1b), 2aα, (2aβ), 2b-34; 45:1, 4-5a, 16-28; 46:1aα, 5b, 28-34; 47:1-5a, 6b, 13-26, 29-31 ... ; 50:1-10a ... 14a, (14b) ...

EXODUS

1:8-12, 22; 2:1-3, (4), 5-6, (7-10aα), 10aβb, 11-14, (15a), 15b-23aα;[3:1-4a, 5, 7, 8aα, (8aβb), 16,17aα, (17aβb), (18-22); 4:1-4, (5), 6-7, (8-9), 10-12, (13-16)], 19-20a, (21-23), 24-26, (27-28), 29, [30-31]; 5:1-3, (4), 5-23; 6:1; 7:14-16, 17abα, 18, 20aβ, 21a, 23-29; 8: ... 4-5a, (5b), 6-11aα,16-21a, (21b-24a), 24b-28; 9:1-7, 13, (14-16), 17-22a, (22b), 23, 24aα,(24aβ), 24b, 25aα, (25aβ), 25b-30,

114

(31-32), 33-34, (35); 10:1a, (1b-2), 3-19,(20-27), 28-29; 11:(1-4aα),
4aβb-8; 12:21-23, 27b, 29-34, (35-36), 37-39; 13:20-22; 14:5b-6,
9aα, 10bα, 13-14, 19b-20, 21aβ, 24, 25b, 27aβb, 30-31; 15:(20-21),
22aβb, 23-25a; 16: ... 4abα, 5 ... 29-31 ... 35b-36; 17: ... 1bβ,
2, 4-16; 19: ... 2b, 10-12a, (12b-13a), 14-15a, (15b), 16aα, 18,
(20-25); [24:12-13a,(13b), 14-15a; 32:1a ... 4b-6, 15-20, (25-29),
30-33, 34aα, (34aβ), 34b, (35) ...]; 34:1a, (1b), 2-6aα, (6aβb, 7) 8,
(9), 10aα, (10aβb), 11a, (11b-12,[13]),14, (15a,[15b],16), 17, (18),
19a, (19b, 20abα), 20bβ, 21a, (21b-22), 23, (24), 25-28abα, (28bβ),
29aα, (29aβ), 29b-30, 31aα, (31aβb,32a), 32b, (33-35) ...

NUMBERS
10:29-33, (34), 36; 11:1-35; 12:1-16; 13: ... 17b-20, 22-24 ... at
Kadesh (26) ... 27a, (27bα), 27bβ, 28, (29), 30-31; 14:1b, 4, 11a,
(11b-23a) ... 23b-24, (25a), 25b, 39-45; 16: ... 1bα, (1bβ), 2aα
... 12-15 ... 25-26, 27b-32a, (32b), 33abα, (33bβ), 34; 20:1aβ
... 19-20 ... 22a; 21:[1-3], 4aα*β(4b,[5], 6-9) ... ... ; 22:3b-8,
13-19, 21-38aα, 39-40; 23:28; 24:1aα, (1aβ), 1b-10abα, (10bβ),
11-19, (20-24), 25; 25:(1a), 1b-5 ... ...; 32:1, 16 ... 39a, (39b-
40a),40b-42 ...

Note: this listing is to be found in M. Noth, *A History of
Pentateuchal Traditions*, 28-32; it will suffice for rapid reference,
but for closer study Noth's accompanying comments should be
consulted.

4

Reflection on Method
in the Study of the Pentateuch

The study of the Pentateuch, the Priestly Document, and the Yahwist has revealed some of the depths and differences concealed within the text of the Old Testament. It is important to understand as fully as possible why these are "concealed" within the text of the Old Testament and to be aware of the thinking which underlies scholarly research on these texts. As the Note at the end of the last chapter indicated, there is considerable difference of opinion among scholars on important issues concerning sources in the Pentateuch. This makes it all the more necessary to have an understanding of some of the methodological issues involved. Two preliminary points are worth looking at first. One is what I have termed the "phenomena of the text"; the other is the reason why modern translations must conceal much that is evident in the Hebrew text.

PRELIMINARY REFLECTIONS

We have already spoken of "the phenomena" in the text or of the text. By this, I mean simply what we observe in the text which leads us to understand it the way we do. The interpretation of a text is always the outcome of an encounter between what the observer brings to the text and what, within the text, makes an impact on the observer. Responsible interpretation has to identify these factors as clearly as possible. To be at ease with modern scholarship's understanding of the Old Testament, and to preserve a sense of fidelity to the Old Testament as God's inspired word, it is important to be fully aware of the phenomena in the text which have their impact on scholar and reader and which control the way the text is understood. All worthwhile understanding rests on the observation of these phenomena, and they form the textual reality any theory must account for.

The observation of such phenomena has been at the basis of Old Testament scholarship. For example, the recognition that the Pentateuch consistently uses two names for God—Yahweh and Elohim—was one of the observations which led to the identification of sources in these texts. Frequently, the phenomena to be observed are slight: an unusual word order, a change from singular to plural or from 1st person to 2nd or 3rd, repetitions of what has already been said, or references to a person who has not been mentioned.[1] These and others are all tiny traces which may point to the composite nature of a text. They are the seams and stitching which can show where the fabric of a text has been put together from many traditions. They may be there because of the respect the editors of these texts had for their traditions. They changed them as little as possible. In fact, it seems likely that they deliberately left material unchanged so that old and new were not confused.

These are the phenomena which often show us that the present text is not a unified text, that it has been woven together as the product of more than one mind. In itself, this is an exciting discovery. It means that the text is rich lode to be mined, that there is a plurality of experience—and of reflection on it—coming to expression in the text. If, for example, a passage is a combination of the Yahwist and the Priestly Writer, this means that, ideally there is the work of three minds to be explored: the Yahwist, the Priestly Writer, and also the redactor who combined them, creating a third text. Often, it is like the perception of a new

[1] The very helpful work of scholars like Robert Alter (*The Art of Biblical Narrative*) or Meir Sternberg (*The Poetics of Biblical Narrative*) reveals the immense amount of meaning to be quarried from repetitions within a text. But that does not mean that all repetition and similar phenomena can be accounted for on grounds of literary art. There have been exaggerations by source critics; it would be a pity if they were repeated in the reverse direction.

dimension; it adds depth and texture to the reading of the text. It means that there are really three texts available for interpretation: the Yahwist's, the Priestly Writer's, and their combination.

For some people, however, this is a disconcerting discovery. They are uneasy when told about such phenomena. They have not noticed them, therefore have not been puzzled by them—and so do not have the "Aha!" experience of having their puzzlement resolved. Two factors can contribute to this. One is in us, the readers: we read with a certain familiarity and with certain assumptions about the text, and so we quite simply do not perceive phenomena which conflict with these assumptions. A simple example: those people who are convinced that the story of the first sin in Genesis 2-3 involved eating an apple, and who have never noticed that there is no mention of an apple in the biblical text. This is a very common factor in all of our sense experience: we tend to see what we expect to see. The second factor is in the biblical text itself which many people have to use: the significant phenomena simply are not visible in a modern translation. It is a matter of fact that some of these important phenomena are not easily apparent to the reader of a translation, without access to the original Hebrew text.

Before going into reflections on method, it is worthwhile pointing out why this is so and why it should be so. It is not a matter of incompetent translation; it is certainly not a case of translators perpetrating a cover-up and keeping the truth under wraps. It is of the very nature of the task of traslation. The translator has to translate the present text—the Hebrew, Aramaic, or Greek text—which is the canonical text of the Bible. If it is question, then, of a composite text, it is a text which the redactor, who combined it in its final form, wanted to have in precisely this form, and which the community of synagogue or church inherited as its sacred scripture. This is the text which the translator has to translate, and therefore it has to be as smooth and coherent a translation as possible.

A few examples may help to make this clear.
a) In Genesis 15, many scholars attribute vv 13-16 to the Elohist. If we were to check the text to verify this, we would expect to see the name "God" occurring there, translating the Hebrew "Elohim." Instead, we would find that, in v 13, the *JB* has "Then Yahweh said," and the *NAB* and *RSV* both have "Then the LORD said."

Naturally, we would expect these to be translating the Hebrew "YHWH." In fact, the Hebrew just has the 3rd person masculine singular verb, "And he said." Is this a case of clumsy, over-interpretative translation? In the context of v 13, a simple pronoun is out of the question. The "he" would appear to refer to Abraham, who would then be speaking to Abraham, and the sentence would make no sense. It is clearly God who is speaking. In the earlier and later verses, God is named as YHWH (i.e., vv 1,2,4,6,7,8, and 18). So the translators are in a quandary. If they translated literally, "And he said to Abram," it would make no sense; compare this with the beginning of v 9, where it makes perfectly good sense. If they translated, "And God said," they would be endorsing a theory about the origins of the text—and that is not a translator's job. So they translate, "And Yahweh/the LORD said," which is the plain meaning of the text as a unity. It is a good and faithful translation. But it obscures one of the important and significant phenomena of the text at this point.

b) In Deuteronomy 4, Moses is speaking to Israel, and he addresses them as "you," in the plural, of course. But parts of the chapter are in the singular. For example: at the end of v 3, literally, "The LORD thy God destroyed from among thee"; v 9, "Only take heed and keep thy soul diligently, lest thou forgettest . . . "; at the beginning of v 19, the end of v 23, in v 24, and in most of vv 29-40. This alternation between the singular and plural address (i.e., "thou" and "you") is a phenomenon which is considered important for understanding the growth of the text in this chapter. But it creates a difficulty for the modern translator. In modern English, "you" represents both the singular and the plural address. "Thou," "thee," and "thy" would be intolerably archaic, and also absurd in a plural context. So modern English is incapable of accurately reflecting this phenomen of the Hebrew text in an acceptable translation. Good translation just has to obscure the phenomenon.

c) The principal Hebrew conjunction, "*we-*," which occurs in almost every sentence, can have the meanings "and," or "but," or "if," or "then," or "when," and so on. The precise meaning depends on the context, and is usually perfectly clear in the context. But in a composite text, where source materials have been combined, it will often happen that the context in the original source requires the meaning "and," while the changed context, brought about by the combined text, just as clearly requires the meaning "but." A translator, who is rendering the final or combined text, has to translate by "but." Yet a diligent student, attempting to follow the trace of the original source, would expect to find "and"—and would be disappointed.

To sum up. The Hebrew text contains a host of little signals which can be pointers to its origins. Because these are little irregularities or dissonances (inconcinnities, if one likes to continue the musical metaphor), they are a source of puzzlement to the reader until an explanation is provided for them. The task of a modern translation is to render the final, canonical text. It will necessarily involve obscuring a lot of these little signals. Providing an explanation for them, then, becomes a source of puzzlement in its turn. It appears to be explaining what does not need explanation; the problem is never genuinely felt, so the solution to it is neither needed nor appreciated.

It is important to realize why these little signals are present in the Hebrew text. Some of them may be unconscious on the part of the biblical writers. For example, a prophetic text is to be updated to point out its application to a later generation (e.g. Amos 2:4-5). The expansion may unconsciously mirror the attitudes and language of the later generation. But, in many other cases, the signals may have been consciously left in the text. The biblical writers could perfectly easily have smoothed out the account of the flood to have either "two of every sort" of living thing in the ark (cf., Gen 6:19), or "seven pairs of all clean animals ... and a pair of the animals that are not clean" (cf., Gen 7:2). The biblical writers could perfectly easily have smoothed out the text of Deuteronomy 4 so that it was all in the plural address. And so on, for a host of cases. But they did not. They left the material as they found it in their sources, making only those adjustments which were absolutely necessary to produce a combined text. Carelessness and laziness do not seem to have been characteristics of the Old Testament redactors; they give every impression of having been, for the most part, very intelligent and very diligent people. So we may presume that these differences were left in the texts out of fidelity to and respect for the traditional materials being used. We may even go a step further and assume that sometimes, at least, these signals were left as a deliberate indication of the difference between older and newer material.

This means that the reason why modern biblical scholarship is possible is that the biblical writers exercised a high level of fidelity toward the sources they worked with. This fidelity left the phenomena in the text which now serve as signals for modern scholars. The reverse side of this is equally important. Modern scholarship, in its task of elaborating theories and hypotheses to explain these phenomena, is also operating in strict fidelity to the text. It is taking the biblical text seriously, not smoothing over and harmonizing what the biblical writers left as irregularities. It endeavors to understand the text on the text's own terms. Fidelity to the biblical text means permitting the text to unfold its own nature to us; it does not mean imposing on the text our own understanding of what it should be.

THE IDENTIFICATION OF THE SOURCES

The realization that there are several literary sources in the Pentateuch may be perfectly correct. That does not prevent some of the ways of conceptualizing the process of identifying these sources from being quite wrong. In the last century, a great deal of effort went into compiling lists of vocabulary and other features which were thought to identify the various sources. To a very large extent, such lists have been abandoned; their contents could not be shown to be exclusive to the relevant sources.

It is argued that the key evidence for the sources in the Pentateuch is the existence of doublets, that is, of occurrences of the same material twice, in different versions. This view is maintained emphatically by Martin Noth.

> It seems to me that fundamentally only one of the usual criteria for the disunity of the Pentateuchal tradition is really useful, though this one is quite adequate and allows a thoroughgoing literary analysis. I refer to the unquestionable fact, attested time and again throughout the tradition, of the *repeated occurrence* of the same narrative materials or narrative ele-

ments *in different versions.* This phenomenon can hardly be explained in any other way.[2]

By "the old Pentateuchal tradition," Noth means J and E, above all. However, the same principles apply for the distinction between P and JE, with the added advantage that P is characterized by "a marked peculiarity in speech, style and thought-world."[3]

Because of the long and complicated process of the oral transmission of the traditions, Noth dismisses many of the criteria used earlier to distinguish J and E, etc., at least on a broader scale. These were: inconsistencies of content; irregularities of arrangement; differences in the manner of narration; dissimilarities of religious, ethical, or intellectual level; and even the examination of language and style.[4]

One further criterion needs explicit mention because it is one of the most important and yet often is left implicit in discussion of source-critical methodology. It is what I would call the continuity of narrative thread or story line. A couple of general examples may help clarify what is meant. A text might tell a story which clearly represents two versions. The two versions are clearly marked in parts of the text, but there are also verses which are quite neutral. If one version of the story represented in the text is complete, but these neutral verses are needed to complete the thread of the story in the other version, then that is where they belong. The continuity of narrative thread determines their attribution, even though there are no other indicators. In another example, there might be a text with a basic story in it to which a number of additions have been made. Some of these are identifiable by characteristics of language, others by questions of consistency, repetition, etc. But some parts of the text are neutral

---

[2]M. Noth, *A History of Pentateuchal Traditions* (Englewood Cliffs, N. J.: Prentice Hall, 1972) 21.

[3]Noth, *Pentateuchal Traditions,* 20. JE is the symbol used to refer to the text formed by the combination of the Yahwist (J) and the Elohist (E). Given the current doubt about the existence of E as a separate and continuous literary source, JE will be used here to refer fundamentally to the text of the Pentateuch prior to P.

[4]Noth, *Pentateuchal Traditions,* 21. Noth does accept the well-known difference between the divine names, although even this cannot be regarded as a 100% certain criterion.

where such characteristics are concerned and their attribution cannot be decided on these grounds. All else being equal, if they are needed for the continuity of the basic narrative's story line, then they belong to it.

To anticipate a little, we may also note that continuity of narrative thread is a valuable check on the validity of source-critical analyses. One cannot simply pare away unnecessary elements of a text, claiming a basic substratum as the original. Such a process is absurd. But there are often good reasons to believe that parts of a text are later additions. If the continuity of the narrative thread in the remaining text is satisfactory or improved when these suspected additions are removed, then that provides a confirmation and validation of the analysis.

Whatever the reasons adopted for differentiating sources, it is still possible to imagine the process of the combination of the sources in quite different ways.[5] To give some examples:

a) The sources were available to the compilers, who selected from them whatever passages they wished, without trying to preserve any of the sources intact.[6]

b) The sources were combined in such a way that each source was substantially preserved.

c) The compilers took one source, each time, to serve as base narrative, which was then enriched from the other sources(s) or other traditions.

d) There was one source originally, which was substantially enriched by the successive addition of other traditions.

These possible approaches have interesting consequences for the verifiability of the relevant hypotheses. A hypothesis which can be neither verified nor falsified labors under a grave disadvantage. As we have noted, the narrative thread is one of the most effective means available for the verification of a source hypothesis. In an extended narrative, for example, certain happenings within a story require antecedents, which should have been narrated earlier; others demand follow-up which should emerge in the subsequent narrative. So, when a hypothesis is

---

[5] See the treatment in most of the *Introductions*.

[6] This is the impression gained from O. Eissfeldt's *Hexateuch-Synopse* (Darmstadt: Wissenschaftliche Buchgesellschaft, 1962; 1st ed., 1922).

formulated involving a narrative, it is possible to verify the hypothesis by checking whether the narrative thread is adequately represented in the text or not.

In options a) and d) above, such verifiability is not possible. In option a), since there is no attempt in the hypothesis to maintain the sequence of the source, there is no narrative thread to be expected. In option d), since the narrative thread is the basic given, to which other traditions have been later added, it is a construct which cannot be used to verify the hypothesis.

In options b) and c), the narrative thread is present and can be used for verifying the hypothesis. In option b), the possibility of verification or falsification is very good, since the hypothesis presumes the entire narrative of each source to have been substantially preserved. What may emerge, in the process of verification, is that a hypothesis of this kind requires unified and artistically constructed stories to be artificially broken up in order to provide for the continuity of the sources.[7] In other words, the hypothesis fails the verification test. In the case of option c), gaps in the narrative thread will be expected. This need not nullify the possibility of verification. What matters, in such a case, is the plausibility of the gap. If the gap is in the narrative thread of the base source, it would need to have been filled with a particularly attractive tradition from the enriching source, for the hypothesis to be plausible. The gaps in the enriching source, similarly, need to be accounted for by the material present in the base source. Option c) is the one advocated by Martin Noth for the Pentateuch, and it is the one which will be followed here.

Noth understands the P document to have been the base used for the compilation of the Pentateuch.

> The P narrative which arose in this way later became the *literary basis of the Pentateuchal narrative.* Contrary to the usual view, the "redactor" responsible for this literary process did *not* understand it to be his task to combine two formerly separate narratives—in this case the P narrative on the one hand and on the other the narrative combined from old sources in a manner still to be investigated—by simply *adding*

[7]See Noth, *Pentateuchal Traditions*, 24.

them to one another so that through a more or less successful interweaving of the particular narrative elements, aided by some harmonizing redactional additions, the two narratives could be taken up into the resulting literary synthesis in their *entirety*. Instead, he made the P narrative the *basis* of his work and *enriched* it by suitably inserting here and there parts of the other narrative. So viewed, his work becomes far clearer and more intelligible.[8]

To carry through an example of part of the verification process, it is worth our while to give the principal gaps in the base or P narrative, and in the enriching or JE sources, as listed by Noth. There are three principal gaps in P.

i. The P notice of the birth of Esau and Jacob has been suppressed in favor of the concrete description in Gen 25:21-26a.

ii. The P account of the marriage of Jacob has been suppressed in favor of the detailed story in Gen 29:15-30 (although it is presumed by Gen 31:18*).

iii. Only a little of the P form of the Joseph story survives, i.e., Gen 37:1-2; 41:46a; the old sources were otherwise too attractive.[9]

As for the gaps in the older sources, or JE, the following are the principal places listed by Noth where the older material has been replaced by P.

i. The account of Abraham's compliance with his call, replaced by Gen 12:4b-5.

ii. The beginning and end of the old Hagar story, replaced by Gen 16:1a, 3, 15-16.

iii. The account of Isaac's birth, replaced by Gen 21:1b-5.

iv. The account of Abraham's death, replaced by Gen 25:7-11a.

v. The traditions replaced by Gen. 33:18a and 35:6.

vi. The account of Jacob's death and burial, replaced by Gen 49:33; 50:12-13.

vii. The introduction to the story of Moses, replaced by Exod 1:1-7.

[8]Noth, *Pentateuchal Traditions*, 11-12.

[9]Noth, *Pentateuchal Traditions*, 14. With regard to "the old sources," note the recent view of Claus Westermann: "It follows from what has been said about the composition and literary form of the Joseph story in the narrower sense that it is a unity; it therefore has one author. The obvious, self-contained plan in the narrative span from Gen. 37 to 45 demands this view" (*Genesis 37-50* [Minneapolis: Augsburg, 1986] 28).

viii. The stories of the manna (Exodus 16), the spies (Numbers 13-14), and Dathan and Abiram (Numbers 16), replaced largely by P tradition.

ix. Finally, the conquest story, suppressed by P.[10]

The upshot of all this: there are breaks in the thread of the respective narratives, but they can be accounted for in a reasonable and satisfactory manner. The hypothesis as presented is respectable.

It is not necessary to cite all the gaps involved in the combination of the Yahwist with the Elohist.[11] However, Noth's comments on the Abraham traditions are worth quoting in full.

> The situation in the Abraham tradition seems so obvious to me that here, above all, the problem of literary analysis of the Pentateuchal tradition must become clear, leaving only the question as to whether the results gained here are valid also for the whole of the Pentateuch. In the Abraham tradition there are, first of all, the Abraham-Lot stories (the joint migration to Canaan, separation in Canaan, Hebron-Sodom narrative), all of which occur only *once* in an originally compact narrative context. However the remaining Abraham stories, in which Lot is missing altogether, occur *twice in different independent versions,* as for example, the story of God's covenant with Abraham (Gen. 15 which is not a unity in a literary sense); the story of Abraham and Sarah in the territory of a foreign king (Gen. 12:10-20; and Gen. 20); the story of Hagar's banishment (Gen. *16 and Gen. 21:8-21); while the story of Abraham's covenant with Abimelech in Beer-sheba (Gen. 21:22ff.) and the story of the sacrifice of Isaac (Gen. 22:1-19) are again found only *once.* I do not know how this situation could be plausibly

[10]Noth, *Pentateuchal Traditions*, 13-16.

[11]See, however, Noth, *Pentateuchal Traditions*, 25-27. It is appropriate to note here that the work of Westermann in his Genesis commentary has led him to conclude that there is no trace in Genesis of a consecutive Elohist source (see *Genesis 12-36* [Minneapolis: Augsburg, 1985] 571-72). Rather, there is enrichment of the Yahwist narrative from the fund of Israel's traditions. Noth argued for a consecutive Elohist source, against Paul Volz. The debate cannot be pursued here. It does not affect the positions held on the Yahwist and Priestly Document.

explained except by the assumption of two "sources" which together shared a basic fund of Abraham stories and which individually had various special materials, ... [12]

In Noth's argument, it is clear that the understanding of the way in which the sources have been combined is not to be confused with the source hypothesis itself. The two are separate.

It is not the two-source hypothesis itself which is in error, for this has repeatedly proved itself to be sound, but rather the conception of the way in which these two old sources were combined, a conception which is not necessarily inherent in the source hypothesis but is almost always connected with it in practice. [13]

Noth's understanding of the way that the combination of J and E was achieved is the same as with JE and P. The Yahwist was used as the base and was enriched from the Elohist.

The procedure here is evidently similar to that followed later when ... the old sources were worked into the P narrative which was chosen as the literary basis. That is to say, *one* of the sources was used as *the basis,* and was continuously *supplemented* and *enriched* with appropriate elements from the other source. [14]

And there is no doubt that the Yahwist constituted the literary basis in this operation.

A clear grasp of these methodological procedures is important for understanding both the possibilities and the limits of the task of interpreting hypothetical texts like the Yahwist and the Priestly Document. Before looking at this a little more closely, two further points need to be made.

The first of these is emphasized by Noth at the start of his study of the pentateuchal traditions.

[12]Noth, *Pentateuchal Traditions,* 22.
[13]Noth, *Pentateuchal Traditions,* 24.
[14]Noth, *Pentateuchal Traditions,* 24-25.

In this connection, the fundamental issue must be stressed that the literary-critical problem always has to be studied in the context of the *whole* Pentateuch; for a result which seems plausible in regard to only a part of the whole can easily and quickly prove to be incorrect in regard to other parts.[15]

This cannot be regarded as a counsel of perfection; methodologically, it is a necessity. Hypotheses have to account for the phenomena of the whole text in each case. The validity of investigations into limited parts of the text can be accepted when the results have been at least spot-checked against the text as a whole.

Secondly, it is critically important to recognize that the approach advocated by Noth is essentially different from that of many earlier source critics. This difference makes it methodologically wrong to attack source criticism by simply comparing the results obtained by different scholars. The reason for this lies in the different approaches taken. When it is argued that clear criteria of language, style, and thought can be used to identify the various sources, like J, E, and P, it is quite legitimate to compare the results of scholars claiming to use the same criteria. If valid and objective, the application of the criteria should generate substantially the same results for different scholars, give or take a little for margins of error and areas of uncertainty.[16] One would also have to take into account the existence of passages where the relevant criteria are so sparsely represented that agreement and certainty about the precise analysis of the composite text cannot be achieved.

However, in the approach taken by Noth, the situation is quite different. When the narrative thread is being pursued, it is much

---

[15]Noth, *Pentateuchal Traditions*, 6.

[16]In this context, it is worth quoting Noth again. "There are passages which have been handed down in such a condition that it is unlikely that any literary-critical analysis will ever really unravel their literary development. In these cases it must always suffice to offer a *possibility* for explanation on the basis of those results of literary-critical analysis which have proved adequate elsewhere. Such passages are, for example: Gen. 15, Ex. 19, Ex. 24, Ex. 33, Num. 12, and probably also the Balaam narratives in Num 22-24. Those who oppose the literary-critical study of the Pentateuch or specific literary-critical theses brought forth from other quarters can gain an all too easy victory by pointing to the absence of any certain and acknowledged result in the analysis of such passages" (*Pentateuchal Traditions,* 6).

less a question of the search for such objective criteria, and much more a question of the interpretative reconstruction or recognition of a narrative. In this case, the validity of a hypothesis depends on the internal integrity of the solution it provides and the adequacy with which this solution accounts for the phenomena in the text. Theoretically, at least, it would be possible for two hypotheses to be advanced, both internally coherent, both accounting for the phenomena of the text with reasonable adequacy, while attributing quite different sections of text to their respective sources. In such a theoretical case, it would be extremely difficult to judge between the two hypotheses. The composite nature of the text would be clear, and there would be two competing explanations for how it had come to be that way. To seek to invalidate the procedure by pointing to the differences between the two solutions would be nonsense.

While this may seem heavily theoretical, its practical outcome, for our purposes, is significant. It is twofold. Firstly, it legitimates the discussion of the message and the theology of the Yahwist. When the work of the Priestly Writer(s) has been identified, in terms of both narrative thread and characteristics of language, style, and thought, a JE text remains. When the doublets and repetitions have been removed from this, whether they belonged to a separate source or derived from the fund of tradition, a text remains which can be attributed to the Yahwist, or, better, which can be called the Yahwist narrative (J).

What remains is a text, not a person or a theologian. It is a text with a very long prehistory. It may not be possible to ascertain which authors are responsible for the various stages of this text, nor which authors are responsible for the various levels of promise within it, for example. But there is a level of text which is a coherent literary whole, and which deserves to be interpreted and demands to be interpreted. It is a convenient shorthand to refer to this text as the work of the Yahwist. Given its coherence and structure, despite all the diversity contained in it as a result of the incorporation of preexisting traditions, it is reasonable to assume that it took its final shape from the work of an author, whom we call the Yahwist.[17]

---

[17]Arguments against this position have been brought, with varying degrees of validity, by Rolf Rendtorff, *Das überlieferungsgeschichtliche Problem des Pentateuch* (BZAW

Secondly, where the Priestly Document is concerned, there is a text which can be identified by criteria of language, style, and thought, as well as by the continuity of the narrative thread. There are reasonable grounds for affirming the successful identification of a coherent narrative thread running through this text.[18] And, as we have seen, there are reasonable grounds for the hypothesis that this text served as the base for the formation of the composite text of the Pentateuch. It is, therefore, legitimate to interpret this text, as a literary entity, and to try to identify the fundamental message it sought to communicate.

THE COMBINATION OF THE SOURCES

In chap. 1, we argued on grounds of unity of progression, of focus, and of understanding, for the legitimacy of treating the Pentateuch as a literary entity. Given this position, the question still remains how it came to be that way. In my judgment, the processes of compilation have managed to preserve and combine the essential qualities of their sources, even if they have sacrificed some of their particularity. The Yahwist's message of universal blessing has been retained and reinforced. It picks up, now, the blessing that the Priestly Document has made explicit in creation. The combination with other sources has meant that the Yahwist's particular application to early Israel has been largely lost. The Priestly Document's message of God's unconditional commitment has been retained and reinforced in part; Genesis 17 is joined by Genesis 15. It has been diluted by the emphasis on law and perhaps by the introduction of the conditional covenant into the Sinai narrative. The emphasis on the certain and permanent possession of the land is weakened by being brought into the wider text; but it is not lost.

It would seem clear that the compilers had a sure sense for the import of the texts with which they worked, and so have not done violence to their sources. It is as though there has been a growing

---

147; Berlin: de Gruyter, 1977); Hans Heinrich Schmid, *Der sogenannte Jahwist* (Zurich: Theologischer Verlag, 1976); Martin Rose, *Deuteronomist und Jahwist* (AThANT 67; Zurich: Theologischer Verlag, 1981).

[18]See above, chapter 2, as well as the discussion in Noth, *Pentateuchal Traditions*, 8-17.

conviction within the community of Israel about its being and its destiny. Like a river, fed by tributaries, but moving in one direction, J and P and the traditions and laws have been caught up and blended into one. The blending has been skillfully done at all its levels: J with the traditions which formed JE (to use the conventional "E" as a convenient symbol for the non-P parallels and additions to J); JE with P; JEP with the legal traditions (without intending to prejudice the possible stages of this amalgamation); and JEP with Deuteronomy. The central concern of J and P with Israel, and the central concerns of the laws and Deuteronomy, helped maintain unity in the combination. The procedure itself also tended toward unity, at least in Noth's understanding of it. The use of J as a literary basis for JE, tended toward maintaining the literary unity of J. The use of P as the literary basis for JEP functioned in the same way, aided by the different narrative structures of J and P. The appropriate insertion of collections of law, as unbroken collections and in the right places, helped minimize their impact on the unity of the whole. The place of Moses in J and P, and as lawgiver—coupled with the presentation of Deuteronomy as the last actions of Moses' life—facilitated Deuteronomy's incorporation into the unity. A common thread of reflection within the community of Israel and uncommon skill on the part of the redactors in the community of Israel have enabled the creation of the Pentateuch as a literary work, rich and many-splendored.

In the context of the present work, it lies outside our scope to explore whether the understandings presented here as the Yahwist's or the Priestly Document's can be maintained as belonging to the Old Testament text, even if its process of growth were to be pictured quite differently. I suspect that to quite a large degree they would be maintained. The elements drawn on to shape the Yahwist's message of universal blessing, with its implications for Israel's understanding of God and understanding of its own destiny, remain in the Old Testament text, no matter how its composition is reconstructed. Similarly, the elements which delineated the message of the Priestly Document remain in the text. What changes is the extent of the text within which they are situated and the specific time at which they might have been addressed to Israel. As we have seen in the trajectory of our exploration, situation in text and time can be highly significant. It can sharpen and focus the understandings being communicated. Nevertheless, even if different views of the development of the Pentateuch prevail, it is probable that the basic positions claimed for the Priestly Document and the Yahwist can be maintained as integral elements of the present biblical text.

Appendix

THE BIBLICAL TEXT AND THE DISCIPLINES OF O.T. SCHOLARSHIP

Fidelity to the biblical text has been a recurrent theme in much of our discussion so far. It is helpful to recognize how the major stages in biblical scholarship have been controlled by discoveries about the nature of the biblical text.

The first of these, at the time of the Renaissance, was the science of text criticism. From the likes of Erasmus on, the passion to recover the most accurate possible text of the Bible has been a powerful force in scholarship. Such a passion can only be aroused by the comparison of texts, the discovery of differences between them, and the recognition of the need to recover as authoritatively accurate a text as possible. As long as there is only one text, it is *the* text; there is very little ground for entertaining doubts about its accuracy. Comparative study of the available texts changes that picture and gives biblical scholarship a hugely important task.

Source criticism (or literary criticism) is the next major movement in biblical scholarship, with its beginnings in the seventeenth century (e.g., Richard Simon, 1678).[19] It arose from the perception that phenomena in the text, above all of the Pentateuch, pointed

---

[19]We have to note that, in biblical circles, "literary criticism" has long been used as a technical term for an activity which has nothing to do with the study of the Bible as literature. In English, it is an unfortunate term, because of the almost inescapable association with literary studies. Until now, it has been in possession of the field, and no alternative is fully satisfactory. "Component analysis" would be accurate, but unlikely to prevail. "Source criticism" has an ambiguity of its own, suggesting an exclusive concern with sources on the pentateuchal model, which is certainly not the case. We have to be

to a composite text, rather than a single and unified one. One of its pioneer spirits, Jean Astruc, physician to Louis XIV, entitled his study, published in 1753, *Conjectures about the sources which it appears Moses used in the composition of the book of Genesis, (Conjectures sur les mémoires dont il paroit que Moyse s'est servi, pour composer le livre de la Genèse).* Once these phenomena had been seen and these signals had been recognized, they had to be accounted for. The outcome of such work has been the realization that one of the first things to be done in approaching the study of a biblical text is to take an inventory of its phenomena to assess its nature and whether it is a composite text or an original unity.

Form-criticism, emerging at the beginning of this century, is marked by the perception that biblical literature, like all literature, makes use of literary genres. The genre, or literary form, is an innate, yet culturally conditioned, instinct for the shape texts must take in order to perform certain functions. The literary genre is not a classification imposed on texts after they have been created. Instead, it is a necessary precondition which makes it possible for an author to create a text. It also generates the structure of expectation in an audience which makes it possible for a text to be understood. All literature is an interplay between the typical structures of the ideal of the literary genre (in German, "Gattung") and the individual features of the text which is actually produced (in German, "Form"). Much of the communicative creativity of great literature emerges out of this tension between the typical and the individual, between the expectation of the genre and the specific fulfillment found in the actual text.

A quotation from outside the biblical sphere confirms this understanding for both literature and art.

> In his brilliant book *Art and Illusion,* E. H. Gombrich speaks of artistic conventions as keyboards of relationship and says that we cannot hope to understand the art of the past without

concerned with the sources of material in all sorts of other texts. Despite this ambiguity, source criticism may be the least unsatisfactory term, as being open to less harmful confusion than literary criticism. Particularly in view of the increasing contribution of literary criticism, properly so called, to the understanding of biblical texts, source criticism will be the term adopted here for what has classically been labelled literary criticism in O.T. studies.

being aware of the systems it is based on. 'Where we have no matrix, no keyboard, we cannot assess the meaning of an individual feature', he says. I think this is often even more true of literature than of the visual arts which Gombrich is discussing.[20]

Form-criticism sprang from the realization of the significant role such systems and matrices played in the generation of the Old Testament texts, especially in so tradition-conscious a society as ancient Israel. It is critically important for the understanding and interpretation of a text to know, for example, whether it is story, or historical report, or fictive account, or liturgical text; and if, for example, it is story, whether it is story as entertainment, story as theology, story as history, or story as fiction. Insofar as an answer can be reached, it must be sought primarily through form-critical study.

Tradition history and redaction history are the two most recent advances emerging from observations about the texts themselves. (I believe it fair to say that structural and sociological approaches to the biblical text are inspired by discoveries and perceptions made outside the Bible; the case of canonical criticism falls somewhere in the middle, drawing both on a reality of the biblical text and a focus of ecclesial concern.) Although they are differently understood by different authors, both tradition history and redaction history, as they concern the Old Testament, have in common the perception that it is possible to trace the development of either a theme or an actual expression in literary form, from its early beginnings down toward its final form. Tradition history tends to be used to describe the process up to the incorporation of texts into a major literary unit. (Some scholars use tradition history for the oral stage of tradition, before the formation of a written text.) Redaction history tends to be used to describe the subsequent modifications of such literary units. Both have in common the discovery that the phenomena in the biblical text permitted such investigations to be undertaken—and therefore demanded them.

[20]Sean Lucy, "What is Anglo-Irish Poetry?" *Irish Poets in English* (The Thomas Davis Lectures; ed., S. Lucy; Cork: Mercier, 1973) 13-29, see p. 21.

The ever-deepening discovery of the nature of the biblical text has led to the emergence of the various classical disciplines of Old Testament scholarship. It has led to a far deeper understanding of the intellectual and theological activity going on within ancient Israel. The better informed our picture of ancient Israel is, the better we are able to reconstruct aspects of its thinking. If, for example, we treated the Yahwist narrative, the Priestly Document, and the Deuteronomic code as three rare books into which were distilled most of the wisdom and traditions about the past of Israel, we would have a vastly different image of the intellectual possibilities in ancient Israel than, for example, if we thought of each sanctuary and each community cherishing the traditions which were significant to it and actualizing them afresh for each generation. The latter picture is far closer to what we believe to have been the reality.

This has profound implications for source criticism. We assume that traditions were handed down in many centers, whether family, court, sanctuary, or city. This "handing down" we might think of as the vertical transmission of tradition from one generation to another. A narrative like the Yahwist or the Priestly Document is culled from these traditions, through a process of selecting, arranging, and interpreting. It has a message directed at its own generation. As such, it might be thought of as the horizontal presentation of tradition, insofar as part of the tradition is being put before a particular generation in a particular way. We must remember that this compiling of a horizontal cross section of the tradition into a source document does not close off the vertical process of transmission. Traditions will still be handed down in their various centers; they will still be represented in liturgies; they will be actualized and made real for each new generation. In due course, the enrichment or transformation of these traditions may come to be reflected in one or other of what are now the great pentateuchal sources. There was an extensive and living process going on among the community of ancient Israel. Explanations of the phenomena in the text and hypotheses about the growth of the text have to be sensitive to the size and complexity of this whole process. Our understanding of source criticism has been profoundly modified by our understanding of tradition history, and many of the implications of this modification are still to be worked out.

RECOMMENDED FURTHER READING

John Barton, *Reading the Old Testament: Method in Biblical Study*. London: Darton, Longman and Todd, 1984.

Simon J. De Vries, "A Review of Recent Research in the Tradition History of the Pentateuch." Pp. 459-502 in *Society of Biblical Literature 1987 Seminar Papers*, edited by Kent H. Richards (Atlanta: Scholars Press, 1987).

Jeffrey H. Tigay (ed.), *Empirical Models for Biblical Criticism*. Philadelphia: University of Pennsylvania, 1985.

Claus Westermann, *Genesis 1-11*, 567-600. Minneapolis: Augsburg, 1984.

R. N. Whybray, *The Making of the Pentateuch: A Methodological Study*. JSOTSup 53. Sheffield: JSOT, 1987.

In the Guides to Biblical Scholarship, Old Testament Series (Fortress Press):
P. Kyle McCarter, Jr., *Textual Criticism* (1986)
Ralph W. Klein, *Textual Criticism of the Old Testament* (1974)
Norman Habel, *Literary Criticism of the Old Testament* (1971)
Gene M. Tucker, *Form Criticism of the Old Testament* (1971)
Walter E. Rast, *Tradition History and the Old Testament* (1972)
also
James A. Sanders, *Canon and Community* (1984)
Robert R. Wilson, *Sociological Approaches to the Old Testament* (1984)
Daniel Patte, *What is Structural Exegesis?* (1976)

Deuteronomy to
2 Kings

5

The Deuteronomistic History

Recommended preliminary reading

Before reading the body of the chapter, it will be helpful to have read the following passages:
Joshua 1:1-6; 23:1-16
Judges 2:6-16, 18-19
1 Samuel 12:1-25
1 Kings 9:1-9; 11:1-13
2 Kings 17:1-23

The idea of the Deuteronomistic History is a relative newcomer among the hypotheses which are part and parcel of biblical scholarship.[1] It is also among the most helpful of them, for it reveals a unified conception holding together the otherwise extremely diverse traditions of the books from Deuteronomy to 2

---

[1]In what follows, the term "Deuteronomist" will be used without prejudice to the question of whether there were one or more Deuteronomists. In chap. 7, we shall see that the existence of a deuteronomistic circle or school is almost certain. In this context, however, it would seem pedantic to insist constantly on the plural; it will be used only where it seems especially appropriate. As far as the adjective is concerned, not all authors make the distinction between deuteronomic and deuteronomistic, especially in English writing. Where the distinction is made, the normal usage is for "deuteronomic" to be used in relation to Deuteronomy and the reform and "deuteronomistic" in relation to the history.

Kings. As a hypothesis, it was first formulated by Martin Noth, in a monograph published in 1943.[2] Language which had been marked by the style and theology of the book of Deuteronomy had long been recognized in the other narrative books of the Old Testament.[3] It is a language that is marked by the repetitive style of the preacher. It reflects a theology which is concerned with the statutes, ordinances, and laws of God, and the blessing and fullness of life which flow from their observance.

What Martin Noth recognized was that the passages where this language predominated marked out the structure of a unified literary work. Instead of being just comments on the collected traditions of Israel, there was a sense of continuity and of plan in these key passages. For the most part, they were speeches, put into the mouths of the leading characters in the history. The sense of continuity came from the way these speeches looked back over what had preceded them, and looked forward to the period to come. The sense of plan came from the positioning of the speeches: they were either at the end or the beginning of major periods, organizing the traditions of Israel. The sense of unity came from the deuteronomic theology and the deuteronomic language so evident in these passages.

The significance of Noth's discovery lies in the difference between editors, who make comments on the traditions they are collecting and preserving, and an author or authors, who organize the traditions available to them into a work of literature. The editors may have a single viewpoint; they express it, where appropriate, in the different traditions at their disposal. The author, on the other hand, takes the traditions and selects from them, organizes them, and out of their diversity forges a single whole. So a literary work comes into being, with all the challenge of its interpretation.

---

[2] *Überlieferungsgeschichtliche Studien* (2nd ed.; Tübingen: Max Niemeyer, 1957); ET (of Part I only): *The Deuteronomistic History* (JSOTSup 15; Sheffield: JSOT, 1981) and (Part II and the Appendix) *The Chronicler's History* (JSOTSup 50; Sheffield: JSOT, 1987).

[3] For example, around the turn of the century, S.R. Driver wrote that "the influence of Dt. upon subsequent books of the OT is very great" (*Introduction to the Literature of the Old Testament* [9th ed.; Edinburgh: T. & T. Clark, 1913] 102; see also pp. 102-3, 104, 166-67, 170-71, 183, 185, 199-203).

A further intriguing aspect of the literary work, identified by Noth, is the chronological structure underlying it. It is noted that Solomon began to build the temple in Jerusalem "in the four hundred and eightieth year after the people of Israel came out of the land of Egypt" (1 Kgs 6:1). Such a round figure certainly would not be understood as a matter of chance—it is 40 x 12, forty being the significant number for a period of time, whether days or years, and twelve being also a significant number, e.g., the tribes of Israel, etc. A count of the biblical chronology from the exodus down to the start of the temple in the fourth year of Solomon's reign does *not* give the figure 480. So the figure has not been built into the very fabric of Israel's history, as it were. On the other hand, if the figures which belong in the Deuteronomistic History are counted, and those which are not part of the Deuteronomistic History are left aside, then the final total of 480 emerges. It is not there by chance; it is there by the careful calculation of the Deuteronomist.[4]

Because the Deuteronomistic History is a vast work, we will deal with it in three stages. First of all, after a structural overview, we will look at the key passages which mark out its organization and plan (this chapter). Then, having acquired some feeling for the work as a whole, we will look at its sources: specifically, at least some of the earlier levels in the books of Joshua and Judges, 1 & 2 Samuel and 1 & 2 Kings (chap. 6). Then, after this has given us some idea of the material that the Deuteronomist was working with, and having seen the way that he planned and structured it, we can return to the Deuteronomistic History, as a whole, to explore its meaning and the message it was composed to express (chap. 7).

Just as we began the Pentateuch with the level of the present text and then moved to the earlier stages, so here we will proceed in a similar fashion. A great deal of work has been done on the

---

[4]It does not change the significance of this observation when we note that three different ways of making this calculation have been proposed: by Noth himself, of course (*Deuteronomistic History*, 18-25), by W. Richter (*Die Bearbeitungen des "Retterbuches" in der deuteronomischen Epoche* [BBB 21; Bonn: Hanstein, 1964] 132-41), and by G. Sauer ("Die chronologischen Angaben in den Büchern Deut. bis 2. Kön.," *TZ* 24 [1968] 1-14). The three different ways involve three different conceptions of the Deuteronomistic History. Their conclusion remains the same: there is a unified conception underlying the work.

Deuteronomistic History since Martin Noth first proposed the hypothesis. It now seems unlikely that the work emerged as the product of one person in the sixth century (Noth's proposal); it probably reached its present state in several stages. However, it is important to have a feel for the overarching vision of the hypothesis, before looking at issues of fine tuning. For that reason alone, a study of Noth's presentation of the hypothesis is well worth while. But more important than that, the task of interpretation should always begin with the final text, as we have it now. It is the phenomena in the present text which push us back to earlier stages. Practically speaking, Noth's view of the Deuteronomistic History substantially coincides with the level of the present text. So, from both aspects of convenience and method, this chapter will deal with Noth's understanding of the Deuteronomistic History, looking at its structure as it is found now in the biblical text of Deuteronomy to 2 Kings; the question of earlier and later stages will be considered in chapter 7.

At this stage, it will be helpful simply to give a bare structural outline of the composition of the Deuteronomistic History. (This analysis is based on the final level of the Deuteronomistic History, not on the present text of Deuteronomy to 2 Kings; while they coincide substantially, there are significant differences.)

THE DEUTERONOMISTIC HISTORY: A STRUCTURAL OVERVIEW

I. THE PREAMBLE: Moses' presentation of
   the law of God for life in the land   Deuteronomy
II. A HISTORY of Israel's life in the land, with
    particular reference to this law of God   Joshua-Kings
        A. UNDER JOSHUA: account of the conquest Josh 1-12;23
        B. Reflection: transition of generations   Judg 2:7-10
        C. LIFE IN THE LAND: a history continued   Judges-Kings
            1. UNDER THE JUDGES   Judg 2:11-1 Sam 7
            a. Up to Abimelech   Judg 2:11-9:57
            b. After Abimelech   Judg 10:1-1 Sam 7
            2. Reflection: transition of institutions   1 Sam 8-12
            3. UNDER THE KINGS   1 Sam 13-2 Kgs 25
            a. Up to the building of the temple   1 Sam 13-1 Kgs 8

1) Up to the coming of the ark	1 Sam 13-2 Sam 6
2) After the coming of the ark	2 Sam 7-1 Kgs 8
b. After the building of the temple	1 Kgs 9-2 Kgs 25
1) To the fall of the north	1 Kgs 9-2 Kgs 17
2) To the fall of the south	2 Kgs 18-25

A glance back over this structure will help us to recognize the plan and conception of the Deuteronomistic History. It falls into two parts. The first (I) is the book of Deuteronomy. It is presented as a series of speeches by Moses in which, on the last day of his life, he puts before Israel the law of God which will enable them to live long and fully in the land (cf., Deut 12:1 and 30:20). This exposition of the law, the last great deed of Moses' life, is given to Israel when they had reached the brink of the promised land, which lay just beyond them across the Jordan (Deut 4:44-49). This law is the first part of the Deuteronomistic History, because it is the key to the whole understanding of Israel's history, in the eyes of the Deuteronomist.[5]

The second part (II) of the Deuteronomistic History is the history of Israel's life in that land across the Jordan. It unfolds in three stages. Firstly (A), there is the conquest of the land; without that, there would be no history of life in it. Secondly (B), there is a brief and dense reflection on the transition from one generation to another and what may happen to profound religious experience in the process. The third stage (C) embraces the rest of the history: gifted with the knowledge of the law and in possession of the land, this is how Israel lived in it.

Within this history of life in the land there are, once again, three stages: (1.) the period of the judges, in which Samuel is included as the last great deliverer-judge; (2.) a moment in which the transition is achieved from the institution of judgeship to that of monarchy; and then (3.) the history of the Israel under the kings. This, too, is again carefully structured. There is a first part (3.a.), leading up to the united monarchy and the building of the temple, 480 years after the exodus from Egypt. The structure here is twofold: firstly (3.a.1), around the establishment of David, culminating in the

---

[5]J.D. Levenson has argued that the deuteronomic lawcode was not part of the original Deuteronomistic History ("Who Inserted the Book of the Torah?" *HTR* 68 [1975] 203-33). It is not possible to go into detail here on the reasons militating against this view.

coming of the ark to Jerusalem; then (3.a.2), the story of the kingdom until the building of the temple, in which the ark was housed. After that (3.b.), the history is fundamentally one of failure, moving in two phases. It begins (3.b.1) with an even-handed note of both encouragement and warning (1 Kgs 9:1-9). All too soon, that becomes a note of ominous threat (1 Kgs 11:1-13). Then the united kingdom of David and Solomon splits apart in political turmoil (1 Kgs 12:1-20). The first phase comes to an end with the destruction of the northern kingdom in 722 (2 Kgs 17:1-23). The history is carried on (3.b.2), through the reform of Josiah with its upsurge of hope (2 Kgs 22:1-23:25), until it reaches its conclusion with the destruction of the southern kingdom in 587. It is a sad and somber end to a mighty work of history and theology.

For a moment, it is important to pause and look closely at the situation in which the Deuteronomistic History was composed. It adds immensely to its significance. Scholars have not reached a consensus on the question of the unity of the history or on the precise period in which it was composed. On the unity issue, views vary from one edition (Noth, Hoffmann), to two editions (Cross, Nelson, Gray), and three editions (Dietrich, Veijola, Smend). On the composition issue, the options defended are: one edition, written in the time of exile (Noth, Hoffmann); two editions, one supporting Josiah's reform, the other completing the history down to the exile (Cross, Nelson); two editions, both after Josiah's reform, one shortly before the exile, the other during it (Gray); three editions, all in the period of exile (Dietrich, Veijola, Smend).[6] While we will look at the reasons for this later, there is one feature common to all these views: the Deuteronomistic History was composed at a very late stage in ancient Israel's

[6]The references are:
M. Noth, *Deuteronomistic History*; H.D. Hoffmann, *Reform und Reformen* (AThANT 66; Zurich: Theologischer Verlag, 1980); F.M. Cross, *Canaanite Myth and Hebrew Epic* (Cambridge: Harvard, 1978); R.D. Nelson, *The Double Redaction of the Deuteronomistic History* (JSOT Sup 18; Sheffield: JSOT, 1981), J. Gray, *I & II Kings* (OTL: 2nd ed.; London: SCM, 1970); W. Dietrich, *Prophetie und Geschichte* (FRLANT 108; Göttingen: Vandenhoeck & Ruprecht, 1972); T. Veijola; *Die ewige Dynastie* (Helsinki: Suomalainen Tiedeakatemia, 1975) and *Das Königtum in der Beurteilung der deuteronomistischen Historiographie* (Helsinki: Suomalainen Tiedeakatemia, 1977); R. Smend, *Die Entstehung des Alten Testaments* (2nd ed.; Stuttgart: Kohlhammer, 1981) 110-24.

existence as a free and independent nation or just after its end.

Freedom, for Israel, blossomed with the exodus from Egypt. But its full flowering on a national level did not occur until the united monarchy, under David and Solomon. For a short time, Israel experienced national freedom, independence, and power, while the great empires of Egypt and Assyria, like the jaws of a vise on either side, were uncharacteristically dormant. It was short-lived. After Solomon (c. 922), the nation divided into two unequal parts, the northern and southern kingdoms. In 722/21, the north fell to the dreaded might of the Assyrians and was incorporated as a province of their empire. In 587, the south fell to the Babylonians, who had arrogated the Assyrian empire to themselves. Throughout the rest of Old Testament history, despite the stirrings of the Maccabean revolt, Israel never regained its full freedom, but was always the vassal in somebody else's empire.

The immense literary achievement of the Deuteronomistic History was realized in very close proximity to this final crumbling of Israel's political freedom. At the earliest, it was written in support of Josiah's reform. If so, it was looking at the fate of the northern kingdom in 722 (cf., 2 Kings 17), the very close call suffered by the south in 701 (cf., 2 Kings 18-19), and it sought to rally Israel to the cause of reform and renewal in order to restore a kingdom like David's and avoid the fate of conquest and exile. At the latest, it was written in the very time of exile, and it sought to understand and explain how this bitter fate had come upon God's people. In either case, it is written at a quite critical moment in Israel's history. The moment is critical not only for Israel's existence, but also for Israel's faith. The Deuteronomist assembled the great traditions of Israel's past and organized them in order to interpret Israel's present. It is this setting and the critical urgency of the endeavor which we need to keep in mind as we pass in review the structure of the Deuteronomistic History.

As we noted above, the organization and plan of the Deuteronomistic History can be seen from the location of the key deuteronomistic passages at the beginning or end of the major periods. Before we turn to a study of the sources used in the composition of the History, we can get a good feel for its contours by looking at these key passages.

THE PREAMBLE

In a sense, the first of them is the book of Deuteronomy itself. Not that it was the composition of the Deuteronomist. He inherited Deut 4:44-30:20, as part of the tradition which inspired both Josiah's reform, around the year 622, and also the Deuteronomistic History as a literary work. Deuteronomy is a key to the History, since it is the speech of Moses which sets the guidelines for the living of Israel's history, and so, too, for its interpretation. It emerges out of the spirit of what is known as the deuteronomic reform. This was a movement of reform, initiated in the reign of Josiah (640-609). Its spirit is expressed in the deuteronomic law code (Deut 12-26): absolute loyalty to the LORD, the god of Israel's ancestors, the god of Israel's history; the shunning of the worship of foreign gods; the centralization of all of Israel's sacrificial worship at the temple in Jerusalem (cf., Deut 12). The reform must have involved major disturbance and change in Israel's life. Sanctuaries outside Jerusalem ceased to function as places of sacrifice, high places deemed idolatrous were destroyed (cf., 2 Kgs 23:4-20). The centralization of sacrifice in Jerusalem would also have had enormous ramifications in the economic and fiscal sphere, channelling funds from the country centers into Jerusalem (cf., Deut 14:24-26).[7] It is assumed that this reform was preached throughout Judah, and that the exhortations and admonitions in Deuteronomy 5-11, introducing the law code, probably reflect much of the substance of that preaching.

The deuteronomic reform sought to catch Israel up in the present moment of "this day," relegating seven centuries of infidelity and failure to the past, and starting afresh in this moment before God. That is the immense significance, in the seventh century, of the words given to Moses in the thirteenth century: "The LORD our God made a covenant with us in Horeb. Not with our fathers did the LORD make this covenant, but with us, who are all of us here alive this day" (Deut 5:2-3). The generation of the desert had died, and this is another generation. Yet the salvation offered at Sinai is still theirs for the accepting. Seven centuries later, it was still theirs for the accepting. It is remarkable testimony to Israel's faith in the unconditional commitment of God.

[7]See W.E. Claburn, "The Fiscal Basis of Josiah's Reforms," *JBL* 92 (1973) 11-22.

The law code of Deuteronomy 12-26 spelled out what that acceptance involved. The introductory chapters (Deuteronomy 5-11) provided the motivation for that acceptance. The Deuteronomistic History is to be a history of the acceptance or rejection of that salvation. So the Deuteronomist placed this great collection of tradition at the head of his work. To it, he simply prefaced chaps. 1-3 and part of chap. 4, to trace Israel's story from Sinai/Horeb to the plains of Moab, by the Jordan, where this final great act of Moses' life is played out. At the end of the collection, which probably formed the book of the reform, the Deuteronomist prepared for the transition into the history which was to be his work. Moses' death is foreshadowed, and the succession is to pass to Joshua, with a view to the conquest of the promised land (Deut 31:1-2, 7-8). The details are worth noting. Their destination is "the land which the LORD has sworn to their fathers to give them" (v 7a). With this, there is the frequent deuteronomistic linkup with Israel's ancestral traditions; it is indeed a "promised land." "And you shall put them in possession of it" (v 7b). There is a subtle interplay between divine word ("to give them," v 7a) and the human action needed to bring that word to fulfillment. At the same time, the key to the Deuteronomist's understanding of the conquest is clearly expressed: "It is the LORD who goes before you; he will be with you, he will not fail you or forsake you; do not fear or be afraid" (v 8).

UNDER JOSHUA

The first of the Deuteronomist's speeches takes up this theme (Josh 1:1-6, 10-18). There is the reference back to the death of Moses, and the continued emphasis that the land is God's gift to Israel (v 2). The extent of the land to be possessed is described. Then the promise, previously on Moses' lips (Deut 31:8), is now given directly to Joshua: "As I was with Moses, so I will be with you; I will not fail you or forsake you" (v 5).

It is worth pausing on the significance of this association with the traditions of Deuteronomy. We take for granted that the book of Deuteronomy is the end of the Pentateuch and that it follows naturally into the historical books, beginning with Joshua. But if the deuteronomic lawcode was the book of the reform, then this state of affairs was not always so. The Yahwist, as we have seen, probably ended at about Numbers 24. The Priestly Document will end (for it is not yet written) with the traditions of the death of Moses, much as we have them now in Deut 34:1*, 7-9. The deuteronomic lawcode, as it existed at the time of Josiah's reform, had no literary connection with Genesis to Numbers, beyond its attribution to Moses; it had no literary connection with the traditions we now find in Joshua to Kings. It is therefore a remarkable and significant move on the Deuteronomist's part to forge this link. It is a theological statement which places the whole of Israel's subsequent history under the aegis of the deuteronomic law. That is, the history which the Deuteronomist's contemporaries looked back to, from the seventh or sixth centuries, was to be interpreted in terms of the law which was the centerpiece of the seventh-century deuteronomic reform. Whatever Israel's understanding of the relationship between law and history earlier in their traditions, from the point of view of a literary work, this step was a radical innovation.[8]

This understanding is developed in a passage which is considered by Noth to be a secondary expansion of the Deuteronomistic History (i.e., Josh 1:7-9; note the duplication of v 6 in vv 7 and 9).[9] Joshua is exhorted to be careful "to do according to all the law which Moses my servant commanded you. . . . This book of the law shall not depart out of your mouth, but you shall meditate on it day and night" (vv 7-8). In such an understanding, the role of the law is being pushed to a theologically radical extreme.

---

[8]Two factors led to the establishment of Deuteronomy in its present position as the conclusion of the Torah. Firstly, the Priestly Document ended with the death of Moses, so overlapping with Deuteronomy at the beginning of the Deuteronomistic History. Secondly, the deuteronomistic introduction in Deut 1-3 recapitulates the history from Sinai, therefore pointing back into what is now the Pentateuch. In Noth's view, the combination of the pentateuchal sources into a single text, using P as its basis, was separate from and preceded the amalgamation with the Deuteronomistic History. This amalgamation occurred in two stages, since the existence of the Samaritan Pentateuch indicates that, initially at least, Deuteronomy alone was incorporated into the combined pentateuchal sources, without the inclusion of Joshua-Kings (Noth, *Überlieferungsgeschichtliche Studien*, 211-16; ET: *The Chronicler's History*, 143-47). More recently, see A.D.H. Mayes, *The Story of Israel between Settlement and Exile: A Redactional Study of the Deuteronomistic History* (London: SCM, 1983) 139-49.

[9]For the identification of the complete text of the Deuteronomistic History (according to Noth), and the reasons for this identification, see Noth, *Deuteronomistic History*.

At the end of the conquest, after the Deuteronomist had incorporated his selection of the available traditions (i.e., Joshua 2-11), there is a second speech by Joshua (Joshua 23). The Deuteronomist has Joshua look back over the whole period, "You have seen all that the LORD your God has done to all these nations for your sake" (v 3). The whole conquest is summed up: what has been conquered, and the division into inheritances of the territory which remains to be conquered (vv 4-5). Then the Deuteronomist has Joshua turn to the future, to enjoin steadfast obedience to the law of Moses, with two areas of specific emphasis. Israel is not to mix with the remaining nations and become involved with their gods (vv 7-8). Israel is not to intermarry with the remnant of these nations (v 12). The consequences of disobedience are explicit: "Know assuredly that the LORD your God will not continue to drive out these nations before you; but they shall be a snare and a trap for you, a scourge on your sides, and thorns in your eyes, till you perish from off this good land which the LORD your God has given you" (v 13). Two things have happened here. Firstly, Israel has been given clear and adequate guidance for their future conduct in this land which is God's gift. Secondly, the possibility of exile, "till you perish from off this good land," has been raised. For the Deuteronomist's contemporaries, the significance of that possibility is inescapable. Their conduct and their fate are almost inextricably bound together.[10] Just as Moses left Israel with the freedom to choose blessing or curse, life or death (cf., Deut 30:15-20), so too does Joshua. The alternatives of blessing and curse, here of "good things" and "evil things" (Josh 23:14-16), are placed before Israel. The freedom of choice is theirs; the consequences of the choice are known. The Deuteronomist is careful to make this clear.

[10]According to Noth, Joshua 13-22 did not belong to the original version of the Deuteronomistic History, but were added shortly after its completion; he considered Joshua 24 to have been an independent passage which was also added to the history later. More recently, Rudolf Smend has argued that Josh 13:1-21:45 and Joshua 24 belonged to the original Deuteronomistic History, with 23:1-16, together with 1:7-9; 13:1b*, 2-6; and Judg 1:1-2:9, belonging to a slightly later, but still deuteronomistic, redaction (*Probleme biblischer Theologie* [ed., H.W. Wolff; Munich: Kaiser, 1971] 494-509). In that case, of course, Joshua 24 would have been the farewell address of Joshua to the people, committing them to absolute fidelity to God. Note the duplication in Josh 24:28-31 and Judg 2:6-9, which would be related to the insertion of Judg 1:1-2:9.

THE TRANSITION OF GENERATIONS

Judg 2:7-10 provides a fascinating reflection on the transition between generations (v 6 forms the conclusion of Joshua's speech). The people are portrayed as remaining faithful to God, "all the days of Joshua, and all the days of the elders who outlived Joshua, who had seen all the great work which the LORD had done for Israel" (v 7). But when that generation died, the next generation "did not know the LORD or the work which he had done for Israel" (v 10). The tragic consequences of this are evident in the next verse: "And the people of Israel did what was evil in the sight of the LORD and served the Baals" (v 11). In the dense juxtaposition of vv 7 and 10 lies the explanation of the tragedy of v 11. The difference between the faithful generation and the unfaithful generation, between those who served the LORD and those who served Baal, was simply the knowledge of the LORD and the works the LORD had done. That "knowledge" had not been passed from one generation to the next. For the Deuteronomist, this "knowledge" was almost certainly not just the words and the traditions. As in the prophets, "knowledge" in this sort of context has to mean that deep inner experience which is part of the appropriation of values and which profoundly influences conduct. In the transition of generations, this experience has to be handed on, otherwise the reason for commitment to the LORD is lost and, with it, the meaning of life. Here, too, the Deuteronomist is speaking directly to his contemporaries.

UNDER THE JUDGES

In Judg 2:11-16, 18-19, instead of a speech, since there was no leader figure available to deliver it, there is a reflective passage in which the Deuteronomist sums up and interprets the next period in the history. The conquest has been achieved. The land has been occupied. This was a necessary prelude to the history of Israel's life in the land: first occupy your land. Now, after the transition of generations, there begins the history of their life in that land. We remember that it is to be judged by the criteria of the deuteronomic law, of which the central and primary requirement is absolute fidelity to God (cf., Deut 5:6-10; 6:4-9; 12:1-3).

Its start is somber, but not totally so. The picture is the

Deuteronomist's composition, but it is not his invention; it is drawn from the traditions. Israel, at the very beginning of their settled life in the land, did what was evil in God's sight and served the Baals (Judg 2:11). "They forsook the LORD, the God of their fathers, who had brought them out of the land of Egypt" (v 12). This is a typically dense deuteronomistic sentence. In two clauses, it sums up the whole of Israel's previous experience of God; here is knowledge of God in a nutshell. "The God of their fathers" evokes the entire sweep of Israel's ancestral traditions; "who had brought them out of the land of Egypt" recalls the whole history of the Mosaic generation. So the Deuteronomist encapsulates all that had been particular to Israel in a sentence summing up the portrayal of what Israel had abandoned. "They went after other gods." A sequence is then unleashed: God is angered and hands Israel over to their enemies, then raises up judges to save them, and this deliverance is effective through the lifetime of the judge (vv 14-16, 18). But the sequence becomes ominously like a cycle: whenever the judge died, it started again (v 19). From the tradition, the Deuteronomist had the stories of Israel's periodic oppression and deliverance. What he has added is, as it were, a preface giving an interpretation of this oppression and deliverance. The oppression results from Israel's forsaking the LORD and turning to other gods. The deliverance is God's gracious act. The tradition has Israel cry to God in their suffering, as they had done under the oppression in Egypt (cf., Judg 3:9, 15; 4:3; 6:6). Here, in the preface, the Deuteronomist has left out this element. Such an omission is hardly accidental. The reason God delivered the people is expressed: "for the LORD was moved to pity by their groaning because of those who afflicted and oppressed them" (v 18b). The omission of the specific reference to Israel's crying to the LORD, although it is mentioned at all four places in the tradition, has to mean that, in the Deuteronomist's understanding of God, gracious divine response is triggered simply by the reality of Israel's need. If this is so, it is an intriguing theological position. It runs counter to much of Israel's experience, as well as ours; yet, paradoxically, it expresses a longing which is deeply rooted in faith.

There is a double significance here for the Deuteronomist's contemporaries. Firstly, Israel's misfortunes are explained by Israel's apostasy and infidelity. So Israel knows why they are where they are. That is one thing. But secondly, there is the gracious nature of Israel's God. The cyclic movement of experience could push one toward despair, because of the constantly recurring cycle of sin. But there is also ground for hope, since there is also the experience of God's constantly recurring deliverance. The outcome for those the Deuteronomist is addressing may depend on where the cycle stops—if it stops.

The Deuteronomist then records the deliverer stories of Othniel, Ehud, Deborah and Barak, and Gideon, followed by the disastrous episode of Abimelech's three-year kingship. This is followed by another brief interpretative passage in deuteronomistic language (Judg 10:6-16). It echoes themes from the first introduction (Judg 2:11-16, 18-19), and yet it is still obviously within the period of the judges. At first sight, its position and purpose are puzzling. Noth understands it as meaning to "accentuate what was said in previous introductions."[11] The two lists of gods and peoples are not entirely helpful (i.e., vv 6 and 11-12).[12] However, in v 6, the "Baals and the Ashtaroth" take us back to 2:13; the gods of Syria, Sidon, and Moab, recall Cushan-rishathaim (3:7-11), Jabin and Sisera (chaps. 4-5), and Eglon (3:12-30) respectively. It is possible that the gods of the Ammonites and the gods of the Philistines refer to the forthcoming stories of oppression, the Ammonites referring to the story of Jephthah and the Philistines to the time of Samuel and Saul. The passage, then, may be both looking back over what has happened so far and looking forward to what is to come. While it is not creating a new period, it does suggest a midway stage in the period of the judges.

It is illuminating to recognize that the passage comes directly after an abortive attempt at kingship in Israel; and it precedes the period which is to lead to the establishment of kingship in Israel. This is probably the source of its significance. It follows a sequence of three stories of deliverance in Israel (the Othniel episode, 3:7-11, is not strictly a story). In each of these three stories, when Israel was in trouble, they cried to God, and God raised up a deliverer and gave them peace. It is a safe assertion to make that, for the Deuteronomist, this was a model of how Israel should act when in trouble, and also of how God responds to

[11]Noth, *Deuteronomistic History*, 46.

[12]Noth regards the text in vv 11-12 to be corrupt, *Deuteronomistic History*, 120.

Israel's need. What follows it, in chap. 9, is a story of an episode of kingship which brought no peace and did nothing but harm. It begins with Abimelech's slaughter of his brothers, the seventy sons of Jerubbaal/Gideon. The parable of Jotham, the youngest son and sole survivor (vv 7-21), ironically points to the uselessness of kingship. It is borne out in the history of treachery and violence which leads ultimately to Abimelech's death, avenging his brothers' deaths, and vindicating Jotham (9:56-57).

With an example of such social strife and violence at his disposal to lead into the Ammonite oppression, it is a mark of the singlemindedly theological intent of the Deuteronomist that Israel's apostasy is still depicted as the motivating force. "We have sinned against you, because we have forsaken our God and served the Baals" (10:10). This is the cry that the Deuteronomist has Israel address to God. Then, in a quite unexpected development, he has God turn them down: "You cried to me (in the past) and I delivered you out of their hand. Yet you have forsaken me and served other gods; *therefore I will deliver you no more. Go and cry to the gods whom you have chosen; let them deliver you in the time of your distress"* (10:12-14). The cycle of sin, oppression, deliverance, and peace has been stopped at oppression. It is not, however, a theological statement about God, but a narrative tactic on the part of the Deuteronomist. The interpretative passage continues with two moves on Israel's part. Firstly, they ignore God's refusal; they continue to cry, not to "the gods whom you have chosen," but to the LORD. "We have sinned; do to us whatever seems good to you; only deliver us, we pray you, this day" (v 15). Secondly, the Deuteronomist depicts them repenting and acting on their repentance: "So they put away the foreign gods from among them and served the LORD" (v 16a). The result is that instead of turning the people down, God "became indignant over the misery of Israel" (v 16b). The Deuteronomist then introduces the story of Jephthah and the deliverance of Israel.

Deuteronomistic theology is expressed in narrative and not in discourse. That is why the Deuteronomist wrote the story of the people of Israel and not a theological treatise about religious infidelity and political disaster. What sort of theology lies behind a passage like the one we have just seen (vv 10-16)? Put in modern terms, it has to be a theology of paradox, surely. The paradox of God's unconditional love, on the one hand, and human responsibility for existence, on the other. If Israel is to take responsibility for its existence—and we for ours—it is impossible to trade on God's unconditional love by living any which way. Israel has chosen a certain path, and it involves certain consequences, and Israel must live with those consequences—"I will deliver you no more." Responsible, then, for its own existence, Israel must repent and do what is right—with no guarantees of what that will bring. Yet there is the unconditional love of God which can be trusted not to reject, but to turn and deliver: "and he (the LORD) became indignant over the misery of Israel." It is the same understanding passionately proclaimed in Hosea:

> How can I give you up, Ephraim,
>   how surrender you, Israel? ...
> My heart is changed within me,
>   my remorse kindles already.
> I will not let loose my fury,
>   I will not turn round and destroy Ephraim;
> for I am God and not a man,
>   the Holy One in your midst.... (Hos 11:8-9; tr. *NEB*)

The action of Israel portrayed here may be a paradigm for the contemporaries of the Deuteronomist. The response of God's unconditional love to Israel's plight cannot be predicted, only trusted. Israel's responsibility is to repent and to trust.

THE TRANSITION OF INSTITUTIONS

As the structural outline indicated, the period of the judges ends at 1 Samuel 7.[13] It is followed by an interpretative reflection on the transition of institutions, from the judges to the kings. The deuteronomistic key passage marking the end of the transition is the speech given to Samuel (1 Samuel 12). In between Judg 10:6-16 and the end of the period of the judges, Israel has been

---

[13]The introduction of the two interpretative reflections on transition (Judg 2:7-10 and 1 Sam 8-12) is an innovation in this treatment. It is a slight variation on Noth's position, who sees the last "judges" story in 1 Samuel 7, while Samuel's "valedictory speech" has to be postponed until 1 Samuel 12 (cf. *Deuteronomistic History*, 49-51).

portrayed as oppressed by the Ammonites and delivered by Jephthah, and then oppressed by the Philistines and delivered by Samuel.[14] The use of traditions in the interpretative reflection (1 Samuel 8-12) is very complex; that use will be looked at a little more closely when we deal with the Deuteronomist's use of sources. At the moment, it will be enough for our purposes to look at the speech which marks the conclusion of the transition from judges to kings.

Within this speech the Deuteronomist has to reconcile the traditions he has chosen to use. These traditions fall into two major groups: those which concern the people's demand for a king (1 Sam 8:1-22 and 10:17-27); those which concern God's gift of a king (1 Sam 9:1-10:16 and 11:1-15). The Deuteronomist has the demand for kingship portrayed as a wrongful rejection of God (cf., 8:7-8; 10:19). Against the background of the deuteronomistic passage in Judg 10:6-16, it would seem likely that, in the Deuteronomist's theology, Israel should have repented, trusted, and waited. The nature of the response is then God's free choice. The demand made by Israel conflicts with God's freedom and reveals absence of trust. The demand is, therefore, viewed negatively. Also, we must be aware that the Deuteronomist's experience of kingship, viewed through the deuteronomistic interpretation of Israel's history, was a highly negative one. Yet there were also the traditions in which kingship was God's gracious gift for Israel's deliverance. All this the Deuteronomist endeavored to reconcile in the great speech given to Samuel in 1 Samuel 12.

As in almost all these key passages, the speech looks back over the past and forward to the future. The retrospective section covers firstly Samuel's own stewardship. He is given a clean bill of health (12:1-5). Then Samuel's address, with the tone of a legal proceeding (cf., v 7), sweeps over Israel's history from the exodus to the present. While some of the details are obscure, the main point is clear: throughout this sweep of history, when the Israelites cried for deliverance, they received it. All the more reprehensible, then, their behavior when Nahash, the Ammonite king, became a grave threat to them. Instead of trusting in God, they demanded a

---

[14]For Noth's reasons why the Samson stories should not be included in the Deuteronomistic History, see *Deuteronomistic History*, 52-53.

king (v 12). The Deuteronomist then has Samuel draw the
threads of the traditions together in one sentence: "And now
behold the king whom you have chosen, for whom you have
asked (demand for a king); behold, the LORD has set a king over
you (gift of a king)" (v 13). The tensions of the past have reached
reconciliation in the present.

The speech now turns to the future. In two lapidary sentences,
the Deuteronomist has Samuel provide Israel with guidance, of
an almost constitutional caliber, for life in the land under the
kings (vv 14-15). The two sentences are very closely balanced and
they point in the direction of the deuteronomic options of blessing
and curse. The close parallelism is worth maintaining.

V 14 (blessing)	V 15 (curse)
If you will fear the LORD and serve him and hearken to his voice	But if you will not hearken to the voice of the LORD,
and not rebel against the commandment of the LORD, THEN both you and the king who reigns over you will be loyal to the LORD your God.[15]	but rebel against the commandment of the LORD, THEN the hand of the LORD will be against you and your king (Heb: your fathers).

Moving out of the present situation, Israel's future is defined in
terms of a clear either-or option. The transition of institutions,
from judgeship to kingship, has not broken Israel's relationship
with its God. It is evidently understood by the Deuteronomist to
have been wrong, but it has not severed relationships between
God and Israel. King and people can still be loyal followers of

[15]The translation of this verse is important. The phrase "it will be well" in the *RSV* does
not exist in the Hebrew. It is understood as elliptical, in a sentence where it is thought that
the conclusion had been left unexpressed. The sentence construction, in the Hebrew, has
the hinge between protasis and apodosis exactly where the THEN is in our translation.
The apodosis in v 14 says literally: "then both you and the king who reigns over you will be
after the LORD your God." At first sight, this appears to be a tautologous repetition of the
early part of the verse. Hence the resort to "it will be well." However, the expression "to be
after" has the meaning "to be loyal to," "to be of the party of," which gives good sense here.
Israel has been accused of rejecting God. Now, they have it in their power to be loyal
followers of God. Cf., D.J. McCarthy, *Treaty and Covenant* (AnBib 21a; new edition,
completely rewritten; Rome: Biblical Institute, 1978) 215.

God, if they are careful to serve the LORD and keep the commandments. But if this does not happen, then God's hand will be against them.

Since Israel has mistrusted God's power to save, Samuel calls for a miraculous demonstration of that power (vv 16-18). The Deuteronomist's idea of the demand for a king as a grave and serious evil is clearly expressed in v 19. Samuel's response to the people confirms this judgment, yet provides assurance, coupled with the promise of his intercession and instruction (vv 20-23). For the Deuteronomist, this is a critical moment in Israel's history. The new institution is to prove fatal to Israel, yet it need never have been so. From the very first, Israel was given a clear understanding of how to live with kingship. They had been instructed by Samuel, promised his prayers and his guidance. For the Deuteronomist, Israel had been set on the right track (v 24). We may note the recurrence of the two themes of God's unconditional commitment and our human responsibility. God's commitment is expressed by Samuel: "For the LORD will not cast away his people, for his great name's sake, because it has pleased the LORD to make you a people for himself" (v 22). And the issue of human responsibility is equally there: "But if you still do wickedly, you shall be swept away, both you and your king" (v 25).

This speech is of immense importance for understanding the theological context of the Deuteronomistic History. The Deuteronomist attributed Israel's disasters, the downfall of the northern kingdom in 722 and of the south in 587, directly to the conduct of its kings. Paradoxically though, one of the great figures in the deuteronomistic gallery of heroes was David, anointed by the prophet Samuel. Also in the tradition available to the Deuteronomist was the story of Saul's anointing, in which kingship came from God's initiative as a gracious, saving gift (1 Sam 9:15-16). Had God then established the fateful institution which ultimately destroyed the nation? The Deuteronomist also had traditions which portrayed kingship as the result of demand from the people. In that case, had God yielded to their demand, and so sealed the people's fate? In Samuel's speech, the Deuteronomist blends all these traditions, and plots a course for the future where life and blessing lie within Israel's grasp. The new institution was not a canker at the nation's core. To fear God, serve God, hearken to the voice of God, and not rebel against God's commandments, that was what Israel had to do. And, having been very carefully prepared by Samuel, Israel, both king and people, knew that this was what they had to do to secure their future.

Just as the Deuteronomist has had Moses confront his generation with the choice between blessing and curse, and exhort them to choose life (Deut 30:15-20), and just as he has had Joshua make the same options clear in his farewell speech (Joshua 23), so too he has had Samuel place Israel squarely before the options of loyally following God or being swept away. In this way, the Deuteronomist expresses his conviction that, at each major stage in its history, Israel received instruction and guidance from God to preserve them "in the good and the right way" (1 Sam 12:23). It may be well to pause and notice at least three theological concerns which underlie this deuteronomistic approach. One is the concern for God's good name: God has done everything for the people that it was possible to do. A second is the concern about Israel's responsibility for their own fate: they were well informed and well aware of the choices which lay before them and the consequences of their actions. The third concern is for their future: what should Israel do now? Latent in the Deuteronomist's exposition is the understanding that what Israel needs to do in its present situation is to make the right choice, the choice that it was exhorted to make at all of the past junctures in its history: "therefore choose life, that you and your descendants may live, loving the LORD your God, obeying his voice, and cleaving to him; for that means life to you and length of days" (Deut 30:19-20).

UNDER THE KINGS

The Deuteronomist's traditions take the history onward, to David's kingship, capture of Jerusalem, establishment of a palace there, and the coming of the ark to David's city (2 Samuel 5-6). Here two deuteronomistic themes come together: David, the ideal king; Jerusalem, the place where God's name dwells. 2 Samuel 7 functions as a key passage for the Deuteronomistic History, even though most probably very little of it derived from the Deuteronomist.[16] What his tradition provided suited his needs admirably. It looked back over Israel's history, from the time of the judges down to the time of David; it looked forward to Israel's future, with the promise of a secure dynasty for David. If we set aside the question of David's prayer, the Deuteronomist needed to make only three additions to the text he received. In vv 1b and 11a, he inserted the references to "rest from enemies." From a deuteronomistic viewpoint, v 1a would have explained why David thought fit to make the proposal to build a temple; yet David's kingdom was far from having rest from enemies, both within and without. The reference in v 11a, however, promises rest for the future, so looking to the time when the temple could be built. And that permitted the Deuteronomist to make a major change to the text of Nathan's speech, when he added to the promise of a son: "He shall build a house for my name" (v 13a). Here, at last, the Jerusalem temple is in certain view.

The construction of the temple, begun 480 years after the exodus, brings this major section of the Deuteronomistic History to an end. Again there is a deuteronomistic key passage, in the form of Solomon's prayer at the dedication of the temple (1 Kgs 8:14-66). Its length alone makes it obvious that this is a passage of major concern for the Deuteronomists.[17] It, too, has its retrospective aspect: it takes in swiftly the perspective from Egypt to David to the present (8:16-21). The pivot to the future is modulated by a passionate prayer: LORD God, there is none like you; as you kept your word to David, keep that word in our future (vv 22-26). Not inadvertently, but because it is linked to that future, the Deuteronomist has Solomon take a brief detour into speculative theology: can God dwell in a temple? "Behold, heaven and the highest heaven cannot contain you; how much less this house which I have built!" (v 27). So God is not to be contained. But there can be presence without containment, and deuteronomic theology expressed that presence of God as the presence of God's name. So the temple is that place of which God has said: "My

---

[16]For a valuable discussion of the place of 2 Samuel 7 in the Deuteronomistic History, see D.J. McCarthy,"II Samuel 7 and the Structure of the Deuteronomic History," *JBL* 84 (1965) 131-38.

[17]"Deuteronomists" is appropriate in this context, since it is likely that this prayer reflects some quite late concerns.

name shall be there" (v 29). The centrality of the Jerusalem temple is crucial to the deuteronomic reform and to deuteronomic theology. It is central, too, to deuteronomistic spirituality: the Deuteronomists have Solomon envisaging Israel at prayer, praying "toward this place" (v 30). The response asked of God: hear in heaven, your dwelling place; and when you hear, forgive (v 30).

In Solomon's prayer, the Deuteronomists then marshal a whole series of situations in which Israel will turn "toward this place" in prayer to God. These situations, with the responses desired of God, are:

—sin against a neighbor:

act and judge, condemning the guilty by bringing his conduct upon his own head, vindicating the righteous (vv 31-32);

—defeat before the enemy:

forgive, and bring them again to the land (vv 33-34);

—drought:

forgive, and grant rain upon your land (vv 35-36);

—famine, pestilence, blight, etc., siege, or whatever plague:

forgive and act, rendering to each, whose heart you know, according to all their ways (vv 37-40);

—foreigner who comes from a far country:

do according to all for which the foreigner calls to you (vv 41-43);

—in time of battle:

maintain their cause (vv 44-45);

—in time of exile:

maintain their cause, forgive your people, and grant them compassion in the sight of those who carried them captive, that they may have compassion on them (vv 46-53).

The sequence totals seven; the fourth is all-inclusive, as if it were once a conclusion to the prayer. But it is not easy to sort the sequence out along these lines. The sixth and seventh items are usually considered later expansions.[18] It may be that the fourth, with its multiple possibilities, summed it up for Israel "that they may fear you all the days that they live" (v 40); and the fifth cared for the foreigner, "in order that all the peoples of the earth may

---

[18]If anyone were interested in creating a series of seven, it may well have been a later editor. The sixth item (vv 44-45) has all the marks of a filler, to make up the sacred number: it does not deal with a disaster and it asks for precious little (cf., v 49b).

know your name and fear you, as do your people Israel..." (v 43). More important than the ordering principle is the underlying theology. The disasters of defeat, drought, and exile are all attributed to sin (vv 33, 35, 46). God is asked for very little. For the most part, it is simply the restoration of the status quo. In some cases it is less than that. It is as if the Deuteronomist's theology of prayer was: it is incumbent on us to cry to God; it is incumbent on God to choose how our prayer will be answered.

Immediately following this prayer, the Deuteronomist has God appear to Solomon (9:1-9). His prayer has been heard. In a quite lovely phrase, God responds: "I have consecrated this house which you have built, and put my name there for ever; *my eyes and my heart will be there for all time"* (9:3). My eyes and my heart—my attention and my love. It is a gorgeous touch, without doubt worthy of God, but quite a surprise coming from the Deuteronomist! He has God go on to place blessing and curse before Solomon. Integrity of heart and obedience will bring Solomon an unfailing future (vv 4-5). Infidelity and idolatry will have Israel cut off from the land and the temple reduced to ruins (vv 6-9). As at the end of the period in the desert, the period of the conquest, and the period of the judges, the Deuteronomist had Moses, Joshua, and Samuel place this option before Israel, so here now, with the temple built and consecrated, the ark installed in it, and the monarchy thoroughly established, this same option is again put to Israel, for the last time. The Deuteronomist is nothing if not painstaking. But then, the stakes are very high: the glory of God and the fate of Israel.

A sadder passage follows very shortly, again from the Deuteronomist (11:1-13). "For when Solomon was old his wives turned away his heart after other gods" (v 4). The consequence is God's anger and the announcement that the kingdom will be divided in two (vv 9-13). It is a dark and ominous note.

The Deuteronomist pieces together the history of both northern and southern kingdoms. The northern kingdom comes to an end in 722/21, a victim of Assyrian might (cf., 2 Kgs 17:1-6). A major interpretative passage from the Deuteronomist's pen addresses this catastrophe (17:7-23). "And this was so, because the people of Israel had sinned against the LORD their God (v 7) ... and walked in the customs of the nations ... (v 8). And the people of Israel did secretly against the LORD their God things that were not right (v 9). . . . Yet the LORD warned Israel and Judah by every prophet and every seer, saying, 'Turn from your evil ways and keep my commandments...' (v 13). But they would not listen ... (v 14). They despised his statutes and his covenant ... and the warnings which he gave them. They went after false gods and became false" (v 15). This is the Deuteronomist's last word of interpretation. It spells out what has become increasingly clear throughout the Deuteronomistic History: the concern of the history is to point to the sins of Israel, to point to the warnings which they had been given at every turn, to let it be seen how, abandoning the LORD, they had gone after false gods and so themselves become false. "False" here is the same word as Qohelet's "vanity of vanities"; it is emptiness and worthlessness. Jeremiah uses the same thought and the same word: "They went far from me, and went after worthlessness, and became worthless" (Jer 2:5).

> For my people have committed two evils:
>   they have forsaken me,
>   the fountain of living waters,
> and hewed out cisterns for themselves,
>   broken cisterns,
>   that can hold no water. (Jer 2:13)

The Deuteronomist will take the story on down to the final catastrophe for Jerusalem, its siege and destruction and the end of the southern kingdom in 587 (2 Kings 25). Before this, there is the reform of Josiah, in the end outweighed by all the evil done by Manasseh (cf., 2 Kgs 23:26-27). The issues of these chapters will be discussed in chapter 7 on the intention of the Deuteronomistic History.

For now, it is enough to have a clear vision of the kind of procedure involved in the composition of the Deuteronomistic History, and the structure which emerged in the process. As to the procedure, the Deuteronomist—as understood by Noth—took the traditions available to him, and organized them into the significant periods, prefaced or concluded them with key passages of his own composition, expressing his own theological perception. It is these which we have just finished reviewing. The structure places the whole of Israel's history in the promised land under the sign of the law of Deuteronomy, seeing that history in the triple movement of conquest, judges, and kings, and observing in it how Israel's sin brings on Israel's downfall, how Israel's cry brings God's response, and noting, above all, that right throughout its history Israel was guided, exhorted, and warned by God's word. Israel's fate has always been within its grasp. "For this commandment which I command you this day is not too hard for you, neither is it far off. . . . But the word is very near you; it is in your mouth and in your heart, so that you can do it" (Deut 30:11-14).

Today

Certain aspects of the deuteronomic movement are remarkably impressive and can stand as models for us today. Others are theologically far less desirable. The reflection on the transition of generations points to issues of the expression of faith. The transition of institutions is a good example of the continuity of faith in differing circumstances. The theological realism of the Deuteronomists is admirable. On the other hand, the particular articulation they give to the theology of covenant, above all its association with the invocation of blessing and curse, has theological implications which are highly questionable.

For the Deuteronomists, "there arose another generation . . . who did not know the LORD or the work which he had done for Israel" (Judg 2:10). Given the massive patterning in the stories which follow, this is hardly a mere historical observation. It reflects, surely, not simply the generation seven hundred years before the Deuteronomist, but emerges out of the experience of generation after generation since. Faith is extremely difficult to hand on. Yet one of the impressive achievements of the deuteronomic movement was the ability to encapsulate the essentials of faith in a phrase or two or a verse or two. Something of the power of the movement's rhetoric is due to this ability to put so much in so short a compass. The short credos (e.g., Deut 6:20-25; 26:1-11) sum up admirably the core of the relationship between God and Israel. Simple clauses call on vast depths of religious experience (e.g., "the God of their fathers, who brought them out of the land of Egypt" [Judg 2:12]).

The Deuteronomists were no strangers to sophistication, but they were able to put their faith powerfully into simple words. In the midst of the pluralism and sophistication of today's theology, it is equally important to be able to confess faith in simple and direct language. To each their own, where such language is concerned. My conviction is that faith is more than adequately expressed in the belief that ultimately life is best understood as a love affair with God. A major pillar of Jewish and Christian faith is belief in the universal love of God for us, both as peoples and as individuals. Given such faith, the ultimate meaning of our lives can only be found in the acceptance of God's love for us and our response to that love. The metaphor of the love affair can provide us with an analogy and a context for much of our language about God.

The unique and ineffable reality of the Creator and Deliverer may never be lost sight of. But, at the level of analogy, the metaphor of human love can serve as a touchstone or control situation for our religious language, as well as offering dimensions of depth and tangibility for our expression. If something could not be said between human lovers, should it be said of God? On reflection, perhaps so; but perhaps not. In human life, the power of love is one of the great driving forces of personal experience. The power of this experience can be harnessed for the expression, in life and in word, of the meaning and significance of God in our lives.

For the Deuteronomists, the transition from the values of peasant life and village or tribal society to the much more complex realities of kingship and nation-state threatened the understanding of faith, but it did not destroy it. Possibilities were not closed off: "If you will fear the LORD and serve him and hearken to his voice and not rebel against the commandment of the LORD, then both you and the king who reigns over you will be loyal to the LORD your God" (1 Sam 12:14). In the midst of the complexity of institutional change, there is a certain directness of insight which is gifted with the perception of what is central and unchanging. With such insight, it is possible to accommodate to the needs of a pluralist and fast-changing society, without losing sight of the essentials of faith which alone give meaning and value to life. The Deuteronomists chronicled change and its impact on their people, but they never despaired of the possibility of faith.

The honest realism of Israel's theologians is always one of their more attractive qualities, and none more than the deuteronomistic historians. Confronted with the national disasters of 722, the loss of the northern kingdom, and 587, the destruction of the south, the Deuteronomists did not flinch. The fault was not that of forces beyond their control, nor was it the inability of their God to protect them. A survey of their history showed simply that it was their own evil which led them into trouble; a close examination of their own recent past pointed to the same cause at work. Jeroboam's sin destroyed the north: part of the failure to observe the centralization law and worship in Jerusalem is possibly to be seen as an affront to national unity and integrity. Manasseh's sin destroyed the south: it is portrayed as a complete erosion of all that faith in the LORD meant in Israel (2 Kgs 21:1-9). For all the rigidity of some of their categories, there is a readiness in these deuteronomistic historians to look plainly and openly at the failings of their society as they saw them. We might sometimes doubt the rightness of their interpretation of history. But their honesty and willingness to come to grips with the reality of experience is admirable and worth emulation.

On the other hand, the deuteronomic movement seems to have been the locus where Israel's relationship to God, particularly formulated in terms of covenant, came to be expressed in the language and thought-world of international treaties.[19] There is always a risk of compressing the mysterious and infinite reality of God into all-too-constricting human categories. The fullness of the God-Israel relationship cannot be exhausted by the metaphor of covenant. The idea of covenant is itself far from simple; it has a rich diversity of application as it is used in Israel. In introducing the legalism of the treaties, and above all the language of blessing and curse, the deuteronomic movement ran a definite risk. The language has a wealth of rhetorical power, but it also brings with it implications that are theologically dangerous.

When one is certain that the law is going to be observed, it may be all very well—although prudentially unwise—to attach the sanctions of divine blessing and curse to it. In the excitement of reform, that seems to have been the deuteronomic experience. Observance of the law was felt to be sure; they had it in their grasp: "For this commandment which I command you this day is not too hard for you, neither is it far off. . . . But the word is very near you; it is in your mouth and in your heart, so that you can do

---

[19]The literature in this area is immense. Reliable and very insightful guidance is given by the completely rewritten 1978 edition of D.J. McCarthy's *Treaty and Covenant*.

it" (Deut 30:11-14). Blessing must have seemed certain. When circumstances change and the zeal for reform has gone cold, the theology of blessing and curse is disastrous. The implications of its language are clear and theologically intolerable: God's curse has been called down upon the people. This is very difficult to reconcile with the language of a loving God. The recognition of the consequences of a people's acts is one thing (see below, chap. 13); the naming of experience as the curse of God is quite another.

To their credit, the Deuteronomists do not go so far as to name their experience in this way. But they generated a powerful rhetoric, imbued with the atmosphere of treaty legalism and the sanctions of blessing and curse. By association rather than by affirmation, this moves the image of God in the direction of the judge, rather than the image of creator and deliverer who had entered into an almost familial relationship with the patriarchs. The power of the deuteronomistic language and the industry of the deuteronomistic movement have left their stamp on the Pentateuch and the prophetic books. The focus on blessing and curse is a theological emphasis which is highly susceptible to misunderstanding. It is important to realize that, with the deuteronomic movement, it originated in a very special set of circumstances and there is reason to regret that it outlived those circumstances.

RECOMMENDED FURTHER READING

Peter R. Ackroyd, *Exile and Restoration,* 62-83. London: SCM, 1968.

A. D. H. Mayes, *The Story of Israel between Settlement and Exile: A Redactional Study of the Deuteronomistic History.* London: SCM, 1983.

E.W. Nicholson, *Deuteronomy and Tradition,* 107-118. Oxford: Blackwell, 1967.

M. Noth, *The Deuteronomistic History.* JSOTSup. 15. Sheffield: JSOT, 1981.

G. von Rad, *Old Testament Theology,* 1.327-47. Edinburgh: Oliver and Boyd, 1962.

W. Zimmerli, *Man and His Hope in the Old Testament,* 70-85. London: SCM, 1971.

6

The Sources of
the Deuteronomistic History

Recommended preliminary reading

In this chapter, the preliminary reading will be noted at the start of each section.

❧

The Deuteronomists selected and arranged traditions and information available from quite a number of sources. In our present context, it is not possible to examine all the sources which contributed to the Deuteronomistic History. Our concern will be to look at some of the major ones, in an effort to identify what they had to say to their generation, before the time of the Deuteronomistic History. What were they? Why were they preserved? Did they constitute literary works? If so, what message were they created to express? By pressing an investigation of this kind, we can glimpse something of the various theologies which existed in Israel over the centuries and so give texture and depth to the process which produced our biblical texts.

The Ideology of Conquest
(Joshua 2-11)

Recommended preliminary reading
Joshua 3-4;11

THE INTENTION OF JOSHUA 2-11

Martin Noth's comment on the source available to the Deuteronomist for the account of the conquest runs as follows.

> For this Dtr. had access to a self-contained and detailed account, already existing in a fixed literary form. This account was composed long before Dtr.; a series of separate aetiological stories relevant to the Israelites' successful incursion was combined into a well-rounded whole with a few heroic legends. Dtr. obviously took the whole of this over and altered it only by adding an introduction and epilogue and some supplementary material.[1]

In Noth's opinion, this well-rounded, literary whole came into existence in Judah about 900.[2] It was made up from separate stories about happenings in the area of Gilgal—principally, the story of the spies in Jericho, the crossing of the Jordan, the capture of Jericho, the story of Achan, and the story of the Gibeonite covenant—and, beyond these, the accounts of the military campaigns in chaps. 10 and 11. The basic perception is

---

[1]Martin Noth, *The Deuteronomistic History* (JSOTSup 15; Sheffield: JSOT, 1981) 36. The introduction and epilogue are, of course, Joshua 1 and 23. Apart from these, the other major contributions by the Deuteronomist are Josh 8:30-35 and Joshua 12. "Dtr." in the quotation refers to the Deuteronomist.

[2]There is little material available in English on these issues. Noth's position is given in *Das Buch Josua* (HAT 7; 2nd ed.; Tübingen: Mohr, 1953) 11-13. Also important is S. Mowinckel, *Tetrateuch-Pentateuch-Hexateuch* (BZAW 90; Berlin: Topelmann, 1964); he is in substantial agreement with Noth on the analysis of Joshua 1-11 (pp. 33-43). In English, there is J.A. Soggin, *Joshua* (OTL; London: SCM, 1972). As background material, there is also *Israelite and Judaean History* (ed. J.H. Hayes and J.M. Miller; OTL; Philadelphia: Westminster, 1977) 213-45, esp. pp. 230-34. No helpful purpose would be served here by a comparison with the treatment in R.G. Boling and G.E. Wright, *Joshua* (AB 6; Garden City: Doubleday, 1982). The interested reader may make their own.

that from these limited localized stories an understanding of Israel's possession of the land was generated which was applied to the whole people and the whole territory. About the time of Saul, Gilgal became a sanctuary of major importance (cf., 1 Sam 10:8; 11:14-15; 13:4, 7; 15:12, 21, 33) and it retained its significance (cf., Amos 4:4; 5:5). So it would not be surprising to find that stories preserved at Gilgal came to be applied to the whole of Israel.

Before looking at the evidence for this insight into the nature of Joshua 2-11, it is worth exploring the insight itself more fully. Fundamentally, it makes Joshua 2-11 far more of a theological text than a historical one. In a few stories and liturgies, restricted to a very limited geographical locality, God's gracious action on Israel's behalf was celebrated and retold. The people's success did not come from their own shrewd tactics or their own military prowess; it came as the direct gift of God. In bringing these stories together and shaping them as a literary whole, and especially in expanding them with the accounts in 10:28-11:14 to take in almost the whole territory of Israel, the compiler has applied the local understanding to the whole land. The text is a theological statement about the nature of Israel's possession of the land: their land came to them as the direct gift of God.

Because of the significance of such an insight, the evidence supporting it needs to be examined as closely as space and context permit us. The first observation is form-critical. The texts in Joshua 2-9 are localized stories or texts deriving from liturgies. They are the kinds of traditions which are kept alive by constant retelling or liturgical celebration at a sanctuary; they relate incidents which are connected with the immediate locality. The texts in Joshua 10-11 are of a quite different character: there is a battle story in 10:1-27 (28) which leads into the expanded list in 10:29-39, an account of battle in 11:1-14, and considerable editorial comment. A second observation is geographical. The stories concern the Jordan crossing, Gilgal, Jericho, Ai, and Gibeon—all within the territory of Benjamin, forming a small sliver of land from the Jordan valley to Gibeon in the central hill country of Israel. It is a very limited block of territory. The other texts extend the territory to the south (10:29-39) and to the north (11:1-14). A third observation is comparative. This presentation of Israel's arrival in the promised land is quite different from other biblical traditions. After referring to Genesis 34, Numbers 13-14,

Joshua 1:1-10:15 and 11:1-14, Judges 17-18 (cf., Josh 19:47-48), Judges 1, and Judges 9, J. A. Soggin comments:

> The elements taken together furnish a fresh proof that the unitary conquest of the country under the sole command of Joshua is a fictional construction, which was perhaps already to be found, even before the Deuteronomic preaching, in the pre-exilic cult. The very complicated history of the conquest is reduced to a handful of typical elements largely drawn from Benjaminite tradition and placed under the aegis of Joshua, because he was a well-known person who had been active either militarily or in resolving controversies between the regions.[3]

So we are looking at separate stories of local significance which have been gathered together to form a larger work of national significance. The statement made by this work—that the land is God's gift—is important for the question of Israel's self-understanding. Israel's understanding of itself and of its existence is closely tied up with its relationship to the promised land. The land is God's gift; so, in a very real sense, is Israel's own existence.[4] Bearing on so central an issue, it is hardly surprising that these chapters were subjected to close attention by Israel's theologians. The process of the text's growth to its present shape is a correspondingly complex one. For a better understanding of the whole, we can focus on two further aspects: the move from separate stories to a unified collection; the nature of the stories themselves.

---

[3]Soggin, *Joshua*, 17-18. There are other pieces of evidence, besides the texts cited by Soggin, for building up a picture of Israel's occupation of Canaan which is quite different from the one depicted in Joshua 1-12. For this issue, see any of the standard histories of Israel, or a work such as Norman K. Gottwald, *The Tribes of Yahweh* (New York: Orbis, 1979) 3-233.

[4]In case we are tempted by too miraculous a theology, it is a good corrective to note that "Joshua made war a long time with all those kings" (11:18). While God may have done the fighting for Israel, the compiler was also convinced that nevertheless it was a long grind for Israel. This is no "wave of the wand" theology: it is tough-minded and down-to-earth—and to my way of thinking, all the more interesting for exactly that reason.

THE GATHERING OF THE COLLECTION

The first evidence for these stories having been gathered together and united under the leader figure of Joshua is provided, according to Noth, by the following verses: 5:1; 6:27; 9:3-4a*; 10:2, 5, 40-42; 11:1-2, 16-20. A glance at these will help to explain the nature of the argument.

a) In Josh 5:1, the kings of the Amorites and all the kings of the Canaanites are reported to have heard of the miraculous Jordan crossing and so to be afraid of the people of Israel. The mention of all these kings obviously suggests a campaign for total conquest, and the people of Israel as a whole are pictured participating in it.
b) 6:27 gives a similar picture. Joshua's fame has spread through the whole country. It is understood that the campaign will follow the same course.
c) 9:3-4a* associate the stories of the capture of Jericho and Ai, thus pointing to the existence of a collection.
d) 10:2 and 5 link Gibeon with Ai, so providing evidence of the wider extent of the collection. They also depict a major southern coalition against Joshua.
e) 10:40-42 describe a total conquest of southern Israel by Joshua.
f) 11:1-2 have Jabin hearing what has happened, so giving evidence for the further extent of the collection; now it is a coalition of northern kings that is mustered, thus preparing the way for a campaign in the north.
g) 11:16-20 puts together a picture of total conquest of Palestine.

The stories are considered to have been separate, not connected with one another beyond the fact that they were associated with localities in the same area. There are several pointers toward this state of affairs. First of all, the story of the spies who entered Jericho could be expected to have been followed by a story of military conquest, employing surprise tactics. An echo of the same sort of story that one would expect here can be found for Bethel/Luz (Judg 1:22-26). A further pointer to the separate origin of the spies' story and the story of the capture of Jericho is the way that Rahab is first mentioned at 6:17b. The mention is secondary. In v 16b, Joshua gives the people the command to shout; but their shout is not reported until v 20. In between, there are several sentences on the ban, i.e. the devoted things. In telling the story, the command, "Shout; for the LORD has given you the city!" (v 16b) would have to be followed immediately by something like "and the people raised a great shout" (v 20b*). The collector, who is going to bring in the Achan story (chap. 7), inserts the note about the ban in v 17a, and then, because of the spies' story, has to make an exception for Rahab in v 17b. (The Hebrew sentence construction makes it likely that vv 18-19 have been added later still.) Another pointer is there in the introduction of the ban as late in the story as v 17a. It prepares for the Achan story, in which, remarkably enough, there is no mention of the devoted things having come from Jericho. The procedure here should be clear: there is an assumption that such stories would originally have been preserved independently; these pointers merely confirm the assumption.

It is probable that a number of these stories were preserved in association with the places that figure largely in them. One pointer to this is the attachment of etiological elements to traditions, seeking to create an association between the tradition and some notable feature of the locality. So, for example, the liturgical responses, now incorporated into the larger narrative, are associated with the two sanctuaries of twelves stones, in the Jordan and at Gilgal (cf., Josh 4:6-7, 21-24). The place name, "the hill of the foreskins" (Gibeath-haaraloth, 5:3), was associated with the traditions of 5:2-9; the name of Gilgal was also linked with it (5:9). Josh 5:13-15, with its echo of Exod 3:5, looks as though it should be attached to a sanctuary, but the text leaves this aspect undeveloped. Both the Jericho and the Ai stories could have been associated with the uninhabited ruins of the two cities. The reference to Rahab's dwelling in Israel "to this day" (6:25) is likely to have been secondary, but may have arisen because of some local association. The Achan story has come to be linked with the valley of Achor and also with the great pile of stones (7:26). The Gibeonite story may be tied to specific customs reflecting the particular status of these people (9:27). These associations now point to the restricted area of Benjamin, and particularly the vicinity of Jericho and Gilgal. An earlier view that such stories arose to explain local phenomena of this kind has been shown to be unfounded. The genuine etiologies relate to relatively short units and tend to be attached to the longer stories secondarily. It is likely that these traditions were gathered together at a major sanctuary, probably Gilgal.[5]

THE NATURE OF THE STORIES

The Jordan Crossing. It is time now to turn to the question of the nature of the stories. When we look at the story of the Jordan crossing (Joshua 3-4), it is obvious that it is a composite story. For example, five sets of instructions are given before the move toward the Jordan: the officers to the people (vv 3-4), Joshua to the people (v 5), Joshua to the priests (v 6), God to Joshua (vv 7-8), and Joshua to the people (vv 8-13). There are numerous references to the people passing over the Jordan: the people passed over opposite Jericho (3:16); when all the nation had finished passing over (4:1); the people passed over in haste (4:10); when all the people had finished passing over, the priests passed over (4:11); the sons of Reuben, Gad, and the half-tribe of Manasseh passed over armed (4:12); about forty thousand ready armed for war passed over (4:13); the priests came up from the midst of the Jordan (4:18).

While some of these might be attributed to a repetitive narrative style, there are three pairs where the duplication is quite obvious. Firstly, the tone of the whole passage is of a stately and leisured procession. The ark is carried by the priests. There is a space of 2,000 cubits (c. 3,000 ft.) between the people and the ark. While the people passed over, the priests, with the ark, stood on dry ground in the middle of the Jordan, until all had passed over; the priests emerged from the Jordan last, according to Joshua's command, received from God (4:15-17). This solemn procession, with men taking up stones from the Jordan to commemorate the event, is in sharp contrast with the short note that the people passed over in haste (4:10b). The reference to armed men, coming so late in the story (4:12-13), is in strange contrast to the more liturgical pattern of the preceding.

Secondly, there are two different sets of commemorative stones, and they are located in two quite different places. One set is put, by Joshua, in the middle of the Jordan, where the feet of

[5]See Soggin, *Joshua*, 9-10.

the priests had been (4:9). The other set is taken from the middle of the Jordan, where the feet of the priests had been, and is set up in Gilgal (4:20).

Thirdly, there are two different little liturgical explanations of these sanctuaries. In one, the central focus is on the ark of the covenant: before it, the waters of the Jordan were cut off (4:7). In the other, the central focus is on God, who dried up the waters of the Jordan like those of the Reed Sea, that the power of God might be known to all the peoples of the earth (4:23-24). So not only are there two explanations, but two theologies. One focuses on the importance of the ark as the intermediary of God's presence. The other focuses on God, and the unity of divine action in Israel's history: as God did to the Reed Sea, so God has done to the Jordan; as God brought us out of Egypt, so God is bringing us into Canaan.

It is quite clear that traditions have been compiled in this text. There is the crossing in haste, and the crossing in stately solemnity; there is the concern with two sanctuaries; there are the two explanations. While it might be possible to arrange all this into a coherent order, it is clear that the text does not. What is very far from being clear is how this text came to be exactly the way it is. There have been a number of suggestions and none of them is fully satisfactory.[6] Our interest will not be to try and trace all the details of the process by which the text came into being. Much more interesting, it seems to me, is to understand the inner workings of such a process, to see what was seen and how it was expressed. We can do this, without having to recover the whole process in detail.

The more liturgical aspects of the text are clear enough. The story or stories which may have been behind the liturgies do not appear so clearly. It may help to include an example of the kind of scholarly reconstruction which is possible. There was, presumably, a text which described a hurried crossing by armed men. We have a good pointer to it in 4:10b, and vv 12-13, but we cannot be sure how much else belonged to it. The reconstruction by Ernst Vogt is an interesting one, recovered from elements in the present text.[7]

---

[6]See the discussion in Soggin, *Joshua*, 43-54.

[7]E. Vogt, "Die Erzählung vom Jordanübergang, Josue 3-4," *Bib* 46 (1965) 125-48, see esp. p. 129.

3:1) Early in the morning, Joshua rose and set out from Shittim, with all the people of Israel; and they came to the Jordan, and lodged there before they passed over. 3:14a) And, when the people set out from their tents, to pass over the Jordan, 3:16) the waters coming down from above stood and rose up in a heap far off, at Adam, the city that is beside Zarethan, and those flowing down toward the sea of the Arabah, the Salt Sea, were wholly cut off; and the people passed over opposite Jericho. 4:10b) The people passed over in haste (more literally: and the people hastened and passed over). 4:13) About forty thousand ready armed for war passed over before the LORD for battle, to the plains of Jericho. 4:19b) And they encamped in Gilgal on the east border of Jericho.

Vogt's reconstruction is simple and satisfying.[8] For completeness' sake, we may note how he accounts for the rest of the text. According to Vogt, the remainder comes from liturgical texts. The part leading up to the arrival at the edge of the Jordan is from a single tradition (i.e., 1:10-11; 3:2-6, 8-11, 13, 14b-15a). The wonderful crossing and the commemorative stones have been taken from two traditions (i.e., version 1—3:12, 17; 4:4-7, 9-10a; version 2—4:1b-3, 8, 11, 20-24).[9] While this may not be the definitive solution to the text's difficulties, it is a good example of the sort of process of growth which has to be envisaged. The process is important: it moves from the event to a story narrating the event; then from the story to a liturgy celebrating what the story narrated; and finally, from the liturgy to the final form of the narrative which historicizes the liturgy.[10]

---

[8]Both Vogt and Noth agree that 3:7 and 4:12, 14 (which Vogt prints in brackets in his text of the story) come from the Deuteronomists. I have not included them here.

[9]The identification of Vogt's text can be found in Soggin, *Joshua*, 52. Soggin has reproduced a misprint in Vogt's article: for 4:13a and 13b, read instead 4:13 and 19b. Note that Vogt considers 3:15b and 4:15-19a to be later additions to the text. When following a reconstructed text like this in an English translation, we need to remember that the choice of verbal forms, from the rich possibilities offered by English, has been made by the translator in the light of the context of the present text. Such choices, naturally, have to change if the context changes. The range of explicit possibilities in the Hebrew verbal system is much more limited.

[10]"Historicizing," in this context, means reporting the liturgy as though it were a reenactment of the actual events. As a parallel, one might try to imagine describing the

Vogt's reconstructed story, starting in 3:1, has Israel camped at Shittim, so linking back to chap. 2 (cf., 2:1) and the old traditions (cf. Num 25:1; 33:49: Mic 6:5). Its conclusion would link up with Josh 6:1. It might have been part of a narrative sequence involving the spying out of Jericho, the crossing of the Jordan, and the capture of the city by stealth or ruse. It is important to note that while, in Vogt's reconstruction, there is no preparation for the miracle (as there is in 3:5, 8, 13), nevertheless the miracle is still the center of the story. But the story is quite different in tenor from the tone of the present text: this is a story of armed men crossing for battle in the plains of Jericho (4:13). The recovery of the older story is not an attempt to remove the element of wonder from the narrative; it is concerned to account for the phenomena of the text. It is worth being aware that the miracle was not necessary. There were fords available for crossing the Jordan (see Josh 2:7). The wonder has a far profounder significance than the mere facilitating of a river crossing.

The liturgical aspects of the present text need to be recognized. The ark and the priests play a central role: they lead the way (3:3, 11), a respectful distance is maintained (3:4), the miracle occurs when the soles of the feet of the priests touch the water (3:13), the waters do not resume their flow until these priests come up on to dry ground (4:18). It is not in the least difficult to picture a liturgical procession from the sanctuary of the twelve stones at Gilgal, down to the riverbank, at the spot where the twelve stones were visible in the riverbed. One would imagine the priests, who have been in the lead, stopping right at the brink of the water, and all the participants passing by, until the priests bring up the rear on the return.

The significance of the liturgy is given by the two explanations. If the ark were at the Gilgal sanctuary at some time, or at least some representation of it, this liturgy would remind the people of the role and power of the ark: before it, once upon a time, "the waters of the Jordan were cut off" (4:7). Then, while that might have been a feature of the riverside ceremony, at the main sanctuary the emphasis was on the mighty deeds of God and the unity and purpose of God's action in history, from Egypt to

sequence of events at the Last Supper, based on a modern eucharistic liturgy; it could give rise to the strangest results. Liturgical worship is a celebration, not a reconstruction.

Canaan, from the Reed Sea to the Jordan (4:23-24).

This unitary, almost cyclic, movement has become highly developed. While still in Egypt, Israel celebrated the Passover (Exodus 12). Then, in the deliverance from Egypt, Israel was brought unscathed through the dangerous obstacle of the sea (Exodus 14). That deliverance was incomplete until Israel reached the promised land. So they were brought unscathed through the dangerous obstacle of the river (Joshua 3-4). And the passover was celebrated in the land (Joshua 5). What was there in promise at the beginning, is now there in fullness at the end. The Song of Miriam foreshadowed this (Exodus 15:13-17): leading your people to your holy abode, causing fear in Philistia, Edom, Moab, and Canaan, your people passing by (the same word as "passing over"), being brought in and planted on your holy mountain, where you have made your abode and your sanctuary.[11] What was then begun is now on its way to achievement. When this is celebrated in full possession of the land, exodus and Jordan-crossing blend into the one saving act of a gracious God, who brought Israel out of the oppression of Egypt into the freedom and life of Canaan. This is the God who is celebrated in this liturgy. This is the understanding of its life which Israel celebrated in the liturgies of the sanctuary at Gilgal.

The capture of Jericho. A similar, though slightly different, process is visible in Joshua 6. We begin by looking at the phenomena in the text. This is the story of the Israelites capturing the great walled city of Jericho by marching around it once a day for six days, and on the seventh day marching around it seven times, and on the seventh time raising a mighty shout and bringing the walls down. So, in the text, the people are given their instructions (6:1-7). Then they did what Joshua had commanded, and went around the city once, and came back to spend the night in the camp (v 11). So they did for six days (v 14b). And on the seventh day, they rose early—understandable enough, with seven

---

[11]Whatever echoes of God's heavenly abode, heavenly mountain, and heavenly sanctuary may resound with mythic power behind this text, the present text has to have an earthly referent. The people of Israel are not brought to the heavenly mountain, but to the mountain of Ephraim; the people of Philistia, Edom, Moab, and the inhabitants of the land provide an earthly and historical context.

circuits of the city to do that day. So far, everything has been plain sailing, except that we have had to skip over the text from v 11, at the end of the first day, to v 14b for the remark that this is what they did for six days.

In vv 12-14a, another day has been introduced. When we have noticed this, we can also see that there is a considerable difference between the two days. On the first day, there is not to be a sound out of the people, not until the day when Joshua gives the word (v 10). But on the second day, without any word being given by Joshua, seven priests are blowing seven trumpets continuously (v 13). So we are left to ponder which pattern they followed for the six days—or five days!

In v 16, the lack of an "and" or "when" (in the *RSV* supplied by the translator) suggests that the clause "the priests had blown the trumpets" was not originally in the sentence. In discussing the original independence of the stories, we noted how there has been an insertion between vv 16 and 20. At the end of v 16, Joshua says to the people: "Shout; for the LORD has given you the city." Then he goes on giving instructions for another three verses! Then, finally, we may notice that in v 20, the people's shout is repeated a second time. The second shout is in response to the sound of the trumpet. It looks as though a watchful editor noticed that Joshua's command to shout had been ignored, and so inserted a first shout to comply with it. This difference is the more acute when we read the text in Hebrew: for the first shout, the verb is singular; but for the second, it is plural. We may reach a preliminary conclusion: there is some duality in the text. There may be a difference between a story in which the people marched in silence, and one in which they marched behind trumpet-blowing priests.

If we look at the early part of the story with this difference in mind, we can easily find the trace of the story of a silent march in vv 1-14. It is helpful to look at the reconstructed text in full (including vv 15-20*).

> 6:2) And the LORD said to Joshua, "See, I have given into your hand Jericho, with its kin. 3) You shall march around the city, all the men of war going around the city once. Thus shall you do for six days. 4) And on the seventh day you shall march around the city seven times. 5) And when there is (literal

Hebrew; *RSV*, "When they make") a long blast with the ram's horn, then all the people shall shout with a great shout; and the wall of the city will fall down flat, and the people shall go up every man straight before him." 7) And he (Joshua) said to the people, "Go forward; march around the city," 8) And it happened (literal Hebrew; *RSV*, "And") as Joshua had commanded the people. 10) But Joshua commanded the people, "You shall not shout or let your voice be heard, neither shall any word go out of your mouth, until the day I bid you shout; then you shall shout." 12) Then Joshua rose early in the morning . . . 14) and they marched around the city once, and returned into the camp. So they did for six days. 15) On the seventh day they rose early at the dawn of the day, and marched around the city in the same manner seven times: it was only on that day that they marched around the city seven times. 16) And at the seventh time, Joshua said to the people, "Shout; for the LORD has given you the city." 20) And (literal Hebrew; *RSV* omits "And") the people raised a great shout, and the wall fell down flat, so that the people went up into the city, every man straight before him, and they took the city.[12]

Even in this story, not everything is perfectly smooth; for example, in v 5, Joshua calls for a long blast from the ram's horn, while in v 16 he simply gives the command. But it is useful enough as a basis for beginning to understand how the story has grown to the form it has in the present text.

A glance at the material omitted from the reconstructed story shows that it elaborates on the procession. The main emphasis is on the seven priests with ram's horn trumpets, who were to go before the ark. Then, as a subsidiary interest, there are the armed men who precede the priests and also form a rear guard (vv 7 and

---

[12]This analysis follows Noth, *Das Buch Josua,* 40–43. The reader will have noticed that Noth has skipped v 11, deriving the first day's march from a combination of vv 12 and 14. Thus the ark has no place in this reconstructed story. This is not arbitrary or prejudiced; there are reasons for it. The ark is not mentioned in vv 16–20. The ark is associated with the trumpet-blowing priests (cf., vv 4, 6, 8, 9); the exception is v 7, where it is mentioned in association with the armed men. The armed men and the trumpet-blowing priests and the ark are all together in v 9. (Note: the *RSV's* "armed men" translates a different Hebrew word from the "men of war" of v 3.) So the ark appears to be associated with the noisy circuits, not the silent ones. We may note, in conclusion, that the beginning of v 11 is uncomfortable Hebrew and does not translate smoothly.

9). At least two explanations have been offered as to why this material should have come into the text. As the level of the composition of the Deuteronomistic History, the processional crossing of the Jordan with the ark pointed to an equally solemn procession with the ark around Jericho. So the Deuteronomist expanded the available source about Jericho to include the ark and the priests, and this account has subsequently been expanded as well (so Noth). Alternatively, the final text comes, not from the composition of the Deuteronomistic History, but from the combination of elements to form a liturgy which, then, either the early compiler or the Deuteronomist historicized (so Soggin).[13]

To get a sense of the literary genres involved in the two texts, we have only to evoke two names: Alfred Hitchcock and Cecil B. de Mille. There can hardly be any doubt that Cecil B. de Mille would prefer the liturgical text, with all the clash and color of armed men, the fanfare of trumpets, and the ritual splendor of priests and ark. On the other hand, Alfred Hitchcock would be intrigued to exploit the symbolism, mystery, and suspense of the silent circuits of the city, on seven successive days, without a sound, until on the seventh day and the seventh circuit the expectant or ominous silence is shattered by the shout—and so are Jericho's walls. It seems likely, to me, that the older text is a story. No liturgical group could maintain the kind of silence required. The same silence, however, would serve a narrator well to build up the suspense of the story. Here, Israel, fresh out of the desert; there, Jericho, a massively walled Canaanite city. The siege weapons of the wandering tribesmen: silence! And the denoument: thunderous and devastating! For a good narrator, there is potential for great storytelling. When the story is enacted in liturgy, transformations have to happen. The ark has to be incorporated. The sense of the power of sound can be extended by introducing the continual trumpet blasts—which would also help cover the participants' inevitable chatter. The procession has to be organized, with the sequence of armed men, priests, ark, and rear guard.

What process have we observed here? The miraculous act of

---

[13]On the concept of "historicizing," see note 10 above. For Soggin, incidentally, only a minimal part of the original narrative has been preserved, perhaps only vv 1-3a and 24ff. (*Joshua*, 83).

God is present in the old story of the silent marches as well as in the noisy liturgy. The recognition of the transformation of story into liturgy means recognition that most of the details are unlikely to be historical. The details have been introduced to heighten and intensify, in the liturgical celebration, the faith and emotion enkindled by the story. The text, as we have it, reflects Israel's celebration of faith.[14]

In both narratives—the crossing of the Jordan and the capture of Jericho—we observe that the texts which have come to us are concerned with the celebration of Israel's faith. Such are the texts which probably served as sources for the Deuteronomist, within the larger collection of Joshua 2-11. Note the Deuteronomist's achievement: in adding chaps. 1, 12, and 23, he has placed this action completely under God's will and direction. But in this he has not really gone beyond his earlier source. He has merely placed that source within a larger context. What God had promised Israel has been delivered. They are in possession of the land, and they know the laws by which they are to live in it.[15]

CONTRIBUTION TO THE DEUTERONOMISTIC HISTORY

Within its own horizon, Joshua 2-11 appears to contribute to Israel's understanding of itself and its relation to its land. The gracious action of God, celebrated in the stories and liturgies of Benjamin, is extended to apply to the whole country. The disparate stories are unified under the figure of Joshua. Israel is treated as a whole. The land is possessed as a whole. The

---

[14]The origin of the older story is outside our certain reach. In theory, there is no reason why it could not derive from an eyewitness account. In practice, the current state of archaeological knowledge suggests that the walls of Jericho had crumbled and been abandoned before any Israelites' arrival; or, at least, those of Joshua's time have been eroded beyond trace (cf., Soggin, *Joshua*, 84-86). To date, all that has survived of late Bronze Age Jericho is an oven, a juglet, and about a square meter of floor.

[15]Within Joshua 1-12, one must also account for another element, the allegedly total elimination of the Canaanite population (e.g., Josh 9:24; 11:19-20). The issue is complex. The Deuteronomists were certainly aware of the continued existence of the Canaanites and the dangers they posed (e.g., Josh 23:6-13; Judg 2:1-5; 2:20-3:6). It is very difficult to say how much of the emphasis on extermination in Joshua 1-12 is unfortunate theological theory and how much goes back to older tradition.

relationship of Israel to the land is one of gift, gracious divine gift. Israel must understand itself as being freely graced by God.

At the level of the Deuteronomistic History, the incorporation of Joshua 2-11 into a wider horizon adds further dimensions to its meaning. For one thing, it follows the exposition of the law in Deuteronomy. For another, Joshua's generation is portrayed as faithful in their adherence to God (Josh 24:31; Judg 2:7). Joshua 2-11, therefore, presents a superb example of how Israel is successful in all it does when it remains faithful to its God. From the fateful example of failure given by Achan through to the successful completion of the conquest, the whole text is a shining example of what the people of Israel can do when, in their fidelity, they let God work for them. Joshua's generation is an ideal which Josiah's might do well to emulate.[16]

The Experience of Deliverance
(Judges 3-9)

Recommended preliminary reading
Judges 2:11-19; 3:12-30; 4:17-22; 7:1-23

Judges 3-9 contains three stories of deliverance, by Ehud, by Deborah and Barak, and by Gideon, followed by the story of Abimelech's short-lived attempt at monarchy. In the Joshua material, we were able in some cases to see a movement from event to story to liturgy to historicized narrative. Here it is possible to see a similar movement from event to story, to a collection of similar stories, to different levels of theological understanding derived from the collected stories.[17]

---

[16]The significance of Joshua as a prototype for Josiah is advocated by R.D. Nelson, "Josiah in the Book of Joshua," *JBL* 100 (1981) 531-40.

[17]My treatment here is largely dependent on two very detailed monographs by Wolfgang Richter (*Traditionsgeschichtliche Untersuchungen zum Richterbuch* [BBB 18; 2nd ed.; Bonn: Peter Hanstein, 1966] and *Die Bearbeitungen des "Retterbuches" in der deuteronomischen Epoche* [BBB 21; Bonn: Peter Hanstein, 1964]). Unfortunately, Richter's work on Judges has not been given the attention it deserves by some subsequent commentaries on Judges in English. This may be the result of the difficulty of his German, which even Martin Noth complained about. Whatever the cause, it is regrettable.

THE STORIES

The events, of course, lie out of reach in the past. We have access to them only through the stories. The stories have first to be looked at in their own right. Considerations of space do not permit us to go into detail.

Ehud. The story of Ehud (Judg 3:15*-29) is almost totally secular.[18] Its beginning is now blended into the framework (in vv 13-15). It is a story of the assassination of a tyrant. Moab has imposed the payment of tribute on Israel. The opportunity to be delivered from the tyranny comes when the tribute is to be presented by a left-handed Benjaminite, Ehud. He makes a special sword for himself, which he can strap to his right thigh, where no one would expect a weapon. Gaining audience with Eglon, the Moabite king, he stabs him in the act of ceremonial embrace, demoralizing Moab and giving Israel victory over their oppressors.

The story is told with obvious interest in the graphic details. The sword is described (v 16). The visual image of Eglon as a very fat man is emphasized (v 17) and put to quite gross effect (v 22). The tension is heightened when the tribute is delivered and the messengers depart with nothing accomplished. But Ehud returns and manages to have the king dismiss his attendants by claiming to have a secret message for the king (v 19). There is a first irony here. The word for message in Hebrew is *dābār,* with the double meaning of word or thing. The secret thing is the hidden sword. The words which then bring Eglon out of his throne are doubly ironic. It is now: "I have a message from God for you" (v 20)—the "message" from God for Eglon is a two-edged sword! While Ehud makes good his escape, the narrator enjoys some byplay at the expense of the servants of the dead king, portrayed assuming their sovereign is responding to a call of nature and wondering why he is taking so long (vv 24-25). One can imagine a skilled storyteller delighting his audience with the dialogue among the confused Moabite courtiers. In the meantime, Ehud has been able to raise an Israelite force and profit from the moment to lead them to a victory over the Moabite intruders.

[18]A helpful treatment is given by Robert Alter, *The Art of Biblical Narrative* (New York: Basic Books, 1981) 37-41.

The story is almost totally secular. There is a trace of a faith context in the ironic "message from God" (v 20). It is confirmed by the rallying cry in v 28: "Follow me; for the LORD has given your enemies the Moabites into your hand." The storyteller hints that in the daring act of a courageous Benjaminite the action of God is to be perceived. This hint will be developed by the redactor who placed these stories in an interpretative framework (see below).

Deborah and Barak. The story of Deborah and Barak (4:4-22) has a stronger element of awareness of divine action in it. It too is a story of deliverance from oppression: Jabin, the oppressor, is to be defeated in battle, and Sisera, his general, is to be killed in his sleep. The story begins with the summons of Deborah, the prophetess, to Barak. The commission she gives him is from God, and God gives assurance of victory (vv 6-7). God is also implicated in the killing of Sisera (v 9). The theme of divine assistance is still to the fore in the account of the battle (vv 14-15). But when the narrative moves to the episode of Sisera's death, the storytelling skills come to the fore and the role of God moves completely into the background.

The storyteller has Sisera head for a house where he can expect peace (v 17)—but will find death. Jael greets him reassuringly, almost seductively: "Turn aside, my lord, turn aside to me; have no fear" (v 18). Portrayed as a caring woman, she covers him with a rug, even gives him milk when he asks for water, sees that he is covered. A further irony: Sisera asks her to stand guard at the opening of the tent. If anyone asks whether there is a man there, she is to answer, "No" (v 20). And soon there will not be—only a body. The storyteller lingers over the details of her actions in the killing: her name, the tent peg, the hammer, her soft approach, the tent peg into his temple, then into the ground, during his weary sleep. And abruptly: "So he died" (v 21). Finally the denouement: the woman shows the military commander the body of Israel's enemy.[19]

There is no mention at all of where Jael got her courage from.

---

[19]For a good discussion of the poetic version in Judges 5, including some insightful comparisons with the prose story, see Robert Alter, *The Art of Biblical Poetry* (New York: Basic Books, 1985) 43-49.

Only the earlier reflective comment in v 9 indicates the narrator's belief that such courage comes from God.

Gideon. The Gideon story (chaps. 6–8, omitting 6:1-2a, 6-10; 8:27b-28, 33-35) has a far more complex history, which we cannot consider here. It is again a matter of deliverance from oppression. The role of divine assistance is much more highly developed than in the other two stories. Gideon receives a special call from God to "Go in this might of yours and deliver Israel" (6:14) and is assured by special signs. The importance of seeing that in such situations it is indeed God who delivers becomes the central theme of the traditions in 7:2-7. Even the episode of Gideon's spying out the Midianite camp and overhearing a Midianite say, "Into his hand God has given Midian" (vv 9-14) is commanded by God. The battle cry is to be: "For the LORD and for Gideon" (v 18).

For all this insistence on God's place in the action, it has to be noted that Gideon's tactics in the commando skirmish were daring and brilliant. They were daring. It was a night attack, with all the difficulties of communication and coordination in the days before hand-held radios. They were brilliant. The small force needed to coordinate such a night attack used sight and sound to confuse and terrify the larger encamped army. In the middle of the night, there was the noise of jars shattering, then flaming torches being waved in the dark, the blaring of trumpets, and the screaming battle cry from all around the camp (vv 19-21). Small wonder the Midianites panicked and fled.

For all the guarantee of God's assistance, with which the narrative is replete, Israel's narrators delight in the best tactics being used. God is not discovered coming in power to supply for the gaps of human weakness. God is discovered empowering people to use the talents that they have.

THE COLLECTION

There is good reason to think that these stories of deliverance, together with the Abimelech story, were quite early on formed into a single collection.[20] The purpose of the collection may well have been to provide three examples of how God worked within

[20]See Richter, *Untersuchungen*, esp. pp. 319-43.

Israel for their deliverance, and one horribly clear example of how God did not. Israel's well-being and security, in the collector's view, was assured by God's empowering people to heroic deeds when they were needed. The last thing Israel needed, again in the collector's view, was the self-imposed oppression of a despotic king like Abimelech.

Dating a collection like this is difficult. The similarity between Abimelech's tactic in burning the tower of Shechem on his foes (Judg 9:46-49) and the death of Zimri in the burning of the royal palace at Tirzah (1 Kgs 16:15-18) suggests a possible ninth-century date. Zimri's seven-day reign is dated to 876. The contemporary political climate in northern Israel would also have provided a most apt context for such a collection. The northern kingdom went through a series of violent and bloody revolutions: Baasha killed Nadab and all his house (1 Kgs 15:27-29); Zimri killed Baasha's son Elah and all his house (16:9-11); Omri drove Zimri to suicide in the burning palace (16:15-18); Tibni fought a civil war against Omri, but lost and was killed, leaving the throne in Omri's bloodied hands (16:21-22).

The link between the Judges collection and the political events of 1 Kings is tenuous. It is not possible to claim any certainty. But these political events do provide a good context for exemplifying the potential significance of the collection in Judges. Early in the story of Abimelech's reign, there is the parable of Jotham (Judg 9:7-21). Its message: kingship is useless. The political chaos and bloodshed in northern Israel were close to the beginnings of kingship. The united kingdom was established shakily enough under David, survived under Solomon, and was dissolved at his death. The first king in the north was Jeroboam, father of the Nadab assassinated by Baasha. With the continued revolutionary bloodshed under Zimri, Omri, and Tibni, small wonder the cry might be raised again: kingship is useless—this is not how God has been experienced providing deliverance in Israel. If this is indeed the message of the collection, it is discreetly expressed. Perhaps diplomatic expression was a condition for the collector's survival. All the same, no Israelite at the time would have missed the point. As a theological exercise, it is a very practical reflection on two quite different sorts of experience, drawing conclusions as to where God is present and how God operates in such events. The storyteller is never far from being a theologian.

The point of a collection of stories is that it reinforces the message, which might be overlooked in individual stories. As the role of God becomes more and more explicit, from Ehud through to Gideon, so the message becomes correspondingly clearer: Israel can rely on God to empower deliverers in time of need. Once this lesson has been fully learned, the point of the Abimelech episode becomes painfully obvious. An insurgent king, in the mold of Abimelech, far from delivering Israel from need is himself the source of oppression and social disaster.

THE LEVELS OF THEOLOGICAL UNDERSTANDING

The framework. As the first three stories stand in the text now, together with the passage on Othniel (3:7-11), they are placed within a framework which is patterned and theological. There are five elements in the framework, which recur around the Othniel episode and all three stories.

1) THEY DID EVIL	3:7	3:12	4:1	6:1
2) ISRAEL WAS OPPRESSED	3:8	3:12	4:2	6:1
3) THEY CRIED TO GOD	3:9	3:15	4:3	6:6 (7)
4) FOE WAS SUBDUED	3:10	3:30	4:23	8:28
5) LAND HAD REST	3:11	3:30	5:31	8:28

Even a quick glance at this table makes one conclusion evident: the Othniel episode is not a story. As the sequence of verses shows, it is no more than an exemplification of the framework pattern. The framework ends with the Gideon story. Elements 1 and 2 recur in 13:1, but that is all.

The framework takes several steps beyond the stories. It looks at the oppression inflicted upon Israel in all three cases, and has a theological explanation for it: the people of Israel did what was evil in the sight of God. The oppression was no chance political occurrence: it was sent by God. The emergence of the hero-deliverer was no chance occurrence either. The people had cried to God and, in response, God raised up the deliverer for them. As a result, their foe was subdued and their land had rest for forty years. Forty years is a round figure for a generation; in this case, for the life of the deliverer and his generation. What the framework has done is bring into a single theological context three otherwise quite separate stories and generalize them as models of Israel's experience.

Out of reflection on the experience of these three stories, a cyclic understanding has been distilled, in which Israel's evildoing is met by the punishment of political oppression; Israel's oppression is met by their cry to God; the cry is heard and a deliverer raised up; the experience of deliverance is adequate for a lifetime, but with the change of generations the cycle starts all over again. This is the result of theological reflection on human nature and the divine response, culled from the stories in which human experience is crystallized. There is no prophetic voice or divine word here to explain to the author the why and the how of what had happened. The perception has to be based on reflection on experience. Once or twice may be chance; what happens three times establishes a pattern and a truth.

The overall interpretation of this cyclic pattern can be pessimistic or optimistic, depending on where the cycle stops or where the emphasis is placed. There is a pessimistic perception of the human capacity for living wrongfully, above all for failing to keep alive the understanding of God's place in their world. There is an optimistic understanding of God as the one who is ready on each occasion to come to Israel's assistance.

The preface. The deuteronomistic understanding of this collection of stories was spelled out in what is, practically speaking, a preface to them (Judg 2:11-16, 18-19). Noth believed that both this preface and the framework were established together by the Deuteronomist. The careful study by Wolfgang Richter shows that this is unlikely to have been the case.[21] Instead, the preface offers a second level of interpretation of the collection of stories in their framework.

A detailed analysis of the language of the deuteronomistic preface and the framework of the stories shows noteworthy differences.

---

[21]See Richter, *Bearbeitungen*, esp. pp. 113-42.

1) The framework has: they did evil (for all three stories).
The preface has a specification of that evil: they served the Baals and forsook the God of Israel.

2) The framework uses three verbs: God strengthened Eglon against Israel, sold them, or gave them into the hands of oppressors.
The preface adds the note that God's anger was kindled against Israel, and concludes that they were in sore straits.

3) The framework has Israel cry to God.
The preface has no cry for help, and, instead of a deliverer (3:15), God raises up a judge.

4) The framework uses the term that the oppressor was subdued.
The preface has no formula here, simply a note that God saved them from the plunderers, the same word used in 2:14 and exclusive to the preface.

5) The framework has: the land had rest for forty years (eighty years for Ehud, which probably includes Shamgar's generation too).
The preface has: all the days of the judge.

While the thought is much the same, there is a distinct difference of language. The evil is now explicitly apostasy, breach of the exclusive fidelity to Israel's God on which deuteronomic theology insisted so strongly. The reference to the judge, in place of the deliverer, is a mark of deuteronomistic theology. The concept of the judge, taken from the two lists of so-called minor judges (Judg 10:1-5; 12:7-15), is a key to the deuteronomistic composition of the book of Judges. Richter's conclusion is that the collection of deliverer stories, with their framework, may well have been in existence before—if only shortly before—the actual Deuteronomistic History itself, and thus been available as a source for the history.

Inclusion in the Deuteronomistic History widens the context of the collection in two respects. Firstly, the evil is identified as part of the apostasy which is depicted bedevilling Israel from the desert down to the failure of the monarchy. Secondly, the deliverer-judges are now placed within a context which extends from Ehud to Samuel. Judg 10:6-16, similar in its own way to the preface, forms something of a bridge to the rest of the period. Obliquely, it confirms the conviction of God's unconditional commitment to Israel. The dismissal of 10:14 is followed by the deliverance that is adumbrated in 10:16 and provided by the story of Jephthah.

CONTRIBUTION TO THE DEUTERONOMISTIC HISTORY

The stories of Judges 3-9 provide three examples of how deliverance is effected in Israel through courage, enabled by trust in the saving power of God, as well as a striking example of how self-sufficient human arrogance can have a disastrous impact on the social community.

At the level of the Deuteronomistic History, the understanding of the collection has to be colored by the intense focus on kingship and kings later in the history. Here, in these stories, Israel's deliverance is obtained without recourse to the institution of kingship. To the contrary, the episode of kingship under Abimelech points to some of the worst features of Israel's later experience: injustice, strife, and instability. As the last verses make clear, the consequences of royal evil redound upon the people (9:55-57). In terms of the deuteronomistic perception, the power of fidelity to God's spirit could enliven the institution of monarchy; but without that fidelity, the institution would wreak havoc within the structures of Israel's society.

The Ark Narrative
(1 Samuel 4-6; 2 Samuel 6)

Recommended preliminary reading
1 Samuel 4:1-22; 5:1-5; 6:19-7:2aα
2 Samuel 6:2-19

The Ark Narrative is about as good an example as one can get of ancient Israel's use of narrative as a vehicle for theological communication. It is deceptively simple in its content, yet a remarkably artful piece of storytelling with an equally remarkable theological conviction to express. It is worth close consideration. Opinions differ about the precise extent of the text belonging to it and about the date of its origin. For our purposes, we will regard the Ark Narrative as probably a composition from tenth-century Jerusalem, comprising 1 Samuel 4-6 and 2 Samuel 6.[22]

We can make two preliminary observations. Firstly, whatever diversity there may be in the stories and traditions which constitute these four chapters, they have in common a single-minded concentration on the ark as the symbol through which God's power and purpose are manifested. The ark is the central and exclusive focus of these traditions. This is quite remarkable, and occurs nowhere else. Secondly, we find that these stories raise important questions within their narrative. For example: "Why has the LORD put us to rout today before the Philistines?" (1 Sam 4:3); "Who is able to stand before the LORD, this holy God?" (1 Sam 6:20); "How can the ark of the LORD come to me?" (2 Sam 6:9); or the implied question, "And watch; if it goes up on the way to its own land, to Beth-shemesh, then it is he who has done us this great harm; but if not, then we shall know that it is not his hand that struck us, it happened to us by chance" (1 Sam 6:9). When the narrative itself asks questions like this, we can be sure that we are being faithful to the horizon of the narrative in looking to it also for answers.

The narrative thread which binds the Ark Narrative together can be followed by noting the question which each section raises

---

[22]More precisely, in my understanding the Ark Narrative begins at 1 Sam 4:1b, "Now Israel went out to battle against the Philistines." The first part ends at 1 Sam 7:2aα, "From the day that the ark was lodged at Kiriath-jearim, a long time passed." The narrative resumes at 2 Sam 6:2-23, translating v 2 literally, "And David arose and went with all the people who were with him from the citizens of Judah to bring up from there (i.e. Kiriath-jearim) the ark of God."

The understanding of the Ark Narrative to be proposed here is the subject of my study, *The Ark Narrative (1 Sam 4-6; 2 Sam 6): A Form-critical and Traditio-historical Study* (SBLDS 16; Missoula: Scholars Press, 1975). A somewhat different understanding has been proposed by J.J.M. Roberts and P.D. Miller Jr., *The Hand of the Lord* (Baltimore: Johns Hopkins, 1977); they begin the narrative with 1 Sam 2:12-17, 22-25, 27-36*, and conclude it with 1 Sam 7:1. Miller and Roberts have been followed by P. Kyle McCarter, Jr., *1 Samuel* (AB 8; Garden City: Doubleday, 1980). In my opinion, in neither publication has the case for the continuation of the narrative into 2 Samuel 6 been adequately appreciated and evaluated. However, this need not hold us up here, since both positions can be reconciled, at least sufficiently for our purposes. In my view, the Ark Narrative continues into 2 Samuel 6; for Miller and Roberts, 2 Samuel 6 was composed somewhat later, but with 1 Samuel 4-6 in mind. Therefore, in either case, it is necessary to look at the significance of both parts, whether they have been composed in one stage or two (cf., A.F. Campbell, "Yahweh and the Ark: A Case Study in Narrative," *JBL* 98 [1979] 31-43).

and seeing how the next section responds to that question. This is
the procedure we will follow. As we have seen, the narrative
opens with a question. Israel has faced the Philistines in battle and
lost, with casualty figures of 4,000.[23] The question the story asks
explicitly is: "Why has the LORD put us to rout today before the
Philistines?" (4:3). Translated more literally, this would be: Why
has the LORD defeated us today before the Philistines? The
question has to be faced in its starkness, and not evaded. It is left
hanging, dominating the whole movement of the story. It only
receives its answer when the whole narrative has fallen into place
and reached its conclusion.[24]

The first section of the story, then, is in 4:1b-11. Israel goes out
to battle, and is defeated, with the loss of 4,000. It is told tersely
and without detail. It is told simply of Israel; no tribes or
commanders are mentioned. Just Israel. The story is about Israel
in history, rather than the history of Israel. The storyteller has the
elders of Israel attribute the defeat to God: Why has the LORD
defeated us? (v 3). It is taken for granted that God was responsible.
The question asked is "Why?" The proposal is made to bring the
ark from Shiloh to the battlefield, so that they may be saved from
the power óf their enemies (v 3b). The Hebrew is delightfully
ambiguous. It can be construed either as "so that he (the LORD)
may come among us" or "so that it (the ark) may come among
us." However, since the ark is a symbol of God's presence to the
people, the ultimate meaning is the same. It is worth noting two
aspects of the story at this point. It does not say that the absence
of the ark was the cause of the first defeat. It is possible to imply

[23]The best understanding of numbers like this is offered by G.E. Mendenhall ("The
Census Lists of Numbers 1 and 26," *JBL* 77 [1958] 52-66): "There is certainly no doubt that
the term *'elef* [thousand] did refer to some subsection of a tribe, though it is not now
possible to identify it more closely.... It is here suggested that the same term was then
applied to the military unit which went to war from the subsection under its own
commander" (p. 61). Confusion arose later, because in David's time the *'elef* or "thousand"
became "a unit whose normal strength was a thousand men" (p. 57). The earlier units,
those related to subsections of a tribe, were much smaller. The involvement of the now
outmoded amphictyony in Mendenhall's treatment leaves a possible query over some
aspects. However, in this text, the concern is less with the absolute numbers than with the
proportional increase of the second defeat.

[24]In my initial study, I thought that the narrative left this question unanswered (*Ark
Narrative*, 66). I failed to see that the answer is provided by the narrative as a whole, visible
only from the vantage point of its conclusion (see below).

this as the reason why the ark was sought, but it is by no means the only possible reason. And, as the story will make clear, it is certainly the wrong reason. Secondly, the story says nothing to imply that Israel was again defeated because they endeavored to manipulate God through the presence of the ark. Such an understanding leaves the first defeat unexplained, leaves the rest of the narrative unexplained, is insensitive to the horizon of the story, and is fundamentally unsympathetic to the significance of the symbols of worship in the ancient world. (Bluntly, it obtrudes a Christian debate on sacramental efficacy into an ancient Israelite story where it has no place.)

Instead of dealing with the question it has raised, the narrative leaves it aside and builds up the expectation of Israel's imminent victory. As we reflect on this, we must remember that the storyteller knows perfectly well that the next stage in the story is Israel's redoubled defeat. Yet an immense expectation of victory is created: Israel expects it (v 5); the Philistines expect it (vv 6-9). The storyteller, in a rather ironic touch, has the Philistines provide the reason for this joint expectation: "Who can deliver us from the power of this mighty God?" (v 8; the Hebrew can be read as singular or plural). Through the Philistines, the storyteller is reminding us of what we should already know: this story is about the power and purpose of this mighty God. The speech, put in the mouths of the Philistines by the storyteller, ends with a note of encouragement (v 9); otherwise, there would be flight and no battle.

Instead, battle is joined for a second time, and Israel is defeated in definitive fashion: the casualties are increased almost sevenfold, the ark is captured, and its priests are dead (vv 10-11). This sudden turn of events in the story leaves us with two questions. There is the one raised explicitly at the outset: Why did the LORD defeat us? With the second defeat, that question echoes all the more insistently: Why? But the emphasis, in the Philistines' speech, on the power of Israel's God, cannot but raise another question: Did our God defeat us or was our God defeated? In the understanding of the ancient Near East, when armies battled, victory went to the army of the stronger god (for example, 1 Kgs 20:23, 28; 2 Kgs 18:32b-35, cf., also v 25). In a moment, the narrative will answer this question.

Before addressing this issue, the narrator appends two poignant little stories, both reflecting the impact of the loss of the ark (4:12-18, 19-22). As any soldier knows, in military campaigns you win some and you lose some (cf., David's comment in 2 Sam 11:25). These two little stories address the issue of how seriously these defeats are to be taken. Is this simply a momentary fluctuation in the fortunes of battle? Or is something more serious at stake? And the message of both stories is: something deadly serious is at stake. In a beautifully told vignette, the messenger runs to Eli from the battlefield. We, the hearers, know from the outset that his news is bad, for his clothes are rent and there is earth on his head, signs of mourning and grief (v 12b). From the second verse of the story, Eli knows that something is up, for there is an outcry in the city (v 13). The storyteller's skill holds up the disclosure till the very last moment, when finally Eli is told: Israel has fled, there has been a great slaughter, your two sons are dead, and the ark of God has been captured (v 17). The storyteller underlines the point of it all: "When he mentioned the ark of God," then it was that the old man fell over and died. Eli here is a symbol of an era in Israel; his death sets a tone of ominous foreboding, of disastrous finality.

The second story reinforces the first. Eli's daughter-in-law is about to give birth. She hears the news of the capture of the ark, and of the death of her father-in-law and her husband. The weight of the words is on the ark. The news precipitates her labor, and she dies in giving birth. The storyteller puts in the mouth of this dying mother the statement of what these events mean: "The glory has departed from Israel" (vv 21, 22). This child, newly born to Eli's line, bears a name given in a most symbolically powerful moment, a name which says "the glory has departed from Israel, for the ark of God has been captured" (v 22). The loss of the battles and the loss of the ark are not just a passing downturn in Israel's military fortunes. The storyteller endows it with a note of despairing finality.

So it becomes all the more pressingly urgent to return to the question of who was responsible for it all. Did God indeed defeat Israel? Or was Israel's God defeated? The answer is given in the brief account of the events in the temple of the Philistine god, Dagon, in the Philistine city of Ashdod. The ark, as the spoils of victory, is placed in the temple, beside Dagon. The narrator has the ark placed beside Dagon, not before him. Perhaps we can sense, in this touch, the Israelite storyteller's reluctance to speak of the ark before Dagon in language evocative of worshipful reverence. Or perhaps there is the dramatist's sense for location. The statue of Dagon is about to fall forward on its face; the ark can hardly be placed before it. Whatever the motive, the symbols of vanquished and victor, ark and statue, are side by side. The only question is which is which, which victor and which vanquished?

The answer is given in the morning: "Dagon had fallen face downward on the ground before the ark of the LORD" (5:3). Here Dagon is prostrate in worshipful reverence before the LORD. The issue is far too serious to be left in any uncertainty. The statue of Dagon is restored to its place. Who knows, its fall may have been chance. The following morning, the answer is definitive: Dagon is once again prostrate before the ark (v 4). Only this time, his head and his hands are cut off and are at the threshold of the temple. There is a grim sense of drama in the story, as the Philistines rise early and race expectantly to their temple, only to be greeted by the sightless eyes and powerless hands of their god. The symbolism is all too clear: headless and handless, Dagon is powerless to think or act. His submission to the God of Israel is complete. This is no time for the listener, whether Israel or ourselves, to be chuckling at the discomfiture of the idol-worshipping Philistines. The message of the story for Israel is far too grim for humor. For if God is victor in the temple of Dagon in Ashdod, then God was victor on the field of battle at Ebenezer. The message is unavoidably clear: Israel's God defeated Israel. And worse: symbolized by the ark, God has departed from Israel.

The question which now confronts the hearers of this story is whether this departure is temporary or permanent. If permanent, has God chosen another people? If temporary, then for how long? The next stories quickly answer the first question: God has not chosen the Philistines. The ark's presence among them is a source of pain and deathly panic (5:6-12). God is not disposed to bless the Philistines, and the Philistines are not disposed to keep the ark in their midst (5:11). The narrator has the Philistines turn to their priests. Two questions are raised. One is what sort of an offering is to be sent back with the ark, since evidently the God of Israel has been outraged and must be appeased (6:2-3). The other is subjacent to this: was what has happened the God of Israel's doing, or was it chance? (6:9).

The Philistine priests set up an experiment in divination to discover God's will. A situation is created in which one outcome is most unlikely. If that outcome eventuates, then God is clearly at work. In this case, local cows, which have never been yoked, are attached to a cart with the ark on it, while their calves are tied up at home. It is unlikely that untrained cows will take kindly to the yoke; it is unlikely that cows will leave their calves; it is unlikely that local cows will leave their familiar surroundings. And, of course, the unlikely happens: mooing all the way, the cows head straight for the border of Israel (6:12).

The answer to the Philistines' question has been given: it was the God of Israel who has done them this great harm. It was the God of Israel who has been in complete control on Philistine territory. This knowledge reinforces the impact of the story of Dagon's temple for Israel: the defeats and the loss of the ark have been God's doing. Israel will welcome the return of the ark with rejoicing; it obviously bodes well for Israel. But a prescient Israelite could not avoid the question whether God's presence in Israel will be benevolent as of old, or whether some radical change has been taking place. What does this sojourn in Philistine territory mean? Was it a divine whim or has it deeper meaning? The references to the Egyptians (4:8; 6:6) evoke memories of the Exodus; the ark afflicts the Philistines with plagues and undertakes a journey out of Philistia into Israel. If something new is afoot, where will this journey end?

One of the fascinating aspects of this Ark Narrative is the way it often lets us know what specific questions it intends its hearers to have been asking themselves when it provides the answers. So it proceeds to answer two questions. On the arrival of the ark in the field of Joshua of Beth-shemesh, the cart is split up and the cows offered as a sacrifice. In narrative terms, the journey is over. The ark has returned to remain in Israel. But the story of the death of seventy of the men of Beth-shemesh means, in narrative terms, that the ark is not yet a sign of God's benevolent presence in Israel. The ark may have returned to Israel, but Israel has not yet returned to favor. The rejoicing at the return of the ark (6:13) is promptly turned into mourning (6:19).

It is a harsh and jarring note. Yet the storyteller has included it, not simply because it happened, but because it contributes to the story. No interpretation of the Ark Narrative can be considered adequate which does not come to terms with this episode and its companion piece, the death of Uzzah (2 Sam 6:6-10). There is a certain mystery about the reason for both incidents. The cause in 1 Sam 6:19 is most mysterious.[25] The Hebrew translates literally: And he killed among the men of Beth-shemesh for they looked at the ark of the LORD, and he killed among the people seventy men, fifty thousand men. If the *RSV's* rendering of "looked into" is right, it is the only occurrence of this meaning in the Hebrew Bible. The Greek text provides a different version: And the sons of Jeconiah did not rejoice among the men of Beth-shemesh when they saw the ark of the LORD (followed by the *JB, NAB,* and *NEB).* It gives the impression of having been coined to explain the disaster, being based on the Hebrew consonants of the first occurrence of the verb "he slew" *(wayyak).* There are problems with these positions. If the slaughter was clearly motivated by an equally clearly defined crime, the act of the people of Beth-shemesh i ı sending away the newly returned ark is one of consummate folly. If the deaths occurred because people opened up the ark and looked into it, or because the Jeconiah clan kept aloof from the celebrations, the question of the Beth-shemesh people is easily answered. "Who is able to stand before the LORD, this holy God?" (6:20). The answer is: Those who are not sacrilegiously curious, looking into the ark; and those who are not coldly unresponsive to God's return to Israel. Something more than the easily explicable seems necessary to account for this unseemly haste to get rid of their God. Their mourning is understandable, but their dismissal of the ark is much less intelligible—in terms of storytelling. It may be necessary to leave space for a certain mystery.

What is quite clear in the narrative is that the ark is causing the same sort of distress in Israel as it caused in Philistine territory. As a result, it is practically banished to Kiriath-jearim. In terms of tradition, or as a sanctuary, Kiriath-jearim is no place. It is a cultic backwater, out of the mainstream of Israel's life. At Kiriath-

---

[25]On the text-critical problems here, consult D. Barthélemy, *Critique textuelle de l'Ancien Testament* (Orbis Biblicus et Orientalis 50/1; Fribourg: Éditions Universitaires, 1983). Barthélemy considers the Greek rendering a translator's midrash; he accepts the translation "looked into"; he suspects that "70 out of 50,000" makes the best sense of the numbers.

jearim, the ark is effectively out of touch with all that happens in Israel. Ark Narrative or no, there is no mention of it at all until 2 Samuel 6.[26] We will need to examine this, when looking at the meaning of the narrative as a whole.

In 2 Samuel 6, however, David goes to bring up the ark to his newly acquired capital city of Jerusalem. Everything is going splendidly until Uzzah is struck dead. The precise nature of Uzzah's error is again unclear. He took hold of the ark, when the oxen stumbled. As one of the sons of Abinadab, he was in some sense a guardian of the ark, so who in Israel was better placed to touch the ark? The Hebrew of v 7 does not enlighten us as to the reason. I cannot help thinking that it is shrouded in mystery, because that is exactly how it ought to be. However, for all the obscurity of its cause, its function in the narrative is quite clear. The storyteller takes three entire verses to describe David's reaction to what happened: David was angry (v 8), David was afraid of God (v 9), and David was unwilling to take the ark into his city (v 10). So the ark is once again put out of the way, for safe keeping, parked in the house of a foreigner, Obed-edom the Gittite.

The significance of this becomes clear in the next section of the narrative. Over the next three months, the ark was in his house; and Obed-edom and all his house were blessed (v 11). When the narrator has this repeated to David, he sharpens the point by adding that Obed-edom and all his household were blessed "because of the ark of God" (v 12a). So David went and brought the ark to the city of David with rejoicing (v 12b). The rest of the story tells of the successful installation of the ark in Jerusalem. Almost as an appendix, there is the story of Michal, Saul's daughter, who holds herself physically and psychologically aloof from the proceedings, and is left barren because of it. She surely symbolizes the house of Saul.

What is the significance of Uzzah's death and Obed-edom's being blessed? Why does the narrator include these things in a story to be told for generations to come? Because Israel's theology

---

[26]There is a single reference to it at 1 Sam 14:18. The occurrence is odd. Saul seems to be intending to ask for an oracular response, such as would make sense for the ephod rather than the ark. The passage is too obscure and too isolated to alter the picture to any significant degree.

is told in story, not in discourse. When David arose and went to collect the ark, its coming to Jerusalem was to be David's doing. After all, Jerusalem was David's city (vv 10, 12, 16); the ark's coming would have crowned David's military and political achievements with a religious coup of no small significance. David would have focused the worshipping life of the new political entity of Israel on his new capital, Jerusalem. This is how many interpreters understand the text. Yet this is precisely how the narrative does not permit itself to be understood.

The control over the coming of the ark to Jerusalem was not exercised by David. It was exercised by God. When David wanted to bring the ark to Jerusalem, God stopped him dead— with the death of Uzzah. For three months, David has to wait. Finally, God's willingness is indicated by the blessing bestowed on Obed-edom and his house. Now the move can be made. But it is no longer being made on David's initiative; the initiative is with God. This is a matter of narrative grammar. How else does a storyteller get the message across that it was not David's doing which brought the ark to Jerusalem but it was God's choice willingly to come? The psalmist is much closer to theological discourse, and so can say: "He rejected the tent of Joseph he did not choose the tribe of Ephraim; but he chose the tribe of Judah, Mount Zion, which he loves" (Ps 78:67-68). For the narrator-theologian, it has to be communicated differently. "Stop and go" is one way of expressing the exercise of divine control. But the "Stop" has to be miraculously dramatic, in order to make clear that it comes directly from God. From the storyteller's point of view, if that has to cost Uzzah his life, so be it. The point is made with complete clarity: after leaving Israel with full freedom of will (1 Samuel 4) and returning to Israel with full freedom of will (1 Sam 5-6) and after waiting offstage in Kiriath-jearim, God has freely chosen to come to Jerusalem. The ark is once more at the center of the stage of Israel's liturgical life. That says something of the quality of God's presence to the new institution established by David.

It is valuable to step back and see what has happened here. The narrator has taken a number of traditions and woven them into a single story. Certain tensions are evident in 1 Samuel 6, between the concerns about what expiatory gift the ark was to be returned with and about whether in fact the God of Israel was responsible for what had been happening. Also in the beginning of 1 Samuel 5, there is some overlapping. These are just some of the pointers to the composite nature of the whole. Yet, out of the diversity of tradition, there has been woven a story sequence with a relentless narrative thread that moves from Ebenezer and Shiloh to Kiriath-jearim and Jerusalem.

In the fashion of storytelling, the narrator has gone to great pains to make quite clear that God's departure from Israel, in the defeat of the second battle at Ebenezer, was entirely under God's own control. But there was no return to Shiloh. Nor was the returned ark a source of blessing in Israel. Instead of a glorious, triumphant, and joyful return, the ark was shunted off to Kiriath-jearim, at the bottom of the hills leading up to Jerusalem, and on the fringe of Israel's territory. When, finally, the ark does move back into the mainstream of Israel's life, it moves to the newly captured Jerusalem. And once again, the narrator has gone to great pains to make quite clear that the move to Jerusalem was entirely under God's own control.

What does this mean? Reduced to basics, the ark, as a primary symbol of God's presence to Israel, withdrew from the mainstream of Israel's life after the battle at Ebenezer. It did not return into the mainstream of Israel's life until after David was established on the throne of all Israel and had captured Jerusalem as his city. In the meantime, a radical change had taken place in the institutions of Israel. Whatever form of leadership existed in the era of Shiloh had been replaced by the, for Israel, almost totally new institution of monarchy. From a tribal people, Israel had become a national state. From the diversity of northern and southern traditions, a precarious unity had been welded. It is probably not too much to say that the face of Israel had changed.

The Ark Narrative is saying something about this change. It draws a line across the history of Israel, bringing a period to an end, allowing a new era to unfold. The only interpretation which accounts for the total text of the narrative is one which sees the preceding period as having been drawn to a close by God's withdrawing of the ark, and one which sees that the appropriate stability and order in Israel, which would permit the ark to dwell in their midst, was not achieved until the establishment of the Davidic monarchy in Jerusalem.

We can now return to the question with which the Ark

Narrative began: "Why has the LORD put us to rout today before the Philistines?" (1 Sam 4:3). The answer is: because God was withdrawing the ark, and the divine presence which it symbolized, from the center of Israel, and would not return until David was king in Jerusalem. It says in narrative prose what Psalm 78 says in poetry:

> When God heard, he was full of wrath,
>   and he utterly rejected Israel.
> He forsook his dwelling at Shiloh,
>   the tent where he dwelt among men,
> and delivered his power to captivity,
>   his glory to the hand of the foe. . . .
> Then the LORD awoke as from sleep,
>   like a strong man shouting because of wine.
> And he put his adversaries to rout;
>   he put them to everlasting shame.
> He rejected the tent of Joseph,
>   he did not choose the tribe of Ephraim;
> but he chose the tribe of Judah,
>   Mount Zion, which he loves. . . .
> He chose David his servant. (Ps 78:59-70)[27]

This is an interesting reflection of the possibilities for a pluralist theology in ancient Israel. Both the Ark Narrative and Psalm 78 ignore the theological approach of the Story of David's Rise, in which God is with David in all the vicissitudes that stand between him and the throne. They also ignore the place of Samuel, who rose at Shiloh to be a prophet to all Israel, who anointed Saul, announced to him his rejection, and anointed David in his stead. Before we close these reflections on the sources of the Deuteronomistic History, we will have reason to return to this issue. For the time being, it is enough to see that, probably in tenth-century Israel, there existed a theological viewpoint which understood Israel's recent history as God's withdrawal from and rejection of a past era—the era symbolized by Shiloh—and God's election of

---

[27]For a discussion of the parallel between Psalm 78 and the Ark Narrative, see A.F. Campbell, "Psalm 78: A Contribution to the Theology of Tenth-Century Israel," *CBQ* 41 (1979) 51-79.

and return to the new era initiated with the kingship of David in Jerusalem.

This is a highly theological reflection on political events. How widely it was shared we do not know. As far as the Ark Narrative is concerned, we must recognize that the expression of theology through narrative has both advantages and disadvantages. It can be open to a rich plurality of meaning. But it also precludes many possibilities of nuance. In discourse, one could deal with the modalities of God's presence to Israel in the interim period between Shiloh and Jerusalem. The grave limitation of the ark as a revelatory symbol of God's power and purpose is that when the ark is excluded from the life of Israel so, it would appear, is God. Of course we know and Israel knew that God's power and presence can be manifested in many and various ways. But the narrative took the ark as its central focus; its capacity for theological expression is correspondingly narrowed and restricted.

CONTRIBUTION TO THE DEUTERONOMISTIC HISTORY

As presented here, the Ark Narrative sought to interpret the recent events of Israel's history in terms of God's purpose and will. The departure of the ark from Israel was interpreted as symbolic of God's rejection of an epoch in Israel. The return of the ark to Jerusalem was equally interpreted as signifying God's initiation of a new era in Israel's history.

At the level of the Deuteronomistic History, this delineation of epochs was particularly suitable, even if it meant breaking up the original unity of the Ark Narrative in order to make chronological sense. The Deuteronomistic History is itself structured according to an understanding of the major epochs in the history of Israel. The first part of the Ark Narrative (1 Samuel 4-6) helps bring one of these epochs to a close, preparing the way for the transition from Judges to monarchy. Coupled with the portrayal of the sins of the Elides, it was particularly suited to the deuteronomistic presentation with its emphasis on sin and its consequences. The second part of the Ark Narrative (2 Samuel 6) portrays in especially vivid fashion God's choice of Jerusalem and favorable disposition toward David. A new era has indeed dawned. The monarchy is now established in Jerusalem, the city of God's choosing, and the move to the establishment of the Jerusalem temple is now in sight (2 Samuel 7).

The Story of David's Rise
(1 Samuel 9—2 Samuel 5)

Recommended preliminary reading
1 Samuel 16:14-18:16; 23:1-18; 25:1-44
2 Samuel 5:1-12

Despite the fact that it contains some brilliant storytelling, much of it probably close to the time of David and Solomon, the story of David's rise to power has always been a bit of a Cinderella among the works of Israel's literature. This is largely due to the fact that it appears as a collection of all sorts of stories and traditions from these early years of David's, without a sense of unity and a clear beginning and an end.[28] It is clear that the material in the Story of David's Rise is a collection of disparate traditions and stories. Some of the stories would have been handed down independently. Some of the traditions look as though they were collected or put together for the purpose of this document (e.g., 1 Sam 22:1-5; 27:1-7). The key question is whether, in amongst this collection, it is possible to see a sense of unity and purpose, guiding the collector and transforming the collection into a composition, making of it a literary work. I believe that it will be possible to answer that question affirmatively. Different interpretations suggest different dates, but an origin in tenth-century Jerusalem is not unlikely.

---

[28]The Story of David's Rise has been begun, for example, in 1 Sam 15:1, or 16:1, or 16:14. And it has been concluded at 2 Sam 5 or 7 or 9. The classical position has it beginning in 1 Sam 16:14 and ending with 2 Sam 5:10 or 12. In connection with the hypothesis of the Prophetic Record (to be discussed in the final section of this chapter), I have argued that the Story of David's Rise may well have begun in 1 Samuel 9, at the earliest levels of these traditions (A.F. Campbell, *Of Prophets and Kings: A Late Ninth-Century Document (1 Samuel 1-2 Kings 10)* [CBQMS 17; Washington: Catholic Biblical Association of America, 1986] 125-38).

These traditions and stories about David have been preserved by someone who supported David. The tendency throughout the narrative is evident: David achieved eminence because God was with him. As the narrative presents him, David was not an ambitious schemer who grabbed for power, but a loyal Israelite who responded to circumstances and his people's need, and who ended up being presented with the crown, which he accepted. Though certain people died, who happened to stand between David and the throne, their deaths were in no way David's doing. They are, of course, Saul and his three sons, who died on Mt Gilboa; and Abner, the commander of Saul's army; and Ishbosheth, one of Saul's sons who succeeded him. As the narrative portrays it, the men of Judah came to David at Hebron and anointed him king over Judah (2 Sam 2:4a); there, too, the men of Israel came to him and anointed him king over Israel (2 Sam 5:1-3).

To all intents and purposes, the kingship is depicted as handed to David on a platter. Not everybody in Israel shared that view. The most eloquent expression of the opposition opinion is preserved for us in the taunt hurled at David by Shimei ben Gera, of the family of the house of Saul. As David wearily and hastily departed Jerusalem, facing potential defeat at the hands of his eldest son, Shimei screamed at him:

> Begone, begone, you man of blood, you worthless fellow! The LORD has avenged upon you all the blood of the house of Saul, in whose place you have reigned; and the LORD has given the kingdom into the hand of your son Absalom. See, your ruin is on you; for you are a man of blood.
>
> (2 Sam 16:5-8)

It is quite possible to see in the traditions about David the kind of reality described by Martin Noth.[29]

> Unlike Saul, David set out on the road to political power quite deliberately and consistently from the very beginning (p. 179)

---

[29]The two quotations which follow are from Martin Noth, *The History of Israel* (2nd ed.; New York: Harper & Row, 1960). For the details of Noth's understanding, see pp. 179-193.

And, after the death of Saul:

> In fact it appears that he (David) had evidently already con-
> sidered and prepared for what he would do if the event which
> he expected actually occurred. He now acted very methodically
> and skilfully, making first of all for the one goal that was within
> his immediate reach, thereby making a move forwards which
> he certainly did not regard as the final stage in his progress. He
> was skilled in the great art of waiting until things came within
> his grasp, and this was the way he created the great empire
> which represents the climax in the development of political
> power in the history of Israel. (p. 181)

With the aid of an equal blend of imagination and prejudice, it is
not difficult to develop this a stage further. Instead of being
"skilled in the great art of waiting until things came within his
grasp," it could be inferred that David was not unskilled in
arranging for things to happen the way he needed, so that what he
wanted came into his possession. In our present context, we will
not pursue these historical quests. Our concern is with the texts as
sources available to the Deuteronomist. At the same time, we
should not be blind to the variety of possible historical recon-
structions.[30]

The text of the Story of David's Rise is too extensive to be
treated in full here. A bird's-eye view can be provided through the
following remarks on the structure of the composition. The
introductory section consists of the earliest pre-Samuel levels of 1
Sam 9:1-10:16 and 11:1-15; then 14:52 and the earliest level of 1
Sam 15:1-35 (for these early levels, see my *Of Prophets and
Kings*, chap. 4). The body of the story extends from 1 Sam
16:14 – 2 Sam 5:12. David's charisma, as deliverer in Israel, is
demonstrated by 1 Sam 16:14-18:16*, the text of the David and
Goliath story to be discussed below. The traditions tracing
David's trajectory from the defeat of the Philistine to the throne

---

[30]Three helpful studies in this area may be found in the same issue of *JBL*: P.K.
McCarter, Jr., "The Apology of David," *JBL* 99 (1980) 489-504; J.D. Levenson and B.
Halpern, "The Political Import of David's Marriages," *JBL* 99 (1980) 507-18; J.C.
Vanderkam, "Davidic Complicity in the Deaths of Abner and Eshbaal: A Historical and
Redactional Study," *JBL* 99 (1980) 521-39.

of Israel are grouped as follows: the conflict at court (1 Sam 18:20-21:11a* [*RSV*, 10a]); the open rupture (22:1-27:12*); the ultimate failure of Saul (28:1-31:13*); the recognition of David as king (2 Sam 1:1-5:12*).[31]

The unity of this narrative complex cannot be demonstrated beyond doubt. However, a good case can be made for it. Early in the text, there is a major story which contains the movement of the whole narrative, in microcosm. That, in itself, constitutes an argument for an author-compiler in whose vision the entire work could be seen as a single and unified whole. At least two more of the stories in the text bear witness, in their intrinsic structure, to the same understanding of David and his rise to power that is present in the text as a whole. Taken together, these constitute a fairly suasive argument for the integrity of the Story of David's Rise as a literary work.

DAVID'S COMBAT WITH THE PHILISTINE (GOLIATH)

The first of these stories concerns David's single combat with a Philistine champion, named in the text as Goliath.[32] Before examining the story as story, there are some questions to be

---

[31]It is not possible here to discuss what may have been original to the body of the Story of David's Rise and what were subsequent additions and why. The following verses would be fairly generally regarded as secondary: 1 Sam 19:18-24; 21:10-15; 23:6; 25:1 (?); 28:17-19a; 2 Sam 2:10a, 11; 3:2-5; 4:2b-3, 4; 5:4-5. Beyond these, I would also argue for omitting as secondary: in 1 Sam 16-18, all the text which is found exclusively in the Hebrew, reading only what is attested in both Hebrew and Greek (see below); also, 1 Sam 19:3a; 20:14-23, 37-39; 23:19-24a; 24:1-22. With these omissions, the remaining text of the Story of David's Rise makes good sense as a smooth and connected composition, consisting basically of originally independent stories, short notices collected by the compiler, and some stories probably shaped by the compiler. Unfortunately, we cannot go into the reasons for these omissions here.

[32]Throughout the story, he is referred to as the Philistine. He is named as Goliath only twice (vv 4,23), that is, at the start of each of the two stories (see below). The proper name does not fit smoothly into the Hebrew syntax of the two sentences. And in 2 Sam 21:19, among the stories and traditions of David's heroes, the killing of Goliath is attributed to Elhanan from Bethlehem. So it seems highly likely that, while David distinguished himself in single combat against a Philistine, the name of Goliath, the giant Philistine from Gath, has been introduced into the story later. As we will see, the story acquired almost legendary significance very early on; the identification of David's opponent with one of the four legendary Philistine giants is simply an extension of this process (cf., 2 Sam 21:15-22).

cleared up about the text. It is a compiled text, not a unity.[33] What
is most unusual is that, for once, the identification of two stories
in the text is confirmed by the different texts transmitted in
Hebrew and Greek. There is a marked difference between the
transmitted text of the Hebrew and the Greek in chaps. 17-18.
The Greek text is about 45% shorter than the Hebrew, 49 verses
to 88.[34] When the text common to both Hebrew and Greek is
read, it can be understood as a complete and smoothly flowing
segment of homogeneous narrative. The additional material,
which is exclusive to the Hebrew text alone, also can be viewed as
homogeneous and witnessing to a different version of the story.[35]

[33]Without going into detail, the main points of tension may be noted.

1) 17:12 looks like the beginning of a story, rather than merely a new paragraph.

2) 17:15 appears to be a harmonizing addition, intended to bring this story into line with 16:14-23.

3) 17:16 tries to reconcile the earlier appearance of the Philistine (vv 1-11) with the later arrival of David (vv 17-23).

4) 17:19 repeats specific information already given in vv 1-3.

5) 17:23 repeats the introduction of the Philistine already given in v 4.

6) 17:24 gives the impression that this was the first time that the Philistine had appeared; flight and fear scarcely occurred twice a day for forty days, and the battle cry (v 20) also suggests a single occurrence.

7) 17:50 has a different conception of the death of the Philistine from that of vv 49 and 51.

8) 17:55 has Saul see David go forth, whereas in v 37, Saul sent him forth. And from 16:14-23, David was known to Saul.

9) Finally, we may notice that 17:57 has David with the Philistine's head in his hand, while in v 54 it has been taken to Jerusalem.

There is a very full treatment of aspects of the text in D. Barthélemy, D.W. Gooding, J. Lust, and E. Tov, *The Story of David and Goliath: Textual and Literary Criticism* (OBO 73; Fribourg, Suisse: Éditions Universitaires, 1986). It is to be noted that not only are textual and literary (or source) criticism closely interlocked, as this volume demonstrates; the form-critical judgment about the kind of story involved and the extent of its text is equally critical—and too often ignored.

[34]One of the three great manuscripts of the Greek Bible, Alexandrinus, does contain this material. However, the difference in translation style shows that it is an addition, which has been made up later from the Hebrew. A study which pays attention to the two textual traditions is S.J. De Vries, "David's Victory over the Philistine as Saga and as Legend," *JBL* 92 (1973) 23-36. De Vries overlooks the contrast being drawn between Saul and David, and does not take adequate account of the material in chap. 18. For a presentation of the different texts and further discussion, see McCarter, *1 Samuel*, 284-314 and Ralph W. Klein, *1 Samuel* (WBC 10: Waco, TX: Word Books, 1983) 168-91.

[35]See A.F. Campbell, "From Philistine to Throne (1 Samuel 16:14-18:16)," *AusBR* 34 (1986) 35-41.

The story we will be looking at is the one common to both Hebrew and Greek texts. We need to omit the following verses, which are not present in the Greek: 1 Sam 17:12-31, 41, 48b, 50; 17:55-18:6aα; 18:10-11, 12b, 17-19, 21b, 29b-30. Once these verses are omitted, the tensions in chap. 17 disappear. It will be noticed that the difference between the Hebrew and Greek texts continues into chap. 18. Contrary to the opinion of most scholars to date, when these are examined closely, they will be seen to coincide fully with the two different traditions begun in chap 17. Again, we cannot go into detail here. The picture will emerge as we go along.

The story of David and Goliath is almost invariably told as the story of the defenseless little shepherd boy facing the monstrous great Goliath. The little lad has no chance against the giant warrior, except for his faith in God, who miraculously gives him victory. Quite bluntly, that picture is wrong and misleading. While one can see where it has come from, it is a fascinating example of how a traditional image of a story can completely ignore the reality of its details. In this case, the text is explicit. Saul says to David: You cannot fight against that Philistine (v 33). David, in his reply, describes himself and his experience: I have been a shepherd. When a lion or a bear raided my flock and took a lamb, I would chase it and catch it, and clout it till it let the lamb go. And if it turned on me, I would get it by the beard, clobber it and kill it. I have done that to lions and bears; I can do it to this brute of a Philistine (vv 34-36). Whatever we may wish to discount to youthful enthusiasm, David is claiming to be very quick on his feet, very fast in his reflexes, and just plain tough.

There is another piece of information we have to bring into play. David is equipped with a sling. In the traditional picture, this is about as effective against an armed warrior as a peashooter against a tank. But around David's day, slingers were elite troops: "Among all these were seven hundred picked men who were left-handed; every one could sling a stone at a hair, and not miss" (Judg 20:16; cf., 2 Chron 26:14). The sling was a deadly weapon. In this case, against a fighter whose primary advantage was in his fearsome size and awesome armor, it was the ideal weapon. It was like the longbow of the English archers against French cavalry. It was like the street-fighter's Molotov cocktail against a tank. With a little bit of luck, it could be devastatingly effective. The little bit of luck is important. And that is where David's trust in God comes in. "The LORD who delivered me from the paw of the lion and from the paw of the bear, will deliver me from the hand of this Philistine" (v 37; the Hebrew has *yad* three times, for both "paw" and "hand"; cf., the *NAB*'s "claws" and "clutches"). It is typical Davidic theology: have complete faith, but leaving nothing to God except trust.[36]

There is one more obstacle to be disposed of, and then we can get to the story. The obstacle is the verse which the whole traditional picture of David and Goliath comes from. "And Saul said to David, 'You are not able to go against this Philistine to fight with him; for you are but a youth, and he has been a man of war from his youth'" (v 33). The Hebrew word for "youth" is *na'ar*. It has a wide range of meanings: infant, lad just weaned, youth, with special stress on youthfulness, of marriageable age, warrior, servant, retainer.[37] In any single case, the meaning has to be dependent on the context. We might check some contexts. The term is used in 2 Sam 2:12-17, so a *na'ar* can kill. It is used in 1 Sam 21:2-5, so a *na'ar* can have sexual intercourse. It is used in 2 Sam 18:5, 12, so a *na'ar* can head a rebellion. It is used in 1 Kgs 11:28, so a *na'ar* can serve as a royal overseer. The precise meaning has to depend on the context.[38] Youthfulness or dependence, especially in the ancient world, can connote inexperience. It is precisely this meaning which makes excellent sense in 1 Sam 17:33. It also permits this level of the story to be associated with the tradition in 1 Sam 16:14-23.[39] David has just come to

---

[36]Ignatius Loyola, founder of the Jesuits, is sometimes quoted as saying: Pray as if everything depended on God and work as if everything depended on you. In effect: pray like fury and work like fury. In an official Jesuit collection, the saying is quoted quite differently: Pray as if everything depended on you and work as if everything depended on God. That is, pray tranquilly and work trustfully. I am told that neither version can be traced to Ignatius; but the latter is more like him. David might have found it hard to decide between them, but I fancy he would opt for the latter too.

[37]These are taken from Brown, Driver, Briggs, *A Hebrew and English Lexicon of the Old Testament* (Oxford: Clarendon, 1907).

[38]There is a monograph devoted to the term, tracing its meaning to the two basic senses of dependence within the family or dependence in service (H.-P. Stähli, *Knabe-Jüngling-Knecht* [BET 7; Frankfurt a.M.: Peter Lang, 1978]). On 1 Sam 17:33, unfortunately, Stähli does not escape the traditional picture of a "half-grown youth."

[39]See H.J. Stoebe, *Das erste Buch Samuelis* (KAT 8/1; Gütersloh: Gerd Mohn, 1973) 335. It is possible that the highly stylized 16:18 replaces an earlier and less formal verse which identified David by name—in view of v. 19.

Saul's court and camp; he has just been made Saul's armor-bearer (16:21). As a warrior, he is inexperienced, a recent untried recruit, whereas the Philistine is a combat-hardened veteran. There is a further pointer in the same direction. Saul put his armor on David (v 38). Now Saul was a big man, head and shoulders above the crowd (1 Sam 9:2; 10:23). If David were assumed to be a little shepherd boy, from the viewpoint of narrative plausibility the offer would have been absurd. David's "I cannot go with these" (v 39) has to be understood as: I am not used to handling this sort of gear; it cuts down my mobility. And so now, at last, we can get down to the story.

It starts with all the formal trappings of a battle story. Armies on one side and the other, in the valley of Elah, between Socoh and Azekah, in the low hills between Judah and the coast. A grand spot for a fight, and a most appropriate setting for a story like this. A wide, flat valley bottom for fighting space; a small stream meandering down the middle, to provide the five smooth stones for David's sling. The hills rising up on either side would almost provide grandstand viewing. The storyteller sets the scene and then brings the Philistine champion on stage: he is enormous, with imposing armor, and massive weapons. That spear, "like a weaver's beam," was legendary (cf., 2 Sam 21:19). He hurls an awesome challenge against Israel: Stake everything on a single combat—with me! This is storytelling, of course; the terms of the challenge are forgotten at the end. But like all good storytelling, it has its roots in reality. What is at stake here is quite simply everything: will Israel survive as a people, or will they be forced into submission to the Philistines? It was for this sort of situation that Saul had been made king (cf., 1 Samuel 11).

And now we get the first shock in the story. When the Philistine has said his piece, the narrator points to Saul and all Israel: "they were dismayed and greatly afraid" (v 11). Something is amiss. Instead of the noble bearing of king and deliverer, Saul's knees are knocking. Rather than the king steadying the ranks of his people, the king himself looks distinctly shaky and in need of steadying.

And now we get the second shock in the story. King Saul has his nerves steadied from a most unexpected quarter. Remember that vv 12-31 are omitted from this version of the story. So as soon as the narrator has told us that Saul and all Israel were dismayed and greatly afraid (v 11), he has young David, Saul's new armor-bearer at his side, speak up to his king and say: "Let no man's heart fail because of him; your servant will go and fight with this Philistine" (v 32). And right there is the key moment of the story. The Davidic tradition will have seen in this moment the instant when David accepted his destiny. Saul's heart has failed him, but not David's. Saul, the king, is powerless to deliver Israel. David will deliver Israel, in Saul's place. It is because David did it so well that Israel made him king (cf., 2 Sam 5:2).

This is a story of single combat between David and the Philistine. But that is secondary to its main point: it is a story of the contrasting destinies of Saul and David. The Philistines are the great threat to Israel. Faced with the Philistine threat, Saul quailed and David stepped into the breach. The storyteller, who can so brilliantly condense the political and military threat, which the Philistines constituted, into the chilling language of the giant challenger, is not likely to leave the contrast between Saul and David undeveloped. And indeed, the contrast is pursued. Saul was afraid (v 11); David courageous (v 32). Saul said, "You cannot" (v 33); David said, "I can" (vv 34-37). Saul based his denial on military experience (v 33); David based his affirmation on his experience of faith in God (vv 36-37). The narrator here is making a very shrewd narrative move. He has cast Saul in the role of trusting in arms, while David trusts in God. It was a dogma of Israel's wars that trust is put not in arms but in God. So the narrator pursues this theme when the story has Saul put his armor on David. Whatever the reasons, the symbolism is there. David discards armor in favor of trust in God. And, being David, he has his sling in his hand—probably behind his back, where the arrogant Philistine will not notice it. Faith does not exclude good tactics.

The focus in the story shifts for the third time. First of all, it was on the massive Philistine and the fearful Saul. Then it shifted to the contrasting figures of the impotent Saul and the willing David. Now it moves to the grizzly Philistine and the youthful David. The storyteller has the Philistine take up the same line of thought as Saul: trust in arms. "Am I a dog, that you come to me with sticks?" (v 43). David is kept in character, trusting in God (vv 45-47). The last words given him point up the difference between David and the Philistine—but between David and Saul too:

"That all this assembly may know that the LORD saves not with sword and spear; for the battle is the LORD's and he will give you into our hand" (v 47). Saul should have known that and been able to act on it. It was because Saul was unable to act that David had to become king.

The actual combat scene is very quick. We omit vv 48b and 50. As the Philistine approached, David slung a stone between his eyes and dropped him to the ground. A quick sprint, a tug at his sword, and David killed the Philistine and cut off his head with his own sword—not the work of a fledgling. The Philistines fled; the Israelites pursued them well into the coastal plain and plundered their camp (vv 52-53; v 54 is an anachronism, and how it got there remains an enigma).

The narrator has done a superb job, and, after having dwelt on the contrast between Saul and David, can now maintain the story's momentum and bring it to its climax and its close. We omit 17:55-18:6aα. So, when David returned from slaying the Philistine, the women came "out of all of the cities of Israel" (18:6), and sang of the victory.

> Saul has slain his thousands,
> and David his ten thousands.

Saul noted it, and did not like it. The storyteller gives it emphasis: "And Saul was very angry, and this saying displeased him. . . . And Saul eyed David from that day on" (vv 8-9).

"From that day on." With that, the narrator shifts the focus one final time, to look into the future. We omit 18:10-11, 12b. The story, which began in 16:14, has really ended here at 18:9. But the narrator forges a link into the stories to come, which will take what has happened here, in the microcosm of the battlefield in the valley, and expand it into the plane of Israel's history—the Story of David's Rise. There are just four verses (vv 13-16). Probably, v 13 should join v 9 in concluding the story proper. Vv 14-16 point to the future. They deal succinctly with the three figures of the story of David's rise to power in Israel.

DAVID: he had success in all his undertakings, for the LORD was with him (v 14).
SAUL: he stood in awe of David, when he saw that he had great success (v 15)

ALL ISRAEL AND JUDAH: and they loved David; for he went out and came in before them (v 16).

This is scarcely romantic love; it is the fidelity of those who are ready to follow a leader. "He went out and came in before them" means that he led them out to battle and brought them home victorious. He provided leadership. It was effective leadership that brought David to the throne of Israel. "In times past, when Saul was king over us, it was you that led out and brought in Israel. . . . And they anointed David king over Israel" (2 Sam 5:2-3).

The narrator of this battle between David and the Philistine has had the contrast between David and Saul in the center of the story. The story of single combat has been, in microcosm, the story of David's rise to power. When the narrator brings this story to a close, the Story of David's Rise is just beginning. But the narrator has made sure that its end is in sight. Such is the stuff of great storytelling, with a depth of vision and purpose that renders narrative a vehicle for exploring experience and giving it theological expression. "For the LORD was with him" (1 Sam 18:14). And the spirit of the LORD had departed from Saul (1 Sam 16:14).

1 SAMUEL 23

A second story which can exemplify a similar understanding of David's coming to power is to be found in 1 Sam 23:1-14. The biblical version of the story is extremely compressed; a little expansion may be helpful. David is told that the Philistines are attacking the Judean town of Keilah and robbing the threshing floors there. The robbing of the threshing floors means that the food supply is threatened, and therefore the people's lives are at stake. The storyteller has David inquire of God as to the course of action to be taken, and he is told to go "and save Keilah" (v 2). Very sensibly, David's men protest that they are in a dangerous enough situation where they are, without seeking trouble by taking on the Philistine army. David again consults God, who assures him, "I will give the Philistines into your hand" (v 4). So David takes up the challenge and succeeds. He captures the Philistine flocks, so restoring the balance in the food supply, and is victorious over the Philistines themselves. The first part of the story ends: "And David saved the inhabitants of Keilah" (v 5).

In miniature, this is the story of the combat between David and the Philistine all over again. The Philistine power is life-threatening; the robbing of the threshing floors is evidence for that. The Philistine power is also vastly superior to David's; the protest of David's troops attests to that. Their argument, with its reference to the "armies of the Philistines," implies an assessment on the grounds of comparative military strength—i.e., trust in arms. David's response is to take the matter back to God—i.e., trust in God. So, just as in the earlier story David vanquished the superior Philistine champion, here he and his men are victorious over the superior Philistine army. Twice, the narrator uses a very significant word of David, *yāša'*, "to save." God declares that David shall save Keilah (v 2); the narrator says that he did save Keilah (v 5). In all this, David is doing the work of a king; he is portrayed saving his people from life-threatening danger. And he is portrayed as God's agent. The forces against him are overwhelming, so that his primary weapon is trust in God. To sum up: just as in the story of chap 17, David did the work of God's king in delivering Israel from the threat of the Philistine champion, so here he is depicted doing the work of God's king in delivering townspeople in Judah from the threat of the Philistines.

The irony is in the second part of the story, which turns its focus on to Saul. As the king, he should have been the one to deliver Keilah. For whatever reason—geographical, military, political, or theological—he did not. David went to war to deliver the town; Saul is presented going to war to destroy the deliverer. The irony is patent. According to the storyteller, Saul's response to the news of David's being at Keilah is, "God has given him into my hand" (v 7), followed immediately by a reason which is one of military strategy. He believes he has David trapped. Saul's villainy is intensified by the storyteller: he is not only out to destroy the deliverer, but also the delivered as well—he will destroy the city on David's account (v 10). This puts Saul in much the same category as the Philistines. The introduction of this theme helps explain the ungrateful attitude attributed to the people of Keilah, ready to surrender David and his men to Saul. They are obliged to, in order to save their own skins. David and his men escape in good time, and Saul gives up the expedition.

The central thrust of the story is clear: God delivered David. It is picked out in the first and last sentences. Saul said, "God has given him into my hand" (v 7); the narrator notes, "And God did not give him into his hand" (v 14).[40] It is all the more evident when we look at the situation more closely. David is not forewarned by God; he knew about it (v 9a), and then turned to God for counsel. The counsel that he sought was on an issue where he might have been expected to turn to reliable military intelligence: "How are the locals disposed toward us?" Instead, the story has David take his counsel from God, act on it, and escape.

In this second section of the story, we are presented with the shadow side of the first section. There, David was acting as God's king should have. Here, God's king is reported as acting despicably. Saul believes that God and military tactics are on his side. The storyteller makes clear that they are not. Here again, in a nutshell, is the central theme of the Story of David's Rise. God is no longer with Saul. God is with David. David is acting as deliverer on behalf of the people.[41]

1 SAMUEL 25

A third story with a similar theme is the story of David's encounter with Nabal and Abigail. It is a wonderful story, richly

[40]Although the *RSV* has "give" in both verses, the Hebrew uses two different verbs. The text-critical status of the first is uncertain. However, for our purposes, the similarities of the rest of the phrase makes the deliberate counter-balance more than adequately clear. McCarter takes v 14 with the next section, vv 14-18 (*1 Samuel*, 373). It is correct that the action of the story ends with v 13; v 14 is the narrator's conclusion . It picks up two points from v 13. David's men scatter, so David's location is given. Saul gave up the Keilah expedition, but he did not give up the pursuit. The Keilah episode is but one instance of a more general pattern: God did not give David into Saul's hand. V 15 makes more sense as an independent beginning to the little story of the encounter with Jonathan. V 15b has all the marks of an editorial bridge, linking the passage into the present context.

[41]A rather different interpretation of this passage is given by McCarter (*1 Samuel*, 371-72). He places primary weight on the presence of Abiathar, suggesting "The Value of a Priest" as a subtitle for the section. This is a correct interpretation of the sequence of the stories in the Story of David's Rise. Saul's folly in chap. 22 rebounds to David's benefit in chap. 23. Yet Abiathar and the ephod are only a means of knowing God's will, and the central figures in the story are David and God. It is also correct that vv 7-14 appear to expand on the original story in vv 1-5. Vv 7-14 function to cast Saul in a negative light, and to emphasize God's assistance to David. The use of the ephod is a means to this end. Even including the later v 6, Abiathar's place in the story is peripheral.

and artfully told. All that we can do here is to note its impact for the Story of David's Rise. Both Nabal and Abigail have to deal with David, and they do so very differently. Nabal's contempt is contained in his opening words, "Who is David?" (v 10). He does not recognize David; he does not acknowledge the services David has rendered; he spurns David. Abigail's attitude is portrayed as the exact opposite. Prostrate before David, she gives him recognition as her lord; the gifts she brings are due acknowledgment of his services.

This is not a lesson in the appropriate tactics for dealing with a guerrilla leader who is looking for supplies for his men. The story does not continue in that vein. We are not told what Abigail whispered in Nabal's ear in the soberer light of dawn (cf., v 37). It might have been that the man he had spurned was to be the future leader of Israel. It might have been that the man he had ignored as a runaway had had something like six hundred armed men under his command. The storyteller has moved to another plane. It is God who brings Nabal to his death (v 38). And this act enables Abigail to become David's wife. By God's doing, what decides the fate of Nabal and Abigail is the way they have reacted to David. Nabal's failure to recognize David costs him his life: Abigail's recognition of David brings her to the court. Yet it is not David who took Nabal's life, but God.

As the story portrays it, people's fate is determined by the attitude they take to David. Those who favor him are favored; those who spurn him are ill-fated. Such is the understanding of the overall narrative of the Story of David's Rise. David's foes, whether Saul, or Abner, or Ishbosheth, fall in battle or at the assassin's hand. Those who are with David prosper. Those who invite David to be their king are blessed by his rule. To a less obvious degree than the previous two, this story of David, Nabal, and Abigail also reveals in microcosm the overall theme of the story of David's rise to power.

CONTRIBUTION TO THE DEUTERONOMISTIC HISTORY

Within its own horizon, the Story of David's Rise was a collection of stories, many of them originally independent, which

had as its aim the presentation of a particular understanding of
how David came to power in Israel. The stories are presented as
distilling the significant reality from the raw events of those years.
These events did not result from the combination of human
cunning and remarkable luck. Instead, they were due to God's
guidance and God's will. The spirit of God was with David,
empowering him; it was not with Saul. That was why David
increased and Saul decreased. That was why David rose to royal
power in Israel. Whether one shares its viewpoint or not, it is a
sustained example of the theological interpretation of human
reality.

At the level of the Deuteronomistic History, another dimension
is added to its significance. David is one of the model kings who
meets with approval in the History. In the Story of David's Rise,
he is portrayed as one who trusts totally in God and, while acting
decisively when it is appropriate, he is also portrayed as one who
knows how to wait. "As the LORD lives, the LORD will smite him;
or his day shall come to die; or he shall go down into battle and
perish. The LORD forbid that I should put forth my hand against
the LORD's anointed" (1 Sam 26:10-11). In words like these, there
is an attitude of utter respect for the will of God. It is later visible
in David's response to the prophetic word as well (2 Sam 7:18-29;
12:13). Here are some of the foundational images for the
deuteronomistic picture of a model king.

The Succession Narrative
(2 Samuel 11-20; 1 Kings 1-2)

Recommended preliminary reading
2 Samuel 11; 13; 15

The Succession Narrative, generally designated as 2 Samuel
9-20 and 1 Kings 1-2, is the greatest monument of Hebrew prose
narrative. It is bedevilled by its title, "The Succession Narrative,"
assuming that its purpose is to respond to the question, "Who
shall sit on David's throne?" (cf., 1 Kgs 1:20, also 1:48). A more
neutral and more accurate title is the Story of David's Later

Years.[42] This concern with succession is also largely responsible
for beginning the Succession Narrative in 2 Samuel 9 or earlier.
Its peculiar style and concerns are most evident from 2 Samuel
11 on.

Usually, but by no means universally, its composition is
situated at the court of Solomon. The richness of its narrative is
too magnificent to be followed up in detail here, and it is visible to
the sensitive reader without special explanation. One aspect of its
intention is worth further exploration. Scholars differ on the
nature of the narrative and whether it is to be seen as favorable or
unfavorable to David and Solomon.[43] It is possible, in my
opinion, that a major reason for this lies in the central purpose of
the text: it is a narrative meditation on statecraft, stories exploring
and reflecting on the art of conducting state affairs. The stories
constantly ask or invite questions which they do not answer. The
questions lead one below the surface of reality into the navigation
of its murkier depths. They would make very good sense as case
studies for the education of young courtiers, destined one day to
be the counsellors of the king. The counsel of Ahithophel and
Hushai is contrasted at a critical turning point in the narrative (2
Sam 17:1-14). But at any number of points in the stories, similarly
contrasting counsel could be elicited. If the story of David and
Bathsheba is given its due place, a major theme of the narrative
would be the relationship between the private behavior of the
king and the public conduct of his kingdom. This is certainly the
view of those prophetic editors who inserted 2 Sam 12:7b-12 into
Nathan's accusation of David. Constantly in the background of
the other stories is the question whether the king acted rightly or
wrongly, did too much or too little. At stake are matters of state:
assassination and revolution and the protection of the monarchy.
Whoever wrote the Story of David's Later Years was certainly

---

[42]The emphasis on the succession aspect comes from Leonhard Rost, in his classic study
in 1926, now available in English (*The Succession to the Throne of David* [Sheffield:
Almond, 1982]). The alternative title derives from the Chadwicks in their monumental
study of literature (H.M. and N.K. Chadwick, *The Growth of Literature* [3 vols;
Cambridge: Cambridge University, 1932-40] 2.645).

[43]Among the extensive literature, we may single out R.N. Whybray, *The Succession
Narrative: A Study of II Sam. 9-10 and I Kings 1 and 2* (SBT 2/9; London: SCM, 1968)
and Charles Conroy, *Absalom Absalom!: Narrative and Language in 2 Sam 13-20*
(AnBib 81; Rome: Biblical Institute, 1978).

familiar with the royal court. The narrative would be an admirable instrument for initiating others into the ambiguities of human situations, the questions to be asked and the conflicting demands to be weighed in giving counsel, as well as awareness of the awesome weight of royal responsibility.

The narrative consists of a series of stories. Allowing for a certain presumption of background knowledge, they could be thought of as independent. Like many a family saga, they are intertwined nevertheless. There is the story of David and Bathsheba (2 Samuel 11-12), the story of Amnon, Tamar, and Absalom (2 Samuel 13-14), the story of Absalom's rebellion (2 Samuel 15-19), the story of Sheba ben Bichri's rebellion (2 Samuel 20), and the story of Solomon's accession to David's throne (1 Kings 1-2*).

In the story of David and Bathsheba, motives are not explored.[44] The *RSV*'s "It happened" (2 Sam 11:2) gives the impression that David's seeing Bathsheba was a matter of chance. The Hebrew does not support that nuance. It says simply that toward evening David rose, went up on the roof, and saw Bathsheba. The narrative does not say whether it was chance. It does not say whether David went up on to the roof with a view to seeing Bathsheba. It does not say whether Bathsheba was bathing with a view to being seen from the palace roof. It does not say whether Uriah was alerted to what may have happened, although there had been quite a deal of traffic between the two establishments by messengers and servants. It does not say whether Uriah was an upright man and scandalized, or whether he was a scheming man who saw a chance for himself. It does not say that the only place in Jerusalem where Uriah could sleep out under the stars was on the palace doorstep. It does place David in a very bad light, as having quite ruthlessly ordered the killing of one of his own men in order simply to protect his own name. It also shows different aspects of God: angered at David's wrongdoing (11:27); forgiving the sin but not commuting the sentence (12:13-14); loving the infant Solomon (12:24-25).

In the story of Amnon and Tamar, no comment is made on the

---

[44]A valuable treatment is given in Meir Sternberg, *The Poetics of Biblical Narrative: Ideological Literature and the Drama of Reading* (Bloomington: Indiana University, 1985) 186-229.

fact that Jonadab and Absalom both knew of Amnon's passion for Tamar, while David was apparently unaware of it. Nor is any comment made on the cruel irony that it was David who delivered Tamar into Amnon's grasp. The narrator puts the criticism of Amnon's folly on Tamar's lips; he does not step out of the story to pass judgment. The narrator does let it be known that David knew and was angry (13:21). There is no comment on the fact that David did nothing, nor are his options canvassed by the narrator. The story paints David in a cruel light as repeating his mistakes. After delivering Tamar into Amnon's power, he later delivers Amnon into Absalom's power (13:25-27). Again, the conniving Jonadab knew just what was going on (13:32)—but not David. There is a remarkable portrait of David's ambivalence. David had got over Amnon's death (cf., 12:20-23) and was longing for Absalom (13:39). But he did nothing about it. It was left to Joab to move the king to action, with the help of a wise woman. But even so, the reconciliation is not complete, and Absalom is not admitted to the court (14:24, 28). When finally the reconciliation is consummated (14:33), it is the prelude to revolution. Moral judgments are not passed. David's options are not canvassed. Questions are invited rather than asked. Through it all, reality is revealed not concealed.

The story of Absalom's revolution is a story that is centered on David, his prudence when he is finally forced to action, his capacity to generate loyalty in his subjects. The central pivot in the story is the defeat of the counsel of Ahithophel, so ordained by God in order to bring evil upon Absalom (17:14). The battle strategy, the death of Absalom, the action of David and the rebuke from Joab, and the negotiations with Judah and Israel are studies in the problem of restoring order after such a civil disaster. Sheba's rebellion is settled on the counsel of a wise woman. There is plenty here for reflection and pondering by those destined to bear the burden of giving counsel themselves.

In the story of Solomon's accession, much again is left unsaid. What is the link between the king's impotence (1 Kgs 1:4) and his eldest surviving son's move for the throne? What are the patterns of power within the palace that align Joab and Abiathar with Adonijah, and Benaiah, Zadok, Nathan, Shimei, Rei, and David's mighty men against him? Why are Shimei and Rei and the mighty men not mentioned again in the story? Is the king so senile that he can be duped by them, yet alert enough that he plans the counter strategy down to its last details? How wise were the instructions given Solomon (2:5-9)? How wisely did he act upon them? One thing is certain. The storyteller was gifted with the insightful eye of one who is wise, as well as with a remarkable capacity for literary expression. Taken together, these stories form a masterpiece.

CONTRIBUTION TO THE DEUTERONOMISTIC HISTORY

At their original levels, these stories might have served as a subtle polemic against Solomon, or as not quite so subtle propaganda on Solomon's behalf. Or perhaps, as suggested here, their purpose leaned more to the exploration of the ambiguities of human experience and reality.

Their contribution to the Deuteronomistic History is less clear. They are hardly flattering to David, the model king. On the other hand, at the level of the deuteronomistic text, they do provide a graphic illustration of the accuracy and power of the prophetic word. The expansions of Nathan's speech promise that, as a consequence of David's adultery and murder, the sword would never depart from his house and his own wives would be publicly violated (2 Sam 12:7b-13). As one might expect, the narrative fully validates these predictions.

The Prophetic Record
(1 Samuel 1 — 2 Kings 10)

Recommended preliminary reading
1 Samuel 9:1-10:16; 16:1-13
1 Kings 11:26-40; 14:1-13; 21:17-24
2 Kings 9:1-13

The Prophetic Record is the last of the sources available to the Deuteronomist which we will be able to look at briefly.[45] Its

---

[45]The Prophetic Record is a hypothesis proposed by the present writer in *Of Prophets*

recovery, as a hypothetical document from northern prophetic circles in the late ninth century, is based on three sets of observations. Firstly, there are marked similarities in the accounts of the anointing of Saul (1 Sam 9:1-10:16), David (1 Sam 16:1-13), and Jehu (2 Kgs 9:1-13). The rite of anointing with oil is done by a prophet, in private, to be either *nāgîd* or king over the people of Israel. There are no other cases in which a king is anointed by a prophet in this fashion. Samuel's anointing of Saul has been superimposed over an earlier story in 1 Sam 9:1-10:16, in which the prophet was anonymous and there was no mention of anointing. The anointing of David appears to be a later preface to the Story of David's Rise; there is no reference to it in any of the subsequent stories. So, it is reasonable to assume that these are not independent accounts, controlled by three separate events. Instead, it is probable that they come from one and the same prophetic group.

Secondly, there is a series of accounts of prophetic encounters with kings, either designating or rejecting them, in which the prophet has a role similar in authority to the accounts of anointing. These encounters are the designation of Jeroboam by Ahijah (1 Kings 11:26-40*) and his rejection by Ahijah (1 Kings 14:1-13*), the rejection of Ahab by Elijah (1 Kings 21:17-24*), and the commission given Jehu in the account of his anointing (2 Kings 9:1-13*). Despite considerable deuteronomistic editing, there are strong similarities binding these accounts together which are untouched by deuteronomistic thought or phraseology. Prominent among these similarities is the language: I will bring evil upon the house of X; I will consume the house of X; I will cut off from X every male, both bond and free; anyone belonging to X who dies in the city the dogs shall eat, and anyone who dies in the open country the birds of the air shall eat. There is nothing deuteronomistic in this strongly formulaic and richly metaphoric language. The accounts give the prophets the same role as in the anointings: they are God's instruments in the establishment and deposition of kings. In both sets of passages, actions are directly attributed to God: I (God) have anointed you, I will bring evil upon you, etc. The fact that both

and Kings. The detailed substantiation for what is said here will be found there, along with the full text of the Prophetic Record and two subsidiary documents.

sets overlap in the account of Jehu's anointing suggests that both come from the one source.

Thirdly, there are certain intervening passages in which the same thought and language is to be found. They are the rejection of Saul (1 Sam 15), an insertion in the story of the medium of Endor (1 Sam 28:17-19a), and the prophecy of Nathan (2 Sam 7:1-16). Taken in combination with the other two sets of observations, these point to a text edited in a prophetic circle interested in legitimating Jehu's revolution and his abolition of the worship of Baal in Israel (cf., 2 Kings 9-10).

When later material, both deuteronomistic and other, is omitted, and when material of southern or non-prophetic interest is put aside, a text remains that is coherent, structured, and that makes very good sense as the document originating from this northern prophetic circle, in the late ninth century. It begins with 1 Sam 1:1 and ends with 2 Kgs 10:28. In its first section, the figure of Samuel is established as a prophet, effective in all Israel (1 Sam 1-7*). The rest of the text is structured around the kings. There is Saul, anointed by Samuel and rejected by Samuel. There is David, anointed by Samuel, confirmed in his kingship by Nathan, and succeeded by his son Solomon. There is Jeroboam, designated as king by Ahijah and rejected by Ahijah. There is Ahab, rejected by Elijah. And there is Jehu, anointed by the disciple of Elisha, and commissioned to strike down the house of Ahab.

The prophetic claim is to have been God's instruments, guiding Israel's destiny from the beginning of the monarchy. They established Saul and replaced him with David. They made David the promise of a sure house, and they transferred this promise to Jeroboam (cf., 1 Kgs 11:38b). They rejected Jeroboam when he proved unfaithful and condemned Ahab who introduced foreign ways and foreign worship into Israel. So it was natural and right that they should anoint Jehu king and commission him to execute God's sentence against the house of Ahab. Jehu's commission does not specifically include the abolition of Baal worship. It is probable that the Prophetic Record was composed after this had been achieved. The task of the Prophetic Record, then, was to legitimate Jehu's revolution and the prophetic contribution to it, by placing it within the long history of prophetic guidance of Israel's monarchy.

There is reason to believe that this Prophetic Record was

expanded by a brief expression of judgment on each of the northern kings, from Jehu down to Hoshea and the fall of the north in 722. There is also a reasonable possibility that a brief account of the monarchy in the separate kingdom of Judah, from Rehoboam to Hezekiah, was composed under the influence of the Prophetic Record's example. The principal evidence for this northern expansion of the Prophetic Record and the analogous southern document is found in the variations in the formulaic patterns in which judgment is passed on each king. These judgments begin as a rule with the statement: He did what was evil or what was right in the eyes of the LORD. A very strong similarity binds together the judgment formulas for the northern kings, from Jehu to Hoshea: they did not depart from the sins of Jeroboam the son of Nebat, which he made Israel to sin. A different pattern of expression binds together the judgment formulas for the southern kings, from Rehoboam (Judah, cf., 1 Kgs 14:22a, 23a) to Hezekiah. A third pattern exists for the northern kings, from Jeroboam (Israel, cf., 1 Kgs 14:15-16) to Joram. This third pattern would derive from the Deuteronomist, when combining the Prophetic Record, its northern expansion, and the southern document into the unified text of the Deuteronomistic History.

The Prophetic Record is a quite remarkable document. It implies that the prophets—probably those associated with Elisha—at a critical time for Israel's survival as a believing people made a powerful political claim, which they substantiated by a sustained reflection on two centuries of Israel's history. Never before in the history of Israelite literature had there been such an intellectual achievement. Other documents spanned shorter periods of time or may have looked into the more distant past of Israel. The Prophetic Record is the first text in the history of Israelite literature to provide a structured account of Israel's existence in the promised land, from the late eleventh to the late ninth century. It covers a period of immense transitions: from the pre-monarchical era exemplified by Shiloh to monarchy and statehood; from a threatened, fledgling kingdom to a major power; from a united kingdom to divided states. On this diversity of time, situation, and tradition, the Prophetic Record imposed an ordered conceptual structure, with a unified picture of God's guidance in these events, and a clear sense of causation in the understanding of the role played by sin in the downfall of kings. It is an intellectual and literary achievement of considerable power.[46]

Those responsible for the Prophetic Record first set up the figure of the prophet, embodied in the person of Samuel. For the first time, a prophet is portrayed as having an authority recognized by all Israel (1 Sam 3:19-21). A huge claim is staked for this prophetic authority. Their claim was to have designated and rejected the kings of Israel, under God's guidance. The situation that called forth the claim was the threat to the faith of Israel posed by the rising influence of Baalism and the prophets of Baal. Under Ahab and Jezebel, his Phoenician queen, Baalism became a significant force in Israel. The clash of irreconcilable opposites is symbolized in the story of Elijah on Mt. Carmel (1 Kings 18). The political resolution of the struggle came in the rebellion of Jehu. Anointed by a disciple of Elisha, after a ruthless seizure of power, he "wiped out Baal from Israel" (2 Kgs 10:28).

Drawing on their traditions, of which we can perceive traces, the prophetic redactors legitimated their instigation of Jehu's revolt by painting a picture of the history of Israel's monarchy in which similar power was wielded by the prophets at critical moments. It is a fascinating claim, because it brings together prophetic word and political reality. Samuel anointed Saul, but the people made the victorious Saul their king (1 Sam 11:15). Samuel anointed David, but he was not spared the struggles and political difficulties of the rivalry with Saul, and eventually first the men of Judah anointed him their king (2 Sam 2:4) and then the elders of Israel anointed him as king over Israel (2 Sam 5:3). Ahijah designated Jeroboam as king, but again it was the political process of the assembly at Shechem which brought him to the throne (1 Kgs 12:1-20). Elisha's disciple anointed Jehu, but it was Jehu's political acumen and military ruthlessness which enabled him to seize and hold power (2 Kgs 9:14-10:17). In the Prophetic Record, the prophets make the claim that the trajectory of all this political and military activity was determined by the all-powerful word of God. Their claim was to perceive and name the action of God within the human realities of their world.

The prophetic word guided Israel in the establishment of the new institution of the monarchy. The prophetic word functioned continually to call the kings to account for their obedience before God. And the prophetic word not only raised its voice in effective protest against the radically destructive menace of Baalism, but also was responsible for instigating the revolutionary transfer of power which resulted in the extirpation of Baal worship from Israel.[47]

CONTRIBUTION TO THE DEUTERONOMISTIC HISTORY

The Prophetic Record had the task of setting up the figure of the prophet, in the person of Samuel, and then of organizing the history from Saul to Jehu around the figures of the principal kings. In this way, God's guidance, through the prophets, could be seen at work in the unfolding history of Israel, until Jehu's seizure of power and his purification of Israel from the threat of Baalism.

The contribution made by the Prophetic Record to the Deuteronomistic History may have been considerable. There is, first of all, the notion of conceptualizing the sweep of history under a single dominant idea: for the Prophetic Record, the prophetic word; for the Deuteronomistic History, the deuteronomic law. The Prophetic Record offered an example of history conceptualized in periods, in this case the grouping of traditions around each of the kings concerned. It constituted a solid core of already organized tradition, around which the Deuteronomistic History could be relatively easily composed. It provided the model of the prophet-king relationship, with the destiny of the king depending on obedience to the prophetic word. The focus in the northern expansion on the sin of Jeroboam, leading to the end of the northern kingdom, set the stage for the Deuteronomists to attribute the destinies which overtook Israel and Judah to the failures or fidelity of their kings. In the Prophetic Record, the rise and fall of kings were effected by the will of God, manifested through the prophets. These texts prepared the way for the Deuteronomists to review the whole history of Israel's life in the land under the criterion of the will of God expressed in the deuteronomic law. The interplay in the Prophetic Record between the pronouncement of the prophetic word and its realization in the reality of history may well have prepared the way for the deuteronomistic insistence on the pattern of prophecy and fulfillment as integral to the warp and woof of the fabric of Israel's history.

Today

A good story is seldom exhausted by a single understanding. In the many good stories which make up the sources of the Deuteronomistic History, there is much that asks for understanding and interpretation. They provide glimpses into human experience; they open up vistas on to Israel's theologians at work. For me, two reflections are especially valuable. One is the recognition that in Joshua 2-11 and Judges 3-9 particular insights are generalized to illuminate a broader canvas of human life. The other is the way in which divine action and human initiative are so intricately interwoven in Israel's narrative theology. In much of this theology, the power of God enters into partnership with human prowess.

INSIGHT

For most of us, the "long littleness of life" is illuminated by flashes of insight and is given continued depth and meaning by peaks of experience. From these moments, the whole takes on a fuller and grander reality. In the private sphere, memory and story can serve us well in giving permanence to what is often fleeting. In the public religious sphere, it is liturgy above all that has the task of celebrating and keeping alive that illumination for the believing community.

The work of Israel's narrator-theologians in Joshua 2-11 and Judges 3-9 seizes on moments of specific insight and broadens them out to apply to a whole understanding of Israel's life. What God had done at the Jordan and Jericho, celebrated in story and liturgy, was extended to the whole land that Israel occupied. It reflected, surely, not only on the land but also on the lives of those who lived in it. If the land was God's gift, then life is also gift from the hand of God and must be lived accordingly. There is a strong desire in us to "be like God" and determine our own destinies. But if our life is gift, then we are not the giver. The quality of our living is controlled by that insight. Along with the gift of life comes the even greater gift of a Creator's love—and that gives depth and meaning to life beyond all expectation.

Judges 3-9 functions in a similar way. Each of the deliverers has been empowered by God for their task. Only glimpsed in the Ehud story, this understanding receives full emphasis in the Gideon stories. The gathering together of the stories gives them force as paradigms. The framework that was put around them and the preface put before them both universalize these stories as examples of how God works in Israel. These are not chance occasions on which deliverance has been wrought. Rather, they are symbolic of how God can bring about deliverance from the trammels of oppression.

POWER AND PARTNERSHIP

It is surprising that the story of David and Goliath is so often read as the story of the small and apparently defenseless shepherd lad who, having no real hope in force of arms, must rely on God to bring victory over the gigantic enemy champion. God gives victory to the weak in order that the power of God may be manifest. Yet David's description of himself in the text makes it clear that he is far from small and weak. Gideon is portrayed having to whittle down his forces, lest Israel overlook God's role in their victory and boast that "my own hand has delivered me" (Judg 7:2). On the other hand, the recognition of God's role in Gideon's victory should not detract from the imaginative and daring guerrilla tactics that he used.

In the deliverer stories of Judges 3-9, human courage and initiative are at a premium. The story of David and Goliath is typical of the stories of David in the course of his rise to the throne of Israel: human weakness is not replaced by divine power; instead, the spirit of God has the role of empowering human beings to use their talents and prowess where timidity might have held them back. A similar understanding is present in the

Prophetic Record where the realization of the prophetic word or action still has to be worked out within the sphere of human history.

Such stories raise the theological question of which is the more helpful way to envisage divine-human relations. Is it more helpful to conceive of God supporting us by filling the gaps left by human weakness? Or is it more helpful to see God empowering us in the use of our talents and strengths? If David is the small and defenseless shepherd lad, then God is left to fill the gaps of his weakness. As an understanding of God, it is uncongenial and unsatisfactory. It can generate expectations of God which are demeaning for the creature and unfair for the Creator. It not infrequently leaves the image of God in considerable need of redemption. On the other hand, the theological understanding which is able to recognize that David was the right person with the right equipment for the task puts God in the role of partner. As partner, what God did for David was to enable him to do what he could do for himself, to do what already lay within his power but needed the spark of spirit to be achieved.

The enabling power of God can be spoken of in many ways. There is the power of basic trust, and the Old Testament speaks of a God who is worthy of trust. There is the power that comes from the acceptance of another's solidly deep commitment, and the Old Testament witnesses to a God who is deeply committed. There is the power that derives from the attraction and challenge of high ideals, and the Old Testament presents a God whose being and love can challenge us to the highest ideals of human living. The combination of basic trust and committed love with the challenge of high ideals is surely enabling and empowering for full human living.

RECOMMENDED FURTHER READING

IDEOLOGY OF CONQUEST

Brevard S. Childs, *Introduction to the Old Testament as Scripture,* 239-53. Philadelphia: Fortress, 1979.

Norman K. Gottwald, *The Tribes of Yahweh,* 191-233. New York: Orbis, 1979.

Gerhard von Rad, *Old Testament Theology,* 1.296-305. Edinburgh: Oliver and Boyd, 1962.

J. Alberto Soggin, *Joshua,* 7-18. London: SCM, 1972.

Manfred Weippert, *The Settlement of the Israelite Tribes in Palestine.* SBT 2/21. London: SCM, 1971.

EXPERIENCE OF DELIVERANCE

Childs, *Old Testament as Scripture,* 254-62.

James D. Martin, *The Book of Judges,* 1-15. CBC. Cambridge: University Press, 1975.

von Rad, *Old Testament Theology,* 1.327-34.

J. Alberto Soggin, *Introduction to the Old Testament,* 175-84. Philadelphia: Westminster, 1976.

ARK NARRATIVE

Antony F. Campbell, *The Ark Narrative (1 Sam 4-6; 2 Sam 6): A Form-critical and Traditio-historical Study.* SBLDS 16. Missoula: Scholars Press, 1975.

_____, "Yahweh and the Ark: A Case Study in Narrative," *JBL* 98 (1979) 31-43.

Patrick D. Miller, Jr., and J. J. M. Roberts, *The Hand of the Lord: A Reassessment of the "Ark Narrative" of I Samuel.* The Johns Hopkins Near Eastern Studies. Baltimore: Johns Hopkins, 1977.

STORY OF DAVID'S RISE

David M. Gunn, *The Fate of King Saul: An Interpretation of a Biblical Story.* JSOTSup 14. Sheffield: JSOT, 1980.

P. Kyle McCarter, Jr., "The Apology of David." *JBL* 99 (1980) 489-504.

Tryggve N. D. Mettinger, *King and Messiah.* Lund: Gleerup, 1976.

SUCCESSION NARRATIVE

Charles Conroy, *Absalom Absalom!: Narrative and Language in 2 Sam 13-20.* AnBib 81. Rome: Biblical Institute, 1978.

David M. Gunn, *The Story of King David: Genre and Interpretation.* JSOTSup 6. Sheffield: JSOT, 1978.

R. N. Whybray, *The Succession Narrative: A Study of II Sam. 9-10 and I Kings 1 and 2.* SBT 2/9. London: SCM, 1968.

PROPHETIC RECORD

Antony F. Campbell, *Of Prophets and Kings: A Late Ninth-Century Document (1 Samuel 1-2 Kings 10).* CBQMS 17. Washington: Catholic Biblical Association of America, 1986.

7

The Intention of
the Deuteronomistic History

Recommended preliminary reading

Before reading the body of this chapter, it would be helpful to reread the passages noted at the beginning of chapter 5.

We have seen the picture presented by Martin Noth of a masterful literary work, marshalling numerous sources, to present a grand outline of Israel's history in the land, structured into its significant periods, and all placed under a single overarching criterion, the deuteronomic law. What is the intention of this literary work? What message did it seek to communicate? What was the aim which inspired and guided its composition? For so clearly articulated a work, it would seem that these should be easy questions to answer. Surprisingly, they are not, and there is still considerable disagreement among scholars about them. Such disagreement is a fairly sure pointer to a complex text with a complex history of growth. Martin Noth's hypothesis of a unitary Deuteronomistic History will, in fact, prove to be an over-simplification. As we noted in chapter 5, a great deal of work has been done since Noth, and it now seems unlikely that the Deuteronomistic History emerged as the product of one person in the sixth century. It probably reached its present state in several stages.

232

Before touching briefly on the likely levels in the Deuteronomistic History, it will be helpful to review some of the classic answers that have been given to the question of its intention. As the first three of these address themselves to Noth's hypothesis without major modification, they apply to what is substantially the present text.

MARTIN NOTH

According to Martin Noth, the Deuteronomist sought to teach the true meaning of Israel's history from the conquest to the fall of Jerusalem in 587.[1] This meaning, as Noth understood it, was the perception of God's action in Israel's history, recognizable in God's response to increasing infidelity and apostasy by warning, by punishment, and finally by destruction. The Deuteronomist recognized in the fate of the nation, rather than of individuals, the just action of God. The Deuteronomist prefaced his work with Deuteronomy because it demonstrated the special role given Israel by God, and Israel's corresponding obligations. Above all, the deuteronomic law was aimed at preventing apostasy and achieving exclusive fidelity.

Noth points out that, in the time of the Deuteronomist, the idea of a new hope for the future was in the air (cf., Jeremiah, Ezekiel, Second Isaiah). For Noth, therefore, the absence of hope from the Deuteronomistic History indicates that the Deuteronomist clearly saw the judgment of God, manifested in the national collapse, as definitive and final. There is no expression of any hope for the future, not even in the simplest form of the hope for a gathering of the scattered exiles. The threat of exile is present (cf., for example, Deut 4:25-28 [note that vv 29-31 are considered to be later]; Josh 23:15b-16; 1 Sam 12:25). If some hope existed for the Deuteronomist, it would have been easy to express it. Yet all the Deuteronomist has is 1 Kgs 8:46-53—a plea to be heard and forgiven (vv 49-50) and to find compassion in the sight of the captors (v 50). There is no return or restoration here. According to Noth, 2 Kgs 25:27-30 does not suggest the dawn of a new hope,

---

[1]For what follows, see M. Noth, *The Deuteronomistic History* (JSOTSup 15; Sheffield: JSOT, 1981) 89-99.

for two reasons: it cannot itself be apt to carry such an interpretation, and there is nothing in the Deuteronomistic History to
prepare for such an interpretation.

Such hope, however, is expressed in Deuteronomy. It occurs in
Deut 4:29-31 and 30:1-10. But both passages are considered by
Noth to be later additions. In Deut 4:29-40, there is a change to
singular address and there is the reference to the conquest as a
past event (v 38). In Deut 30:1-10, there is a change in theology,
expressed in the promise that "the LORD your God will circumcise your heart and the heart of your offspring, so that you
will love the LORD your God" (v 6). The Deuteronomist took for
granted that Israel could obey: "But the word is very near you; it is
in your mouth and in your heart, so that you can do it" (30:14).
The metaphor of circumcision, in which God will change the
people's hearts, is much closer to the thought of Jeremiah (cf., Jer
31:31-34) and Ezekiel (cf., Ezek 36:22-32; 37:14). Noth argues that
since this expression of hope occurs in Deuteronomy alone, when
there was ample opportunity to insert such ideas in Joshua-
Kings, the passages must have been added when Deuteronomy
had been removed from the Deuteronomistic History and added
to the Pentateuch. As the canonical scripture of the post-exilic
community, it could scarcely conclude without an appropriate
expression of the hope promised Israel from other sources.

GERHARD VON RAD

Gerhard von Rad saw the matter differently.[2] On the negative
side, he was in substantial agreement with Noth. The Deuteronomistic History was Israel's confession that they had forfeited
salvation. The guilt was theirs; the fault was not God's. In this
confession, the Deuteronomistic History stood within a respectable theological tradition in Israel, referred to by von Rad as the
"doxology of judgment." So, for example, when Achan's sin is
about to be revealed, he is exhorted: "My son, give glory to the
LORD God of Israel, and render praise to him; and tell me now

[2]For what follows, see G. von Rad, *Old Testament Theology* (2 vols; Edinburgh: Oliver
and Boyd, 1962-65) 1.327-47; *Studies in Deuteronomy* (SBT 9; London: SCM, 1953)
74-91.

what you have done; do not hide it from me" (Josh 7:19). Or, early in the great confession of sin, attributed to David, we find the admission: "You are justified in your sentence, blameless in your judgment" (Ps 51:4). So von Rad sees the Deuteronomistic History as a massive and extended doxology of judgment on the part of Israel. In von Rad's view, the Deuteronomist also set great store by the fulfillment of God's word. In the destruction of Israel as a free and independent nation, the word of the covenant curse had attained its goal. Yet von Rad insisted on the positive side: there was the word of the Davidic covenant which was still open. The promise of salvation expressed in Nathan's prophecy was also God's word. It had yet to attain its goal.

Two quotations catch von Rad's position remarkably well.

> One has to appreciate the dilemma into which the Deuter-
> onomist was driven by the actual course of the history, in that
> it ended with the catastrophe of 587. On the basis of his
> theological presuppositions he had certainly no reason to
> lighten the darkness of this judgment. On the other hand, he
> could never concede that the saying about the lamp which was
> always to remain for David had now in fact "failed." As to any
> goal to which this saving word was coming he had nothing to
> say: the one thing he could do was just, in this direction, not to
> close the door of history, but to leave it open. This he did in the
> reflective conclusion of his work (II Kings XXV. 27ff.).[3]

Returning finally to this theme, von Rad expresses himself with powerful eloquence.

> In conclusion, we have once more to look at the question of the
> peculiar aim which the author of this great work has in mind.
> Is it likely that the sole purpose to be served by a work of such a
> comprehensive range was buttressing a theological judgment,
> namely that the calamity of the year 587 was just ("ge-
> rechtes"—as in justice) divine punishment, and would this
> word of explanation have been directed to a generation which
> Jahweh had in fact written off? It is much more likely that the

[3] Von Rad, *Old Testament Theology*, 1.343, n. 22.

purpose of all its theological expositions was to deliver to its contemporaries what is at bottom a simple religious message. In our historian's eyes the period of the Judges ended in disaster also. But the fact that Samuel delivered Jahweh's word of judgment (I. Sam XII) and Israel was about to enter on a totally different kind of existence did not mean that Jahweh had finally abandoned his people. The Deuteronomist's verdict on the great cleft made in 587 would have been similar. The determinative thing which Jahweh was now waiting for from Israel was "turning" (I Sam. VII. 3; I Kings VIII. 33, 35; II Kings XVII. 13, XXIII. 25). . . . Thus in our historian's view, the judgment of 587 did not mean the end of the people of God; nothing but refusal to turn would be the end.[4]

HANS WALTER WOLFF

The position advocated by Hans Walter Wolff takes the discussion a step further.[5] Wolff first of all parts company with von Rad, dismissing any hope based on the Davidic covenant. As he points out, whenever the Deuteronomist speaks of Nathan's prophecy to David, its fulfillment is made conditional upon obedience to the law of Deuteronomy. So, if the law has not been observed, the prophecy of Nathan can hold out no hope. However, for Wolff, 2 Kgs 25:27-30 makes it impossible to view the Deuteronomist's conclusion as intended to be the just and definitive judgment of God concluding the history of Israel. So, on this point, Wolff disagrees with Noth and moves in the direction indicated by von Rad. In Noth's view, there was nothing in the history to prepare for this final paragraph as an expression of hope. Wolff argues that the ground is prepared for this hope.

Wolff looks to the full sweep of the Deuteronomistic History to provide a clue to its intention. Why would the Deuteronomist have reached back to Deuteronomy and Moses, unless perhaps to show the pattern of apostasy, repentance, and forgiveness so strikingly evident in the period of the judges, but present also in

[4]Von Rad, *Old Testament Theology*, 1.346.

[5]For what follows, see H.W. Wolff, "The Kerygma of the Deuteronomic Historical Work," *The Vitality of Old Testament Traditions* (ed. W. Brueggemann and H.W. Wolff; 2nd ed.; Atlanta: John Knox, 1982) 83-100.

the transition to the monarchy. In Judges 2, "the LORD was moved to pity by their groaning because of those who afflicted and oppressed them" (v 18). In 1 Samuel 12, the people ask for Samuel's intercession, confessing their sin, and they receive Samuel's assurance (vv 19-22). "For the LORD will not cast away his people, for his great name's sake, because it has pleased the LORD to make you a people for himself" (v 22).

For the Deuteronomist's contemporaries, a third such moment in Israel's history has arrived. The pattern would indicate that, as in Judges 2 and 1 Samuel 12, Israel must confess its guilt and pray, if it is to be saved again. Wolff insists that if this is the message of the Deuteronomist, it would have to have been given prominence in the great interpretative speeches. The confession and prayer is summed up by Wolff in the theme of returning to God. This occurs first in 1 Sam 7:3. It is found then at 2 Kgs 17:13 and 23:25. Above all, it is a key part of the great prayer of dedication in 1 Kgs 8:33, 35, 46-53. So the Deuteronomist implies that what the exiles must do is "to turn back to Yahweh with all one's heart and all one's soul" (p. 93), to cry to the LORD. He gives no hope for what might occur, but a new era is not excluded. There is no programme of hope. There is simply the picturing of a situation in which one must turn to God and pray.[6]

FRANK MOORE CROSS

The position of Frank Moore Cross moves toward a synthesis of what has been considered so far.[7] Cross argues for two editions of the Deuteronomistic History. In his view, a first edition in the time of Josiah had two themes: the sin of Jeroboam, and the faithfulness of David. Thus, there is both threat and promise, and so a platform for the Josianic reform. "In this edition the themes of judgment and hope interact to provide a powerful motivation both for the return to the austere and jealous God of old Israel, and for the reunion of the alienated half-kingdoms of Israel and

---

[6]Note that for Wolff, Deut 4:29-31 and 30:1-10 are from a later hand in the deuteronomistic school. So they show how the school saw the call to repentance as central to the Deuteronomistic History ("Kerygma," 93-97).

[7]For what follows, see F.M. Cross Jr., *Canaanite Myth and Hebrew Epic* (Cambridge: Harvard University, 1973) 274-89.

Judah under the aegis of Josiah" (p. 287). A second edition in the time of the exile introduces a sub-theme: the sin of Manasseh is responsible for the demise of Judah. In this understanding, Cross seeks to draw together the threads of Noth, von Rad, and Wolff's positions.

> Little or no hint of inevitable disaster is found in the deuter-onomistic historian's framework and transitional passages in Joshua, Judges, and Samuel. Yet the Book of Kings and the Deuteronomistic history in its final form offer little hope to Judah, as Noth has correctly maintained. In the retouching of the original work by an Exilic hand, the original theme of hope is overwritten and contradicted, namely the expectation of the restoration of the state under a righteous Davidid to the remembered greatness of the golden age of David. Von Rad's instincts were correct in searching here for an element of grace and hope. The strange shape of the Exilic edition with its muted hope of repentance (as Wolff has described it) and possible return (Deuteronomy 30:1-10) is best explained, we believe, by the relatively modest extent of the Exilic editor's work and his fidelity in preserving intact the work of the Josianic Deuteronomist.[8]

SUBSEQUENT RESEARCH

Research into the Deuteronomistic History has continued with considerable intensity. It is not possible to discuss the various positions in detail. Frank Cross's two-edition theory was first proposed in 1968. It was supported by the work of R. D. Nelson, and has been widely adopted.[9] In 1971, Rudolf Smend pointed to the presence of later deuteronomistic editing in Joshua and Judges 1-2. He attributed this to a nomistically interested Deuter-

---

[8]Cross, *Canaanite Myth and Hebrew Epic*, 288.

[9]R.D. Nelson, *The Double Redaction of the Deuteronomistic History* (JSOTSup 18; Sheffield: JSOT, 1981), based on a 1973 thesis. Note also the extension of the implications of Cross's thesis to other areas: R.E. Friedman, *The Exile and Biblical Narrative: The Formation of the Deuteronomistic and Priestly Works* (HSM 22; Chico: Scholars Press, 1981) and Steven L. McKenzie, *The Chronicler's Use of the Deuteronomistic History* (HSM 33; Atlanta: Scholars Press, 1984).

onomist (i.e., one interested in the law, the *nomos),* whom he called DtrN. Smend's work was followed up by Timo Veijola for the books of Samuel and Walter Dietrich for the books of Kings. Their consensus was that an exilic Deuteronomistic History (perhaps c. 580) had been further edited by a Deuteronomist concerned with prophecy (= DtrP) and later again by a nomistically interested Deuteronomist (= DtrN, perhaps c. 560).[10] This position too has been widely supported. A valuable review of these developments is provided by A. D. H. Mayes, *The Story of Israel between Settlement and Exile.*[11]

At this point, it will be helpful to sketch the results of a comprehensive reevaluation of the Deuteronomistic History undertaken in a doctoral thesis by Mark O'Brien.[12] According to O'Brien, the basic Deuteronomistic History was written in Josiah's time, in support of the deuteronomic reform. It was perhaps influenced by the Prophetic Record in its emphasis on the role of the leader and on the prophet-king relationship in the latter part of the history. It is structured in three parts: Israel under Moses and Joshua (Deut 1:1-Judg 2:10); Israel from the Judges to the Monarchy (Judg 2:11-1 Sam 11:15); Israel under the Prophets and Kings (1 Sam 13:1-2 Kgs 23:23). Each of these periods is marked by a different form of leadership. In the section devoted to the monarchy, a four-part pattern is discernible in the treatment of those few kings who are viewed favorably, i.e., David, Hezekiah, and Josiah. Firstly, a critical event occurs during the reign of the king. Secondly, the king consults a prophet about what has occurred. Thirdly, a favorable prophecy is pronounced. Finally, a significant development follows which functions as a fulfillment of the prophecy. For David, it involved the entry of the ark into Jerusalem and the prophecy of Nathan; for Hezekiah, the threat

---

[10]For a recent summary by Smend, with bibliography, see R. Smend, *Die Entstehung des Alten Testaments* (2nd ed.; Stuttgart: Kohlhammer, 1981) 110-25. For the monographs of Dietrich and Veijola, see above, chap. 5, n. 6.

[11]A.D.H. Mayes, *The Story of Israel between Settlement and Exile* (London: SCM, 1983). See also Helga Weippert, "Das deuteronomistische Geschichtswerk. Sein Ziel und Ende in der neueren Forschung," *TRu* 50 (1985) 213-49.

[12]Mark A. O'Brien, O.P., *The Deuteronomistic History Hypothesis: A Reassessment* (D. Theol. thesis, Melbourne College of Divinity, 1987). I am particularly grateful to Fr. O'Brien for permission to quote from his thesis. It is to be published in the series Orbis biblicus et orientalis (Fribourg).

to Jerusalem and the prophecy of Isaiah; for Josiah, the discovery of the book in the temple and the prophecy of Huldah.

The overall thrust of this first edition of the Deuteronomistic History was to promote the deuteronomic reform undertaken by Josiah. So it intends to set up the deuteronomic law as Israel's guide, to interpret Israel's history in its light, and to bolster Josiah's reform by an emphasis on the consequences of observance of the three key deuteronomic criteria: fidelity to the exclusive worship of the God of Israel; fidelity to the centralization of this worship; fidelity to the relationship of prophet and king. The deuteronomic ideal had been realized at one stage in the reign of Solomon, with the construction of the temple. The ideal could be recaptured through whole-hearted commitment to the deuteronomic reform.

A major contribution by O'Brien is the identification in the subsequent development of the Deuteronomistic History of three redactional stages with fairly clearly marked cores, although allowing for some overlap at the edges. Firstly, probably early in the exile, the history was completed by a straight-forward account taking it from Josiah's death to the exile. It dealt with the reigns of the last four kings of Judah in a uniform and relatively limited way.

Secondly, the need was seen for an attempt to account for the death of Josiah and the subsequent exile of Judah in terms of deuteronomistic theology. The death of Josiah required some reshaping of Huldah's prophecy, separating Josiah's fate from that of the people. Responsibility for the exile was focussed on Manasseh, censured by the prophets and accused of causing Judah to sin, so that the exile was taken into the schema of prophecy and fulfillment (2 Kgs 21:10-15). A number of the additions concerned with prophecy and fulfillment may have derived from this second stage, tracing the reasons for Judah's fall back beyond Manasseh to earlier Davidic kings. While anti-monarchical, this redaction did not invalidate the promise of the Davidic dynasty. For this reason, it may be associated with the time of uncertainty connected with Jehoiachin's release into apparently favorable house arrest.

Thirdly, in the early post-exilic period, a further stage of editing involved a far more extensive revision of the history. This redactional work is marked by specific theological concerns and some identifiable characteristics of legal or nomistic vocabulary. In this revision, the blame for what happened to Israel and Judah is moved away from an exclusive focus on the kings and placed on the shoulders of the people. It is at this late stage that there is an insistence on the warning and guidance given the people in Deuteronomy 4 and 29-30, Joshua 23, 1 Samuel 12, 2 Kings 17:7-19, and also Judges 2:12-13, 17, 20-21, 23a; 6:7-10; and 10:10-16. These major redactional interventions transformed the Deuteronomistic History from a story of Israel's leaders to a story of the people and their ultimate failure to observe the deuteronomic law. The role of the prophets is transformed so that they become preachers of the law.

Alongside these identifiable stages of expansion, a number of other additions were made by the deuteronomistic circles. These do not appear to have had an overarching redactional purpose.

The validation of any such hypothesis lies in the way that it copes with and accounts for the phenomena in the key blocks of text involved. O'Brien's work makes a great deal of sense of a number of areas in which it has always been difficult to account for the text. It so happens that it accommodates the phenomena noted by Cross which point to a Josianic edition of the Deuteronomistic History. At the same time, there is a certain correlation between the three stages of redaction and the positions of the Smend school, especially in their concerns with prophecy and the law.

What is ironic about this proposal is that the speeches which identified the structure, which was heuristically so important to Martin Noth, emerge as the work of the final stage of redaction. While ironic, this should not be surprising. It is natural that the later generation saw with clarity the structure which the initial Deuteronomists sought to impose on Israel's history. It is not surprising that in their endeavor to bring out an underlying aspect of the history—the responsibility of the people—they should have inserted speeches or passages of warning and guidance at the appropriate places. The irony is only that the latest structural markers became the first heuristic pointers to the discovery of the Deuteronomistic History—and by this fact may have masked its original construction for quite some time.

CONCLUSION

The direction in which, in my judgment, matters are moving in research on the Deuteronomistic History suggests a blending of the insights of both the Cross and Smend schools of thought. A Josianic origin for the history seems highly likely. There is little doubt that the account of the last four kings of Judah is a separate expansion. A redaction which sought to extend the impact of the prophetic word within the history makes very good sense and accounts for many of the phenomena in the text. A redaction which reshaped the history in terms of the people's responsibility under the deuteronomic law also makes good sense of a number of passages. While this hypothetical model of the growth of the text may attract a consensus, there is little doubt that the attribution of a number of texts will have to remain uncertain. A deuteronomistic school clearly treasured and worked over the masterpiece of theological thought which we call the Deuteronomistic History. It is not surprising that some of their contributions cannot be clearly identified with one or another specific redactional stage.

The picture of the basic (Josianic) Deuteronomistic History is one of a great effort of intellect and faith to muster Israel's traditions behind a national reform. The traditions of Deuteronomy, Joshua, Judges, and the Prophetic Record were drawn on to provide the underpinning for a new upsurge of faith and hope. Hezekiah had shown that the downward trajectory of the kings could be halted. Josiah would show that the glories of the past could be retrieved. Behind this confidence and behind the appeal to the deuteronomic law lies the conviction of a God who was ready to overlook generations and centuries of failure in order to bring about blessing in Israel's midst.

With the failure of that hope, shattered by Josiah's death and laid to rest by his successors' apostasy, the deuteronomistic historians were confronted with the task of accounting for the disaster. One move was toward the political and religious sphere. The evil of Manasseh's reign had been so deeply rooted within the people that it had not been eradicated by Josiah's generation. This can be understood in the deuteronomistic language of God's great wrath (2 Kgs 23:26-27). It can also be understood in terms of the impact of Manasseh's policies on the people. The two understandings need not be so far apart.

Another move was to look back into the full sweep of the Deuteronomistic History and find there pointers to the possibility of the ultimate disaster. One aspect of this was to focus on the words of the prophets, which were understood to point clearly to the disastrous consequences of disobedience. The kings who followed Josiah failed to obey. The other aspect of this retrospective search was a focus on the deuteronomic law and a shift of emphasis to include the people's failure to obey among the causes of the catastrophe. In all of this, these later Deuteronomists maintain a strong faith in God's commitment to Israel along with a remarkable honesty in their appraisal of their nation.

Overall, then, there is a marked ambiguity within the Deuteronomistic History, across its total trajectory. Its original composition was imbued with the hope inspired by the Josianic reform. It then has to find the causes to be blamed for the failure of these hopes and the destruction of the nation. At the same time, avenues are left open for hope. The cycle of the Judges did not lead to despair; God's commitment could be counted on. It will be worth our while to explore something of the reason for this ambiguity, as well as identifying and circumscribing its limits.

The deuteronomistic theology itself contributes to this ambiguity. For better or worse, the deuteronomic reform movement and the deuteronomistic historians adopted a theology of blessing and curse. This may well have been taken over from the structures of the Assyrian treaties. The Assyrians were the major imperial power of the time; their dominance was not only military and political, but also cultural and economic. It would be expected that a smaller power would protect and bolster its own beliefs and cultural institutions by clothing them in the language or thought patterns of the dominant power. That may have been the origin of the deuteronomic theology's expression in terms of blessing and curse. While the Deuteronomists may have understood God to be unconditionally committed to Israel (e.g., Judg 10:15-16; 1 Sam 12:22), nevertheless, this commitment did not alter the realm of reality in which the consequences of Israel's actions were unfolded. For the Deuteronomists, if Israel held fast to the guidance it had been given—if it observed the law—its life would unfold in blessing. If, to the contrary, it violated the guidelines that had been given, its life would unfold in curse. The Deuteronomists were convinced of Israel's capacity to live in conformity with the wise guidance of the law (cf., Deut 30:11-14). But a person with the Deuteronomists' acquaintance with history would have had to have been equally well aware of Israel's all-too-human propensity for turning aside from the divinely appointed path. Therefore, Israel's fate is always, to some degree, in the balance. No matter how confident one may be of blessing, history is a reminder that curse may lurk around the corner. The Deuteronomists' constant concern with these two potentialities contributes to the ambiguity of the Deuteronomistic History.

In the light of these considerations, it is worth returning to some of the key points which have been built into the Deuteronomistic History over the course of its composition. They help to highlight the ambiguities of the present text, and are themselves illuminated when they are seen to reflect the processes of growth which the history had undergone in periods from Josiah's reform, through the exile, to the early post-exilic period.

Deuteronomy 1-3* was intended to situate the deuteronomic code within its apparent historical situation, resuming Israel's narrative from Sinai to the plains of Moab. Deuteronomy 4, on the other hand, places massive emphasis on the word of God's command, which Israel is to obey and which is to be found in the statutes and ordinances of the deuteronomic law. The danger of apostasy to the graven images of other gods is particularly stressed, with the threat of consequent exile. The possession of the land will be God's gift and therefore God's commandments must be obeyed. Similar concerns are visible in Deuteronomy 29-30.

The ninth-century story of the conquest had built upon the stories of the tribe of Benjamin to portray an occupation of the land in which God's action and God's will were paramount. This is the aspect which the Deuteronomists picked up in the preface to the conquest (Joshua 1). The land is God's gift to the people of Israel (v 2). It is God's power which will make Israel, under Joshua's leadership, irresistible (v 5). The later redaction balances this with an emphasis on Israel's obligation to observe the law (vv 7-9). The later redactor returns to these themes in the review of the conquest (Joshua 23). "You have seen all that the LORD your God has done to all these nations for your sake, for it is the LORD your God who has fought for you" (v 3). The theme of God's action on Israel's behalf is strong. Yet here the issue of the remaining nations surfaces, and with it the observance of the law (v 6). At first, it is part of the assurance of God's continuing assistance (vv 4-5). But then it becomes a threat to Israel. Intermarriage and apostasy loom as threats (v 7). Intermarriage will deprive Israel of God's help (vv 12-13); apostasy will trigger God's anger and Israel's exile (v 16). In the balance of blessing and curse, the curse is taking concrete shape.

The Deuteronomists' reflection on the transition of generations foreshadows difficulties in Israel's future. Those "who had seen all the great work which the LORD had done for Israel" (Judg 2:7) remained faithful to God all their lives. Those who came after them did not, for they "did not know the LORD or the work he had done for Israel" (v 10). There is an experience of God which can take deep root in human hearts and be a permanent guiding force in people's lives. But it is a difficult task to recreate that experience for another, whether another person or another generation. The Deuteronomists saw this in Israel's history. It bears an ominous foreboding for Israel's future.

To some extent, this is offset in the deuteronomistic interpretation of the Judges stories (Judg 2:11-19). Here the apostasy is reported and its consequences described. Whenever the people's apostasy led them into oppression, God came to the rescue, raising up judges to deliver them. This became the message of the collection of deliverer stories, once the framework was put in place. When the people cried to God, God raised up a deliverer for them. The Deuteronomists heighten the graciousness of this deliverance by omitting the element of Israel's crying to God; it would appear that it was enough that Israel was "in sore straits" (Judg 2:15).[13] While this would seem to be a sign of sure and certain hope, the Deuteronomists sound a note of warning after the Abimelech story. The people cry to God and their cry is rebuffed, "I will deliver you no more" (Judg 10:13). Israel repents, ignoring the rebuff, and the outcome is favorable. The later redactor has here created cause for both hope and anxiety. The fear has been spoken that God may not always deliver the people from the consequences of their actions. That is cause for anxiety. At the same time, the text portrays God as "indignant over the

---

[13]Wolff and others (*BHK* and *BHS*) emend the text, to insert "When they cried to the LORD" at the beginning of Judg 2:16 (cf., "Kerygma," 87 and n. 19). There is no textual support for this, so that it may be an arbitrary alteration to deuteronomistic theology.

misery of Israel," and that is cause for hope. The ambiguity is inescapable, because it is rooted in reality.

The conclusion to the transition to kingship contains the same ambivalence. While the original deuteronomistic presentation of this transition may have been favorable to the monarchy (O'Brien), in setting up the conditions for kingship, the later redactor gives voice to a sharp either-or: either "you will follow the LORD your God" (1 Sam 12:14), or "the hand of the LORD will be against you" (v 15). Yet the people's request for Samuel's intercession is met by his assurance that God will not abandon them (v 22). And it is balanced by the strong language of v 25, picking up the theme of v 15. The alternation of hope and threat may reflect the Deuteronomists' profound insight into the reality of the human condition before God. Given God's unconditional commitment, there is ground for hope. Given that Israel is responsible for its actions and must normally bear their consequences, there is ground for anxiety.

Solomon's prayer of dedication (1 Kgs 8:14-53) is situated at a high point of the Deuteronomistic History. The temple in Jerusalem, begun 480 years after the exodus from Egypt, is now completed and houses the ark of the covenant. There is an extraordinary sense of physical unity pervading this prayer. The temple is the place toward which God's eyes are to be open night and day (v 29), so that all Israel's prayer is directed toward this one place. Just as the Shema—"Hear O Israel: The LORD our God is one LORD; and you shall love the LORD your God with all your heart, and with all your soul, and with all your might" (Deut 6:4-5)—is an extraordinary spiritual unification of all of human life, providing a center and a core that radiates out upon the whole, so too the deuteronomic insistence on the centrality of the temple in Jerusalem is a remarkable endeavor to duplicate this spiritual unity in physical terms. The temple is to give a spiritual unity to all of Israel.

Yet in the midst of this, the knife-edge balance is still there. The Deuteronomists have Solomon pray that God's promise to David will be kept for the future, but a condition is present in the prayer: "if only your sons take heed to their way, to walk before me as you have walked before me" (1 Kgs 8:25). The prayers that follow, from a later hand, are double-edged: they assume God's forgiveness; they also assume Israel's sin. The opening and closing prayers of the first series of four place emphasis on human responsibility, on the correspondence of act and consequence. Condemn the guilty, bringing their conduct on their heads; vindicate the righteous according to their righteousness (v 32). Render to each, whose heart you know, according to their ways (v 39). Given the assumption of sin—if they sin against you, for there is no one who does not sin (v 46)—this insistence on the association of act and consequence looks to an uncertain future.

Immediately following the dedication of the temple, the Deuteronomists have God appear to Solomon (1 Kgs 9:1-9). At such a moment, we would expect a ringing endorsement of hope for the brave new future now ahead. Instead, it is remarkably muted. God replies to Solomon's prayer. The temple has been hallowed: I have put my name there for ever; "my eyes and my heart will be there for all time" (v 3). Yet where Solomon is concerned, the conditional aspect of the promise is to the fore (v 4), and the positive aspect receives only a verse (v 5). The later redactor devotes four verses to the negative aspect, going so far as to portray the exile from the land and the temple being reduced to a heap of ruins (v 7-8). When one compares vv 3 and 8, there is ambiguity indeed and contrasting theologies emerging from contrasting experiences.

The Deuteronomists' judgment on Solomon is handed down in 1 Kgs 11:1-13. It is negative. The fears of Joshua 23 have been realized. Intermarriage has led Solomon into apostasy. As a consequence, the kingdom will be divided; one tribe will remain to the Davidic dynasty, for the sake of David and Jerusalem (vv 11-13). Again the ambiguity. Solomon is punished, yet fidelity to David remains. In contrast to 9:6-9, there is no reference to exile or a final destruction. But an ominous enough note has been sounded. It is reinforced by the later deuteronomistic comment on the fall of the northern kingdom (2 Kings 17:7-23*).

One of the puzzling imbalances in the structure of the Deuteronomistic History is the absence of any comment on the fall of the south.[14] Even the concluding passage on the release of

---

[14]R.D. Nelson partially alleviates this by attributing 2 Kgs 17:7-20, 23b to his second editor. His reasoning is that, at the time of the Josianic reform, the fall of the north would have seemed a temporary setback, soon to be set right. When Judah and Jerusalem have fallen too, the situation of the north is seen as a fateful warning that went unheeded (see *Double Redaction*, 61-63).

Jehoiachin has its ambiguities. There is a ray of hope in the favorable treatment of Jehoiachin. It is dimmed by the sense of enduring inevitability, expressed in the repeated *tāmîd* ("always," 2 Kgs 25:29-30; *RSV*, "regular(ly)") and the references to "every day of his life" (v 29) and "as long as he lived" (v 30).

Perhaps a key to the later deuteronomistic understanding was given us in the interpretative passage, at midpoint in the period of the judges.

> "You have forsaken me and served other gods: therefore I will deliver you no more. Go and cry to the gods whom you have chosen; let them deliver you in the time of your distress." And the people of Israel said to the LORD, "We have sinned; do to us whatever seems good to you; only deliver us, we pray you, this day." So they put away the foreign gods from among them and served the LORD; and he became indignant over the misery of Israel. (Judg 10:13-16)

Today

Despite all the ambiguity we have been discussing, some themes stand out clearly. For the Deuteronomists, the deuteronomic law stood as the guide to Israel in its history and the criterion by which that history was to be judged. There is the evidence of God's unchanging commitment to Israel through the changing institutions of their national life. There is the Deuteronomists' evident conviction of God's will for Israel's good. The shadow side of this is the deuteronomic theology of blessing and curse, with the human propensity for incurring the latter.

There are certain fascinating social reflections. Among these, I would count the reflection on the transition of generations—the difficulty of communicating religious experience from one generation to the next. Then there is the concept of the sin of Jeroboam, of a structural sin that is built into the life of the community and that wreaks its havoc from generation to generation. It is the sin of institutions. There is the sin of Manasseh, the force of habit and weight of attitude and expectation, that has too much momentum to be stopped in a single generation of reform. There is the whole deuteronomic passion for centralization: the spiritual centralization expressed in the Shema, looking to the inner eye of the person; the physical centralization focused on Jerusalem and the temple, caught in the gaze of the eye of God.

There is also the deuteronomic theology of blessing and curse, balanced by the deuteronomistic insistence on sin and forgiveness. Blessing and curse are closely associated with the understanding of human acts which bring their consequences in their train. For us, there is a theological option. We may understand Israel's fate as decided by God's will, by divine judicial sentence. Or we may understand Israel's life as determined for good or evil by the wisdom of following God's guiding law or the folly of rejecting it. The language of the Deuteronomists, at one time or another, embraces both options. It is likely that, for the Deuteronomists, they were but two sides of the same coin. The Deuteronomistic History is a magnificent achievement as a literary work. Part of its greatness as a theological document is its refusal to give up on the ambiguity and inherent messiness of the human situation. The Deuteronomists may not always have seen grounds for clarity and hope. But, in their view, it would be unbelievable that one should give up on God.

If there is no particular word of God in the Deuteronomistic History from which an openness to the future can be derived, one has to fall back on the basic insight into the fundamental nature of God presented within the history. This is where its vast sweep makes such very good sense. God is portrayed guiding and warning the people, but never abandoning them. When they sin, God is always there waiting for their return. The commitment of God to Israel appears unconditional. Not that the aspect of curse is evacuated, but that the commitment of God is not broken by the people's breaches of the law. This is the message, above all, of the history of the judges. Within the movement into monarchy, there is the portrayal of God walking with the people in these profound institutional transitions, whether they are wise or not. Even when the Deuteronomists have God refuse any further rescue for the people, still Israel's misery moves God to compassionate indignation, and so they are delivered (Judg 10:10-16). It is this understanding of God which provided the basis for the call to reform under Josiah. It is this understanding of God which makes sense of the completion of so massive a work in the dark days of exile. It is right to see the possibility for hope latent within the Deuteronomistic History, for all that it deals unflinchingly with the tough realities of human sin and failure. At the base of it all, it portrays a picture of God who is "a merciful and gracious God, slow to anger and rich in kindness and fidelity, continuing his kindness for a thousand generations and forgiving wickedness and crime and sin; yet not declaring the guilty guiltless" (Exod 34:6-7, *NAB*).[15] It is this perception of a God who is ultimately unconditionally committed to Israel which makes sense of Israel's history and makes it possible for a literary work such as the Deuteronomistic History to have been written. The Deuteronomistic History is not the outcome of facile optimism or blank despair; it is the product of a nation's long experience and deep faith.

RECOMMENDED FURTHER READING

Frank Moore Cross Jr., *Canaanite Myth and Hebrew Epic*, 274-89. Cambridge: Harvard University, 1973.

Terence E. Fretheim, *Deuteronomic History*. Nashville: Abingdon, 1983.

A. D. H. Mayes, *The Story of Israel between Settlement and Exile*. London: SCM, 1983.

Martin Noth, *The Deuteronomistic History*. JSOTSup. 15. Sheffield: JSOT, 1981.

Robert Polzin, *Moses and the Deuteronomist: A Literary Study of the Deuteronomic History. Part One: Deuteronomy-Joshua-Judges*. New York: Seabury, 1980.

Gerhard von Rad, *Old Testament Theology*. 1.327-47. Edinburgh: Oliver and Boyd, 1962.

---

[15]The text goes on, "but punishing children and grandchildren to the third and fourth generation for their fathers' wickedness" (Exod 34:7) It can seem difficult to reconcile this with the forgiving of wickedness and crime and sin. In my understanding, what is present here is the recognition that acts have their natural consequences, whose reality is not taken away by either love or forgiveness; and that the deeds the fathers have done may have their effect on society for generations to come. The merciful aspect, at this point, is the limiting of those effects to the third and fourth generation, those generations which might live together as a single family.

Hans Walter Wolff, "The Kerygma of the Deuteronomic Historical Work." Chap. 5 in *The Vitality of Old Testament Traditions* edited by W. Brueggemann and H. W. Wolff. 2nd ed. Atlanta: John Knox, 1982.

The Pre-Exilic
Prophets

8

The Forerunners to the Emergence
of the Pre-Exilic Prophets in Israel

Recommended preliminary reading

Before reading the body of the chapter, it will be helpful to have
read the following passages:
Numbers 23:1-12
1 Samuel 3:1-21
2 Samuel 12:1-15a
1 Kings 11:16-40; 21:1-24

❧

The phenomenon of pre-exilic prophecy in Israel is particularly
remarkable in that it emerges in full flower with Amos in the
middle of the eighth century and concludes with Ezekiel in the
early sixth century. The major figures of pre-exilic prophecy—
Amos, Hosea, and Micah, Isaiah, Jeremiah, and Ezekiel—all
have a similar task to perform and operate out of similar
convictions. These convictions are sufficiently shared by their
audience to enable them to function and be heard. Such a cultural
phenomenon does not emerge in a vacuum. In order to understand these prophets themselves, and to understand how they
were understood in their own society, it is necessary to examine
their forerunners. Two aspects in particular will come out of this
examination: the conviction in Israel that prophets spoke the

word of God; the conviction in Israel that prophets came on the scene when the ordinary institutions of society were ineffectual.

BALAAM

The figure of Balaam is a fascinating one. The texts, Numbers 22-24, reach back into remote antiquity. The poems are thought to be earlier than the monarchy; a substantial part of the stories may be as early as the tenth century. Balaam is a foreigner. He was to be found at Pethor, near the Euphrates, in the Land of Amaw, in rough figures some 400 miles or 600 kilometers northeast of Israel. The scene of the stories is set on the brink of the promised land, with the people of Israel "encamped in the plains of Moab, beyond the Jordan at Jericho" (Num 22:1). This is Moabite territory, and Balak, the king of Moab, is portrayed as most unhappy at the presence of the intruders. He also feels powerless to do anything about it (22:3-4). So he sends off an embassy to Balaam, to hire him to curse Israel on Balak's behalf. The storyteller lets us know that Balaam has a reputation for being at the top of his profession; "for I know that he whom you bless is blessed, and he whom you curse is cursed" (22:6).

We might pause a minute here on this understanding of the power of the word. Clearly Balaam's word is understood to be effective of what it says: "he whom you bless is blessed, and he whom you curse is cursed." The classic formulation for this understanding in the case of God's word is given by Second Isaiah.

> For as the rain and the snow come down from heaven,
>   and return not thither but water the earth,
> making it bring forth and sprout,
>   giving seed to the sower and bread to the eater,
> so shall my word be that goes forth from my mouth;
>   it shall not return to me empty,
> but it shall accomplish that which I purpose,
>   and prosper in the thing for which I sent it. (Isa 55:10-11)

One will often hear it explained that "those people in those times" believed that the word of a spirit-person effectively changed reality. The phenomenon is thus attributed to a primitive mentality, or at least to a world-view far different from our own. The fact that the Hebrew word *dābār* can mean both "word" and "thing" is pointed to as evidence for this understanding, which, of course, makes it special to Israel. Whatever of other societies in which the magical word may flourish, it is worth being aware of the power of the word in our own society. In society as we experience it, the word has a power to effect what it signifies, to change reality. In a situation of general fear, a leader's words of courage can transform that reality. That is what we mean by inspiring leadership. We know, too, the power some people have to name a situation for what it is; they do not alter the reality of the situation itself, but in changing how it is perceived they have changed reality as a whole. Whether it is Cato's "Carthage must be destroyed," or Churchill's "We will never surrender," or Kennedy's "Ich bin ein Berliner," or King's "I have a dream," words have a power to effect reality. Since Dante and Shakespeare wrote, reality has never been the same. In Israel and other cultures, this perception may have been enhanced and taken further. We will be unsympathetic to the phenomenon, if we do not see the roots that it has in our own understanding of the world.

Back, however, to Balaam. The storyteller goes to great pains to make it absolutely clear, beyond any possible doubt, that the only word Balaam can speak is the word which God gives him. First of all, there is the episode of the embassy. The messengers arrive, money in hand, and give Balaam the message from Balak. Instead of giving them an answer, Balaam has to wait for God's will to manifest itself, during the course of the night. And God's answer is negative; Balaam is not to go with them. "You shall not curse the people, for they are blessed." With that message, the disappointed embassy returns to Moab (Num 22:7-14). The narrative then has the king of Moab send off a second embassy to make a more impressive offer to Balaam. Again Balaam waits for the word of God at night, and this time he is allowed to go, but on one condition: "But only what I bid you, that shall you do" (22:20).

At this point in the present text, which is a composite one, we have the story of Balaam's ass. It is an independent story, and one in which clearly Balaam was going without God's blessing. The angel of God, therefore, stood over against Balaam with drawn sword. Throughout the little story, the ass is perceptive and

Balaam blind. The ass turns off the road into the field, and gets beaten for it; the ass moves to the side of a narrow road and squeezes Balaam's foot against the stone wall, and gets beaten for it; and finally, with no place to go and the angel of God dead ahead, the ass just lies down, and gets beaten again. Stories do things in threes, so with this third occurrence, the ass speaks up and calls Balaam to his senses. The angel of God then makes himself known. The outcome of the story is identical with the result of the second night vision. Balaam is told, "Go with the men; but only the word which I bid you, that shall you speak" (22:35).

The story of the embassies and the story of the ass present different pictures of Balaam. In the first, he would not move without first ascertaining God's will. In the second, he apparently moved prematurely and had God's will brought home to him on the road, in the encounter with the angel of God. However, the message in both stories is identical: Balaam can only speak the word that God gives him to speak. That is why the two contrasting stories are set side by side. Now, when Balaam reaches Moab, the same message is expressed a third time. The king of Moab complains of Balaam's delay in coming. Balaam's reply could be paraphrased, "Now that I am here, you are no better off." The reason is: "The word that God puts in my mouth, that must I speak" (22:38). So, in three separate ways, the narrative has made abundantly clear that the word Balaam will speak is God's word and only God's word.

The reason for this insistence will be seen as the narrative continues: Balaam does in fact speak God's word and Balak is taken by surprise. As in any good storytelling, it will happen three times. Balak and Balaam go up to a high point, Bamoth-baal (literally: the high place of Baal). There Balaam has seven altars built, with a bull and a ram sacrificed on each. Then Balaam goes aside and is met by God, "and the LORD put a word in Balaam's mouth, and said, 'Return to Balak, and thus you shall speak'" (23:5). Balaam returns and speaks his word, and it is practically a blessing. When Balak remonstrates with him, Balaam replies, "Must I not take heed to speak what the LORD puts in my mouth?" (23:12). The point is made for the first time.

Balak has a lot invested in this, and the storyteller is not going to spoil a good story by cutting it short. So a second attempt is

made, this time from the top of Pisgah. Again the sacrifices, again
the encounter with God, and again the word put in Balaam's
mouth and the same instruction (23:16). The second word is more
emphatic than the first. In the course of the first oracle, Balaam
said, "How can I curse whom God has not cursed?" (23:8) In the
second, it is, "Behold, I received a command to bless: he has
blessed, and I cannot revoke it" (23:20). Again Balak expostulates,
and again he gets the same reply: "Did I not tell you, 'All that the
LORD says, that I must do'?" (23:26). The point is made for the
second time.

The third attempt is made from the top of Peor. Balak is
portrayed as aware that God is in control of the word being
spoken. He hopes that God may relent: "Perhaps it will please
God that you may curse them for me from there" (23:27). Balaam
knows better than that, and this third time he does not need to go
off to look for omens. He speaks his blessing on Israel, ending in
the formula that was picked up for Genesis 12:3, "Blessed be every
one who blesses you, and cursed be every one who curses you"
(24:9). Balak explodes in anger. Balaam makes the rejoinder that
he had told Balak's messengers that he would not be able to go
beyond the word of God; "what the LORD speaks, that will I
speak" (24:13). The point has been made for the third time. And
then, for good measure, he pronounced a fourth favorable word
over Israel (24:15-24). And then he went home.

There is a very good reason for this massive insistence in the
stories on the divine origin of Balaam's word. Whether as
independent stories, or as the conclusion to the Yahwist's narrative, Balaam's blessing is immensely important. Israel is on the
brink of crossing the Jordan. Like Jacob before the crossing of
the Jabbok (Gen 32:22-32), Israel is poised before the promised
land. With the crossing, life will change. So the blessing comes at
a significant moment. Hence the emphasis that this word of
blessing comes from God and from God alone. Whatever the
reasons for the emphasis, it allows us to see Israel's conviction
that the prophet spoke God's word.

This was not a naive conviction. Israel was well aware that false
prophets were about who spoke their own word, not God's. The
question of discernment between prophets is at the center of

several of Israel's stories.[1] The question of knowing the word
which God has spoken or, conversely, "How may we know the
word which the LORD has not spoken?" (Deut 18:21), is one
which must have been often discussed in Israel. From the different answers given, it is clear that Israel was well aware that
there is no simple answer to such questions. We will look more
closely at this a little later. For the moment, it is enough to
recognize that, despite all the uncertainty, Israel was convinced
that when the prophets spoke truly, they truly spoke God's
world.

The last two poems of Balaam begin with three formulaic lines
that are almost a prophetic self-description. The claim is a very
striking one. The prophet is one who hears the words of God,
who knows what the Most High knows, and who sees what the
Almighty sees, (24:4, 16). The impression given is of an ecstatic
trance; the claim made could hardly be higher. For Jeremiah, the
prophet stands in the council of God to perceive and to hear
God's word, to give heed to God's word and listen (cf., Jer 23:18).
The understanding is the same: the prophet has intimate access to
the mind of God. It is all the more striking that Israel has
canonized this claim on the part of a non-Israelite prophet. The
Balaam stories are a witness to the universal power of God and to
the prophetic claim to speak God's word.

SAMUEL

Samuel is the first great prophetic figure within Israel itself.
As we mentioned in passing, when discussing the Prophetic
Record earlier, it is quite possible that some of the elements in
the picture of Samuel have been painted by the authors of the
Prophetic Record, late in the ninth century. Since this is still well
before the emergence of the pre-exilic prophets, it will suit our
purposes here to look principally at the figure of Samuel as it is
portrayed in the pre-deuteronomistic texts.

Samuel has the image of a figure of national status. This is a

---

[1]In this context, two monographs are particularly helpful: J.L. Crenshaw, *Prophetic
Conflict* (BZAW 124; Berlin: de Gruyter, 1971); S.J. De Vries, *Prophet against Prophet*
(Grand Rapids: Eerdmans, 1978).

little puzzling, as nothing is reported which might justify such status. Samuel comes to Shiloh as a newly weaned child (cf., 1 Sam 1:22-28). The notices concerning Samuel, interspersed between the anti-Elide passages, are repetitive and not very informative about Samuel himself. "Samuel was ministering before the LORD" (2:18); "and the boy Samuel grew in the presence of the LORD" (v 21); "and the boy Samuel continued to grow both in stature and in favor with the Lord and with men" (v 26); "and the boy Samuel was ministering to the LORD under Eli" (3:1); "and Samuel grew, and the LORD was with him and let none of his words fall to the ground" (v 19). The three occurrences of "boy" translate *na'ar,* which can range from an infant to an adult, according to the context. But prior to the report that none of Samuel's words fell to the ground (v 19), the only tradition we have about Samuel is the revelation he received at Shiloh directed against the Elides (3:2-18). This he told Eli, and then only on Eli's express demand. The episode hardly seems sufficient to catapult Samuel to national prominence.

Yet national prominence is what he is portrayed as enjoying. "All Israel from Dan to Beer-sheba knew that Samuel was established as a prophet of the LORD.... And the word of Samuel came to all Israel" (3:20-4:1a). This particular statement of Samuel's status may derive from the redactors responsible for the Prophetic Record, establishing from the outset the figure of the prophet. In 1 Samuel 7, it is likely that vv 2b, 5-6a, 7-12, at least, are pre-deuteronomistic. The issue of Samuel's judgeship is much more difficult to situate. The pre-deuteronomistic verses, however, provide a picture of Samuel as a figure of national significance.

The story of the anointing of Saul is of major importance.[2] Here Samuel is portrayed as the direct instrument of God, designating a man to be the future king of Israel. The immediacy of the prophet as instrument of God is fascinating. Samuel does not say, "Have not I anointed you" or "Has not the LORD

___

[2]Whatever the age of the various traditions involved may be, I am inclined to see the picture of the Samuel who puts up resistance to the notion of kingship as the work of the Deuteronomists. So 1 Sam 8; 10:17-27; and 12 will not be taken into account at this point. They would not make any fundamental change in the picture. Note that, according to the work of Mark O'Brien, the Josianic Deuteronomist is not unfavorable to kingship in these passages; the opposition to God's will is stressed by the later deuteronomistic redaction.

commanded me to anoint you," but "Has not the LORD anointed
you" (10:1). The anointing is immensely significant. It claims to
set up a process which will fundamentally change the national
structures of Israel, from a tribal organization to a national
monarchy. One tends to assume that this action would also
point to Samuel's having enjoyed national prominence. However
that need not be the case. The figure of Samuel, in 1 Sam
9:1-10:16, appears to have been grafted on to that of an older
and unnamed man of God. This man of God gave Saul a
prophetic commission, which led to his demonstration of valor
in the relief of Jabesh-gilead, and so to his establishment as king.
If the unnamed local seer could do this, there is no reason why
Samuel would have needed national status to anoint Saul. The
anointing of Jehu, for example, was the work of one of Elisha's
disciples. For all that, the act itself is highly significant and
stakes a claim to an authority of the highest level.

Surprisingly enough, in the coronation of Saul at Gilgal,
Samuel is not given a major role. It happens at his instigation
(11:14), but that is all. There is no mention explicitly of any
further part that Samuel played.

The next major passage is a very significant one (1 Samuel 15).[3]
Samuel is depicted revealing to Saul a word of God on a matter of
national policy: a war of extermination against the Amalekites.
And Saul is portrayed as accepting that word as a matter of
course. This puts the prophet, at least in the role of God's
instrument, in a position practically superior to that of the king
himself. When Saul fails to carry out his orders to the letter,
Samuel rebukes him for the violation and communicates his
rejection as monarch.[4] The phrase has become classic: obedience

---

[3] 1 Sam 13:7b-15a is secondary in its context and paints the same sort of picture of
Samuel as 1 Samuel 15.

[4] Samuel's confrontation with Saul over this incident is a narrative gem. In the report of
the expedition, it is said that Saul and the people spared Agag and the best of the spoil
(15:9). When Samuel and Saul meet, Saul volunteers, "I have performed the commandment of the LORD" (v 13). Samuel asks about the sounds of sheep and cattle he can hear.
Saul replies, in a vain attempt at ingratiating diplomacy: *they* (indeterminate) have
brought them along; for *the people* (slipping out of his own responsibility) spared the best,
to sacrifice to the LORD, *your* God (ingratiating himself with Samuel). The final
"everything else we destroyed" has Saul including himself in the good deed, blithely
bypassing the fact that the order was to destroy everything (cf., vv 14-15). When Samuel
renews the charge, Saul makes a classic attempt at evasion: I obeyed, I went on the

is better than sacrifice (v 22), followed by, "Because you have rejected the word of the LORD, he has also rejected you from being king" (v 23). This story puts the prophet in the exalted role of being God's instrument for the establishment and deposition of kings.[5] This is heightened by the immediately following story of the anointing of David in Saul's place.

Finally, the story of the medium of Endor points to the significant role of Samuel as prophet (1 Samuel 28). Saul is about to engage in a national life-and-death struggle with the Philistines. The figure the king wants to consult is Samuel. Vv 17-19a are most probably a prophetic insertion, since they refer back to the concerns of the Prophetic Record in 1 Sam 15:1-16:13. Nevertheless, without that, Samuel is still the figure Saul seeks to consult and the message he delivers is fundamentally the same.

Overall, then, whether at the level of the Prophetic Record or at the level of the earlier stories, Samuel is portrayed as a prophet with authority and prominence in Israel. His prophetic stature is sufficient to enable him to give God's orders on matters of national policy as well as to rebuke the king severely and publicly. To this, the prophetic redactors have added the task of anointing and rejecting kings. Even if it is a composite picture, it is one of very considerable authority within the nascent Israelite monarchy.

GAD

Gad is an interesting figure insofar as he is the only one amongst these early prophets who has kept a pretty low profile.[6] He was with David in the early days of the guerrilla band in the

---

mission, I brought Agag (made to sound like an achievement instead of disobedience), and I utterly destroyed the Amalekites (which is true, since Agag has already been mentioned and the sheep and cattle are not Amalekites). After this litany of his own obedience, Saul tries again to evade his responsibility: but *the people* took the best of the spoil, to sacrifice to the LORD *your* God (cf., vv 20-21). This is storytelling in the tradition of Gen 3:11-13.

[5]This role in 1 Samuel 15 is very closely associated with the whole theme of anointing, and it is almost certainly the work of the prophetic redaction. Even so the older story (vv 1*, 2-9, 13-15, 17a, 18-22, 24-25, 31-34 (35a) still has Samuel rebuke Saul, and also slay his royal captive in the very public situation of the Gilgal sanctuary. Such a public rebuke attributes high standing and independence to the prophet.

[6]Gad would also appear to be the only one whose image has not been touched up by the redactional activity of those responsible for the Prophetic Record.

wilderness of Judah, when "every one who was in distress, and everyone who was in debt, and everyone who was discontented, gathered to him; and he became captain over them" (1 Sam 22:2). The only information we have on Gad, from this period, is that he advised David not to remain in the stronghold but to go into the interior of Judah (22:5). David's stronghold was close to the Philistine border; Gad suggested pulling back to well within Judah's boundaries. The text gives no indication as to the origin of this strategic advice. Was it a word from God, or Gad's own instinctive strategic sense, or the result of some intelligence gathering in the area? Did it come from Gad as prophet or Gad as private individual? We do not know.

Gad appears again in the rather mysterious story of 2 Samuel 24. Gad is described as "David's seer" (24:11). When David is in trouble with God over his census taking, Gad is sent to present David with God's options (vv 12-14). When the plague stops at Araunah's threshing floor, Gad comes to David again to tell him to build an altar to God at that place (vv 18-19). And there, just outside Jebusite Jerusalem, David built his altar. Gad is a gentle reminder of the figures around the king of whom we see and hear little, a reminder of all the activity in Israel that has never reached our texts. As prophet, his exercise of the messenger function is intriguingly literal. Not only does he bring God's message to David, but he must take back David's answer. "Now consider, and decide what answer I shall return to him who sent me" (v 13). While he had unpalatable options to present to David, nevertheless his role appears to have been one of cooperation rather than confrontation.

NATHAN

Nathan is another prophet at David's court. He appears in the text three times. The first time, he gives his assent to David's proposal to build a temple; he then has to tell David that God declines the temple, but that instead it is God who will build a sure dynasty for David (2 Samuel 7). The second time, he confronts David with his crime of adultery compounded by murder (2 Samuel 12). And the third time, he is part of the palace intrigues which determine whether Adonijah or Solomon will manage to succeed to David's throne (1 Kings 1). Beyond these three occasions, for all we know of David's court with its comings and goings, there is no more mention of Nathan than there is of Gad. While the priests, Abiathar and Zadok, for example are mentioned in the lists of officials (cf., 2 Sam 8:15-18; 20:23-26; 1 Kgs 4:1-6) and on other occasions, the prophets are passed over in silence. This may be simple chance. We know nothing, for example, of Ira the Jairite, who was also David's priest (2 Sam 20:26). On the other hand, it may indicate something of their status or their style. It would be consonant with their appearing when needed or sent, rather than residing at or frequenting the court. But again, we do not know.

Rather than Nathan, the court prophet of 2 Samuel 7, or Nathan, the prophet caught up in palace factions of 1 Kings 1, it is the Nathan of 2 Samuel 12 who points to a direction that will be important to later prophecy. In this, he is following in the footsteps of Samuel in his rebuke of Saul. We need to recall the story briefly. It is told in 2 Samuel 11, and it does nothing to spare David's reputation. Uriah is out of town with David's army. His wife takes a bath rather too openly, and David takes a fancy to her rather too passionately. He commits adultery; she becomes pregnant. David summons Uriah from the front, to have him spend a couple of nights' leave in the marital bed that David had violated, and so cover David's tracks for him. Uriah demurs. So David cold-bloodedly has him killed. The strategy costs the lives of some of David's soldiers as well, but no matter. "Do not let this matter trouble you, for the sword devours now one and now another" (2 Sam 11:25). When Bathsheba's mourning was over, David made her his wife, and she bore him their son. "But the thing that David had done displeased the LORD" (11:27).

So God sends the prophet Nathan to the scene. Nathan tells David his parable of the rich man with extensive flocks, and the poor man with one ewe lamb that was like a child to him. The rich man had a visitor to entertain, and instead of killing one of his own flock, he slaughtered the poor man's lamb and served it to his guest (2 Sam 12:1-4). David reacts with anger, menaces death, and decrees fourfold compensation. But Nathan cuts him off, with a single line that echoes still: you are the man (12:7).

Two aspects are significant here: the prophetic role, and the punishment prophesied. The king is the highest instance of justice in the nation. When the king commits crime, there is no higher tribunal to which to appeal. In these circumstances, the prophet appears on the scene, sent as God's intermediary, to confront the king with the judgment of a higher authority. When the unfettered power of the monarchy is taken into account, it says a great deal about the fundamental attitudes among the people that a prophet could even be portrayed standing in condemnation before his king. The only grounds on which that portrayal can be based is the conviction that the prophet speaks a word that is not his own, on an authority that is not his own. The prophet is understood to speak God's word, on God's authority. It is with this understanding that the later prophets will speak to the people as a whole.

It is widely held that the material in vv 7b-12 is an expansion of Nathan's speech to David. In that case, Nathan's "You are the man" would have been followed by David's confession, "I have sinned against the LORD" (v 13). With surprising abruptness, Nathan assures David that God has forgiven his sin and his life will be spared, although the child of his adultery will die. There are two sets of tensions here. One is between Nathan confronting the guilty David with his sins and the same Nathan so promptly extending to David God's forgiveness, with only David's confession as a mediating factor. The other is between the mercy of God shown to the repentant David and the harsh fate of the child. These tensions are not easily resolved; we can only hint at possibilities here. Perhaps there are two basic convictions being held in tension. One is the conviction of God's love, which longs to forgive. The immediacy of David's confession opens the way to immediate forgiveness. The other is the conviction that in many cases human actions have inevitable consequences, which are not eliminated by forgiveness. Why the death of the child should be picked out as such a consequence defies explanation, unless it reflects the historical reality of the child's death.

For an understanding of prophetic theology, it is the intervening verses, vv 7b-12, which are enlightening. Here the conviction that many human actions have inevitable consequences comes to the fore. There are basically two prophetic utterances which have been inserted here, one in vv 7b-10 and the other in vv 11-12. The first has its emphasis on David's responsibility for the death of Uriah by the sword. As a consequence, "the sword shall never depart from your house" (v 10). This reflects the fate of David's own children. His eldest son, Amnon, will fall to the sword of his brother Absalom (2 Sam 13:20-29); Absalom himself will die ingloriously in the course of his rebellion against David (2 Sam 18:9-15); Adonijah too will die, a victim of his brother Solomon's despotism (1 Kgs 2:13-25). The second utterance (vv 11-12) picks up the crime of David's adultery, unmentioned in the other. The episode in which Absalom makes the breach with his father irrevocable (2 Sam 16:20-22) is portrayed as the consequence of David's sin. In his private life, David has been guilty of sexual and homicidal transgression. In the public life of his kingdom, David's family will be pursued by sexual and homicidal violence.

Here there is evidence for the widespread conviction in Israel that human acts have their inevitable consequences. There are two ways, at least, of understanding this conviction. One attributes the consequences to the judicial act of God, judging the sinner guilty and apportioning the penalty. The other attributes the consequences to the order of the universe, imprinted within it by God at creation and sustained still by the creator, but not requiring or involving divine judicial intervention. We will look more closely at this issue when we discuss the theology of the prophets. It is as well to be aware of it now, so that we do not attribute too naively interventionist a view to the prophetic proclamation. In this particular case of David, there is another factor at work. The behavior and well-being of the king is reflected in the fate and well-being of his people. This is a belief shared by the surrounding peoples and present, too, in Israel. So it is all the more likely that the behavior of the king will have its repercussions on the broader level of the nation.

AHIJAH

Ahijah of Shiloh appears in the biblical text twice, functioning in totally private contexts, yet performing acts of major significance for the history of Israel (1 Kgs 11:26-40; 14:1-18). The first story tells of an encounter between Ahijah and Jeroboam, alone in the open country outside Jerusalem. Jeroboam was an able and energetic man to whom Solomon had given responsibility for the forced labor from northern Israel used in Solomon's construction projects. Ahijah goes through the symbolic action of tearing his garment into twelve pieces and giving ten of these to

Jeroboam. In a prophetic speech, Ahijah interprets this sign for Jeroboam. The ten pieces of the garment are a sign that God will establish Jeroboam as ruler over ten of the tribes of Israel.[7]

The importance of the act and the claim it embodies can hardly be overemphasized. Ahijah claims, as God's intermediary, the authority to transfer to Jeroboam the legitimacy and the divine promises given to David (1 Kgs 11:37, 38b). The kingdom over which God had established David is now to be broken up and divided in two. The lion's share is to be given to Jeroboam; only a rump is left to the dynasty of David in Jerusalem. And the guarantee of a sure house, once given David by the prophet Nathan, is now given Jeroboam by the prophet Ahijah. The prophetic story claims for the prophets the authority and responsibility for the division of the united kingdom of Israel.

What makes this case particularly interesting is that the text also gives us the story of how this prophetic word was realized in history. In 1 Kgs 12:1-20, the division of the kingdom after Solomon's death is narrated. The fate of the kingdom is depicted turning on the sole issue of the burden of labor and tax policies. In 1 Kgs 11:26-40, we have the theological view, advanced by the prophets. In 1 Kgs 12:1-20, we have the political account, now put forward as the realization of the prophetic word in history.

The second Ahijah story attributes equal authority to the prophet, even if the consequences are not quite so nationally momentous (1 Kgs 14:1-18). Jeroboam's wife is sent by the sick king to consult the aged Ahijah. His prophetic power is indicated by his recognition of the disguised woman. His word to her for her husband gives God's judgment on the king. Jeroboam's infidelity will cost him his kingdom. His dynasty will not retain control of the kingdom of northern Israel. It will be wiped out and replaced by another. As God's intermediary, the prophet claims the authority to elevate and depose kings. And in the narrative, the course of events validates the prophetic claim.

In these stories, the prophet is portrayed standing not merely over the king but also over the nation. They are fitting forerunners to the figures of the classical prophets to come.

---

[7]On the text itself, see A.F. Campbell, *Of Prophets and Kings: A Late Ninth-Century Document (1 Samuel 1-2 Kings 10)* (CBQMS 17; Washington: Catholic Biblical Association of America, 1986) 25-32.

ELIJAH

The status of the prophet as one able and obliged to confront the king, when he is guilty of wrongdoing, is confirmed in one of the great stories about Elijah. It is the story of Naboth's vineyard (1 Kings 21). Summarized briefly, it is the story of Naboth who has land adjoining the royal garden, which Ahab, the king, would like to purchase to extend his property. Ahab makes Naboth a reasonable offer: a cash deal, or an exchange of equivalent land (21:2). Naboth turns the king down. His reason, "The LORD forbid that I should give you the inheritance of my fathers" (v 3), suggests the conviction that the land has been distributed among the people by God, the owners are therefore stewards of the land that is ultimately God's, and trafficking in real estate is for that reason out of the question. (Cf., Lev 25:8-34, where the jubilee legislation points to a similar understanding.) Ahab, influenced by Jezebel, his Phoenician queen, commits judicial murder so that he can take over Naboth's land. At that point, enter the prophet Elijah.

Like Nathan, Elijah is sent by God. He is to confront Ahab and say: "Thus says the LORD, 'Have you killed and also taken possession?' Thus says the LORD, 'In the place where dogs licked up the blood of Naboth shall dogs lick your own blood' " (21:19).[8] Here again, royal wrongdoing is confronted by prophetic condemnation. Ahab's evil is particularly grave, because it has involved the judicial system. It is corrupting justice at its source. Justice, in the towns of Israel, was administered by a meeting of the citizens of the town, in the open space at the gate. Under royal pressure, Naboth's fellow citizens have betrayed him and breached the solidarity that members of a community owe to one another. According to the text as it stands, Jezebel sent her letters to the elders and the nobles, so that they were all in the know, guilty of complicity in the corruption of justice. The text lays ironic

---

[8]The repetition of the introductory phrase, "Thus says the LORD," suggests that two pungent prophetic sayings have been juxtaposed here. The figure of Elijah is a towering one in the landscape of Israel's prophecy and there has been considerable accumulation within the tradition. Another saying from this occasion, which must be old and probably circulated independently, is preserved in v 20: "Ahab said to Elijah, 'Have you found me, O my enemy?' He answered, 'I have found you.'" There is here the same terseness as Nathan's "You are the man."

emphasis on this breach of citizenly solidarity: Jezebel wrote to the elders and nobles "who dwelt with Naboth in his city" (v 8); "and the men of his city, the elders and the nobles who dwelt in his city" (v 11) complied with the royal intrigue. A little of that sort of conduct and the fabric of mutual trust, which is the secure foundation of society, will be irrevocably eroded. Hence the importance of Elijah's intervention. The gravity of the crime is reflected in the gravity of the punishment. Ahab's actions threatened to destroy the social fabric; the punishment is the destruction of Ahab's dynasty. The text notes that Ahab repented, and so was himself spared (vv 27-29); it is possible that this is a later addition.

The major issue of interest, from our present point of view, is the perception of the role of the prophet. When grave crime has been committed, at the highest level in the land, it is the prophet who is sent to proclaim God's judgment. It is done on the spot, in direct confrontation with the guilty party. It is an understanding that is important for the later tradition of prophecy in pre-exilic Israel.

There is another tradition in the Elijah cycle which is a witness to the convictions about the prophetic role in Israel. That is the story of the confrontation with prophets of Baal on Mt. Carmel (1 Kings 18). It is now associated with traditions about Elijah's role in a drought and the bringing of rain; it is not certain that Ahab was originally a figure in the story of the confrontation on Carmel, since he is not mentioned in vv 21-40. But as the story stands now, and probably from the time of the eighth century, Elijah's call to decision was enacted before the king and all the people.

Elijah stands alone, over against 450 prophets of Baal. The story emphasizes this aspect (cf., v 22). There is a sense in which Elijah is typical, here, of the prophetic role of lone opposition to practices and policies which were destroying the nation. Elijah also is portrayed standing on the firm conviction that the LORD, the God of Israel, and the god Baal are incompatible. This may not have been so obvious earlier in Israel. Saul and Jonathan had sons called by names involving Baal (i.e., Ishbaal/ Ishbosheth and Meribaal/ Mephibosheth; later tradition changed the "baal" element to "bosheth," meaning shame); and David gave names involving El to some of his sons born in Jerusalem (i.e., Elishua, Elishama, Eliada, and Eliphelet, 2 Sam 5:16). In no sense was apostasy intended. But for Elijah, it is clear that Baal and the God of Israel are incompatible. The refusal to perceive this and act upon it can only hobble the people. "How long will you go limping with two different opinions?" (v 21). There is a choice to be made, and the story pictures it very dramatically. The outcome is the people's commitment: the LORD is God, the LORD is God (v 39). In this classic scene, Elijah stands as a type of the pre-exilic prophets, constantly calling the people to a true allegiance to their God, constantly reminding them that only in fidelity to its God can Israel walk freely on the path of its destiny.

ELISHA

The figure of Elisha stands apart from these forerunners, so much so that he might not seem to belong in a chapter like this. At least two important elements focus attention on the significance of Elisha. Firstly, there is the anointing of Jehu which was commanded by Elisha and carried out by one of his disciples (2 Kgs 9:1-10). In itself it is important as a prophetic claim to responsibility for the political and religious transformation effected by Jehu's revolution. Since it is very probable that the accounts of the anointing of Saul and David depend on this anointing of Jehu, there is a link here that claims to go a long way back in prophetic tradition. Secondly, if the hypothesis of the Prophetic Record is correct (see above, chap. 6), it is likely that Elisha and the group around him have to be reckoned not only as heirs but also as shapers of the tradition which gave prophets authority to designate and depose Israel's kings.

> The numerous stories which have been preserved from the Elisha circle, coupled with their ability to bring the Elijah traditions into continuity with their own, witness to this prophetic group's potential for literary activity, extending over a significant period of time. The hypothesis of the Prophetic Record points to such a group functioning as both bearers and shapers of their national traditions. It provides evidence of intellectual power, literary skill, and a concern for the interpretation of tradition, as well as its preservation for posterity.[9]

[9]Campbell, *Of Prophets and Kings*, 115-16.

Their insistence on the national status and authority of the
prophets has to have been a major contribution to the idea of
what it meant to be a prophet and what it meant to speak to Israel
in the name of God.[10]

The image of Elisha as a legendary wonder-worker, associated
with a prophetic band, can lead to his not being as highly
esteemed as other major prophetic figures. We have to realize
how little we know of Elisha and the nature of the prophetic
association he led. Careful study of the literary additions to the
Elijah traditions and of the Elisha stories themselves show
evidence of remarkable theological acumen and perceptive reflection in this quite extensive redactional and narrative activity.[11]
Much of this requires too much detail to be discussed here. But
we might mention briefly the story of Elisha's succession to Elijah
(2 Kgs 2:1-15).

Whatever its origins, in its present form it is a highly stylized
story. From the outset, we are informed of Elijah's imminent
departure in a whirlwind. Three times Elijah suggests that he
separate from Elisha; each time Elisha insists on remaining with
him (vv 2, 4, 6). At Bethel and at Jericho, the sons of the prophets
speak to Elisha about Elijah's departure and both times are
answered, "Yes, I know it; hold your peace." Elijah and Elisha
cross the parted waters of the Jordan, away from the prophetic
band. Elisha asks for a double share of Elijah's spirit and is told
that he can only have such a hard thing if he sees Elijah in the
moment of his being taken away. In that moment, they are
separated by a chariot of fire and horses of fire, but Elisha's cry,
"My father, my father! the chariots of Israel and its horsemen!"
indicates that he saw him—only to see him no more. Elisha rends
his own clothes and takes up instead the mantle of Elijah. As
Elijah had parted the waters of the Jordan, so does Elisha and
returns to the prophetic band.

[10]See Von Rad, *Old Testament Theology* (2 vols.; Edinburgh: Oliver and Boyd,
1962-65) 2. 25-32.

[11]The best treatment of this material that I am aware of is by Georg Hentschel, *Die
Elijaerzählungen: Zum Verhältnis von historischem Geschehen und geschichtlicher Er-
fahrung* (Erfurter Theologische Studien 33; Leipzig: St. Benno, 1977) and "Die geschicht-
lichen Wurzeln der Elijatradition," *Dein Wort Beachten: Alttestamentliche Aufsätze* (ed.
J. Reindl and G. Hentschel; Leipzig: St. Benno, 1981) 33-57. See also R.R. Wilson,
Prophecy and Society in Ancient Israel (Philadelphia: Fortress, 1980) 202-6.

There is here narrative exploration of prophetic discipleship and the qualities that make for a prophet. There is persistence, even against the words of the master. There is the experience that comes at a time not of the prophet's choosing. There is the aloneness of the prophet, unwilling even unable to accept assistance from the band, crossing the river away from them. There is the need for insight, to be able to see what ordinary people do not see. There is finally the experience of insight and the transfer of prophetic power, with echoes of the Exodus and Mosaic authority. The whole story moves at a level above that of ordinary human existence, until the succession is assured, the spirit of the master will live on, and Elisha can return to the side of ordinary life.

Regrettably, we know all too little of Elisha and the people around him and after him who nurtured these stories. But if they were responsible for the keeping of Israel's prophetic traditions and the shaping of a document like the Prophetic Record, they are important among the forerunners of Israel's pre-exilic prophets. Not only did they retail the prophetic traditions concerning Samuel, Nathan, Ahijah, and Elijah, they appear to have pondered them and elaborated them to bring their meaning into full clarity. They arranged and structured these traditions, integrating them with other narratives from Israel's stock, to offer a coherent presentation of the thread of authoritative prophetic guidance in Israel's history from Samuel and Saul to Elisha and Jehu. Our ignorance of their activities should not lead us to underestimate their influence in contributing to the prophetic tradition in Israel.

The Exploration of the Prophetic Experience in Israel's Storytelling

In ancient Israel, storytelling was one of the favorite vehicles for theology, one of the best ways of provoking and communicating theological reflection. As we noted earlier, Israel pondered long over the discernment between true and false prophecy. It is small wonder that there are several stories which explore this theme. As background to the understanding of pre-exilic prophecy, they will be well worth our while considering here. We will look at 1 Kings 13, 1 Kings 22, and Jeremiah 28. Like all good

stories, they are rich and full of meaning; our discussion here will
have to be restricted to the light they throw on Israel's understanding of prophecy.[12]

1 KINGS 13

The story in 1 Kings 13 begins very dramatically. In the
historical context, King Jeroboam has established centers of
worship at Dan and Bethel, for the newly created northern
kingdom. At Bethel, the king is standing by the altar to burn
incense when a man of God comes suddenly on the scene, with a
devastating word directed against the altar. When the king hears
it, gesturing to the man he says, "Lay hold of him." Instantly, the
king's arm is frozen in the outstretched gesture. At the same time,
the altar splits open and spills its ashes, just as the man of God had
said. This is high drama and a great start to a story: a shattered
altar, and a king with his arm paralyzed in a dramatic gesture. He
turns to the man of God, and at his prayers the king's arm is
healed. So right at the start of the story, we have absolutely no
doubt as to the power of this prophetic figure. The source of his
power is God, for, at the very start, the story is insistent that he
came out of Judah to Bethel "by the word of the LORD" (13:1),
and he cried against the altar "by the word of the LORD" (v 2).

Therefore the man of God from Judah is set before us as a
prophet sent by God, who has spoken God's word, and has done
so with immense effectiveness. He falls into the "true prophet"
category, if anyone does. Against this background, the story can
unfold. The king, with his hand restored, is naturally grateful and
offers the man of God refreshments and a reward. Now a new
element enters the story. When the man of God was sent by God,
he was given three commands, "You shall neither eat bread, nor
drink water, nor return by the way that you came" (v 9). So he
declines the king's offer of hospitality and goes on his homeward
way by another route.

---

[12]For other aspects of these stories, the insights of scholarship and the literature
concerning them, see the studies of Crenshaw and De Vries (above, note 1). We will
prescind from most of those questions here. The issue of date is not a primary concern for
us either; what matters at this point is the exploration of the phenomenon of prophecy and
the reflection on it which existed in Israel.

The story's scene shifts to a second prophet, an old prophet who lived in Bethel. His sons came and told him about all these dramatic events. So he has his ass saddled and rides after the man of God. He finds him resting under an oak tree, and the storyteller makes sure that we have got the right man (v 14). Notice that we are dealing with two anonymous figures; the story is moving in the realm of the typical. The old prophet then invites the man of God to come back and share a meal with him. Naturally the man of God declines, repeating the three commands that had been given him. The old prophet replies, "I also am a prophet, as you are" (v 18). And now the story has brought us to the center of a drama, for we have two prophets present and the words they claim to have received are about to conflict. For the old prophet now tells the man of God that he has received a word from God to bring the other home for some bread and water. In an aside, the storyteller adds: "He lied."

The story is told very sparingly, with total concentration on the two figures and the drama being enacted between them. We are not told whether the man of God was beginning to feel the need for some food. The offer is kept to bread and water, partly in counterbalance to the word from God, but partly too in order not to distract from the central drama. The old prophet has prophesied falsely, and the man of God who had prophesied truly has been deceived and has obeyed the false prophecy. Not a word is said about the motivation for what has happened.

They are sitting at table when the word of God comes to the old prophet from Bethel (v 20). He then proclaims to the man of God from Judah that, since he has disobeyed the command he was given by God, his body shall not come to the tomb of his fathers (v 22). That said, he saddled the ass for the man of God, here referred to as "the prophet whom he had brought back" (v 23, cf., v 20; the two men are intended to have equivalent status). The storyteller does not linger for a moment on what might have been thought or said by either party. There is no distraction from the central action. The man of God goes his way and is met by a lion on the road, which kills him. It is no chance occurrence. The storyteller paints the tableau: the body lying in the roadway, the ass standing beside it, and the lion standing by them both. The ass has not bolted; the lion is not interested in prey. Without doubt, the finger of God is here. The prophet who prophesied truly permitted himself to be deceived by the prophet who prophesied falsely, and as a result he has met his fate.

In the final stage of the story, the old prophet is informed of what has occurred. He rides out and finds the tableau unchanged: the body, the ass, and the lion (v 28). He brings back the body of the man of God and buries it. He mourns him as a colleague, "Alas, my brother" (v 30). And he gives instructions that he himself is to be buried in the same grave, "for the saying which he cried by the word of the LORD . . . shall surely come to pass" (v 32). The man of God, who died for his disobedience, is honored for the truth of his prophecy. And the old prophet, who deceived him with false prophecy, now not only honors him but prophesies truly about him.

While there are all sorts of aspects of this story which cry out for explanation, there is only one which we need to emphasize here.[13] Israel was aware that the true and false prophet are not necessarily distinguished by external signs. The one who prophesies truly can be led astray. The one who prophesies falsely can recognize truth and error and can prophesy truly. It is likely enough that the story was told the way it is in order to raise questions for discussion and reflection. It is also told in such a way as not to distract attention from its central issue.

1 KINGS 22

The story in 1 Kings 22 begins with the kings of Israel and Judah making an alliance to go out to war (vv 1-4).[14] The alliance agreed on, the king of Judah asks that God be consulted. This would be quite normal procedure before going to war. So far so good; nothing is unusual. The prophets are summoned, about four hundred of them, and they all favor the war, assuring the kings that God will give them victory (v 6). And now the

[13]For further discussion, see particularly S.J. De Vries, *1 Kings* (WBC; Waco, TX: Word Books, 1985) 164-74.

[14]De Vries, in *Prophet Against Prophet*, postulates two earlier stories which have been combined to form the text we now have in 1 Kings 22 (see also De Vries, *1 Kings*, 259-72). The analysis is not problem-free. It will be sufficient for our purposes to interpret the present text. In my judgment, it is not correct to say that "the story has no meaningful structure as it now stands" (against De Vries, *1 Kings*, 265).

storyteller springs the first surprise on us. The king of Judah asks for another prophet. As if four hundred were not enough, there is need for one more. This is the first inkling we are given that this is a special story. The king of Israel admits that there is one more prophet, Micaiah ben Imlah, but he is in disfavor, because his prophecies do not please the king. And here we are given another little hint about the direction of the story: is the purpose of prophecy to please the authorities or to reveal the truth?

A messenger is sent to summon Micaiah. While the messenger is on his journey, the storyteller provides us with two pieces of byplay. One sets the scene for the subsequent action. A little imagination can set it all in place. There are the two kings, in all the splendor of their royal robes, enthroned on the level area at the gate of Samaria, the towers of the gate and the walls of the city forming the backdrop. Around the kings, who have been preparing for war, are their army commanders and the royal guards. On the land sloping gently away from the walls of the city, built on a low hill, the four hundred prophets perform before the kings and their troops. In a symbolic gesture, beloved of prophecy, Zedekiah ben Chenaanah makes horns of iron and dramatizes the thrusting back of the Syrian foe. And the four hundred join in the chant foretelling victory (vv 10-12).

Against the mass of color and sound, with all the pride and pomp of military might and royal power, and the shouts and ecstatic demonstration of the four hundred prophets, the storyteller shifts the focus to two individuals, the messenger and Micaiah. The messenger urges Micaiah to back the campaign, like the others. Micaiah replies, with echoes of Balaam, that "As the LORD lives, what the LORD says to me, that I will speak" (v 14).

And so the storyteller has another surprise in store for us. The king of Israel puts the same question to Micaiah that he put to the four hundred. And Micaiah gives him the same answer that they gave: "Go up and triumph; the LORD will give it into the hand of the king" (v 15). What on earth has made Micaiah change his mind? We are not told. Was it the awe-inspiring spectacle of the two kings on their thrones, and the masses of troops around them, and the four hundred prophets roaring their approval of the royal plans? It is hardly likely, even though prophets are human. With the lone individual and the mass of four hundred, there is too much resemblance here to Elijah's confrontation on Carmel; fear does not seem fitting. It is more likely that the storyteller took this liberty in order to make possible the next surprise.

The king of Israel rejects Micaiah's prophecy. Instead of saying, "Thank God, good news for once!", he fulminates against Micaiah: "How many times shall I adjure you that you speak to me nothing but the truth in the name of the LORD?" (v 16). So when it comes to prophecy, the king knows where truth lies—not with his four hundred. What he will do with that truth is delayed a little in the story. Meanwhile, Micaiah gives the king the truth he has asked for. Micaiah reports a vision of "all Israel scattered upon the mountains, as sheep that have no shepherd; and the LORD said, 'These have no master; let each return to his home in peace'" (v 17). The meaning is limpidly clear: Israel's army will be scattered in defeat; they have no master for the king will be dead. So naturally the king of Israel points out angrily to the king of Judah that he knew that Micaiah would not prophesy good concerning him. He appears to have completely forgotten his interest in the truth. Perhaps he knows that he has it, but he certainly does not like it.

Confronted with this royal displeasure, Micaiah has to defend his prophecy. He does so by appealing to his vision of the heavenly council. There God asked who would entice Ahab to his death at Ramoth-gilead. Various counsels were offered, until one spirit proposed to go and be a lying spirit in the mouths of his prophets. With that Micaiah has impugned the prophecy of the four hundred. Their leader, he of the iron horns, Zedekiah ben Chenaanah, is not one to take that quietly, so he gives Micaiah a backhander across the mouth, with the challenge: "How did the Spirit of the LORD go from me to speak to you?" (v 24). There is only one defense left to Micaiah, and he uses it. It is the appeal to fulfillment: You will see! The king of Israel, who had been so concerned to hear the truth, now orders Micaiah thrown into jail, with hard rations, to be dealt with on the king's return. Consciously or not, the king is going to put Micaiah's prophecy to the test. Micaiah has the last word, as he is about to be led off: "If you return in peace, the LORD has not spoken by me" (v 28).

The king of Israel, of course, dies in battle, despite disguising himself. But that is almost beside the point. The story opposes authority and true prophecy. The authorities know where truth is to be found: not in the four hundred, but in the one. Yet knowing that, they will not accept it. The king prefers to go to his death on the field of battle than to defer to the word of a prophet which he himself has implied is true. Folly as this may sound, it is no more foolish than the behavior of Israel, turning a deaf ear to the proclamation of the prophets. There is also here the conflict between prophet and prophet, each claiming to speak by the spirit. Micaiah can claim his vision and his presence in the council of God (cf., Jer 23:18, 22). Zedekiah can still claim the spirit as his own. And so the storyteller has Micaiah fall back on fulfillment as the decisive criterion. Yet that criterion, too, cannot be absolutely certain (cf., Deut 13:1-5). The story is witness to Israel's contemplative reflection on the interaction between king and prophet and also prophet and prophet.

JEREMIAH 28

This story is set at a critical time in Judah.[15] In 597, there has been a first taste of exile, with many of the leading classes and skilled workers taken in exile to Babylon. Nebuchadnezzar, king of Babylon, had put his own nominee, Zedekiah, on the throne in Jerusalem (cf., 2 Kings 24:10-17). The moment is critical. What policies will the new king follow? Is the disaster of 597 a foretaste of worse to come? Can one break with Babylon or must one bow to Babylon? Jeremiah has received God's word for the kings of the surrounding nations, Edom, Moab, Ammon, Tyre, and Sidon, to be communicated to their ambassadors who have been presenting their credentials to Zedekiah. The word is basically: one must bow to Babylon (cf., Jer 27:1-15). Then Jeremiah had spoken to the priests and the people, prophesying that what has happened is only a foretaste of worse to come (27:16-22). At stake in all of this: the fate of the king, the people, and the treasures that have been taken off to Babylon.

The story begins with Hananiah, the prophet from Gibeon, which was a major sanctuary (cf., 1 Kgs 3:4), confronting

---

[15]There is a very good treatment in Crenshaw, *Prophetic Conflict,* and also in R.P. Carroll, *Jeremiah* (OTL; London: SCM, 1986) 537-50.

Jeremiah in the temple, in the presence of the priests and the people (28:1). Hananiah's message: God will break the yoke of Babylon. It is important, by the way, to notice the apparent evenhandedness of the storyteller throughout this story. It is always Hananiah the prophet and Jeremiah the prophet. We may know the end result and who was truly the prophet, but it is not allowed to distract from the real tension of the moment. Both speak in God's name; both use the prophetic messenger formula, "Thus says the LORD." Externals do not guarantee discernment.

The response given Jeremiah by the storyteller is remarkably mild. "Amen! May the LORD do so; may the LORD make the words which you have prophesied come true . . . ." (v 6). But Jeremiah points to tradition. The accepted tradition of prophecy speaks of war, famine (Hebrew: evil), and pestilence (28:8). The prophet of peace must await the criterion of fulfillment before that prophet will be accepted as having been sent by God. The issue of self-interest may be a key to this. There is little to be gained by prophesying war, famine, and pestilence; a prophet who prophesies peace is far more likely to find both self and prophecy accepted.

The storyteller has Hananiah respond with a symbolic act. Jeremiah was bearing a yoke across his shoulders, as a symbol of the yoke of Babylon which was to be borne. Quoting a word from God, Hananiah breaks the yoke before Jeremiah's eyes. In the full public glare of the temple, before priests and people, it is a most dramatic confrontation. The storyteller's "Jeremiah the prophet went his way" (v 11) leaves us to imagine Jeremiah's humiliation and frustration. He has proclaimed God's word to ambassadors, to the king, to priests and people. Now, confronted in the temple, he has little to say: I hope you are right, but we will have to wait and see. There is no fulminating word from God to put Hananiah in his place and restore the preeminence of truth. Jeremiah went his way. Clearly, the word of God was not a tool at the prophet's disposal.

It is only sometime after that the word of God comes to Jeremiah, countermanding Hananiah's symbolic action (vv 12-15). Then Jeremiah knew that Hananiah had not been sent by God. Hananiah has made the people trust in a lie. Their trust may cost them their lives; his lie will cost Hananiah his, within the year. The criterion of fulfillment is on the side of Jeremiah. The narrator drily notes: "In that same year, in the seventh month, the prophet Hananiah died" (v 17).

The story is told with surprising objectivity: prophet versus prophet. It is a remarkable reflection on the difficulties of discernment. Here is Jeremiah the prophet, who has received God's word and proclaimed it, saying of the contrary word of Hananiah, "Amen! May the LORD do so." Here is Jeremiah the prophet appealing to tradition, but unable to tell Hananiah on the spot that God has not sent him. When Jeremiah receives the word, Hananiah is unmasked—but not before. So carefully told and carefully balanced a story is witness to the amount of thought and reflection given in Israel to the phenomenon of prophecy, experienced in their midst. Any consideration of the message of the prophets must keep this background in mind.

Today

Our own age is well aware of the existence of cranks, crackpots, and religious soothsayers. Our age must also come to terms with the reality that the fads and whims of society at large and the directions taken by political society in particular have to stand under the judgment of God. Human life and culture is not at the totally free disposal of human beings. That has been the lesson of the Old Testament since Genesis 3. If one believes that God exists and that God is concerned for the welfare of all humankind, then no human society and no human authority can withdraw itself from the reality of God and the origin and purpose of our human world. We may or may not wish to appeal to God's design, but unquestionably we may in faith appeal to God's desire.

It is not that a loving God will be transformed into a cosmic judge, intervening in human history to mete out reward and punishment. But the spirit of God can move in groups or individuals to speak out what is elemental truth and to protest what smooth words and self-interest can clothe in acceptability. It can be that the churches are disinterested groups, with the capacity to see clearly and speak powerfully. It can be that, when the churches are entrammelled in their own interests, others come forward to speak with clarity and power. It is difficult to classify the Old Testament prophets neatly between those who were central and parties to power and those who were on the periphery and apparently powerless. So it is always difficult to discern who can claim to be speaking God's word.

One thing, however, the figures of Samuel, Nathan, Ahijah, and Elijah will not let us forget. We do not have complete control of our destiny. We cannot create our universe, no more can we create the universal context and backdrop of our lives. All human actions, all human policies are to be judged against a context and a backdrop which is the existence of a loving God who is concerned for the welfare of all humankind. The thought may seem abstract and empty. As the prophets have always shown, its consequences are concrete and very real. In the long run, truth has a habit of being heard.

RECOMMENDED FURTHER READING

Joseph Blenkinsopp, *A History of Prophecy in Israel,* 13-79. Philadelphia: Westminster, 1983.

Antony F. Campbell, *Of Prophets and Kings: A Late Ninth-Century Document (1 Samuel 1-2 Kings 10),* 114-23. CBQMS 17. Washington: Catholic Biblical Association of America, 1986.

James L. Crenshaw, *Prophetic Conflict: Its Effect Upon Israelite Religion.* BZAW 124. Berlin: de Gruyter, 1971.

Simon J. De Vries, *Prophet against Prophet: The Role of the Micaiah Narrative (I Kings 22) in the Development of Early Prophetic Tradition.* Grand Rapids: Eerdmans, 1978.

Klaus Koch, *The Prophets: The Assyrian Period,* 1-35. Philadelphia: Fortress, 1982.

Gerhard von Rad, *Old Testament Theology,* 2. 3-98. Edinburgh: Oliver and Boyd, 1965.

Robert R. Wilson, *Prophecy and Society in Ancient Israel.* Philadelphia: Fortress, 1980.

9

The Prophetic Books as Literary Works

Recommended preliminary reading

Before reading the body of the chapter, it will be helpful to have read the following passages:
Amos 1-2
Hosea 1-3
Isaiah 5

The prophets of Israel did not write books. They spoke directly to their people. Their address was generally in short sayings, not in long discourses. Their sayings were gathered into collections, by the prophets themselves or by their disciples. In due course, the collections of sayings were arranged into prophetic books. Varying principles governed the ordering of the collected sayings; literary force and impact was certainly a consideration. The ordering of the collections into books came in time to reflect Israel's understanding of the nature of the prophetic experience. The main task of this chapter will be to throw light on the process which brought the prophetic books into being. The process begins with individuals sayings and poems, continues with the gathering of these into collections, and concludes when the collections are arranged to form a prophetic book. Aspects of this process can be seen in different ways in the different books. Our task will be to get some insights into this process, rather than to trace it comprehensively through the prophetic corpus. However, an understanding of the process will reveal some of the limits to the search for literary artistry at the level of the book as a whole, while bringing to light the considerable literary skills involved at other levels.

NOTE: It will help our discussion to point out here that the structure of a prophetic saying, in what might be called its ideal form, consisted of an accusation or censure linked to an announcement or threat by the messenger formula, "Thus says the LORD," or its equivalent. The accusation or censure denounced the particular evil with which the prophet was confronted or concerned. The announcement or threat proclaimed the disaster which was imminent as a result of the evil.[1]

THE BOOK OF AMOS

The book of Amos stands out among the prophetic books by the obvious clarity with which it falls into three separate sections or collections. The book starts off with a heading, indicating something of who Amos was, and naming the kings under whom he prophesied (Amos 1:1). Similar headings occur for all the prophetic books, and the similarity of their style suggests that they derive ultimately from the group responsible for the final editing of the books. One thing is certain. Since they name all the kings the prophet operated under, they have to belong after the end of the prophetic activity and not at the beginning. They are an indication of Israel's view of the prophetic books as literary units. The second verse of the book of Amos is also intended as part of the title or as a brief overview, summarizing in two lines the whole message of Amos. But, since it talks about God roaring from Zion and speaking from Jerusalem, it is unlikely that it is from Amos himself. Although from Tekoa, south of Bethlehem, Amos directs his words entirely to the northern kingdom. References to Zion and Jerusalem are not part of his style.

Once we set these two headings aside, we come to the block of patterned sayings which form the first collection in Amos (i.e., chaps 1-2). We will examine these more closely later. For now, it

---

[1]See Claus Westermann, *Basic Forms of Prophetic Speech* (Philadelphia: Westminster, 1967).

is enough to recognize that there is a word for each of the
countries surrounding Israel: Damascus to the northeast, Gaza to
the southwest, Tyre to the northwest, Edom to the southeast,
Ammon adjoining to the east and a little north, Moab adjoining
to the east and a little south. We may note that the sayings against
Tyre and Edom are slightly different from the others, and that the
saying against Judah is certainly a later addition. So we arrive at
the proclamation to Israel: "Behold, I will press you down in your
place . . . . " (2:13-16). The collection is complete in itself. There is
a short, pithy oracle for each of the neighbors; then there is a
longer oracle, centering on Israel, its faults and its fate. If we
compare this with Amos 3-6 and 7-9—and we will, a little
later—this section contains the whole of Amos's message in a
nutshell. There is the denunciation of the breaches of social justice
within Israel. There is the proclamation of the future fate of Israel.
It is placed within an artfully constructed whole, in which the
reverberations of Amos's message echo around the periphery of
Israel, before its full force implodes upon the center of Israel, like
a hammer crushing the kernel of the nut.

Chapter 3 starts afresh. There is a call to all Israel to hear God's
word. In chapter 2, Israel has just heard it, so at least here a new
section begins. The introduction sums up the identification of
Israel in a single line: "the whole family which I brought up out of
the land of Egypt" (3:1). There is a tightness of thought in this
clause, as well as its language, which is suggestive of the typically
deuteronomistic theology. The saying which follows expresses, in
two taut poetic lines, the whole message conveyed in the previous
two chapters.

> You only have I known
> > of all the families of the earth;
> therefore I will punish you
> > for all your iniquities. (3:2)

The previous two chapters surveyed Israel's neighbors in a series
of six sayings, with the seventh destined for Israel. "Of all the
families of the earth" sums up that series of six and universalizes
it. "You only have I known ... therefore I will punish you"
expresses the meaning and content of the saying to Israel, in the
seventh and climactic position.

This opening saying, almost a headline, is followed by a carefully structured series of sayings which have a completely different concern (3:3-8). There are seven questions in a row. The first five are identically formulated: they refer to an effect and ask about its natural cause. Do you see two people walking alone in the fields (the effect), and they have not planned it that way (the cause)? Do you hear a lion roaring (the effect), and it has not caught its prey (the cause)? Any lion that was fool enough to give warning of its coming, by roaring at the start of the hunt, would soon enough starve to death. Does a bird in full flight plummet to earth entangled in a net (the effect), unless somebody set a trap for it (the cause)? Does a flexible sapling suddenly spring up straight (the effect), unless some poor animal, running along the path, has blundered into the noose and triggered the snare (the cause)?

After these five questions, the form in the Hebrew changes for the next couplet. But the gist is the same. The first line of the couplet remains in the natural sphere, like the previous five. If the alarm trumpet is sounded in the city (the cause), are not the people afraid (the effect)? The sequence up till now of effect first, followed by the cause, is reversed here. This is the sort of device used in Hebrew poetry to alert the listener to a change which is about to occur. Here the change is that the second line shifts from the natural to the theological sphere. Does evil befall a city (the effect), unless God has done it (the cause)? And so the sequence of seven questions is complete, ending on a theological note. The next verse (v 7), a line of prose, breaks into the movement of the poem; we will leave it aside for a moment.

The climax of the poem is in the next couplet, and it demonstrates this with a notable change in the syntax. Instead of opening with a question, each line in the couplet opens with a statement and then follows it with a question. The first line picks up the natural sphere of the first six questions: the lion has roared, who will not fear?—the cause is posited and the effect necessarily follows. The second line, like the seventh question, shifts to the theological sphere: God has spoken, who can but prophesy?—the cause is posited and the effect necessarily follows.

It is obvious that it is a very carefully thought out and well structured little poem. Its message is clear: since God has spoken, Amos has to prophesy. It is a defense of the prophetic message, and it is placed here, immediately following the terribly harsh summary of that prophetic message in v 2. It is a fearful message—"You only have I known ... therefore I will punish you"—but, since God has spoken (the cause), Amos has to say it (the effect). We need to remind ourselves that Israel's prophets did not sit studiously in seclusion, writing for publication in the media. They were out in the streets and the marketplace, in direct confrontation with their people. And, for good reason, as we can see, their message was not welcome and they themselves met with opposition. In this context, it is not difficult to imagine the sort of exchange which might have originally provoked Amos's poem. Amos has gathered a crowd around him and has proclaimed his message. Someone in the crowd shouts out: "Shut up, prophet! You make us afraid." Amos begins his sequence of seven questions, and brows furrow as the crowd wonders what he is getting at. The last couplet makes it clear: You have to be afraid, and I have to prophesy.

In its present context, in the book, the poem is no longer an exchange with one angry and fearful listener. It says something about the prophetic message and the whole phenomenon of prophecy. The message is a fearful one, which Israel did not want to hear. Its proclamation is not the prophet's free choice; it is something he is obliged to do. God has spoken; the prophet has no choice but to prophesy. The sequence is as inevitable as cause and effect.

The people who were inspired by the deuteronomic reform (under Josiah) and who were responsible for the composition of the Deuteronomistic History, were very impressed by the phenomenon of prophecy. They probably based their history on the Prophetic Record (see above); they incorporated into it a number of stories about the prophets. They were also convinced that the prophets had been God's instruments in God's endeavor to spare the people of Israel the fate that lay in wait for them.

> Yet the LORD warned Israel and Judah by every prophet and every seer, saying, "Turn from your evil ways and keep my commandments and my statutes, in accordance with all the law which I commanded your fathers, and which I sent to you by my servants the prophets." But they would not listen, but were stubborn, as their fathers had been, who did not believe in the LORD Lord their God. (2 Kgs 17:13-14)

These same deuteronomistic circles, therefore, deeply valued the sayings of the prophets and made sure that they were preserved in Israel. We can spot traces of deuteronomistic editing and commentary in almost all the prophetic books. It is to them, for example, that we attribute many of the introductory superscriptions at the beginning of each prophetic book. Here, in v 7, we have the equivalent of a deuteronomistic footnote, making one additional point about Amos's poem.[2] When God had spoken, the prophet had to prophesy. And, in deuteronomistic theology, God never did anything without revealing it to the prophets. Hence, Amos knew and therefore had to speak.

This second collection, in the book of Amos, has opened with a call to Israel to hear the word of God spoken against them, expressed in a powerful summary of the prophet's message (3:1-2). This has been followed by a poem, justifying the prophet's speaking out, especially given the fearful nature of the message. The poem is followed, in turn, by a classic example of Amos's sayings (3:9-11). It begins with the kind of instruction that would be given to messengers or ambassadors: Summon the people who live in the fortified palaces of Ashdod and Egypt to come to Samaria.[3] They are to come in order to see the great tumults and oppressions in the midst of Samaria. It is not quite clear exactly what function they are being invited to perform: whether as judges, jury, witnesses, or observers.[4] It does not matter very much, since Amos's summons is rhetorical only. But what it

---

[2]Footnoting was not in vogue among the writers of scrolls. Words left out or comments to be made could be written in the margins or between the lines. An added comment could easily be mistaken by a later copyist for words of the original, which had been left out by oversight and written in when the omission was discovered. Quite a few comments seem to have come into the text this way.

[3]The Hebrew text has Ashdod and Egypt, while the Greek has Assyria and Egypt. The textual shift is a good example of how later generations interpreted the biblical text. For Amos, the two legendary enemies of Israel's past were the Philistines and the Egyptians. Ashdod, a Philistine city, stands for the Philistines. For later generations, Assyria and Egypt were the two great hostile forces, so Amos's text came to be updated in the tradition represented by the Greek text. Assyria and Egypt, as a pair, occur several times in Hosea.

[4]Judge and jury are not as anachronistic for Israel as it might seem at first sight Dispensing justice, the king served as judge. There appear to have been judges in other circumstances. When justice was dispensed in the gate, the elders of the town combined the functions of judge and jury. The jury as such was not known in Israel. Probably, in this saying, Amos had observers in mind, those who would corroborate the denunciation he was about to utter.

means is clear and the irony very powerful. The two prime villains of Israel's history, unsurpassed for oppression and brutality, would be appalled at what they would see in Samaria, would certainly pass sentence of condemnation. In the corruption of its society, Samaria has become first among the worst.

The censure that follows is as fundamental as it is possible to be. Those people in Samaria who store up the benefits of oppression and violence in their fortress-like houses simply do not know how to do what is right. They have lost all moral sense. Property and persons are their prey, without thought or remorse, just so long as they put them to service in the accumulation of wealth. To them, Amos proclaims the old law of the biter bit: a stronger than they will come and plunder their strongholds. In terms of the structure of the collection, this is a headlining saying. Its accusation is fundamental and comprehensive, and its threat is no less so. The land will be overrun by the enemy, rendered defenseless, and plundered. The life of wealthy Samaria will be at an end. In terms of the prophetic theology, it is interesting to note the relationship between cause and effect in this saying. The proclamation is introduced: "Therefore thus says the LORD God" (v 11). But that is all. Amos does not have God claim responsibility for the adversary's coming, nor describe the adversary as an instrument of divine punishment. Rather, the image of the plunderers plundered suggests the sequence of cause and effect, of act and consequence. This aspect we will leave until chapter 13.

Again, in terms of the wider context of the collection of Amos's sayings, the next saying follows appropriately on its predecessor. Defences are to be torn down and strongholds plundered. Ah well, worse has happened, and plenty of people have survived a siege or two. It probably will not be too bad. The saying in v 12 is there to deflate any such illusory optimism. When a lion destroys a sheep, perhaps the shepherd will get hold of a couple of legbones or a bit of an ear to bring back to the owner as evidence of the total destruction of the beast (cf., Exod 22:13). And that is how it will be with the inhabitants of Samaria. The following saying, too, reinforces this image (3:13-15). The destruction will extend beyond Samaria; the altars at Bethel will be desecrated. No sanctuary will be granted there. The destruction around Samaria will be extensive, summer house and winter house, the luxury dwellings with their ivory furnishings, all shall come to an

end. For the inhabitants of Samaria, it is a far-reaching proclamation. If Amos is right, they are in for a very hard time, besieged
by an enemy, their defenses breached, their houses pillaged, and
everything so thoroughly demolished that there would be nothing
left to show for it.

The final saying in this group, representative of what Amos
proclaimed in Samaria, is directed at the wealthy women of the
capital. The accusation of oppression of the poor and maltreat-
ment of the needy is hurled directly at the women. They may call
to their lords to bring on the drinks, but they are portrayed by
Amos as quite capable of carrying out their own oppressive
behavior. In Amos's proclamation, the imagery of siege and
destruction is carried through. The walls protecting the city will
be breached, and Samaria's leading ladies will be forced out over
the rubble, prodded on by alien soldiery, and dragged off,
probably beyond Mt. Hermon into exile in Syria.

If Amos 3-6 form a separate collection of the prophet's sayings,
these four sayings (3:9-11, 12, 13-15; 4:1-3) are remarkably well
placed. Coming after the introductory material (3:1-2, 3-8), they
bring together a striking selection of the sayings uttered by Amos
in the capital city. He spoke of the coming downfall of the
northern kingdom. This collection of sayings begins with that
message, proclaimed at the center of the kingdom, in the capital.
It is carefully structured and well put together.

The sayings which follow seemed to be grouped around the
denunciation of the two sanctuaries of Bethel and Gilgal. Bethel
was set up by Jeroboam as the northern rival to Jerusalem (1 Kgs
12). Of itself, it was an ancient and hallowed place in Israel's
tradition, as was Gilgal. We do not know what was going on there
to deserve Amos's fulmination, we can only surmise. In the
present text, there is a series of five catastrophes which God has
brought on Israel, without being able to achieve the goal of
repentance and reform; therefore, the time has now come for
Israel to meet its God (4:6-12). On the grounds of style and points
of contact with the Holiness Code (Lev 17-26), Hans Walter
Wolff considers that 4:6-12 are not from Amos. He suggests that
the "*thus* I will do to you, O Israel, because I will do *this* to you" (v
12) might refer to the destruction of the altar at Bethel by Josiah.[5]

---

[5]See H.W. Wolff, *Joel and Amos* (Hermeneia; Philadelphia: Fortress, 1977) 212-18.

Since the two hymnic passages here (4:13; 5:8-9) are generally considered not to be from Amos either, the closing section of this collection may be considerably reduced.

There are three sayings which relate to the worshipping life of northern Israel (4:4-5; 5:4-5, 14).[6] Whether 4:6-12 are from Amos or from a later redactor, they have been attached to the saying about coming to Bethel and Gilgal and transgressing in 4:4-5. It is a mockery of the priestly call to worship: come to the sanctuary—and sin! The five passages which follow portray God's endeavor to bring Israel out of that sin and persuade them to return to their God. Taking the sequence as it is, the saying in 4:4-5 pours scorn on Israel's worship at Bethel and Gilgal. Vv 6-11 then catalog God's attempts to compel the people to return, with v 12 summing up the failure and its consequences for Israel: "prepare to meet your God."

The saying in 5:1-3 gives emotional color and concrete detail to what is involved in this meeting with God. The lament over fallen and forsaken Israel provides the emotional color. The city that was a thousand and will be a hundred provides a concrete sense of the disaster envisaged; this is not decimation, it is annihilation. 5:4-5 hammers home what has to be done to reverse this situation. It is the theme that is at the back of 4:6-11. Life is to be found with God, not in the worship at Bethel and Gilgal. For Amos, life with God is utterly inseparable from justice in the community. So, quite rightly, some denunciations of the injustice visible in Israel are appended to this appeal to seek God and live (5:7, 9-12). Perhaps 5:16-17 closed off this sequence.[7] The wailing which Amos proclaims leads into the saying portraying the day of the LORD as darkness and not light (vv 18-20). The section began with the denunciation of worship at Bethel and Gilgal; it concludes with an even broader censure of Israel's worship, with a strong final call for justice.

J.L. Mays does not share this view (*Amos* [OTL; Philadelphia: Westminster, 1969] 77-83).

[6]For Wolff, 5:6 is seen as an interpretation of vv 4-5. Instructive in his comments is the suggestion that the term "house of Joseph" became more prominent as a designation for northern Israel after the fall of Samaria in 722, when the term "Israel" was being used for the people of God as a whole (*Joel and Amos*, 240). Mays accepts the authenticity of Amos 5:6 (*Amos*, 89-90).

[7]V 13 is considered a later addition. Wolff attributes vv 14-15 to one of Amos's disciples (*Joel and Amos*, 249-51; cf., Mays, *Amos*, 96-102).

> But let justice roll down like waters,
>   and righteousness like an everflowing stream. (5:24)

Four more sayings bring the collection to a close. 6:1-7 returns
to the theme of the wealthy in Samaria, with the proclamation
that they shall be the first to go into exile.[8] The three sayings
which follow (vv 8-11, 12, 13-14) reinforce the certainty of the end
which is coming.

Chapter 7 begins something quite different: the sequence of
visions. The first four visions are very closely patterned into two
pairs. In the first two, Amos is shown something that is visibly
destructive, and instantly he intercedes, and his intercession is
successful. In the second pair, the situation changes. The significance of what Amos sees is no longer immediately evident, so
God asks him what he sees. When he has said it, before he is even
aware that he needs to intercede, God tells him what he has seen
and said and what its significance is. By the time Amos is aware of
what he has seen and what he has said, it is uttered, it is out there,
and there is no place for intercession. However one understands
this sequence, it is clear that, at first, Amos was able to intercede
and did so successfully, while with the second pair of visions, the
pattern was changed and Amos no longer interceded. With the
fifth vision, the end is clearly visible (9:1-4).

We will look at these visions later, as a possible report of the
experiences which first triggered Amos's prophetic ministry. In
the report of these visions, Amos himself is much more to the fore
than in the other parts of the book. There is no command to
proclaim the message of the visions. Why then were they narrated?
One aspect of this narrative sequence may be the self-defense of
the prophet against the charge of inadequacy or callousness. One
of the roles of the prophet was intercession. We find it in the
image of Samuel (1 Sam 12:19, 23). Abraham is cast in the role of
the archetypal prophet, and his intercessory ability with God is
portrayed in legendary fashion (Gen 18:23-33). Moses is depicted
as having to intercede with God constantly on behalf of the

---

[8]On the question of whether the mention of Zion (Jerusalem) is from Amos or a later
addition, see Wolff, who deems it later (*Joel and Amos*, 269-70), and Mays, who attributes
it to Amos (*Amos,* 115). Wolff suggests that 6:6b and 6:2 are later additions (*Joel and
Amos*, 273-74); v 6b would make explicit what is already implicit in the words of Amos.

people (e.g., Exod 32:7-14, deuteronomistic). In several of the deuteronomistically influenced passages in Jeremiah, the prophet is forbidden to intercede for the people (e.g., Jer 7:16; 11:14); the implication behind the prohibition is that intercession would be the right and proper thing for the prophet to do, in normal circumstances. So it is quite possible that, confronted with the unexpected harshness of Amos's message, the people reproached the prophet with not having interceded on their behalf. The response conveyed by this sequence of vision reports: I tried, and initially my intercession was successful; but then, the nature of the visions I was shown changed, and it was no longer possible for me to intercede anymore. At this point, the message becomes that of 3:3-8—I must prophesy and you must be afraid.

There is another aspect, however, which is also significant. The message conveyed in the narrative of the vision sequence and the message conveyed in the patterned formulas of the oracles in chaps. 1-2 have an element in common. In both cases, Israel is depicted at the last stage of the legal process: appeal is denied. In chaps. 1-2, the anger of God has gone forth, for the statement now is, "I will not cause it to return" (1:3 ... 2:6). In terms of the legal process, Israel has been found guilty, sentence has been uttered, and now it will not be revoked. The refusal to revoke implies the appeal which is denied. All that is left now is execution of the sentence. In chaps. 7-9, the visions of locusts and fire imply a verdict passed and sentence about to be executed. Amos appeals on compassionate grounds, "How can Jacob stand? He is so small!" (7:2, 5). The next two visions circumvent the possibility of appeal and bring Israel to the situation of the fifth vision: the execution of the sentence has been commanded. The message of Amos in chaps. 1-2 and in chaps. 7-9 is identical.

We can take these reflections a step further. If we only had one of the sets of chapters within the book of Amos—either chaps. 1-2 or 3-6 or 7-9—we would still have a very clear idea of Amos's message. From chaps. 1-2, we know that God's anger has reached the point of no return, because of the social injustice and transgression in Israel. Therefore they will be crushed by the ancient Near Eastern equivalent of a steamroller; only the mightiest of the mighty will save his skin that day (2:13-16). In chaps. 3-6, we have basically the same message. The denial of appeal is not explicitly present, but it may be implied from the certainty of the proclamation; only 5:4-5 unambiguously leaves open a possibility of escaping the inevitable. The message is explored more fully and more colorfully than in chaps. 1-2 or 7-9, but it is the same message. In chaps. 7-9, as we have seen, the message to Israel is that they are past the stage of appeal and intercession and the execution of the sentence has been ordered. The reason for it is clearly expressed in the saying denouncing transgressions of social justice, appended after the fourth vision (8:4-8).

What conclusions are we to draw from these phenomena? Firstly, it is hardly likely that such a carefully structured collection of sayings as chaps. 3-6 reflects the precise sequence of Amos's discourse on any particular occasion. It is more likely to be literary reminiscence, distilling the quintessential message of the prophet. The series in chaps. 1-2 and 7-9 would lend themselves best to proclamation on single occasions. But even there, both show how they have been subsequently expanded with additional material. They may well have been proclaimed originally in much more fragmentary fashion. It is possible, at least in theory, that the prophet himself undertook the organization of these reminiscences, which were to contain his message. We see that happening with Isaiah (Isa 8:16) and Jeremiah (Jer 36). It is equally possible that it was the work of the prophet's disciples: they are explicitly mentioned in Isa 8:16, and Baruch and also the deuteronomistic circles are visible in Jeremiah 36. In theory, again, it is possible that prophet or disciples arranged Amos's sayings into the three collections we now have, as the most effective or aesthetically satisfying way of going about it. But this would not explain how a saying like 8:4-8 came to be where it is and not among the sayings of chaps. 3-6. The savage exchange between Amos and Amaziah, the priest of Bethel (7:10-17), which is recounted about Amos not by him, is where it is because of the saying in v 9b which Amaziah quotes in his dispatch to the king (v 11). But the material in 8:4-14 and 9:7-10 need not be here, distracting from the central impact of the vision sequence. It is, therefore, quite possible that collections of a prophet's words were maintained in different circles or in different places. They have been collected, structured, and preserved to give the clearest possible expression of the message of the prophet.

When we recognize this, the prophetic books take on an added dimension. They are not merely the memory of the oral preaching of the prophet. They give evidence of being a careful and deliberate attempt to communicate the message of the prophet as effectively as possible. We have seen this careful structuring evident in Amos 1-2 and 7-9. We have noted that it is particularly clear in the beginning of Amos 3-6. There is the call to attention and the initial striking summary of the whole prophetic message (3:1-2). This is followed by the poem justifying the prophet's proclaiming so fearful a message (3:3-8). Then comes the most comprehensive of Amos's sayings against Samaria (3:9-11), followed by two more sayings about the extent of the devastation to come (3:12, 13-15), and finally another saying against Samaria, this time directed against the women there (4:1-3). This is more than merely the record of a good day's prophesying. And so the collection continues. There is a picture emerging of a skillful editorial effort, directed at selecting and arranging the sayings of the prophet in the way that would most effectively communicate the message. It was not simply a case of stringing together prophetic sayings by catchword association and other mnemonic links; thoughtful planning and structuring seems to have been the order of the day. It would seem likely that this effort began with the smaller collections within what is now a prophetic book; later, the collections were combined to form the books as we have them. The process need not have applied in equal measure to all the prophetic books; yet it appears to have been fairly general. While we have given particularly close attention to the process in the book of Amos, it will be worth while surveying some of the evidence in other prophetic books.

THE BOOK OF HOSEA

The situation for the book of Hosea is, in some respects, quite different from that of Amos. Above all, the material in Hosea is not divided off into clearly marked sayings in the way that the Amos material is. This has led Hans Walter Wolff to put forward the suggestion that the traditions in the book of Hosea derive from sketchy outlines of the various moments in the prophet's activities, noted quite soon after the events occurred. Wolff points out that, after Hosea 1-3, there is a call to hear God's word in 4:1 and a concluding formula, "says the LORD," in 11:11, but otherwise there are no formulas which introduce or conclude smaller units. For guidance in where sections of discourse begin and end, we have to look to elements like the naming of the addressee, or the adoption of a new theme, the absence of a syntactical link to the preceding passage, or a change in style from a speech of God to a speech of the prophet, or from second person to third person, and so on. Careful use of these criteria, it is suggested, can identify a series of sayings which were proclaimed by the prophet on one and the same occasion. Wolff refers to such a series of sayings as a "kerygmatic unit." He comments, "The peculiar way the sayings have been strung together, as described above, is explicable only if these kerygmatic units present sketches of scenes which were written down soon after the prophet had delivered his message."[9] The proposal is attractive, but it has not been widely endorsed.

Whatever of the manner in which the units of Hosea's sayings came into being, there is good evidence for identifying three collections within the book of Hosea. These are chaps. 1-3, 4-11, and 12-14. In each, the same movement is to be found, from initial condemnation to a final message of hope. The first collection is grouped around the theme of Hosea's marriage. Chap. 1 is a report by a third person about the beginning of Hosea's activity as a prophet—"when the Lord first spoke through Hosea" (1:2). The careful note that this is what happened when God first spoke through Hosea implies someone looking back over a longer period of time, and quite possibly also aware of a change in what Hosea was saying later. Hosea 1 could be from the compiler of chaps. 1-3. As we will see, its message is structured on the commands from God: to marry and have children; to name the children Jezreel, Not Pitied, and Not My People. Censure is secondary in the chapter; it has a place in explaining the initial command and, barely, the name of Jezreel. The message of the chapter is summed up in the reason for the

---

[9]H.W. Wolff, *Hosea* (Hermeneia; Philadelphia: Fortress, 1974) xxx, for this and the above discussion. J.L. Mays remains skeptical: "H.W. Wolff in BK calls these compositions 'kerygmatic units' because he thinks they are made up of sayings (divine and prophetic) which derived from one appearance of the prophet and were spoken in sequence, sometimes in response to reactions of the audience. But composition by similar theme or catchword, or perhaps the same general period in the case of 5.8-6.6, explains the larger units adequately; and so much does not have to be imagined" (*Hosea* [OTL; Philadelphia: Westminster, 1969] 6, n. a).

name of the third child: "For you are not my people and I am not
your God" (1:9—literally: and I am not "I am" for you).

Hosea 3 is in the first person, so from Hosea himself. There is a
radical shift in the message. Love is to be restored, despite
infidelity. There is a period of difficult times to be endured, but at
the end of it all the relationship between God and Israel will be
renewed and strengthened (3:5). What might have seemed like a
definitive breach in chap. 1 can now be seen as a distancing, with a
deliberate purpose of restoring the relationship. In between these
two chapters, the compiler has skillfully placed those sayings of
Hosea which make use of the wife-husband metaphor. Within
these sayings, the same trajectory is travelled, from rejection ("she
is not my wife"), through punishment ("I will punish her for the
feast days of the Baals"), to renewed courtship ("I will allure her").
Two further series of sayings have been added to these: 1:10-2:1
(MT,2:1-3) and 2:16-23 (MT,2:18-25). Doubts have been raised
as to whether they come directly from Hosea or from disciples. It
has been suggested that 1:10-2:1 originally belonged after 2:23
(Wolff); others have placed it after 3:5 (*JB, NAB*). It was put
where it is now, presumably by the compiler, so as not to leave 1:9
echoing too long, without the counterbalance of the hope Hosea
later expressed.

Certainly, after the hope expressed in Hosea 3, the sharp blast
of God's controversy with the inhabitants of the land, in 4:1-3, is a
marked change of tone. We will discuss it at length as a remarkably comprehensive and far-reaching prophetic saying. What we
may note here is its aptness to begin a collection of Hosea's
sayings. In much the same way as Amos 3:9-11, Hosea 4:1-3 is
one of the most effective and all-embracing of the prophet's
sayings. As the first saying in a collection, it is well chosen. The
conclusion to this second collection of Hosea's sayings has long
been revered as one of the most exalted passages of the Old
Testament (11:1-11). Coming from the prophet who fought so
uncompromisingly against the nature religion of Baalism, it is
remarkable for the freedom with which it speaks anthropomor-
phically of God. But far more remarkable is the depth of
tenderness and the strength of feeling which Hosea dares to depict
in God.

The relationship between God and Israel is set up from the
outset as one of love. That, for Hosea, was the force which
motivated the Exodus.

> When Israel was young, I loved him,
>   out of Egypt I called my son. (11:1)[10]

Such was the beginning and yet, as the relationship unfolded, the more God reached out to Israel, the more they withdrew and turned toward Baal. There, in a nutshell, is Hosea's complaint with Israel, expressed here in a speech by God. In its history, and above all in the exodus, Israel has come to know the LORD as the God who can give full richness to the meaning of human life. Instead of living deeply into the mystery of life, Hosea's Israel has chosen to turn aside to the shallow emptiness of Baalism. They did not have the insight to discern the presence of God in their experience, to recognize the action of God in their midst.

> Yet it was I who taught Ephraim to walk
>   and I took them in my arms.
> But they did not perceive
>   that I cared for them.
> With humane cords I drew them,
>   with ropes of love.
> And I was to them
>   as those who lift a small child to their cheek,
>   and I bent down to him to feed him. (11:3-4)

It is the most incredibly lovely imagery for the God-Israel relationship. The metaphors are marvelous in their daring. God teaching the infant to walk; Israel cuddled in the arms of God. The summary of salvation history: drawn with humane cords, with ropes of love; they have been led along their way, but lovingly. Even Hosea holds back from depicting infant Israel actually lifted to the very cheek of God, but he pursues the image as far as analogy will permit. He compensates by having God bend down to Israel—to feed him! The tender intimacy of these images contrasts so sharply with the harsh reality Hosea sees as Israel's present state.

---

[10]The translation of the passages quoted from chap. 11 will be taken from Wolff (*Hosea*, 190-93).

He returns to the land of Egypt,
  but Assyria is (and remains) his king.
  For they refuse to return.
Thus the sword surges throughout his cities
  and destroys his braggarts,
  it devours because of their schemings.
But my people are bent on apostasy from me,
  to Baal they call,
  but he by no means raises them up. (11:5-7)

What a sad and sorry picture. Israel reverses salvation history by seeking liberation with the help of Egypt. Assyria remains their oppressor. So they turn from the God who liberated them from Egypt, and call on Baal for help.[11] And there is none. The very wretchedness of the picture impinges emotionally on God.

How shall I surrender you, O Ephraim?
  give you up, O Israel?
How can I surrender you like Admah?
  treat you like Zeboim?
My heart turns against me,
  my remorse burns intensely.
I will not execute my burning anger,
  I will not again destroy Ephraim.
For I am God
  and not a man,
the Holy One in your midst,
  and I will not become enraged. (11:8-9)

Admah and Zeboim are the twin cities of Sodom and Gomorrah, symbols of devastation and destruction. So intense is the emotion, it is expressed in terms of the body language of movement and heat, the interior churning and the warmth of feeling. "I will not again destroy Ephraim" is an unfortunate translation. It conveys the sense that it has been done once and will not be done a second time, yet Wolff explicitly denies this

[11]We cannot take up the various translational difficulties here. Help can be found in either Wolff or Mays.

meaning. "Had Yahweh once before brought about Israel's destruction? Certainly not in the sense of vv 8f. What had befallen Israel up to this time was the consequence of Israel's own intentional actions, the harvest of what had been sown (4:9; 8:7; 10:13). . . . Israel's situation would be totally different if Yahweh were to destroy with the heat of his wrath rather than to draw with cords of love." The verb cannot indicate a second destructive action. . . . It denotes, however, "not only the repetition of an action, but also the restoration of previous conditions, or the nullification of a deed."[12] The sense has to be something like "I will not turn around and destroy Ephraim" *(NEB),* or more precisely, I will not turn history back in destroying Ephraim, they shall not be as they were before I saved them. God's love for Israel remains dominant. From Egypt and Assyria, where they may have gone suing for alliances or seeking refuge or taken into exile, they will return to the security of their own homes (v 11).

> The restoration does not cancel judgment. This description of salvation assumes that refugees have fled to Egypt while deportees are living in exile in Assyria. The nations to which Israel turned in frantic search for a solution to her national crisis have become the places of punishment and humiliation. Chastened and awed, they shall come back to the land like a bird returning to its nest. But the return is not their achievement; it is the action of Yahweh. Once again he is the subject of Israel's history and once again by his act they are brought to their homes.[13]

After the power and feeling of this passage, with its passionate affirmation of restoration and salvation, it is a rude awakening to encounter the denunciation of Ephraim in the following verse.

> Ephraim has encompassed me with lies,
>   and the house of Israel with deceit. (11:12; MT, 12:1)

This can hardly be anything else but a third collection, including words of Hosea's that were probably pronounced within a year or

---

[12]Wolff, *Hosea,* 202.

[13]Mays, *Hosea,* 159. V 10 is regarded as an explanatory supplement to v 11.

two of the fall of Samaria (e.g., 13:10). This collection, too, ends with the promise of restoration. Once again, true to Hosea's style, it is lovely in its language and its metaphor. It speaks beautifully of God's grace.

> I will heal their faithlessness;
>> I will love them freely,
>> for my anger has turned from them. (14:4; MT, 14:5)

As in Amos, so too in Hosea the same message is repeated in all three collections. In the first of them, Israel's infidelity predominates as the evil denounced, but there is also the reference to the bloodshed in the valley of Jezreel (1:4). In the second collection, 4:1-3 is a strong statement of total social collapse, while there is a hint of oppression and social injustice in the third (12:7-8; MT, 8-9). The evil which is incessantly denounced by Hosea is Israel's infidelity to the God of Israel and their turning to the worship of Baal. From first to last the theme of infidelity is dominant. "Plead with your mother, plead—for she is not my wife, and I am not her husband" (2:2; MT, 2:4); "Samaria shall bear her guilt, because she has rebelled against her God" (13:16; MT, 14:1).

Hosea denounces the blind stupidity of Israel's religious infidelity. He does not try to spell out the vision he sees Israel abandoning; his concern is to pillory the Baalism to which they have turned. Elements of that vision can be glimpsed nevertheless. It contains a very strong relationship with God, tender, passionate, and intimate. In its extraordinary breadth, it encompasses a mutually enlivening relationship with the natural environment. Social breakdown causes the land to mourn (4:3). Restoration includes a covenant with the beasts of the field, the birds of the air, and the creeping things of the ground (2:18; MT, 20). Social breakdown culminates in the overlapping shedding of blood (4:2). Restoration banishes the bow, the sword, and war, and replaces them with safety (2:18). Restoration is pictured as betrothal to God, "in righteousness and in justice, in steadfast love, and in mercy. I will betroth you to me in faithfulness; and you shall know the LORD" (2:19-20; MT, 21-22).[14] In this is visible

[14]The authenticity of 2:16-23 (MT. 18-25) has been contested. For Mays, "the work was done by a contemporary disciple of Hosea, if not by the prophet himself. The inner

both the knowledge of God, which for Hosea clearly encompassed a deep insight into the mystery and richness of human life, and the social conditions which necessarily flowed from that knowledge and insight. The tenderness here is echoed in the passion of chap. 11 and the delightful imagery of chap. 14.

Restoration is the other aspect that is common to all three collections in Hosea. Each speaks of the restoration of Israel. What is to happen to Israel is not punitive so much as restorative, and the cause of the restoration is the free love of God. If the beginning of Hosea's proclamation of doom was to be founded in the command to marry a prostitute and have children by her (1:2), it is to be expected that the promise of future salvation would also have been founded in the command to go love again a woman who is an adulteress (3:1). If so, it is a fascinating reflection that Hosea, who inveighs so strongly against the naturalistic worship of Baal, god of fertility and the storm, should be possessed of so profoundly incarnate a theology. It is Hosea who gives particularly striking emphasis to the interweaving of the consequences which are to befall Israel with the acts of Israel that bring these consequences in their train. It is all the more striking that Hosea can proclaim a God who beyond these consequences will bring salvation.

Before we leave Hosea, it is worthwhile looking more closely at Hosea 1-3 as an example of the way in which a prophetic collection was formed. In Hosea 3, the report in the first person is presumed to be from Hosea himself. The arrangement of the sayings in 2:2-15 (MT, 4-17) is also attributed to Hosea. These two pieces of tradition from the prophet are the building blocks around which the collection has been formed. The account in Hosea 1 is in the third person. While it is likely to have been an old tradition, probably the person who gave it its place here is the one who had the idea for this collection. With this, the frame is set for the collection: the beginning of Hosea's experience of God's word, concluding with the name, "Not-My-People"; the words of Hosea protesting Israel's adultery; the experience of the command

---

connection of the material in every verse with the rest of Hosea's prophecy leaves no reasonable basis for doubting that the sayings are his" (*Hosea*, 47). Wolff assesses the passage critically, and concludes to the compiler of this first collection as the one who added 1:2-6, 8-9, and this section from Hosea's more recent sayings (*Hosea*, 47-49).

to go love again. The compiler, presumably one of a circle around Hosea, is probably the one who built on this framework, putting the oracles of salvation (i.e., 1:10-2:1; MT, 2:1-3) after the menacing conclusion to the report of Hosea's initial experience, and arranging a number of Hosea's sayings to expand and fill out the conclusion to the middle section (i.e., 2:16-23; MT, 18-25).

1:5, with its own introduction and "Israel" instead of "the house of Israel" (cf., vv 4, 6), probably did not belong originally in this context. The same compiler may have added it, particularly in the light of Tiglath-pileser's control of the Esdraelon valley (valley of Jezreel) in 733. Two more verses remain to be accounted for. There is 1:7, a clear interruption in the context, seeking to emphasize that Hosea's message applied exclusively to the northern kingdom and certainly not to Judah. This is quite different from the Judean update of Amos, which sought to bring Judah in under the proclamation of Amos's prophecy (Amos 2:4-5). A later Judean update did the same thing for Hosea (cf., Hos 4:5a*, 15; 5:5b*; 6:11a). 1:7 would have to be earlier than the fall of Jerusalem; it could be related to Sennacherib's failure to capture Jerusalem in 701. Finally, there is the superscription of the whole book, added in 1:1.

While one or two details have been passed over, this picture provides a sense of the way in which the prophetic books were formed: first the sayings of the prophet, and also the reports about the prophet from those in the prophetic circle; then the arranging of these into collections to give greater impact or better order. Finally, the gathering of the collections together to form the book as we have it.[15] In such a book, we have not only the words and actions of the prophet, but also the record of their impact on the prophet's disciples and on subsequent generations. Recognition of the process permits us to see, at least to some extent, into the movements of theological thought and reflection within Israel.

---

[15]For further discussion of the growth of the book of Hosea, see especially Wolff, *Hosea*, xxix-xxxii; also Mays, *Hosea* 15-17.

THE BOOK OF MICAH

While the book of Micah, as a whole, presents a complex and lengthy process of growth, our scope here will be adequately served by paying attention to the construction of Micah 1-3, most of which is attributed to Micah. The discussion will be simplified if we restrict it to what is understood to have been the original text, quite possibly arranged by Micah himself.[16]

The key events for understanding Micah's message are the fall of Samaria in 722 and Sennacherib's campaign in Judah and siege of Jerusalem in 701. Of the latter, Sennacherib records: "As to Hezekiah, the Jew, he did not submit to my yoke, I laid siege to 46 of his strong cities, walled forts and to the countless small villages in their vicinity and conquered (them).... Himself I made a prisoner in Jerusalem, his royal residence, like a bird in a cage."[17] Sennacherib's sudden lifting of the siege was so remarkable as to have been regarded as miraculous (cf., 2 Kgs 19:35-37).

The beginning of the original collection remains uncertain. It may have had a brief title and it may have begun with the saying against Samaria (v 6).[18] If so, the first saying of Micah's is a blunt and direct word of God threatening the levelling of the northern capital and its conversion to arable land. Even in the south, its directness had to shock.

It leads into a lament that eliminates any southern complacency. The lament is ominous for Judah and Jerusalem (1:8-16). The towns known to us among those named are near Micah's hometown of Moresheth (v 14), on the southwest fringes of the Judean hills. Located diagonally across Judah from the Assyrian threat in the northeast, they suggest an extensive catastrophe.

So far, while catastrophe is threatened, no cause or reason has been clearly named. The woe saying now makes the causes

[16]My understanding of the structure and formation of the book is taken from J.L. Mays, *Micah* (OTL; Philadelphia: Westminster, 1976, see esp. pp. 21-29) and H.W. Wolff, *Micha* (BKAT 14/4; Neukirchen: Neukirchener Verlag, 1982, see esp. pp. XXI-XXIX).

[17]From the Annals of Sennacherib, *ANET*, 288.

[18]Mays favors seeing the Samaria oracle as a later addition (*Micah*, 25, 45-48); Wolff considers it original (*Micha*, 16-17, 21-23). The blunt shock of this oracle may have contributed to attracting the addition of the introductory verse(s). The introduction now provides an opening to the book which is one of the most dramatic in prophecy: the call to all peoples and the whole world before God's emerging from the heavenly temple and the earth-shaking theophany.

explicit (2:1-2). It is a classic prophetic utterance, combining censure with threat. The censure is hurled at the social injustice of a situation so corrupt that there are people immoral enough and powerful enough to put into action whatever schemes they can dream up to increase their wealth. Specifically, properties—fields and houses—are being expropriated, and the independent citizens of Israel are being oppressed and deprived of their inheritance, the source of life and security.

> Woe to those who devise wickedness
>   and work evil upon their beds!
> When the morning dawns, they perform it,
>   because it is in the power of their hand.
> They covet fields, and seize them;
>   and houses, and take them away;
> they oppress a man and his house,
>   a man and his inheritance. (2:1-2)

This is the same sort of situation pictured in Isa 5:8 or 10:1-2. There is a massive transfer of wealth from the independent peasant owners to the wealthy and land-hungry ruling classes. The wickedness being thought up overnight is the variety of ways of expropriating the rightful owners: foreclosure on debts, bribing of witnesses, establishing unjust laws to justify seizing land. Israel saw the land as God's gift, an inheritance that could not be alienated. The whole social fabric of Israel was being transformed and eroded by the emergence of new classes of a wealthy elite— clustered around the capital cities and associated with the royal courts, royal administration, and standing army (cf., 1 Sam 8:11-17; 22:7-8).[19]

The threat follows (vv 3-5). Just as these powerful figures have been devising wickedness against those they have dispossessed and expropriated, so God is now devising evil against them. Their haughty style will change to taunted lamentation, and the land holdings they have unjustly amassed will be distributed to others.

Immediately following that programmatic utterance, there is a quotation of the resistance which it met: "Do not preach . . . One

---

[19]For Mays, this saying is pronounced in Jerusalem (*Micah*, 62); for Wolff, it is directed against the powerful people of the towns of vv 8-16 (*Micha*, 44).

should not preach of such things; disgrace will not overtake us" (2:6). The prophet explodes against this reaction. The iniquitous oppression of men and women substantiates his word (2:8-11).[20] The despoiling of the peaceful and trusting, the expropriation of the homes of women and children call for prophetic truth, not hot air and lies.

Following this attack on unspecified powerful figures, Micah's word is addressed directly to the heads of Israel who preside over this oppression. He uses the most savagely vivid imagery in his denunciation of these rulers. They reverse the fundamental law of human behavior: they hate good and love evil (3:2). So rapaciously grasping is their conduct, it can be likened to skinning people, scraping the flesh of their bones, cannibalizing God's people, chopping them up like stew in a pot (v 3).

In this context, Micah turns again to the prophets who, in such a situation, have the gall to proclaim peace, whose prophecy is determined solely by their stipend. He stands over against them, consigning them to darkness and disgrace. For himself, he claims the spirit of God, enabling him to function with justice and power, and "to declare to Jacob his transgression and to Israel his sin" (v 8).

A final saying brings the collection to its climax and close. In the present text, it balances the initial threat to Samaria. The threat concerns Jerusalem. The censure is directed at its rulers who abhor justice and pervert right order: its judges who can be bribed, its priests who teach for hire, and its prophets who divine for money (v 11). Because of them, Zion shall be ploughed like a field and Jerusalem shall become a heap of ruins (v 12). As far as Jerusalem is concerned, what began as a lament (1:8-9) ends as a prophecy of its total devastation. The collection mounts steadily from an ominous beginning, through the social evils that beset the community, to the fearful climax of prophesied destruction.

There are some intriguing aspects to this prophetic collection. The structuring is obviously well done. There are two ways of looking at its overall movement, depending on a couple of disputed points of interpretation. In one scenario, with Wolff, the Samaria oracle is included and 2:1-11 are addressed to the people of southwestern Judah. In this case, the collection is structured to

---

[20]There is general agreement that 2:12-13 is an addition from the exile or later.

begin with the northern capital, sweep through the Judean countryside, and culminate in the sayings of chapter 3 against the southern capital, Jerusalem. In the other scenario, with Mays, the Samaria oracle is excluded as an addition, and 2:1-11 are addressed to the people in Jerusalem, along with 3:1-12. In this case, the collection moves from the broad lament over Judah, through the general attack against unspecified powerful evildoers, to the specific classes pilloried in the capital, and the prediction of its destruction.

According to tradition, Hezekiah's repentance won a reprieve for Jerusalem, and so Micah's prophecy was not fulfilled. A century later, when after the collapse of Josiah's reform the Babylonians threatened Jerusalem, Micah's words were pondered afresh. Whether the Samaria saying was inserted then or was already there, to the later generations Micah's prophecy must have seemed a perfect mirror of the course of events: Sargon's capture of Samaria, Sennacherib's devastation of the Judean countryside, and the encampment of his armies at the gates of Jerusalem. The disaster was averted in Hezekiah's time. The threat remained.

THE BOOK OF ISAIAH

Isaiah 1-12 provides insight into a different aspect of these processes in the growth of a prophetic book. There, the inter-meshing of collections can be seen, rather than their simple juxtaposition.[21] So our exploration can be started almost at the middle of the collection. Isaiah 5 begins with a song. It is sung for the beloved and it is a love song about his vineyard. There are levels of ambiguity in the possible identifications here: is the singer the prophet, God, or someone else? Is the beloved a person, the nation, or God? Is the vineyard a real one, or a metaphor for a bride, or something else? These arise out of the interlocking of the settings in which this song might have been sung: in the context of

[21]The understanding presented here is basically that given by G. Fohrer, *Introduction to the Old Testament* (Nashville: Abingdon, 1968) 363-73. While scholars may differ on particular points, it is representative of the kind of process involved in the composition of Isaiah 1-12. A markedly new approach is offered by O. Kaiser in the completely rewritten second edition of his commentary, *Isaiah 1-12* (OTL; 2nd ed.; London: SCM, 1983).

a wedding, where the vineyard would have been a metaphor for
the bride; in the context of a harvest festival, where the vineyard
would have been the fertile land; in the context of salvation
history, where the vineyard would have been the chosen people.[22]
While the poem exploits all of these, it sets the tone at the
beginning of a love song, a relationship of love. To speak directly
of God's love for Israel would be to anticipate the identification at
the end of the song. So, instead, the context and mood of a loving
relationship are created.

The poem begins with the interaction between the beloved and
his vineyard, in the third person (5:1b-2). The address to the
inhabitants of Jerusalem and the men of Judah modulates a shift
to the first person, where the interaction is now between the
speaker and the vineyard (vv 3-6). The interaction is moved to a
new context; not marriage, or harvest, or history, but law: "Judge,
I pray you, between me and my vineyard" (v 3b). The poet
becomes the plaintiff in a lawsuit. First the complaint (v 4), then
the punitive action proposed as a just settlement of the case (vv
5-6). Only with the reference to control of the clouds in v 6, does it
finally become clear that the speaker is God. In the final couplet (v
7), all the ambiguities melt away as the whole poem is focused on
its one central statement.

> For the vineyard of the LORD of hosts is the house of Israel,
>   and the men of Judah are his pleasant planting;
> and he looked for justice (*mišpāṭ*), but behold, bloodshed
>   (*mišpāḥ*);
>   for righteousness (*ṣĕdāqâ*), but behold, a cry (*ṣĕ'āqâ*)! (v 7)

With these two lines, the whole situation has changed and
become clear. The prophet stands outside the love song and
interprets it. The tender warmth of the love song is replaced with
the anguished cry of the unjustly oppressed. The uncertain identification of the vineyard is now all too painfully clear: it is Israel
and Judah. The plaintiff's metaphor in the complaint about
grapes and wild grapes is now transparent: the field is not
agriculture but social justice. "He looked for justice, but behold,

---

[22]Cf., R.E. Clements, *Isaiah 1-39* (NCB; Grand Rapids: Eerdmans, 1980) 56-58.

bloodshed; for righteousness, but behold, a cry!" The proposal for actions against the vineyard (vv 5-6) are revealed as metaphors for the fate of the land of Israel. The power of the word play in the couplet—justice (*mišpāṭ*) and bloodshed (*mišpāḥ*), righteousness, properly understood as right order and right relationships (*ṣĕdāqâ*), and the cry of the oppressed (*ṣĕʿāqâ*)—focuses all the feeling of the poem into one burst of outrage. What should be, justice and right, has been replaced by what should not be, bloodshed and a cry.

Isaiah's interpretation of the poem points to bloodshed and the cry. It supplies no specifics. These are provided in the series of seven woe sayings which follow. The opening exclamation (*Hôy*, Woe) expresses dissatisfaction and pain; it has its place in dirge and lament, but also to introduce denunciation and the declaration of judgment. The seven sayings are primarily accusations of social evil; the proclamation of the consequences for Israel is more muted. First in the series, there are those "who join house to house, who add field to field" until all of the land is theirs and there is no room for others (v 8). Then there are the carousers, whose passion for alcohol and fine food blinds them to the vision of God in their history and their world (vv 11-12). Thirdly, there are the sceptics, who work hard at their wrongdoing. Their scoffing response to the prophet's proclamation may be paraphrased: "We will believe it when we see it. Have your God hurry it up—we would hate to die before it happens" (cf., vv 18-19). This is aggressive agnosticism with a vengeance. The fourth, fifth, and sixth sayings touch on the destructive attitudes which are wreaking havoc: the reversal of values (v 20), the failure of wisdom (v 21), and the use of power and wealth only for intoxicating oneself and distorting justice for others (vv 22-23).

However, our concern in this chapter is not so much with Isaiah's message as with its literary organization into the form we possess in the biblical text. So we have surveyed the six woes in the series, and we have to look for the seventh which provides the climax. It is several chapters away.

> Woe to those who decree iniquitous decrees,
>   and the writers who keep writing oppression,
> to turn aside the needy from justice
>   and to rob the poor of my people of their right,

> that widows may be their spoil,
>> and that they may make the fatherless their prey. (10:1-2)

It is an appropriate climax to the series. It seizes not on individual acts of oppression but on the manipulation of the whole system of law to do wrong, so that the law, which should be the bulwark of justice, becomes the instrument of oppression. It points to the needy and the poor, the widow and the orphan. These are the criterion of the justice of a society. They are powerless and must look to society to assure their due. Their cry goes straight to God's heart (cf., Exod 23:23, 27b; Deut 24:15b). The threat that goes with this accusation is also a very appropriate conclusion to the sequence of seven sayings (10:3-4). It is now the oppressors who will be helpless and powerless—"Nothing remains but to crouch among the prisoners or fall among the slain" (v 4).

But the question has to be answered: what is the seventh woe saying doing here, at the beginning of chap. 10? Before we address this question directly, there is one more phenomenon to be observed in the text. The threat concluding the seventh woe saying ends with a formulaic line:

> For all this his anger is not turned away
>> and his hand is stretched out still. (10:4b)

The same refrain occurs earlier in 9:12b, 17b, and 21b. And it also occurs back in 5:25b. We noted that the element of threat concerning the fate to befall Israel, as a result of the evils denounced, was not a prominent element of the woe sayings. It occurs in only three of the seven (5:9-10, 13-17; 10:3-4). In the series of sayings, on the other hand, each of which ends with this refrain, the element of threat is to the fore. The sequence would have begun with the announcement of the word sent against Jacob/Israel (9:8). It is presumed that it concluded with 5:25-30. God's anger is not turned away; God's hand is stretched out still. 5:26-30, with its picture of the relentless approach of the harsh and disciplined Assyrian army, portrays the consequences of that divine anger.

It would have been highly appropriate to combine these two sequences of Isaiah's sayings. The woe sayings have a primary emphasis on the censure of evil; the sayings with the refrain have a primary emphasis on the announcement of the fate that lies ahead. Together, they provide a balanced presentation of the main thrusts of Isaiah's message. That presentation is now sundered by the presence of Isa 6:1-9:7. And that phenomenon may throw a little more light on the way in which prophetic books were put together.

Isaiah 7 opens with a formal introduction of the king of northern Israel and the king of Syria and their joint compaign against Jerusalem. The historical situation is well known (cf., 2 Kgs 16:1-9). Rezin of Syria and Pekah of northern Israel were planning to shake off the Assyrian control of their kingdoms, on the western fringes of the Assyrian empire. They first turned their attention to Judah, with a view either to forcing Ahaz to join their coalition or to securing their southern flank against possible attack. Ahaz, very frightened, shaking "as the trees of the forest shake before the wind," wanted to appeal to Tiglath-pileser III, the Assyrian emperor, for help. Isaiah wanted him to hold out and place his trust in God. The oracles which are gathered in 7:3-8:15 are, for the most part, directed to this end.[23] Ahaz turned down Isaiah, turned to the Assyrian, and among the consequences were the Assyrian campaigns in Palestine of 734, 733, and 732— sweeping down the Mediterranean coast to Gaza (734), over-running Galilee, the plain of Esdraelon, and much of Transjordan (733), and subjugating Damascus and Syria (732). The short-term danger to Judah was relieved, but with Judah an Assyrian vassal the long-term danger had begun (cf., 8:5-8).

So the sayings which concern this dramatic episode in Judah's history were brought together in this collection (chaps. 7-8). The conclusion is in 8:16-22, with the reference to the testimony to be kept among Isaiah's disciples. Since God is "hiding his face from the house of Jacob" (8:17) and Isaiah speaks of waiting for God, one can conclude that a period of Isaiah's prophetic activity had drawn to a close. It was therefore written down on the testimony or scroll, to be sealed and preserved among the disciples. Thus the core of the collection was formed.

---

[23]"For the most part," since there are considerable doubts and uncertainties. Kaiser comments on 7:14-17, "The interpretation of the sentences that follow is among the most disputed in all scripture" (O. Kaiser, *Isaiah 1-12* [OTL; 1st ed.; Philadelphia: Westminster, 1972] 100). For Kaiser's present position, see the 2nd edition.

It is presumed that Isaiah 6 was prefaced to this collection, being understood as the account of the prophet's call.[24] There is a link formed by the dating of the vision in the year King Uzziah died and the genealogy of Ahaz traced back to his grandfather, Uzziah. 9:1-7 (MT, 8:23-9:6) rounds off the collection with a prophecy of hope addressed to those northern territories subjugated in the Assyrian campaigns of 734-32. The collections of Hosea's sayings had each concluded with a note of hope. Whether a tradition was already forming, or whether it simply seemed appropriate, this collection of Isaiah's words was also concluded with the powerful and splendidly ringing words of 9:1-7. As always for the hope of the prophets, the future salvation will not be Israel's doing; "the zeal of the LORD of hosts will do this" (9:7; MT, 9:6).

Our understanding of the growth of the Isaiah traditions, toward the shape of the book we have today, assumes that the collection constituted by 6:1-9:7 was inserted into the middle of the earlier collection, which had been formed around the song of the vineyard, the woe sayings, and the sayings marked by the repeated refrain. That is what the evidence we have looked at would suggest. It is not certain why this should have been done. Perhaps a desire not to break up the collection of 6:1-9:7, coupled with a feel for the chronological reference of the sayings. It is possible that, given the harshness of the proclamation in chap. 6 and the references to the Assyrians as future adversaries (7:18, 20; 8:7), 5:25-30 was brought forward to its present place as a fitting introduction to this collection. Then the word addressed to Jacob/Israel in 9:8 (MT, 9:7) would be a warning that, despite the hope expressed in 9:1-7, salvation was not yet at hand. "For all this his anger is not turned away and his hand is stretched out still." We cannot trace with certainty the precise moves made in the intermeshing of these collections.

The movement toward the completion of Isaiah 1-12 may be quickly sketched. 2:1 indicates the beginning of another collection of Isaiah's sayings, concerned with Judah and Jerusalem. This

---

[24]Whether as call narrative or vision of judgment, it sits somewhat uncomfortably with the initial message of comfort addressed to Ahaz. Ahaz's refusal to heed that message smacks of the commission given Isaiah in 6:9-10. The message of judgment is more consonant with later proclamations in the collection (i.e., 7:18-25; 8:5-8).

collection consisted of at least chaps. 2-4, with 4:2-6 being provided at some stage as the note of hope, appropriate for concluding a prophetic collection. A similar note of hope, much more extensively expressed, is to be found in chap. 11 and the hymnic conclusion in chap. 12. They bring the assembled collection to a satisfactory close. There remains simply Isaiah 1 to be considered. The superscription (1:1) is in the usual style for the prophetic books; it duplicates some of the information in 2:1, for example. Chap. 1 may have been a separate collection of Isaiah's sayings, or it may be a selection made to introduce the collections which had been brought together so far. There are ways in which it is representative of his message.

> They (the sayings) constitute a planned composition; the train of thought passes through the themes of sin, the judgment that follows upon sin, possible deliverance from the judgment, and a possible realization of this deliverance. The collection has the nature of a compendium of Isaiah's message or a cross-section of it and has therefore been placed at the beginning of the book[25]

It should be clear by now that, in the prophetic books, we are dealing with the end products of careful and reflected development. Apart from the matter of later additions, expanding or interpreting the prophetic tradition, there is the basic movement from the sayings of the prophet to collections of these sayings, and finally to the assembling of the collections to form the prophetic books. As has become obvious, the collections are, for the most part, carefully arranged with a view to making the most of the sayings available. Various concerns have governed the arranging of the collections into the shape of a single book. In its turn, the shape of the prophetic book has come to reflect Israel's understanding of the shape of prophecy.

---

[25]Fohrer, *Introduction*, 366. So Clements: "The first chapter of the book of Isaiah has been intentionally formulated for a selection of the prophet's sayings in order to provide a general preface and guide to his preaching"(*Isaiah 1-39*, 28). For Kaiser, the picture is now more complex (*Isaiah 1-12*, 2nd ed.)

THE BOOKS OF JEREMIAH AND EZEKIEL

There is a structure in the books of Jeremiah and Ezekiel which provides a valuable insight into Israel's overall perception of prophecy, as a phenomenon in their religious experience. Broadly speaking, the book of Ezekiel falls into three parts. There are the sayings addressed to Israel, denouncing evil and proclaiming doom, which are to be found in Ezekiel 1-24. The last of these is dated to the very day that the king of Babylon laid siege to Jerusalem (24:2). These are followed by compositions directed against Israel's neighbors, condemning them for gloating over Israel's downfall or for contributing to it, and proclaiming the judgment which will befall them in turn (Ezekiel 25-32). These are Ammon (25:1-7), Moab (25:8-11), Edom (25:12-14), Philistia (25:15-17), Tyre (26:1-28:19), Sidon (28:20-23), and Egypt (29:1-32:32).[26] Then, beginning with the reflection upon the prophet as watchman (chap. 33), the remainder of the book is substantially concerned with hope for the future (Ezekiel 33-48).[27]

Much the same arrangement is to be found in the Septuagint version of the book of Jeremiah. The sayings against Israel occupy Jer 1:1-25:13(14). The sayings against the other nations extend from Jer 25:15-32:38 (= LXX numbering). Then there follows the material which builds up to the book of consolation, Jeremiah's expression of future hope for Israel (LXX, chaps. 33-40 = RSV, 26-33). This means that, just as for the book of Ezekiel, the traditions from Jeremiah are arranged with the sayings against his own people first, followed by the sayings against other nations, and then moving to the expression of future hope for Israel. There are other traditions of a different nature after that.

In the Hebrew version of the book of Jeremiah, the introduction to the sayings against the nations is to be found in Jer

[26]These sayings are directed against a total of seven nations or cities; there are seven sayings directed against Egypt or Pharaoh; the other sayings, against Ammon, Moab, Edom, Philistia, Tyre, and Sidon, reach a total of nine (cf., W. Zimmerli, *Ezekiel 1* [Hermeneia; Philadelphia: Fortress, 1979] 60-62). Such numerical groupings are not a matter of chance.

[27]The expressions of hope in Ezekiel are not restricted to these chapters; see Ezek 11:14-21; 16:42, 53-63; 17:22-24; 20:32-44; and 28:25-26 (cf., Zimmerli, *Ezekiel 1*, 62). However, they clearly constitute the principal location for sayings of hope in Ezekiel.

25:15-38 (which in LXX is now at 32:15-38). It lists those who are to be given the cup of God's wrath to drink (25:17-26). But the actual sayings directed against most of these are placed together at the end of the book (Jer 46-51). Instead of these sayings, the chapters which follow this introduction have the story of Jeremiah's trial because of his temple sermon, and the story of his confrontation with Hananiah, material which publicly authenticates Jeremiah as a prophet of God before the introduction of his expression of hope for the future (Jer 30-33).[28]

The significance of these observations is that they point toward an understanding in Israel of the totality of the phenomenon of prophecy: of what it meant to be a prophet, at least in terms of those prophets whose activities generated the books which bear their names. What did these prophets do? They spoke God's word against their own nation, censuring its evident evils, announcing its imminent downfall. In the fall of Samaria and Jerusalem, they were substantially vindicated. They also spoke out in condemnation of other nations (beyond the passages noted in Jeremiah and Ezekiel, see Isaiah 13-23 and Zeph 2:4-15, and as a forerunner Amos 1-2). This aspect appears to be a relatively late element in the tradition. Finally, they spoke of a hope for their own people, which lay in the future. There may be doubts about the authenticity of some of the pronouncements of hope (especially in the cases of Amos and Jeremiah). Nevertheless, they form part of the prophetic experience, and were clearly generalized by the later community to all prophets.

The precise role of the oracles against other nations remains unclear. There is anger at the brutality of the oppressing foes; God's instruments have gone beyond their commission. There is anger at the neighboring countries who rejoiced at the downfall of Israel. Zimmerli speaks of "the view that in the judgement upon the nations the turning point of Israel's destiny is reached."[29] Whatever of the details here, an understanding of prophecy appears to have emerged in which there is a clear turning point. The word of God, addressed to Israel—both northern and southern kingdoms—spoke of the disaster which was to come

---

[28]For a more detailed outline of the contents of the book of Jeremiah, see for example Robert P. Carroll, *Jeremiah* (OTL: London: SCM, 1986) 86-88.

[29]Zimmerli, *Ezekiel 1*, 72.

upon them, resulting from the evils which they had perpetrated. After this, a period was promised in which there would be hope and restoration. In the case of the northern kingdom, some of this hope would have been focused in the reform movement under Josiah. After the fall of Jerusalem, the hope needed to be extended to embrace both north and south. The function of prophecy has come to be seen as the proclamation of both judgment and restoration. This conviction is reflected in the literary shape of the prophetic books.

Today

The task which confronts us in coming to grips with Israel's pre-exilic prophecy is reconciling the understanding of God with the experience of history. These prophets, who spoke God's word to their people, spoke of disaster which would and did strike both northern and southern kingdoms. Often in quite gruesome terms, this disaster is attributed to God. Yet when the promises of future hope are formulated, they are not based on the certainty of reformed behavior on Israel's part; they are based on faith in God's commitment to Israel.

It is not easy to find language which is adequate for discussing God's action in history. What may seem simple and straightforward can have troubling theological implications, once set within a broader context. If we were to speak of punishment and purification followed by gracious restoration, there is the difficulty of explaining why the prophecies of punishment were fulfilled to the letter while those of restoration were not. Generally, the chastising parent metaphor does not prove helpful in relating God to Israel's or our historical experience. While it was taken for granted in the ancient Near East that the gods went out to war with the armies of their peoples, the violent intervention of God in the history of Israel provides problems for faith's experience of the immense respect God shows for the divine gift of human freedom. The realm of mind and spirit gives appropriate scope for the action of God, while the realm of power and violence seems less apt. The shaping of language in this area is not a task to be taken lightly.

As we consider the prophetic sayings more closely in the next couple of chapters, it will become evident that the evils which the prophets censured in Israel were such that of themselves they might well have brought about Israel's downfall. Certainly, they created a state of affairs such that there is no question of thinking that, if only God had been merciful and turned a blind eye, nothing would have happened. There is an inevitability in certain situations which seems to tap into the forces of cosmic order—and of course it is God who is responsible for the structures of cosmic order.

The task confronting us is twofold. One aspect is the attempt to understand as clearly as possible just how the prophets in Israel understood their pronouncements and the actions which followed in their train. The other aspect is our own attempt to understand them today, and how we maintain congruence with all the elements of a broader theological canvas. These twin concerns will need to be present in our closer examination of the prophetic message.

RECOMMENDED FURTHER READING

Robert Alter and Frank Kermode, (eds.), *The Literary Guide to the Bible,* 165-233. London: Collins, 1987.

Otto Eissfeldt, *The Old Testament: An Introduction,* 146-50. Oxford: Blackwell, 1965.

_____, "The Prophetic Literature." In *The Old Testament and Modern Study,* edited by H. H. Rowley, 126-34. Oxford: Clarendon, 1951.

Georg Fohrer, *Introduction to the Old Testament,* 358-62. Nashville: Abingdon, 1965.

Otto Kaiser, *Introduction to the Old Testament,* 297-305. Oxford: Blackwell, 1973.

Marvin A. Sweeney, *Isaiah 1-4 and the Post-Exilic Understanding of the Isaianic Tradition.* BZAW 171. Berlin: de Gruyter, 1988.

Emanuel Tov, "The Literary History of the Book of Jeremiah in the Light of Its Textual History." Pp. 211-37 in *Empirical Models for Biblical Criticism,* edited by Jeffrey H. Tigay. Philadelphia: University of Pennsylvania, 1985.

10

The Prophetic Censure of Israel

Recommended preliminary reading

Recommended preliminary reading

Before reading the body of the chapter, it will be helpful to have read the following passages:
Isaiah 1:1-9
Jeremiah 7:1-20

Nathan, Ahijah, and Elijah confronted individual kings whose crimes were such as could threaten to erode the social structure of the nation. Samuel confronted Saul with an evil which would have been seen as a source of danger to the nation. The great pre-exilic prophetic figures, whose work has been enshrined in the prophetic books which bear their names, stood in the same tradition. But their circumstances were different. For these prophets—Amos, Hosea, Micah, Isaiah, Jeremiah, Ezekiel—it was not the individual crimes of kings which had to be confronted. It was the nation as a whole. It was not so much the threat to the social structure which had to be addressed, as the consequences which would flow from the already evident decay of society. The time has come to look more closely at their prophetic message.

Two dates in Israel's history are immensely significant for understanding the pre-exilic prophets. They are 722 and 587. Their import is described in the biblical text.

For 722:

> Then the king of Assyria invaded all the land and came to
> Samaria, and for three years he besieged it. In the ninth year of
> Hoshea the king of Assyria captured Samaria, and he carried
> the Israelites away to Assyria, and placed them in Halah, and
> on the Habor, the river of Gozan, and in the cities of the
> Medes.
>
> (2 Kgs 17:5-6)

For 587:

> And in the ninth year of his reign, in the tenth month, on the
> tenth day of the month, Nebuchadnezzar king of Babylon
> came with all his army against Jerusalem, and laid siege to it;
> and they built siegeworks against it round about. So the city
> was besieged till the eleventh year of King Zedekiah. On the
> ninth day of the fourth month the famine was so severe in the
> city that there was no food for the people of the land. Then a
> breach was made in the city; the king with all the men of war
> fled by night by the way of the gate between the two walls, by
> the king's garden, though the Chaldeans were around the city.
> And they went in the direction of the Arabah. But the army of
> the Chaldeans pursued the king, and overtook him in the
> plains of Jericho; and all his army was scattered from him.
> Then they captured the king, and brought him up to the king
> of Babylon at Riblah, who passed sentence upon him. They
> slew the sons of Zedekiah before his eyes, and put out the eyes
> of Zedekiah, and bound him in fetters and took him to
> Babylon.
>
> In the fifth month, on the seventh day of the month—which
> was the nineteenth year of King Nebuchadnezzar, king of
> Babylon—Nebuzaradan, the captain of the bodyguard, a
> servant of the king of Babylon, came to Jerusalem. And he
> burned the house of the LORD, and the king's house and all the
> houses of Jerusalem; every great house he burned down. And
> all the army of the Chaldeans, who were with the captain of the
> guard, broke down the walls around Jerusalem. And the rest
> of the people who were left in the city and the deserters who
> had deserted to the king of Babylon, together with the rest of

the multitude, Nebuzaradan the captain of the guard carried into exile. But the captain of the guard left some of the poorest of the land to be vinedressers and ploughmen. (2 Kgs 25:1-12)

With these two disasters, the free and independent national life, first of the northern kingdom of Israel, and then of the southern kingdom of Judah, came to an end.

The pre-exilic prophets were sent to address a nation whose decay was like a vast landslide moving inevitably toward these disasters. The range of the dates generally suggested for the periods of activity of each of the prophets shows how closely they were associated with the national collapses of 722 and 587. Amos's activity can be located within the decade from 760-750; Hosea's somewhere in the period 750-724. That is from some thirty or more years before the fall of Samaria to just a few years from it. Isaiah was active from either 742 or 736 to 701; and Micah perhaps from 734 or 725 to 701. So both saw the fall of Samaria, and the last evidence of their prophecy comes at the time of Sennacherib's threat to Jerusalem and its deliverance in 701. Jeremiah's activity was located within the period 627-586 and Ezekiel's from 593-571. So Jeremiah was active from before the reform of Josiah until just after the fall of Jerusalem; Ezekiel was deported with the first exiles in 597 (cf., 2 Kgs 24:14-16) and functioned among the exiles in Babylon.[1]

The Task of the Pre-Exilic Prophets

It is difficult for us to get a sense for just how stark and awesome was the task which confronted the pre-exilic prophets, in proclaiming the word of God to a people far down the track on the way to disaster. Having noted the association of their prophetic activity with the end of the northern and southern kingdoms, it may help to bring their task home to us if we confront the impact of some key statements from their message.

[1]It is not possible within the context of this book to deal with all the texts or all the figures of the Old Testament. So, here, we have to leave aside Zephaniah (c. 630) and Nahum and Habakkuk (between 628 and 612). Also, it must be recognized that some of these dates are approximate estimations. It is possible, for example, that the activity of either Amos or Micah lasted no more than a year.

AMOS

> You only have I known
>> of all the families of the earth;
> therefore I will punish you
>> for all your iniquities. (3:2)

> Not one of them shall flee away,
>> not one of them shall escape. (9:1)

HOSEA

> Call his name Not my people,
>> for you are not my people
>> and I am not your God. (1:9)

> They shall be like the morning mist
>> or like the dew that goes early away,
> like the chaff that swirls from the threshing floor
>> or like smoke from a window. (13:3)

MICAH

> I will make Samaria
>> a heap in the open country,
>> a place for planting vineyards. (1:6)

> Therefore because of you
>> Zion shall be ploughed as a field;
> Jerusalem shall become a heap of ruins,
>> and the mountain of the house a wooded height. (3:12)

ISAIAH

> Your country lies desolate,
>> your cities are burned with fire;
> in your very presence
>> aliens devour your land;

it is desolate, as overthrown by aliens.
The daughter of Zion is left
  like a shanty in a vineyard,
like a shed in a melon patch,
  like a besieged city. (1:7-8)

Nothing remains but to crouch among the prisoners
  or fall among the slain. (10:4)

JEREMIAH

For, lo, I am calling all the tribes of the kingdoms of the north, says the LORD; and they shall come and every one set his throne at the entrance of the gates of Jerusalem, against all its walls round about, and against all the cities of Judah. (1:15)

I will do to the house which is called by my name, and in which you trust, and to the place which I gave to you and to your fathers as I did to Shiloh. And I will cast you out of my sight, as I cast out all your kinsmen, all the offspring of Ephraim.
(7:14-15; cf. 26:6, 9, 18)

EZEKIEL

A third part of you shall die of pestilence and be consumed with famine in the midst of you; a third part shall fall by the sword round about you; and a third part I will scatter to all the winds and will unsheathe the sword after them. (5:12)

Behold, I will profane my sanctuary, the pride of your power, the delight of your eyes, and the desire of your soul; and your sons and your daughters whom you left behind shall fall by the sword. (24:21)

It is a harsh message that the pre-exilic prophets had to proclaim. No wonder Jeremiah burst out in pain:

For whenever I speak, I cry out,
  I shout, "Violence and destruction!"

For the word of the LORD has become for me
a reproach and derision all day long.
If I say, "I will not mention him,
or speak any more in his name,"
there is in my heart as it were a burning fire
shut up in my bones,
and I am weary with holding it in,
and I cannot. (20:8-9)

The harshness is eased to some degree by the realization that repentance and forgiveness are always possible. The prose sermon in Jer 7:1-15 is, in many ways, an ideal summary of the whole message of pre-exilic prophecy.[2] The first exhortation of that sermon is: "Amend your ways and your doings, and I will let you dwell in this place" (v 3).[3] At one level, it is inaccurate to categorize the prophetic message as a call to repentance. Exhortations to repent or reform are relatively rare in the prophetic speeches. At another level, the possibility of repentance may be assumed to have been constantly present. At this level, every threat and every menace is, in its own way, a call to that repentance which alone may avert the disaster. The book of Jonah expresses this con-

---

[2] It is among the prose passages in Jeremiah which resemble aspects of deuteronomistic thought and language. This is generally attributed to editing or transmission in deuteronomistic circles. There are differences of opinion as to the degree to which they represent Jeremiah's message or deuteronomistic convictions. The recent study of R.P. Carroll favors deuteronomistic creativity: "On the other hand it must be acknowledged that there is as strong, if not stronger, a case to be made for the view that the deuteronomists present Jeremiah in their own words completely. As a paradigm of prophecy they show him to have spoken and acted in the way the authentic prophet of Yahweh would have spoken and acted" (*From Chaos to Covenant: Uses of Prophecy in the Book of Jeremiah* [London: SCM, 1981] 86). Certainly, we need to be aware of the deuteronomistic overtones in the picture presented. They are reflected in the emphasis on repentance. As Carroll comments: "The perspective of the editors is a different one from the prophet's, because most of his work was done before the fall of Jerusalem, but the deuteronomists worked through the exile. Jeremiah failed to turn the community of his time, but the deuteronomists were determined to use him in their scheme to turn the exilic community and to secure the future. . . . The overriding concern of the editors is with the community in exile, rather than with presenting a historically accurate account of the prophet (*From Chaos to Covenant*, 79). On Jer 7:1-13, and a valuable comparison with chap. 26, see *From Chaos to Covenant*, 85-95, and now Carroll, *Jeremiah* (OTL: London: SCM, 1986) 206-12.

[3] A slight change in the vowels of the Hebrew gives the attractive rendering, "so that I may remain with you in this place" (*NAB*, similarly *JB*).

viction brilliantly. Jonah's message is utterly unconditional: "Yet forty days, and Nineveh shall be overthrown!" (Jon 3:4). And the people of Nineveh believed God, fasted and did penance, with the expectation that "Who knows, God may yet repent and turn from his fierce anger, so that we perish not?" (Jon 3:9). Which is exactly what God did. Which is exactly what Israel knew all the time.[4] The possibility that repentance could always have averted the disasters mitigates the harshness of the prophetic proclamation, but only to some degree.

The Example of Amos

It may help us create a certain empathy with the situation of the prophets if we walk a mile in Amos's moccasins. Von Rad has a very perceptive reflection on the visions of Amos, reported in chapters 7-9.[5] Amos reports a series of five visions. The fifth (9:1-4) varies slightly from the others in form, but it is almost certainly intended to be the climax of the series. In these visions, the approaching end of Israel is revealed to Amos. As von Rad observes, there is no command given Amos to proclaim what he has seen. The visions are for Amos alone. In the first two (7:1-3, 4-6), natural disasters threaten and Amos successfully intercedes. In the next two visions (7:7-9; 8:1-3), Amos is shown a symbol, and the symbol is interpreted for him as signifying the destruction and the end of Israel. This is vividly clear in the fifth vision, where he sees the command being issued for that destruction. What searing impact a visionary experience of this nature would have had on Amos! In von Rad's words:

---

[4]A little later, we will need to examine what understanding of reality is associated with this conviction that repentance can bring forgiveness and thus avert threatened evil. For the present, it is enough to be aware of this conviction in Israel. With it, one must also examine the meaning of God's refusal to listen to intercession from the prophets. J.M. Ward considers that the view of the prophets as exhorting Israel to repentance was first promulgated in the sixth century (*Amos & Isaiah: Prophets of the Word of God* [Nashville: Abingdon, 1969] 155). While this may be put too strongly, it is timely caution against reading later attitudes back into the thought of earlier generations.

[5]G.von Rad, *Old Testament Theology* (2 vols.; Edinburgh: Oliver and Boyd, 1962-65) 2. 131-132.

> What is even more important, however, is that intensive intellectual process which must have followed such a revelation. *Amos went about amongst a people who had been condemned to death; and as a result his environment at once assumed a different appearance and he became acutely aware of the abuses around him.*[6]

Whether the visions came all at once, or were spread over a period of time, one can imagine that Amos's initial reaction would have been a desperate search for the reason why. Why? Why? Why on earth should so disastrous a fate be about to befall northern Israel?

If, as von Rad assumes, these five visions triggered Amos's prophetic activity and are to be associated with his call, we might wonder whether they led him to trek north in an effort to find out why this disaster was imminent.[7] We can imagine how, as Amos moved from village to village, he noticed the poor trampled into the dust, the righteous and needy being sold (2:6-7), the poor and needy being oppressed and crushed in the northern capital (4:1), grain being demanded from those who could scarcely spare it and any word of honest protest being muzzled (5:10-11), and what he saw in the villages and cities appeared in an ominous and baleful light, after what he had seen in his visions. No longer need Amos ask why. Now he knew why. Instead of the questioning search for reasons, he became possessed by indignation at the abuses and by an urgent compulsion to bring Israel to a clear understanding of what was happening to them. A society that behaved in so destructive a fashion would inevitably be destroyed. There is the source of the destruction which he had seen in his visions. And there is the source of Amos's prophetic message.

[6]Von Rad, *Old Testament Theology*, 2. 132. Emphasis mine.

[7]"The peasant Amos's call is almost certainly to be connected with the reception of the five visions" (von Rad, *Old Testament Theology*, 2. 131).

The Form of the Prophetic Message

This understanding can give us insight into the form of the prophetic message in the pre-exilic period, and why it was that these so-called "writing prophets" generated books, while their predecessors left only stories behind them. The figures like Samuel, Nathan, Ahijah, Elijah, and Micaiah confronted individual kings, on single occasions, about specific matters. When they had had their say, all that was to be said had been said. The guilty party, the king, had been confronted with his crime or with the truth; he had been made aware of the consequences which would flow from it, so that the link between crime and punishment would be acknowledged. There was no more to do. Perhaps it was necessary that others should know that an errant king had been reproved, that a headstrong king had ignored the truth; for that reason, the stories were told. The stories were individual stories, because the situations were individual situations; in themselves, apart from their ramifications, they extended no further.

For the prophets from Amos to Ezekiel, the situation is very different. It is not an individual person who has to be confronted, but the nation. It is not an individual crime that has to be condemned, but the whole web and tissue of evil acts which corrosively erode the structure and soul of society. Only rarely did the pre-exilic prophets address this evil globally, inveighing against it at the royal court or in the temple (for example, Jeremiah's temple sermon). Instead, they dealt with it at the concrete level, wherever they met it. The global assault came, not in the form of the discourse, but in its presentation: in collecting all of the individual utterances so that, in their very mass, they communicated a sense of the totality of what had gone wrong.

The clearest example of this being actually portrayed for us, rather than deduced by us, is to be found in Jeremiah 36. The text speaks for itself.

> In the fourth year of Jehoiakim the son of Josiah, king of Judah, this word came to Jeremiah from the LORD: "Take a scroll and write on it all the words that I have spoken to you against Israel and Judah and all the nations, from the day I spoke to you, from the days of Josiah until today. It may be

that the house of Judah will hear all the evil which I intend to do to them, so that every one may turn from his evil way, and that I may forgive their iniquity and their sin." (Jer 36:1-3)[8]

It is in the fourth year of Jehoiakim. That is four years after the death of Josiah in 609, and the consequent collapse of his reform movement. Jehoiakim had been placed on his throne as a puppet of the Egyptian Pharaoh Neco. Jehoiakim's fourth year, 605, is the year when the Babylonian forces broke the power of the Egyptian empire (cf., Jer 46:2). There is, therefore, a new political situation in Palestine, and the possibility of critical decisions for Judah. Jeremiah must be ready to throw the full weight of his words into the balance. He is therefore portrayed gathering the spoken words, uttered on various occasions over the past twenty years, and having them written on a scroll. In this concentrated form, they are all the more likely to have a powerful impact. According to the narrative, they were read by Baruch the following year. We are not told their impact on the people, but a clear picture is given of the impact they had on the princes of the royal court (vv 11-19). Then it was the king's turn to hear the prophet's words, and with royal contempt he cut the scroll into strips, as it was read, and burned it in the brazier beside him. We are given a sense here of what the narrator thinks the king should have done, and also some insight into the didactic purpose of the narrative.

> Yet neither the king, nor any of his servants who heard all these words, was afraid, nor did they rend their garments. Even when Elnathan and Delaiah and Gemariah urged the king not to burn the scroll, he would not listen to them. (36:24-25)

[8] Jeremiah 36, like Jeremiah 7 quoted earlier, is among the prose material in the book of Jeremiah which has affinities with deuteronomistic theology and language. Carroll comments: "It is a very dramatic narrative, redolent of ironic observation and unstated power struggles, which many commentators have taken to be an account of how the Jeremiah tradition was created. However that aspect of the matter is to be adjudged, the involvement of a scribe in the proceedings gives fair indication of the scribal origins of the story. It is a story created by the deuteronomists, which accounts for their part in the construction of the tradition. Whether it is an accurate historical account or a story created by the redactors to justify their place in the tradition is a matter much debated by scholars" (*From Chaos to Covenant*, 15). With due caution on the historical details, it may stand as a helpful example of the way in which collections of prophetic utterances were put together and the purposes they served.

Jehoiakim is not like his father, Josiah. When Josiah heard "the words of the book of the law, he rent his clothes" (2 Kgs 22:11); he set out promptly to implement all the words of the book. Jehoiakim is pictured in the mold of the king of Israel, typified in the Micaiah story: even if he knew the truth, he did not want to act upon it. Jeremiah and Baruch had to be hidden in order to avoid the royal prison, which had been Micaiah's fate. With all of its drama and the wealth of its implications, the chapter is a valuable pointer to the way the prophets' words were brought together and the sorts of purpose that they served.[9]

Our understanding of the situation in which the prophets found themselves helps us also to grasp the fundamental structure which was archetypal for prophetic speech.[10] Amos had seen, in his visions, the end that was coming upon Israel. Amos had learned something of the reasons why that end was coming upon Israel, either through his own experience or directly through the word of God.[11] Each in their own way, the pre-exilic prophets

[9]There has been much speculation about the contents of Baruch's scroll. "It must have been fairly short, in order to have been read three times in the one day, and it must also have contained curses and threats exclusively to have warranted the king's complete rejection of it. As such it may have consisted of the bulk of threat oracles in chs. 2-6 and possibly 8.4-9.1 (Hebrew 8.23), but as Georg Fohrer wisely observes, 'It is probably hopeless to try to reconstruct an original scroll'" (Carroll, *From Chaos to Covenant*, 15).

[10]On this subject, the classic study is Claus Westermann, *Basic Forms of Prophetic Speech* (Philadelphia: Westminster, 1967). The elements of prophetic speech are there termed "accusation" and "announcement." "Reproach" and "threat" have also been used. The most appropriate and vivid words in English are probably "censure" and "threat." In what follows, the terms "accusation," "censure," and "denunciation," on the one hand, and "announcement," "proclamation," and "threat," on the other, will be treated as interchangeable.

[11]There is a delicate distinction here, and it should not be drawn too sharply. Most of the time, the word of God *comes* to the prophet, and we are not told how. Did it come as insight, conviction, understanding or image? We are not told. Some people have a mental picture of a voice speaking out of the heavens, as in the story of Jesus' baptism (Mt 3:17; Mk 1:11; Lk 3:22). The Old Testament never speaks of the prophetic experience in this way. The closest parallel is 1 Sam 3:1-18, but it is not the same; to interpret it in such terms would be to distort the point of the story. There is perhaps a very thin line between conviction divinely engendered in the human mind through insight or experience and divine communication granted to a person. Elijah speaks not of wind, earthquake, or fire, but "a still small voice" *(RSV)*, "a tiny whispering sound" *(NAB)*, "the voice of a gentle breeze" (LXX)—certainly, no overwhelming experience here (1 Kgs 19:12). Jeremiah could be uncertain of the word: "then I knew that this was the word of the LORD" (Jer 32:8)—but only at the end of the story (vv 6-8). And the prophets could also be ruthlessly certain. We should be careful not to impose a straitjacket on the ways of God's communication nor to strip it of its mystery. Some of the mystics remind us that divine

reached similar convictions. And that was the brunt of their communication to Israel: the proclamation of the end, and the hammering home of the reasons for it. The announcement of the end could be simple enough; it was a statement of fact. It is sometimes clothed in horrific language. Perhaps the vividness was needed to break through the dullness of apathy and lethargy; perhaps through shock they sought to stir repentance. The reasons, on the other hand, took the form largely of accusations addressed to the people. As the sins of Saul, David, and Ahab brought about their punishment, so the evil of the people was bringing about their end. It is often in these censures that we find the profound insight and depth of religious passion which have come to be associated with Israel's prophets.

The structure of a prophetic statement, in what might be called its ideal form, consists of an accusation or censure linked by the messenger formula, "thus says the LORD," to an announcement or threat. The censure specified the particular evil with which the prophet was either confronted or concerned. The threat declared the disaster which was imminent. The link between them could be forged in various ways—a simple "therefore," or "thus says the LORD," or "oracle of the LORD"—but for the most part it expressed the conviction that the prophet was the messenger of God. The messenger had always a formulaic identification of his message. For example, the embassy from Balak, king of Moab, to Balaam began their message: "Thus says Balak the son of Zippor"(Num 22:16). One of the fundamental aspects of prophecy is the image of the prophet as messenger of God.[12]

The structure in which the censure is linked by the messenger formula to the threat makes it tempting to argue that the divine message was the threat alone, with the censure stemming from the prophet's own insight. Our reflections on Amos could point in the same direction. It is probably not a prudent path to take. Either censure or threat can stand alone. The messenger formula in its various guises can stand at the beginning, middle, or end, or be

communication can occur without words and is most easily betrayed on being transformed into words.

[12]This image says little of the concrete forms and social situations of prophetic activity (see R.R. Wilson, *Prophecy and Society in Ancient Israel*, [Philadelphia: Fortress, 1980] esp. 10-13).

repeated. The process of growth of Israel's tradition often involved the accumulation of utterances or traditions, and their updating through redaction. While it is always a challenge to reconstruct an original simple form and trace the development of subsequent forms from it, it is also a precariously insecure undertaking. In the present state of our knowledge, such a venture must be treated with caution.

We have looked at the literary structures of the prophetic books. It is very important to keep in mind the association of censure and threat, of accusation and announcement, in the structure of the prophetic oracles. As long as this is remembered, the task of getting a close feel for the components of the prophetic message may be best served by a running survey of the prophetic texts, looking first in this chapter at the censures which the prophets pronounced over Israel, then in the next at the threats which it was their hard duty to announce.[13]

The Prophetic Censure

AMOS

The book of Amos begins with a series of highly structured sayings, addressed first of all to the surrounding nations, culminating in the saying about Israel.[14] They begin with the messenger formula: "Thus says the LORD." Then there is a proverbial play with numbers, marking intensification toward a climax: for three and for four (cf., Proverbs 30). Here the intensification is focused on the transgression, which elicits the next element of the saying. The literal translation of this element is: I will not revoke it, or I will not cause it to return. The "it" most

---

[13]The following sections, in particular, should be read in conjunction with the biblical text.

[14]The ministry of Amos, from Tekoa, is located in the northern kingdom, approximately in the decade 760-750. Among the most helpful commentaries on Amos are: J.L. Mays, *Amos* (OTL; London: SCM, 1969); J.M. Ward, *Amos & Isaiah* (Nashville: Abingdon, 1969); and H.W. Wolff, *Joel and Amos* (Hermeneia; Philadelphia: Fortress, 1977).

probably designates God's anger.[15] It has been dispatched; it will not be called back. Then comes the specific accusation in each case, perhaps to be understood as the climactic transgression. Finally, there is the proclamation of the judgment, with a standard formula recurring ("So I will send a fire upon...,") which is then further developed in certain cases. The oracle formula, "says the LORD" closes off each saying.[16] Experience of several realms of knowledge is evident in this structure: prophetic, proverbial, legal, and of course historical.

With the exception of the later update to include Judah (2:4-5), all the accusations are concerned with what appears to be excessive brutality in the prosecution of war. Damascus threshed Gilead with threshing sledges of iron; the image is of harsh and cruel treatment. Gaza delivered a whole people into exile to Edom; selective exile seems to have been a common practice, but here it is a whole people. The same is repeated for Tyre. For Edom, the accusation is general, but the theme of excess is maintained, since he "cast off all pity and his anger tore perpetually" (1:11). Ammon mutilated pregnant women in a mere border dispute. Moab burned to lime the bones of the king of Edom, denying him decent burial. These are offences of one nation against another, as well as crimes against humanity. In the prophetic indignation against these crimes, there is not only a sense of the universal sovereignty of God, but also a feel for some form of international law. There is also a remarkable knowledge of international affairs on Amos's part; his horizons are far wider than the village of Tekoa.

These nations are the neighbors of Israel: Damascus to the NE, Gaza to the SW, Tyre to the NW, Edom to the SE, and Ammon and Moab nearer at hand to the East. Perhaps in this geo-

---

[15]See R.P. Knierim, "'I will not cause it to return' in Amos 1 and 2," in *Canon and Authority: Essays in Old Testament Religion and Theology* (ed. G.W. Coats and B.O. Long; Philadelphia: Fortress, 1977) 163-75.

[16]The final "says the LORD" is missing for the sayings against Tyre and Edom. Tyre's transgression repeats that of Gaza; Edom's is couched in general terms. The proclamation for both is left undeveloped. Opinion differs as to whether these differences are simply variations (cf., Mays, *Amos*), or indicate a secondary expansion of the series (cf., Wolff, *Joel and Amos*). The saying against Judah not only has no development of the proclamation and no final "says the LORD"; it also speaks of a totally different kind of transgression. It is generally considered to be a later updating of Amos's message.

graphical grouping we can see a reason for the addition of Tyre and Edom. Whatever of that, Israel lies at the center. The accusation directed against Israel is internal, not in the area of international affairs like the others. Yet they have a common theme: for the others, it was the dealings of peoples with peoples; for Israel, it is the dealing of people with people. Amos speaks of the innocent and the needy who are sold.[17] We are not told the whys and wherefores of the sale. The pair of shoes may be symbolic for a mere bagatelle; it may, instead, be symbolic of land transfer transactions. The selling probably is as slaves, with a view to recovering debts. The central issue is innocence and need. The innocent have not had their rights respected in court, in the gathering of the elders in the open space at the gate (cf., Ruth 4:1-12). Their fellow citizens have handed them over unjustly. The needy have not had their need respected. Perhaps their crops failed, perhaps their flocks were raided; their fellow citizens looked at their legal obligations and not to their human need.

So Amos generalizes: they trample the head of the poor into the dust of the earth; they "turn aside" the way of the afflicted. The image of trampling on people's heads is clear enough and vivid enough. Turning aside the way of the afflicted employs a technical metaphor we can recognize from its contexts. It denotes the failure to give due process of law in the courts. Perhaps the metaphor is from the turning aside of the course of justice. Or perhaps it derives from the body language of those who turn their heads aside to deny justice or so as not to see the rightness of a cause.[18] Whatever the details, justice is being denied to those who need it. In the ancient Near East, as in any society, the poor and the needy are the touchstone of justice in society. Where might is right, the mighty are never unjustly treated. Where the weak and

---

[17] The two Hebrew words *ṣaddîq* and *rāšā'* are frequently and correctly translated "righteous" and "wicked" respectively. It is important to recognize that, at their base, there is the legal status of innocent and guilty. It is not a claim that one makes of oneself; it is a declaration that is made by the legal authority, just as the declaration of clean and unclean is made by the priestly authority.

[18] Such body language is very clear in the case of the king or judge. When the head and eyes remain cast down, the plea is denied. When the face is lifted up to the plaintiff, the plea is granted. Hence the blessing: "The LORD make his face to shine upon you, and be gracious to you: the LORD lift up his countenance upon you, and give you peace" (Num 6:25-26).

powerless are justly treated, one may be certain of the justice of the society. Amos is certain: the society is unjust.

The details of the next cases are rather more obscure. The "maiden" would be a woman of marriageable age; nothing else is defined. If a man has intercourse with her, he must marry her (cf., Deut 22:28-29), and be responsible for her honor and her rights, her support and protection. It was forbidden for a father to have intercourse with his daughter-in-law (cf., Lev 18:15; 20:12). In the deuteronomic law, the necessities of life cannot be taken in pledge; a garment cannot be taken from a widow (Deut 24:17), and the poor man's cloak must be restored to him before nightfall (Deut 24:12-13). The matter of pledges or monetary damages is not an occasion for revelry and carousing, and not in the sanctuary and at the altar, which should be special symbols of justice.[19]

This sense of outrage at the oppression of the poor and the powerless is very strong in the sayings of Amos. In the saying in 3:9-11, the censure is about as fundamental as it is possible to get: "They do not know how to do right ... those who store up violence and robbery in their strongholds" (3:10). The unbridled pursuit of material wealth has so dulled their sensibilities, that they do not know how to do right. No accusation could be more basic. Violence has the connotation of harm done to persons, robbery the connotation of harm done to property. So Amos takes in the broad sweep of personal injury and injury to property, the proceeds amassed in the fortresslike homes of the city rich of Samaria.[20] Here Amos pillories, in global fashion, the outcome of the individual cases mentioned in 2:6-8. These are not the exceptions; these have become the rule on which society is run and wealth is won.

The same theme is present in the saying in 4:1-3. This time it is addressed to the wives of the wealthy. Samaria was the capital of the northern kingdom. The "cows of Bashan" was probably not a pejorative form of address, since the lords at court can be referred to as the rams and bulls. Since Bashan was rich grazing land, it probably has overtones of well-fed, well-heeled, and well-groomed. They are the wealthy women of the capital, and Amos

[19]On these issues, see Wolff, *Joel and Amos*, 165-68.

[20]Cf., Wolff, *Joel and Amos*, 192-94.

denounces them for oppressing the poor and crushing the needy in order to maintain their lifestyle. There is a deliberately cruel irony in the juxtaposition of the oppression of the poor and the crushing of the needy with the order for more liquor. There is clear evidence in these accusations of a pattern of luxurious living built up at the cost of the impoverishment of others. Amos has a grim reminder: when the besieging forces breach the walls, the first of the land will be the first to go out into captivity.

The theme recurs in more fragmentary sayings. In their grammatical form, 5:7 and 10 belong together. They have been separated by the hymnic passage in vv 8-9 (cf., 4:13; 9:5-6). Both vv 7 and 10 refer to the distortion of the processes of justice. In the Israelite and general ancient Near Eastern understanding, justice was the foundation of society. When justice failed, society foundered (cf., Ps 82:3-5). When justice has turned sour and innocence is ground into the dirt, the fabric of human society is rotted. When honest protest is not upheld and truth is not respected, the social bonds are irreparably weakened. The words of v 10 need to be turned into the picture of the citizens of a town, gathered in the gate to transact the legal cases of the day. When false evidence is taken for true, when the rights of citizens are not respected, the one who rises in protest becomes the focus of hate and abhorrence. In such circumstances, the full human life of the free Israelite is impossible. The details recur: the extortionate demands for grain (v 11), the bribes offered and taken in order to be sure that one's fellow citizens nod in one's favor when one's case is false (v 12), and those who are in need can find no recourse in the law which should protect them (v 12). It is worth noting, in this context, that in the story of Naboth (1 Kings 21) the narrator takes for granted that the elders were all in the know about the falsity of the trumped up charges; the letters are sent to the collectivity (v 8). The narrator brings home the perfidy of it all, with references to "the men of his city" (v 11), his fellow citizens, "who dwelt with Naboth in his city" (vv 8, 11), who knowingly sacrificed a fellow townsman to the greed of royal convenience.

There is also in Amos the condemnation of cultic abuse. Bethel and Gilgal were great sanctuaries of the northern kingdom. Yet Amos says: "Come to Bethel, and transgress; to Gilgal, and multiply transgression" (4:4). We may need to paraphrase in order to feel the force of the irony: come to church, and sin; to the cathedral, to break the law. God is not present in their liturgies: "I hate, I despise your feasts, and I take no delight in your solemn assemblies" (5:21). In the context of what Amos censures, this incredibly strong statement can only be a total condemnation of liturgical celebration in an unjust society. Sacrificial worship is a communal worship, a celebration of social community in grateful recognition of the God who has made it possible. Where the core of society is incurably corrupt, there can be no cause for celebration. So the concluding cry: "let justice roll down like waters, and righteousness like an everflowing stream" (v 24).

As Amos looked closely into the life of his community, and as the details accumulated to fill out the general picture of social depravity, perhaps Amos came to understand why his intercession on behalf of his people was hopeless (cf., 7:1-6), and why their end was certain (cf., 7:7-9; 8:1-3; 9:1).

HOSEA

In general, the censure in Hosea takes a different tack.[21] But similar concerns are present there too. When we turn to the names of Hosea's children, there are possibly three reasons alleged for the name of his firstborn, Jezreel. There is the triple word-play: the blood of Jezreel, the house of Israel, and the valley of Jezreel (1:4-5). "The blood of Jezreel" must refer to the wholesale bloodshed which accompanied Jehu's revolution (2 Kings 9-10). In pursuit of his coup, Jehu killed Joram, king of Israel, and Ahaziah, king of Judah (2 Kgs 9:24, 27). Then he had Jezebel killed (9:33), followed by all the sons of the king of Israel, his lords, his friends, and his priests (10:1-11). Meeting kinsfolk of the king of Judah on the road, he had them killed too (10:12-14). Finally, in one great slaughter, he wiped out the worshippers of Baal (10:18-27). Although the circle around Elisha, whose disciple anointed Jehu and triggered the coup (9:1-13), presumably ap-

---

[21]The ministry of Hosea is located in the northern kingdom, approximately in the years 750-724. Among the most helpful commentaries on Hosea are: J.M. Ward, *Hosea: A Theological Commentary* (New York: Harper & Row, 1966); J.L. Mays, *Hosea* (OTL; Philadelphia: Westminster, 1969); and H.W. Wolff, *Hosea* (Hermeneia; Philadelphia: Fortress, 1974).

proved—considering the bloodshed a small cost to pay to exterminate the destructive influence of the worship of Baal—Hosea thought quite differently. Perhaps the fruitlessness of it impacted on him. A hundred years later, he still had to struggle against the seductive attraction of Baal. Or perhaps he was acutely sensitive to the irreparable damage done to the social fabric by such murderous disregard for the sanctity of human life. It was obvious enough to Hosea's disciples that they added no explanation.

In pleading the case against Israel as wife (Hos 2:2-15; MT, 4-17), Hosea's accusations all turn on the false understanding of life, which attributed natural fertility to Baal, the nature god. The imagery for Israel and its gods is that of the prostitute and her clients. To these clients, the Baals, Israel attributed its bread and water, wool and flax, oil and drink (v 5; MT, 7). The error of this understanding is underscored as Hosea has God cry: "She did not know that it was I who gave her the grain, the wine, and the oil, and who lavished upon her silver and gold which they used for Baal" (v 8; MT, 10). Fertility and prosperity come from the God of Israel, not Baal. Hosea's principal accusation against Israel is that they did not live by this understanding, and so they eroded the very foundation of their existence. The sustained use of the husband and wife image for this understanding of life is one of the marked characteristics of Hosea. It speaks of the inner depth of intimacy and passionate attachment which colors Hosea's understanding of the relationship between Israel and God.

The saying which begins the next collection in Hosea is remarkable for its comprehensiveness (4:1-3). It opens God's case against Israel:

> Hear the word of the LORD,
>   O people of Israel;
> for the LORD has a controversy
>   with the inhabitants of the land. (v 1)

The language is legal, the sort of speech that would have its place in the gate, where the rights of the inhabitants were decided. Here, Hosea details the complaint that God has against the people. The censure itself is spread over one long line and two short ones. The long line spells out the good which is absent from Israel; the short

ones hammer home the evil that is present. The translation below
is literal, to approximate to this poetic force.

> There is no trustworthiness and there is no loyalty,
>   and there is no knowledge of God in the land;
> cursing and lying and killing,
>   and stealing and adultery;
> they break out
>   and bloodshed follows bloodshed. (4:1-2)

The primary balance is between the goodness that is absent and
the evil which is present. There is also the possibility that there is
further balance between the relationship to God, which is defective, and the correlative breakdown in human relationships as
well. Faithfulness/trustworthiness (*'emet*) and kindness/loyalty
(*ḥesed*) are the qualities which go with strong relationships. They
are expressive of reliability and commitment, of loyalty and trust.
"Kindness/loyalty/steadfast love" (*ḥesed*) is one of the central
elements in the description of God. See, for example, the formulaic
words of Exod 34:6, where the same pair recur (*RSV*, "steadfast
love and faithfulness"). This fidelity and loyalty is a strong part of
the God-Israel relationship: of God's commitment to Israel, and
of Israel's accepting response. But fidelity and loyalty are also
immensely important qualities within human relationships. We
should probably not try to polarize the saying into qualities of the
relationship to God which are missing, and defects in the relationship to people which are all too painfully evident. At the same
time, it would be an unwarranted simplification to hear these
words solely on the human plane. If the faithfulness and kindness,
referred to in v 1b, are primarily directed to human relationships
(so Wolff), nevertheless for Hosea it would be unthinkable for
these qualities to be flourishing in Israel's relationship with God
while being so devastatingly defective at the human level.

In a similar way, it would be unnecessarily restrictive to
describe what Hosea meant by "no knowledge of God" in terms
of the breaches of law listed in v 2. We have already seen the
deuteronomistic reflection on the transition between generations
and the difficulty of passing on the knowledge of God in that
transition (i.e., Judg 2:7-10). There is no significant human
difficulty involved in passing on the knowledge of law. There is a

vastly different situation encountered when we seek to pass on the values engendered by the experience of God. Those who had "seen all the great work which the LORD had done for Israel" (Judg 2:7) had a deeply felt experience of God. Their human lives are portrayed as marked by this experience.[22] Something of this experiential quality is almost certainly to be understood as part of the background to the use of this phrase in Hosea.

Given these general considerations, the specifics of God's accusation against Israel depict a society that has broken down. No trustworthiness, no loyalty, no knowledge of God: those are the traits of an anarchic rabble, not a richly human society. Society cannot exist long without trust and truth, without the reasonable certainty that commitments made will be responsibly met. Self-interest can rapidly cease to be enlightened and turn to self-seeking and the avaricious hunger for power and possession, unless the image of full human potential is etched by the guiding hand of the law and brought alive by the felt experience of God. Cursing, lying, killing, stealing, adultery: five verbs point to concrete instances of the factors which are eroding society. Cursing is not just the use of foul language. It is the attempt, through the manipulation of words and rites, to bring down evil and misfortune on another. In a society that believes it efficacious, it is most unneighborly behavior. Lying destroys the bonds of trust on which society relies. Above all, in cases of law, in the gate, it destroys the foundation of justice in society. Killing is the ultimate in social disruption; it takes the life of the victim, and the peace and security of everyone else. In societies fairly close to the survival line, theft may threaten personal existence; in certain contexts, it actually means kidnapping. Adultery poisons the wellsprings of both personal and family life. This heinous mess has burst across society. Hosea concludes the denunciation with a vivid metaphor: and blood touches blood. It may mean that the acts of bloodshed are so frequent that they are piled up against

---

[22]At least that is how the Deuteronomist portrays it in Judg 2:7-10, where fidelity and infidelity are directly correlated to the knowledge of God and the work God had done. It is, perhaps, more of a theological construct than a historical reality. The picture of the desert generation, who had also seen all that God had done, is a picture of rebellious and unfaithful conduct. The Deuteronomist seems to want to project a different image for life within the promised land.

one another. Or it may convey the vivid image of the bloodstains which spread and touch and mingle, and cover the country.

Hosea's censure is not concerned with blemishes in a healthy society. He portrays a society in its death throes. The threat that follows it is equally catastrophic (v 3). The land mourns, its inhabitants grow feeble; the very animals, the birds, and even the fish in the sea are taken away—they are gathered up and removed, they perish (to run the gamut of the meanings of the verb). This is too sweeping and far-reaching a disaster to be fobbed off as a drought. "But the description really outruns the limits of a drought or any other empirical situation; it portrays a loss of vitality by land and population that affects every creature, even the fish."[23] It is a picture of the wholesale contraction of life, touching the land itself, those who live on it, above it, and in its seas—for all, life is to be lessened, if it is not to vanish.

This is a very significant saying, and it is worth our while to dwell on it a little longer. We need to notice the link made between what Hosea censured and the threat he spoke. The link is not divine intervention or divine judgment, but a simple "therefore." The breakdown of society, for Hosea, involves the breakdown of nature. It seems clear that Hosea sees this not as a punishment meted out to the guilty, but as the natural consequences of what they have done. At first sight, this seems rather strange and overly naturalistic, coming above all from Hosea. It seems much too close to the Canaanite understanding, in which the fertility of nature depended on Baal, and was somehow connected to the fertility of human sexuality and to human behavior. That is Hosea's point precisely: it is not Baal but the God of Israel who is the source of fertility and life.

It is remarkable, though, that in this key position, at the start of a new section in the book of Hosea, what Hosea censures is not infidelity to God but social iniquity. Chapters 1-3 dealt with

---

[23]Mays, *Hosea*, 65. Wolff speaks of a great drought, but expands it to a universal catastrophe more grievous than the flood (*Hosea*, 68). Whether the verb here translated "mourn" is better read "wither/dry up" (with Wolff and Mays) is not significant for the drought issue. Wolff adds: "It is noticeable that the judgment results not from the direct actions of Yahweh himself, but from an 'organic structure of order,' 'a sphere in which one's actions have fateful consequences,' which Yahweh puts into effect. This conception results from a 'synthetic view of life'" (*Hosea*, 68). We will discuss this more fully in chapter 13.

infidelity, and it will remain the major thrust of Hosea's message. But here it is submerged by the passionate denunciation of the total social breakdown. Of course, the two are not separate. For Hosea, the right attitude to God simply cannot exist in a society in which all bounds are broken and the bloodstains merge across the land. As we will see in Hosea, fidelity to God is not a matter of words, but of that depth of inner conviction which motivates and sustains action. The society Hosea describes, then, is not a society capable of fidelity to God. The Israel Hosea denounces in 4:1-3 is as unfaithful to God as the Israel decried as an adulterous wife in chaps. 1-3.

Much the same concern recurs in the denunciation of the priests. The rejection of knowledge by the priests, their forgetting the law of their God, has led to the destruction of God's people (4:6). 4:1 deplored the absence of the knowledge of God. Hosea now turns against those responsible for that absence. It is the priests' task to keep alive in the community the vital respect for God and the living and celebrating of commitment to God. They failed. They rejected that task. Instead, they gloried in the evil that was spreading among the people. "They feed on the sin of my people; they are greedy for their iniquity" (4:8). Whether or not this means that the priests were delighted to be doing so well out of the people's sacrificial practices, it certainly expresses a terrible irony. The priests are foremost among those professionally responsible for protecting and promoting religious values among the people. Yet: "they are greedy for their iniquity." It shall be like people, like priest. The religious and the secular are not separable within Hosea.

Wine has taken away their understanding (4:11). Instead of a grasp of the meaning of God in their lives, they turn to superstition and idol worship, led astray by the seductive attraction of Baalism. The seduction has been pervasive in Israel: priests and people and court, Tabor and Mizpah and Shittim (5:1-2). Mizpah, probably in Benjamin, Tabor to the north, and Shittim further south just beyond the Jordan valley; why these three are singled out, we do not know, but they cover a wide sweep of the country. Israel's attachment to Baal has become attractive enough that a terrible thing has happened to them: "Their deeds do not permit them to return to their God" (5:4). The theme will recur in Hosea. Israel has become mired in the bog of its own religious behavior.

The habits and traditions of Yahwism are lost to it, replaced by the newfound spirit of Baalism. Israel could not return to its God, even if it wanted to. And that is tragic. The spirit that Hosea calls harlotry has taken over the way they see themselves and their world. They do not know their God: the word, the name of the LORD, the experience and the traditions can no longer strike a chord for Israel.

The implications of that ignorance are that even when Israel thinks of repentance, it can strike no roots. Hosea's denunciation of this fickleness comes in a context that is rich with theological understanding. After the images of God as pus and rottenness (5:12) and as lion and young lion (5:14) to Israel and Judah, Hosea presents a quite different aspect. God will withdraw, apparently leaving Israel to its fate, until they turn back in repentance (5:15). Here there is no image of active aggression on the part of God, but of a withdrawal which leaves events to take their course. God's words for Israel to say, in Hosea 6:1-3, are a lovely expression of what repentance should mean; they give us insight into the trust and understanding which were part of Israel's relationship with God.

> Come, let us return to the LORD,
>> for he has torn, that he may heal us;
>> he has stricken, and he will bind us up.
> After two days he will revive us;
>> on the third day he will raise us up,
>> that we may live before him.
> Let us know, let us press on to know the LORD;
>> his going forth is sure as the dawn;
> he will come to us as the showers,
>> as the spring rains that water the earth. (6:1-3)

The sure confidence is marred by Israel's inability to give any sort of lasting effect to this change of heart. Israel is confident of God's love, but their response of love "is like a morning cloud, like the dew that goes early away" (6:4). Israel's failure to grapple seriously with the meaning of life before God is at the core of much of Hosea's denunciation.

The evils Hosea censures in 6:11b-7:2 are left very general: corruption, wicked deeds, within and without. Yet the reflection on them gives a further insight into Hosea's understanding of human behavior before God. Earlier it was: "their deeds do not permit them to return to their God" (5:4). Here it is rather: their deeds do not permit their God to heal them. No short statement can compass a total theology. Hosea will later speak of God healing their faithlessness (14:4). But, in this saying, the reality is brought out that, where human attitudes are fixed and human minds are closed, it may be impossible to bring people to a vision they have abandoned. Here, Hosea has God confronted with the frustrating reality of human dullness, stubborn selfishness, and the ingrained habits of self-justifying evil. The attitudes result in a mesh of specific acts which prevent God from reaching the people to heal and restore.

The target of 7:3-7 is not clear to us. Perhaps it is connected with the coup in which King Pekah was assassinated and King Hoshea seized the throne of northern Israel (cf., 2 Kgs 15:30); perhaps its reference is wider, to the whole series of assassinations and coups (cf., 2 Kgs 15:8-30). Two aspects of the evil denounced by Hosea come out clearly. Government is profiting from wickedness and approving it (7:3). Government has got its priorities wrong, and is wrapped up in its own jealousies and intrigues rather than working for the good of the country (7:6-7). The reference to a royal celebration where the drunkenness got out of hand (7:5) is a reminder that Hosea is not reflecting in the abstract, but is close to the harsh hurly-burly of the actual events of the capital. When government forgets its responsibilities, the welfare of the nation is threatened.

The interplay of act and consequence is very strong in Hosea's thinking. His accusations point to a situation in which Israel's turning away from the ideals on which it was founded has brought about a set of inevitable consequences.

> Woe to them, for they have strayed from me!
> Destruction to them, for they have rebelled against me!
> I would redeem them,
> but they speak lies against me. (7:13)

This is a particularly good example of the ambiguity latent in much of the prophetic language. Is the cry of woe and destruction a statement of punishment to be inflicted by God, because Israel has strayed and rebelled? Or is it a lament over the fate of a people who have gone astray? James L. Mays opts for the latter.

> A woe-saying is spoken over those who are doomed or dead. It is not an invocation of disaster, but rather a statement of sorrow and warning that the consequences of some act or situation are impending and inevitable.[24]

The question remains open as to Hosea's understanding of the origin of the coming disaster: natural consequences, or divine causation, or are they inseparable in Hosea's thinking? The second half of the verse does not resolve the ambiguity. Is God's will to save impeded by the falsehood in Israel which demands punishment? Or is God's will to save frustrated by the false security in Israel which makes it impossible for God to reach them? My understanding of Hosea favors the latter interpretation. The verse then opens with a cry of sorrow and frustration: Woe is theirs, destruction is theirs! They have strayed far from the wellsprings of their life. They have rebelled against the directions which safeguard that life. The lies spoken against God close them off from the source where life is available. "Israel has spurned the good; the enemy shall pursue him" (8:3). They are out of redemptive reach.

"They made kings, but not through me. They set up princes, but without my knowledge" (8:4a). In the context, hardly a rejection of kingship as such, but a denunciation of the series of destructive political coups which have controlled the succession of kings. "With their silver and gold they made idols for their own destruction" (8:4b). Not only have they set up their own kings and princes, they have set up their own gods. The fabric of the nation, political and religious, is corroded. The folly of it all, "silly and without sense" (7:11), has embroiled Israel in the turmoil of the

---

[24]Mays, *Hosea*, 111. Wolff implies rather God's judgment: "After the first stage of weighing the evidence (6:4) and then examining Israel's transgression, Yahweh reaches a decision" (*Hosea*, 127). His understanding of the second half of the verse is adversative: "And am I supposed to redeem them" (*Hosea*, 127). Mays, too, continues from the quotation given above: "In prophetic speech it becomes a dirge for those under the sentence of Yahweh's judgment. The 'woe' is provoked by the 'devastation' which Yahweh has decreed against his people who have fled from him to another, and so rebelled against his lordship" (*Hosea*, 111).

constantly boiling cauldron of the politics of the fertile crescent. "Israel is swallowed up; already they are among the nations as a useless vessel!" (8:8).

> Like grapes in the wilderness,
>   I found Israel.
> Like the first fruit on the fig tree in its first season,
>   I saw your fathers.
> But they came to Baal-peor,
>   and consecrated themselves to Baal,
>   and became detestable like the thing they loved. (9:10)

Political turmoil and religious or ideological folly are the ruin of Israel. They have lost their sense of identity. The greater their prosperity, the greater their failure to understand the meaning of their lives.

> Israel is a luxuriant vine
>   that yields its fruit.
> The more his fruit increased
>   the more altars he built;
> as his country improved
>   he improved his pillars. (10:1)

For Hosea, Israel's understanding of its well-being is clearly mistaken. Yet the thinking and understanding which lies behind Hosea's accusations is never fully elucidated. It would seem, from the wordplays of the saying just quoted, that the increase in produce and the output of the land led to an identification of divinity with the forces of this prosperity. In turn, then, the God of Israel, whose embodiment of divinity drew on personal relationships, extending over a long historical development and challenging human beings to freedom and full richness of life, must fade in significance, with higher values relinquished for a crasser level of life.

Two sayings of Hosea may sum this up. One uses the agricultural metaphor of ploughing, reaping, and consumption.

> You have ploughed iniquity,
>> you have reaped injustice,
>> you have eaten the fruit of lies. (10:13)

And the other speaks, with infinite sadness, in the historical context of the exodus.

> The more I called them,
>> the more they went from me. (11:2)

The gist of Hosea's censure is just that: Israel has abandoned God. And in doing that, they have abandoned the true vision of themselves and the significance of their lives and their world. Unguided by any worthwhile vision, they have fallen into political turmoil and social and religious disintegration. As a result, their independence and their freedom will be short-lived.

MICAH

Micah is the prophet whose name is associated with the lapidary formulation of what is good and what is required by God: "to do justice, to love loyalty, and to walk wisely with your God" (6:8).[25] It is not surprising that the evils denounced by Micah around whose sayings the book has formed are primarily the evils of social injustice.

> Woe to those who devise wickedness
>> and work evil upon their beds!
> When the morning dawns, they perform it,
>> because it is in the power of their hand.
> They covet fields, and seize them;
>> and houses and take them away;
> they oppress a man and his house,
>> a man and his inheritance. (2:1-2)

---

[25]The ministry of Micah is located approximately in the years 725-701. Among the most helpful commentaries on Micah are: J.L. Mays, *Micah* (OTL; Philadelphia: Westminster, 1976) and H. W. Wolff, *Micha* (BKAT 14/4; Neukirchen: Neukirchener Verlag, 1982); also H.W. Wolff, *Micah the Prophet* (Philadelphia: Fortress, 1981).

The picture is clear, appalling, and all too well known in any day or age. Fields and houses are expropriated; family heritages are wiped out. Those who have power put all their energies into elaborating schemes to strip their assets from those who are less powerful. People are deprived of their livelihoods and their dignity; society is deprived of its reason to exist. People are stripped of security, women driven from their homes, and children deprived (2:8-9).

Micah condemns with fierce savageness the leaders in government whose duty was to protect the innocent and powerless, and who instead have totally reversed the moral order.

> Hear, you heads of Jacob
>   and rulers of the house of Israel!
> Is it not for you to know justice?—
>   you who hate the good and love the evil,
> who tear the skin from off my people,
>   and their flesh from off their bones;
> who eat the flesh of my people,
>   and flay their skin from off them,
> and break their bones in pieces,
>   and chop them up like meat in a kettle,
>   like flesh in a cauldron. (3:1-3)

The image could scarcely be harsher; the censure could scarcely be more fundamental. The heads and the rulers are those responsible for justice; they are the ones who hate good and love evil. Such is their greed and avarice; they are metaphorically cannibalizing their own people.

It is not only the political rulers who come under Micah's condemnation. The corrupting influence has spread to priests and prophets so that the steadying influence of the nation's religious traditions has been replaced by the avaricious pursuit of wealth.

> Its heads give judgment for a bribe,
>   its priests teach for hire,
> its prophets divine for money;
>   yet they lean upon the LORD and say,

> "Is not the LORD in the midst of us?
> No evil shall come upon us." (3:11)

The traditional sources of stability and security in Israelite society have failed. Unjust verdicts can be bought by bribery. The decisions and teaching of the priests, who are the guardians of the nation's traditions, can be influenced by money. The prophets, who once confronted the wrongdoing of kings, will now discover God's will in accordance with the payment offered them. To add insult to injury, they all rest secure in the certainty that God is in their midst. They cannot see that the holiness of God and the injustice of society are utterly incompatible.

There are five moments of censure (2:1-2, 8-9; 3:1-3, 5, 9-11), with the vehement denunciation of the blood and the wrong linked to Jerusalem, its heads, priests, and prophets, leading to the announcement of its total destruction. It is remarkable that this should be associated with the Jerusalem of Hezekiah, and that the so manifestly unfulfilled prophecy should be so clearly remembered. The deuteronomistically influenced story in Jeremiah 26 remembers this final saying (3:9-12), and uses it as a clear example of royal repentance and entreaty winning a last-minute reprieve from God. But Micah's accusation in 3:9-11 provides a markedly different picture of Hezekiah's Jerusalem from the image of the pious and god-fearing Hezekiah of the Deuteronomistic History. All of this is a valuable reminder of the complexity of the real life situations in ancient Israel, and the folly of thinking that our biblical text adequately reflects the whole spectrum of Israelite thought and literature.

Midway Reflection

At this point, after observing the evils denounced by Amos, Hosea, and Micah, it is worth our while to reflect a little on the state of the society in which these pre-exilic prophets were operating. It will help to have some sense of what Israel saw as an ideal structure of society, and to understand what was happening within Israel to make possible the evils so bitterly denounced by the prophets. What will be said here looks back over the sayings of Amos, Hosea, and Micah. It will be confirmed by the words of

Isaiah, Jeremiah, and Ezekiel.

We are presented with a picture of a society in transformation, with changes taking place which are extremely profitable to some, and humanly disastrous to others. Part of it, certainly, is the movement from an egalitarian peasant society to a stratified society of landowners and landless, exacerbated by the emergence of the cities as centers of wealth and power.

The egalitarian roots of Israel's concept of society can still be seen in the program for the jubilee year, outlined in Leviticus 25. There is no indication in the literature of the Old Testament that this program was ever put into action. Nevertheless, it is a very clear indication of the ideological convictions of one school of thought within Israel about the basis for a secure and just society. The idea is fundamentally very simple. Every fiftieth year, owners shall return to their land, and those who have been slaves shall return to their families (25:10). The underlying concept, where land is concerned, is of a stable society in which every family unit is endowed with land. This corresponds with the picture of the distribution of the land by lot to each of the tribes and families (cf., Josh 13-19). The society is thought of as stable. Land is only sold because of crop failure, drought, or other delinquencies which bring on debt. So there is amnesty from all debts every fiftieth year. Land returns to its original owners; those sold into debt slavery return to their families. Society is off to a fresh start.

The jubilee, as a program, is trying to deal with the problem of inherited wealth. The problem is one that many modern societies have tried to resolve through legislation, and so far no solution has won a wide measure of acceptance.[26] The theory of the jubilee was based on certain assumptions which are erroneous; these errors would have crippled its implementation. The population is assumed to be stable, so that there is always approximately the same ratio of families to land and the land is able to support those families. The transfer of land is associated only with debt or its equivalent. As a workable economic and political program, the jubilee year was probably not practicable. It stands, however, as

---

[26]The issue is primarily one of maintaining a certain level of equality of opportunity within each generation, while allowing for the differences created in each generation by aptitude, application, and fortune. For a discussion of some of the philosophical aspects of the problem, see J. Rawls, *Theory of Justice* (Cambridge: Harvard University, 1971).

witness to Israel's commitment to the ideals of an egalitarian society. Furthermore, it is a witness which comes from a relatively late stage in Israel's history and a late stage of a society in transition.

What Micah and the other pre-exilic prophets pillory is this transition, above all in its destructive impact on human lives and destinies. In particular, what we find the prophets placing under condemnation is the scheming to force this transition forward for personal profit and gain, regardless of either justice or truth; the pursuit of such aims, regardless of their terrible cost in human happiness and well-being; the wallowing in luxurious living of those who have benefited from this social change, coupled with the desertion of the values and religious faith which have been the traditional mainstay of their society.

A corresponding picture of what was involved in Israel's loss of faith is not easy to construct. Despite the immensely valuable discovery of the Ugaritic mythic literature, we still do not know enough about the beliefs and practices of the Canaanites to be able to document what Israel found attractive in Canaanite religion. Nor can we be certain about many of the particular features which prompted prophetic condemnation.

Eighth- and seventh-century Israel lived at the end of a long and remarkably change-filled history. Behind them lay the transition from semi-nomadic to settled existence, or at least from non-Palestinian to Palestinian life; the transition from dependence and oppression experienced in Egypt to independence and freedom in Israel; the transition from a basically tribal society to monarchy and nationhood; the transition from united kingdom to the division between north and south; the shifting emphasis from a variety of patriarchal shrines to the royal sanctuaries of Jerusalem, Bethel, and Dan. Every change in the surrounding world would require an adjustment to the complex of Israel's religious beliefs, their self-understanding, and their articulation of their relationship with God.

We have already noted that Israel did not initially experience Canaanite religion as hostile or antipathetic. The Baal and El names among the children of Saul and David point to an apparent appropriation of these divine names. By the time of Elijah, the impact of Baalism had been felt as deleterious and destructive. The reasons for this are not easy to isolate. Hans

Küng has made the comment that "every religion in the concrete is certainly a mixture of faith, superstition and unbelief".[27] There is, of course, the natural tendency when entering a new environment to assimilate to the beliefs, customs, and practices that are in vogue there. The unsettling nature of many changes may have propelled Israel toward seeking security in conforming to local traditions rather than confronting them. The strong deuteronomistic concern with intermarriage suggests that it may have played a role at various times.

There is a tendency also to blame the policies of the Assyrian empire, requiring the worship of Assyrian gods. Recent research has shown that this factor has probably been overemphasized.[28] A stronger influence may well have been the desire to imitate the behavior patterns of the more powerful and sophisticated of the surrounding nations. There is also latent in much of the prophetic denunciation the implication that prosperity had dulled Israel's religious sensibilities and had generated a self-sufficiency and pride that became contemptuous of faith. A clear expression of this danger is preserved in Proverbs.

> Give me neither poverty nor riches;
>> feed me with the food that is needful for me,
> lest I be full, and deny thee,
>> and say, "Who is the LORD?"
> or lest I be poor, and steal,
>> and profane the name of my God. (Prov 30:8-9)

Fear and physical need are base causes for belief in God. Pride and physical security and well-being are equally base causes for unbelief. It would seem, however, that they were at work in ancient Israel.

Israelite society, therefore, was caught up in changes which affected both its social structure and the structures of its religious belief. The injustice and oppression and the unbelief and religious apostasy which resulted are the principal targets of the pre-exilic prophets. What we have seen in Amos, Hosea, and Micah will be

[27]*On Being a Christian* (Garden City: Doubleday, 1976) 91-92.

[28]See M. Cogan, *Imperialism and Israelite Religion* (SBLMS 19; Missoula: Scholars Press, 1974).

reinforced by the sayings of Isaiah, Jeremiah, and Ezekiel. Because of their greater extent, we will be forced to greater selectivity.

ISAIAH

The book of Isaiah opens with a saying which powerfully deplores the failure of religious faith in Israel.[29]

> The ox knows its owner,
>   and the ass its master's crib;
> but Israel does not know,
>   my people does not understand. (1:3)

The central core of Israel's being as a people is its relationship with God—and that it does not know nor understand.

> They have forsaken the LORD,
>   they have despised the Holy One of Israel,
>   they are utterly estranged. (1:4)

As an accusation, it is the most central one on the religious plane. The whole of Israel's history has been interpreted in terms of its election, guidance, and protection by God—and they have forsaken God, despised the Holy One of Israel. Nothing could be more central.

We have to be careful not to be naive in reading such an accusation. It is all too easy for a modern to hear behind this charge the jealousy of a god whose devotees have apostatized, or the pain of a prophet whose nation has become bored with God. Yet the picture Isaiah paints resembles a surfeit of religiosity: multitudes of sacrifices, the swarming of crowds in the sanctuaries,

---

[29]The ministry of Isaiah is located in Jerusalem, approximately in the years 742/36-701. Our treatment here will be restricted to Isaiah 1-12. Among the most useful commentaries for Isaiah are: J.M. Ward, *Amos & Isaiah* (Nashville: Abingdon, 1969); O. Kaiser, *Isaiah 1-12* (OTL; Philadelphia: Westminster, 1972); and *Isaiah 13-39* (OTL: Philadelphia: Westminster,1974); R.E. Clements, *Isaiah 1-39* (NCB; Grand Rapids: Eerdmans, 1980); there are radical changes in the completely rewritten second edition of Kaiser's *Isaiah 1-12* (OTL; London: SCM, 1983). See also J.H. Hayes and S.A. Irvine, *Isaiah, The Eighth-century Prophet: His Times & His Preaching.* (Nashville: Abingdon, 1987).

the observance of sabbaths and festivals (vv 11-14). All of this speaks of plenty of attention being given to God—but not enough to justice in the community.

> When you spread forth your hands,
>> I will hide my eyes from you;
> even though you make many prayers,
>> I will not listen;
>> your hands are full of blood.
> Wash yourselves; make yourselves clean;
>> remove the evil of your doings from before my eyes;
> cease to do evil,
>> learn to do good;
> seek justice,
>> correct oppression;
> defend the fatherless,
>> plead for the widow. (1:15-17)

This is what it means to have forsaken God and despised the Holy One of Israel. It is to have turned God's people from a people gifted with freedom, security, and justice into a people under oppression, unable to find justice, riddled with evil.

It would be foolish to read such texts as though a jealous God was upset because a favored people had taken their affections elsewhere. Not to know God, not to understand, to forsake and to despise God describe a total state of affairs within the people. Lack of knowledge of God is not a matter of religious doctrine but of attitude to and outlook on the world. Not understanding, then, is seeing themselves and their world in a light which does not reflect the faith-understanding distilled by Israel from their experience of God. Forsaking God can go hand in hand with plenty of expressions of religious devotion—but they do not mirror an Israelite perception of reality. Despising God may not take the form of a calculated affront to the deity, but is more likely to be evident in the injustice and oppression which erode the foundations of society.

Of course, Isaiah does not offer us a theological discourse on the interplay of religious infidelity and social injustice in the fabric of Israelite society and Israel's relationship with its God. As so often in the prophetic collections, Isaiah 1 offers us a series of utterances which may well have been independent of each other. What is said is short and pungent; the underlying theology is latent, but is left unexpressed. Within these sayings, the themes of Israel's infidelity to God, of the social injustice in the community of Israel, and of God's disdain for Israel's sacrifices are intimately connected. This connection is not simply the work of the collectors who compiled the prophetic books; it can be found within individual sayings, and it is of the very nature of things.

The link is multifaceted but easily understood. God chose Israel as a people and delivered them from danger and oppression so that they might exist in freedom and security. Oppression and injustice within Israel, negating that freedom and security, are therefore an effective denial or rejection of God's action and election. Israel's worship celebrated God's election and God's action on Israel's behalf. But if it were denied within the social life of the community, it could have no meaning within the liturgical life of the sanctuary. One category of Israel's sacrifices, the communion-sacrifices, were shared among the worshippers in the sanctuary, expressing the social ties which bound them to one another in their relationship with their God. When injustice had destroyed the reality of those ties, the sacrificial worship had worse than no meaning—it acted out a lie. Another category of Israel's sacrifices, the holocausts, expressed the utter dependence of Israel upon God. Infidelity, which denied that dependence, would also transform these sacrifices into effective lies.

The saying in Isa 2:6-17, which really begins the collection 2:1-4:6, draws a picture of Israel's wealth and power being coupled with religious debasement.[30] The outcome will be divine action against them and the humbling of human pride. The economy is thriving and Israel's military power is at its peak:

> Their land is filled with silver and gold,
>   and there is no end to their treasures;
> their land is filled with horses,
>   and there is no end to their chariots. (2:7)

---

[30]Isa 2:2-5 and 4:2-6 are seen as later additions, when the collection was used in the context of community worship. 2:1 may have been the heading for this and the following collection, which begins with 5:1-7 (see Kaiser, *Isaiah 1-12*, [1st ed.] 23); a different view is presented in the 2nd edition, pp. 48-52.

The saying reflects the prosperity under Jeroboam II in the north and Uzziah and Jotham in the south; it probably just antedates the three humiliating Assyrian campaigns of 734-32. The picture of power and prosperity is sandwiched between accusations of idolatry. Not only is the land full of wealth; it is also full of foreign religious soothsayers (v 6) and full of idols (v 8). The verses are carefully constructed around the key verb of being "full," with the fullness of idolatry surrounding the fullness of prosperity.

The accusation of idolatry is balanced toward the end of the collection by a strong censure of the injustice occurring in the nation (3:12-15). Those responsible for national well-being—leaders, elders, princes—are taken to task, indeed taken to court by God. They devour the vineyard, metaphor for the people of Israel and Judah. The wealth accumulated in their houses has been plundered from the poor. They have crushed God's people, grinding the faces of the poor. What Isaiah censures is not petty injustice between individuals. It is the transfer of resources on a national scale from those who are in need to those who have no need at all. The injustice is laid to the charge of the ruling class. Isaiah will later accuse them of furthering this inequitable social transition by the enactment of unjust laws (10:1-2).

The metaphor of the vineyard is developed in detail in the Song of the Vineyard (5:1-7) which opens the collection in 5:1-10:4*. We considered it in detail in chapter 9. Here we may simply note the primary thrust of the censures levelled against Israel and Judah. The Song culminates in the charge of bloodshed and oppression (5:7). The first woe attacks the grabbing of land—so social injustice. The second woe castigates the luxurious living that blinds people to the reality of God—so religious infidelity. The next three censure the cynics, those who have reversed the basic values of society, and those who have decided to be the arbiters of their own self-interested standards. The sixth returns to decry luxurious living at the cost of social justice (5:22-23). The seventh and final woe saying pillories those who busy themselves enacting unjust legislation which will facilitate the expropriation or exploitation of the poor. Their victims are the poor and needy, the widows and orphans. In the ancient Near East, these typical cases of the powerless are the criteria and touchstones of justice in any society. By these criteria, the society censured in Isaiah 1-12 is radically unjust.

JEREMIAH

After the account of Jeremiah's call, and the two visions which go with it, the book of Jeremiah has two sizable collections of sayings, one on the theme of apostasy (2:5-4:4), the other on the foe from the north (4:5-6:26).[31] The outcome of religious infidelity is pungently summarized: "they went after worthlessness, and became worthless" (2:5).

These sayings have particular importance, since they offer us some flashes of insight into what the prophets valued so highly in the faith of Israel and why they lamented its loss so vehemently. The issue of apostasy is put at its starkest.

> Has a nation changed its gods,
>   even though they are no gods?
> But my people have changed their glory
>   for that which does not profit.
> Be appalled, O heavens, at this,
>   be shocked, be utterly desolate, says the LORD,
> for my people have committed two evils:
>   they have forsaken me,
> the fountain of living waters,
>   and hewed out cisterns for themselves,
> broken cisterns,
>   that can hold no water. (2:11-13)

---

[31] The ministry of Jeremiah is located in Jerusalem, approximately within the period bounded by 627-586. Among the more helpful books on Jeremiah are: J. Bright, *Jeremiah* (AB 21; Garden City: Doubleday, 1965); E.W. Nicholson, *Preaching to the Exiles: A Study of the Prose Tradition in the Book of Jeremiah* (Oxford: Blackwell, 1970) and *Jeremiah 1-25* and *Jeremiah 26-52* (CBC; Cambridge: University Press, 1973); W.L. Holladay, *Jeremiah: Spokesman out of Time* (Philadelphia: United Church, 1974); T.M. Raitt, *A Theology of Exile: Judgment / Deliverance in Jeremiah and Ezekiel* (Philadelphia: Fortress, 1977); R.P. Carroll, *From Chaos to Covenant: Uses of Prophecy in the Book of Jeremiah* (London: SCM, 1981) and *Jeremiah* (OTL; London: SCM, 1986); W.L. Holladay, *Jeremiah 1: A Commentary on the Book of the Prophet Jeremiah, Chapters 1-25* (Hermeneia; Philadelphia: Fortress, 1986). As a more technical resource, see W. McKane, *Jeremiah* (Vol. 1: Introduction and Commentary on Jeremiah I-XXV; ICC: Edinburgh, T. & T. Clark, 1986).

On the two collections, see Carroll, *Jeremiah*, 115-18. For Carroll, Jeremiah is addressing the Jerusalem community. Holladay suggests a first recension may have been addressed to the north (*Jeremiah 1*, 62-77).

Religious infidelity, as understood by Jeremiah, means exchanging what is glorious for what is profitless. In forsaking their God, the people have forsaken the source of their life, "the fountain of living waters." Instead, they have turned for inspiration to sources of their own making, "broken cisterns, that can hold no water," and that give no life. The image is a strong statement about what God meant to Israel—no more nor less than the source of life. Israel lived closely enough to barren land to know the life-giving and transformational power of a well or a water-supply.

Israel was gifted with freedom and is losing it (2:14-16). The loss is a cruel irony, for its cause is Israel's cry of rebellion, "I will not serve" (2:20) and Israel's claim to its own freedom (2:31). The loss of freedom is in the process of becoming political reality, and Israel has brought this on itself. (2:17)

Jeremiah puts Israel's religious infidelity into the language of human infidelity (3:1-5). After divorce and remarriage, what possibility is there of reconciliation? Can Israel return to God? The whole countryside is mute witness to just how widespread their worship of Baal has been. As happens quite often in the book of Jeremiah, a prose passage is put next which sets out to interpret the poetic saying. It develops the image in the direction of the divergent histories of Israel and Judah (3:6-11).

The images of family and marriage, illustrating Israel's infidelity, are taken up in another strongly metaphorical saying.

> I thought
>> how I would set you among my sons,
> and give you a pleasant land,
>> a heritage most beauteous of all nations.
> And I thought you would call me, My Father,
>> and would not turn from following me.
> Surely, as a faithless wife leaves her husband,
>> so have you been faithless to me, O house of Israel,
>> says the LORD. (3:19-20)

In the beauty of the images, there is a vision of the meaning of faith—becoming part of the family of the God of Israel. In the poignant sense of loss, there is all the sadness resulting from infidelity.

The hint of universality, "I would set you among my sons," is taken up in the final saying of this collection focused on infidelity (4:1-2). The impact of its infidelity is not felt by Israel alone. The theme of Gen 12:1-3 returns: Israel as the destined mediator of blessing to all the world. If Israel were to return to their God, "in truth, in justice, and in uprightness,"

> then nations shall bless themselves in him,
> and in him shall they glory. (4:2)

Israel's infidelity is not merely Israel's loss. Israel's wholehearted returning to God would bring blessings on Israel, surely, and redound to the benefit of all nations.

The note of censure recurs in the middle of 4:5-6:26, the collection on the foe from the north—probably to be identified with the Babylonians (so Carroll and Holladay). In the streets and squares of Jerusalem, it is apparently impossible to find one ordinary person who "does justice and seeks truth" (5:1, 4). Among the aristocracy, it is no better: "they all alike had broken the yoke, they had burst the bonds" (5:5). The themes of infidelity and injustice return. There is no fear of God in Judah (5:20-25). Injustice is rife in the treacherous accumulation of wealth, probably through the seizure of goods or property in satisfaction of debt, to the detriment of the rights of the orphan and the needy (5:26-29).

The so-called temple sermon (Jer 7:1-15) begins a series of sayings on cultic abuse. It is all the more remarkable then that it contains strong emphasis on both elements of religious infidelity and social injustice. It is a carefully and concisely structured passage which serves almost as a summary of the prophetic message. It is often seen as a later deuteronomistic reflection on Jeremiah's message; but it need not be regarded as later.[32] Close comparison with Jeremiah 26 shows the quite different intentions of the two passages. Jeremiah 7 sets out the prophetic message as a call for reformation; Jeremiah 26 is a study in how the word of God is received when proclaimed by the prophet, as well as the public authentication of Jeremiah as a prophet of God.

It is presented as a word of God to Jeremiah, and not as the delivery of this message by Jeremiah. This may be an intentional

[32]See Holladay, *Jeremiah 1*, 240.

device to place an important word in as close an association with its divine source as possible. Its location is significant: at the entry to the temple, so that it is addressed to the people of Judah probably as they come to a festival. Jer 26:1 places its timing as the beginning of the reign of Jehoiakim, the son of Josiah. In this case, it is intended to portray Jeremiah's address as a comprehensive attempt to swing Israel over to God, at a critical time when the death knell appears to have been sounded for the deuteronomic reform and Egypt's Pharaoh Neco has imposed his own man on the throne of Judah (cf., 2 Kgs 23:29-35).

The message is presented as an order from God for change in the nation of Judah. Its basic expression is caught in two formulations: a positive command, "Amend your ways and your doings"; a negative prohibition, "Do not trust in these deceptive words" (7:3-4). Each of these formulations is taken up and developed in turn.

The positive command is unfolded in vv 5-7. Amendment of Judah's ways and doings would involve establishing social justice (7:5b-6a) and religious fidelity (7:6b). Interestingly enough, in this temple context, it is the social injustice aspect which is further developed. Truly executing justice with one another involves not oppressing the stranger, the orphan, or the widow and not shedding innocent blood (cf., 2 Kgs 21:16; 24:4). Note that religious infidelity is specifically described as being self-destructive for Judah.

The negative prohibition is unfolded in vv 8-10. It has the same concerns for social justice and religious fidelity. Stealing, murder, adultery, and perjury are all evils that strike directly at the fabric of society; burning incense to Baal and going after other gods return to the theme of religious infidelity.

As the sermon stands, this call for national change modulates through vv 11-12 to a threat to the national existence in vv 13-15. Whether from Jeremiah or a later follower, it is a reflection on the sweep of prophetic tradition. The prophets pointed to the social injustice and religious infidelity in Israel. They pointed out that these evils constituted a threat to the national existence of Israel. Implicit in the prophetic proclamation was the conviction that amendment would turn aside the threat. But as amendment remained an illusory hope, the threat became an increasingly inevitable reality. So Jeremiah is forbidden even to intercede for the people; the time for that appears to be past (cf., Jer 7:16; 11:14; 14:11).

The censure of social injustice recurs again in Jeremiah. Sweepingly in Jer 9:4-6; as an order in 21:12; in terms that echo the temple sermon in 22:3; in a condemnation of Jehoiakim, with strong implications for the role of king or government, in 23:13-17; and, in the context of broken promises for social justice reform, in 34:8-22. For the most part, the accusation of religious infidelity repeats the basic charges: cultic abuse, disobedience, apostasy in which the nation has abandoned its God and turned to other gods.[33] Censure does not seem to loom as large in Jeremiah as in some of the earlier prophets. Perhaps in the context of his time, the deterring power of threat was judged the more necessary emphasis.

EZEKIEL

Ezekiel was in a different situation from his prophetic colleagues when it came to censuring his people.[34] He had been taken to Babylon with the first exile from Jerusalem, in 597. His prophetic ministry began in 593, in this decade of exile before the final catastrophe of 587. He was therefore not in the same sort of position to confront his people's evil directly.

Within Ezekiel's call narrative itself, Israel is characterized as rebellious and stubborn (2:3-4, etc.). The rebellion is specified as breach of God's law, "rejecting my ordinances and not walking in my statutes" (5:5-7). A comparison is made with the other nations around about, emphatically to Israel's detriment: "And she has wickedly rebelled against my ordinances more than the nations" (v 6a). The comparison with the nations has been already begun

[33]Cf., Jer 7:18-19; 8:4-9; 9:13-14; 11:1-17; 13:8-11; 16:10-13; 17:21-22; 18:13-17; 19:4-5; 23:9-14; 25:3-7; 26:4-5; 35:12-17.

[34]The ministry of Ezekiel is located in the Babylonian exile, in the years 593-71. Among the most helpful commentaries on Ezekiel are: J.W. Wevers, *Ezekiel* (NCB; London: Nelson, 1969); W. Eichrodt, *Ezekiel* (OTL; London: SCM, 1970); K.W. Carley, *The Book of the Prophet Ezekiel* (CBC; Cambridge: University Press, 1974); M. Greenberg, *Ezekiel 1-20* (AB 22; Garden City: Doubleday, 1983); and the monumental work of W. Zimmerli, *Ezekiel 1: A Commentary on the Book of the Prophet Ezekiel, Chapters 1-24* and *Ezekiel 2: A Commentary on the Book of the Prophet Ezekiel, Chapters 25-48* (Hermeneia; Philadelphia: Fortress, 1979 and 1983).

in 3:6. As with Amos 1-2, other nations are also in the prophet's view and Israel's wrongdoing exceeds theirs. There is a certain tension within 5:6-7. At first sight, the comparative emphasis suggests concern with the sorts of laws and behavior that are common to all peoples; but v 7b reverses this direction, accusing Israel of adopting the ordinances of the nations. For W. Zimmerli, vv 5-6a connect directly with vv 8-9 and 14-15, and vv 6b-7 comprise two additions, emphasizing the reproach in v 6a.[35] Perhaps then Ezekiel was looking toward the kinds of evil castigated in chap. 22, while the redactor was looking rather to that of chaps. 8-11. We might look at both.

In chap. 22, Ezekiel gathers the evils of Jerusalem under two heads, bloodshed and idolatrous defilement (22:3-4). Bloodshed is censured three times, once attributed to the princes of Israel, associated with slander and with bribery (22:6, 9, 12). Contempt is the lot of father and mother, extortion for the stranger, and wrongdoing is visited on orphan and widow (22:6-7). Holy things and sabbath are profaned, sexual evils are common (22:10-11). Interest rates and extortion are the means of acquiring one's neighbor's wealth (22:12). The overall picture is one of rampant social injustice and gross disorder in the sacral realm. In fairness to the citizens of Jerusalem, we should note Zimmerli's comment.

> A certain trait of doctrinaire speech, which derives from an overall view, and which simply makes affirmations, without enumerating individual facts, is not to be denied here (as also in another way in ch. 20). Ezek 22:1ff. also introduces into the process the spiritual understanding of judgement upon Jerusalem by those already sitting in the darkness of judgement. For those in Jerusalem Ezek 22 could only be an immense exaggeration.[36]

Whatever the exaggeration, it is clear that Ezekiel is concerned with crimes against both the social and the sacral order. All of this Ezekiel sums up with the phrase, "you have forgotten me" (22:12). This is the ultimate and basic failing: Israel has forgotten its God.

The great vision of the departure of God's glory from the

[35]Zimmerli, *Ezekiel 1*, 175.

[36]Zimmerli, *Ezekiel 1*, 456.

temple, in Ezekiel 8-11, lists sacral evils in ascending order of seriousness. The first abuse is an altar placed before a guardian figure ("the image of jealousy") protecting the temple gate (8:4-5). The second abuse is the burning of incense by the elders before wall carvings of unclean animals and idols (8:10-11). The third abuse is women weeping for Tammuz, the dying-and-rising god of ancient Near Eastern fertility myths (8:14). The crowning wrong is a group of men, at the door of the temple, worshiping the sun, with their backs to the temple and so to the God whose temple it was (8:16). Zimmerli raises the possibility that the participants might have seen these practices as legitimate and orthodox ways of extending the worship of the God of Israel.[37] For Ezekiel, they were an abomination of the first order, of such magnitude that it was no longer possible for the glory of God to remain within the temple (cf., 10:18-19; 11:22-23). Israel is left bereft of the presence of its God.

Beyond these two major presentations, Ezekiel's sense of the evil which brought disaster upon Israel is vividly expressed in the extended allegories of Ezekiel 16 and 23, as well as the recapitulation of Israel's history in Ezekiel 20.

Ezekiel 16 develops the metaphor of the wife into an allegory of God's relationship with Israel; Ezekiel 23 allegorizes the history of the northern and southern kingdoms under the metaphor of two daughters. In chap. 16, the figure of the woman is the vehicle used by Ezekiel to accuse Jerusalem of its sins and pass judgment upon them.[38] The basic wrongdoing is the adoption of Canaanite cult practices, culminating in child sacrifice (cf., vv 15-23). As Zimmerli puts it:

> The root of the sin of the woman who had been so lavishly favored by Yahweh lies in her false trust in her own beauty and the reputation gained from this. The gift replaces the giver.[39]

---

[37] For this material, see Zimmerli, *Ezekiel 1*, 236-46.

[38] Zimmerli (*Ezekiel 1*, 335) points out that this use of a woman as allegorical figure for Israel has its beginnings in metaphors such as "virgin Israel" (Amos 5:2), then the development of Hosea 1-3, taken up in Isaiah (Isa 1:21) and continued in Jeremiah (Jer 2:2; 3:6-25).

[39] Zimmerli, *Ezekiel 1*, 342.

16:26-29 have much the same characteristics as chap. 23. In Ezekiel 23, the concern is no longer with Canaanite cult practices but with the folly of Israel's political alliances, with Egypt, with Assyria, and with Babylon, pictured as desirable and smartly turned-out warriors. As recent background to all this, there was Josiah's death while trying to prevent Egypt aiding the Assyrians against Babylon, after which their king was imposed on them by the Egyptian pharaoh; then Judah's subjection to Babylon, and their unsuccessful attempt to break away and find support from Egypt (2 Kgs 24:1-7). Such political promiscuity did little to further Judah's chances of survival in the maelstrom of changing imperial destinies.

In Ezekiel 20, as Zimmerli puts it, "the 'accusing' of the people is wrapped up in a narrative of Israel's history," with its credal summary in the background. Rebellion is begun in Egypt (v 8) and continued twice in the wilderness (vv 13, 21); in the promised land it culminates in idolatrous Canaanite worship (v 28).[40] Before each of the three occasions of rebellion, Israel has been duly graced and instructed in their relationship with God (cf., vv 5-7, 10-12, 17-20)—but still they rebelled. Ezekiel takes the catastrophe which threatens his contemporaries and traces its roots to the very beginnings of their existence as a people. The destructive force which ultimately brought Israel low was there from the beginning: the rebellious refusal to accept their destiny as people of God. In the same way, the seeds of our human destruction have been there from the beginning, in the refusal to accept our human destiny as creatures of God.

Today

In their charge against their people, the pre-exilic prophets censured their failure in the fundamentals of religion and society. The prophetic accusations were not restricted to peripheral matters or to breaches of outmoded religious laws; they went straight to the heart of what is central for any society, then and now. They dealt with religious infidelity and social injustice.

---

[40]According to Zimmerli, 20:27-29 is an addition, so that the original picture did not extend to the gracious gift of the promised land *(Ezekiel I* 405).

It might seem strange to speak of religious infidelity in the context of modern secular and pluralist societies. But any society which is without a faith in its meaning and value is a society that is slowly dying. Understanding the word as neutrally as possible, there needs to be a certain ideology in any society which justifies the sacrifices the members of society have to make for the common good. Without the conviction that there is a benefit to be had, however altruistic, through its members' sacrifices— through their taxes—a society can scarcely hope to flourish.

It is perhaps too facile a reading of history to say that England was held together by the hopes embodied in Magna Carta, or that the French Revolution rallied to the benefits of Liberty, Equality, and Fraternity, or that American society finds its cohesion in a faith in the advantages and values of democracy. But they certainly generated a faith which made its contribution.

> There has so far always been a need in human societies to possess a sense of worth and of value. This, of course, may be provided in non-historical ways—by the quality of life that is experienced, by the sense of identification with the aims and purposes of a group or community. Some men and women can derive it from the richness of their own instinctive lives; for many, the will to live is sufficient justification for being alive. The majority of men and women, however, need the dimension of time because they are conscious of it. They realize that they are a part of an historical process that has changed over the centuries; that time for men and women and their societies can never be static, or at least has never been static; that the process of change has accelerated and is accelerating so that they require to know what the nature of this process has been and is. They need an historical past, objective and true.[41]

The faith of Israel was in their God, to whom they owed their past and from it their present. As that faith waned, so the fabric of Israel's society weakened.

The prophetic accusations of infidelity have their relevance for modern society precisely in this sense of the faith that gives a

---

[41]J.H. Plumb, *The Death of the Past* (London: Macmillan, 1969) 16.

society its vision and cohesion. When this is lost, the society's grip on life has gone. In secular and pluralist societies, we can scarcely speak directly of faith in God. But there has to be something which is close to its equivalent. Central to any social ideology which is going to be effective must be a sense of the value of human life which can never be subordinated to other social goals. Absolute respect for human life can be founded in instinctive insight, or it can be founded on faith in the created dignity of each person, loved by the creator God. When society loses sight of the values of every individual, society is losing sight of its aims and purpose. When a society loses faith in the richness and value of human life in community, that society is gravely threatened.

Social justice is as central to the well-being of any society today as it was to the survival of ancient Israel. A society that lacks the basics of social justice is one in which the rot has set in at the core. Justice is often a matter of perception, and history is witness to how laggardly perception can sometimes be. But once injustice is perceived, it is a corrosive force that gnaws incessantly at the vitals and conscience of society. It can be silenced by mindless indulgence or false mythologies, but it is not stilled. The quest for justice can be stopped by armed force, but like a rivulet moving down a hillside it is likely eventually to find a way through or around or under the barrier.

It may be that a perfectly just society lies outside our human grasp. But the continued struggle for social justice has to be a substantial element in society; the passion for justice has to be kept alive in society. Philosophers may differ about the ways of speaking of a just society, but the ultimate goal is denied by none. In the ancient Near East, the justice of society was tested by the lot of those who were powerless: the widow, the orphan, and the foreigner. In today's world there is no neat triad of the powerless, but in our experience we can each select our own. The lot of those who are powerless in our society can tell us much about its justice—and therefore its vitality and its worth.

Israel's pre-exilic prophets sometimes spoke in superb poetry and sublime images; at other times, their voices sound harsh and raw, from a distant past. What they had to say came from their experience of God moving in the midst of their people. What they had to say came also from the very core of social experience and it has meaning today wherever there is social living.

RECOMMENDED FURTHER READING
GENERAL

Joseph Blenkinsopp, *A History of Prophecy in Israel*. Philadelphia: Westminster, 1983.

Léon Epsztein, *Social Justice in the Ancient Near East and the People of the Bible*. London: SCM, 1986.

Klaus Koch, *The Prophets*. 2 vols. London: SCM, 1982-83.

Gerhard von Rad, *Old Testament Theology: Vol. 2. The Theology of Israel's Prophetic Traditions*. Edinburgh: Oliver and Boyd, 1965.

Claus Westermann, *Basic Forms of Prophetic Speech*. Philadelphia: Westminster, 1967.

Robert R. Wilson, *Prophecy and Society in Ancient Israel*. Philadelphia: Fortress, 1980.

AMOS

J.L. Mays, *Amos*. OTL. London: SCM, 1969.

J.M. Ward, *Amos & Isaiah*. Nashville: Abingdon, 1969.

H.W. Wolff, *Joel and Amos*. Hermeneia. Philadelphia: Fortress, 1977.

HOSEA

J.L. Mays, *Hosea*. OTL. Philadelphia: Westminster, 1969.

J.M. Ward, *Hosea: A Theological Commentary*. New York: Harper & Row, 1966.

H.W. Wolff, *Hosea*. Hermeneia. Philadelphia: Fortress, 1974.

Extensive, technical, and often speculative:

F.I. Andersen and D.N. Freedman, *Hosea*. AB 24. Garden City: Doubleday, 1980.

MICAH

Delbert R. Hillers, *Micah*. Hermeneia. Philadelphia: Fortress, 1984.

J.L. Mays, *Micah.* OTL. Philadelphia: Westminster, 1976.

H.W. Wolff, *Micah the Prophet.* Philadelphia: Fortress, 1981.

_____, *Micah.* Minneapolis: Augsburg, forthcoming.

ISAIAH

R.E. Clements, *Isaiah 1-39.* NCB. Grand Rapids: Eerdmans, 1980.

O. Kaiser, *Isaiah 1-12.* OTL. Philadelphia: Westminster, 1972. Completely rewritten second edition: OTL. London: SCM, 1983.
_____, *Isaiah 13-39.* OTL. Philadelphia: Westminster, 1974.

J.M. Ward, *Amos & Isaiah.* Nashville: Abingdon, 1969.

JEREMIAH

i. Commentaries

Traditional:
J. Bright, *Jeremiah.* AB 21. Garden City: Doubleday, 1965.

E.W. Nicholson, *Jeremiah 1-25* and *Jeremiah 26-52.* CBC. Cambridge: Cambridge University, 1973-75.

Innovative, readable, and interpretative:

R.P. Carroll, *Jeremiah.* OTL. London: SCM, 1986.

Innovative, detailed, and reconstructive:

W.L. Holladay, *Jeremiah 1: A Commentary on the Book of the Prophet Jeremiah, Chapters 1-25.* Hermeneia. Philadelphia: Fortress, 1986.

Detailed and a more technical resource:

W. McKane, *Jeremiah.* Vol. 1: Introduction and Commentary on Jeremiah I-XXV. ICC. Edinburgh: T. & T. Clark, 1986.

ii. Other

R.P. Carroll, *From Chaos to Covenant: Uses of Prophecy in the Book of Jeremiah.* London: SCM, 1981.

W.L. Holladay, *Jeremiah: Spokesman out of Time*. Philadelphia: United Church, 1974.

E.W. Nicholson, *Preaching to the Exiles: A Study of the Prose Tradition in the Book of Jeremiah*. Oxford: Blackwell, 1970.

T.M. Raitt, *A Theology of Exile: Judgment/Deliverance in Jeremiah and Ezekiel*. Philadelphia: Fortress, 1977.

EZEKIEL

K.W. Carley, *The Book of the Prophet Ezekiel*. CBC. Cambridge: Cambridge University, 1974.

W. Eichrodt, *Ezekiel*. OTL. London: SCM, 1970.

M. Greenberg, *Ezekiel 1-20*. AB 22. Garden City: Doubleday, 1983.

J.W. Wevers, *Ezekiel*. NCB. London: Nelson, 1969.

Vastly comprehensive:

W. Zimmerli, *Ezekiel 1: A Commentary on the Book of the Prophet Ezekiel, Chapters 1-24* and *Ezekiel 2: A Commentary on the Book of the Prophet Ezekiel, Chapters 25-48*. Hermeneia. Philadelphia: Fortress, 1979-83.

11

The Prophetic Threat to Israel

Recommended preliminary reading

Before reading the body of the chapter, it will be helpful to have read the following passages:
Amos 2:12-16
Hosea 8:4-11
Micah 1:1-7
Isaiah 5:26-30
Jeremiah 6:1-8
Ezekiel 24:1-14

The pre-exilic prophets in Israel were entrusted with a truly fearful mission. It was their task to speak to a nation that was on the verge of being defeated in war and incorporated into the Assyrian or Babylonian empires respectively—with all the agony, suffering, and death that was part and parcel of such national upheavals. The upshot would be loss of freedom, loss of population, and loss of national independence. The prophets' task was to communicate God's message to the people, to make them aware of their impending fate, in the hope that it might be averted by a radical change of national attitude. What made that task ever more burdensome was the growing realization for each prophet that the message was not being heard or accepted, that their proclamation of God's word was being treated with contempt and rejected.

The prophetic word consisted of accusation and announcement, or censure and threat. We have looked closely at the prophetic censure in the preceding chapter. Now, for a full understanding of Israel's pre-exilic prophets, we need to hear clearly the threat they levelled against their people. Confronting a people on the brink of national disaster, they did not mince their words. Without hearing the harshness of their announcements, we will not understand the reaction of their contemporaries against them. Without grappling with the harshness of their announcements, we will not be forced to come to terms with the reality of God experienced in the Old Testament, nor will we have struggled adequately with the reality of today's experience.

AMOS

The book of Amos begins with a series of very strongly patterned sayings.[1] Each has its threat. Israel's is in 2:13-16. It is military in its meaning, rich in the imagery of its symbolism. The Hebrew of the first line (v 13) sounds heavy, with the clumsy crushing weight of the loaded cart. Two triadic lines follow, each with their own set of images: the swift, the strong, and the mighty shall not escape (v 14); the bowman, the runner, and the rider shall not save their lives (v 15). The mightiest of the mighty may just save his skin that day (v 16). The power of the poetry reinforces the weight of the message: that day will be a terrible day; almost nobody will escape from it. The closing dyadic line has a terrible finality to it. Literally: the mighty of heart among the valiant, naked will he flee that day (v 16).[2]

By contrast, the proclamation in the second verset of Amos 3:2 is stark and abstract: "therefore I will punish you for all your

[1]For the most helpful commentaries on the prophetic books discussed in this chapter, see the references and recommended reading in chapter 10.

[2]It may be helpful to clarify the poetic terminology we will need occasionally. "Verset" is used for the parts of a poetic line (often called stich or colon elsewhere). A dyadic line contains two versets; a triadic line contains three. There is normally a progression from one verset to the next within a line, either a narrative progression, or a progression of intensification through focusing, heightening, or sharpening of the image. It is a pleasure to acknowledge my debt to Robert Alter in deepening my appreciation of the art and richness of biblical Hebrew poetry (see R. Alter, *The Art of Biblical Poetry* [New York: Basic Books, 1985]).

iniquities." There is a major saying in 3:9-11. It is deliberately general, like the headline over a newspaper report. Its threat (v 11) is equally general; like 2:13-16, it is military in character. Your land will be surrounded by your foe, your defensive power will be overcome, your strongholds will be plundered. V 12 is a separate saying, but it reinforces the point: all that will be left is the minimal evidence of total destruction (cf., Exod 22:13). The saying in vv 13-15 is straightforward threat. When Israel's transgressions are sheeted home, it will fall on the sanctuary at Bethel, winter and summer house, luxury construction and great house—it will be total.

In Amos 4:1-3, the saying zeroes in on the wives of the wealthy in the capital, Samaria. The focus is narrowed from the surrounding of the land (3:11) to the siege of the city. While the precise military imagery is unclear (*RSV:* hooks and fishhooks; *NEB:* on their shields, in fish-baskets), the meaning is perfectly plain: in the siege, the protective city walls will be breached, and you will go out through the broken rubble of the walls and into captivity. Much the same tone is maintained in the proclamations which follow: you will be reduced to a tenth of what you are now (5:3); the houses you have built, you will not live in, and you will not drink the wine from the vineyards you have planted (5:11b); in town and country, there will be mourning and lamentation (5:16-17). 6:1-7 turns the focus back to the capital, Samaria: those who revel in thoughtless luxury will be the first to go into exile.

As we saw earlier, the visions Amos received have the same message. First destruction that is held off by intercession, then destruction that is inevitable, and the order for the actual destruction in the final vision. "Not one of them shall flee away, not one of them shall escape. . . . I will set my eyes upon them for evil and not for good" (9:1, 4). The proclamation Amos had to make to Israel is, undeniably, about as tough as it is possible to get. Small wonder the priest Amaziah told him, "Never again prophesy at Bethel" (7:13). The saying hurled against Amaziah, for setting himself in opposition over against the word of God, is of a piece in harshness with the rest of the book (7:17).

HOSEA

The book of Hosea is structured differently from that of Amos, as we have seen. Its passages are longer and more complex; it is not so easy to identify the individual sayings. But while the imagery of Hosea is much richer, the initial message is no gentler. The first threats in the book of Hosea take the form of symbolic actions: the names given his children, Jezreel, Not pitied, and Not my people. They are explained; yet, apart from the first, they need no explanation. They are chillingly clear. The only explanation needed is the origin of the names. And that is given too. On each occasion, the command is explicitly attributed to God. There is a fascinating little phenomenon in the Hebrew. It begins with the divine command which started Hosea's ministry and continues through to the name of the third child. The Hebrew phrase becomes progressively shorter: And the LORD said unto Hosea (v 2); And the LORD said unto him (v 4); And He said to him (v 6); And He said (v 9). The full impact of the Hebrew is made in the first command. As the impact of God's word becomes clearer and clearer, the actual attribution of it can be made shorter and shorter. It does not have to be spelled out at length, for it is clear. The word is from God. The narrator has all four instances in view, and they articulate the message of Hosea, when the LORD first spoke through him. Amos may be paraphrased:because you are my people, therefore I will punish you for your iniquities (3:2). Hosea is harsher: "Call his name Not my people, for you are not my people and I am not your God" (1:9—literally: and I am not "I am" for you).

The next threats are within the metaphor of the husband suing for the affections of his alienated wife (2:2-15; MT, 4-17).[3] He will fence her in and prevent her pursuing her lovers, so that she may return to him (vv 6-7; MT, 8-9). She will say, "For it was better with me then than now" (v 9); so there are hard times ahead, but the purpose is to effect a reconciliation. It is the hard times which are in sight in vv 9-13 (MT, 11-15). The fertility of nature—grain and wine, wool and flax, fig tree and vine—will be at an end; the

---

[3]In Hosea 1-2, differences in the verse numbering are further complicated by reordering of the text in some translations. The numbering of the Hebrew (= MT) is therefore added. The *NAB* follows the Hebrew; the *JB* gives both numberings. Both *JB* and *NAB* rearrange the sequence of the text to some degree.

religious festivals, which had been distorted into Baalism, will be stopped. This announcement is followed by a third, where she will be allured into the desert and there successfully wooed (vv 14-15; MT, 16-17).

The imagery is quite different from that of Amos. Hosea's images are not military, but agricultural. This may reflect their respective concerns. Amos 1-2 is overwhelmingly concerned for social justice, appalled by the oppressive cruelty of people to one another; by people they will be punished. Hosea 1-3 is concerned with the pervasive influence of Baal worship in Israel, and the growing belief in Israel that its agricultural fertility and prosperity could be best assured through Baal; by nature they will be punished. But Hosea also differs from Amos in the explicit orientation of God's action toward reconciliation.

This is evident in the autobiographical account in Hosea 3. There is God's command to Hosea (v 1); Hosea's compliance with that command (v 2); and Hosea's speech to his wife (v 3) and the interpretation of it all (vv 4-5).[4] The interpretation contains the threat: for many days Israel will be deprived and restricted; then they shall return, and be restored to their God (vv 4-5). It is a message of reconciliation through discipline. The message of hope and salvation does not do away with the discipline; it is after it, not instead of it.

The saying which begins the next section is vastly comprehensive (4:1-3). The announcement suggests a devastation of universal scope (v 3). It touches the land, its dwellers, the animals, the birds, and the fish. There is an extraordinary ecological and environmental consciousness here. But that does not take away from the impact of the saying for Israel: they will languish. Where the concerns in Hosea are so predominantly with matters of

---

[4]Much has been written about the identity of the woman. The logic of the situation demands that she be Gomer. Mays concludes: "The symbolism is best served if the woman is Gomer; its point is that Yahweh's love will find a way with Israel even though this people has turned away from him to other gods. Just so, Hosea is to seek out a woman who has deserted him" (J.L. Mays, *Hosea* [OTL; Philadelphia: Westminster, 1969] 56). Wolff explains: "It lies beyond the scope of chap. 1 to provide a glimpse of the marriage's continuation. As the writer of chap. 3, Hosea does not presuppose any knowledge of chap. 1. With regard to the time it was written, chap. 3 is probably older than the third person account of chap. 1, which summarizes Hosea's previous experiences" (H.W. Wolff, *Hosea* [Hermeneia; Philadelphia: Fortress, 1974] 59). Whether vv 4-5 were intended to be understood as part of Hosea's speech or not is immaterial.

religious faith, in this saying the decay of the social structure is at least equally to the fore. Hosea returns to matters religious in the next saying, where he turns on the priests, whose dereliction implicates the people in their fall. "The priests' sin and shame consist plainly in their eagerness for the people's transgressions."[5] "They feed on the sin of my people; they are greedy for their iniquity" (4:8). And so, in the threat, "They shall eat, but not be satisfied; they shall play the harlot, but not multiply" (vv 8, 10). Crime and punishment are intimately related.

There are several of Hosea's proclamations which speak out of the political context of Israel's dealings with Assyria and Egypt. The context can be quite clearly identified. Northern Israel formed an alliance with Syria against the imperial power of Assyria; they had backing from Egypt. They wanted to assure their southern flank by bringing Judah into the alliance. When Judah refused, they were brought under military pressure from Syria and northern Israel (cf., Isa 7:1-6). Ahaz, king of Judah, appealed to Assyria for help and got it (cf., 2 Kgs 16:5-9). The Assyrians dealt with the western boundaries of their empire in three successive campaigns, 734, 733, and 732. In the first, they swept down the Mediterranean coast as far as Gaza. In the second, they overran Galilee, the plain of Esdraelon, and much of Transjordan. In the third, they subjugated Damascus and Syria.[6] During the course of these three years, the king of Israel, Pekah, was assassinated and replaced as king by Hoshea, his murderer (cf., 2 Kgs 15:29-30; perhaps also Hos 7:7b, "all their kings have fallen," and 7:3). Hoshea followed the example of Ahaz, king of Judah, in binding himself to Assyria (cf., 2 Kgs 16:7-9; 17:3; and Hos 5:13; 7:11). About this time, it appears too that Ahaz took advantage of the weakness and preoccupation of the northern kingdom in order to recover territory earlier lost to Judah. The sequence in Hos 5:8, from Gibeah, to Ramah, to Bethel moves from the south northward, through Benjamin toward Ephraim.

---

[5] Wolff, *Hosea*, 81. Wolff considers v 9 an insertion, because of the change to third person singular (p. 74; the *RSV* maintains the plural).

[6] For a graphic presentation of these campaigns, see Y. Aharoni and M. Avi-Yonah, *The Macmillan Bible Atlas* (New York: Macmillan, 1968) map 147. For further details, see the commentaries of Mays and Wolff, as well as the standard histories of Israel.

It seems that Ahaz was bent on pushing his border to the north.[7] A number of Hosea's sayings seem to be closely linked to the events of this period. They are illuminating for our understanding of the prophetic mission.

The first proclamation is directed against Judah, the aggressor from the south. "Upon them I will pour out my wrath like water" (5:10). It is interesting for the fact that there is nothing specific that Hosea refers to by way of punishment for Judah. It would appear that Hosea was outraged by Judah's hostilities against northern Israel and therefore condemned those responsible. But it would also appear that he had nothing more specific to say than condemnation in general terms, the pouring out of God's wrath upon them. As prophet, therefore, he may speak without either a clear knowledge or a general sense of what the future holds. So, in this case, Hosea appears to speak in ignorance of the future, but in intense indignation at the present. Such political conduct clearly incurs God's wrath; the outcome of that wrath is not revealed.

The saying which follows is of particular interest for the insight it offers into the prophet's understanding of God's action.

> Ephraim is oppressed,
>   justice is crushed.
> For he persisted in following
>   what is worthless.
> But I am like pus to Ephraim,
>   like rottenness to the house of Judah. (5:11-12)[8]

The oppression of Ephraim and crushing of justice probably refer to the Assyrian campaign of 733, ravaging Galilee, the broad fertile plain of Esdraelon, and sweeping across the Jordan into Gilead.

> Hosea further concedes that Ephraim already has 'suffered violence,' namely, the violence of those very weeks when Tiglath-pileser III advanced into the northern and eastern

---

[7]See Wolff, *Hosea*, 111-12; Mays, *Hosea*, 88.

[8]The translation is from Wolff, *Hosea*, 104.

provinces. As a result, Ephraim's 'legally established borders were overthrown.'[9]

Hosea attributes this to Ephraim's following "what is worthless," a reference, probably, to the alliance with Rezon of Syria.[10] In that case, Ephraim's oppressive entanglement with Assyria is the result of their own shortsighted and bloodyminded politics. One does not have to be a modern political analyst to see that; one may assume that Hosea saw it and meant it. But he goes on to have God speak in the first person: I am like pus and like rottenness within Ephraim and Judah (v 12). The thought is as astonishing as the metaphors. The political folly of Ephraim and Judah is described as God's corrosive destruction from within. Such a statement invites us to great caution in our reflections on how the prophets saw God at work in their history. It points to a remarkable identification between the natural factors of politics and war and the claim of divine action.[11] The subsequent alliance with Assyria only brought Israel closer to the maelstrom in which it would ultimately be engulfed (cf., Hos 5:13).[12] And Hosea intensifies his emphasis on its being God's doing.

> For I will be like a lion to Ephraim,
>   and like a young lion to the house of Judah.
> I, even, I, will rend and go away,
>   I will carry off, and none shall rescue. (5:14)

---

[9]Wolff, *Hosea*, 114.

[10]So Wolff, *Hosea*, 114; and Mays, "All this because Ephraim had turned to an enemy for an ally. Syria is undoubtedly in mind. How could Ephraim make common cause with this ancient foe against its brothers?" (*Hosea*, 90). In pursuit of their coalition, Syria and northern Israel together attacked Judah (cf., Isaiah 7; 2 Kgs 16:5).

[11]"God is putrefaction and bone rot in the body of both peoples. The comparisons are drawn to the extreme limit, but their boldness is meant to reveal how God in hiddenness is already at work, sapping away the vitality of Ephraim and Judah *through the very actions which they initiate and execute.* The debilitating effects of their policy is not to be thought of as separate from the effect of his presence in their history" (Mays, *Hosea*, 90-91, emphasis mine).

[12]Tiglath-pileser III gives himself most of the credit for it. "They (the inhabitants of Israel) overthrew their king Pekah ... and I placed Hoshea ... as king over them. I received from them 10 talents of gold, 1,000 (?) talents of silver as their (tri)bute and brought them to Assyria" (*ANET*, 284).

When Hosea returns to the theme of Israel's folly in pursuing alliances, now with Egypt, now with Assyria, he also returns to the hunter metaphor: "I will spread over them my net; I will bring them down like birds of the air" (7:12). There follows a cry that is part dirge and part denunciation.

> Woe to them,
>> for they have strayed from me!
> Destruction to them,
>> for they have rebelled against me!
> I would redeem them,
>> but they speak lies against me. (7:13)

In the last of the three poetic lines, there is the contrasting polarity between God and Ephraim/Israel. The first verset has a marked "I" for the God who would redeem them; the second verset has an equally marked "they" for the people whose refusal of truth impedes redemption.[13] Human falsehood can stand in the way of divine redemption. The following verses spell out what these lies are. Israel is interpreting its world in terms of Baal, and not turning to its God. And so, Hosea's proclamation: "Their princes shall fall by the sword because of the insolence of their tongue. This shall be their derision in the land of Egypt" (7:16). Death to the rulers and derision from the Egyptians at the failure of Israel's strategies.

Another saying of Hosea's reflects much the same situation (8:7-10). The threat itself is textually difficult. Wolff translates: "I will now gather them up, so that they soon writhe under the burden of the officials' king" (v 10). The "officials' king" is the king of Assyria, the great king, the king of kings; the "officials" are his viceroys and representatives. Of great interest is again the thinking which leads to this proclamation. First of all, a proverb with an agricultural background to it: "For they sow the wind and they reap the whirlwind" (v 7). There is a twofold progression in the line. There is narrative progression from "they sow" to "they reap"; there is progressive intensification from "the wind" to "the

---

[13]Wolff treats the first verset as a question, and adversative at that (*Hosea*, 108, 127). There is nothing in the syntax to require it. Mays comments: "But the divine will to redeem is frustrated by the treachery of his subjects" (*Hosea*, 111).

whirlwind." The intellectual context to this is again the broad conviction that acts bring their consequences in their train; that as you sow, so you are likely to reap.[14] The second line has a similar proverb: grain that does not sprout into a head will provide no flour (v 7). "Grain without head yields no bread" (Mays, also Wolff) catches the Hebrew accurately. Israel's political strategies are not going to assure its security. The third line adds: "If it were to yield, aliens would devour it" (v 7; literally: would swallow it up). The image is of Israel surrounded by its enemies; if there is anything in the land worth taking, they will take it. The saying may be meant concretely, referring to the foraging activities of the Assyrian troops. Or it may have a wider application. Certainly, two statements are taken for granted: whatever you have, they will know about; if you cannot stop them, they will take it. These are only pointers to the climate of thought, but they will be important for a consideration of the prophetic theology.

Hosea picks up the swallowing metaphor and goes on: "Israel is swallowed up; already they are among the nations as a useless vessel" (v 8). The reference may well be to Tiglath-pileser III's subjugation of much of northern Israel in 733. And Hosea places the blame on Israel's own political activity: "For they have gone up to Assyria, a wild ass wandering alone; Ephraim has hired lovers" (v 9). "Israel herself relinquished her freedom in that she 'went to Assyria.' . . . Israel took the initiative in offering tribute, even before Assyria's conquest forced its necessity."[15] So here Hosea is drawing a picture of Israel tirelessly enmeshing itself in the web of its own undoing. And, at the same time, he will attribute the responsibility for it to God: "I will now gather them up, so that they soon writhe under the burden of the officials' king" (v 10). Israel's fate is the same: subjugation to Assyria. But the agent responsible is now God. It is important to note how, in the prophet's use of language, he can modulate effortlessly from a disastrous situation which is the result of Israel's own doing to an

---

[14]This is a realm of thought which we will discuss in detail later (chap. 13). However, it is so frequently misunderstood, that one caution should be stated here. "As you sow, so you reap" cannot be generally reversed. Whatever limits have to be put on the saying itself, its reverse is patently untrue. One cannot say: "As you reap, so you must have sown." That is precisely the error of Job's friends, who are convinced that since he is suffering he must have sinned. And that is unequivocally wrong.

[15]Wolff, *Hosea,* 142.

equally disastrous situation which is the result of God's doing. Clearly, Hosea sees both in the same light. The different forms of expression do not reflect different realities; rather, they reflect different aspects of the one reality.

The theme of exile occurs in several of Hosea's threats against Ephraim (cf., 9:3, 6, 17). The announcement can be directed against the king (10:7) or against the royal sanctuary at Bethel (10:8), or, in all probability, against the cocksure confidence of the military (10:13-15). Hosea 11 has already been treated (above, chap. 9). Here we may note that the proclamation in vv 5-7 points to Assyrian domination, sieges and destruction, and submission to foreign power.[16] 12:14 (MT, 12:15) is a particularly clear case of the act-consequence thinking in a prophetic announcement. Ephraim's blood guilt is left upon him; his own reproach is brought back upon him. The hunting metaphor recurs once more, with the images of the lion, the leopard, and the bear (13:7-8). It is one of the harshest images among Hosea's proclamations. Its metaphor is parallelled only by the literal reality of the final proclamation, with its reflection of the terrible and inhuman cruelty of war and conquest (13:16).

MICAH

The first three chapters of the book of Micah open and close with a proclamation of destruction for a capital city, Samaria at the start (1:6-7) and Jerusalem at the end (3:12).[17] The image is

[16]The meaning of the "return to Egypt" in Hosea is not simple. It can have the sense of the literal return there of exile groups; or the turning to Egypt for political help; or the spiritual return to Egypt which blots out the significance of salvation history (cf., the constant refrain of the wilderness murmuring, from Exod 16:3 to Num 14:2-4). It is the third which is predominant here, contrasting with v 1, although the overtone of seeking help can also be present. On this, see Wolff, *Hosea*, 145-46. Mays places more emphasis on the literal sense of the groups in exile.

[17]As for Isaiah, so for Micah the depth of his impact on his community can be gauged by the amount of material which accumulated in the book which bore his name. There is general agreement on the attribution to Micah of: 1:8-16; 2:1-11; 3:1-12. Wolff considers there is good reason to attribute 1:6-7 and some of 4:9-5:4 (MT, 5:3) and 6:9-16 to Micah (H.W. Wolff, *Micah the Prophet* [Philadelphia: Fortress 1981] 17). Mays attributes to Micah substantially: 1:3-5a, 8-15; 2:1-11; and 3:1-12 (J.L. Mays, *Micah* [OTL; Philadelphia: Westminster, 1976] 13). So there is some doubt concerning the authenticity of 1:6-7. Mays comments, "The verses are clearly part of a redactional pattern whose concern

much the same for both. Samaria is to be made a heap in the open country, a place for planting vineyards; it will be levelled to its foundations, its images and idols destroyed. Jerusalem is to become a ploughed field, a heap of ruins, a wooded height. Micah envisages the destructive conquest of the country (although "conqueror" and "captors" are both textually uncertain in 1:15 and 2:4). The evil ahead is inescapable (2:3-4). Escape is not to be had by praying to God (3:4). And as for the prophets who deny all this by crying, "Peace," they shall be disgraced, shamed, and silent (3:5-7). As far as the criterion of fulfillment is concerned, the fate forecast for Samaria was not long in coming, if the saying is authentic; that of Jerusalem was delayed more than a century. Poetic license has to be granted on the dramatic details. Neither city was reduced to vineyard or forest.[18]

ISAIAH

Isaiah 1:7-8 is less an announcement or threat than a description of what has actually happened.[19] It refers to the devastation during the campaign of Sennacherib, king of Assyria. In his own annals, Sennacherib paints much the same picture, with much the same sort of metaphor:

> As to Hezekiah, the Jew, he did not submit to my yoke, I laid siege to 46 of his strong cities, walled forts and to the countless small villages in their vicinity, and conquered (them) by means of well-stamped (earth-) ramps, and battering rams brought (thus) near (to the walls) (combined with) the attack by foot soldiers, (using) mines, breeches as well as sapper work. . . .

is the Samaria-Jerusalem scheme of judgment specified in the title and introduced in v 5b. The style and the concern with idolatry are found together elsewhere only in 5:10ff., itself a later piece. The language seems in part to have been drawn from material already at hand and it would also appear to have been composed as a companion piece to 3:12" (*Micah*, 47).

[18]Sargon claimed to have rebuilt Samaria better than it was before (according to the text reconstructed in *ANET*, 284). The account in 2 Kings 25 points to extensive destruction—temples, palace, great houses, walls (vv 9-10).

[19]Our treatment here will be restricted to Isaiah 1-12.

> Himself I made a prisoner in Jerusalem, his royal residence, like a bird in a cage.[20]

Isaiah's image of Jerusalem as a shanty or a shed in the midst of a desolate landscape gives concrete details to the more general proclamation of wrath, such as 1:24-26. He picks up the theme of the proud and the haughty whom the prophesied disaster will humble (2:9, 17-22). The details are filled out there, too, with the picture of Jerusalem in helpless anarchy, stripped of the mainstays of its society, the consequence of defeat and its aftermath (3:1-7). It is given unpleasantly concrete shape in the frightful details of siege, defeat, and devastation (3:17-4:1). The catalog of aristocratic finery (vv 18-23, perhaps added to Isaiah's text) makes a fearfully stark contrast with the marks of a defeated populace, rottenness and the rope, hairless heads and sackcloth, shame and death.

The woe sayings of Isaiah 5 contain two specific threats. One points to an abandoned land, with empty houses and no productive farming (5:9-10). The other speaks of exile, death, and collapse (5:13-17). The source of all this is depicted in two superb, but frightening, passages (5:26-30; 10:27-32). In the first, the irresistible might of the fiercely disciplined Assyrian troops—as menacing in Isaiah's poetry as in their own murals! Swift and untiring, in perfect order and perfectly equipped, bowmen and chariotry; the rumble of their approach is like the roar of lions or the surge of the sea. They bring darkness and distress to the land. After the picture of the troops themselves, the other passage turns to the relentless, unstoppable speed of their approach. Along the backbone of the hills north of Jerusalem they come. Michmash, Geba, Ramah, Gibeah—these are the towns just to the immediate north—until at Nob, the might of Assyria can look down on Jerusalem and shake its fist.

There is some difference of opinion today as to whether or not the vision of judgment in Isaiah 6 constitutes the report of Isaiah's call, as is generally assumed.[21] Whatever the conclusion on this

[20]*ANET,* 288.

[21]See R. Knierim, "The Vocation of Isaiah," *VT* 18 (1968) 47-68; M. Tsevat, "The Throne Vision of Isaiah," in *The Meaning of the Book of Job and Other Biblical Studies: Essays on the Literature and Religion of the Hebrew Bible* (New York: Ktav, 1980) 155-76; J.M. Ward, *Amos & Isaiah* (Nashville: Abingdon, 1969) 144-45; and O. Kaiser, *Isaiah 1-12* (2nd ed.; OTL; Philadelphia: Westminster, 1983) 118-23.

issue, it is clear that the vision contains a proclamation of judgment. The vision is dated to the year King Uzziah died. He was a king of northern Israel. The dates given for his death, by various authorities, range from 747/46 to 735/34.[22] The proclamation is addressed to "this people" (v 10); there is no specification as to whether Israel or Judah is intended. The implication of it is that Isaiah's message will confirm the people in the contrary views they already hold. The outcome is what constitutes the sharpest aspect of the threat:

> Until cities lie waste
>   without inhabitant,
> and houses without men,
>   and the land is utterly desolate,
> and the LORD removes men far away,
>   and the forsaken places are many in the midst of the land.
>
> (6:11-12)

The faint hope expressed at the end of v 13, whatever its date of origin, would have been meager solace for a people confronted with the prophecy of such devastation.

The message Isaiah is to announce to the people contrasts strangely with the one he delivered to Ahaz, when the Judean king quailed before the combined military power of northern Israel and Syria, bent on removing him from his throne (Isa 7:1-6). Isaiah brings the king good news: "Take heed, be quiet, do not fear, ... thus says the LORD God: 'It shall not stand and it shall not come to pass'" (vv 4-7). The irony of it is that Ahaz did not want to accept such good news. It is a prompt confirmation of the announcement of chap. 6: even the good news they did not want to hear or understand. Whether the last line of the saying (v 9b) called on Ahaz to believe Isaiah and stand firm politically, or to believe in God and stand firm in faith, neither was acceptable to Ahaz.[23] The confrontation between prophet and king continues

---

[22]Cf. Ward, *Amos & Isaiah*, 147, n. 4.

[23]The options, as discussed by Ward, may be paraphrased: 1) Do not panic and you will stand fast; 2) Believe Isaiah and you will stand fast; 3) Trust God and you will stand fast. For Ward, the last is the least likely (*Amos & Isaiah*, 184-91). For most interpreters, it is the option they choose. For Kaiser, "the present narrative does not come from the prophet

with the Immanuel oracle. Isaiah's idea of good news did not sit
well with Ahaz. The king, of course, by enlisting the assistance of
the Assyrian, Tiglath-pileser III, effectively blocked any test of
Isaiah's prophecy through fulfillment. The following text, which
is difficult and has a complex history of growth, concludes with
oracles which are distinctly unfriendly (vv 18-20, 23-25). The
theme of devastation has returned.

When God sent Isaiah to speak to Ahaz, he was told to take
with him his son, *Shear-jashub* (A-Remnant-Shall-Return) (6:3).
Later he is told by God to name the next son *Maher-shalal-hash-
baz* (The-Spoil-Speeds-The-Prey-Hastens) (8:1-4). In the tradition
of Hosea, the prophet's children are living witnesses to their
father's message. One wonders if the neighborhood ever grew
used enough to those dread-sounding names not to shudder
whenever a parental voice summoned the Isaiah children to their
home. For the prophet, the proclamation of devastation was
something to be lived with, in the heart of his family.

A series of sayings, marked by the refrain "For all this his anger
is not turned away and his hand is stretched out still," begins in
5:25 and continues with 9:8-10:4. There is a threat in 9:11-12
which is directed against the northern kingdom: their political
foes will devour them. A final woe saying, in 10:1-4, completes the
series begun at 5:8, and, in the present text, is blended in with the
refrain. It is a fitting finale for the threat of Isaiah to the people of
Israel and Judah

> What will you do on the day of punishment,
>   in the storm which will come from afar?
> To whom will you flee for help,
>   and where will you leave your wealth?
> Nothing remains but to crouch among the prisoners
>   or fall among the slain.
> For all this his anger is not turned away
>   and his hand is stretched out still. (10:3-4)

Isaiah but is heavily influenced by Deuteronomistic theology, and presumably belongs
only to the late sixth or early fifth century BC" (*Isaiah 1-12* [2nd ed.] 143).

There is one final threat in Isaiah 1-12 of which mention has to be made. It is 10:5-15(16-19), directed against Assyria. Assyria is accused of going beyond the commission it received from God and of arrogating to itself what was a delegated authority. Therefore, when God's work with Jerusalem is done (v 12), Assyria's boasting and pride will be punished. From one aspect, it is a word of encouragement to those under the oppressive burden of Assyrian hegemony. From another, it is in some sense a theodicy, justifying God who did not stand behind the barbarous cruelty and brutality of the Assyrians. It may also serve as a reminder to us, here, of a whole category of prophetic utterance which circumstances will force us to ignore: the prophetic judgments against foreign nations. It is one of the areas of the prophets' activity that is seldom brought to the fore. Yet it is a feature of the sayings of Amos and Isaiah, of Jeremiah and Ezekiel. If nothing else, such sayings serve as a reminder of the broader international perspective that was part of prophecy in Israel.

JEREMIAH

In the book of Jeremiah, we have already discussed the phenomenon of extensive passages of prose, with resemblances to deuteronomistic language and thought.[24] So as to keep our present discussion within bounds, we will restrict it principally to the poetry of chaps. 1-25. It is worth noting that often the deuteronomistic prose passages pick up a theme from one of the lines in the preceding poetry and develop it. The deuteronomistic themes which are woven into the development include the emphasis on Israel's sins as apostasy and injustice, the emphasis on prophecy as call to repentance, and also the use of language redolent of the curses, part of the panoply of deuteronomistic covenantal expression. We also need to remember that, during the years of Jeremiah's activity (627/609-586), first the Assyrians, then the Egyptians, and finally the Babylonians made the exercise

---

[24]See above, chap. 10, n. 2.

of their power felt in Judah.[25] Often what for earlier prophets might have been in the category of proclamation or foretelling, for Jeremiah becomes actual description of the present or the recent past.

The announcement of judgment in the prophecy of Jeremiah is an integral element of his call narrative (cf., Isaiah 6). After the gesture of God's hand touching Jeremiah's mouth has been reported, its significance is unfolded (1:9-10). God's words have been placed in Jeremiah's mouth. His destiny as a prophet is now effectively realized; he is set over nations and kingdoms. His task: "To pluck up and to break down, to destroy and to overthrow, to build and to plant" (v 10). Three pairs of infinitives, in a beautiful enumeration, but with a fearful message. Before there can be talk of building and planting, there must first be tearing up and breaking down, destruction and demolition. These key verbs occur a number of times through Jeremiah's sayings. In other places, the listing is not so complete or not so well balanced.[26] Here, either the best and most balanced statement has been distilled from the others, or it has been chosen as the prime example, to feature in the call narrative and open the collection of Jeremiah's sayings. In either case, it is a pointer to the degree of reflection which went into the formulation of a prophetic call narrative.

[25]A glance through the relevant chapters of 2 Kings gives a good indication. Josiah died trying to stop Pharaoh Neco from assisting the Assyrians (23:29). Neco put Jehoahaz, Josiah's son and successor, in bonds at Riblah and laid a tribute on the land; he installed Jehoiakim as king, and exacted tribute from him (23:33-35). Nebuchadnezzar, king of Babylon, came on the scene to establish his power in the region, and Jehoiakim became his vassal for three years (24:1). Then, when Jehoiakim threw off the Babylonian yoke, Babylonian troops and Syrians, Moabites, and Ammonites attacked Judah (24:2). The king of Babylon had taken all that belonged to the king of Egypt from the Brook of Egypt to the river Euphrates (24:7). Nebuchadnezzar's troops besieged Jerusalem; the king gave himself up, and much of the city's wealth and its upper classes and skilled workers were taken into exile to Babylon (24:10-16). Nebuchadnezzar put Zedekiah on the throne in Jerusalem (24:17). When Zedekiah attempted to escape the Babylonian yoke, the Babylonian army besieged and sacked Jerusalem (24:20-25:12). All this between 609 and 586. Note that the view that Jeremiah's ministry began in 627 is rejected by all three of the most recent commentators: R.P. Carroll, *Jeremiah* (OTL; London: SCM, 1986), W.L. Holladay, *Jeremiah 1: A Commentary on the Book of the Prophet Jeremiah, Chapters 1-25* (Hermeneia; Philadelphia: Fortress, 1986), and W. McKane, *Jeremiah* (Vol. 1: Introduction and Commentary on Jeremiah I-XXV; ICC; Edinburgh, T. & T. Clark, 1986).

[26]Cf., Jer 12:14-17; 18:7-10; 24:6; 31:27-28; 42:9-10; 45:4-5.

The call narrative is extended by two vision reports. The second sounds a note which will reverberate through Jeremiah's message—the evil from the north. "Out of the north evil shall break forth upon all the inhabitants of the land" (v 14). Jeremiah's proclamation is that God is bringing the tribes of the kingdoms of the north (primarily the Babylonians) and setting them up as besieging adversaries, around the walls of Jerusalem and all the cities of Judah (v 15).[27] No wonder that with a message like that to utter, Jeremiah needed to be toughened against his people— kings, princes, priests and people (v 18). The prophet had no possibility of modifying his message just a little. God's command was: "Arise, and say to them *everything* that I command you. Do not be dismayed by them, lest I dismay you before them" (v 17). Jeremiah knew exactly what it was like to be between a rock and a hard place.

For our purposes, it is possible to get a further sense of the threats in Jeremiah by looking over some of the quite extensive passages in which he sketches the picture of devastation caused by war and military campaigns. There is the cry to get into the walled cities for safety, for the destroyer of nations has set out from the north to make the land a waste and cities ruins (4:5-8). The following prose passage reflects on the bitter irony of those who have been assuring Judah that "It shall be well with you" (vv 9-10). There is the image of chariots as swift and destructive as the whirlwind, of horses swooping faster than eagles, as the besiegers come from a distant land (vv 13-17). The anguish of the situation is mirrored in the personal anguish of Jeremiah as he hears the alarm signals of war and knows that disaster will follow on disaster and the land will be laid waste (vv 19-20).

> O my bowels, my bowels! I writhe!
> O walls of my heart!
> My heart is in storm within me
> I cannot be still. (4:19)[28]

---

[27]The passage is understood differently by Carroll and Holladay.

[28]Translation from J. Bright, *Jeremiah* (AB 21; Garden City: Doubleday, 1965) 30. The *RSV's* "My anguish my anguish" catches the meaning perfectly. But it fails to express the concomitant body feelings, which go with the personal anguish, and which Bright's more literal translation brings out. The expression of joy and suffering in the great poets of Israel

This section, which began with the summons to seek safety within the city walls (v 5), now pictures the flight from the cities to seek shelter in the dense forests and the rocky fastnesses (vv 29-31). The imagery evokes the situation: the desperate fugitives slipping out of the towns, dodging their way through the attacking forces, dashing for cover among the trees and undergrowth at the foot of the hills, forced in fear higher and higher beyond the vegetation to the rocks and crags of the summits. And the cities are deserted.

The Babylonians are an enduring nation, an ancient nation, a fearsome nation, for their language is foreign and unknown (5:15). Their quiver is like an open tomb, eating up the food supply, vines and fig trees, flocks and herds, sons and daughters, even the fortified cities which promised security (vv 16-17). Again and again, the picture is relentlessly repeated. For Jerusalem (6:1-5, 6; 9:11), with frightening images of the merciless destroyer (6:22-26; 8:16). Because Israel has abandoned its God, their acts have dragged their consequences in train, and they, Israel, have made their land "a horror, a thing to be hissed at forever. Everyone who passes by it is horrified and shakes his head" (18:16). Then Jeremiah changes his image and has God say:

> Like the east wind I will scatter them
>> before the enemy.
> I will show them my back, not my face,
>> in the day of their calamity. (18:17)

A little later, the prose picks up the theme of the city of horror, to be hissed at (cf., 19:8, followed by the awful reality of the inhuman misery of a siege).

Jeremiah's announcements are not restricted to threats to the whole nation. There is a triad of sayings directed to three among the last kings of Judah. In 22:10, there is a dirge for Jehoahaz (Shallum), with an explanation of the dirge in vv 11-12. Pharaoh Neco had put him in jail in exile, and put his brother on the throne of Judah in his place (cf., 2 Kgs 23:33-34). In 22:13-17, there is a reproach hurled at this brother, Jehoiakim, for his vain injustice

makes it perfectly clear that they address their emotions in terms of the impact they have, physically, upon their bodies.

in building extensions to his palace at the cost of the poor of his kingdom. For him, there will be no dirge or lament (vv 18-19). Finally, there is Jehoiachin (Coniah, short form of the king's personal name, Jeconiah, cf., 1 Chron 3:16): he is in exile, he may as well be childless, he will be the first of David's line to have no successor on his throne (22:29-30). The prose account is given before the poetic oracle (vv 24-27). For Jehoiachin, there is no hope of return (cf., 2 Kgs 24:11-15 and 25:27-30).[29]

EZEKIEL

While Ezekiel was among those exiled before the fall of Jerusalem, he too has announcements to proclaim against Israel and Jerusalem. Like most exiles, those in Babylon hankered for news of their homeland. They would have known of the prophecies, circulating in Jerusalem, that within two years they and the treasures of Israel would return (cf., Jeremiah 27-29). Ezekiel's verdict on Jerusalem was a harsh counterblast to such hopes. Ezekiel's language alternates between imagery which hews close to the literal reality of siege and conquest, and imagery more traditional and general.

In a symbolic action, Ezekiel shaves his head and beard at God's command. The hair is weighed out and divided: a third burned in the fires of the captured city; a third struck with the sword round about the city; a third scattered to the winds, with the sword unsheathed after them (5:1-2; cf., also v 12). The message is as harsh as that of Amos. There will be those dying, trapped in the burning city. There will be those dying in their attempts to escape the fallen city. No rest for those who manage to get away; they will be pursued by the sword. Side by side with this siege imagery, Ezekiel can speak of famine and wild beasts which will ravage the people (5:17). The traditional triad of sword, famine, and pestilence is part of his armory (6:11-12; 7:15). In the image of general devastation, these are expanded by a fourth.

---

[29]On these passages, see the helpful treatment by Carroll, *From Chaos to Covenant* (London: SCM, 1981) 138-49. The reflections on fulfillment are important (p. 145).

> For thus says the LORD God: How much more when I send
> upon Jerusalem my four sore acts of judgment, sword, famine,
> evil beasts, and pestilence, to cut off from it man and beast!
> (14:21)

At other times, Ezekiel's proclamation is very general, but very
final: "An end! The end has come upon the four corners of the
land" (7:2). The most dramatic aspect of Ezekiel's proclamation is
his vision of God departing from Jerusalem. There, the end is
terribly vivid. "The glory of the God of Israel had gone up from
the cherubim on which it rested to the threshold of the house"
(10:4). "Then the glory of the LORD went forth from the threshold
of the house and stood over the cherubim, ... and they stood at
the door of the east gate of the house of the LORD" (10:18-19).
"And the glory of the LORD went up from the midst of the city,
and stood upon the mountain which is on the east side of the city"
(11:23). There could hardly be a more powerful image of a city
abandoned by its God.

The city will be abandoned by its people too. Ezekiel is
commanded to perform the symbolic action of the exile, getting
out through a hole in the wall, taking only what could be carried
on the shoulder (12:1-16). Ezekiel has no doubt that it is to
happen, and happen soon. A couple of sayings are doing the
rounds among the people. "The days grow long, and every vision
comes to naught" (12:22); "The vision that he sees is for many
days hence, and he prophesies of times far off" (12:27). Ezekiel's
proclamation counters such self-delusion: "Thus says the LORD
God: I will put an end to this proverb, and they shall no more use
it as a proverb in Israel" (12:23). "Thus says the LORD God: None
of my works will be delayed any longer, but the word which I
speak will be performed" (12:28). The false prophets, whose
prophetic activity succeeds in reinforcing the people in their
illusions of security, also come under condemnation (Ezekiel 13).
"They shall not be in the council of my people nor be enrolled in
the register of the house of Israel, nor shall they enter the land of
Israel; and you shall know that I am the LORD God" (13:19). The
illusions will be shattered.

Toward the end of these proclamations of judgment against his
own people, Ezekiel proclaims the coming disaster in general
terms of the flashing sword (21:1-17). Then suddenly, he turns to

the picture of the king of Babylon, planning his campaigns and standing at the parting of the ways. "Into his right hand comes the lot for Jerusalem, to open the mouth with a cry, to lift up the voice with shouting, to set battering rams against the gates, to cast up mounds, to build siege towers" (21:22-23). The proclamations end with the poem written on the day the king of Babylon laid siege to Jerusalem (24:2). The city is likened to a cooking pot: its inhabitants are the contents, and the besieging Babylonians are the fire.

> Therefore says the LORD God: Woe to the bloody city, to the pot whose rust is in it, and whose rust has not gone out of it . . . Heap on the logs, kindle the fire, boil well the flesh, and empty out the broth, and let the bones be burned up. . . . I the LORD have spoken; it shall come to pass, I will do it; I will not go back, I will not spare, I will not repent; according to your ways and your doings I will judge, says the LORD God.
>
> (24:6, 10, 14)

These are harsh and gruesome words. No wonder the prophets' contemporaries gave them a most grudging hearing. It is certainly not a pleasant experience for us, even at this distance, to be confronted with this message. We have so far left aside the prophetic promise of hope for the future, but not with any intention of playing it down. It is simply that without having experienced the full burden of the proclamation of judgment, it would be almost meretricious to delight in the promise of salvation. That is why it has been necessary for us to work our way through these proclamations, to be shaken by their grimness, and at times appalled by their imagery.

Today

The prophetic threats bring into sharp focus the question whether we can legitimately speak of the Old Testament's witness to a loving God. Closely allied to this is the question whether in the face of the world's suffering it makes sense to speak of a loving God.

There are two ways we can approach the prophetic threats which speak of God's punitive action against Israel or Judah. One way is to assume that they are to be understood literally as threats of divine intervention guiding the course of human history, and that the prophets themselves understood them in this way. This assumption would imply, in the limit case, that without God's action the course of history might have unfolded in other ways or that without God's action Israel's evil might have gone unpunished.

In such an understanding, there is obvious difficulty in speaking of witness to a loving God. There are various ways of lessening the difficulty, first and foremost among them being to point out, quite rightly, that all human language about God ultimately enters the realm of mystery and we should never err by eliminating mystery from its place in our understanding of God. Appeal can be made to the necessity of divine justice, or to the analogy of loving parental chastisement, and so on. Under close scrutiny, most such approaches fail to be fully satisfactory, and the final appeal must be to divine mystery. One may also query the correctness of the initial assumption.

Another way of looking at the prophetic threats is to assume that the prophets were perfectly well aware of the political and military factors involved in the situation they addressed. This assumption would imply that they believed that the policies and national attitudes within Israel and Judah would inevitably bring about the disasters they announced. In the hypothetical limit case, had God turned a blind eye to Israel's evil, the Assyrians and the Babylonians would still have pursued their imperial policies and subdued these fractious nations on their south-western borders. In this case, the prophetic threats of God's punitive action against Israel understand the action of God to be within the natural course of history's unfolding. God is creator and sovereign of the universe and what happens in accordance with the procedures of that universe is legitimately and rightly described as God's action.

In this understanding, language of a loving God is necessarily coupled with language of an angry God and a grieving God. Within the limits and inadequacies of human speech, God must of necessity be described as angered by the evils of Israel, which caused so much social suffering and sacral ugliness and folly. Equally within the limits of human speech, God must of necessity be described as grieving over the suffering of the chosen people, whom God loves, being bent beneath the savage yoke of the Assyrian and Babylonian empires. The Old Testament has no hesitation in speaking of God as loving, as angry, as grieving or compassionate. These emotions are all compatible within our human experience. Used of God, they must be transformed by analogy and they too must partake of the realm of mystery. But they may offer a language which more appropriately honors God's self-communication and which more appropriately mirrors the understanding of the Old Testament. We will need to consider this more closely in chapter 13.

RECOMMENDED FURTHER READING

See the reading recommended at the end of chapter 10.

12

The Prophetic Hope for Israel

Recommended preliminary reading

Before reading the body of the chapter, it will be helpful to have
read the following passages:
Hosea 14:1-8
Isaiah 43:14-21
Jeremiah 31:31-34
Ezekiel 37:1-14

Any consideration of Israel's pre-exilic prophets has to take
serious account of their promise of hope for their people's future.
It is an integral part of most of the prophetic books. It is a
necessary balance to the grim picture of the prophetic threats
against Israel. Above all, it reveals an important aspect of Israel's
faith and their understanding of their God.

The strikingly new element that appears in the prophecies of
salvation is the repeated insistence that the new future will be
God's doing and will depend on God alone. For Hosea, there is
still the call to return to God, alongside the promise of God's
gracious action. In the prophets who were closest to the final
catastrophe of Jerusalem's fall—Jeremiah, Ezekiel, and Second
Isaiah—faith in the new future as God's doing has become
paramount. As Gerhard von Rad puts it, "Jeremiah and Ezekiel
take Israel's total inability to obey as the very starting-point of

their prophecy."[1] Perhaps this reflects the experience of hopes raised high by the deuteronomic reform and dashed by the cruelty of its aftermath.

What this new element reveals is the depth of Israel's faith in the unconditional commitment of God. It may be that this faith finds expression in all-too-human hopes for prosperity and power, but the faith itself is remarkable and should not be underestimated. The deuteronomic reform, with its emphasis on "this day," was confident that God was ready to overlook centuries of failure so that the blessing available in the time of Moses was available too in the time of Josiah. The prophets, who announced and even witnessed the loss of Samaria and Jerusalem, were sufficiently firmly convinced of the sure commitment of God's love for Israel that they could speak confidently of a new and hopeful future beyond these two major breakdowns. It is in these prophecies of a new future that Israel gives us its most eloquent witness to God's unconditional love.

AMOS

It might seem strange to start a chapter on prophetic hope with a section on a prophet who originally expressed no such hope. But it has the advantage of showing what a prophetic book without hope might look like. It looks pretty grim. The message from the fifth vision of Amos is:

> Not one of them shall flee away,
> not one of them shall escape. (9:1)

The next three verses unfold the seriousness of that message and there is no relief. It is always difficult to judge how literally a vision is to be taken, but there is no doubt that this one does not bode well for Israel. As we have seen, it is possible that these visions came early in Amos's prophetic experience. From that point of view, it is interesting that the rest of his proclamation (2:13-16; 3:11; 4:2-3 for example) is not so universally annihilating. A

---

[1]G. von Rad, *Old Testament Theology* (2 vols.; Edinburgh: Oliver and Boyd, 1962-65) 2.270.

fearful fate awaits the nation certainly. Does it also imply that God has abandoned Israel? Symbolically, the vision is on a par with Hosea's "You are not my people and I am not your God" (Hos 1:9). To my sensibility, there is something a fraction more final about Hosea's verbally explicit rupture of relationship. There is always the lingering hope that the visionary words are not to be taken with utter literalness to mean an end of all life in Israel and all relationship with Israel.

Hope for the future is expressed in the last two sayings of the book of Amos (9:11-12, 13-15). There is a broad consensus that these cannot have come from Amos himself. In vv 11-12, the references to restoring the booth of David and possessing the remnant of Edom make most sense after the fall of Jerusalem in 587. The same is true of the ruined cities and need for restoration in vv 14-15. Elsewhere, Amos shows no concern with the hopes of Judah and the Davidic dynasty. Comparison with the other redactional layers in the book of Amos suggests that these sayings are independent, the final addition bringing the perspective of hope to a prophetic book which had lacked it.

HOSEA

The baneful message of threat which Hosea delivered to Israel, culminating in that fearful "You are not my people" was grounded in the commands of God reported in Hosea 1. In the same way, the expression of hope in the prophecy of Hosea comes first and foremost from God's command as reported in Hosea 3. The divine command is clear and direct:

> Go again, love a woman who is beloved of a paramour and is an adulteress; even as the LORD loves the people of Israel, though they turn to other gods and love cakes of raisins. (3:1)

The "again" is the counterbalance to the "first" of 1:2—"When the LORD first spoke through Hosea." There is a conscious awareness of the relationship between these two sets of divine commands. Hosea is to reestablish a relationship of love with a sinful woman, just as God still loves sinful Israel. The meaning is present in all succinctness in this divine command. It is unfolded in the report of Hosea's speech to the woman (3:3-5). Their conduct will reflect the events in Israel's future. For many days Israel will be deprived, politically, in worship, and in divine guidance. But afterwards, Israel's relationship with God will be restored. The message is spare; there is none of the lovely imagery and eloquence usual in Hosea. For all that, the message is enormously significant.

In Jeremiah, Ezekiel, and Second Isaiah, as we have noted, the new emphasis is on the unilateral action of God to bring about the future state of salvation for Israel. It is foreshadowed here, where the initiative comes spontaneously from God. The text gives no indication of any move on the part of Hosea or the woman. The command comes directly from God, erupting into their lives. Like the call of Abraham, this action commanded of Hosea symbolizes God's gracious saving initiative. While in Jeremiah, Ezekiel, and Second Isaiah, the perception of human failure may have played its role (heavily emphasized by von Rad), in Hosea Israel's perception of God's commitment to salvation is clearly the major factor.

It is a safe assumption to make that this experience of God's command is the origin of Hosea's conviction that God would again save Israel. In the arrangement of the first collection of his sayings, this conviction is repeated twice more. After the terrible utterance, "You are not my people and I am not your God," whoever compiled the collection immediately added the sayings which reversed that all-too-final verdict (1:10-2:1; MT, 2:1-3). Israel shall be numerous as the sands of the sea, echoing the promises to the patriarchs of numerous descendants. That saying of decisive rupture, "You are not my people," will be replaced by a saying of full relationship, "Sons of the living God." Divided Israel will regain its political unity. Once again Israel will be known as "My people" and as "Pitied." Nothing is directly said as to the source of this transformation; God is not mentioned. But so direct a reversal can only be effected by God.

God is very powerfully present in the sayings of the second part of chapter 2 (2:14-23; MT, 2:16-25). The metaphor is of lover and beloved: the image one of seduction, the goal one of marriage— my husband and not my Baal (2:16; MT, 18). The relationship between God and Israel will return to the honeymoon status of Egypt and the wilderness—a vision shared by Jeremiah (2:1-3) but not by some other O.T. writers, such as the Yahwist. All trace of idolatry will disappear from Israel and it will be God's doing: "For I will remove the names of the Baals from her mouth. . . . " A covenant will be established, surprisingly not between God and Israel but between Israel and beasts, birds, and creeping things. The disharmony traced back to Genesis 2-3 is to be replaced by perfect harmony. There will be harmony between peoples, so that war will cease. The relationship with God will be securely reestablished.

> And I will betroth you to me for ever; I will betroth you to me in righteousness and in justice, in steadfast love, and in mercy. I will betroth you to me in faithfulness; and you shall know the LORD.   (2:19-20; MT, 21-23)

In all of this superb harmony between God and the world, the message of the God-given names of Hosea's children will be totally reversed. God will indeed sow, God will have pity, and God will say to Israel, "You are my people" and Israel will reply, "You are my God" (2:23; MT, 25). Here it is quite clear that all of this is God's doing and only God's doing.

There is a subtle progression in the collection, from the neutral formulation of 1:10-2:1, to the divine "I" of the seduction (2:14-23), ending finally in the divine command of 3:1. It may be intended, it may not. But it has the effect of bringing gently on to the scene the total commitment of God to Israel. At first, God is not explicitly in the text, but clearly between the lines. Then, after the censure of faithless Israel, fidelity and harmony are promised for a future time, as the result of God's wooing and restoring Israel. Finally, the divine action is initiated in the present, through the command to Hosea, even though its fulfillment is for the future. Furthermore, in 3:1 it is explicitly clear that God's commitment is to Israel, even in their sinfulness and infidelity— "though they turn to other gods."

We have already considered Hos 11:1-11, in chapter 9, so it is enough simply to draw attention to it in this context. It expresses so powerfully the tender emotion and compassion of God. It is a love and compassion which is expressed in a context that is emphatic about Israel's sinfulness: "The more I called them, the more they went from me; . . . my people are bent on turning away from me" (11:2, 7). It locates Israel's certainty of salvation in the inner being of God: "for I am God and not man, the Holy One in your midst, and I will not come to destroy" (11:9). The homecoming is indeed the work of God (11:11).

The final chapter of Hosea juxtaposes two themes: Israel's repentant return and God's gracious healing of their infidelity. Wolff points out that the reference to Israel in the third person, "their faithlessness," is typical of a divine decree rather than an assurance of salvation which would be directly addressed to Israel.[2] 14:1-3 can be seen as Hosea's address to Israel, calling them back to God, before he proclaims over them God's gracious decree: "I will heal their faithlessness; I will love them freely..." (14:4). The primary demand of unconditional love is to be accepted rather than returned, but the return of such love is ultimately inevitable. The fullest repentance is the return of accepted love. The most powerful motive for it is the recognition of God's spontaneous and gracious love reaching out toward us in our faithlessness.

JEREMIAH

There is considerable uncertainty about the attribution of the passages of hope in Jeremiah. John Bright express one position:

> All in all, the safest conclusion is that chapters xxx-xxxi contain genuine sayings of Jeremiah addressed to northern Israel and uttered relatively early in his career (xxxi 2-6, 15-22), together with other words of his uttered much later, and that the material has in certain cases subsequently been expanded and supplemented in such a way as to apply Jeremiah's prophecies more directly to the situation of the exiles living in Babylon.[3]

[2]H.W. Wolff, *Hosea* (Hermeneia; Philadelphia: Fortress, 1974) 233.

[3]John Bright, *Jeremiah* (AB 21; Garden City: Doubleday, 1965) 285.

The more skeptical position is put forward by Robert Carroll:

> As the cycle shows the marked influence of Hosea and Second Isaiah in places (e.g. 30.9, 10-11; 31.2-6, 7-9, 10-14, 18-20) and shares some common elements with the Ezekiel tradition (e.g. 31.29-30, 33, 38-40), it is preferable to attribute it to the anonymous circles during and after the exile which cherished expectations of restoration.... The vagueness of this attribution is balanced by the lack of information available for determining the issue in a reliably historical manner and the contradictions inherent in crediting Jeremiah with the authorship of the cycle.[4]

While clearly caution is required, we may at least look on these passages as evidence of the faith of Israel, which the community of Israel esteemed highly enough to incorporate into the book of the prophet Jeremiah.

The classic passage for the expression of future hope in Jeremiah is the saying about the new covenant (Jer 31:31-34). Probably the majority of exegetes regard it as coming from Jeremiah.[5] It looks to a future time, and the new covenant to be made with Israel and Judah will be God's doing. It will be different from the broken Sinai covenant. The difference is that God will put the law within the people and write it upon their hearts. The broken relationship will be restored and God will effect full reconciliation: "I will be their God, and they shall be my people.... I will forgive their iniquity, and I will remember their sin no more."

It would appear that the law will remain the same; no change to it is suggested. The change is that the law is to be placed within, written on the heart. It would be a false emphasis to see internalized appropriation of the law being opposed here to mere external observance. The Shema stands as eloquent witness to the extent to which the law was internalized and permeated the whole of human existence in the preaching of the deuteronomic reform (cf., Deut 6:4-9). Rather, the emphasis here is on the action of

---

[4]Robert P. Carroll, *Jeremiah* (OTL; London: SCM, 1986) 569.

[5]Carroll, *Jeremiah*, 613. The rendering of Jer 31:32 in the *JB*, and to a lesser degree the *NAB*, is regrettably chauvinistic.

God placing the law within the human heart. There is to be a new future, and it is God's action which will bring it about.

A quite different expression of the same hope is found in Jer 32:6-15. Here Jeremiah receives a word from God indicating that he would be offered the right of purchase of family land in Anathoth, just to the north of Jerusalem. At a time when Jeremiah is prophesying Babylonian victory, the purchase of land would seem madness. Why buy land when an enemy army is in possession of it or about to occupy it? The text has no command from God to buy the offered land, but clearly that is how Jeremiah understood it. There was an obligation to keep such land within the family (cf., Lev 25:25). Yet there is a suggestion in the text—"Then I knew that this was the word of the LORD" (v 8)—that Jeremiah was unsure about the origin of the word until it was confirmed by his cousin's coming with the offer. Is it meant to have seemed so impossible to Jeremiah that he doubted his own experience?

Once the word is clearly recognized as being from God, Jeremiah is portrayed complying with it in a fully public ceremony. Money is weighed out, deeds signed, sealed, and witnessed. The deeds are to be stored with great care. The meaning of the whole is given in the last saying.

> For thus says the LORD of hosts, the God of Israel: Houses and fields and vineyards shall again be bought in this land. (32:15)

No details are offered, no extravagant promises made. Just the bare statement that here in this land of Israel social life will one day be resumed. "The family land bought by Jeremiah is like the field of Ephron which Abraham bought in order to bury his dead (Gen 23), an earnest of the future and a land claim legitimately acquired. . . . Its purchase by *the* prophet is what matters because it stakes a claim to the future *in the land* for the people."[6] All is not lost. And the initiative for this came from the word of God.

---

[6]Carroll, *Jeremiah*, 623.

EZEKIEL

As a prophet of visions, it is appropriate that Ezekiel's message of hope for the future should be communicated to him in visions. The well-known vision of the dry bones might have been foundational in this regard (Ezek 37:1-14). God's hand comes upon Ezekiel, as in 1:3; 3:22; 8:1 and 40:1; the prophet is seized by the power of God. The experience is a visual one, and we need to let our imaginations have full play in order to be possessed by the imagery. Ezekiel sees a valley and it is full of bones—very many and very dry. Not a pleasant sight. In fact, a horrific one! Ezekiel is in a valley of death, an open charnel house on a massive scale. In the midst of this testimony to death, the question is raised: "Son of man, can these bones live?"

The answer will be that they can. Ezekiel receives his command to prophesy (vv 4-6). The life will come to the bones from God; the action is entirely God's. Ezekiel complies with God's command and prophesies (vv 7-8). Movement and sound enters the valley: the bones come together and there is a rattling sound as they fit, bone to bone. Sinews, flesh, and skin cover them. Imagination is stretched to the utmost to recapture this image of reconstruction, still recumbent on the valley floor. For all the movement, life has not yet come into the valley. Ezekiel is again commanded to prophesy and again he complies (vv 9-10). At the prophecy, breath enters these strange beings and they become alive and come to their feet—and there is a vast number of them.

When the vision is interpreted, there is no wonder the number is vast: "these bones are the whole house of Israel" (v 11). And here we have quoted the misery of Israel: "Behold, they say, 'Our bones are dried up, and our hope is lost; we are clean cut off.'" Here is the expression of Israel's despair. Dried up, lost, clean cut off: it is as if the triple hammer blows of misery reflected the disasters of 722 when the northern kingdom was lost to Assyria, of 701 when most of Judah was devastated by Assyria, and to the final disaster of 587 when Judah itself was swallowed up by the Babylonians. Small wonder Israel feels itself bereft of all hope. Its despair is countered by the fresh command to prophesy.

This new prophecy interprets the meaning of the vision and is a promise for the future. From its graves, Israel will be brought home to its land. This is not a matter of personal resurrection but of national reconstruction. This is not a matter of Israel's future achievement, but of God's action, promised in God's word: "I will open your graves ... O my people ... and I will bring you home" (37:12). In fact, so much will this be God's own doing that through it Israel will recognize their God (v 13). The ultimate gift and the ultimately new—going beyond the breath of life of Genesis 2:7 and beyond the breath from the four winds of the world (v 9)—is to be the gift of God's own spirit.

> I will put my Spirit within you, and you shall live, and I will place you in your own land; then you shall know that I, the LORD, have spoken, and I have done it, says the LORD. (37:14)

Clearly inner renewal is intended, as well as political restoration. No trace of detail is given on Ezekiel's understanding of this inner renewal. But one thing is abundantly clear: it is to be God's doing. Given all that has happened to Israel and the depth of despair expressed in v 11, it is a remarkable expression of faith in God's unconditional commitment to Israel. This is to be the action of a truly loving God.

In the preceding chapter, possibly the work of Ezekiel's disciples rather than Ezekiel himself, there is a reflection on the promise of inner renewal (36:22-32). At first sight, it does not sound in the least bit loving. "It is not for your sake, O house of Israel, that I am about to act, but for the sake of my holy name, which you have profaned among the nations to which you came" (36:22). The motive for God's action is portrayed as concern for God's own reputation (cf., v 20); it is not loving at all. Harsh as this may seem, there are understandable grounds for Israel to appeal to it. Recent history had given Israel every reason to distrust their own ability to reform, to put their house in order, to behave in ways that might have seemed to make it possible for them to be spoken of as lovable (cf., v 31). On the other hand, to appeal to God's reputation, God's name, was to rest the future hope on sure ground. It rests, as it were, unshakably on the nature of God. Nothing could be surer than that.

The dependence on God for what is to come is made unmistakably clear (vv 24-28). God will gather Israel into their own land. God will sprinkle clean water on them and cleanse them from their uncleanesses—this is the "I will heal their faithlessness" of Hosea 14:4. The inner renewal is to be complete. A new heart and a new spirit will be given them: a heart of flesh to replace their heart of stone, and God's spirit to enable them to live according to the law. The upshot of all this divine activity is the full restoration of God's relationship with Israel:

> You shall dwell in the land which I gave to your fathers; and you shall be my people, and I will be your God. (36:28)

Ezekiel's final great vision portrays the renewal of the temple (40:1-42:20), the return of the glory of God to dwell there (43:1-7a), and the life that was to flow out from the temple (47:1-12). Again the hand of God is upon the prophet (40:1). What he is shown is a remarkable image of the future restoration. He sees in his vision a renewed and reconstructed temple. Nothing is said about its building; one may assume that it is from God.

> There is nothing to suggest that it should have a human builder. The entirely miraculous character of the dwelling place of God described in the following passage must therefore be kept in view in estimating its significance as a whole; the same is true of it as of the descriptions scattered through Isa. 40-55 of the miraculous journey home across the wilderness by the returning exiles, or the statements made about the new Jerusalem in Isa. 60. Already they all shine with the colours of the new age, and are images of the future blessedness which transcends all the limits of history. In this way they are better fitted to represent the magnitude and steadfastness of the divine compassion than some course of events which can be measured and expressed by the petty inadequacies of earth.[7]

Such an architectural blueprint of the dwelling place of God in Israel's midst is an expression of sure faith in God's commitment. God's departure, in the vision of Ezekiel 8-11, is now cancelled by God's return (43:1-5).

> And behold, the glory of the LORD filled the temple. (43:5)

---

[7] Walther Eichrodt, *Ezekiel* (OTL; London: SCM, 1970) 542.

Israel will be brought home to their land. God will come home to their temple. "This is the LORD's doing; it is marvellous in our eyes" (Ps 118:23).

The meaning of God's presence in Israel's midst is expressed in an unusual and striking image: the water flowing out from the temple (Ezek 47:1-12). God's return to Israel is permanent; the gate through which God entered the temple is shut to symbolize this permanence (cf., 44:1-2). Now from this gate, water is seen trickling out. The trickle deepens and deepens until it becomes a mighty river. Such is its power that it can even freshen the Dead Sea. Its waters will teem with fish. On its banks, fruit trees will bear every month—"because the water for them flows from the sanctuary" (v 12).

For anyone aware of the barrenness of much of the land and hills leading to the Dead Sea, this is an incredible affirmation of the life-giving power of God. What is totally out of human reach will be brought about by the power of the presence of God—that is the faith of Israel.

SECOND ISAIAH

The most eloquent prophet and poet of future hope was the prophetic figure of the exilic period known as Second Isaiah (Isaiah 40-55). It is only possible for us to pick up some of the key images and metaphors and to underline the prophet's insistence that what is to come will be God's doing. The dominant image is of a committed God who cares deeply, for whom Israel is indeed precious, honored, and loved (Isa 43:4).

The opening lines of Second Isaiah's collection are justly famous, reflecting the prophet's call and the message to be delivered. "Comfort comfort my people, says your God. Speak tenderly to Jerusalem, and cry to her that her warfare is ended, that her iniquity is pardoned..." (40:1-2). The image which follows is of a great highway thrown up across the wilderness, a highway over which in due course the exiles will return to Israel. Such are the dimensions of this undertaking that it can only be from God: every valley shall be lifted up, every mountain and hill made low, uneven ground levelled, and rough terrain made smooth. The highway is first and foremost for God, but not for God alone.

> He will feed his flock like a shepherd,
>> he will gather the lambs in his arms,
> he will carry them in his bosom,
>> and gently lead those that are with young. (40:11)

For all the grubbiness of the real flocks, the imagery of the shepherd is used very tenderly to portray God's action on Israel's behalf.

As in Ezekiel, so here too Israel's agony of despair can be glimpsed: "My way is hid from the LORD, and my right is disregarded by my God" (40:27). Second Isaiah's response is the confident affirmation of the impossibility of wearying God. God does not grow faint or grow weary, God's understanding is unsearchable (40:28). That "unsearchable" hints at the theological turmoil of trying to account for the events of Israel's recent experience. But the affirmation is clear. God's commitment is not faint or feeble. God's commitment does not grow weary.

The expression of that commitment returns in 41:8-10. Second Isaiah has God address Israel:

> You whom I took from the ends of the earth,
>> and called from its farthest corners,
> saying to you, "You are my servant,
>> I have chosen you and not cast you off";
> fear not, for I am with you,
>> be not dismayed, for I am your God.... (41:9-10)

I will not cast you off, reject you; I am your God. Such is the commitment Second Isaiah proclaimed. The proclamation is repeated with a wealth of imagery to give color, texture, and life (41:17-20). For God will answer the poor, needy, and thirsty; the God of Israel will not forsake them. God will open rivers on the heights, fountains in the valleys, pools in the wilderness and springs in the desert, plant cedar, acacia, myrtle, and olive in the wilderness, and cypress, plane, and pine in the desert. Dull would they be of soul who did not realize that such ecological abundance would be matched by fullness of inner renewal.

God's motivation is beautifully spelled out in 43:1-7. The saying begins, as so often in Second Isaiah, with an appeal to the identity of God as creator—one who can create has also the power to redeem (v 1). Israel has no cause to fear, for they may look to God for redemption. The reason is clear.

> I have called you by name, you are mine....
> Because you are precious in my eyes,
>   and honored, and I love you. (43:4)

And so Israel will be brought from the ends of the earth, redeemed by the God who created them—to whom they are precious, by whom they are honored and loved.

Second Isaiah conjures up powerful images to picture God's commitment to Israel, an Israel that fears it is forgotten by its God. Can a woman forget her nursing infant? Even if this should happen, "yet I will not forget you" (49:15). Israel will be as ever-present to God as the upturned palms of the hands. The metaphor of a troubled marriage accurately mirrors Israel's recent past, but is rich with promise of fidelity for the future.

> For the LORD has called you
>   like a wife forsaken and grieved in spirit,
> like a wife of youth when she is cast off,
>   says your God.
> For a brief moment I forsook you,
>   but with great compassion I will gather you.
> In overflowing wrath for a moment
>   I hid my face from you,
> but with everlasting love I will have compassion on you,
>   says the LORD, your Redeemer. (54:6-8)

The combination of creative power and redemptive action is continued in 43:14-21. The creator God of Israel is also the redeemer God of the exodus who made a path in the sea. Yet these former things are not to be remembered, although they constitute Israel's salvation history. God is now doing a new thing, effecting a new exodus—the chosen people are still God's chosen (43:19-21). A superb verse hymns God's forgiveness:

> I, I am He who blots out your transgressions for my own sake,
>   and I will not remember your sins. (43:25)

The strongest imagery combining creation and redemption is in 51:9-11. There Second Isaiah appeals to the creative power of God, subduing the sea dragon in the act of creation, and—caught by the force of the image—associates it with the drying up of the waters of the sea at the exodus. This creative and redemptive power of God is harnessed to support the hope of the exiles. Second Isaiah is, probably, the contemporary of the Priestly Writer for whom the creation account of Genesis 1:1-2:4a is so important. The creator God of the universe is also the redeemer God of Israel, and what God has begun God will bring to conclusion.

The final sayings of the collection emphasize the certainty of this future hope. It rests on the word of God. God's word, once pronounced, does not return empty but accomplishes its purpose. So it will be God's doing that Israel will go out in joy to return to their home (55:12). What is brought about then will be "an everlasting sign which shall not be cut off" (55:13). Israel's future will be sure.

Yet, while all of this witnesses to faith in the love and forgiveness of God, it is not divorced from the realities of human life and history. The oppression of Babylon is to be broken by the power of Cyrus, the Persian. One empire is substituted for another, a burdensome oppression by one more benevolent (45:1-7). It is a remarkable appeal to the universal power of God and a faith in God to operate among those who have no knowledge of God's name.

> I call you by your name,
> > I surname you, though you do not know me.
> I am the LORD, and there is no other,
> > besides me there is no God;
> I gird you, though you do not know me,
> > that men may know, from the rising of the sun and from the west,
> > that there is none besides me;
> I am the LORD, and there is no other. (45:4-6)

Today

The prophecies of hope and salvation in the Old Testament are superbly eloquent witness to Israel's faith in the unconditional commitment of their God. So it is with deep sadness that we have to face the reality that these prophecies remain unfulfilled. For Christian faith, Israel's faith in God's unconditional commitment has been fully verified in the incarnation of Jesus Christ. But the prophecies gave a different shape to the working out of God's commitment, and it is that which remains unfulfilled. It is epitomized by a line found in both First and Third Isaiah, surely among the saddest words in the whole Old Testament.

> They shall not hurt or destroy
> in all my holy mountain. (Isa 11:9; 65:25)

Ever since the word was spoken, they have never ceased to do just that. Of course Israel returned to the land, and of course Israel survived, and of course God's relationship with Israel was shown to be irrevocable. But the hopes and visions of which the prophets spoke remain unrealized.

One might wonder whether, if the prophetic picture of the future were brought anywhere near close to realization, it would not signal the end of humanity as we know it. The prophetic concern with faith and justice was strong. The prophetic hope embodies such perfect faith and justice that we are left to wonder. It is perhaps characteristic of our humanity that unwavering faith and unspoiled justice lie always just beyond our reach. Our task is to struggle toward them; our fate may be always to fall just short. Should we give up on the struggle, we would be giving up on ourselves. Is it, perhaps, not for our achievement but for our struggle that God conceived of us, created us, and loves us?

It would be a total misunderstanding of what I am suggesting to read it as relaxing the prophetic demands and the gospel demands for faith and social justice within our human community. If we accept God's commitment to us and God's love for us, then we accept God's commitment to and love for every individual human being. If our acceptance of love is genuine, it is impossible for us to rest content while another human being suffers injustice or want. This is an ideal to which we are committed, toward which we strive, which has to be the goal of our social endeavors. To give up on the struggle for faith and justice would be to give up both on our own humanity and on God's love with which we have been gifted. But just as we are of necessity endlessly restless for God, it may be that the necessity of the human condition requires us to be endlessly discontent—because the justice of our world remains imperfect. We may never complacently come to terms with that imperfect justice. Perhaps we may never come to the end of our struggle for fully realized social justice and fully committed faith.

There is an important implication in all of this for our acceptance of God's love for us. If we see the ideal of God's creation as radically different from what we are, then we run the risk of believing God loves us not for who we are, but for who we might have been or might become. In human relationships, to love someone for the person they may become is a sure recipe for disaster. In the relationship with God, it is likely to be equally theologically and personally disastrous. The mystery of God's love for us will always be mystery—but it would be evacuated of meaning if it did not mean love for us as we are. Anyone who has ever been deeply loved knows that this is no license to settle for mediocrity of being. Nothing can so challenge us to live our lives to the full as the gift of unconditional love. In the fragility of our human state, we seldom attain to love without condition. Yet rare is the human person who has not been loved at some time in some way. If we can find the spark of the lovable in each other, should we think it beyond God?

RECOMMENDED FURTHER READING

Ronald E. Clements, "Patterns in the Prophetic Canon." In *Canon and Authority: Essays in Old Testament Religion and Theology,* edited by G.W. Coats and B.O. Long, 42-55. Philadelphia: Fortress, 1977.

John L. McKenzie, *A Theology of the Old Testament,* 267-317, esp. 270-85. Garden City: Doubleday, 1974.

Gerhard von Rad, "The New Elements in Prophecy in the Babylonian and Early Persian Period." In *Old Testament Theology,* 2. 263-77. Edinburgh: Oliver and Boyd, 1965.

Thomas M. Raitt, *A Theology of Exile: Judgment/Deliverance in Jeremiah and Ezekiel.* Philadelphia: Fortress, 1977.

Claus Westermann, *Elements of Old Testament Theology,* 141-48. Atlanta: John Knox, 1982.

Walther Zimmerli, *Man and his Hope in the Old Testament.* SBT 2/20. London: SCM, 1971.

13

The Theology of the Pre-Exilic Prophets

Recommended preliminary reading

Before reading the body of the chapter, it will be helpful to have
read the following passages:
Amos 3:9-11
Hosea 4:1-3; 8:7-10; 13:1-3
Jeremiah 2:4-19

✣

A full treatment of the theology of the pre-exilic prophets
could easily fill a book in itself. From the ideals which the
prophets put before their people, the understandings involved in
the censures they utter against evil, and from their lament over
what is absent from Israel, one may gain an immensely profound
understanding of human life before God. The task we must set
ourselves in this chapter has to be a more limited one. It is
fundamentally concerned with the image of the God of the Old
Testament. We have seen the two principal elements of the
preaching of the pre-exilic prophets: the censure of the evils in
Israel; the threat of the consequent fate of Israel. We have seen
that this threat included the destruction of the northern and
southern kingdoms of Israel, the end of their existence as
independent nation-states, the exile of substantial sections of the
population, and a great deal of suffering. The language in which
these proclamations are couched is often harsh and even
shocking. Yet it is understood that this message is from God and
the judgment it expresses is God's judgment. The question cannot

be evaded: what image of God is painted by the pre-exilic prophets?

Without any doubt, the prophets have splendid words and lovely images for the tender, compassionate love of God. But that love either does not mitigate the announcement of punishment, or it is expressed in connection with the situation after the punishment has been visited on Israel. Suffering Israel might have been consoled by the thought that the pain and misery of it all was educative and restorative in intent. But that does not completely eliminate the problem. We have to reflect whether such a parent-to-child metaphor is appropriate and adequate for describing God's relationship with Israel or with us. We also have to ask whether, as an educative measure, such social and national catastrophes were in any way effective enough to be commensurate with the suffering involved. Certainly the fate of the north failed to educate Judah. Is the educative effect to be reduced to this: that the evils previously perpetrated by the rulers of Israel and Judah were now perpetrated by the subsequent imperial powers? In these circumstances, Abraham's plea reverberates:

> Far be it from you to do such a thing, to slay the righteous with the wicked, so that the righteous fare as the wicked! Far be that from you! Shall not the Judge of all the earth do right?
>
> (Gen 18:25)

The difficulty is not a modern one. Israel was well aware of it and Ezekiel 18 and 33 are an attempt to come to terms with it. For example:

> Yet you say, "The way of the Lord is not just." Hear now, O house of Israel: Is my way not just? Is it not your ways that are not just? When a righteous man turns away from his righteousness and commits iniquity, he shall die for it; for the iniquity which he has committed he shall die. Again, when a wicked man turns away from the wickedness he has committed and does what is lawful and right, he shall save his life. Because he considered and turned away from all the transgressions which he had committed he shall surely live, he shall not die. Yet the house of Israel says, "The way of the Lord is not just."

> O house of Israel, are my ways not just? Is it not your ways that are not just? (Ezek 18:25-29)

Life in this context is equivalent to well-being and prosperity. Ezekiel has advanced matters in two areas. Firstly, there is a denial that responsibility extends beyond a generation (18:3-20). Secondly, there is a denial that one's present state is irrevocably determined by one's past behavior (18:21-32). But the approach does not really help with situations of national downfall, such as the catastrophes of 722 and 587.

A far more evidently just solution is offered in Ezekiel's vision. There, all those in the city who "sigh and groan" over the evils being committed have a mark placed upon their foreheads. The executioners are then instructed to "touch no one upon whom is the mark" (Ezek 9:4-6). Unfortunately, the discrimination which could occur in the circumstances of a vision was not possible within the circumstances of Nebuchadnezzar's siege.

However, the sharp difference between the prophetic vision and the historical reality helps to raise the question of just how *literally* the prophets intended their words to be taken in their attribution of the coming disasters to the *direct* action of God. We will return to it.

As we noted at the end of chapter 11, there are two ways we can approach the prophetic threats which speak of God's punitive action against Israel or Judah. One way is to assume that they are to be understood literally as threats of divine intervention guiding the course of human history, and that the prophets themselves understood them in this way. This assumption would imply, in the limit case, that without God's action the course of history might have unfolded in other ways or that without God's action Israel's evil might have gone unpunished.

The other way of looking at the prophetic threats is to assume that the prophets were perfectly well aware of the political and military factors involved in the situations they addressed. This assumption would imply that they believed the policies and national attitudes within Israel and Judah would inevitably bring about the disasters they announced. In the hypothetical limit case, had God turned a blind eye to Israel's evil, the Assyrians and the Babylonians would still have pursued their imperial policies and subdued these fractious nations on their south-western borders.

In this case, the prophetic threats of God's punitive action against Israel understand the action of God to be within the natural course of history's unfolding. God is creator and keeper of the universe and what happens in accordance with the procedures of that universe is legitimately and rightly described as God's action.

In exploring this area, we are dealing with two questions, which we need to keep separate. One is what the Old Testament prophets thought about God's actions. The other is what we ourselves think. The background to the utterances of the prophets is never systematically spelled out. We have to read between the lines and divine what we can. The interpretation of the thoughts of a generation long dead is always an extremely risky business. At the same time, the clarification of our own beliefs is no easy process either. Yet neither question can be responsibly left unanswered.

My own approach to this issue is a mixture of exegesis and common sense. The exegesis helps in understanding precisely what the prophets said. The common sense comes into play in helping to explain how they could have said it, trying to discern what attitudes and mindsets might have generated such utterances. It would be desirable to be able to bring the skills of anthropology or sociology to this inquiry, but these lie beyond our present scope. It is also important to observe the other cultures of the ancient Near East, to gather whatever data they may have to contribute. While I am aware of the ancient Near Eastern background, I have not surveyed it systematically. The proposals put forward here, therefore, are necessarily tentative.

Fortunately, there is a basis of earlier scholarship which can contribute helpful insights. Scholars have studied the association of act and consequence in Israelite thought and language, and have reflected on the implications of this for Israel's self-understanding and world-view.[1] One of the early studies, by

---

[1] Much of this discussion has gone on in German-language circles, without touching English-speaking scholarship. A recent study of the prophetic texts with implications for this act-consequence understanding is P.D. Miller, Jr., *Sin and Judgment in the Prophets* (SBLMS 27; Chico: Scholars Press, 1982). Prior to that, it had been mainly available in English through G. von Rad's *Old Testament Theology* (Edinburgh: Oliver and Boyd, 1962-65; consult the index: in vol. 1, under "fate-charged sphere, fate-effecting act"; in vol. 2, under "fate: act which creates, sphere of") and his *Wisdom in Israel* (London: SCM, 1972; consult the index under "Act-Consequence"). Much of the earlier German scholarship has been conveniently gathered in a single volume, *Um das Prinzip der Vergeltung in*

K.H. Fahlgren, examined the Israelite use of language and observed that the classic Hebrew words for sin covered a semantic range coextensive with three different concepts in European languages, namely, sin, guilt, and punishment. From the Hebrew use of a single word for these three, Fahlgren concluded to the Israelite perception of the world as a synthetic one, that is, one in which elements which the European perceives separately were perceived in a synthesis, as a unity.[2] Klaus Koch built on this observation, examining the etymological origin of a number of verbs which express the bringing of punishment, and concluded that the Hebrew Old Testament had no concept of retribution. Instead, Koch argued for an Israelite synthetic perception of the world, in which each person was surrounded by the sphere of influence created by their deeds. Koch spoke of this in almost mystical terms as a particular way of thought, which he called "Tatsphäredenken"—a literal translation would be "deed-sphere thinking."[3]

Two difficulties stood in the way of these ideas gaining wider acceptance. The first was Koch's claim that there was no concept of retribution in the Hebrew Old Testament. The claim was exaggerated and based on the mistaken priority of etymology over context in the determination of the meaning of a word. Several studies were published arguing that, despite a non-retributive etymology, the verbs in question were to be found in retributive contexts and therefore could have a retributive

---

Religion und Recht des Alten Testaments (ed. K. Koch; Wege der Forschung 125; Darmstadt: Wissenschaftliche Buchgesellschaft, 1972). An excellent treatment is also available in R. Knierim, *Die Hauptbegriffe für Sünde im Alten Testament* (Gütersloh: Mohn, 1965) 73-112.

[2]Fahlgren's study is reprinted in the Koch volume, *Um das Prinzip der Vergeltung.* A modern echo of this understanding could have been noted earlier, (above chap. 10, n. 23) in the quotation from H.W. Wolff which referred to the act-consequence connection being the result of a "synthetic view of life."

[3]This study was originally published as "Gibt es ein Vergeltungsdogma im Alten Testament?" *ZTK* 52 (1955) 1-42, reprinted in *Um das Prinzip der Vergeltung*; it is available in English, "Is There a Doctrine of Retribution in the Old Testament?" in *Theodicy in the Old Testament* (Issues in Religion and Theology 4; edited by J.L. Crenshaw; Philadelphia: Fortress, 1983) 57-87. According to Koch, the concept of retribution was introduced into the Old Testament with the Septuagint; the Greek translators used retributive words to translate the Hebrew which, Koch claimed, did not have that retributive connotation.

meaning.[4] The second difficulty, I believe, was the use of a quasi-mystical language of "deed-sphere thinking," with an almost physical material sphere of influence being woven around the doer by the deeds, and so on. It is interesting to note, in von Rad's publications, that there is a shift away from this mystical language toward the more commonsense language of the connection between act and consequence.[5]

Nevertheless, when these difficulties in Koch's presentation are put to one side, two important elements remain. There is the conviction, stressed in Israelite wisdom, that good is rewarded and evil punished, the conviction that the consequences of acts are in some way sheeted home to the doer. And there is Fahlgren's observation that the Hebrew language points to a unitary perception of sin, guilt, and punishment, that is, of the act and what we would see as two distinct consequences of it.

The suggestion to be discussed in this chapter proposes contributory factors for the origin of Israel's conviction that good is rewarded and evil punished, and its reflection in the language of sin. It allows for a basic correctness in the original perception, but demonstrates the error of extending the idea beyond the limits of the situation in which it developed. Israel's wisdom tradition committed this error of overextending the connection between act and consequence. An understanding both of what is right in the original perception and of what is wrong in its subsequent generalization will be helpful for the treatment of the book of Job. In our present context, this understanding will be helpful toward a deeper insight into the prophetic proclamation and the prophetic picture of Israel's God.

The suggestion will be proposed in its commonsense aspect first. The exegetical underpinning will appear as the discussion proceeds. The conviction that the consequence of an act eventually caught up with the doer of the act was deeply embedded in Israel's thinking. For example: "The one who digs a pit falls into it, the stone comes back on the one that rolls it" (Prov 26:27). Yet when this line of thought is developed to the point of claiming that "misfortune pursues sinners, but prosperity rewards

---

[4]These studies are reprinted in *Um das Prinzip der Vergeltung*.

[5]Compare the index entries quoted above, n. 1.

the righteous" (Prov 13:21), it runs up against the very different evidence of experience. There has to be strong motivation in effect to account for its widespread acceptance.

One aspect which should not be ignored is the natural human desire for order in life. There seems to be an innate human resistance to chaos and the unpredictable. We want a level of order and predictability in our lives, even if it is only to the point of being able to predict where chaos will set in. For many people, there is a comforting assurance in the affirmation that the righteous will be rewarded; they take for granted that they are among the righteous. If misfortune in the world is a random occurrence, my neighbor's catastrophe is a grim reminder of what might happen to me. But if misfortune is correlated with wrongdoing, I can feel smugly superior and secure, while I wonder what my neighbor has been hiding which deserved this catastrophe. There seems to be a certain inner sense in many which would prefer that the good be rewarded and the evil punished. It makes for security and a tidier world.

There is a second aspect at work as well. That is the question of inner personal existence. If I do good, I am by that very fact a better human being. I may die for it, I may be despised for it, I may lose money because of it—but I am a better human being. And if I do wrong, I have irrevocably diminished my own humanity. I may remedy the damage, but I can never recapture that particular lost opportunity or nullify that particular harm done the fabric of my being. In this sense, the good are rewarded by their very goodness, and the evil are deprived by the very fact of wrongdoing which lessens their selfhood—but none of this need show up in the external theater of our lives.

A third aspect reinforces both of these, and it is the centerpiece of this suggestion. Life in ancient Israel was, for the most part, lived in small communities: family, clan, and village. In a small community, when good is done it benefits the whole community: trust is heightened, generosity is appreciated, friendship is enjoyed. The person responsible for the good is rewarded by participation in the total benefit, in the heightened quality of the life of the community. On the other hand, when evil is perpetrated in a small community, the damage is felt throughout the community. Levels of fear and hate increase, readiness to contribute to the good of the community is lessened, trust is eroded. The one responsible for the evil will share in the burden of that heightened hate or vanished trust. This is, surely, one of the reasons lying behind the legitimation of retribution, whether personal or social. Retribution redresses the balance of society, upset by evil. When retribution further aggravates the imbalance, it ceases to be functional and will cease to be legitimate.

As an observation of small community dynamics, it would seem clear that good is rewarded and evil punished by the simple functioning of the community, for better or for worse. A couple of proverbs may exemplify this understanding.

> When it goes well with the righteous, the city rejoices;
>   and when the wicked perish there are shouts of gladness.
> By the blessing of the upright a city is exalted,
>   but it is overthrown by the mouth of the wicked.
>
> (Prov 11:10-11)

It is well to be aware that the "city" here is no metropolis. Our village would be more exact—a town, perhaps, at most. Without doubt, a small and close community. In the towns of Israel, people lived so closely together that when it was necessary to speak confidentially they went out into the fields.

As a lapidary summary of the social dynamics of small communities, "good is rewarded and evil punished" is probably accurate enough. But it is strictly limited. The bond linking goodness to reward and evil to punishment is the quality of life in the community—which is a totally blind force. It is unable to cope with or account for the element of chance. Those who have done most good in a community may still have their fields set on fire by a lightning strike and be impoverished. The avenging arrow, aimed at an evildoer, may veer and strike an innocent neighbor. The social dynamics operate blindly, at the general level of the community. They cannot, therefore, be particularized to account for the fate of specific individuals. This is the error of the so-called friends of Job. It is the error of much of the wisdom tradition.

A similar attitude at the level of practical morality is equally circumscribed. The assertion that the industrious benefit, while the lazy are unrewarded is a truism at a general level. But it does not take into account factors of chance, circumstance, or structure. It cannot be made universally applicable to individual cases. For example, "Whoever tills the land will have plenty of bread, but the one who follows worthless pursuits has no sense" (Prov 12:11) is perfectly true at a general level. But it does not allow for drought or flood. Nor does it allow for the cunning of the lazy in filching the bread of the industrious. It is general; it cannot be particularized.

Nevertheless, it is not unreasonable to assume that these reflections contributed to the attitude in Israel that acts engender consequences which follow necessarily upon them. What is involved is not a mystical perception of the world; it is a matter of peculiarly ordinary common sense, the fruit of day-to-day experience in small community living. The indeterminate operation of the social dynamics in sheeting home reward and punishment to those responsible is implicitly acknowledged in the institution of law. The law has as one of its goals, the bringing of conscious awareness to the operation of community dynamics. Specifically, the evil effects of crime are to be felt by those who committed it; the law is established to bring this about.

At a further level, there is the issue of the divine action in the maintenance of right order in creation. Does divine justice oblige God to reward the good and punish the evil? Where the association of crime and punishment or goodness and reward are concerned, an important difference must be grasped. There is all the difference in the world between the association which is *internal* and *natural* and the association which is *external* and *legal*. In the first case, when a deed is done, the consequences follow automatically. In the second, when a deed is done, it is necessary for an external agent to operate before the consequences will be felt. A hand placed on a hot stove will have the automatic consequence of pain; this is internal and natural. Disobedience of a traffic signal will have no external consequences, unless an agent of the law intervenes.

If the action of God to maintain justice in creation is thought of as the kind that is internal and natural, it acts within the structuring order of the cosmos. To this degree, it is blind; it cannot be particularized to the cases of individuals. It has its effects in broad general ways. If the action of God to maintain justice in creation is of the kind that is external and legal, it would require divine intervention in the created order to duly reward or punish. Which is accepted as the better description of God's action in reality is a matter of belief, informed and shaped by experience. My personal conviction favors the former. My observation of experience has shown the rewards and punishments of life as far too arbitrary and capricious to be attributed to the intervening justice of God. The issue still to be determined is which understanding of divine justice colored the prophetic proclamation.

To recapitulate for a moment. Israel held the conviction that acts committed had consequences which came back upon the doer. So, for example:

> The wicked man dug a pit, hollowed it out,
>   only to fall into his own trap!
> His spite recoils on his own head,
>   his brutality falls back on his own skull.
>
>   (Ps 7:15-16, MT 16-17)

It seems highly likely that, among other factors, this conviction was supported by the observation of social dynamics within small communities. For this reason, it can be true only at a general level, and cannot be particularized to account for individual experience. When speaking of God's action in the world, it is important to be clear whether the consequences of an action are attributed directly to God's intervention, or whether they are seen as the natural outcome of the created order. The difference has a great deal to do with one's understanding of the place of forgiveness. If the connection between act and consequence is internal and natural, then the consequence will follow the act according to the immutable order of the universe. But if the connection between act and consequence is external and legal, the consequence only follows on the act when the supreme lawgiver and judge holds court and passes sentence. Were the Almighty only to turn a blind eye, there would be no punishment. As Job implores:

> Will you never take your eyes off me
>   long enough for me to swallow my spittle?
> If I sin, what do I do to you, you watcher of men?
>   Why have you made me your mark?
>   Why have I become a burden to you?

> Why do you not pardon my transgression
> and pardon my iniquity. (Job 7:19-21)

And later, in the natural consequence of this logic, Job accuses:

> It is all one, and this I dare to say:
> innocent and guilty, he destroys all alike. (Job 9:22)

What impact do these attitudes have for understanding the prophetic message and the God the prophets represented?

Before we can ask whether the pre-exilic prophets understood that the consequences of Israel's acts were brought upon Israel by the internal and natural processes of the created order, we need to determine whether such processes are within the realm of the possible. I submit that they are. Two aspects of such natural forces will be discussed in a moment. The discussion is not intended as exhaustive but as illustrative. While the two factors chosen for discussion are central to Israelite society, they are far from providing a comprehensive description of it. Social processes are almost unfathomably complex. It is hoped, simply, that the analysis of these two factors may point in a direction which is fruitful.

The two factors concerned are those most central to the prophetic accusations: the social injustice in Israel, and the religious infidelity of Israel. The situation within which these factors are being evaluated is the central element of the prophetic announcement of the coming judgment: military defeat and political subjugation. The argument is that both factors, social injustice and religious infidelity, could in the natural order of things contribute to Israel's defeat and subjugation.

Where social justice is concerned, the issue is the morale of a conscript army. While there was a core of professional mercenaries in Israel's armies, the bulk of the national army was made up of men obliged to serve for the duration of a campaign. Many factors impinge on the morale of an army. Few armies fight more valiantly than those defending homes and fields and loved ones. The social injustice pilloried by the prophets included the forced and unjust acquisition of houses and lands, and the sale of loved ones to provide payment of debt. As these practices became widespread, it would seem certain that the morale of the popular

422 Theology of the Pre-exilic Prophets

army must have plummeted. There is little purpose in fighting for king and country, when king and country have deprived you of your ancestral lands. There is little purpose in fighting for hearth and home, when avaricious landowners have seized your house and sold your family.

Something of the feelings of the troops in a popular army may be gauged from the list of exemptions to service. Exempt from service are: whoever has built a new house and not yet dedicated it; whoever has planted a new vineyard and not yet enjoyed its fruits; whoever has betrothed a wife and not yet taken her (cf., Deut 20:5-7). For the man who is newly married shall not join the army; he shall be left at home free of all obligations for one year to bring joy to the wife he has taken (Deut 24:5). Clearly, the soldiers in Israel's armies could be expected to have their thoughts constantly on home and family and fields. When homes and families and fields had been confiscated, whether as a consequence of misfortune or by calculated miscarriage of justice, then conscripted soldiers had nothing to fight for. We may note that Israel was well aware of the importance of morale.

> And the officers shall speak further to the people, and say, "What man is there that is fearful and fainthearted? Let him go back to his house, lest the heart of his fellows melt as his heart."
> (Deut 20:8)

The prophetic accusations, which we have seen, make it abundantly clear that in times of rampant social injustice there would have been every reason for the morale of the popular army to have been at the lowest possible ebb.

The issue of religious infidelity might not seem so immediately associated with military morale. Yet the passage from which we have just quoted in Deuteronomy points to a direct connection.

> And when you draw near to the battle, the priest shall come forward and speak to the people, and shall say to them, "Hear, O Israel, you draw near this day to battle against your enemies: let not your heart faint; do not fear, or tremble, or be in dread of them; for the LORD your God is he that goes with you, to fight for you against your enemies, to give you the victory."
> (Deut 20:2-4)

It was a standard idea, in the ancient Near East, that a nation's god went out to war with its national army. The Assyrian murals depict the god Assur hovering above the front-line troops. A waning faith in the God of Israel will, therefore, be a potential factor for weakening morale. A transfer of allegiance from the God of Israel to Baal might have had different effects. It would at least have deprived the men of Israel's armies of much support from tradition. Should guilt or uncertainty have been involved, an erosion of morale might be expected.

From all that we know of the emergence of Israel as a unified nation in Palestine, a very considerable diversity was forged into a remarkable unity. The figure of Israel's God, god of the fathers and god of the exodus, seems to have been of central importance in the process of forging this unity. At least to some degree, therefore, whatever weakened allegiance to the God of Israel would have weakened allegiance to the cause of the nation. In a similar way, any human society which transcends the natural bonds of family or tribe is reliant upon some focal point of attachment to provide a sense of identification with the larger society, its aims and goals. A common history and a national god provide just such a central identifying focus. The rehearsal of God's saving deeds formed part of Israel's liturgical worship, and through it a sense of their identity as Israel, people of God, was passed on from generation to generation. Any derogation from commitment to God meant a weakening in Israel's sense of identity and national unity.

This unifying impact of Israel's faith in God is visible in a number of areas. First and foremost is the creating of a united people out of the diversity of tribes; the acknowledgment of the LORD as the God of Israel was apparently central to this process. Similarly, the defensive wars which Israel fought to maintain its existence, and in which its sense of identity must have been reinforced, were God's wars, fought and won in God's name. The immense social and economic significance of Israel's worship of the LORD—festivals, sacrifices, sanctuaries, and temple—can hardly be underestimated in forging and keeping alive a sense of unity among the people. The law by which Israel lived was God's law. In so many spheres of Israel's life, Yahwism was a unifying and vivifying force. Faith in their God, it seems, was the keystone in the building of Israel. When the key stone is corroded and crumbles, the whole structure is doomed to collapse.

Israel's idolatry—its turning to a different understanding of its existence and its world in the worship of Baal and other gods— was not just a fickle toying with other attractions. It struck at the very roots of Israel's own existence. As with social injustice, religious infidelity weakened the fiber of Israel's national strength, and so of itself could contribute to Israel's downfall.

Of course, this presumes that Israel's enemies were aware of the question of military morale, and were informed about social and religious conditions in the countries they sought to subdue. While I have no knowledge of records from the deliberations of the Assyrian imperial council of war, I have no doubt that there was such a body and that it regularly weighed the relative administrative, military, and financial benefits of punitive raids to extract annual tribute over against the incorporation of a country into the Assyrian empire, with consequent costs of occupation and administration. What we know of the close communications and surveillance maintained by kings and commanders with regard to subordinates in the field gives every reason to believe that information on the morale and preparedness of potential foes or targets would have been gathered regularly and evaluated in the imperial capitals.[6]

All this talk of morale, and its association with social injustice and religious infidelity, may sound too modern and too farfetched by half for an ancient and supposedly more primitive society. It is interesting, therefore, to have an Israelite document allegedly reporting the speech of a senior Assyrian official, made in the hearing of the inhabitants of besieged Jerusalem (2 Kgs 18:17-37). Such a document is witness both to the views held within Israel itself, and also to the views Israel believed the Assyrians would have shared. The Assyrian official, the Rabshakeh, is concerned to weaken the morale and achieve the defection of the populace in Jerusalem. A direct tie to our reflections on social justice is provided by his words:

---

[6]The Lachish letters are evidence of the communications between an Israelite garrison commander and his commanding officer. Letters from Ras Shamra (Ugarit) provide evidence of similar control exercised by the king over his generals in the field.

> Do not listen to Hezekiah; for thus says the king of Assyria:
> "Make your peace with me and come out to me; then every
> one of you will eat of his own vine, and every one of his own fig
> tree, and every one of you will drink the water of his own
> cistern; until I come and take you away to a land like your own
> land, a land of grain and wine, a land of bread and vineyards, a
> land of olive trees and honey, that you may live, and not die."
> (18:31-32)

Apart from the desperate misery of a besieged city, to anyone
deprived of land and livelihood such an offer is calculated to
sound alluringly tempting. With remarkable irony, the Rabshakeh
is depicted addressing the religious issue too.

> But if you say to me, "We rely on the LORD our God," is it not
> he whose high places and altars Hezekiah has removed, saying
> to Judah and to Jerusalem, "you shall worship before this altar
> in Jerusalem"? (18:22)

After that unkind sally, directed to the popular ill-feeling caused
by Hezekiah's religious reforms, the Assyrian turns to the issue of
brute force. The sensibilities of the Israelite author have the
Assyrian refrain from referring explicitly to the god of Assyria.

> And do not listen to Hezekiah when he misleads you by
> saying, The LORD will deliver us. Has any of the gods of the
> nations ever delivered his land out of the hand of the king of
> Assyria? Where are the gods of Hamath and Arpad? Where
> are the gods of Sepharvaim, Hena, and Ivvah? Have they
> delivered Samaria out of my hand? Who among all the gods of
> the countries have delivered their countries out of my hand,
> that the LORD should deliver Jerusalem out of my hand?
> (18:32-35)

The evidence seems adequate to assert that the primary evils
denounced in Israel by the pre-exilic prophets—namely, social
injustice and religious infidelity—would have been significant
influences in the military and political collapse of northern and
southern Israel.

So much for commonsense analysis. There remains the

exegetical task of identifying the degree to which these considerations were influential in the thinking and theology of the pre-exilic prophets.

Before turning to this, however, there is one last preliminary reflection needed. Does this picture of a natural process of history, by which the acts of injustice and irreligion lead automatically toward military defeat and political subjection, leave any room for Israel's repentance and God's forgiveness. I believe that the answer is clearly affirmative. A project of social reform, committed to undoing the injustices of recent generations, would clearly give immense stimulus to popular morale. In the same way, a project of religious reform, rallying the nation to the enthusiastic worship of their God alone, would also serve to raise national morale. There is no reason to doubt that reports of such reforms would reach the ears of the Assyrian king. They could well have swung the balance toward a campaign aimed at forcing the payment of tribute to be resumed, rather than a campaign of subjugation, with incorporation into the Assyrian empire and the forced exile of much of the population. These are, again, only pointers toward possibilities in a vastly more complex social and political situation. But they point to a reality: repentance and reform could, even in military and political terms, stave off the fate which the prophets had proclaimed.

Of course the appeal for repentance and reform is precisely the sort of occasion in which we might assume there would be expectations of divine intervention on a scale similar to that of the exodus—at least as portrayed in the present O.T. text. Such expectations and their possibility cannot be denied. At the same time, Israel was well aware that the avenues open for the exercise of divine power were not limited to such displays of force. There was also the realm of heart and mind and spirit. The God who was understood to have hardened the heart of Pharaoh at the exodus (e.g., Exod 11:10) was quite capable of softening the heart or enlightening the mind of any would-be foreign oppressor. And if national downfall could be the result of the processes of history, the reversal of those processes could contribute to survival. It is remarkable that Judah retained its sovereignty for almost a century and a half after the fall of the northern kingdom.

In turning to the actual texts of the prophets, we will not attempt a systematic and exhaustive survey. A limited number of selected texts will be examined which seem helpful in fathoming more fully the prophetic understanding of their own threats. In selecting these passages, we are not looking for texts in which God simply is not mentioned; we are looking for texts which seem to reflect an act-consequence understanding or an understanding which focuses on the internal processes of history.

AMOS

In Amos 3:9-11, there are two aspects worth noting in this connection. While the censure (v 10) is linked to the threat (v 11) by the messenger formula, "Therefore thus says the LORD," the threat itself is not expressed as the direct action of God. It says simply, "An adversary shall surround the land"; it does not say, as other examples do, "I shall bring an adversary against you." It suggests that God's message is declaring the consequences which follow on Israel's acts.

The second aspect which supports this understanding is the repeated use of the word "stronghold." It is used twice in the summons to Ashdod and Egypt; it is used once each in the censure and the threat. The stronghold dwellers of Ashdod and Egypt gather to see how just and right it is that those who quite unjustly and wrongly are filling up their strongholds will have those same strongholds emptied out by an enemy. The wheel of justice has turned full circle and the robbers will be robbed, the plunderers plundered. The consequences of their evildoing will come home to the evildoers. God declares, God announces; God need not do.

HOSEA

In Hos 4:1-3, the only link between the accusation and the announcement is a simple "therefore." Of course, the saying is introduced as part of God's legal proceedings against Israel, but that does not prejudice the understanding of the relationship between its parts. What makes it particularly likely that the normal processes of the cosmos are envisaged here is the involvement of the whole ecology: land and those who dwell in it, beasts, birds, and fish. Just as in certain ancient Near Eastern understandings there was a correlation between the sexual potency of the king and the fertility of the land, so here there appears to be a correlation between the proper conduct of the people and the vitality of the land. The sequence of act and consequence, in such an understanding, does not require particular divine intervention.

Hos 8:7-10 employs two act-consequence metaphors from the wisdom tradition: who sows the wind reaps the whirlwind; grain without head yields no bread (Mays). Catchword association leads on to the next two sayings. Whatever yield Israel produced aliens would swallow. In fact, Israel is already swallowed up among the nations as a useless vessel. The historical reference is taken up into the image of a natural process. True, direct reference to God's action occurs in v 10: "I will soon gather them up." There is no bar to understanding this within the context of God's participation in the natural process, which is, of course, a God-given process. There are similar echoes in Hos 7:8-10, where aliens devour Ephraim's strength. The understanding is again situated within the context of natural processes.

Hos 10:13-15 also begins with an act-consequence metaphor: "you have ploughed iniquity, you have reaped injustice, you have eaten the fruit of lies." Trust in military strength brings destruction by military means. The context of natural processes is emphasized by the impersonal formulation of v 15: "Thus it shall be done to you." The Septuagint rendering, "Thus I shall do to you," brings divine action into the context of natural process—perhaps unnecessarily. It must be clear that there is no question in these reflections of denying God's responsibility for what happens. What is at stake is only how that responsibility was understood to be exercised: whether directly or through the processes of the cosmos.

Hos 13:1-3 has guilt followed by death, as an act is followed by its consequences. Their sin continues and increases. Its consequence is depicted in the natural images of morning mist and dew, wind-blown chaff and smoke. An act-consequence understanding is likely. Such language is quite common in Hosea, although one cannot say that it predominates. A clear example of brutally direct imagery follows closely on these:

> So I will be to them like a lion,
>> like a leopard I will lurk beside the way.
> I will fall upon them like a bear robbed of her cubs,
>> I will tear open their breast,.... (13:7-8a)

The prophets are ready to use every resource of language to drive their message home. The act-consequence metaphor returns in the natural image of the birth process (13:12-13). God's action is seen as refraining from intervention and allowing the natural processes to have their effect (13:14). Different theological languages are intermingled at will.

MICAH

Micah too portrays God as refraining from intervention. The horrible deeds of the heads of Jacob and rulers of Israel are such that, when they cry to God, they will not be heard (Mic 3:1-4). When the consequences of their acts catch up with them, they will cry to God for help—and not be heard. The denial of intervention of course leaves open its theological possibility. But the denial also puts emphasis on the place given to the natural processes of history in the prophetic understanding. In Mic 3:9-12, again there is no appeal to divine intervention. Those who "abhor justice and pervert all equity" believe God to be in their midst. Reading between the lines, one realizes that God is in the forces of history which will overwhelm them.

ISAIAH

In Isa 3:9b-11, a wisdom saying has been introduced to argue that the people have brought evil upon themselves (vv 9b, 11). While the opinion does not come from Isaiah, it is a pointer to the way the prophet's words were heard in Israel. It is an example of the act-consequence mentality being applied to the threats spoken by the prophets. The editor may be applying wisdom teaching to Judah's history "in such a way as to see the collapse of the kingdom of Judah and its consequences as a disaster which the people brought upon themselves."[7] While the expression is from

[7] O. Kaiser, *Isaiah 1-12* (OTL; 2nd ed.; London: SCM, 1983) 73.

the wisdom tradition, the understanding of act and consequence
is not foreign to the prophets.

Isaiah portrays God signalling for a nation from afar and
bringing it from the ends of the earth (Isa 5:26-30). From one
point of view, the metaphor of God's signal and whistle suggests
direct intervention. However, the overall impact of this and
similar passages (cf., 8:5-8; 9:8-11; 10:27b-32) is to make quite
clear that God's action is envisaged occurring through the
unfolding of the course of history. It is the armies of aggressive
empires which form the instruments of God. The prophetic
language assimilates the forces of history to the vehicles of God's
anger. We should not equate this with direct divine control of
these forces. A saying such as Isa 10:5-15, which accuses Assyria
of overreaching its mandate, is an indication that God's action is
understood to be mediated by the ordinary forces of history.

JEREMIAH

In much of Jeremiah 2, especially vv 4-19, the imagery is of the
fate that has come upon Israel as a consequence of their foolish
actions. They "went after worthlessness, and became worthless"
(v 5). They forsook the source of living water and hewed out
broken cisterns for themselves (v 13). As a result, the freedom
they had been given has been lost, and the question has to be
asked: "Have you not brought this upon yourself?" (v 17). "Your
wickedness will chasten you, and your apostasy will reprove you"
(v 19) is very much in the line of act-consequence language.

What is happening to Israel is the result of forsaking their God
(2:13, 19). But, in the language of its portrayal, this result comes
about naturally; it does not require God's direct intervention.
Similarly, in vv 26-28, Israel has turned its back on its God, and
now in its time of trouble has no one to turn to. The "time of
trouble" appears as the natural consequence of the act of
apostasy.

EZEKIEL

Most of the time, Ezekiel's language is very strongly marked by
the divine "I." But in the allegories of the lament in Ezekiel 19 a

different possibility emerges. The lioness and the vine fall from glory into ruin—and God's action is nowhere mentioned. This could, of course, be simply the result of the allegorical nature of the poem. Bringing God into the allegory might have been judged out of place. On the other hand, such allegories may have been chosen because they mirrored an act-consequence perspective, one that was different from most of Ezekiel's sayings. However, Ezekiel's vision of direct divine judgement (Ezekiel 9) provides a portrayal of just what God's direct intervention might look like. It will be taken up again below.

CONCLUSION

The outcome of this discussion should not be formulated more strongly than the evidence permits. The passages discussed do not constitute all the evidence available; there are others whose treatment would be too complicated to be undertaken here. But when all that is taken into account, the evidence is not remarkably strong. Nevertheless, there are grounds enough for concluding that one should not assume too easily that the pre-exilic prophets were convinced their people's fate depended entirely on God's direct intervention in their history.

There is plenty of prophetic language which points toward such direct intervention. But it must be remembered that the prophets spoke in terms of great feeling and urgency at a time of crisis. There are also traces in the prophetic language which point, as we have seen, to another way of envisaging God's action. In my judgment, it is not a matter of opting for one side or the other. Rather, the prophetic understanding perceived reality as a totality, two aspects of which could be expressed in these two approaches to language—like two sides of the one coin.[8] What holds them together is the belief that God is working in the forces of the universe, not in a forensic and external fashion but in an intrinsic and natural way.

The basic issues are how we understand the prophetic language

[8]As Miller notes in his final paragraph: "There remains a mystery to this interaction of divine act and human agency behind which one cannot go, but its reality and centrality for the prophetic word are always assumed" (*Sin and Judgment*, 139).

and the stance we take toward it in our own understanding of God today. From the sayings of the pre-exilic prophets, one might easily conclude that they were convinced of God's direct intervention in history to bring about Israel's punishment for the evils which the prophets so roundly condemned. The corollary for the understanding of God is that the suffering inflicted upon Israel is to be laid directly at God's door.

Against this, we need to recognize the intellectual and theological context within which the prophets operated. Firstly, there is the dynamic of act and consequence perceived by Israel to be operative in reality. As we have said, there is a sound basis for this in the dynamics of small community living. It is only in its unnuanced generalization that it is falsified and unjustified. Its significance is that it creates within the intellectual universe of Israel—and of the prophets—the expectation that evil acts will be met by evil consequences. There is the greater chance of this being true on a national level. It is an understanding which does not appeal to the direct intervention of God, since the dynamic of act and consequence is part of the inbuilt operation of the universe God has created.

Secondly, there is the strong likelihood that the prophets were aware that the particular evils which they pilloried in Israel—social injustice and religious infidelity—were contributory factors to the weakening of the national fabric of Israel. As we have seen, it is highly probable that social injustice sapped the readiness of a peasant conscript army to defend the land of which they were deprived and where they were unjustly treated. Equally, it is highly probable that apostasy from the traditional God of Israel also eroded unity and national morale in Israel. Not only can we observe it, but it would appear from the speech put on the lips of the Assyrian official (2 Kings 18) that Israel perceived it and, furthermore, believed the Assyrians perceived it. It would be strange if such insightful individuals as the prophets did not share this perception.

Thirdly, we are aware of the remarkable degree of political awareness among the prophets. Amos 1-2 show Amos as well-informed on the international affairs of his day. Isaiah addresses God's word to the king of Judah on the handling of the highly political affair of the Syro-Ephraimite war (Isaiah 7). Jeremiah is portrayed addressing the envoys sent to the enthronement of

Zedekiah (Jeremiah 27) and held strong views on the attitude to be taken in the political crisis of the fall of Jerusalem. In the extraordinarily sensitive story of Elisha's encounter with Hazael, the prophetic circle responsible displays an informed political consciousness of the destinies of Israel and Syria and similar small nation-states (2 Kgs 8:7-15). The prophets were surely aware of the fate of small nations which did not have the strength or wisdom to keep themselves aloof from the struggles of empires. All of this was part of the divinely ordained processes of history and needed no direct intervention by God. In it the hand of God was already discernible.

Finally, it is worth reflecting how the prophets might have spoken and the sort of picture that they might have painted had they perceived God acting directly for the punishment of Israel. In Ezekiel's vision, there is a description of just such direct divine action (Ezek 9:1-8). The foreheads of all those "who sigh and groan over all the abominations that are committed"—i.e., all those who do not participate in the evil—are to be marked. The executioners are then to go through the city slaying all, but touching no one upon whom is the mark. There are echoes here of the final plague of the exodus, with the angel of God sparing all those houses marked with the blood of the passover lamb (Exodus 12). This direct and selective action is a totally different scenario from that of the massed armies of the Assyrian and Babylonian empires. These latter represent the action of God through the intrinsic dynamics of history. It is with these latter that the prophets deal.

Today

There is violence in the language of the prophets and it raises problems for our understanding of God. We live in a generation that is increasingly aware of the extensive presence of forms of coercion or violence in all sorts of human relationships and just as aware of the destructive effect of violence on almost any relationship. Violence can be as unsubtle as the manifestation of superior physical force. Or it can be as subtle and sophisticated as a raised eyebrow or downcast eye. Violence or coercion does not respect the integrity of a person, and that is why it is destructive of relationship. The deeper and more valued the relationship, the more damaging the effect of violence.

We set as the ideal of a loving human relationship one in which violence has no part. Would we be dishonoring God to expect less in God's relationship with us? As always when dealing with God, we enter the realm of mystery and we are enclosed within the limits of human understanding and human language. But human language is all we have with which to speak of God. So use it we must—but use it with care. Between God and creature, there is of course the analogy of parent and child. A parent must often do violence to a child's will for its own good. A toddler heading out across a busy street has to be swept up into the security of protective arms. I would not want to deny the possibility of applying the parent-child or similar analogies for language about God. There are other analogies: violence may be appropriate to prevent worse violence. But I believe that in most cases where we use these analogies, on reflection, they do not help us speak rightly of God. They neither honor God nor correspond with experience.

If we accept that we are precious in God's eyes, honored and loved by God, and if we accept that possibly what God values most in each of us is the integrity of our personal God-given freedom by which we are most fully ourselves, it would seem we have to conclude to a certain powerlessness in God. One could appeal to deepest mystery and affirm that in gifting us with freedom God did not surrender the slightest trace of effective sovereignty—that we are completely free and God is completely in control. Such mystery would reduce us to silence. If we honor God's love and believe God treasures our freedom, our language must recognize that God refrains from violence against our will—and that to this degree God has chosen a certain power-lessness. The use of coercive power in human personal rela-tionships is demeaning; is it any less inappropriate to attribute it to God?

There are many ways in which we can influence each other without doing violence to our freedom. There are at least as many ways in which God can be spoken of as influencing us, while maintaining full respect for our freedom and integrity. In the whole vast area of mind to mind, will to will, and spirit to spirit, there is enormous scope for the exercise of influence without coercion. There is encouragement and enlightenment, the simple awareness of presence, the consciousness of love, the challenge of ideals, the certainty of support, and much more.

If one concedes belief in a creator God, then physical or moral intervention with overwhelming power has to remain within the realm of possibility. But in our experience, it is outside the scope of the ordinary dispensation within which our human lives are lived. The common tendency is to speak and think in terms of the omnipotence of the all-powerful God. Due reflection may suggest that God's infinite respect for the integrity of the created person may render God almost infinitely powerless. This means that we have to take seriously the language of divine anger and frustration.

When those who are deeply loved by God are subjected to misery and injustice because of the greed, blindness, or cruelty of others, it is impossible not to think of God as angered. Yet love is not driven out by anger. It is hardly conceivable that God should be believed to love us and to want fullness of life for us and not be thought of as hugely frustrated by our human inability to rise above our selfishness and our pettiness. Just as we can be frustrated by powerlessness in our longing to lift others out of their depression or their personal entrapment, so it seems not only legitimate but absolutely necessary to speak of the frustration of God. It is frustration that derives from a divine powerlessness which is self-imposed, chosen out of respect for the personal integrity of the creature, based therefore on God's love.

These reflections may seem to have strayed a long way from the theology of the prophets. It is simply that we are reduced to the use of models and analogies in our language and thought about God. If we permitted the violence of the prophetic language to be universalized as a model for our language about God or as a base for our language about God, we could well be doing God a disservice. The historical reality which the prophets had to deal with was indeed a violent reality. Small wonder their language too was violent. In other times, we have need to reflect on other models. Language which emphasizes the power and omnipotence of God risks reducing our appreciation of the qualities of love and respect in God. Models in which there are no limits to what God can achieve run the risk of dishonoring God, since they raise the issue of God's responsibility for what is not achieved. It is humanly essential to be aware that there is no place for coercion and violence in fully mature and loving human relationships. It is theologically wise to transport that awareness into the realm of the divine.

RECOMMENDED FURTHER READING

Patrick D. Miller, Jr. *Sin and Judgment in the Prophets: A Stylistic and Theological Analysis.* SBLMS 27. Chico: Scholars Press, 1982.

Gerhard von Rad, *Wisdom in Israel.* London: SCM, 1972.

K. van der Toorn, *Sin and Sanction in Israel and Mesopotamia: A Comparative Study.* SSN 22. Assen/Maastricht: Van Gorcum, 1985.

Jonah and Job

14

The Book of Jonah
A Reflection on Prophecy

Recommended preliminary reading

Before reading the body of the chapter, it will be helpful to have
read the following passages:
Jonah 1-4

After we have read the prophetic books, the book of Jonah
comes as a surprise.[1] It is quite different from the books of Amos
and Hosea, or Isaiah, Jeremiah, and Ezekiel. It contains stories
about Jonah and a prayer or psalm of thanksgiving, but—unlike
the other prophetic books—it does not contain any prophetic
sayings. At best, there is one, perhaps we should say half a one,
which is reported within a story about Jonah. This saying reads:

> Yet forty days, and Nineveh shall be overthrown! (3:4)

It is an unconditional proclamation about the future; there is no
accusation or censure levelled against Nineveh—that is why we
can speak of it as half a saying. A prophetic book with hardly any
prophetic sayings is remarkable.

A close examination reveals that the book of Jonah is not a

---

[1]For a helpful discussion of the book of Jonah, along with extensive bibliography, see
B.S. Childs, *Introduction to the Old Testament as Scripture* (Philadelphia: Fortress, 1979)
417-27. Its discussion is a useful complement to the position proposed here.

prophetic book like the others at all; rather, it is a story about the prophet Jonah. Stories told about the prophets are quite common. We find them embedded in the narrative books as well as in the prophetic books themselves.[2] The book of Jonah has a story about Jonah's unsuccessful attempt to evade a divine command to go and prophesy against Nineveh. At the end of this story, there is the song of thanksgiving for Jonah's deliverance. Then there is the story of Jonah's mission to Nineveh, the outcome of his mission, and the exchanges between God and Jonah about Jonah's reaction to what happened. In fact, if 4:2 is given due weight, it is clear that there is really only one story in three acts. Its structure can be laid out as follows:

I.	Jonah's attempt to evade a prophetic mission	1:1-2:10
	A. The unsuccessful attempt at evasion	1:1-17
	B. A song of thanksgiving	2:1-9
	C. The conclusion of the story	2:10
II.	Jonah's carrying out of his prophetic mission	3:1-10
	A. The performance of the mission itself	3:1-4
	B. The outcome of the mission	3:5-10
III.	Jonah's exchanges with God about his mission	4:1-11
	A. The first exchange	4:1-4(5)
	B. The second exchange	4:6-11

To grasp the message of a story, especially an Old Testament story, we must always read the text very closely. The story of Jonah is not only unusual, it is unique in the Bible. It merits close study.

The first part of the story begins with God ordering Jonah to go and "cry against" Nineveh because of its wickedness (1:2). We need to notice that no message is given for Jonah to proclaim; he is simply to cry against Nineveh. The emphasis of the text is not on Jonah's message. Instead, it emphasizes the commission from God. The story moves to the abrupt statement that "Jonah rose to flee to Tarshish from the presence of the LORD" (1:3). The contrast is sharp. God says: "Arise, go to Nineveh"; the narrator says, Jonah arose to flee to Tarshish. God says, "Go east," and

---

[2] For example, in the narrative books there are stories such as 1 Sam 3; 15; 2 Sam 11-12; 1 Kgs 13; 20; 21; 22; 2 Kgs 1. Examples from the prophetic books would be Jer 26; 28; 36.

Jonah promptly heads due west. No reasons are given, no circumstantial details offered. It is bare and clear: Jonah has been given a job by God and Jonah is in full flight from both job and God.

Once this has been established, the narrator is free to indulge in details, mentioning the port, the ship, the fare, and the embarkation. The detail continues in a spirited portrayal of the events of the storm with which God will put a stop to Jonah's flight. From the first mention, it is made clear that the storm is from God (v 4). The sailors combine prayer with lightening ship. But from the outset, Jonah is fingered by the narrator. While the sailors are fighting to save their boat, Jonah is fast asleep. The captain summons Jonah to add his prayers to the rest. Lots are cast to discover the culprit responsible, Jonah is identified, and quite a discussion follows. The sailors ask, "What is this that you have done!" and the narrative leaves the question unanswered.[3] Old Testament stories tend to leave the most important answers unspoken. Audiences were expected to be able to do their own thinking.

Asked what they should do with him, Jonah answers directly, admitting that he is responsible, but still not disclosing what he has done. The narrator gives the sailors one more scene before they are forced to follow Jonah's counsel and toss him into the sea. The point of their final efforts is not so much to portray them in a good light as to show the utter inevitability of what was happening. Details become scanty again as God commands a large fish to swallow Jonah and bring him back to dry land.

The second part of the story opens with God's word coming to Jonah a second time, the narrator's quiet reminder that he has disobeyed once. The beginning of the word from God is identical with the first time: "Arise, go to Nineveh, that great city." The message to be given remains unspecified, but it is promised to Jonah. What he will say is what God will give him to say. This time, Jonah complies with the divine command: "So Jonah arose and went to Nineveh," with the compliance explicitly underlined by the narrator, "according to the word of the LORD" (3:3).

---

[3]V 10b is likely to be a comment added to the text later. It does not provide an answer to the sailors' question; instead, it explains why the question was asked, since the sailors knew Jonah was fleeing from God.

We are given no information as to how or when Jonah received his message for Nineveh. Within the context of the story, we must assume that it was communicated to him by God. The message is clear, specific, and extraordinarily blunt: "Yet forty days, and Nineveh shall be overthrown!" (3:4). Two things are missing from this message. Firstly, there is no reason given for the announcement: no evil is denounced, no accusation made. The narrative mentioned it in the first command to Jonah—"for their wickedness has come up before me" (1:2)—and it is not necessary to repeat it again. But it is still significant that the only message the people of Nineveh receive from God is the announcement of the imminent overthrow of their city. They are not confronted with their evil; no accusation is made to bring them face to face with the stark reality of their wrongdoing. In the context of the book of Jonah, the second omission is even more remarkable: there is no call to repentance whatsoever.

There is no call to repentance, and yet the immediate response of the people of Nineveh is repentance:

> And the people of Nineveh believed God; they proclaimed a fast, and put on sackcloth, from the greatest of them to the least of them. (3:5)

The juxtaposition of the two sentences is a strong and stark contrast. God's messenger said Nineveh was about to be destroyed; the Ninevites believed God and repented. The sentence moves emphatically: they believed, they called a fast, they dressed in sackcloth, all of them. The thinking behind it is held back for a little; it will not be disclosed until the end of the royal decree (3:9).

Just as the narrator let the story line take a detour into detail about the episode of the storm, so here there is a detour into the reaction of the king of Nineveh and his royal decree. What is first portrayed as a popular response becomes official. The king hears what is happening and issues a proclamation. It spells out the severity of the fast. Above all, it emphasizes that the fast is to extend to human and beast alike. There is an implicit confession of sin: "yea, let every one turn from his evil way and from the violence which is in his hands" (3:9). And the royal reasoning is spelled out explicitly:

> Who knows, God may yet repent and turn from his fierce
> anger, so that we perish not? (3:9)

Of course, this is precisely what happens. God sees Nineveh's
repentance and with a change of mind does not overthrow the
city (3:10; cf., Exod 32:14; Jer 26:19).

If the book of Jonah were an account of Jonah's prophetic
mission to the foreign city of Nineveh, it would end here. But it
continues, and its continuance is a pointer to its ultimate
meaning.

"But it displeased Jonah exceedingly, and he was angry" (4:1).
The narrator clearly intends Jonah to be aware of God's change
of mind.[4] Jonah's anger is expressed directly to God, revealing
motivation that was left unspoken at the start of the story. Far
from being a surprise, this outcome is portrayed as exactly what
Jonah expected; it was his reason for trying to avoid his mission
by going to Tarshish instead. Jonah knew that God was a
gracious God and merciful, slow to anger, and abounding in
steadfast love, and one who repented of evil (4:2). The implication
is that Jonah knew God's design would not be carried out and
that therefore his own mission was doomed to failure from the
start.[5]

Jonah's anger is portrayed as deep enough to be life-denying:
"it is better for me to die than to live" (4:3). God's response is
simply to query the wisdom of this attitude: "Do you do well to be
angry?" Anger may well be Jonah's feeling, but is it an
appropriate response in the situation? The dialogue goes no
further. Instead God undertakes a parabolic response to bring

[4]This makes it likely that 4:5 should follow 3:4. After delivering his message (3:4), Jonah
leaves the city and settles outside it to await events (4:5). It is quite possible, in the
transmission of manuscripts, for a verse to be left out by oversight, then inserted in the
space between two columns, and later restored to the body of the text but in the wrong
place. Depending on the layout of a manuscript, the number of words which intervene
would be quite adequate to account for such a transposition. The present position at 4:5
sets Jonah up as rebuffing God's overture, but it is not in coherent harmony with the total
context.

[5]There is one logical flaw in this implication: Jonah had no way of foreseeing that the
people of Nineveh would repent. When narrative is used to induce reflection, it is not
possible to account for every aspect of a situation. Of course the narrator knew what the
outcome would be.

Jonah to an awareness of the absurdity of his attitude. A plant is made to provide Jonah with much appreciated shade. The next day a worm is made to attack the plant and it withers. Just to make sure the point gets home, God turns on a scorcher of a day. Jonah returns to his anger and again prays for death. In the new situation, God's query is renewed: "Do you do well to be angry for the plant?" (4:8). Jonah is not one to give up his views lightly; he maintains his anger and his desire to die. At this point, God draws the parallel with the city of Nineveh. If Jonah is so deeply moved over so little a thing as the fate of this plant, should not God be more deeply moved over the fate of so vast a city as Nineveh?

Such is the story of Jonah. The key question, as with any story, is why was it told, what was it intended to say? Any interpretation has to account for all the various elements in the text, placing them in a coherent horizon. Stories like 1 Kings 13 and 22 are clearly reflections on prophetic experience. It makes a great deal of sense to see the whole story of Jonah as a reflection on the experience of prophecy in Israel. Precisely how it reflects this experience has been debated.[6] In my view, two aspects of prophecy in Israel are important for the understanding of Jonah.

It is overwhelmingly evident that the prophetic movement, which now bulks so large in the canonical Old Testament, ran into very considerable resistance in Israel. The priest at the royal sanctuary of Bethel tried to silence Amos (Amos 7:12-13). Hosea was despised and hated (Hos 9:7-8). Isaiah encountered cynical scorn (Isa 5:18-19). Jeremiah was faced by similar unbelief (Jer 5:12-13; 17:15), and was even put on trial for his life because of his prophecy (Jer 26:1-19; note also the fate of Uriah ben Shemaiah, Jer 26:20-23). So strong is this tradition that the resistance of a rebellious people to the prophetic word is a major element in the account of Ezekiel's call (Ezek 2:3-3:11). The prophetic ministry was not one to be undertaken willingly (cf., Jer 1:6-8). It engendered vehement opposition.

---

[6] Traditionally, the two main directions of interpretation have either focused on the issue of unfulfilled prophecy or on the issue of the universality of the message of salvation (cf., Childs, *Introduction to the Old Testament as Scripture*, 419-21). Strong support for the understanding to be maintained here is provided by R. E. Clements, "The Purpose of the Book of Jonah," in the *Congress Volume: Edinburgh, 1974* (VTSup 28; Leiden: Brill, 1975) 16-28.

Such opposition is hardly surprising. While the prophets are sometimes loosely spoken of as preachers of reform, a close examination of the prophetic texts, as we have seen, does not bear this out.[7] Instead the great prophets of the eighth and seventh centuries "passed the sentence of death on their contemporaries."[8] Their task as accusers was to denounce the evils, religious and social, which were destroying their people. Their task as announcers was to proclaim the imminent destruction of their people's national independence. Neither task would have endeared them to their hearers. Neither word was one that any people would want to hear.

The possibility of repentance is not denied; it is just not a central element in the prophetic preaching. Amos calls on Israel, in God's name: "Seek me and live; but do not seek Bethel, and do not enter into Gilgal.... Seek good, and not evil, that you may live"(Amos 5:4-5, 14). These are exhortations to reform, envisaging repentance. Hosea calls for Israel to return to God (Hos 14:1-3). The concept of the prophets as God's messengers, constantly calling Israel to reform, is largely a deuteronomistic one. For example:

> "Yet the LORD warned Israel and Judah by every prophet and every seer, saying, 'Turn from your evil ways and keep my commandments and my statutes, in accordance with all the law which I commanded your fathers, and which I sent to you by my servants the prophets.' But they would not listen, but were stubborn, as their fathers had been, who did not believe in the LORD their God. They despised his statutes, and his covenant that he made with their fathers, and the warnings which he gave them." (2 Kgs 17:13-15)

The same idea is present in deuteronomistic passages in Jeremiah, above all the famous temple sermon (Jer 7:1-15, esp. v 13) or the account of the visit to the potter's house (Jer 18:1-12, esp. vv 7-10).[9]

The heirs of the deuteronomic and deuteronomistic movement

---

[7]See the treatment above, chapters 9-11.

[8]J. Blenkinsopp, *A History of Prophecy in Israel* (Philadelphia: Westminster, 1983) 73.

[9]On these verses, see R.P. Carroll, *Jeremiah* (OTL; London: SCM, 1986) 372-74.

appear to have had a considerable role in the preservation of the prophetic books in the form they have now come down to us. The implications of this are theologically significant. This movement saw its hopes raised to giddy heights in the period of Josiah's reform, only to have them dashed with Josiah's unexpected death in battle and the failure of his successors to maintain the reform. With the fall of Jerusalem and the exile, their dashed hopes must have seemed to sink even more toward despair. Almost all the pre-exilic prophets speak of hope lying beyond the disaster. At the same time, however, all these prophetic collections announced the disaster, announced it as God's doing, and announced it with powerful rhetoric and often horrific images.

To those torn between hope and despair, the power of prophetic rhetoric must have seemed an overwhelming burden. To what purpose had all these fulminations been uttered and preserved, since they might have been felt as the cruel taunts of an all-powerful bully. The deuteronomistic answer to this dilemma was to make explicit what was believed to be implicit in the understanding of the prophets: if we had amended our ways and our doings, then we would have been let dwell in this place and the exile would not have occurred (cf., Jer 7:3).

This implicit understanding is not a later attempt to sanitize an otherwise unholy theology. It had long been part of Israel's understanding that a position attributed to God could be changed, either by human prayer and intercession or by divine fiat. An example of the former is David's prayer for the life of his child, even though it was under prophetic sentence of death (2 Sam 12:14-23). An example of the latter is given in God's own reversal of an earlier sentence, "I will not execute my fierce anger ... for I am God and not man ... and I will not come to destroy" (Hos 11:9). In the deuteronomistic framework of the deliverer stories in the book of Judges, there is a powerful example, as we have noted more than once. God is depicted declaring to Israel, "I will deliver you no more," and Israel refuses to accept the rebuff, praying, "Do to us whatever seems good to you, only deliver us, we pray you, this day" (Judg 10:13-16). And of course they were delivered.[10]

---

[10]Equally, Israel knew that God's unconditional word could be made conditional. The original dynastic promise to David is unconditional (2 Sam 7:14-16); but it is made conditional in the Deuteronomistic History (e.g., 1 Kgs 9:4-9; 11:11, etc.).

While Israel knew that God always retained the freedom to change a decision that had been made and declared, nevertheless, as the collections of prophetic sayings were gathered together and the prophetic books became part of the scriptures of Israel, the impact of these threats of destruction from God's intermediaries could only have been painful and hurtful, a source of discomfort to the community which felt obliged to treasure these books. Israel's sensitivity to the issue can be seen in the compilation of the collections of prophetic sayings. A collection of the prophet's threats against Israel or Judah was never left to end on so dismal a note; the collections always concluded with a prophetic expression of hope for the future. Even in a case like Amos, where it appears that no hope was expressed in the original collections (i.e., chaps. 1-2, 3-6, 7-9), oracles of hope were added at the end of the book (Amos 9:11-15).

The oracles of hope, as we have seen, are a very important aspect of pre-exilic prophecy. Not only do they express Israel's hope; they also express Israel's understanding of God and Israel's faith in God. But they do not wipe out the memory of the prophetic threats. The hope looks to the period after the catastrophes; it does not prevent them. The more the prophetic books moved into the worshipping life of Israel and the more the fulfillment of their hope receded, the more these questions had to come to the fore: What sort of a God would threaten to destroy us? What was the meaning and purpose of threats like those uttered against us by the prophets?

As we have also seen, the possibility of Israel turning to God and finding life was almost certainly implicit in the prophetic threats, and was expressed in some of them. In deuteronomistic theology and in deuteronomistic passages in the prophetic books, this same idea is present. But there is a problem. In comparison with the imagery and eloquence of the prophetic threats, the possibility of repentance seems pale and powerless.

What the book of Jonah brings to this situation is the force and impact of narrative. Vividly and dramatically, the story portrays a prophet in full flight from his message. Brought back dramatically to his task, the prophet proclaims a clear and unequivocally unconditional threat: "Yet forty days, and Nineveh shall be overthrown!" Promptly the people of Nineveh repent of their evil. Just as promptly, God repents of the threatened destruction. In the final exchanges, it becomes transparently clear that God was known to be gracious, merciful, and loving, a God that certainly could be counted on to repent of threatened evil, and a God who cared for people and pitied them.

The argument is one the rabbis called *qal wāḥōmer,* the argument a fortiori: if the people of Nineveh, confronted with an unconditional threat, knew that it was worthwhile repenting and entreating God (3:5, 8-9), then all the more so was it obvious that the people of Israel also knew it. Furthermore, if Jonah was so certain that God was gracious and merciful, slow to anger, abounding in steadfast love, and likely to repent of evil (4:2) that he shirked his mission and fled in the diametrically opposed direction, then it is an intended assumption that his contemporaries held the same conviction.

The God of Israel emerges from the book of Jonah as a God known to be gracious and loving. The threats hurled unconditionally by the prophets of this God were not aimed at the willful destruction of a people, but sought to bring about repentance and a change of heart, eliminating evil and violence. The fulminations of the prophets were not expressed as pleadings to Israel to turn from utterly destructive ways—but Israel knew they were intended to have that effect.

God, the creator, cared deeply for the created world. In the dramatics of the story, Jonah is suicidally angry over a plant which withered. "I do well to be angry, angry enough to die" (4:9). Extravagant as it may seem, Jonah's joy in the plant and his sense of loss at its destruction touched the very vital forces of his will to live. Should not God be vitally touched by the possible destruction of Nineveh and its people. A fortiori, how much more would God surely be touched by the possible destruction of Israel, God's chosen people.

Either side of this dramatic narrative presentation of Nineveh's reprieve, there are the flanking stories of a churlish prophet, either in full flight or angrily sulking. Both serve to ram home the message of the middle section. Jonah fled for Tarshish because he knew of God's capacity to repent of the threatened evil—"Is not this what I said when I was yet in my country?" (4:2). The reason for Jonah's anger at this point is not explained in the text; where the text is silent, we are unwise to push forward with surmise. The effect of this surly anger is to drive home Jonah's certainty that

God would let him down and, paradoxically, to paint sharply contrasting pictures of an angry frustrated creature and a gracious loving God.

The book of Jonah straightens out the theological hurts of an Israel which may have been troubled by the seemingly vindictive threats of God—threats which all too soon became reality. Given Israel's conviction of the gracious and loving nature of God, these prophetic threats could, and can, only be understood as desperate and passionate attempts to turn a people hell-bent on ruin from the ways which were leading direct to their destruction.[11] The attempts failed. But, in Israel's eyes, the responsibility for that failure lay with themselves and not with God.

Today

To my mind, the most striking statement in the book of Jonah is the description which Jonah casts reproachfully at God.

> I knew that you are a gracious God and merciful, slow to anger, and abounding in steadfast love, and repenting of evil.
> (4:2)

The statement is all the more striking for the evidently explosive anger with which Jonah says it. Reading between the lines, there can hardly be any doubt that the final punctuation of the sentence on Jonah's lips was a furiously angry "Damn it!" It is this context of Jonah's being reluctantly and angrily forced to admit to the reality of God's love which makes the book so eloquent a witness to Israel's faith in the love of God. Jonah knew and Israel knew that their God could be counted upon to be gracious and merciful, committed in steadfast love. It is a strong affirmation of faith.

It would be tempting to move a step further and argue from Jonah's position to Israel's conviction of the unconditional love

---

[11]The question what difference it might have made if Israel had repented, given that economic, military, and political forces were already in full swing, is not easily answered, outside of an interventionist framework. A pointer in a possible direction is offered in chapter 13, "The Theology of the Pre-exilic Prophets."

of God. For Jonah claims that he knew God would relent (4:2) and there is no reason whatsoever why Jonah should have believed Nineveh would repent. Therefore, one might argue, Jonah must be witnessing to a faith in God's unconditional love. Regrettably, I believe such a position pushes the story beyond its proper horizon. In the story, Nineveh's repentance does precede God's change of heart. It is explicitly given as the motivation for it, by the narrator (3:10). Furthermore, although Jonah might not have known Nineveh would repent, the narrator certainly knew how the story was going to unfold. And finally, in Israel's own experience the prophetic threat was fulfilled—it was not turned aside.

For all that, the story invites us to ponder the mystery of God's deep and abiding love. The story of Israel begins with the portrayal of God as one who seeks to bring about blessing for all the families of the earth (Gen 12:3). The story of Jonah culminates in Israel's traditional affirmation of the love of God (Jonah 4:2).[12] For the Israel of the Old Testament, the outcome of God's love had to be seen within this world; there was no afterlife in which it might be manifest. The hope of the prophets testifies to Israel's conviction that God's love would ultimately triumph.

As we reflect today upon that love of God, we are compelled to ask whether, in the final analysis, the passion of God's love will prevail over the demands of divine justice. Jonah gives us no answer. But Jonah's affirmation of certainty about the strength of God's love gives us ground for hope. Jonah's surly unreadiness to accept the consequences of God's steadfast love is hardly a paradigm for our own reflections on the acceptance of God's unconditional love. But it is a pointer to a resistance which is often instinctive: God's unconditional love would deprive this life of meaning and seriousness; there would be no benefit to be had from right living. Reflection reminds us that right living carries its own inner benefit within itself. If right living is not richest living, then right needs to be redefined. There is more, however, than that. God's unconditional love does not deprive life of its seriousness. To be unconditionally loved is never a license for

---

[12]In Exod 34:6, almost the identical formula is placed in the mouth of God, as the opening of God's own self-description. It is noteworthy that Jonah replaces the second part of the saying with the single phrase, "repenting of evil," (cf., Exod 34:7).

infidelity. No bond binds more surely than that of love which knows no bounds. There is a mystery here which each of us must ponder. The book of Jonah gives us no answer. The faith of Jonah invites us to reflect and may stir us to hope.

RECOMMENDED FURTHER READING

James S. Ackerman, "Jonah." Pp. 234-43 in *The Literary Guide to the Bible,* edited by Robert Alter and Frank Kermode. London: Collins, 1987.

R.E. Clements, "The Purpose of the Book of Jonah." In *Congress Volume: Edinburgh, 1974.* VTSup 28, 16-28. Leiden: Brill, 1975.

André Lacocque and Pierre-Emmanuel Lacocque, *The Jonah Complex.* Atlanta: John Knox, 1981.

Gerhard von Rad, *Old Testament Theology*, 2. 289-92. Edinburgh: Oliver and Boyd, 1965.

Bruce Vawter, *Job & Jonah: Questioning the Hidden God.* New York: Paulist, 1983.

H.W. Wolff, *Obadiah and Jonah.* Minneapolis: Augsburg, 1986.

15

The Book of Job

Recommended preliminary reading

Before reading the body of the chapter, it will be helpful to have read the following passages:
Job 1-5; 6:1-4; 7:1-21; 9:13-10:17; 13:1-24; 31:35-37; 38-42

The book of Job has always been recognized as one of the great literary masterpieces of the ancient world. It is also one of the most unusual books of the Old Testament. Job, its central figure, is not an Israelite; he was from the land of Uz, usually associated with Edom, east of the Dead Sea. Some of Job's statements about God are unequalled in Israelite literature. For sustained poetic power, the book of Job is unsurpassed in the entire literature of the ancient Near East. For all that, it is a book that has its difficulties and its mysteries; it does not yield its secrets easily.[1] In that, it is only commensurate with its topic. It deals with

---

[1] Commentaries on Job in their own way bear witness to this difficulty. Among the more easily accessible are H.H. Rowley, *Job* (NCB; London: Oliphants, 1970), R. Gordis, *The Book of Job: Commentary, New Traditions, and Special Notes* (New York: Jewish Theological Seminary of America, 1978), N.C. Habel, *The Book of Job* (OTL; London: SCM, 1985), and J.G. Janzen, *Job* (Interpretation; Atlanta: John Knox, 1985). Valuable for their scholarly grappling with the text of Job are S.R. Driver and G.B. Gray, *The Book of Job* (ICC; Edinburgh: T. & T. Clark, 1921), P. Dhorme, *A Commentary on the Book of Job* (London: Thomas Nelson & Sons, 1967), and M. Pope, *The Book of Job* (AB 15, 3rd ed; Garden City: Doubleday, 1973). Particularly helpful is the chapter "Truth and Poetry in the Book of Job," in R. Alter, *The Art of Biblical Poetry* (New York: Basic Books, 1985) 85-110.

the sufferer before God. To be true to that theme, it must plumb mystery and eschew any hint of a facile solution. In that, it does not disappoint.

It is immediately evident that the book begins in prose and ends in prose, and apart from that is entirely poetry. It is also obvious that the prose and the poetry are miles apart where the portrayal of the sufferer is concerned. The Job of the prose bears his suffering in silent patience, for which he is rewarded with twice what he had before. The Job of the poetry speaks out in his anguish, and comes ultimately to rail in fury against God. For this reason, prose and poetry have often been set apart. Yet without both, the book of Job would be impossible.

The figure of Job apparently ranked among the great legendary figures of the pre-Israelite past. Ezekiel speaks of three great figures, evidently renowned for their righteousness: Noah, Daniel, and Job (Ezek 14:20). Noah was "a righteous man, blameless in his generation" (Gen 6:9); his generation, of course, is located in remote antiquity. Ezekiel's Daniel is almost certainly the Daniel or Danel now known to us from Ugaritic legend, also "a well-known figure of ancient time."[2] It is apparent, therefore, that Job was a figure of equal antiquity and equal renown. It is very likely that a story or stories circulated about him. The poet of the book of Job has chosen the story of the suffering of the righteous Job as the frame for the literary work he sought to create; the prose functions as prologue and epilogue, without which the poetry would have no context. The relationship between the prose frame and the poetry has to be evaluated carefully.

Because of the differences between the prose story and the poetry, one can sometimes get the impression that the author of the book of Job took over the story from tradition, even though it was at odds with the message of the poetry. This may be seriously misleading. Certainly the figure of Job and the story of Job are taken from tradition. It is very difficult to decide whether the poet of Job gave the prose story the particular formulation which it has in the book, or whether it was taken over as it is from the stock of narrative tradition. Ultimately, it is not important. What

[2] See W. Zimmerli, *Ezekiel 1* (Hermeneia; Philadelphia: Fortress, 1979) 314-15; cf., "The Tale of Aqhat," *ANET*, 149-55.

is very important is to recognize the elements in the prose story which provide an essential background to the unfolding of the poetry.

The first of these elements concerns the figure of Job himself. He is "blameless and upright, one who feared God, and turned away from evil" (1:1). This comes through again and again. It is present in Job's almost scrupulous care to atone for the possible sins of his children (1:4-5).[3] It is emphasized in the dialogue between God and Satan.[4] God describes Job in the same terms as the introduction in v 1.

> Have you considered my servant Job, that there is none like him on the earth, a blameless and upright man, who fears God and turns away from evil? (1:8)

Satan accepts the description, merely impugning Job's motivation. It is present again in the narrator's comment on Job's reaction to the catastrophes that destroy his flocks and his family: "In all this Job did not sin or charge God with wrong" (1:22). The emphasis is reiterated in God's speech, in the second dialogue with Satan (2:3). And again, in the narrator's comment: "In all this Job did not sin with his lips" (2:10).

This description of Job, so strongly affirmed here, is challenged throughout the whole of the poetry. Job's three friends start gently, but soon enough they all affirm and reaffirm that Job is not blameless and is not upright or free of evil. The prose narrator insists that Job did not sin, or charge God with wrong, or sin with his lips. Yet, in the poetry, under the ceaseless pounding of his friends, Job is brought to charge God with wrong. One might be tempted to add: and sin with his lips. But the charge of injustice which Job levels against God is made in the context of the friends' assertion of Job's guilt. In the context of the prose prologue, Job's

---

[3]Even the number of Job's children, seven sons and three daughters—two symbolic numbers adding up to a third symbolic number, ten—point to the perfection surrounding him. Note that the text's clear statement is that Job is perfect, the limit case of human perfection. Any attempt to interpret these actions as evidence of a scrupulous obsession—the imperfection that brought Job down—is quite contrary to the horizon of the text.

[4]The Hebrew word, śāṭān, means "adversary"; in Job, it is used with the definite article, "the adversary." The word Satan, therefore, denotes a personal figure, but it has not yet become a personal name.

charge is justified, for the prologue affirms his sinlessness and attributes his suffering to God's dubiously justifiable action. In the strange harmony of the aesthetics of expectation, the certainty provided by the framing story creates the possibility for greater freedom on the part of the poet.

The second element of some importance is the image presented of God. As we have just remarked, the actions of God described in the prologue are dubiously justifiable. This is not a matter of modern sensibilities. It is a view shared by the narrator, who has God remark to Satan, "although you moved me against him, to destroy him without cause" (2:3). Of course, we are in the realm of storytelling, but nevertheless it is hard to escape the impression that Job is the victim of God's wounded pride. In the dialogue, it is God who parades Job's virtue like a red rag before Satan. Satan's rejoinder places God on the defensive. Job's well-being is sacrificed to show that he will not curse God. Within the sphere of human morality, it is most improper behavior. And yet it is repeated. In the vehemence of his protest, the Job of the poetry denounces God for taking him as a target. In the context of the prologue, while this may not be wholly accurate, nevertheless, since God has handed Job over to Satan's attack, there is considerable justification for Job's complaint.

There is a third element which is also important. The prose prologue places the whole drama of Job within a storytelling context, in which the relationship between God and Job is assumed by God to be an unshakably strong one. We, the audience, are taken into the secret, in the same way that we are in the story of Abraham and the sacrifice of Isaac. "After these things God tested Abraham" (Gen 22:1). Somewhat in the fashion of the willing suspension of disbelief in drama, the narrative framework permits the poet to explore the full gamut of human anguish, secure as to its outcome. Not that the outcome should be cheapened by the materialistic calculation that Job did remarkably well out of it, doubling his assets. That would be to play Satan's game. Rather, in the grammar of narrative, Job holds fast to the only thing of which he is certain, his integrity, and emerges from his pain with his relationship to God doubly strengthened.

Satan's taunt does more than just cast doubt on God's assessment of Job; it impugns the entire class of the God-fearing.

They do well out of their devotion to God; they are fair-weather friends. In this confrontation, within the prologue's storytelling, the whole issue of the integrity of life before God is at stake. This is no small matter. The wisdom literature of Israel had developed a massive insistence on the profitability of goodness and the bankruptcy of evil. Is one to do good and to fear God in order to profit from it and do well out of it? In such a scenario, mapped out by Satan in the dialogues with God, where is the possibility of human integrity?

In chapter 13, we touched on the allure of this picture of an ordered world. It appeals to the instinctive desire within us for order rather than chaos, reinforced by the self-serving conviction that we ourselves will be found on the side of the angels. It is strengthened by the reality, on the inner personal plane, that goodness is personally beneficial and evil is ultimate human folly. It is borne out, on a general level, by the experience of life within the small communities of family, village, and tribe. But that experience cannot be particularized to account for the fate of individuals; this is the cardinal error perpetrated by the wisdom tradition. Latent within the formulations of the wisdom literature is the invitation to do good in order to reap prosperity, which is destructive of human integrity. Latent within these same formulations is the invitation to see prosperity as a sign of right relationship with God, which is destructive of any true commitment to God.

The prologue sets up the first of these situations: that good is done in order to reap prosperity. Job's friends will move blatantly along this plane: deny your claim to integrity, humble yourself before God, and you will surely be blessed. The poetry explores further into the second situation: can a right relationship with God exist in suffering? Must the integrity of the sufferer be denied in order to remain at one with God?

In the prologue, Job's response remains within the context set by the dialogue between God and Satan. Job's goodness and his relationship to God does not depend on what he gets out of it. That is made clear in Job's first response.

> Naked I came from my mother's womb,
>   and naked shall I return;
> the LORD gave, and the LORD has taken away;
>   blessed be the name of the LORD. (1:21)

It is made even clearer in his second response, addressed to his wife: "Shall we receive good at the hand of God, and shall we not receive evil?" (2:10). It is a passive and accepting theology. There can be a certain aura of stoic nobility attached to it. There is also the risk that human beings come to be seen as pawns, devoid of rights before God, to be gifted or stripped at the divine whim. At one level, human integrity is saved, since Job's goodness is clearly not a manipulative means to prosperity. At another level, human integrity is threatened, if God is identified with the caprice of blind fate and Job must yield submissively before such a God.

The coming of Job's three friends, and the seven days and nights of silence as they sit compassionately with him, brings a pause into the movement of the text. It creates the possibility for the text to move to another and deeper level. The poem of Job 3 provides the entry into this new level. For the first time the personal anguish of Job comes to the fore. The only hint of it before, beyond the description of the tragedies which afflicted Job, was his wife's invitation to "curse God and die" (1:9). Her words are important. They are an assessment of Job's situation, and they embody the conclusion that all that is left to a person in such a situation is to break with God and with life. Given what has happened to Job—his possessions suddenly destroyed, his sons and daughters suddenly dead, his own person suddenly loathsome—it is a reasonable conclusion that he has been abandóned and is accursed, and that life has therefore lost its meaning. In his reply to his wife, Job refrains from attaching any interpretative values to the events that have befallen him; nor does the narrator permit him to give vent to any of the feelings that must inevitably have been pent up within him.

In his utterance before his friends, Job lets those feelings pour forth in a despairing curse. It is not directed at God; it is directed at the moment when his life began. The poem is an outpouring of human agony, the depth of agony which eviscerates life, making it seemingly meaningless to live. The day of birth and the night of

conception are to be blotted out of the calendar.[5] His agony
drives Job to ask: why was I conceived, why was I born, why did I
not die at birth? What purpose is there to life if it is destined for
bitterness and misery.

> Why is light given to one that is in misery,
>   and life to the bitter in soul? (3:20)

> Why is light given to a man whose way is hid,
>   whom God has hedged in? (3:23)

In that second couplet, a hint is given of what is to come. It is not
only that Job's way is hidden and his life misery, but there is Job's
sense that it is God who has hedged him in. "The LORD gave, and
the LORD has taken away" (1:21) is impersonal and unemotional.
"Shall we receive good at the hand of God, and shall we not
receive evil?" (2:10) is more personal, but still untinged by
feeling. Here "hedged in" by God, the calamities that have
happened to Job begin to take shape as the concrete embodiment
of God's relationship to Job.

With this poem, the focus of the book has moved to the
personal situation of Job, the sufferer. Job's three interlocutors,
referred to on their arrival as his friends (2:11), begin with
different approaches to Job. As the book continues, they become
less differentiated, while the position Job is forced into becomes
more and more sharply delineated. The structure of this section of
the book is clearly laid out. In a first cycle, each of the friends
replies to Job, and after each of their speeches, Job replies in turn.
This same procedure is repeated in a second cycle. It would
appear that a third full cycle was intended, but, as the text stands
now, the third cycle is incomplete.

Eliphaz speaks first among the friends (Job 4-5). He affirms
that Job has a long history of compassionate pastoral counselling
(4:3-4). But at no time does the poet permit Eliphaz to appeal to
Job's own words of counsel. That is not part of the perspective.
Instead, the appeal Eliphaz makes to the past is simply to
generalize Job's suffering. It has happened to many others, whom

---

[5]The poem balances day and night in Job's curse. What is not known to human eyes
until the birth can be permitted to the mysterious knowledge of the night.

Job has strengthened and encouraged in the past; now, when it has happened to Job, he is impatient and dismayed. Eliphaz has broken the first rule of counselling. Instead of paying close attention to the individual before him, he has universalized Job's suffering as being one case among many. He breaks the second rule of counselling, by having a solution ready to hand. But at least the solution has the merit of taking Job seriously and accepting him as an upright man.

> Is not your fear of God your confidence,
> and the integrity of your ways your hope? (4:6)[6]

At the beginning, then, Eliphaz accepts the estimation of Job put forward in the prose prologue. However, Eliphaz's acceptance of Job is going to be put to a use that, for Job, is unacceptable. Eliphaz has that confident assurance which is almost a dogma of the wisdom literature. He claims to base it on his own experience; but it is an experience which many do not share. Eliphaz exhorts Job:

> Think now, who that was innocent ever perished?
> Or where were the upright cut off?
> As I have seen, those who plough iniquity
> and sow trouble reap the same. (4:7-8)

So the advice implied for Job is simple: Job may be confident in his fear of God and in his integrity that, since he is innocent and upright, he will not perish or be cut of. It will work out all right in the end. Implicit here, this becomes explicit later.

For the moment, Eliphaz has another string to his bow. He turns from the ordinary observation of human lives in the public

---

[6]In such wisdom contexts, "fear of God" is not a craven or anxious attitude. Rather, it has the connotations of commitment, loyalty, reverence, and love. While awe is associated with the holy, it does not, in these contexts, denote anxiety or terror. The Septuagint is close with its translation by a word connoting piety, reverence, and respect. There have been several extensive studies of fear in the wisdom literature, without reaching full agreement on the finer nuances. This is a good example of the importance of paying attention to the context in which a word is used.

sphere to the inner realm of personal mystical experience. The gist of this communication is:

> Can mortal man be more righteous than God
>   or the creature purer than his Maker? (4:17, *NEB*)

The implication for Job: no matter how blameless and upright Job may be, there is still fault in him to justify his chastisement. The inner perception of reality, according to Eliphaz, recognizes that every human being is flawed, and thus human misfortune can be justified. "Man is born to trouble as the sparks fly upward" (5:7).

After putting before Job the fruit of his public and private experience, Eliphaz ends with some advice, of the "If-I-were-you" category. "As for me, I would seek God, and to God would I commit my cause" (5:8). There is an inescapable irony here: according to the prologue, it is through God and with God's permission that Job's troubles have arisen. Unaware of this, of course, Eliphaz pushes his logic to the limit:

> Behold, happy is the one whom God reproves;
>   therefore despise not the chastening of the Almighty.
> For he wounds, but he binds up;
>   he smites, but his hands heal. (5:17-18)

The irony is complete: blessed is the one whom God corrects, with the sort of calamitous misery which has shattered Job, meted out as correction for one who fears God and is of assured integrity. Eliphaz will torture truth in the pursuit of simple clarity of theology. He piles assurances for the future on Job, without a thought to the present. And he concludes:

> Lo, this we have searched out; it is true.
>   Hear, and know it for your good. (5:27)

Job's response goes directly to the central weakness in all that Eliphaz has said: it has not confronted the reality of Job's suffering. There has been no sympathy, no feeling for Job; just words, to be listened to "for your good." Hence Job's cry:

> O that my vexation were weighed,
>> and all my calamity laid in the balances!
> For then it would be heavier than the sand of the sea;
>> therefore my words have been rash. (6:2-3)

Job concedes that his words are wild, but they are wrung from him by the immensity of his suffering. The refusal of his friends to confront that suffering will force Job to ever harsher language. Eliphaz has counselled Job to wait for the change in his fortunes which will surely come. Job instead longs for an end.

> What is my strength, that I should wait?
>> And what is my end, that I should be patient?
> Is my strength the strength of stones,
>> or is my flesh bronze? (6:11-12)

Job gives superlative expression to the anguish of those whose pain is passed over by smoothly facile words.

> He who withholds kindness from a friend
>> forsakes the fear of the Almighty.
> My brethren are treacherous as a torrent-bed,
>> as freshets that pass away ...
>> you see my calamity, and are afraid. (6:14-15, 21b)[7]

Utterly senseless suffering is terrifying, since it strikes at the heart of our human need for some sense of order. The poet of Job is determined to face that issue, without yielding to any appeasing palliatives. Job is ready to listen to doctrine—if it is honest. But where is honesty, when anguish is ignored? Job turns for vindication to the one thing of which he is certain: his own situation.

> Is there any wrong on my tongue?
>> Cannot my taste discern calamity? (6:30)

---

[7]The rendering of the first line (v 14) is uncertain. Another translation is: "A friend owes kindness to one in despair, though he has forsaken the fear of the Almighty" (cf., *NAB, NEB*). For v 15, compare Jeremiah's reproachful question to God (Jer 15:18).

With this, Job launches into an evocation of his suffering, the months of emptiness and nights of misery (7:3). Eliphaz's promise of blessings to come has no meaning for Job.

> Remember that my life is a breath;
>   my eye will never again see good. (7:7)

So, in anguish of spirit and bitterness of soul, Job speaks out directly to God. Is Job Yamm or Tannin, one of the primeval forces of the creation myths, which had to be subdued by God that order might be brought out of chaos? Is Job a threat to God, that God sets a constant guard over him? (7:12). In a terrible parody of Psalm 8, Job asks what man is that God takes him so seriously, constantly watching and testing him. So oppressive does Job sense his God to be, that he begs for just a moment's respite from God's presence and attention (7:17-19). Job plunges into the ultimate mystery. If this suffering is punishment for sin, why then is forgiveness so totally absent?

> If I sin, what do I do to you, you watcher of men?
>   Why have you made me your mark?
>   Why have I become a burden to you?
> Why do you not pardon my transgression
>   and take away my iniquity? (7:20-21)

The future brings no healing for the present. What lies in the future is already too late. "You will seek me, but I shall not be" (7:21).

It is the turn of the second of the friends, Bildad. No question, even for a moment, of concern for Job's suffering. The words of Job are now the central focus. Bildad has heard them, and he does not like them: "How long will you say these things, and the words of your mouth be a great wind" (8:2). Bildad is the classic caricature of the closed mind: he is secure in the information and attitudes he has derived from the past, and he is quite unable to put these aside in order to look searchingly into the present. But, for all of his outrage, Bildad has picked up the central drift of Job's discourse. Job spoke directly to God, and his words implied injustice. Quite rightly, Bildad saw that as central, and he moves to bring it out into the open.

> Does God pervert justice?
> Or does the Almighty pervert the right? (8:3)

Bildad does not delay over his own question; the answer was sure before the question was put. Instead, he moves to the level of personal attack. By implication, the fate of Job's children is tied to supposed sin (8:4). Where, for Eliphaz, Job's own integrity was his confidence and his hope, for Bildad that too has become open to doubt. If Job is pure and upright, then God will surely arise on Job's behalf. The implicit logic is, of course, that if God does not, then Job is not pure and upright. From the prologue, we know that Bildad is wrong about Job and wrong about Job's children. But Bildad knows nothing of that. He is fortified by the certain knowledge from the past, and nothing will shake that certitude.

> For inquire, I pray you, of bygone ages,
>   and consider what the fathers have found;
> for we are but of yesteryear and know nothing,
>   for our days on earth are a shadow.
> Will they not teach you, and tell you,
>   and utter words out of their understanding? ...
> Behold, God will not reject a blameless man,
>   nor take the hand of evildoers. (8:8-10, 20)

Bildad's doctrine is lucid, but it fails to come to grips with Job's situation. He assures Job that the hope of the godless shall perish (8:13). But this not Job's problem. He promises Job that God will yet fill his mouth with laughter, and his lips with shouting (8:21). But that is no more comfort than the hopes held out by Eliphaz. The impact of Bildad's initial attack on Job remains more striking than his comforting conclusion.

Job's response returns to the point of Bildad's initial attack. Job's "truly I know that it is so" (9:2a) has to refer back to Bildad's fundamental question: "Does God pervert justice? Or does the Almighty pervert the right?" (8:3). Job turns the question back into the realm of human life: "How can a human being be just before God?" (9:2b). Justice is spoken of against the background of human procedures, of proposal and counterproposal, of argument and counterargument. How do you argue with God?

How do you answer God? How do you even question God? Job's dilemma is not the elusive quality of God, but the overwhelming power of God (9:3-12, although cf., v 11, and also 23:8-9). The might of God makes it impossible for someone to seek justice from God. What does it mean to affirm God's justice, with Bildad, if that leaves Job with no way of establishing his own justice. The despairing situation wrings from Job the cry:

> Behold, he snatches away; who can hinder him?
>   Who will say to him, 'What are you doing?'
> God will not turn back his anger;
>   beneath him bowed the helpers of Rahab.
> How then can I answer him,
>   choosing my words with him?
> Though I am innocent, I cannot answer him;
>   I must appeal for mercy to my accuser. (9:12-15)

This is the situation to which Bildad has reduced Job. The insistence on the unarguable justice of God leaves Job deprived of the possibility of justice. God must be just, therefore Job has no case. The cry of human experience is to be silenced before the certainty of the word about God. Rahab is another of the primeval forces subdued in creation, like Yamm and Tannin (cf., Isa 51:9). The awesome power of the creator God negates any possibility of human protest. Bildad's unquestioning certainty about God's justice brings into full light the glaring injustice of Job's situation.

Within the frame of the discussion, initiated by Eliphaz and Bildad, representing the approach of the wisdom tradition to suffering, there is no possible resolution. If suffering is somehow tied to sin, and if the justice of God is not open to question, then the sufferer is sinner, and the justice or injustice of it is not open to discussion. The enormity of it has been brought home to Job.

> If it is a contest of strength, behold him!
>   If it is a matter of justice, who can summon him?
> Though I am innocent, my own mouth would condemn me;
>   though I am blameless, he would prove me perverse.
> (9:19-20)

From the prologue, we know that Job is blameless. From the exchanges, we know that his friends have relativized this till it is of no account. The one quality of Job's which emerges as preeminent in the book is not his patience. The Job of the poetry is not a patient man. It is his total passion for human integrity. Job stands by the truth of his own experience and will let nothing be used to distort the reality of that experience. If the justice of God is being used to manipulate Job's experience, then the justice of God must be assailed. If theology is being formulated so as to distort human life, then theology must be refashioned.

With the reality of his experience being distorted in order to protect God's justice, Job launches into his most blatant charge against God.

> I am blameless; I regard not myself;
> > I loathe my life.
> It is all one; therefore I say,
> > both the blameless and the wicked he destroys.
> When disaster brings sudden death,
> > he mocks at the calamity of the innocent.
> The earth is given into the hand of the wicked;
> > he covers the faces of its judges—
> > if it is not he, who then is it? (9:21-24)

This is the most serious accusation that Job hurls against God. It is important to see how it emerges out of the logic in which his friends have trapped him. The friends argue that God is just, therefore Job cannot be blameless. Job's argument is the reverse: he knows himself to be blameless, therefore God must be unjust. At the bottom of it all is the impossibility of any sort of adjudication in which the rights and wrongs can be resolved. Job cannot bring God into a trial situation, nor is there anyone to see to the fairness of such a trial (9:32-33). Sheer fear keeps Job from speaking freely (9:34-35).

It is difficult at such a point to know whether the poet portrays this situation as the experience of life, or whether it is the straitjacket created by the strictures of an all-too-narrow theology. These lines could result from a sense of the injustice of life, coupled with the frustration of human inability to debate such injustice with God. Or they might well result from the narrowness of a theology which has already set the ground rules of debate and foreclosed the major issues.

For Job, the major issues seem to be that he is condemned, that he feels under attack from God, and that he is convinced of his innocence.

> I will say to God, Do not condemn me;
>   let me know why you contend against me.
> Does it seem good to you to oppress,
>   to despise the work of your hands
>   and favor the designs of the wicked?
> Have you eyes of flesh?
>   Do you see as man sees?
> Are your days as the days of man,
>   or your years as man's years,
> that you seek out my iniquity
>   and search for my sin,
> although you know that I am not guilty,
>   and there is none to deliver out of your hand? (10:2-7)

The brilliance of this plea is that it is reflecting on to God the anthropomorphic conceptions which power the theology of Job's friends. The friends are caught in the trap of being afraid to let God be God, and therefore of being too fearful to examine the human situation fully and fairly. Job is basically asking God: are you like them? Here the beginning of a solution is being hinted at. God is not like the friends, God does not think their way, God does not condemn or oppress the sufferer. Perhaps it is with this in mind that the poet has Job mention, for the first time, God's love and care for him (10:12).

Zophar is the third friend. Like Bildad, he too goes directly to a central issue in Job's discourse and he denies Job's experience of himself.

> For you say, "My doctrine is pure
>   and I am clean in God's eyes." ...
> Know then that God exacts of you
>   less than your guilt deserves. (11:4, 6b)

Zophar appeals splendidly to the limitless mystery of God (11:7-10). There is only one weakness in his argument: in order to uphold that mystery, he has to assert the guilt of Job. And we know that he is wrong. Secure in his argument, Zophar exhorts Job to set his heart aright and to put iniquity far from him. Then Job can be certain that he will be protected and rest in safety. And there is a final warning about the fate of the wicked: "all way of escape will be lost to them, and their hope is to breathe their last" (11:13-20). The cruel irony is that this is the hope Job has been expressing. And the crooked theology is that, by a lie, Zophar promises Job a future security which Job knows to be illusory, for were it true Job would be in possession of that security now.

Job replies with a massive appeal to experience. He claims understanding and wisdom equal to that of his friends, a claim that will be traded back and forth in the speeches to come. But he also points to the reality of his own experience.

> I am a laughingstock to my friends;
>> I, who called upon God and he answered me,
>> a just and blameless man, am a laughingstock. (12:4)

The power of God and the arbitrariness of fate are the background to the picture Job paints of the broader witness of experience, in which the high and the mighty, the wise and the trusted may all be laid low (12:13-25). The force behind all this is God (12:7-10). Job wants to argue this out with God. The time for arguing it out with men is past. Job pronounces the ultimate verdict on his friends: they defend God with lies, speaking falsely and deceitfully on God's behalf. There is hardly a more shameful evil.

> As for you, you whitewash with lies;
>> worthless physicians are you all....
> Will you speak falsely for God,
>> and speak deceitfully for him? ...
> Will it be well with you when he searches you out?
>> Or can you deceive him, as one deceives a man? ...
> Your maxims are proverbs of ashes,
>> your defenses are defenses of clay. (13:4-12*)

468   *The Book of Job*

Here again, the poet anticipates the conclusion of his work. For what Job foretells is exactly what occurs at the end of the book: the friends are rebuked for not having spoken rightly of God. The goal of Job, as of suffering humanity, is to defend its innocence before God. "I have no hope; yet I will defend my ways to his face" (13:15). Job's defense of his ways will not work out the way that he expects. But here his expectation is very clearly expressed.

> Only grant two things to me,
>> then I will not hide myself from your face:
> withdraw your hand far from me,
>> and let not dread of you terrify me.
> Then call, and I will answer;
>> or let me speak, and do you reply to me.
> How many are my iniquities and my sins?
>> Make me know my transgression and my sin.
> Why do you hide your face,
>> and count me as your enemy. (13:20-24)

Job, whom we know to be blameless and who knows himself to be blameless, is suffering. Therefore, according to the theology which opposes him, he must have sinned. If so, says Job, what are my iniquities and my sins? Above all, there is Job's conviction that God counts him as an enemy, that his suffering has estranged him from God. This, too, is an important aspect to remember for the conclusion of the book.

In a very powerful passage, Job reflects on the difference the possibility of an afterlife would make to his situation.

> If a man die, shall he live again?
>> All the days of my service I would wait,
>> till my release should come.
> You would call and I would answer you;
>> you would long for the work of your hands. (14:14-15)

But for Job that cannot be. And for us, it is just as well. For Job's struggle with suffering is all the more stringently honest because it is tied to the issues of this life and this generation. Twice elsewhere, Job speaks of future vindication. One passage expresses his conviction that God will eventually vindicate him.

O earth, cover not my blood,
  and let my cry find no resting place.
Even now, behold, my witness is in heaven,
  and he that vouches for me is on high.
My friends scorn me;
  my eye pours out tears to God,
that he would maintain the right of a man with God,
  like that of a man with his neighbor. (16:18-21)

The other is the famous passage, "For I know that my Redeemer lives" (19:25). Neither refers to a permanent afterlife, and the latter has to remain one of the great mysteries of the book of Job. However, in the book, the struggle to understand human suffering remains within the sphere of this present life.

Now that each of the three friends has been heard from, we may move more swiftly through the book. Regrettably, so much that cries out to be explored must be left aside. All we can do here is point to some of the highlights, as the book moves toward its conclusion.

Eliphaz takes up the word, with a diatribe against Job. The first point is the danger of what Job is saying. The truth of it does not matter. The argument instead is from its consequences. "But you are doing away with the fear of God, and hindering meditation before God" (15:4). And secondly, Eliphaz, who had comforted Job that his fear of God and his integrity was his confidence and his hope, now accuses Job of iniquity and condemns him for his words. It is as though, unable to find sin in him, the friends have provoked Job to the point where his discourse has become sin to him. It is true that Job has been pushed to the point of blasphemy, declaring God the author of injustice. But he has only done so in defense of human integrity and under the pressure of a narrow theological system. Eliphaz clings to the defense of his system. No human being can be free of sin (15:14-16). The implication: therefore, all human suffering can be justified. Proportionality has apparently not entered into Eliphaz's thinking at all.

The theme of the fate of the wicked will be increasingly developed in the following chapters. The blessings awaiting the good were to the fore in earlier chapters. It is as if Job were now convicted of iniquity because of his suffering, so the fate of the wicked becomes an appropriate theme of discourse. "The wicked man writhes in pain all his days, through all the years that are laid up for the ruthless" (15:20). As he is increasingly vilified, Job expresses the conviction that God will ultimately vindicate his cause. We have already noted 16:18-21. But Job continues:

> My spirit is broken,
>> my days are extinct,
>> the grave is ready for me.
> Surely there are mockers about me,
>> and my eye dwells on their provocation.
> Lay down a pledge for me with yourself;
>> who is there that will give surety for me?
> Since you have closed their minds to understanding,
>> therefore you will not let them triumph. (17:1-4)

Bildad returns to the fray with a detailed portrayal of the awful fate of the wicked, so fearful that east and west are appalled in horror (18:5-21). Or rather, so fanciful! Job does not bother to rebut Bildad, beyond reproaching his friends for the torment they impose upon him. His claim still stands against the justice of God.

> Know then that God has put me in the wrong,
>> and closed his net about me.
> Behold, I cry out, "Violence!" but I am not answered;
>> I call aloud, but there is no justice. (19:6-7)

From the prologue, we know that Job is right. The other element is also present, namely Job's interpretation of his suffering as the effect of God's hostility toward him.

> He has kindled his wrath against me,
>> and counts me his adversary.
> His troops come on together;
>> they have cast up siegeworks against me,
>> and encamp round about my tent. (19:11-12)

Job touches then on the personal aspect of his misery. his estrangement from brethren and acquaintances, kinsfolk and friends, guests and servants, even his wife and blood brothers. When all these fail him, there remains the conviction that he will yet see his vindication at the hands of God (19:23-29).

Zophar, in turn, develops the theme of the wretched fate of the wicked. From of old, since man was placed upon the earth, "the exulting of the wicked is short, and the joy of the godless but for a moment" (20:5). Now that all three of the friends have played their variations on this theme, Job turns the full force of his eloquence against it. His reading of experience is not theirs. First of all, look at his own case—it is appalling, and should be enough to silence that line of argument (21:5). Look at the wicked, ripe in age and rich in power (21:7). They are secure, and God does not touch them (21:9). Their flocks and families prosper; they spend their days in prosperity and die in peace (21:10-13). And they despise God.

> They say to God, "Depart from us!
> We do not desire the knowledge of your ways.
> What is the Almighty, that we should serve him?
> And what profit do we get if we pray to him?" (21:14-15)

Job asks how often calamity befalls the wicked. To the supposed reply that their iniquity will be stored up for their sons, he retorts: "Let him recompense it to themselves that they may know it. Let their own eyes see their destruction, and let them drink of the wrath of the Almighty" (21:19-20). Job's case does not rest on his own experience alone. He appeals to the testimony of travellers, who will attest that what he says is a universal phenomenon: "that the wicked man is spared in the day of calamity, that he is rescued in the day of wrath" (21:29-30). So Job brings his observation of experience up against that claimed by the friends. In the presence of such claim and counterclaim, the readers of Job must consult their own experience and that of others. For Job, the conclusion is clear.

> How then will you comfort me with empty nothings?
> There is nothing left of your answers but falsehood. (21:34)

Perhaps it is this last sting which causes the worm in Eliphaz to turn. Eliphaz, who alone of the friends began by paying some tribute to Job's past and his uprightness (4:2-6), had come to find Job's fault in his words (15:5-6). Now, in a slanderous reversal, he accuses Job point-blank of gross evildoing. "Is not your wickedness great? There is no end to your iniquities" (22:5). And the bait is still held out to Job: repent and you will be rewarded (22:21-30).

We may pause a moment to consider one or two of the problems concerning the text of the book of Job. Firstly, it is easy to notice that the sequence of three cycles is not complete. There is the third speech for Eliphaz (22:1-30), a fragment for Bildad (25:1-6), and nothing for Zophar. There are other indications of possible dislocation of the text. It is, of course, possible that the text was never completed to the author's original plan. It is also possible that somehow, in the process of transmission, the middle part of the scroll was damaged and inadequately put together again. Attempts have been made to reconstitute a fuller sequence, but none has won wide acceptance.

In chap. 28 there is a piece in praise of wisdom, which was probably not original to the book of Job. On either side of it, in 27:1 and 29:1, the introduction to Job's speeches differs from those in the earlier chapters. This may not be significant, or it may indicate the presence of some editorial insertion. Above all, with the ending of the words of Job (31:40), there is the sudden introduction of Elihu. Elihu is presented as the sleeper in the group, who has been silent because of his youth, but now bursts into speech, angry at Job for justifying himself rather than God, and angry at the three others for being unable to justify God adequately. So Elihu sets out to rectify the situation (chaps. 32-37).

Very considerable doubts have been expressed about the authenticity of the Elihu speeches in the original composition of Job. Elihu is not mentioned at the arrival of the friends (2:11-13). His speech comes to an abrupt end; after the special introduction (32:1-5), some concluding frame would be expected. Opinions on the worth of what Elihu has to say differ widely. But his speech is repetitive and covers themes both from the friends and from the later divine speeches. At the same time, the Elihu speeches bear a close resemblance to the rest of the book of Job. Perhaps the most tempting hypothesis is to see in the Elihu speeches sketches composed by the author of Job, as experiments along the way to reaching a conclusion to the book. Then discarded in favor of the divine speeches, they would have been introduced into the book by the author's literary heirs. We can surmise; we cannot be certain. As they stand in the text now, they confirm the inadequacy of any human answer to the questions raised by Job's suffering.

To return to the figure of Job, in these final sections he makes clear his longing to confront God. There is a quite remarkable confidence that, were only this to be possible, Job would clear himself before God. From the prologue, we know that Job is probably right. If God were honest, Job would be cleared. Within the context of human life, we can only admire Job's single-minded defense of human integrity.

> Oh, that I knew where I might find him,
>   that I might come even to his seat!
> I would lay my case before him
>   and fill my mouth with arguments.
> I would learn what he would answer me,
>   and understand what he would say to me.
> Would he contend with me in the greatness of his power?
>   No; he would give heed to me.
> There an upright man could reason with him,
>   and I should be acquitted for ever by my judge. (23:3-7)

After Job's earlier speeches, especially in chap. 9, this is remarkably restrained. Perhaps it prepares the way for the conclusion. For all that, Job still clings stubbornly and splendidly to his innocence and integrity (cf., esp. 27:2-6).

Chaps. 29-31 provide almost a summary of Job's experience and may even go some way toward rehabilitating that side of Job which we have heard becoming increasingly strident, angry, and aggressive. There is a mellow wistfulness as he speaks of his past, "the days when God watched over me . . . my autumn days, when the friendship of God was upon my tent" (29:2-4). There is a personal touch to the care for the needy which goes beyond the stock recitals of social virtue (e.g., 31:16-21). When allowance is made for rhetoric, we are perhaps permitted to glimpse a more attractive and sympathetic figure, before the encounter with God and the conclusion of the book.

It is appropriate that Job, who has been steadfast in affirming his innocence and integrity, returns to this theme in his closing words.

> Oh that I had one to hear me! . . .
>> Oh, that I had the indictment written by my adversary.
> Surely I would carry it on my shoulder;
>> I would bind it on me as a crown;
> I would give him an account of all my steps;
>> like a prince I would approach him. (31:35-37)

Finally, God answers Job out of the whirlwind, the storm. It may be this pride which has the creature approaching his creator as a prince, that attracted the opening divine rebuke: "Who is this that darkens counsel by words without knowledge" (38:2). However, what Job has so insistently longed for he now receives. He is face to face with God. In the most magnificent poetry of the book, he will hear what God has to say. Despite his final confidence in his ability to approach God "like a prince," he ends up being almost mute before his Maker. For some interpreters, Job is bullied into silence by God's overwhelming power and eloquence. Were this so, Job's forebodings in chap. 9 would be fully justified. But such an interpretation runs counter to the total horizon of the book. That Job, who has stood his ground for so long, should collapse completely before God's overpowering rhetoric reduces the whole book of Job to an exercise of the most cynical despair. It is impossible to reconcile this interpretation with God's verdict on the friends: "for you have not spoken of me what is right, as my servant Job has" (42:7).

While Job's confidence in his ability to argue his case before God is completely misplaced, Job's certainty that he has been the victim of God's hostility is also completely undermined. At no point does the poet portray God as Job's adversary; at no point does God speak of Job as an enemy or a target for attack. This is immensely significant and cannot be overlooked.

The following movements can be discerned in the poetry: cosmogony (38:4-21), meteorology (38:22-38), and zoology (38:39-39:30). The second divine speech develops the zoological theme in the hyperbolic treatment of Behemoth and Leviathan (the hippopotamus and the crocodile).[8]

---

[8]On the poetic structure and the significance of the divine speeches, see Robert Alter, "The Voice from the Whirlwind," *Commentary*, 1984, pp. 33-41, now chapter 4 in *Art of Biblical Poetry*, 85-110.

Robert Alter argues for the significance of the contrasting correspondence between chaps. 3 and 38. In Job's focus on his suffering, light is blotted out by darkness. The grand sweep of God's evocation of creation opens up vistas beyond human knowledge, bringing the alternation of light and darkness into balance. The contrast is most clearly seen in two passages.

> Job: Let its twilight stars stay dark,
>   let it hope for light and have none,
>   let it not see the eyelids of the dawn. (3:9)
> God: When the morning stars sang together,
>   all the sons of God shouted for joy. (38:7)[9]

The picture of creation may stretch beyond the reaches of human power, but it is an optimistic and a friendly picture, a creation which is ordered and secure.

The meteorological images touch on elements which are vital to the cycle of life: snow and hail, rain and dew, clouds and lightning. This caring for the physical needs of nature is continued in the care for the animal kingdom: their prey and their young, the wild ass and the wild ox, the strange behavior of the ostrich and the mighty power of the war-horse, the soaring beauty of hawk and eagle. The significance of the poetry is tellingly expressed by Alter.

> To be sure, the whole zoological section of the poem is meant to tell Job that God's tender mercies are over all His creatures, but tonally and imagistically this revelation comes in a great storm rather than in a still, small voice, for the Providence portrayed is over a world that defies comfortable moral categorizings. The most crucial respect in which such defiance makes itself felt is in the immense, imponderable play of power that is seen to inform creation. The world is a constant cycle of life renewing and nurturing life, but it is also a constant clash of warring forces. This is neither an easy nor a direct answer to the question of why the good man should suffer, but the imposing vision of a harmonious order to which violence is

---

[9]From Alter, *Art of Biblical Poetry*, 98.

nevertheless intrinsic and where destruction is part of creation is meant to confront Job with the limits of his moral imagination, a moral imagination far more honest but only somewhat less conventional than that of the Friends.[10]

Then there is the image of Behemoth, a peaceful vegetarian and a beast of immense power—yet a creature of God, as Job is (40:15-24). Job asked if he was Yamm or Tannin, that God should set a guard over him (7:12). Here he has his answer. The hippopotamus is practically God's pet. There is no need for a guard. The source of Job's suffering must have been elsewhere. The awesome figure of Leviathan clinches the point. Job cannot tame him or make him his pet. "Will you play with him as with a bird, or will you put him on leash for your maidens?" (41:5). It is, as Alter remarks, "a marvelous fusion of precise observation, hyperbole, and mythological heightening of the real reptile."[11] Yet this fearsome beast—"upon earth there is not his like, a creature without fear" (41:33)—is also part of God's creation. Why should God have needed to take Job for a target or feared Job as an adversary?

In total contrast to Elihu's speeches, the divine speeches do not undertake a logical rebuttal of Job's charges. Nor do they attempt an explanation of the reasons for human suffering. In total contrast to the speeches of the friends, there is not a word from God about sinfulness in Job—just an indication that Job has presumed a little too much on his own knowledge (cf., 38:2, 21). The book of Job is almost entirely poetry. Its resolution, too, lies in the poetic and emotional sphere.

If the divine speeches are read against the context of the book, their emotional impact is totally different from all that might have been expected. God does not confront or admonish Job as the friends' positions would have led us to expect. God is not Job's implacable foe, as Job would have led us to expect. Nor is the situation of Job's suffering open to the kind of understanding that can be hammered out in a court of law, as Job longed to do. Instead, it is placed within the far vaster and more extensive

[10]Alter, *Art of Biblical Poetry*, 106.

[11]Alter, *Art of Biblical Poetry*, 107.

context of creation. Job has a place in creation. Presumably Job's suffering has a place in creation. As there is so much in creation that escapes human understanding, so innocent suffering remains in the realm of mystery, not to be cheapened by glib explanations.

This seems to be Job's interpretation of the divine speeches too. For he replies to God:

> Therefore I have uttered what I did not understand,
>> Things too wonderful for me, which I did not know. (42:3)

What Job had asked for, he has been granted. The meeting with God that he had sought has taken place. Job speaks as though he had met God face to face: "I had heard of you by the hearing of the ear, but now my eye sees you" (42:5). The outcome has been very different from Job's expectation. This brings him to his final words:

> Therefore I retract and I repent,
>> in dust and ashes. (42:6)[12]

This is one of the two key lines in the book of Job. It passes judgment on Job himself; he has to retreat from the position he maintained throughout the poetry. What is the exact nature of this retreat? It is highly unlikely that the poet of Job, who has portrayed Job so carefully as the staunch defender of human integrity, would now have Job recant. Furthermore, situated as we are within the framework of the prose story, Job's recantation of his defense of his innocent integrity would be flatly wrong. In its context, this can only mean that Job retracts his affirmations of God's hostility toward him and his assertions of God's injustice. This interpretation is confirmed by the other key line in the book of Job, which passes judgment on Job's friends: the positions they have held against Job cannot be sustained.

---

[12]This is well rendered by Norman Habel, "Therefore I retract and repent of dust and ashes." Job retracts his case against God and forsakes his position of lamentation among the dust and ashes (Habel, *The Book of Job*, 576). For a full review of the possible translations, see W. Morrow, "Consolation, Rejection, and Repentance in Job 42:6" *JBL* 105 (1986) 211-225.

> "You have not spoken of me what is right, as my servant Job has." (42:7, 8)

Presumably, God is not intended to be ratifying Job's wilder assertions. Rather, the theology of the friends is discredited. They have depicted a God punishing Job for the faults which stem from the human frailty of creatureliness, and they have painted a picture of God's relationship to the world which God here disowns.

These two key lines (42:6-7), side by side in the text, one poetry and one prose, reveal what one may assume to have been the author's conviction throughout the book. Despite appearances, God is not guilty of hostility toward Job. Despite plausibility, the friends' interpretation of experience is inadequate and unjust to God.

Job was right to stand up for human integrity and human dignity. Only so can God be rightly spoken of. Any theology which belittles the integrity of human experience does disservice to the honor of God. An explanation for innocent human suffering is not given. Those inadequate explanations, which only added moral anguish to physical pain, are exposed for what they are—folly.

The book concludes with the ending of the prose story. Not because it is right for Job to receive from God twice as much as he had before (42:10). Not because this is a moral recompense for his unmerited suffering. Rather, because the poetic discourse was inserted within the setting of a story, and the narrative movement of the story must be brought into equilibrium.

The presence of this epilogue (42:7-17) often causes problems for the understanding of the book of Job. It leads some to argue that the book is comedy rather than tragedy; it comes right in the end, and Job is back precisely twice as wealthy and blessed as he was. This might be all very well if the world, or literature, is to be inflexibly divided between comedy and tragedy, and if all works of literature are to be assessed by their final paragraphs. But it has to be seen that the epilogue stands in flat contradiction to the passion of Job in his poetry.

To give the epilogue the last word would be a betrayal of Job: it would be succumbing to the recurrent temptation held out as a final bait by Eliphaz.

> Agree with God, and be at peace;
>> thereby good will come to you.
> Receive instruction from his mouth,
>> and lay up his words in your heart. ...
> Then you will delight yourself in the Almighty,
>> and lift up your face to God. (22:21-26*)

The structure of Eliphaz's thought is clear. The condition is for Job to deny his own experience and yield to God; the consequence is a blessed life before God. Whether v 23a (omitted here) is simply part of the condition—"If you return to the Almighty and humble yourself (so *RSV*, following the Greek)— or whether it contains both condition and consequence—"If you return to the Almighty, you will be built up" (so the Hebrew)—the invitation and the temptation are unmistakable: repent and you will be rewarded. It has been a constant refrain from the friends.

Seen as comedy, the epilogue offers the seductive possibility that Job has done just this. His repentance is portrayed in 42:1-6, where he accepts his instruction from God, laying up God's words in his heart; his reward is portrayed in 42:7-17, where his prayers are heard and, twice blessed, he can lift up his face to God.

Thus Job is betrayed and his whole stance throughout the poetry abandoned. This cannot be: not because we might not like it, nor because it denies the truth of the poetry, but because the epilogue itself will not permit it. If the epilogue were to be seen in this light, then the constant refrain of the friends has been justified and the stubborn insistence of Job is shown up as ignorant arrogance. But the epilogue does not permit this view:

> After the LORD had spoken these words to Job, the LORD said to Eliphaz the Temanite: "My wrath is kindled against you and against your two friends; *for you have not spoken of me what is right, as my servant Job has.* (42:7)

Job's stance is justified, even if it must be modified in the face of the divine speeches. The friends must abandon their arrogant stubbornness in insisting inflexibly on the tenets of the wisdom tradition; instead, they must seek Job's intercession before God.

Another common attitude toward the epilogue is to distance it completely from the poetry. The prose thus becomes but a frame for the poetry; it has no intrinsic link with it. However, we have seen the role of the prologue. It creates an unreal world of utter simplicity in which the tortured questions of the ambiguous world of our reality can be talked out to the end. Because of the prologue, we know that Job is blameless and upright. Because of the prologue, we know that God is responsible for the suffering which has befallen Job—God gave in to Satan. Because of the prologue, Job's stridency is tolerable, and gives vent in clarity to the feelings of tortured ambiguity. Probably, without the prologue the book of Job would never have made it into the canon of scripture.

The unreal situation set up by the prologue has to be brought to closure. The epilogue achieves this, with an equally unreal solution. The unreality of the solution should keep it from contaminating the stark reality of the poem. Prologue and epilogue set a stage within which the drama can be played out. Without the epilogue, the structure would be out of kilter. The disagreeable smugness of the epilogue appropriately balances the insensitive smugness of the prologue. Both are tolerable because they form the setting for poetry which is the utter opposite of smug, which pierces all pretense and claws at the very vitals of human living.

CONCLUSION

An explanation for innocent human suffering is not given. But the book is not silent on the directions an answer must take. Two such directions are intimated. One is pointed to by the power of the poetry; the other lurks in the very silence of the text.

As to the first, one of the values of Robert Alter's treatment of Job has been to ask the question why Job was written in poetry rather than prose and to look for part of the book's resolution in the stuff of the poetry. Alter's observations identify enough echoes between chap. 3 and chaps. 38-41 to suggest that part of the problem and its solution is expressed in the poetry of these chapters. The poetry of chaps. 38-41 probes and lays bare the mysteries of creation, the ordered care in creation, the beauty and power of the animal world—and also the cruel violence necessary for the nurturing of much of the animal world.[13]

There is a terrible paradox here: care for a mysterious infinity of detail; tender beauty nurtured by unreasoning violence. There is a goodness in nature at which the human mind can only gasp; there is a savagery there too at which the human mind can only wonder. But while we wonder, we are also aware of our perception of the natural world as good.

Perhaps it is a similar perception which keeps deeply reflective minds from nihilism. Despite the suffering and misery which we may have experienced personally or known vicariously, those who retain faith have seen a goodness in human beings, human love, and human life. Sometimes it is glimpsed only momentarily, a possibility perceived but never realized. Sometimes it is swamped and overwhelmed by the suffering and misery—but it was there. Having seen it, we cannot deny an ultimate meaning to our world nor an ultimate goodness in it. We cannot understand; we cannot affirm or explain; but we cannot deny. Perhaps, in the infinity of God, all those moments and glimpses of goodness are the deep inner truth of reality. Perhaps, in the timelessness of eternity, what was seen for a flickering instant in life is the substantial stuff of being. But whatever of eternity and infinity, we have glimpsed the goodness in life; we cry out at misery and suffering—and we entrust ourselves to the hope implicit in the goodness we have glimpsed.

In the very silence of the book of Job another direction is intimated. It is an answer which is unsaid; it can only be heard in the context of all that is said. It is heard in the silence left when the

---

[13]"The sequence of beasts [in 38:39-39:30] . . . is loosely associative but also instructive: lion, raven, mountain goat and gazelle, wild ass, wild ox, ostrich, war horse, hawk and eagle. The first two and the last two creatures in the sequence are beasts of prey whose native fierceness in effect frames the wildness of the whole catalogue. . . . This concluding poem in Job is probably one of the most unsentimental poetic treatments of the animal world in the Western literary tradition and, at least at first thought, a little surprising coming from the mouth of the Lord. But the violence and, even more, the peculiar beauty of violence are precisely the point of God's visionary rejoinder to Job. The animal realm is a nonmoral realm, but the sharp paradoxes it embodies make us see the inadequacy of any merely human moral calculus—not only that of the Friends, learned by rote, but even Job's, spoken out of the integrity of suffering. In the animal kingdom, the tender care for one's young may well mean their gulping the blood of freshly slain creatures. It is a daily rite of sustaining life that defies all moralizing anthropomorphic interpretation. And yet, the series of rhetorical questions to Job suggests, God's providence looks after each of these strange, fierce, inaccessible creatures" (Alter, *Art of Biblical Poetry*, 102).

verdict has been reached on all that has been said—and it has been found lacking. It is worthwhile reflecting on that verdict.

The friends are clearly wrong: they earn Job's contempt and God's anger. Their view is that of traditional wisdom morality. It can be summed up under three heads. Misfortune is the punishment of sin, and the wicked come to an unfortunate end through the just judgment of God—which runs counter to experience. Misfortune may fall upon the just, for none is sinless, but it is for their purification and will be of short duration—which fails to take into account the severity of suffering and the random indeterminacy of its occurrence. When misfortune strikes the just, the correct attitude is to hold fast and wait for God to redouble one's reward—which is venal. God rejects their view.

Job is also wrong. Job views his misfortune as the result of God's attack on him. Job insists that it is not the result of any sin. Sin could have been forgiven. His sufferings are incommensurate with any evil he might have done. Nor will any form of purification or reward rectify the wrong that his suffering involves. So Job accuses God of being responsible for the injustice in the world and for mounting a personal attack against Job. So sure of this is Job that he is convinced he could win his case against God in open court. God brings Job to recant.[14]

It would appear that, as so often in human communication, the message of the book of Job lies principally in what is not said. The friends make the claim to be able to justify human suffering in terms of punishment or purification. They are wrong. Job ends up attributing human suffering to divine malice. He is wrong. The message of the book lies in what remains unsaid. The way to an understanding of human suffering is left unspoken, but two blind alleys have been blocked. Neither human sin nor divine anger can be used as general causes for human suffering. Instead, the understanding of suffering has to reckon with a benevolent God and human innocence. In this its mystery may outrun the capacity of the human mind.

[14]The minor figures fare no better. Elihu's dismissal lies in being ignored. Job's wife is prepared to ditch Job's integrity and get it over with quickly: "Curse God, and die" (2.9). Job dismisses the advice as folly. In the overall context, Satan is proved wrong. Technically, while Job rails violently against God, he does not formally curse God. Certainly, with God's final commendation of Job, Satan has lost.

This conclusion, that the opposing ways in which Job and his friends speak of God are both wrong, leaves the option open of another way that is different from both and is right. As an answer, in one sense it is unsatisfactorily negative: it spells out two wrong ways of speaking about God. In another sense, it is very positive, since it leaves only one way open in the end, and so points in a definite direction. The dialogue with the friends has excluded human morals, human goodness and badness, as a way to right understanding of the situation. The dialogue with God has excluded divine malice or failure to care as a way to right understanding. All that is left, within the context of Hebrew thought, is a situation in which God is benevolent and humans are free of guilt. How one is to understand this situation may be more mysterious than the creation of the universe and its control, but at least the parameters of the situation are clear: there is no fault, neither human nor divine.

There is nothing particularly remarkable in the silence of this conclusion. It is often the case that what is most deeply meaningful to us is also most difficult to bring to adequate expression. Left in complete silence, it is condemned to incomprehension. But surrounded with the right parameters, silence may permit mystery to move toward understanding and even more toward acceptance.

Today

A surprising aspect of the genius of the book of Job is that we resonate with Job and not with his friends. It is surprising, for most of us are not made of the stuff of heroes, ready to challenge God. It is surprising, for all too many of us, at some instinctive level, tend to endorse the views of the friends. We want order and predictability in our world. We want the good to flourish—we feel we are to be reckoned among them. We believe that wrong-doing should meet its just deserts. And yet we resonate with Job!

The book of Job is one of the greatest defenses of human integrity and therefore also of the honor of God. Before the mystery of suffering and evil, Job will not permit blame to be allotted where none is due. Job does not allow the claim that the frailties of human conduct can offer adequate reason for the calamities that may befall us. Job dismisses the attempt to deny experience by equating right living with good fortune and misfortune with wrongdoing. So strong is Job's commitment to human integrity that, under the goading of the friends, he moves to positions which impugn the integrity of God. There lies the folly for which he is rebuked.

The honor of God, on the other hand, is never served by the belittling of human integrity or the attempt to reduce the mystery of human life to simple equations. There is suffering in human life and we do not know why it should be. Some we can see as the result of the gift of human freedom. Some we can see as the result of the forces of nature. Some is utterly inscrutable, with an apparent cruelty of fate for which there is no explanation. Some suffering can be ennobling, but not all. Some lives that are burdened with heavy suffering can be rich and fulfilling lives, but why should it have to be so? The denial of God does not alleviate the suffering one whit; all it eases is our inability to comprehend. Railing against God does nothing to help, unless it ventilates an anger that were better directed against the arbitrariness of misfortune.[15] Job's diatribes against God show there is no solution to be sought in that direction.

Instead there is the encounter with mystery. The mystery of human life which in its vulnerability and frailty can be infinitely precious and treasured. The mystery of human love which can surmount extraordinary pain and suffering. The mystery of divine love which must suffer and grieve with us in our hurt and misery, but which—as we can say to each other—says also to us: "you are precious in my eyes, and honored, and I love you." Love is gift. We really know not its why or wherefore. How much more the love of God. The ultimate mystery of our world is not that we are nor that we love. It is not that we suffer. Nor is it faith that

---

[15]Of course, we believe that it is God who created this universe in which we often experience either fortune or misfortune as arbitrary. So the problem remains at one remove but the problem of evil will never simply go away. At least the recognition of the arbitrariness of misfortune places a distance between the responsibility of a loving God and our own experience of misery. It also leaves open the possibility that there is an overall value in the structure of our universe which is not visible in many of the individual situations we encounter. We have no guarantee that God created the best of all possible worlds, but we also have no way of knowing whether it was possible to create a better one.

there is a God. The ultimate mystery of our world is that its creator God should deeply love each human creature. Such mystery calls forth unfathomable wonder. Such love can only be met with unconditional acceptance.

RECOMMENDED FURTHER READING

Robert Alter, *The Art of Biblical Poetry*, 85-110. New York: Basic Books, 1985.

Robert Gordis, *The Book of God and Man: A Study of Job.* Chicago: University of Chicago, 1965.

——————, *The Book of Job: Commentary, New Translation, and Special Studies.* New York: Jewish Theological Seminary of America, 1978.

Moshe Greenberg, "Job." Pp. 283-304 in *The Literary Guide to the Bible,* edited by Robert Alter and Frank Kermode. London: Collins, 1987.

Gustavo Gutierrez, *On Job: God-Talk and the Suffering of the Innocent.* Maryknoll: Orbis, 1987.

Norman C. Habel, *The Book of Job.* OTL. London: SCM, 1985.

J. Gerald Janzen, *Job.* Interpretation. Atlanta: John Knox, 1985.

Gerhard von Rad, *Wisdom in Israel*, 206-26. London: SCM, 1972.

H.H. Rowley, *Job.* NCB. London: Nelson, 1970.

Bruce Vawter, *Job & Jonah: Questioning the Hidden God.* New York: Paulist, 1983.

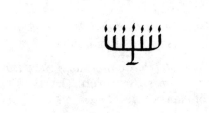

Conclusion

The Christian community distanced itself from certain aspects of the Old Testament quite rapidly. For example, despite the privileged status of the Ten Commandments, the Christian communities altered the observance of sabbath from the Sabbath day to the Lord's day, from Saturday to Sunday. It also set aside the commandment about images. In distancing itself from the synagogue and seeking its own identity, many of the legal practices which bound the Jewish communities together, such as the dietary laws and the rituals of cleanliness, were deliberately discontinued; and with these went circumcision with its roots in the covenant with Abraham (Genesis 17; Acts 15).

Just as much of the law has been allowed to lapse, there may well be doubt as to the wisdom of quarrying the Old Testament in quest of support for details of doctrine. Its theologies are too many and too diverse for this to be a pursuit which is both profitable and honest. The wisdom tradition and the book of Job stand at odds in their understanding of providence. The deuteronomic traditions and the priestly traditions probably stand at odds in their understanding of covenant. The prophets said much that is true in all times and all societies, but the particular announcements they made were for their own day and were fulfilled in 722 and 587. Their faith-filled prophecies of hope—unless radically transformed and redirected toward the person of Christ—remain as far from fulfillment now as when they were spoken.

The Old Testament is a deep and craggy quarry in which to search out the rich ore of the dialogue of God and Israel. In it can be found insight into God's concern for Israel and God's commitment to Israel—and through Israel to all the world. In it can be discovered samples of the manifold aspects of Israel's understanding of God, extracted from the diversity of experience revealed in Israel's history. In it can be glimpsed something of the theological forces at work within Israel, applied to the task of laying language on the experience of God in human life, producing the texts which have become our sacred scriptures. In it are crystallized the many moments of God's relationship with Israel—and through Israel with us.

Scholarly study has changed attitudes to the Old Testament. No longer can its writing be attributed to the great and inspired figures of a distant past: Moses, Joshua, Samuel, David, Solomon, and the prophets—figures of religious genius, who communed in intimacy with God. Rather than a book of the inspired few, the Old Testament has come to be seen as a book of the living community. What was once simply taken as straightforward history, recorded by those close to the events, is now known to be often carefully structured narrative, frequently based on traditions celebrated in liturgy or preserved in story, concerned much more with theological interest than with historical record.

Scientific discovery has changed attitudes to our own world. There are those who believe that Darwin and the advent of scientific investigation cast a shadow over the Old Testament. Whatever may be the truth of this at a popular level, it has little basis in the history of scholarship. The investigation of the Pentateuch was under way at least a century before Darwin; it took its origins from phenomena within the Old Testament text itself. Similarly, while the Copernican revolution and the discovery of countless galaxies beyond our own has enormously increased our knowledge of our universe beyond that of our biblical forebears, nevertheless its ultimate secrets that they did not dream of still remain unknown to us.

Then as now, it was and is part of the human condition to exist in faith. Then as now, some believed in a universe without God, and some believed in a universe with God. Only those who avoid living in faith fail to see that they cannot avoid this decision. Whether or not our universe, in all its infinite intricacy, comes from the hands of God or from the mysteries of chance is as indemonstrable for us as it was for them. Science can investigate what is, what has become. The act of becoming escapes it.

With the discoveries of steam and electricity, of the internal combustion engine and nuclear energy, of the transistor, the computer, and the super-conductor, human life has changed enormously in the last couple of hundred years. Yet as we look back over the trajectory of western civilization—the Renaissance, the Middle Ages, the periods of patristic and classical thought, back to the antiquity of Egypt and Babylon and Sumer—the issues of human spirit and human life remain remarkably the same. We still search for meaning in life. We still face the unknown of death. We are still completed in the love of one another and of God. The restlessness of faith was admirably summed up by Augustine in the fourth century: "you have made us for yourself, O God, and our hearts can find no rest until they rest in you." Today many will express that restlessness in other terms, but restless we remain.

It is my hope that in this book the Old Testament can be clearly seen as magnificent witness to Israel's ponderings of the ultimate mysteries of human life. Myth yes, occasionally, when myth is properly understood. Legend yes, in some cases. Story often, when story is seen as one of the great vehicles of theology, of metaphor and symbol, powerful for interpreting life and passing on its understanding.

The faith which stands on the Bible does not stand on weak foundations. In the Old Testament, such faith stands on the writing of wise and thinking people, matured by the experiences of many generations, pondered and shaped by a believing community—all of this under the power of God's spirit. In its great wisdom, Israel did not sort through and discard its conflicting traditions. Aware of the impossibility of giving adequate expression to the mystery of God's relationship to human history and human life, Israel retained all that it found inspiring and inspired. What may have seemed wise and life-giving to one generation may not have seemed so to another. But who was to know that yet another generation might arise to see more keenly and again discern there life and wisdom.

So Israel retained its scriptures and the Church retained its canon. In them are enshrined the struggle of a human community to interpret its life and experience, to articulate its faith in God. In proclamation, in didactic reflection, in joy or agony of soul, Israel pondered the mysteries of God—its pondering guided by the

Spirit of God. As the foundation of community and faith, the Old Testament is a book with closure and an end. As the pondering of the spirit, it is open—open always to life and to God, never to be finally encompassed, never to be ended as long as the race still runs.

> For my thoughts are not your thoughts,
>> neither are your ways my ways, says the LORD.
> For as the heavens are higher than the earth,
>> so are my ways higher than your ways
>> and my thoughts than your thoughts. (Isa 55:8-9)

Abbreviations

The asterisk (*) refers only to the relevant part of the text cited. Reference is made to a verse or verses where part of the material is clearly not meant to be included in the reference: the asterisk (*) indicates the reference is only to the relevant part of the text cited. For example, if there is a gloss in a text, the asterisk means ignore the gloss; if the text is a combination of J and E and the reference concerns J, the asterisk means ignore the E material.

a, b, α, β etc. Verse halves are denoted by "a" and "b," following the major division of a verse in the Hebrew punctuation (or cantillation marks). Subdivisions within any half verse are indicated by the Greek letters, α, β, γ, etc. following the principal secondary punctuation divisions in the Hebrew. As a rule, this punctuation follows the sense of the verse, so that someone unfamiliar with Hebrew will frequently be able to decide from the context what part of the verse is meant.

AB	Anchor Bible
AnBib	Analecta biblica
ANET	*Ancient Near Eastern Texts Relating to the Old Testament*
AThANT	Abhandlungen zur Theologie des Alten und Neuen Testaments
AusBR	*Australian Biblical Review*
BBB	Bonner biblische Beiträge
BET	Beiträge zur evangelischen Theologie
BHK	*Biblia Hebraica* ed. R. Kittel
BHS	*Biblia Hebraica Stuttgartensia*
BK	Biblischer Kommentar
BKAT	Biblischerz Kommentar: Altes Testament
BZAW	Beihefte zur Zeitschrift für die Alttestamentliche Wissenschaft
CBC	The Cambridge Bible Commentary
CBQ	*Catholic Biblical Quarterly*
CBQMS	Catholic Biblical Quarterly Monograph Series
CRB	Cahiers de la Revue Biblique
E	Elohist

FRLANT	Forschungen zur Religion und Literatur des Alten und Neuen Testaments
HAT	Handbuch zum Alten Testament
HSM	Harvard Semitic Monographs
ICC	International Critical Commentary
J	The Yahwist narrative or the Yahwist narrator
JB	*Jerusalem Bible*
JBL	*Journal of Biblical Literature*
JE	Text derived from the combination of Yahwist and Elohist
JSOT	*Journal for the Study of the Old Testament*
JSOTSup	Journal for the Study of the Old Testament—Supplement Series
KAT	Kommentar zum Alten Testament
LXX	Septuagint—Greek version of the Old Testament
MT	Masoretic text = standard text of the Hebrew scriptures
NAB	*New American Bible*
NCB	New Century Bible
NEB	*New English Bible*
OBO	Orbis biblicus et orientalis
OTL	Old Testament Library
P	The Priestly Document or the Priestly Writer
RB	*Revue Biblique*
RSV	*Revised Standard Version*
SBLDS	Society of Biblical Literature Dissertation Series
SBLMS	Society of Biblical Literature Monograph Series
SBT	Studies in Biblical Theology
SSN	Studia Semitica Neerlandica
TBü	Theologische Bücherei
TRu	*Theologische Rundschau*
TZ	*Theologische Zeitschrift*
VT	*Vetus Testamentum*
VTSup	Vetus Testamentum Supplements
WBC	Word Bible Commentary
WMANT	Wissenschaftliche Monographien zum Alten und Neuen Testament
ZTK	*Zeitschrift für Theologie und Kirche*

Index of Biblical References

References are to the *RSV* verse numbering. Where necessary, adjoining references have been amalgamated.

Old Testament